THE HUNDRED LANGUAGES OF CHILDREN

The Reggio Emilia Approach—Advanced Reflections

Second Edition

THE HUNDRED LANGUAGES OF CHILDREN

The Reggio Emilia Approach—Advanced Reflections

Second Edition

edited by
Carolyn Edwards
Lella Gandini
George Forman

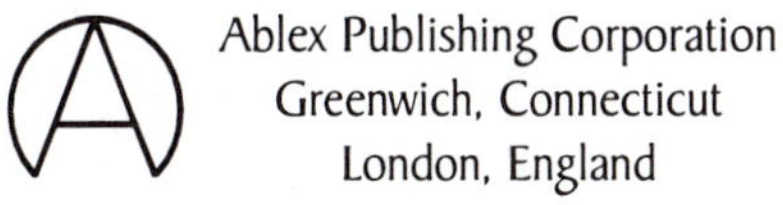

Ablex Publishing Corporation
Greenwich, Connecticut
London, England

The color photograph on the front cover is by Sue Sturtevant.

The photographs appearing in the first 10 chapters and in the conclusion are by teachers in Reggio Emilia schools.

The two photographs included in chapter 11 by Cathleen Smith are, by permission, from the book: *E'Nato un Bambino Down* published by Isituto Italiano di Medicina Sociale Editore, Roma.

Printed in the United States of America

Library of Congress Cataloging-in-Publication Data

The hundred languages of children : The Reggio Emilia approach--advanced reflections / edited by Carolyn Edwards, Lella Gandini, and George Forman. — 2nd ed.

p. cm.

Includes bibliographical references (p.) and index.

ISBN 1-56750-310-1 (cloth). — ISBN 1-56750-311-X (pbk.)

1. Early childhood education—Italy—Reggio Emilia. 2. Early childhood education—United States—Case studies. I. Edwards, Carolyn P. II. Gandini, Lella. III. Forman, George E., 1942–

LB1139.3.I8H85 1997

372.21'0945'43—dc21 97–22318

CIP

Ablex Publishing Corporation
P.O. Box 5297
55 Old Post Road #2
Greenwich, CT 06831

Published in the U.K. and Europe by:
JAI Press Ltd.
38 Tavistock Street
Covent Garden
London WC2E 7PB
England

Contents

Acknowledgments ix
About the Contributors xi
Foreword: Complementary Perspectives on Reggio Emilia xv
by Howard Gardner
Remarks: Malaguzzi's Story, Other Stories xix
by David Hawkins

Part I. Starting Points
1. Introduction: Background and Starting Points
by Carolyn Edwards, Lella Gandini, and George Forman 5
2. What Can We Learn from Reggio Emilia?
by Lilian G. Katz 27

Part II. Reggio Emilia's Educators Describe Their Program: Interviews With Lella Gandini
3. History, Ideas, and Basic Philosophy: An Interview with Lella Gandini
by Loris Malaguzzi 49
4. The Community–Teacher Partnership in the Governance of the Schools: An Interview with Lella Gandini
by Sergio Spaggiari 99
5. Projected Curriculum Constructed Through Documentation—*Progettazione:* An Interview with Lella Gandini
by Carlina Rinaldi 113

6. The Role of the *Pedagogista*: An Interview with Lella Gandini
by Tiziana Filippini in collaboration with Simona Bonilauri 127
7. The Role of the *Atelierista*: An Interview with Lella Gandini
by Vea Vecchi 139
8. The Voice of Parents: An Interview with Lella Gandini
by Gianna Fontanesi, Miller Gialdini, and Monica Soncini 149

Part III. Reflections on the Interplay of Theory and Practice
9. Educational and Caring Spaces
by Lella Gandini 161
10. Partner, Nurturer, and Guide: The Role of the Teacher
by Carolyn Edwards 179
11. Children With "Special Rights" in the Preprimary Schools and Infant–Toddler Centers of Reggio Emilia
by Cathleen Smith 199
12. Curriculum Development in Reggio Emilia: A Long-Term Curriculum Project About Dinosaurs
by Baji Rankin 215
13. Negotiated Learning Through Design, Documentation, and Discourse
by George Forman and Brenda Fyfe 239
14. Theory and Praxis in Reggio Emilia: They Know What They Are Doing, and Why
by Rebecca S. New 261
15. Poppies and the Dance of World Making
by Paul Kaufman 285

Part IV. The Extension of the Reggio Emilia Approach Into American Classrooms
16. The Child in Community: Constraints From the Early Childhood Lore
by John Nimmo 295
17. Existing Frameworks and New Ideas From Our Reggio Emilia Experience: Learning at a Lab School With 2- to 4-Year-Old Children
by Rebecca Kantor and Kimberlee L. Whaley 313
18. Bridge to Another Culture: The Journey of the Model Early Learning Center
by Ann W. Lewin, with contributions from Genet Astatke, Jennifer Azzariti, Wendy Baldwin, Deborah Barley, Amelia Gambetti, and Sonya Shoptaugh 335
19. The City in the Snow: Applying the Multisymbolic Approach in Massachusetts
by George Forman, Joan Langley, Moonja Oh, and Lynda Wrisley 359

20. Looking in the Mirror: A Reflection of Reggio Practice in Winnetka
by Eva Tarini and Lynn White 375
21. The Project Approach Framework for Teacher Education: A Case for Collaborative Learning and Reflective Practice
by Mary Jane Moran 405
22. Stories of Change from the St. Louis–Reggio Collaborative
by Brenda Fyfe, Louise Cadwell, and Jan Phillips 419
23. Reconsidering Early Childhood Education in the United States: Reflections From Our Encounters With Reggio Emilia
by Carol Brunson Phillips and Sue Bredekamp 439

Part V. Conclusion
24. Conclusion: Final Reflections
by Carolyn Edwards, Lella Gandini, and George Forman 457

Glossary of Terms Used by Educators in Reggio Emilia 467
Additional Resources 468
Author Index 475
Subject Index 479

Acknowledgments

We would like first of all to acknowledge our positive dialogue with the chapter authors, who contributed so many valuable ideas to this volume and whose work with parents, teachers, and children we admire so strongly. We feel particularly privileged to have given the ideas of our contributors from Reggio Emilia their first voice in the English language. We know that for Loris Malaguzzi, who used to dash off articles and editorials for *Bambini* (the Italian *Young Children*), it was difficult to commit his thoughts to paper, when they were to be bound in a book. With such a constraint he would continually revise his writing in a constant search for better words and definitions that would win respect for the culture of children and the role of educators. Therefore, we are grateful to all our contributors, particularly to Loris, for entrusting to us the task of presenting these ideas that began with extraordinary developments in the small city of Reggio Emilia and now belong to the world of education beyond Italy.

Several people and institutions have helped to make this book possible in both its first and second editions. Lester Little and Vittoria Poletto helped with the translation, Alison Rogers and Rose Pennington read portions of the manuscript and made excellent suggestions. Vea Vecchi was particularly helpful in finding and selecting wonderful visual material, and the Municipality of Reggio Emilia provided permission to reproduce photographs and drawings from their files and exhibit catalogs. REGGIO CHILDREN S.r.l., the University of Kentucky, the University of Massachusetts, Amherst, and the University of Nebraska, Lincoln, Institute of Agricultural and Natural Resources, have generously contributed institutional resources to help us work together from different home bases on this complex manuscript. Carolyn

Edwards also acknowledges the Centre for Advanced Study at the Norwegian Academy of Science and Letters for providing a fruitful intellectual climate in which to draw the work to a close. Walter and Herbert Johnson, past and present Presidents of Ablex Publishing Corporation, provided abiding faith for the completion of this second edition. We have appreciated working over the years with many excellent staff persons at Ablex, most recently, Andrea Molitor, Kimberly Burgos, and Anne Trowbridge. And finally, but foremost, we wish to thank our respective three families for their sustaining support and encouragement.

About the Contributors

Sue Bredekamp, Director, Professional Development, National Association for the Education of Young Children, Washington, D.C.

Louise Cadwell, *Atelierista* and Consultant, College School, St. Michaels School, and The Family Center, St. Louis, MO

Carolyn Pope Edwards, Professor, Departments of Psychology and Family and Consumer Sciences, University of Nebraska, Lincoln

Tiziana Filippini, *Pedagogista,* Department of Early Education, Reggio Emilia

Gianna Fontanesi, Parent, Reggio Emilia

George Forman, Professor, School of Education, University of Massachusetts, Amherst

Brenda Fyfe, Professor, School of Education, Webster University, St. Louis, MO

Lella Gandini, REGGIO CHILDREN, S.r.l., United States liaison for the dissemination of the Reggio Emilia approach and Adjunct Professor, School of Education, University of Massachusetts, Amherst

Howard Gardner, Professor, Graduate School of Education, Harvard University, Cambridge, MA

Miller Gialdini, Parent, Reggio Emilia

David Hawkins, Professor Emeritus, University of Colorado, Boulder

Pamela Houk, Curator, Experience Center, The Dayton Art Institute, Dayton, OH

Rebecca Kantor, Associate Professor, College of Education, The Ohio State University, Columbus, OH

Lilian Katz, Professor, ERIC Clearinghouse on Elementary and Early Childhood Education, University of Illinois, Urbana

Paul Kaufman, Writer and Television Producer, P.K. Inc., New York

Joan Langley, Teacher, Marks Meadow Elementary, Amherst Public Schools, Amherst, MA

Moonja Oh, Educational Consultant, Seoul, South Korea

Loris Malaguzzi, (deceased), Founder and Director, Department of Early Childhood Education, Reggio Emilia

Mary Jane Moran, Associate Director, Child Study and Development Center, University of New Hampshire, Durham, NH

Rebecca New, Professor, Department of Education, University of New Hampshire, Durham

John Nimmo, Professor, Faculty of Education and Human Development, Pacific Oaks College, Outreach, Bellevue, WA

Ann Lewin, Educator, Memphis, TN

Carol Brunson Phillips, Executive Director, Council for Early Childhood Professional Recognition, Washington, D.C.

Jan Phillips, Principal, The College School, St.Louis, MO

Baji Rankin, Assistant Professor of Education, University of New Mexico, Albuquerque, NM

Carlina Rinaldi, Director of Early Childhood Education, Municipality of Reggio Emilia, and Executive Consultant of REGGIO CHILDREN, S.r.l., Reggio Emilia

Monica Soncini, Parent, Reggio Emilia

Sergio Spaggiari, Director, Department of Education, Municipality of Reggio Emilia

Cathleen Smith, Educational Consultant, Whitehorse, Yukon, Canada

Eva Tarini, Teacher, Crow Island School Winnetka, IL

Vea Vecchi, *Atelierista,* Diana School, Department of Early Childhood Education, Reggio Emilia

Kimberlee Whaley, Assistant Professor, Department of Family Relations and Human Development, The Ohio State University, Columbus, OH

Lynn White, Teacher, Greely School, Winnetka, IL

Lynda Wrisley, Teacher, Marks Meadow Elementary, Amherst Public Schools, Amherst, MA

IN COLLABORATION WITH

Genet Astatke, Teacher, Model Early Learning Center, Washington, D.C.

Jennifer Azzariti, Teacher, Model Early Learning Center, Washington, D.C.

Wendy Baldwin, Teacher, Model Early Learning Center, Washington, D.C.

Deborah Barley, Teacher, Model Early Learning Center, Washington, D.C.

Simona Bonilauri, *Pedagogista,* Department of Early Childhood, Reggio Emilia

Amelia Gambetti, REGGIO CHILDREN, S.r.l. liaison for consultancy to schools in the United States

Sonya Shoptaugh, Teacher, Model Early Learning Center, Washington, D.C.

Thinking about living.
Drawing by 5 year-olds,
Diana School

Foreword: Complementary Perspectives on Reggio Emilia

Howard Gardner

Midst the multitude of books about education issued these days, few stand out. This book that you hold in your hands does. An integrated set of essays on a unique approach to early childhood education, *The Hundred Languages of Children* documents the remarkable set of schools that have evolved over almost 40 years in Reggio Emilia in northern Italy. At the same time, the book constitutes a profound meditation on the nature of early human nature, and the ways in which it can be guided and stimulated in different cultural milieus. Anyone with an interest in the education of children should read it; few who do so will remain unaffected by the experience.

In the opening pages of this book, you will read the remarkable story of how Loris Malaguzzi, an intellectually oriented young Italian teacher, became interested in the building of a new school directly after World War II, and how a momentary infatuation with this new construction turned into a lifelong love affair with young pupils. Without question, Malaguzzi (as he is universally called) is the guiding genius of Reggio—the thinker whose name deserves to be uttered in the same breath as his heroes Froebel, Montessori, Dewey, and

Piaget. But far more so than most other educational thinkers, Malaguzzi has dedicated his life to the establishment of an educational community: a remarkable group of teachers of various stripes and specialties who have worked together for years, even decades, with parents, community members, and thousands of children, to set up a system that works.

The Reggio system can be described succinctly as follows: It is a collection of schools for young children in which each child's intellectual, emotional, social, and moral potentials are carefully cultivated and guided. The principal educational vehicle involves youngsters in long-term engrossing projects, which are carried out in a beautiful, healthy, love-filled setting. Dewey wrote about progressive education for decades but his school lasted a scant 4 years. In sharp contrast, it is the Reggio community, more so than the philosophy or method, that constitutes Malaguzzi's central achievement. Nowhere else in the world is there such a seamless and symbiotic relationship between a school's progressive philosophy and its practices.

Just as Reggio represents the achievement of many individuals and groups, each of which brings to bear its own special gifts, so, too, the present volume is distinguished by the range of individuals who have reflected about Reggio from their own distinctive and complementary perspectives. Within the Reggio family, there are essays by individuals who represent the teaching, the architectural design and layout, the community relations, and the rich curricula of projects. From the American perspective, there are the impressions of a philosopher, a filmmaker, a progressive educator, and several researchers who have explored the cognitive, affective, and social dimensions of the projects carried out by the children of Reggio and their teachers. Of special note is that cohort of educator-researchers who traveled back and forth between Reggio and Massachusetts during the 1980s, sharing experiences and developing their own transoceanic network. These individuals and others have helped to make Reggio Emilia known around the world, even as they have sought to explicate its special nature to interested audiences on both sides of the Atlantic.

Words are necessarily the prime medium in a book. The writers have done a splendid job of recreating the special atmosphere of Reggio, and the various photos and diagrams presented here add the essential visual element to the portrait. The various exhibitions about Reggio that have been mounted have helped to convey its special flavor, and there are now several film and video treatments as well. Of course, there is no substitute for a visit to Reggio Emilia, and without a doubt, the publication of this book will increase traffic to the lush and civilized Emilia Romagna area. Yet, even for those who are quite familiar with the Reggio scene, this book provides a wealth of additional information. As one who had the privilege of visiting in Reggio several years ago, and has remained in touch ever since, I can say that I learned something on nearly every page of this gritty volume.

In reading *The Hundred Languages of Children* I was struck—or struck anew—by many messages, of which I shall mention just a few. So much has been written about progressive methods in education, but so rarely are the ideals of progressive education actually realized. Perhaps one reason why is that one needs a team that is willing to work together for decades in the service of a set of energizing ideas; the team needs to evolve procedures for attaining an education of quality while still encouraging growth for all who participate. So much has been written about the powers of the young mind, and yet so rarely can they be seen in full action. In Reggio, the teachers know how to listen to children, how to allow them to take the initiative, and yet how to guide them in productive ways. There is no fetish made about achieving adult standards, and yet the dedication exemplified by the community ensures that work of quality will result. The effect comes about because of the infinite care taken with respect to every aspect of existence, whether it be the decision to constitute groups of two as compared with three children, the choice of brush or color, or the receptivity to surprises and to surprise. Reggio successfully challenges so many false dichotomies: art versus science, individual versus community, child versus adult, enjoyment versus study, nuclear family versus extended family; by achieving a unique harmony that spans these contrasts, it reconfigures our sclerotic categorical systems.

As an American educator, I cannot help but be struck by certain paradoxes. In America we pride ourselves on being focused on children, and yet we do not pay sufficient attention to what they are actually expressing. We call for cooperative learning among children, and yet we rarely have sustained cooperation at the level of teacher and administrator. We call for artistic works, but we rarely fashion environments that can truly support and inspire them. We call for parental involvement, but are loathe to share ownership, responsibility, and credit with parents. We recognize the need for community, but we so often crystallize immediately into interest groups. We hail the discovery method, but we do not have the confidence to allow children to follow their own noses and hunches. We call for debate, but often spurn it; we call for listening, but we prefer to talk; we are affluent, but we do not safeguard those resources that can allow us to remain so and to foster the affluence of others. Reggio is so instructive in these respects. Where we are often intent to invoke slogans, the educators in Reggio work tirelessly to solve many of these fundamental—and fundamentally difficult—issues.

It is tempting to romanticize Reggio Emilia. It looks so beautiful, it works so well. That would be a mistake. It is clear from the essays in this book that Reggio has struggled much in the past and that, indeed, conflict can never be absent from the achievements of any dynamic entity. The relationships to the Catholic Church have not been easy; the political struggles at the municipal, provincial, and national levels never cease, and even the wonderful start achieved by the youngsters is threatened and perhaps undermined by a secondary and tertiary educational system that is far less innovative. Reggio is distinguished less by the fact that it has found permanent solutions to these problems—because, of course, it has not—than by the fact that it recognizes such dilemmas unblinkingly and continues to attempt to deal with them seriously and imaginatively.

No matter how ideal an educational model or system, it is always rooted in local conditions. One could no more transport the Diana School of Reggio to New England than one could transport John Dewey's New England schoolhouse to the fields of Emilia Romagna. But just as we can now have "museums without walls" that allow us to observe art work from all over our world, so, too, we can now have "schoolhouses without walls" that allow us to observe educational practices as they have developed around the globe.

I have had the privilege of visiting centers of early childhood education in many lands, and have learned much from what I have observed in these diverse setting. Like other educational tourists, I have been impressed by the stimulating children's museums in the big cities of the United States, the noncompetitive classroom environments in Scandinavia, the supportive and sensitive training of artistic skills in China, the well-orchestrated engagement of joint problem-solving activity in Japan, and the sincere efforts now underway in many lands to develop sensitivity in young children to diverse ethnic and racial groups. In its own way, each of these educational environments has to struggle with and find its own comfortable point of repose between the desires of the individual and the needs for the group; the training of skills and the cultivation of creativity; the respect for the family and the involvement in a wider community; attention to cognitive growth and concern with matters of temperament, feelings, and spirit.

There are many ways of mediating among these human impulses and strains. To my mind, no place in the contemporary world has succeeded so splendidly as the schools of Reggio Emilia. When the American magazine *Newsweek,* in typically understated fashion, chose "The Ten Best Schools in the World" in December 1991, it was entirely fitting that Reggio Emilia was its nominee in the Early Childhood category. Reggio epitomizes for me an education that is effective and humane; its students undergo a sustained apprenticeship in humanity, one that may last a lifetime.

Thanks to the efforts of Carolyn Edwards, Lella Gandini, and George Forman, this remarkable educational enterprise can now become better known within—and more effectively emulated by—the community of concerned citizens of our troubled world.

Difficult, zig-zag, intricate, important discussions. Drawing by 5 year-olds, Diana School.

Remarks: Malaguzzi's Story, Other Stories

David Hawkins

The extraordinary story told by Loris Malaguzzi, in his interview with Lella Gandini, has reminded me vividly of my first meeting with him. That was at the great Reggio Emilia conference of March 1990, when he spoke so incisively on the conference theme—the Potentials and Rights of Children. His story has reminded me also of other stories that have been told, or could be told, from different times and places. All speak of successful efforts to create new patterns of educational practice—patterns that can at least begin to match the manifold talents of young children. Most of these other successes have been limited in scale and often, sadly, in duration. Yet brought together, they spin a golden thread through many decades of adult neglect and preoccupation with other matters. Although education is among the oldest and most vital parts of human praxis, the successes typically have been supported only through a minority tradition, ignored by mainstream society, even by the mainstream of scientific curiosity and research. That this should be true is a paradox. Such a brilliant exception as the case of Reggio Emilia should, therefore, bring with it much joy.

I think it is worth reminding ourselves of a few of those other stories. Malaguzzi refers in passing to some of them, mainly to the theorists. Let me mention others. In the field of education, as in many others, good theory—I boldly say—has come mostly as a harvest, a reflection of successful practice.

Harvested from past practice, theory in turn can, then, bring new practical guidance. An outstanding example of this twofold relation was the part played by John Dewey.

In Dewey's time, almost a century ago, a minority tradition of excellent practice in childhood education already existed in the United States. That tradition had evolved, in turn, from the experience of the Froebel Kindergartens. My own mother received a basic part of her education in a Froebel Kindergarten during the 1870s, when the number of such schools in the United States grew by two or three orders of magnitude. Strong women teachers had been supported by Froebel's basic insight into the learning process, but had outgrown the quaint rigidity of his pioneering "system." (Something similar was true, later, of Montessori's influence.) The pioneering teachers involved in this development were looking for new theoretical recognition and guidance. They found it in John Dewey, already a deeply perceptive philosopher and psychologist. But they had to educate him first, a pupil of profound aptitude! Dewey's own practice was that of a university lecturer, deeply reflective but dry as dust except to those who already shared something of his spirit and insight. Although many contemporaries were profoundly moved by his clarity of understanding, his influence has largely been lost in my country as part of the attrition of childhood education. I am happy that this great educational philosopher is still alive and well in Italy. I associate his vitality most with the names of Lydia Tornatore and Nando Filograsso, among several others.

Looking further back, Froebel linked himself theoretically to Hegel; and for practice and commitment to his mentor, Johann Pestalozzi. Not far north of Reggio Emilia, but nearly two centuries ago, Pestalozzi rescued children tragically orphaned in the wake of Napoleon's armies, developing deep insight concerning the nurturance of their life and their talents.

Coming forward again in time, one sees that the fruition of this long development has been irregular. Its practical influences have grown also in Canada and in continental Europe, developing differently in Germany and the low countries, in France and Scandinavia. In the United States it was once powerful but has largely been co-opted by the schools, in which "Kindergarten," for the most part, survives in name only. This whole international story needs to be rescued. Here I shall only add a note about England, where their major developments had a history similar in some ways to that of the United States, starting also from 19th-century small beginnings under such influences as those of Froebel and, later, of Dewey and the McMillian sisters. Whereas in the United States this evolution suffered from neglect or rejection after World War II, in England it flourished. In some regions a large proportion of the Infant Schools (ages 5–7+) were radically transformed, as were smaller proportions of Junior Schools (ages 7–11+). Visitors to some of those good classrooms could find much to delight in and reflect on. Political idealogues, more recently, have suppressed or ignored these forward steps. But the new ways of learning and teaching have not been wholly reversed. They are successful, they persist, and one still can learn from them.

I mention this English phase of our joint history because it attracted great attention from many of us in the United States, suffering from the loss of our own best traditions. The result was a fashion, a seeking to emulate "the English Infant School." This was a kind of emulation that ignored a long history of development, a well-rooted tree that could not simply be put in an airplane and transported. We have our own very strong traditions, and we need to rescue them.

After this circuit of history I come back, finally, to the fascinating history of Reggio Emilia and the other Italian communities in which childhood education has similarly evolved and prospered. We who labor in this particular vineyard have much to learn from the history of Reggio and its still-evolving practice. An evolution with such communal support is an achievement that Americans, in particular, will carefully study. But it can be a great mistake for us, as it was in the case of our desire to emulate the English Infant Schools, to think that we can somehow just import the Reggio experience. By reputation we are prone to look for the "quick fix." Such an attitude would deprecate the very achievement it professes to admire. Among many other institutional and cultural differences, we in the United States do not know such solidarity, such sustaining communality, reshaping itself in the ways Malaguzzi describes, demanding better education for children. Our social landscape is different, so must our battles be.

Although many of us still lack acquaintance with the obvious profusion of Reggio practice, I hazard the opinion that we—we being the United States, England, and elsewhere—have contributions both to receive and to give. I shall mention particularly the practice of developing "projects" for children's inquiry and invention. It is similar to a strategy that we saw well developed, years ago, in California. Frances Hawkins (my co-author of these remarks) taught there and contributed to that strategy, often a great advance over dreary daily "lessons." When based in part on the interests some children revealed in play and discussion, such projects could enlist their commitment and enthusiasm. Yet fundamental questions still remained open: about the degree to which such enthusiasms might support, or merely mask, the more hidden and less developed talents of other children. To recognize and encourage these less articulate ones, on their diverse trajectories of learning, remains a constant challenge.

Such questions and challenges, we learned, must always permeate our intellectual curiosity about the earliest years of learning. We came to see the need to evolve a style of classroom practice that would support a greater simultaneous diversity of work than our project methods, even at their best, could easily maintain. Out of this more pluralistic and richer ambiance, ideas and inventions could, at times (although not often), be shared by all. Out of this sharing, projects did indeed sometimes evolve, with great vitality. But the definition and duration of these projects was always a dependent and restricted variable.

I mention this specific topic—projects—because as I read the very open and charming reflections of Loris Malaguzzi, I thought not only of the wider history of childhood education, but also about the details, the debate, the problems, that must have been involved at every step. I have tried to suggest, as an example, that the etiology and uses of the "project" may still be in that problematic state. For our own benefit, we need to know more of the debate, the retrospective valuations, the successive approximations. We need to join in the debate!

In the meantime, it is quite enough that we salute the achievement and devotion revealed in this remarkable story of a devoted teacher-theorist and a devoted community.

part I

Starting Points

Invece il cento c'é

Il bambino
é fatto di cento.
Il bambino ha
cento lingue
cento mani
cento pensieri
cento modi di pensare
di giocare e di parlare
cento sempre cento
modi di ascoltare
di stupire di amare
cento allegrie
per cantare a capire
cento mondi
da scoprire
cento mondi
da inventare
cento mondi
da sognare.
Il bambino ha
cento lingue
(e poi cento cento cento)
ma gliene rubano novantanove.
La scuola e la cultura
gli separano la testa dal corpo.
Gli dicono:
di pensare senza mani
di fare senza testa
di ascoltare e di non parlare
di capire senza allegrie
di amare e di stupirsi
solo a Pasqua e a Natale.
Gli dicono:
di scoprire il mondo che già c'é
e di cento
gliene rubano novantanove.
Gli dicone:
che il gioco e il lavoro
la realtà e la fantasia
la scienza e l'immaginazione
il cielo e la terra
la ragione e il sogno
sono cose
che non stanno insieme.

Gli dicono insomma
che il cento non c'é.
Il bambino dice:
invece il cento c'é.

Loris Malaguzzi

No way. The hundred *is* there.*

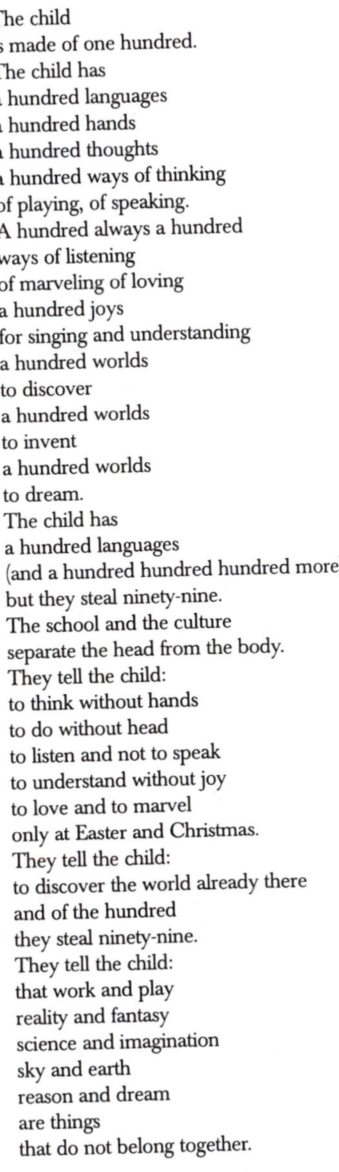

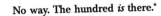

The child
is made of one hundred.
The child has
a hundred languages
a hundred hands
a hundred thoughts
a hundred ways of thinking
of playing, of speaking.
A hundred always a hundred
ways of listening
of marveling of loving
a hundred joys
for singing and understanding
a hundred worlds
to discover
a hundred worlds
to invent
a hundred worlds
to dream.
The child has
a hundred languages
(and a hundred hundred hundred more)
but they steal ninety-nine.
The school and the culture
separate the head from the body.
They tell the child:
to think without hands
to do without head
to listen and not to speak
to understand without joy
to love and to marvel
only at Easter and Christmas.
They tell the child:
to discover the world already there
and of the hundred
they steal ninety-nine.
They tell the child:
that work and play
reality and fantasy
science and imagination
sky and earth
reason and dream
are things
that do not belong together.

And thus they tell the child
that the hundred is not there.
The child says:
No way. The hundred *is* there.

—LORIS MALAGUZZI

* Translated by Lella Gandini

Horse and rider.
Drawing by 5 year-olds,
Anna Frank School.

chapter I

Introduction: Background and Starting Points

Carolyn Edwards
Lella Gandini
George Forman

Reggio Emilia is a small city in northern Italy that shines with a bright light for what it has accomplished and what it stands for in the field of education. For the past 30 years, educators, working together with parents and citizens, have built a public system of child care and education long recognized as a center of innovation in Europe, and now increasingly recognized as a point of reference and a resource and inspiration to educators in the United States and throughout the world (Cohen, 1992; Corsaro & Emiliani, 1992; Kamerman & Kahn, 1994; *Newsweek*, Dec. 2, 1991; New, 1993; Pistillo, 1989; Ross, 1982; Saltz, 1976; U.S. Government Accounting Office, 1995). Programs combine the concepts of social services and education. Children from all socioeconomic and educational backgrounds attend, with children with disabilities receiving first priority and full mainstreaming following Italian national law. Over 10% of the city budget goes to support this early childhood system, which at present includes 13 infant–toddler centers (for children 4 months–3 years) and 19 preprimary schools (for children 3–6), serving, respectively, 47% and 35% of the two age groups.

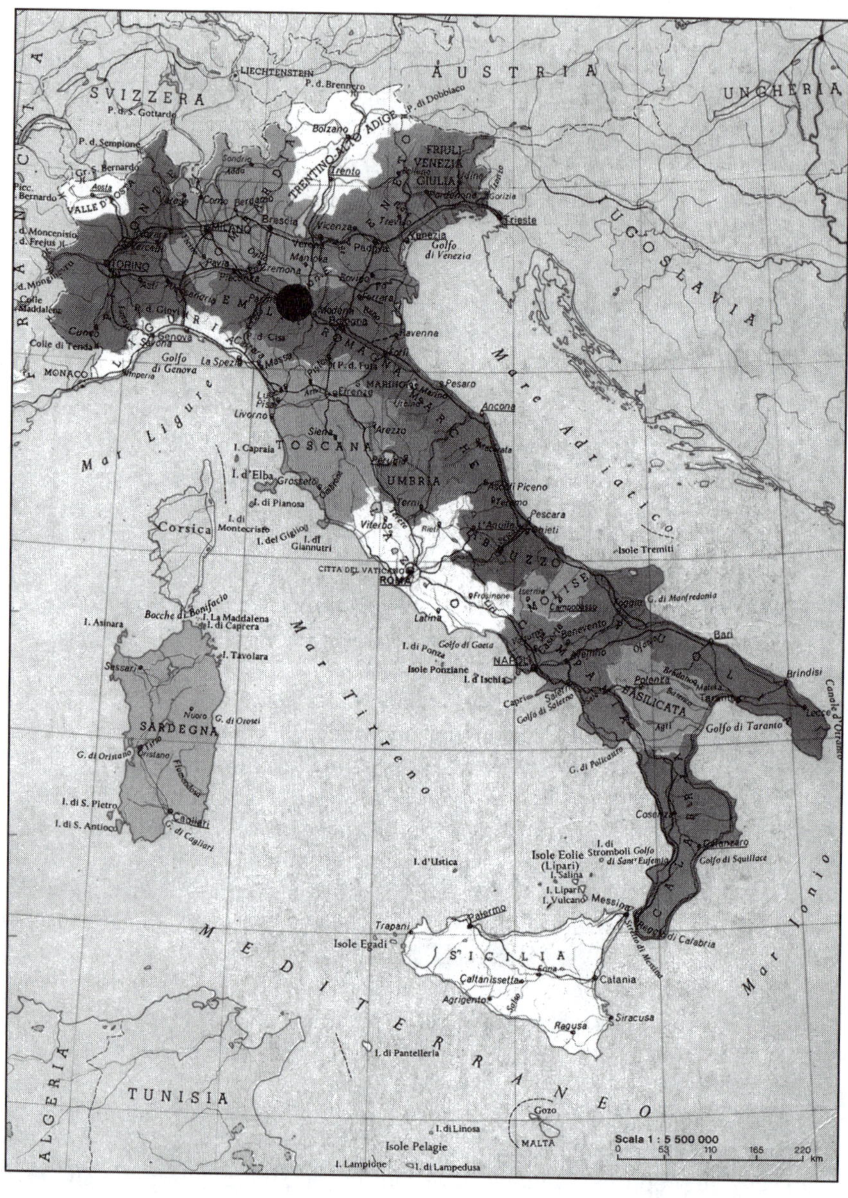

FIGURE 1.1. Map of Italy with indication of the city of Reggio Emilia.

THE REGGIO EMILIA APPROACH

Over more than the past 30 years, this system has evolved its own distinctive and innovative set of philosophical and pedagogical assumptions, methods of school organization, and principles of environmental design that, taken as a unified whole, we are calling *the Reggio Emilia approach.* This approach fosters children's intellectual development through a systematic focus on symbolic representation. Young children are encouraged to explore their environment and express themselves through all of their available "expressive, communicative, and cognitive languages," whether they be words, movement, drawing, painting, building, sculpture, shadow play, collage, dramatic play, or music, to name a few. From the beginning, there has been an explicit recognition of the relationship or partnership among parents, educators, and children. Classrooms are organized to support a highly collaborative problem-solving approach to learning. Other important features are the use of small groups in project learning, teacher–child continuity (two co-teachers work with the same class group for 3 years), and the community-based management method of governance. In Reggio Emilia, education is seen as a communal activity and sharing of culture through joint exploration among children and adults who together open topics to speculation and discussion. The approach provides us with new ways to think about the nature of the child as learner, the role of the teacher, school organization and management, the design and use of physical environments, and cur-

FIGURE 1.2. One of the main squares in the city of Reggio Emilia.

riculum planning that guides experiences of joint, open-ended discovery and constructive posing and solving of problems. Because of all these features, the Reggio Emilia approach is important and exciting to Americans.

A DISTINCTIVE CITY AND REGION

The Reggio Emilia approach to early childhood education is founded on a distinctive, coherent, evolving set of assumptions and perspectives drawn from three important intellectual traditions: European and American strands of *progressive education*, Piagetian and Vygotskian *constructivist psychologies*, and Italian postwar *left-reform politics*. All of these are blended together with elements of past and present history and culture, such as the strong regional traditions of participatory democracy; that is, citizen alliances for solidarity and cooperation. A word frequently heard in discussions among Reggio educators is *civile* ("civil"), and the child is understood to have rights to "civility," "civilization," and "civic conscience." It is important to understand at the outset, therefore, what is special about Reggio Emilia and its surrounding region of Emilia Romagna. Reggio Emilia is known throughout Italy as a livable city, with characteristically low unemployment and crime, high prosperity, honest and effective local government institutions, and ample, high-quality social services (Bohlen, 1995). The Emilia Romagna region, in which the city is located, has been found to have a very high level of civic community—citizens bound together by horizontal relations of social solidarity, reciprocity, and cooperation, as opposed to vertical relations of authority and dependency (Putnam, 1993). Putnam collected data revealing that among the 20 regions of Italy, Emilia Romagna has the highest levels of citizen responsibility and basic trust in local institutions and office-holders (as evidenced by high voter turnouts, newspaper readership, and membership in clubs and associations). Popular concepts of participatory democracy assert that people can and should speak out "as protagonists" on behalf of themselves and their group, on the basis of their own experience and at their own level of consciousness (Hellman, 1987). Citizens revere their traditions of mass organization and people across social class lines come together to solve social problems by means of political parties and economic cooperatives (agricultural, marketing, credit, labor, producer, and consumer unions and cooperatives). These collectivist tendencies are not of recent origin, but rather trace back to the craft guilds and communal republics of the 12th century; they are a strong source of identity and pride to the people of the Emilia Romagna region, in general, and the city of Reggio Emilia, in particular. Clearly, ideas about participatory democracy and civic community are fundamental to what the educators in Reggio Emilia feel about their educational vision and mission (Edwards, 1995).

TABLE 1.1. Schedules and Staffing of the Preprimary Schools in Reggio Emilia

Typical preprimary school composition	
Classrooms	3
Children	75
Teachers	6
Altelierista	1
Cook	1
Auxiliary Staff	4

Typical children's annual calendar	
Opening	September 1
Closing	June 30

Typical staff's annual calendar	
First day of service	Aug. 23
Last day of service	Jul. 5

Summer service
One preprimary school is open during the month of July.

Hours open	
Monday to Friday	8 a.m.–4 p.m.
Extended day service: 7:30–8:00 a.m. & 4:00–6:20 p.m.	

Staff's daily schedule	
1st shift teacher	8:00 a.m.–1:48 p.m.
2nd shift teacher	8:27 a.m.–4:00 p.m.
Altlierista	8:30 a.m.–3:33 p.m.
Cook	7:45 a.m.–2:54 p.m.
1st auxiliary staff	8:30 a.m.–4:03 p.m.
2nd auxiliary staff	9:00 a.m.–4:03 p.m.
Others	12:30 p.m.–6:54 p.m.

Staff's weekly meetings	
36 hours a week of which:	
30	hours spent with children
4½	hours for meetings, planning, and inservice training
1½	hours for documentation and analysis

Adapted from: "An Historical Outline, Data, and Information," page 21, published by the Municipality of Reggio Emilia, Department of Education, 1996. Reprinted by permission.

THE INSPIRATION OF THE EXHIBIT

This book takes it name, *The Hundred Languages of Children,* from the grand exhibit conceived by Loris Malaguzzi and his closest coworkers as a visual documentary on their work in progress and its effects on children. "The Hundred Languages" Exhibit,[1] on tour in the United States since 1987, is a beautiful and

[1] The exhibition and the accompanying catalog (*The Hundred Languages of Children: Narrative of the Possible,* 1987) are the property and publication of the Region of Emilia Romagna and the City of Reggio Emilia, Department of Education. A new, expanded catalog (1996) is available from Reggio Children USA along with a videotape to accompany and introduce the exhibit by Lyon (1995). (see Additional Resouces at the end of this volume).

intriguing display that narrates an educational story and weaves together experiences, reflections, debates, theoretical premises, and the social and ethical ideals of many generations of teachers, children, and parents. It describes and illustrates the philosophy and pedagogy of the Reggio Emilia approach, through photographs depicting moments of teaching and learning; explanatory scripts and panels (many containing texts of children's words); and samples of children's paintings, drawings, collages, and constructions. As a medium of communication, the exhibit is wonderfully suited to occasions such as meetings, conferences, and workshops, where people meet face to face and are able to open themselves up in a full, intense, and focused way to the story that the Reggio Emilia educators want to tell. Created by the Reggio educators to inform both public and professional audiences, the exhibit in several ways exemplifies the very essence of the educational approach.

First of all, the exhibit was authored and designed not individually, but collectively. Loris Malaguzzi, founder and for many years Director of the Reggio Emilia system of municipal early childhood education, led the task of preparing the exhibit, but (demonstrating the quality of results coming from group effort) many of the administrators and teachers from throughout the city contributed time, labor, ideas, and the results of recording project work in their classrooms. Reggio educators believe, as we shall see in detail, that reciprocity, exchange, and dialogue lie at the heart of successful education.

Second, the exhibit plunges the visitor into a form of learning that is multileveled and multimodal. Looking at the large, highly detailed panels, densely embedded with words and images, the mind and senses are overwhelmed with information and impressions coming in on multiple channels all at once. This gives visitors the immediate and tangible experience of learning through "one hundred languages." As Malaguzzi (1984) put it, the exhibit creates "a place of uninterrupted condensation of hundreds of subjective and objective experiences" (pp. 20/22).

Third, wandering at will through the exhibit, visitors find themselves on a circular path as they retrace their steps and return repeatedly to favorite panels or themes, each time with deeper understanding. In just this way, education in Reggio Emilia is anything but linear; it is, instead, an open-ended spiral. Young children are not marched or hurried sequentially from one different activity to the next, but instead they are encouraged to repeat key experiences, observe and reobserve, consider and reconsider, represent and rerepresent.

Fourth, the exhibit as a form of communication grew directly out of what Reggio Emilia educators call *documentation*. Early in their history (Malaguzzi, this volume Chapter 3), the educators realized that systematically documenting the process and results of their work with children would simultaneously serve three key functions: It would provide the children with a concrete and visible "memory" of what they said and did in order to serve as a jumping-off point for next steps in learning; provide the educators with a tool for research and a key

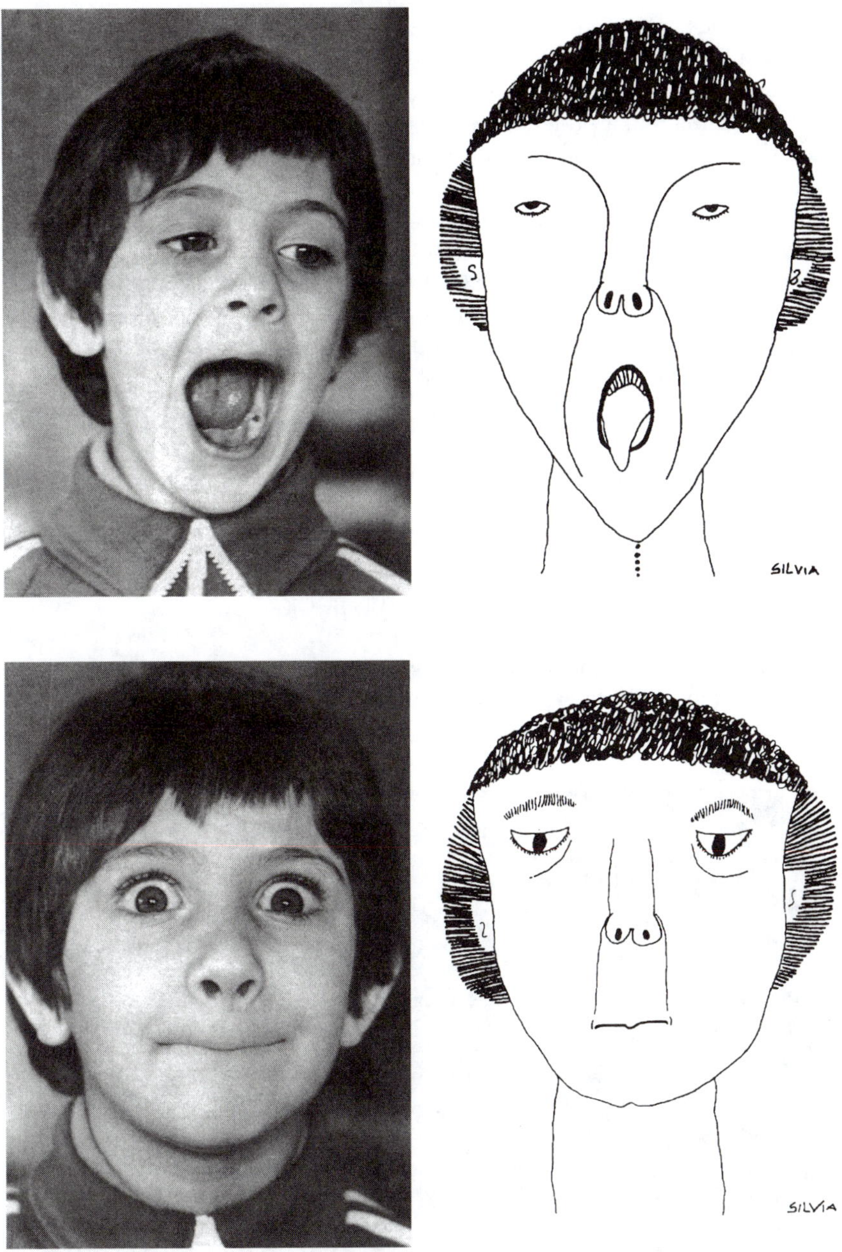

FIGURE 1.3. From the exhibit The Hundred Languages of Children, The importance of looking at ourselves. Silva says: "When I look at myself it is as if I saw another child."

to continuous improvement and renewal; and provide parents and the public with detailed information about what happens in the schools, as a means of eliciting their reactions and support. This bold insight led to the development of documentation into a professional art form in Reggio Emilia, involving use of slide shows, posters, short books, and increasingly, videotapes, to record children's project experiences.

Finally, the exhibit is never completed; it never reaches a state at which the Reggio educators say, "Now, it is perfect." Instead, it undergoes transformations and emerges in one after another versions or editions. The first opened in 1981 and began to travel in Europe under the name, *L'Occhio se Salta il Muro* ("When the Eye Jumps Over the Wall"). The title became *I Cento Linguaggi dei Bambini* ("The Hundred Languages of Children") for the third, fourth, and fifth editions. In just such a way, the educational work in Reggio Emilia never becomes set and routine but instead is always undergoing reexamination and experimentation. For this reason, the Reggio educators refuse the term *model* when talking about their approach, and instead speak of "our project" and "our experience."

THE NEED FOR THIS BOOK

Yet, the exhibit does not accomplish everything. Unlike a book, it cannot be taken home for study and reflection. It cannot answer all of our questions about the history and philosophy of the program; curriculum, planning, and teacher

FIGURE 1.4. Loris Malaguzzi, Sergio Spaggiari and Carlina Rinaldi receive the first copies of the first edition of this book from Lella Gandini.

behavior; work with parents, including those whose children have disabilities; and the administrative organization and structure. Thus, the need for this book was born. It allows for a more extended and analytic treatment of the Reggio Emilia approach in all of its aspects, and it provides a forum for both Italians and North Americans to tell what they know about the Reggio Emilia approach.

The first edition, published in 1993, was intended to be a starting point, and it has succeeded in initiating discussions, introducing readers to the fundamental points of the Reggio Emilia approach, and describing first steps in using and adapting it in this country. Yet, already since 1993, there has been such an upsurge of American interest and such a deepening of reflections about the Reggio approach, as well as increased sophistication in adaptations and applications to the American context, that the need for this second edition became apparent. A measure of the deepening critical reflection and advanced work of adapting and applying insights from Reggio Emilia can be seen in the fact that in Part IV, The Extension of the Reggio Emilia Approach into American Classrooms, all but two of the chapters are entirely new. Another index of the growing interest and involvement can be seen in the new list of Additional Resources at the end of the volume, which has not only tripled in length but also has additional new subsections covering books, slide sets, electronic discussion groups, and dissertations and theses, in addition to articles and chapters, video resources, the exhibit, and the newsletter. Preparing this edition, in turn, allowed our Italian colleagues to respond to the intervening years of contact and dialogue with Americans, by revisiting and revising or expanding their original chapters and making possible new interviews that directly introduce parents' experiences and perspectives and describe more fully ways of working with the parents and children with disabilities.

And yet, as the reader will see, although the Reggio Emilia approach has become widely known in the United States, it has not become just a slogan or formula, a recipe or commercial commodity, a fad or fashion. It has not (indeed, cannot) be thought of as any kind of quick fix, because quick fixes never work in education, and moreover, programs and models from overseas can never be transplanted wholesale from one cultural context to another without extensive change and adaptation. Instead, what we have seen and learned in Reggio Emilia has become a source of energy and inspiration, as we wrestle with our own continuing problems of public school reform and uneven quality, poor coordination, and lack of access and affordability of other kinds of early childhood services. The discourse about the Reggio Emilia experience has entered our pool of common referents and become a source of powerful terms (such as *reconnaissance, documentation, progettazione, image of the child, education as relationship, revisiting, cognitive knots*) as we develop our own shared vocabulary and set of exemplars for talking and arguing in ever more productive ways about theory and practice in education.

THE AUTHORS AND THEIR CHAPTERS

The American Network

This book represents a combined effort by many individuals and groups. First there is the introductory chapter by the editors, who originally worked together on the exhibit and conference, "The Hundred Languages of Children," held at the University of Massachusetts in Amherst in December 1988. It was during and immediately after this conference that Carolyn Edwards proposed that we collaborate to edit a book about the municipal preprimary schools of Reggio Emilia—the first book of its kind. We felt that we had complementary strengths that would yield a useful and significant book. Carolyn Edwards, who also helped host the 1993 exhibit in Lexington, Kentucky, has an extensive background in cultural anthropology and social development, and for many years directed the early childhood laboratory school at the University of Massachusetts. Lella Gandini, bridge to the Italian culture and its people, has consulted to many early childhood systems in Italy, including Reggio Emilia, and has a strong background in art education as well as early childhood education. George Forman has studied constructivism from the beginning of the Piagetian movement in the late 1960s and founded the School for Constructive Play in Amherst, Massachusetts. All three of us had the fortunate opportunity to observe and study these schools during many trips to Reggio Emilia: Lella for more than 20 years, Carolyn since 1983, and George since 1985.

As we worked on the exhibit and conference in Amherst, in collaboration with our Italian friends, we formed a broader network of educators whose work is presented in this book. Major networks have also been established by Baji Rankin, host of the 1989 exhibit in Boston, Massachusetts, and leader of delegations to Reggio Emilia; by Rebecca New, host of the 1988 exhibit in Syracuse, New York, and leader of other delegations; by Rosalyn and Eli Saltz, hosts of the 1991 exhibit in Detroit, Michigan, and founders of the newsletter, *Innovations in Early Education: The International Reggio Exchange,* edited by Patricia Weissman and Judy Kaminsky; and by many others. Brenda Fyfe, host of the 1991–1992 exhibit in St. Louis, Missouri, has with Louise Cadwell and Jan Phillips, codirected a Danforth Foundation Grant to bring the Reggio Emilia approach to teachers in the greater St. Louis area; three sites have now formed the St. Louis-Reggio Collaborative for the Study and Adaption of the Reggio Approach, a place of study for those wishing to study the Reggio approach in the American context. Pamela Houk, who hosted the 1991 exhibit in Dayton, Ohio, serves as Exhibit Curator, assuring quality and educational installments at the many sites of the exhibit. Angela Ferrario has organized and led, with professional and personal care, several study tours for groups of US educators. Eva Tarini, along with Baji Rankin and Louise Cadwell, was one of three Americans to spend a year-long internship in Reggio. Ann Lewin hosted the

1990 exhibit in Washington, DC, and founded the Model Early Learning Center, which was from 1994 to 1996 certified as a reference school by REGGIO CHILDREN S.r.l., International Center for the defense and promotion of the rights and potential of all children. Carol Brunson Phillips and Sue Bredekamp have helped to bring the Reggio approach into the huge professional circle of the National Association for the Education of Young Children (NAEYC) as well as helping to establish Reggio Children USA, under the auspices of the Council for Early Childhood Professional Recognition in Washington, DC.

The Flow of Chapter Topics

Howard Gardner and David Hawkins, distinguished educators whose reflections in the Foreword and Remarks invite the reader into this book, have each been honored guests in Reggio Emilia.This chapter is intended to provide necessary historical background on the book and on the early childhood system in Reggio Emilia. Lilian Katz, a world traveler and past President of the National Association for the Education of Young Children, can better than anyone point out lessons to be learned from the experience of Reggio Emilia. In Chapter 2, she compares and contrasts these ideas with aims and principles she has discovered to be true of education in the United States, where she has been a professional leader since the days of compensatory education in the late 1960s.

Beginning with Part II, we turn quickly to what the Italians say about themselves. What distinguishes this section is that the chapters are written as interviews with the authors. Not only did this process expedite the completion of each chapter, but the interview format itself indicates that this book resulted from lengthy and in-depth dialogue with our Italian colleagues.

The lead chapter in this section (Chapter 3) presents an interview with Loris Malaguzzi, founder of the municipal early childhood system in Reggio Emilia. It is welcoming that Malaguzzi took the first edition of this book as an opportunity to write, for the first time, a comprehensive review of his life's work and the history of the municipal early childhood system in Reggio Emilia. With his passing in January 1994, we dedicate this book to his memory and vision. In the second edition, we have added a new piece about projects and about representation. Sergio Spaggiari, the next director of the municipal early childhood system, lays out (Chapter 4) the organizational structure and how it functions. He has added commentary on recent trends in parent participation and the social fabric of quality education. Carlina Rinaldi, the first *pedagogista* (pedagogical coordinator) to work with Loris Malaguzzi in curriculum theory, explains (Chapter 5) the constructivist base of *progettezione* and documentation, particularly their foundation in observation, dialogue, communication, and joint problem-solving at all levels of the system. Tiziana Filippini, whose fluency in English comes from a high school study abroad experience spent in

Oklahoma, explains in an expanded and clarified Chapter 6 the role and rationale for the *pedagogista* (pedagogical coordinator), a level of staffing uncommon in the United States. The *pedagogista* links the systems of schools and parents into a coherent whole in terms of values, educational objectives, and a shared image of the competent child. Likewise, Vea Vecchi, one of the original *atelieristi* (resource teacher), explains (Chapter 7) how the presence of the *atelier* (studio/workshop) makes possible mutual support with teachers and a deepening of the learning by means of the use of many diverse media and avenues of learning, expression, and communication. Chapter 8, based on a new interview with parents by Lella Gandini, allows parents to give direct testimony of their commitment toward and sense of benefits received from participating in these municipal schools.

Part III, From Theory to Practice, contains chapters by authors who analyze the specifics of classroom practice in Reggio Emilia. This analysis draws from principles avowed by the Reggio teachers or implied by their practice. The chapters lay out these principles in the American idiom and theoretical constructs. Lella Gandini (Chapter 9) describes the way that school environments in Reggio have been built to maximize quality of social encounters and the relation between the local space and its surrounding community. She reminds us that environments are "read" by their users and carry potent messages about our images of children. Carolyn Edwards (Chapter 10), through her video-ethnographic research on teacher behavior and meaning systems in Reggio Emilia, describes the multiple roles of the teacher and presents commentary on transcripts of actual teacher–child interactions. She helps us understand the finesse of teaching based on listening and entering a partnership with children. Cathleen Smith (Chapter 11) interviewed Ivana Soncini, the *pedagogista* for special education. She provides us with information about inclusion as a policy and practice in Reggio Emilia, including the observations of herself and Sharon Palsha, another North American expert in early childhood special education. Baji Rankin (Chapter 12) walks us through a long-term project conducted at the Anna Frank School. As she describes how children are challenged to plan and build a dinosaur 9 feet tall, she reveals the processes of children learning about measurment, as well as the social implications of such a project. George Forman and Brenda Fyfe (Chapter 13) present a synthesis of Italian and American ideas that they call *negotiated learning,* to signify that knowledge is never received, but instead negotiated through a co-constructive process. Rebecca New (Chapter 14) renews the discussion of the social basis of constructivism as a philosophy of education in Reggio Emilia. The final chapter in Part III (Chapter 15) is a lyrical piece by Paul Kaufman, a video producer, who spent a week in Reggio Emilia with his film crew talking with Malaguzzi, conveying his insights on children's power to create images and filming the children exploring the poppy fields—all captured for a segment of the Public Broadcasting System television series *The Creative Spirit.*

In Part IV, we shift to American authors who have applied their respective interpretations of Reggio Emilia in the United States. John Nimmo (Chapter 16) opens the section with a series of reflections about the cultural assumptions that can blind educators to the true potential for community in early childhood settings, and for young children to be active contributors to those communities. Rebecca Kantor and Kimberlee Whately (Chapter 17) suggest how their thinking was changed by visits to Reggio Emilia and how these insights have been used in project work with preschool children (including toddlers) at The Ohio State University laboratory preschool. Ann Lewin and her collaborators (Chapter 18) present the history and messages of one of the most successful and complete adaptations of Reggio Emilia in the United States, constructed with the strong support by Amelia Gambetti who consulted there for three years, at the Model Early Learning Center in Washington, DC. The chapter documents the change process that a program undergoes as transforming new methods are introduced. In Chapter 19, George Forman, Moonja Lee, and four teachers from an elementary school in Amherst, Massachusetts, transform a well-known project from Reggio Emilia, "The City in the Rain," into a New England version, "The City in the Snow," addressing cycles of symbolization to highlight how children need to revisit concepts to broaden and deepen their understanding. In this chapter and the next, we see the upward extension of American interpretations of Reggio principles into the elementary years. Eva Tarini and Lynn White (Chapter 20) apply their insights from Reggio Emilia to work with first graders at the Crow Island School in Winnetka, Illinois, and discuss a reflective activity and a project about fathers' jobs. The final three chapters turn our attention to work with adults. Mary Jane Moran (Chapter 21) extends principles of project work and documentation to the college level where she works with preservice teachers at the University of New Hampshire laboratory preschool. Brenda Fyfe, Louise Cadwell, and Jan Phillips (Chapter 22) report on their ambitious and successful project adapting Reggio principles to professional and staff development in St. Louis. This chapter shows how change needs a professional development plan, designed over time by the very teachers seeking to change their practice. Finally, Carol Brunson Phillips and Sue Bredekamp (Chapter 23) discuss how their growing knowledge of early education in Reggio Emilia has provoked them to reconsider their views on program practice, professional development, and policy. They bring us this perspective from their positions at the national level in Washington, DC.

THE HISTORICAL CONTEXT OF THE REGGIO APPROACH

As we begin to turn to the experience of children and adults in Reggio Emilia, we need to place this experience in perspective, to inquire into the context that made it possible for this educational approach to come together. Doing so will help us better understand those factors that are common to other educational programs in Italy, those that pertain to the Emilia Romagna region, and those that are unique products of the dedication and vision of the educators of Reggio Emilia.

Historically, early education in Italy has been caught in the tangled web of relations between church and state. The enormous power conflicts between the centuries-old Catholic Church and the young Italian state (formed only in 1860) have affected many modern outcomes, including early childhood education.

Around 1820 in the northern and central parts of Italy, charitable institutions began to emerge. These were offshoots of a concern for the poor, emerging throughout Europe at that time, with the intention of improving the lives of the urban populace, reducing crime, and forming better citizens (Cambi & Ulivieri, 1988). For young children, there came into being institutions that were, to some extent, forerunners to the two major public early education programs currently offered in Italy: the infant–toddler centers (*asili nido*, or "safe nests"), serving infants aged 4 months to 3 years; and preprimary schools (*scuole dell'infanzia*, or "schools of infancy"), serving children 3 to 6 years old.

The Infant–Toddler Centers *(Asili Nido)*

The early forerunners to the modern infant–toddler centers were crèches *(presepi)* for breast-fed or newly weaned infants of working mothers. Industrialists set these up at their factories. For example, in Pinerolo, Piedmont, one was started in the silk mill, where the cradles were rocked by the mill's hydraulic engine. Other similar institutions were promoted by the public administrations of the small, separate states that shared the Italian peninsula prior to unification. Still others resulted from initiatives by private benefactors (Della Peruta, 1980).

After the unification of the Italian state, these institutions continued to develop, but with difficulties. It was only toward the beginning of the 20th century that some of the private initiatives began to be supported by public funding, mostly municipal. The idea was to move away from charitable assistance, dispensed only by private means, toward programs combining prevention and assistance and funded by both private and public sectors. For example, next to crèches or shelters for infants there would be a center for dispensing medical instruction and help to mothers with the goal of educating them on child care and reducing infant mortality. All these initiatives eventually culminated in 1925 in the passage of a national law for the "Protection and Assistence of Infancy," which provided for the National Organization for Maternity and Infancy (ONMI). This organization was to expand and organize infant centers under the Ministry of the Interior.

The Fascist regime, which had taken over Italy in 1922, took upon itself all the merits of this innovation, still trying to keep alive the connection with private, philanthropic support. ONMI centers adopted a medical-hygenic model of child care, which was the prevailing trend of the time, and took up the Fascist ideology of motherhood, which in turn was tied to the regime's policy of population growth. Rosalyn Saltz (1976) visited ONMI centers in Rome in 1975 and subsequently remarked, "Psycho-social aspects of an infant's development are assumed to be adequately served if the psychological atmosphere of the center is not harsh, if children are not in obvious distress and if caregivers appear to be reasonably fond of children" (p.130).

The ONMI organization remained in place with some ideological changes for 50 years, even through the social upheavals of the 1960s and early 1970s. In December 1971, however, major national legislation to institute a new kind of infant–toddler center was finally passed, drawing on the strong support of labor unions and the women's movement. In December 1975, the 604 ONMI centers across Italy were officially transferred to city administrations (Lucchini, 1980).

The new law (Law 1044) instituted social and educational services for children under 3 years of age, with the dual goals of ensuring adequate assistance to families and facilitating women's entry into the workplace. Law 1044 further stated that families were to apply for services and make partial financial contributions, but the assistance was a matter of public (as opposed to purely private) interest. During the 1970s and 1980s, as employment opportunities for women increased throughout Italy, infant–toddler services began to be seen by many as a right of every working family. In fact, in locations where the services developed particularly well, they further came to be seen as a quality benefit for children in addition to a service to parents.

Law 1044 made the 20 regional governments of Italy responsible for carrying out the legislation and gave municipal governments the task of establishing standards and regulations, making requests for funds, and constructing and organizing the infant–toddler centers. Inevitably, the network of centers developed in an uneven way across the regions of Italy, influenced by political choices, views about women's roles, financial resources, and norms of administrative effectiveness. Similarly, the law's interpretation and implementation has also varied across municipalities. For example, cities differ in how they have set fee scales and prioritized admission criteria based on maternal employment, family income, and presence of extended family support. By 1986, a total of 1,904 infant–toddler centers had been built, serving some 99,000 children (about 6% of Italian children under age 3), with the lowest percentage (0.7%) in the Campania region of southern Italy, and the highest (19.2%) in Emilia Romagna (Musatti, 1992). In the municipality of Reggio Emilia (where the first infant–toddler center was opened in 1970, in advance of Law 1044), the number of children under 3 who are served reaches 30%.

Since the late 1980s, a general financial crisis has afflicted the economies of Europe, with large budget deficits, unemployment, and lower rates of growth. In the face of diminished financial and political capital to spend on behalf of children, the European Community has established a study committee to assess needs. This committee has elaborated four major objectives, concerning: (a) adequate and assessible services for children, (b) parental leave for working mothers and fathers, (c) reforms in the workplace to support families, and (d) programs to promote more equal sharing of child care between men and women (Ghedini, 1992).

Likewise in Italy, budget crises have led to a reassessment of services for children under 3. Committed educators and policymakers have become concerned that in spite of research pointing to the benefits of quality child care for both children and families, the current trend is once again for responsibility for children's care and education to be put on the shoulders of mothers—mothers who are now also likely to be wage-earners. Responsible administrations have protected their infant–toddler services (indeed, some municipalities are even continuing to add some new centers), but the debate has at least created new awareness about parents' variety of needs in a time of social transformation and the necessity for rationalizing all public expenditures. Building on the knowledge and experience gained in the past, educators and administrators have found ways to offer new types of services. Especially in regions such as Tuscany, Lombardy, Emilia Romagna, and Umbria, some promising innovations offer new kinds of flexibility (e.g., serving parents with part-time as well as full-time needs), and new ways to build on the participation and competence of parents and grandparents.

The Preprimary Schools *(Scuole dell'Infanzia)*

The contemporary preprimary schools also have deep roots in the 19th century. One institution, devoted to children aged 2 to 6 years old and considered outstanding, was founded by Abbot Ferrante Aporti in 1831 in the city of Cremona. Teaching and learning were important there, and play was often replaced by crafts for little boys and domestic activities for little girls (Della Peruta, 1980). After 1867, the influence of Froebel's Kindergarten started to take root. At the beginning of the 20th century, as Italy became industrialized and the Socialist Party, with its progressive agenda, emerged and grew, the needs of working women and the care and education of children came into focus. Progressive educators became involved in early childhood education. Pistillo (1989) described the years around 1904 to 1913 as particularly fertile for early childhood education. During this period, a national law established a teacher training school to prepare teachers of young children. The sisters Rosa and Carolina Agazzi developed a new philosophy and method of early education. Maria Montessori founded her first Children's House in Rome.

However, the Italian Ministry of Education did not directly assist the growth of preprimary education; and while initiative remained in the private sector, it became increasingly controlled by the Roman Catholic church. After 1922, the Fascist regime dismissed Montessori Education and promoted only those school reforms compatible with Church monopoly and control. The Agazzi method, favored by the Catholic church, was proclaimed the official state method for the education of young children. In 1933, at the height of Facism, over 60% of preprimary schools were run by religious orders (Olmstead & Weikart, 1994; Pistillo, 1989).

By the postwar period, however, after all of the years under Fascism, people were ready for change. In 1945–1946, for a short period right after World War II, people took many initiatives into their own hands. The national government was undergoing reorganization. It was in this very period that, in localities with a strong tradition of local initiative, there arose spontaneous attempts to establish parent-run schools, such as Loris Malaguzzi (Chapter 3) describes so vividly for Reggio Emilia.

By the 1950s, many educators and parents had become aware of the critical need for more and better early childhood education. They also knew that the dominant Christian Democratic Party had no intention of changing the status of early childhood education. New ideas about education were entering Italy: the "popular school" movement coming from France; the newly translated writings of progressive educators such as Celestin Freinet and John Dewey. A feverish debate fed people's determination to change education at all levels. In 1951, the Movement of Cooperative Education (MCE) was formed. This organization of elementary teachers had the goal of applying the techniques of Freinet; they achieved cooperation through an Italian style of critical debate. The leader of the MCE was a charismatic educator named Bruno Ciari, who was invited by the left-wing administration of Bologna to organize and direct their city school system. Indeed, it was only in cities with left-wing administrations that progressive municipal early childhood systems were establised in the 1960s and 1970s. In cities in which the centrist Christian Democratic Party was dominant, the Catholic church's monopoly on early education tended to prevail.

Ciari suggested many educational innovations, both in his writings and through the meetings he organized for teachers in Bologna. Like others in the MCE, he was convinced that a more just society could be achieved through the right kind of early childhood education. His books became classics.

The build-up of energy, enthusiasm, and thoughtful concern generated the take-off of early childhood education in Italy. The debates initiated by Ciari activated people, and in turn helped Ciari formulate many of his key ideas. Loris Malaguzzi participated in these lively debates; through them he came to know Ciari. Deeply inspired by Ciari, Malaguzzi (Chapter 3) recalled him as a fabulous friend and as "the most lucid, passionate and acute intelligence in the field of childhood education." The group around Ciari declared the beliefs that education should liberate childhood energy and capacities and promote the harmonious development of the whole child in all areas—communicative, social, affective, and with respect to critical and scientific thinking. Ciari (1961) urged educators to develop relationships with families and encourage participatory committees of teachers, parents, and citizens. He argued there should be two rather than one teacher in each classroom, and that teachers and staff should work collectively, without hierarchy. He thought children should be grouped by age for part of the day, but mix openly during another part, and he wanted to limit the number of children per classroom to 20. Finally, he gave much attention to the physical setting of education (Ciari, 1972).

In 1967 there appeared an explosive pamphlet, *Letter to a Teacher*, by the Scuola di Barbiana. This was a passionate but solidly documented denunciation of selectivity and social class discrimination in the national school system. Widely quoted, the *Letter* became a manifesto in the fight for educational reform. In 1968, the student movement erupted; students occupied the universities and demonstrated in the streets. The next year saw mass mobilization of workers; widespread strikes in the cities arose over the national labor contract negotiations. Women's groups became outspoken and led the protests for better social services, schools, and child care (New, 1993). Often all of these groups marched together through the streets, putting concerted pressure on the political parties and government (Corsaro & Emiliani, 1992).

The 10-year period from 1968 to 1977 saw the enactment of many key pieces of social legislation. During this same period, women were entering the labor force in ever greater numbers and vigorously pressing their demands. Among the most important of the new laws were as follows:

1968: Establishment of government-sponsored preprimary education.
1971: Establishment of paid maternity leave.
1971: Establishment of government-sponsored *asili nido* (infant–toddler centers).
1975: Institution of a new family law.
1977: Institution of work parity (equal pay for equal work) between men and women.

In this changing social landscape, with its notable legislative accomplishments, the educators were rewarded for their vision, responsive to new expectations about care and education for young children. The number of preprimary schools grew rapidly until the mid-1980s, and then more slowly during the following years. Altogether, the percentage of the 3- to 6-year-old population served by state (national), municipal, or private schools reached 88.8% in 1988–1989, and 92.7% in 1992–1993 (Becchi, 1995). During this time period, the resources allocated to state schools rose from about $2,000 to $2,300 per child served, and the teacher–child ratio remained 1 to 11, one of the most favorable among the European countries (Becchi, 1995).

Although the promise of the 1968 law has been largely fulfilled, in terms of free education becoming available to children aged 3 to 6, there still remains unevenness across the regions of Italy in quality and quantity of services for children and in-service training for teachers (Corsaro & Emiliani, 1992;

Olmstead & Weikart, 1994; Pistillo, 1989). Furthermore, the quality of education provided varies widely. A number of municipal systems are known for their excellent systems (e.g., Pistoia, Modena, Reggio Emilia, and some cities in the regions of Piedmont, the Veneto, and Liguria). Private schools based on a strong philosophy and method, such as Montessori or Rudolph Steiner schools, can also be excellent. However, such levels of quality are not typical of the majority of schools, perhaps because the strong, alternative pedagogies do not mix well with traditional methods (based on either family models of nurturant affection, or more often, elementary school methods) that are most familiar.

Trends of innovation have always existed side by side with the traditional methods, however. New ideas have stirred debate, for example, in connection with establishment of national guidelines of good preschool practice (*Orientamenti*) in 1968 and 1991, and community-based management in 1974; and such gradual developments as the inclusion of children with disabilities, and increased immigration of families with children from countries outside the European Community. Recently, attention has turned to the system of state preprimary schools and what can be done to bring these schools to a consistently high level of quality. In 1994, the Italian Ministry of Education launched an experimental program called *Progetto Ascanio* to promote reflection, innovation, and improved organization in the state preprimary schools, with better controlled study and compilation of results so that they can be communicated and transferred.

In Spring 1996, the Ministry of Education further signed a formal agreement with the municipality of Reggio Emilia, entrusting its early childhood system with the authority and funds to improve professionality of teachers in the state preprimary system. This important initiative has four stated objectives: (a) to promote professional development and provide in-service training, (b) to produce training materials, (c) to establish a national documentation center, and (d) to organize an exchange of educational experiences. Reggio Emilia was selected for this task because of its continuous high investment and involvement in education for children under 6, and such well-known innovations as the *atelier* and *atelierista*; methods and uses of documentation; complex functions of the pedagogical team; continuous dialogue among administrators, teachers, and elected officials; and participation of the whole city in development of the early childhood system.

Furthermore, and just at the same time, the Reggio Emilia approach—so extensively studied for what it can contribute to educational improvement around the world—is about to go on display throughout Italy. This is happening because a new version of the "Hundred Languages of Children" Exhibit (1995) has begun its Italian tour with a 1995 opening in Rome. Furthermore, dissemination and training efforts by REGGIO CHILDREN S.r.l., the independent corporate entity formed in 1993 to defend and promote the rights and potential of all children around the world—a private organization owned in part by the city government and in part by private citizens—continue to increase.

All of these recent developments offer opportunities to Americans, as well as Italians, who would seek to know in greater depth and with greater clarity about the Reggio work with young children. They also validate and reward the achievement of the Reggio educators and citizens, for their unique combination of commitment and determination, research and experimentation, renewal and openness—all strengthened by years of work in refining skills of communication and documentation. Let us go now to that story and ask of its implications and possibilities for ourselves.

REFERENCES

Becchi, E. (Ed). (1995). *Manuale della scuola del bambino dai 3 ai 6 anni* [Handbook for the school of the young child, 3 to 6 years of age]. Milan, Italy: Franco Angeli.

Bohlen, C. (1995, March 24). Tell these Italians communism doesn't work. *New York Times International.*

Cambi, F., & Ulivieri, S. (1988). *Storia dell'infanzia nell'Italia liberale* [Childhood history in liberal Italy]. Florence, Italy: La Nuova Italia.

Ciari, B. (1961). *Le nuove tecniche didattiche* [The new teaching techniques]. Rome: Editori Riuniti.

Ciari, B. (1972). *La grande disadattata* [The great maladjusted]. Rome: Editori Riuniti.

Cohen, D.L. (1992, November 20). Preschool in Italian town inspiration to U.S. educators. *Education Week, 12,* pp. 1, 12–13.

Corsaro, W.A., & Emiliani, F. (1992). Child care, early education, and children's peer culture in Italy. In M.E. Lamb, K.J. Sternberg, C.P. Hwang, & A.G. Broberg (Eds.), *Child care in context.* (pp. 81–115). Hillsdale, NJ: Erlbaum.

Della Peruta, F. (1980). *Alle origini dell'assistenza alla prima infanzia in Italia* [At the origins of early childhood assistance in Italy]. In L. Sala La Guardia & E. Lucchini (Eds.), *Asili nido in Italia.* (pp.13–38). Milan, Italy: Marzorati.

Edwards, C.P. (1995, October). *Democratic participation in a community of learners: Loris Malaguzzi's philosophy of education as relationship.* Paper prepared for "Nostalgia del Futuro," international seminar on the educational contributions of Loris Malaguzzi, University of Milan, Italy.

Ghedini, P.O. (1992). *Politiche sociali, famiglia, e servizi per i più piccoli* [Social policies, family, and services for the youngest children]. In T. Musatti (Ed.), *La Giornata del mio bambino: Madri, lavoro e cura dei più piccoli nella vita quotidiana,* pp. 129–136. Bologna, Italy: Il Mulino.

Hellman, J.A. (1987). *Journeys among women: Feminism in five Italian cities.* New York: Oxford University Press.

Kamerman, S.B., & Kahn, A.J. (1994). *A welcome for every child: Care, education, and family support for infants and toddlers in Europe.* Washington, D.C.: ZERO TO THREE National Center for Clinical Infant Programs.

Lucchini, E. (1980). *Nasce l'asilo nido di tipo nuovo* [The birth of the new type of infant-toddler centers]. In L. Sala La Guardia & E. Lucchini (Eds.), *Asili nido in Italia,* (pp. 13–38). Milan, Italy: Marzorati.

Malaguzzi, L. (1984). *L'occhio se salta il muro: Narrativa del possibile.* [When the eye jumps over the wall: Narratives of the possible]. Regione Emilia Romagna, Comune di Reggio Emilia.

Musatti, T. (1992). *La giornata del mio bambino: Madri, lavoro e cura dei più piccoli nella vita quotidiana* [The day of my child: Mothers, work, and care of the youngest children, in daily life]. Bologna, Italy: Il Mulino.

New, R. (1993). Italy. In M. Cochran (Ed.), *International handbook of child care policies and programs.* Westport, Connecticut: Greenwood Press, pp. 291-311.

Olmstead, P., & Weikart, D.P. (Eds.). (1994). *Families speak: Early childhood care and education in 11 countries.* Ypsilanti, Michigan: High/Scope Press.

Pistillo, F. (1989). Preprimary Education and Care in Italy. In P. Olmstead & D. Weikart (Eds.), *How nations serve young children: Profiles of child care and education in 14 countries.* Ypsilanti, Michigan: High/Scope Press, pp. 151–202.

Putnam, R.D. (1993). *Making democracy work: Civic traditions in modern Italy.* Princeton, NJ: Princeton University Press.

Ross, H. (1982). Infants in Italy: An evaluation of other than mother care. *Early Child Development and Care, 9,* 121–154.

Saltz, R. (1976). Infant day care Italian style. In M.L. Hanes, I.J. Gordon, & W.F. Breivogel (Eds.). *Update: The first ten years of life,* (pp. 128–144). Gainesville, FL: University of Florida.

Scuola di Barbiana (1967). *Lettera a una Professoressa* [Letter to a Teacher]. Florence, Italy: Libreria Editrice Fiorentina.

The 10 best schools in the world, and what we can learn from them. (1991, December 2). *Newsweek,* pp. 50–59.

United States Government Accounting Office (1995). *Early childhood programs: Promoting the development of young children in Denmark, France, and Italy.* GAO/HEHS-95-45BR.

Shopper.
Drawing by children of
Ada Gobetti School.

chapter 2

What Can We Learn from Reggio Emilia?

Lilian G. Katz

Although the saying that "travel broadens the mind" is a well-worn cliché, it still has some validity. It seems to me that travel is broadening not only because of the nw things we see, but also because of what they make us think about, for example, reflecting in new ways about old things—those we might have taken for granted, or perhaps never questioned before. Seven visits to Reggio Emilia since my first one in 1990, and many subsequent discussions with the educators in Reggio Emilia and other knowledgable colleagues have provoked me to think again and anew about many aspects of early childhood education. Some of these thoughts are outlined as seven lessons in this chapter.

GRAPHIC LANGUAGES AND PROJECT WORK IN EARLY CHILDHOOD

One of the most impressive features of the Reggio Emilia approach is the way their young children are involved in extended in-depth investigations. The inclusion of long-term investigation projects is not new to preschool or primary education. It was a main feature of the Progressive movement spurred by

Dewey and his colleagues in the early 20th century, widely used during the "Plowden Years" in Great Britain in the 1960s and 1970s, and adopted by many Americans under the name *open education* at that time.

In the book *Engaging Children's Minds:The Project Approach* (1989), written before the Reggio Emilia approach had come to our attention, Sylvia Chard and I presented our rationale for including project work in early childhood programs, and guidelines for its implementation. We use the term *project work* to refer to in-depth studies of particular topics undertaken by groups of young children (Katz & Chard, 1989). From our point of view, project work is designed to help young children make deeper and fuller sense of events and phenomena in their own environment and experiences that are worthy of their attention. Projects provide the part of the curriculum in which children are encouraged to make their own decisions and choices—usually in cooperation with their peers and in consultation with their teachers—about the work to be undertaken. We assume that such work increases children's confidence in their own intellectual powers, and strengthens their dispositions to continue learning (see Katz & Chard, 1989, especially Chapter 2).

In the course of a project, for example, on a topic such as "What happens at the supermarket?" or "How houses are built," children explore the phenomena first-hand and in detail over an extended period of time. The activities of the children include direct observation, asking questions of relevant participants and experts, collecting pertinent artifacts, and representing observations, ideas, memories, feelings, imaginings, and new understandings in a wide variety of ways including dramatic play. Most preschoolers—at least at age 3 or 4—are not yet easily able to represent their observations, thoughts, and new knowledge in writing. They may, of course, dictate their thoughts and observations to others who can write for them.

The first major lesson from Reggio Emilia is the way their young children are encouraged to use what they call *graphic languages* (Rinaldi, 1991) and other media to record and represent their memories, ideas, predictions, hypotheses, observations, feelings, and so forth in their projects. Observations of the children at work in Reggio Emilia reveal how a wide variety of visual media are used to explore understandings, to reconstruct previous ones, to construct and to coconstruct revisited understandings of the phenomena investigated.

Certainly most early childhood educators in the United States have long acknowledged that young children can explore and express their feelings and understandings verbally, visually, and through dramatic play, and typically encourage children to do so. The Reggio Emilia experience, however, demonstrates convincingly that preprimary children can use a wide variety of graphic and other media to represent and thereby communicate their constructions much more readily, more competently, and at a much younger age than we (in the United States and other countries) have customarily assumed. The Reggio Emilia children's work suggests to me that many of us seriously underestimate preschool children's graphical representational abilities, and the quality of intellectual effort and growth it can engender.

FIGURE 2.1. Children's collective drawing of their experience at the supermarket. From the booklet "Noi Bimbi e Lui Gulliver" ("Us Kids and Him Gulliver"), Ada Gobetti School, 1984, Education Department, Reggio Emilia.

Figure 2.3. Children's comments following a visit to the closed supermarket

It is as large as a forest.
You could get lost in it, just like on the Via Emilia.
It is as huge as the whale of Pinocchio.
It looks like a swimming pool.
The man in the supermarket divides things in half, half on one shelf and half on another one.

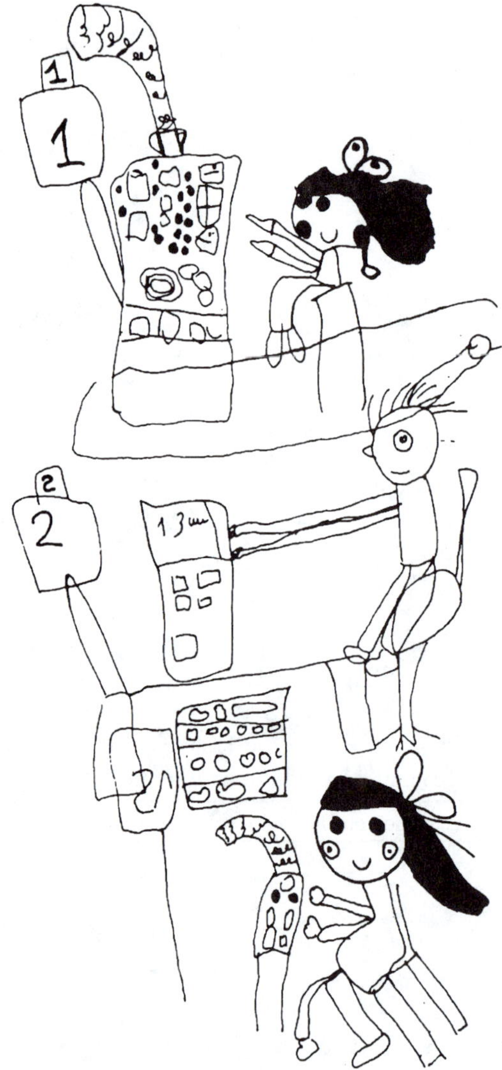

FIGURE 2.4. "The Mystery of the Cashier's"–Detail from Figure 2.1.

By way of example, a group of 4- and 5-year-olds of the Ernesto Balducci school in Reggio Emilia undertook an extended study of an exceptionally large cooperative supermarket in their neighborhood. A study of a store is a fairly popular topic in many preschools and kindergartens in the United States as well. However, several features of the project as conducted by the children in Reggio Emilia are especially noteworthy.

First, the children made several visits to the market, including one when it was closed. In this way, they were able to get a close look at various features of it, sketch many of the objects and elements that impressed them, and run up and down the aisles undisturbed by shoppers, noting anything of interest about the facility, including how their voices sounded in such a large interior space (see Figure 2.1).

Detailed drawings of the supermarket, the rows of shopping carts, the counters with a variety of merchandise, shoppers with or without shopping carts, with or without children under foot, the cashiers (see Figure 2.4), and so forth, are captured in remarkable detail in the composite drawing of the supermarket scene.

However, the drawings alone would mean relatively little without the teachers' documentation of what the children said about what they observed and experienced (see Figures 2.2 and 2.3). The children's recorded comments and discussions provided teachers with knowledge of the children's levels of understanding and misunderstanding of these everyday phenomena.

The children also shopped at the supermarket, giving due attention to preparing the shopping list, paying for their purchases, receiving change, and then using the items for cooking on their return to the school. Some of the children also interviewed the manager and put a barrage of questions to him about what is involved in being the "boss" (sees Figure 2.5 and 2.6).

The children also submitted their "wish list" to the manager reflecting what they thought should be added to the facility: a television viewing room, comfortable rest room facilities, playground, a place to play with dolls, and so forth. Many of the desired additions are beautifully illustrated by a combination of drawings

Figure 2.2. Children's comments about the visit to the supermarket.

What do you like to do at the supermarket?
Push the carts.
Touch the merchandise.
Climb on the shelves.
Run up and down.
Ask questions to everybody.
Eat pieces of cheese.
To know what is behind the closed doors.
Buy everything.
Look at myself in the mirror.

FIGURE 2.5. "Interview with the boss." (From the booklet, *Noi Bimbi e Lui Gulliver.*)

Figure 2.6. Children's comments related to the manager and drawing.

Questions about the manager
Who is the manager?
He is the one who gives money away.
He is the president.
He is the one who watches out to see if anyone steals the money.
He gets up early in the morning, opens the doors, and organizes everything.
Questions to the manager
Are you a boss?
How many people do you direct?
How do you become a manager?
Do you get more money than the others?

superimposed on photographs of furnishings apparently cut out of newspapers or magazines. In addition, many children developed their own designs for packages of cereal, crackers, detergent boxes, and the like. The children also constructed a market in the classroom and enjoyed the dramatic play greatly enriched by their close observation of the objects, people, and events they observed at the market.

Of course, one could ask why bother to undertake a project on such a mundane topic as a local supermarket—something children experience frequently and directly. After all, in a year or two, all the children will know that the cashiers do not take the money home, and that they do not decide the price of an item on the basis of their own personal tastes. So why not study something outside of the children's daily experiences? Many U.S. teachers prefer to introduce esoteric topics with which they hope to capture or excite the children's interests, presumably under the assumption that everyday objects and events are uninteresting. However, the work of preschoolers in Reggio Emilia indicates that the processes of "unpacking" or defamiliarizing everyday objects and events can be deeply meaningful, interesting, and instructive to them.

Furthermore, when the topic of a project is very familiar to the children, they can contribute to the project from their own knowledge, and suggest questions to ask and lines of investigations to pursue; the children themselves can take leadership in planning, and can assume responsibilities for specific observations and information and artifacts to be collected and closely examined. Such projects that involve young children in investigating real phenomena offer them an opportunity to be the natural scientists or anthropologists they seem born to be. On the other hand, if the topic of a project is exotic and outside of the children's direct experience, they are dependent on the teacher for most of the questions, ideas, information, thinking, and planning. Young children are dependent on adults for many aspects of their lives and their learning experiences; however, project work should be that part of the curriculum in which their own interests, ideas, preferences, and choices can be given relatively free reign.

Another value of project work is that extended studies of particular phenomena undertaken in project work give young children early experience of knowing and understanding a topic in depth. As Inagaki (1992) pointed out, having experience of knowing a topic in depth can be highly rewarding for young children. Such early experience of feelings of mastery can also cultivate and strengthen a disposition to seek in-depth understandings of topics—a disposition that can serve children well throughout their development and education.

It should also be noted that sometimes the teachers in Reggio Emilia undertake a project on a topic of unpredictable or uncertain value. Willingness to explore a topic that might not work very well is part of their commitment to experimentation, and to exploring together with the children what kinds of experiences and ideas might emerge from an experiment. In one of the Reggio Emilia preschools, the children engaged in an extended project about the solar system and space travel—phenomena hardly in their direct or immediate experience. The topic was not initiated by the teachers; it grew out of the children's animated response to a large poster of the solar system brought to the school by one of the children. The children's great interest in various *Star Wars* characters seen in films, television, and their toys was evidently partly responsible for their positive reactions to the poster. The paintings, drawings, clay work, and large complex space station made by the children suggest that their understandings of the solar system remained substantially pre-Galilean! However, their imaginings about life on a space station, space travel, rocket launching, space vehicles, space creatures, and so forth were richly and skillfully depicted in drawings, paintings, clay, and papier-mâché, including the large space station constructed with a wide variety of materials.

It seems to me, then, that a first lesson from the Reggio Emilia approach is that preschool children can express and communicate their ideas, understandings, imaginings, observations, and feelings through visual representation much earlier than most U.S. early childhood educators typically assume. The representations the children create with such impressive skill can serve as bases for modifying, developing, and deepening understandings, and as a basis for hypotheses, discussions and arguments, often leading to further observations and fresh representations. Using this approach, we can see how children's minds can be engaged in a variety of ways in the quest for deeper understanding of the familiar world around them.

TREATING CHILDREN'S WORK SERIOUSLY

Observing the care with which such young children use the graphic languages such as drawing and painting suggested another lesson concerning the possible effects of adults' treatment of children's work on its quality. It seems to me that the Reggio Emilia children approach the task of representing what they are studying through drawing, purposefully and assiduously, because they have a lot of experience using their drawings. They are are accustomed to *using* their own field drawings as bases for discussion, argument, and further work, such as making group murals, sculptures, and paintings. Refering to the media of visual representations as graphic languagues, educators in Reggio Emilia speak of children "reading" their own and each others' drawings. Teachers transcribe the recorded comments and the discussions of the children at work; with this documentation, the drawings are read and reread by the teaching staff as a basis for planning the next steps in the project. The care with which the children's work is stored and displayed (as discussed in Gandini's Chapter 9) also surely conveys to children a sense of the importance of their work that further encourages them to attend to it with concentration and care.

In American schools, children's graphic representations may be treated as mere decorative products to be taken home at the end of the day, most likely never to be discussed or looked at again. In Reggio Emilia, graphic representations serve as resources for further exploration and deepening knowledge of the topic.

REALISTIC AND IMAGINITIVE REPRESENTATION

A third lesson from the Reggio Emilia preschools' experience is that children's extensive experience of drawing from observation does not appear to inhibit their desire or ability to draw and paint from the imagination or fantasy. Contrary to the fears of many U.S. early childhood educators, the work of the Reggio Emilia children suggests that an either/or choice is unnecessary: The children appear to be competent in representative *and* creative or unrepresentative, realistic *and* abstract visual expression. In other words, experience of the former does not necessarily damage the competence or desire to engage in the latter.

Because of the high level of competence evident in the Reggio Emilia preprimary schools, it is understandable that many U.S. educators label it art education, or art instruction; some even assume that these schools are art schools. Such characterizations seem to miss a major point: Visual and graphic languages provide ways of exploring and expressing understandings of the world that are easily available to most preschoolers. The visual arts are integrated into the work simply as additional languages available to young children not yet very competent in conventional writing and reading; the arts are not taught as a subject, a discipline, a discrete set of skills, or treated in other ways as a focus of instruction for their own sake.

This not to suggest that the children are not given directions and guidance in the use of the tools, materials, and techniques of graphic and visual representation. Of considerable interest is the way such teaching (vs. instruction) invariably includes giving the child—in simple form—the principle underlying a suggested technique or approach to materials. The inclusion of the principle within a suggestion increases the chances that the child will be able to solve the problem when the adult is not there—an appropriate goal of teaching at every level.

It should be kept in mind that the Reggio Emilia children—especially the younger ones—engage in many other activities besides project work. Opportunity for a whole range of spontaneous play with blocks, dramatic play, outdoor play, listening to stories, cooking, housekeeping, and dress-up activities, as well as "one-shot" activities like painting, collage, and clay work are available to all the children daily. All children are also encouraged to be involved in an extended project throughout their years in the school. Of course, some children draw, paint, and create more skillfully than others. But the extensiveness of early experience of expressing and communicating their ideas and observations graphically during the preschool years helps explain the impressively high level of competence.

In sum, a useful lesson of the Reggio Emilia approach is that there is no reason to believe that teachers must choose between encouraging realistic or imaginative visual expression as two mutually exclusive alternatives.

THE CONTENT OF TEACHER–CHILD RELATIONSHIPS

The fourth lesson to be drawn from observations in Reggio Emilia preprimary schools concerns the content of the relationships between adults and children. My underlying assumption is that individuals cannot just relate to each other: they have to relate to each other *about* something. In other words, relationships have to have content of mutual interest or concern that can provide pretexts and texts for the interaction between them.

In his studies of the Oxford preschools in England, Bruner (1980) showed that the content of the teacher–child interactions was predominantly about managerial issues. He lamented, for example, that of nearly 10,000 units of observation, only 20% contained genuine conversations, and he pointed out that the nursery classes observed were organized so that it was difficult for connected conversations to occur. He also pointed out that "a high proportion of adult-initiated interaction with children was given over to the boring stuff of petty management—housekeeping talk about milk time, instructions about picking up, washing, and the like" (Bruner, 1980, p. 61).

As far as I know, there are no comparable large-scale data on the content of interactions between preschool teachers and children in the United States. However, it is my general impression from observations of early childhood settings all over the United States that the content of teacher–child relationships seems similarly focused on the routines and the rules of classroom life, especially during informal activity periods. When children are painting or drawing, teachers seem very reluctant to engage the children in any kind of conversation at all. When children are filling in worksheets and workbooks, teachers are understandably eager to give positive feedback, and therefore frequently say things to them like "You did well," "That's the right idea," "Very good," and similar general positive comments. In other words, the content of the relationships between our teachers and their pupils tends to be dominated by information about the child's conduct and level of performance. Thus it seems that the content of relationships between teachers and children in our early childhood settings, when not focused on mundane routines, is about the children themselves.

In contrast, my impression of Reggio Emilia practices is that to a large extent the content of teacher–child relationships is focused on the work itself, rather than mainly on routines or the children's performance on academic tasks. Adults' and children's minds meet on matters of interest to both of them. Both the children and the teachers seem to be equally involved in the progress of the work, the ideas being explored, the techniques and materials to be used, and the progress of the projects themselves. The children's roles in the relationships were more as apprentices than as the targets of instruction.

Such relationships have several benefits. The first is that the children's minds are engaged in challenging work, including, for example, discussing their intentions, making decisions about what to represent, how to represent it, how to coordinate the efforts and resolve conflicting views of the various contributors to the project, and so forth. Second, because the teachers and the children's minds meet on matters of real interest to both, teachers' minds are also engaged. They seem intent on listening closely to the children's suggestions and questions, probing their thinking, making suggestions, and encouraging children to respond to each others' ideas. They are also intent on not overassisting the children (Rabitti, 1992).

Because there are no formal prespecified lessons that all children must learn, teachers can create activities that can contribute to developing childrens' more appropriate understandings of the topic. Thus the content of the teacher–child relationship is rich with problem setting and problem solving. The work of the projects provides ample texts, pretexts, and contexts for extensive conversations between the adults and the children, as well as among them. Hawkins (1986) pointed out that the child and his or her behavior is appropriate as the main content of a relationship between an adult and a child only if the adult is a therapist and the child is the patient: "A teacher has a unique role.…It is not the role of mother or therapist or peer, but that of one who values learners and learning professionally" (p.35).

In summary, comparing Reggio Emilia preprimary schools to those I typically see in North America and elsewhere suggested to me that one way the quality of a preschool program can be evaluated is to examine the content of adult–child relationships. A program has intellectual vitality if the teacher's individual and group interactions are mainly about what the children are learning, planning, and thinking about, plus their interest in each other, and only minimally about the rules and routines.

CHILDREN'S SENSE OF WHAT ADULTS THINK IS IMPORTANT

Like most visitors to the Reggio Emilia preprimary schools and viewers of *The Hundred Languages of Children* exhibit, I frequently wondered how such an exceptional level of competence in graphic representation is achieved. One hypothesis is that the children work at their representations with concentration and care because, like all other young children, they sense what is important to the adults around them. At some level we may not be able to specify, the children are aware of what the adults really care about, what they judge to be interesting, worth doing, worth probing, and worthy of their time and serious attention. The children know what the adults take great pains to explain, take pictures of, make notes about, and display very carefully. Because teachers often repeat to children what they might have said during a previous discussion, the children learn to treat their own and others' ideas seriously. The children also seem to sense what the adults talk about to each other, bring to the attention of their parents, and show to a steady stream of interested visitors. Therefore the children know—perhaps at a preconscious level—that the adults take the children's work and ideas very seriously.

However, the ability of young children to sense what the important adults in their lives really care about is likely to be universal. Thus all teachers might ask: What do most of my pupils really believe I take seriously and care deeply about? Awareness of what adults value should not be confused with what provokes adults' praise and flattery; rather, I have in mind children's awareness of what adults take seriously enough to make suggestions about, ask for clarification about, urge children to look at again, reconsider, and perhaps do over again.

Theoretically, of course, it is possible that in some cases, the answer to the question "What does my teacher really care about?" might be "nothing." However, in the absence of any reliable information relevant to this question, let us assume that all teachers convey some messages to their pupils about what aspects of children's effort and behavior really catch their serious attention, deep interest, appreciation, and sometimes true delight. By comparison, my impression is that in the United States we are not as likely as we could be to help children sense that their intellectual quest is of deep interest and importance to us. In many of the early childhood programs I see, adults' serious attention is most likely to be stirred when something among the children is amiss or disturbs routine activities, rather than when the construction of understandings is the main focus of activity. I suspect that because, on the whole, we overestimate children academically and underestimate them intellectually, we miss moments when our attention could convey to children that their ideas are important. This is not to suggest that a sense of what teachers deem important can be conveyed explicitly by lecturing or preaching to the children about it. Rather, even very young children are most likely making inferences about what adults care about based on multiple observations of the adults' actual behavior in context.

An important lesson then, from our colleagues in the Reggio Emilia preprimary schools is that when adults communicate genuine and serious interest in the children's ideas and in their expressions of them, rich and complex work can result, even among very young children.

THE ROLE OF DOCUMENTATION

The sixth lesson, and perhaps the most unique contribution of the Reggio Emilia approach to early childhood education, is the introduction of documentation as a standard part of classroom practice. It seems to me that the careful documentation characteristic of their schools provides four fundamental and equally important improvements to early childhood education.

First, it contributes to the extensiveness and depth of the learning gained by the children from their projects and other work. As Loris Malaguzzi points out (Chapter 3), through documentation the children "become even more curious, interested, and confident as they contemplate the meaning of what they have achieved" (p. 70). Experience and observation of the children in Reggio Emilia also indicates that children learn from and are stimulated by each other's work that is made visible through documentation.

Second—and some might insist that this point be first—the documentation makes it possible for parents to become acutely aware of their children's experience in the school. Again, as Malaguzzi (Chapter 3) puts it,

> documentation introduces parents to a quality of knowing that tangibly changes their expectations. They reexamine their assumptions about their parenting roles and their views about the experience their children are living and take a new and more inquisitive approach toward the whole school experience. (p. 70)

Invariably, alongside the children's work are photographs of the children at work. Transcriptions of their questions and the comments made in the course of their work are also displayed. In this way, the children can easily share their actual school experiences (and not just their products) with their parents. The enthusiasm of the children and the interest of the parents in children's work helps strengthen the involvement of parents in the children's learning, provides a rich basis for parent–child discussion, and deepens parents' understanding of the nature of learning in the early years. The level of involvement of parents in the schools is reminiscent of parent cooperative nursery schools of the United States and of the preschool playgroups of New Zealand and Britain. Perhaps a new model of the parent cooperative nursery school as a way to optimize the needs of children, parents, and teachers should be developed in the United States, combining the needs of working parents with the importance of participating in their children's school experiences.

Third, documentation is an important kind of teacher research, sharpening and focusing teachers' attention on the intentions and understandings of the children as well as their own role in children's experiences. It provides a basis for the modification and adjustment of teaching strategies, a source of ideas, and an impetus for the creation of new ones. Documentation also deepens teachers' awareness of each child's progress. On the basis of the rich data made available through documentation, teachers are able to make informed decisions about appropriate ways to support each child's development and learning. Moreover, teachers and *atelieristi* in Reggio Emilia preprimary schools are often observed in intense discussion with each other about the documentaries around them.

Finally, a fourth value of documentation, of particular relevance to American educators, is that it provides information about children's learning and progress that cannot be demonstrated by the formal standardized tests and checklists commonly employed in the United States. U.S. teachers sometimes gain much important information and insight from their own observations of children, but the documentation of the children's work in such a wide variety of media provides compelling public evidence of the intellectual powers of young children that is not available in any other way I know of.

The powerful role of documentation in these four ways however, is possible because the children are engaged in interesting projects and other activities worthy of documentation. If, as is common in many U.S. classrooms, the children spend large proportions of time making the same pictures with the same materials about the same topic on the same day in the same way, it is unlikely that documented displays would intrigue parents and provide rich content for teacher–parent or child–parent discussion.

MODELS AND METAPHORS FOR EARLY CHILDHOOD PROGRAMS

In the processes of organizing and operating programs in preschools and primary schools, it is natural to use an underlying framework, model, or metaphor taken from other phenomena that have similar parameters. Designs for and deliberations about educational settings and the relationships within them, we use metaphors that betray the underlying models of our interpretive frameworks (Nuthall & Snook, 1973). Based on observations in the Reggio Emilia preschools, discussions with the teachers, and with others involved in them, it seemed to me that their underlying models and metaphors are different from those we customarily use in the United States.

Families and Communities as Models

One of my strong impressions of the Reggio Emilia municipal preschools is that in several ways they are modeled more on the lines of extended families and communities than most of the long-day early childhood programs seen in the United States. To begin with, the buildings in which their preschools are housed are more like large homes than most of our preschools, and certainly more so than our typical kindergartens within elementary schools. Each of the preprimary schools I visited is exceptionally attractive in the quality of furnishings and organization of space and in the displays of the children's work, which together create a comfortable, warm, and cheerful ambience and pleasant environment. The architecture also includes the *piazza* as an element of the community environment.

Although there are approximately 75 3- to 6-year-old children in each school, and about 25 in a class, the quality of life within the classes seems to achieve a homelike closeness and intimacy associated with family life that is especially appropriate for young children. The fact that the children stay with the same teacher throughout the 3 years of their participation in the program enables them, their parents, and their teachers to form strong and stable relationships with each other, as they might if they were members of extended families and small close communities. By the time most U.S. teachers have been able to develop real relationships with parents and to know them well enough to deal meaningfully and frankly with their concerns, it is necessary to move on and get to know the next group of parents. In some of the preschools, the classes are organized into mixed-age groups providing more family-like environments than homogeneous groups can (see Katz, Evangelou, & Hartmann, 1990).

As indicated earlier in this chapter and elsewhere in this volume, a great deal of the work of the children in Reggio Emilia is done in small groups. No evidence was seen of a whole class offered formal instruction at the same time, or of being required to create the same pictures or other art products—a common sight in our schools, especially in connection with holidays like Valentine's Day, Halloween, and Thanksgiving.

The emergent and informal nature of the curriculum lends itself particularly well to cooperative work among small groups of children mixed in age. The informal community-like atmosphere also seems to be enhanced by the comparative freedom from time pressures. The children are free to work and play without the frequent interruptions and transitions so common in most of our early childhood programs. It seems to me that the majority of our early childhood programs are organized into a rigid timetable, and are often one-shot activities started, packed up, and put away within prespecified time periods, usually counted in minutes.

The fact that Reggio Emilia children assume responsibility for some of the real chores involved in group life throughout the long day, such as setting the tables for meals, tidying up afterward, frequently working with the cooking staff, and sharing responsibility for keeping the art materials in good order, strengthens an atmosphere of communal life. The communal feeling is also enhanced by the participation of the entire staff of the preschools in all aspects of the program and the frequent long meetings of all concerned, especially parents.

Extended families are characterized by shared responsibility, intimacy, informality, and participation. The extended family seems to provide a very appropriate model on which to design early childhood programs. Communities are groups of people who can do together what they could not accomplish alone and who have a stake in each others' well-being. Although such models are likely to have their own problems, their appropriateness can be understood when contrasted to the corporate-industrial model that serves as a basis for education in the United States.

Corporations and Industries as Models

Observations in Reggio Emilia reminded me that in the United States, the principal models and metaphors that have been increasingly adopted from the primary and secondary school level come from the industrial and corporate world and its factories. Nursery schools were developed from nurseries that were places in the home devoted to the nourishment and care of the very young. However, during the last several decades, the term *nursery* in the U.S. literature related to young children has been completely replaced by the term *preschool*—as in precooked, and preshrunk!

Child care centers, on the other hand, have often been compared to warehouses in which children were held in custody until their parents could resume their childrearing responsibilities. They are now increasingly referred to as child care programs, or even all-day preschools, as a way to discard the custodial and warehouse metaphors. It seems to me, however, that early childhood programs are increasingly in danger of being modeled on the corporate-industrial or factory model so pervasive at the elementary and secondary levels of education.

Schlechty (1990) pointed out that factories are designed to transform raw material into prespecified products by treating it to a sequence of prespecified standard processes:

> In this vision, students are viewed as raw material to be subjected to standardized processes and procedures to mold them, to be tested against rigid standards, and inspected carefully before being passed on to the next workbench for further processing. (p. 22)

The industrial model assigns teachers the role of technocrats who are responsible for operating the factory machinery according to a prespecified design handed down to them, and for whom "the curriculum must be articulated with the tests that will be used to inspect the students who are the products of this controlled and rational process" (Schlechty, 1990, p. 23).

Concepts frequently used in educational discussion such as delivery systems, cost–benefit ratios, prespecified specific behavioral and learning outcomes, outcome-based curriculum, curriculum packages and kits, teacher-proof materials, and so on, betray the application of the industrial model to the design, operation, and assessment of schooling.

In a similar way, most of our official state and school district curriculum guides reflect an assumption that virtually all children should be subjected to the same sequence of instructional treatments in lock-step fashion in the interests of creating a standard product. Schlechty (n.d.) summed up the implications of this trend toward the factory model by saying that as the school becomes an assembly line where children, as raw material, are differentiated by quality on the basis of family background and measured in terms of "Academic aptitude" or ability to do the school work assigned.

The industrial model as a framework for designing and interpreting education is inappropriate in many ways at every level of education, but especially so for young children. During the early years of children's lives, stability of relationships and the formation of attachment between children and those who care for them is highly desirable and perhaps essential. In institutions designed on the model of a factory, individuals are interchangeable; the only requirement is that the changing individuals carry out the same prespecified functions and roles in standardized ways. An industrial model also implies that education is a unidirectional process: Adults impose instructional procedures on the raw material (i.e., children) in order to change it in predictable ways.

The proliferation of numerous special categories of children and special education programs (e.g., transition classes, learning-disabled and developmentally delayed children, etc.) and the high rates of retention in the early grades are analogous to the recalls of defective products common to U.S. industry (see also Skrtic, 1991).

Optimizing the Strengths of Families and Institutions

A preschool program and pedagogical approach based on an extended family model is likely to have its own problems. Although preschools are not factories or corporations, nor are they families. They are institutions staffed by professionals employed to apply specialized knowledge and skills to their work in the best interests of every client.

Institutions differ from factories in that they are designed to serve people and their needs, and not to produce standardized goods. By definition, public institutions are operated according to rules and regulations to be applied uniformly to all clients, independent of the particular individuals being served or the particular professional providing the service.

Families differ from both factories and institutions in that they are particularistic and responsive to the unique characteristics, needs, wishes, and values of its members in ways marked by relatively high intensity of emotion, involvement, and attachment not possible or desirable in institutional settings. Similarly, the roles of parents and teachers are distinct from each other, and ideally allow each to make complementary but different contributions to the child's growth, learning, and development (Katz, 1995). Professionals are committed to a universalistic ethic that enjoins them to apply all of their specialized knowledge and skills impartially and equally to every child, whether they like the child or feel close to him or her or not. All of these considerations suggest that a preschool must optimize the special and essential benefits of family life to children, and it must do so within the constraints and standards essential to professional practice and institutional regulation.

The municipal preschools of Reggio Emilia show us an optimum combination of the strengths of family relationships and the integrity of professional practices par excellence in several ways. First, the inclusion and involvement of parents in virtually in every aspect of the schools' functioning is deliberate and central to the planning and operation of the preschools. The quality of thought and the amount of energy given to the establishment and maintenance of strong school–parent relationships in these schools are impressive, inspiring, and also daunting.

SUMMARY

I have suggested seven lessons to be learned from colleagues in the Reggio Emilia municipal preschools. First, together children and teachers examine topics of interest to young children in great depth and detail in project work and make excellent use of a variety of visual and graphic forms as they do so. The teachers seem to have higher expectations than most of us in the United States do of very young children's abilities to represent their thoughts, feelings, and observations with the graphic skills they already have at hand, namely drawing, painting, and other graphic arts. The teaching staff act on the assumption we often give lip service to: that children have an inherent desire to grow, to know, and to understand things around them.

Second, when children have experience using their drawing, paintings, and so on, as a basis for further discussion and work, they attend to it with great care. Young children do not have to take work home every day; when they do, the work is not being used for their learning.

Third, early introduction to observational and realistic represention does not necessarily inhibit children's abilities or desire to use the media for abstract and imaginative expression as well. Fourth, the kind of work undertaken by the children in these projects provides rich content for teacher–child relationships. Fifth, many features of the adults' behavior convey to the children that all aspects of their work are taken seriously. This message is not communicated directly by pronouncement or announcement; it permeates the environment indirectly through a variety of actions, provisions, and strategies.

Sixth, detailed documentation and display of children's thought and work enhances their learning, the teachers' learning and the parents' involvement in their children's experiences in fundemental ways. Finally, the underlying model upon which school life is based is closer to family and community relationships than customary in the United States, where I believe early childhood programs are ill-served by the encroachment of an industrial-corporate model for their design.

Much has been accomplished by early childhood educators in Reggio Emilia over a period of a generation. It should be kept in mind as we seek to learn from them and apply some of that learning at home, that the schools are relatively well funded and supported by their community. They show us what can be achieved when a community makes a real commitment to its young children.

REFERENCES

Bruner, J. (1980) *Under five in Britain. Vol. 1. Oxford preschool research project.* Ypsilanti, MI: High/Scope Press.

Hawkins, F.P. (1986) *The logic of action: Young children at work.* Boulder, CO: Colorado Associated University Press.

Inagaki, K. (1992). Piagetian and post-Piagetian conceptions of development and their implications for science education in early childhood. *Early Childhood Research Quarterly,* 7(1), 115–134.

Katz, L.G., & Chard, S.C. (1989). *Engaging children's minds: The project approach.* Norwood, NJ: Ablex.

Katz, L.G., Evangelou, D., & Hartmann, J. A. (1990). *The case for mixed-age grouping in early childhood.* Washington, DC: National Association for the Education of Young Children.

Katz, L.G. (1995). *Talks with teachers of young children: A collection.* Norwood, NJ: Ablex.

Nuthall, G., & Snook, I. (1973). Contemporary models of teaching. In R.M.W. Travers (Ed.), *Second handbook of research on teaching* (pp. 47–76). Chicago: Rand McNally & Co.

Rabitti, G. (1992). *Preschool at "La Villetta".* Unpublished Master's thesis, University of Illinois, Urbana.

Rinaldi, C. (September, 1991) *The Reggio Emilia approach.* Paper presented at the Conference on the Hundred Languages of Children, Detroit, MI.

Schlechty, P. (1990). *Schools for the 21st century.* San Francisco: Jossey-Bass.

Schlechty, P. (n.d.). *Four models paradigms for schooling.* Louisville, KY: Center for Leadership in School Reform.

Skrtic, T.M. (1991). The special education paradox. *Harvard Educational Review, 61*(2), 148–206.

part II

Reggio Emilia's Educators Describe Their Program: Interviews With Lella Gandini

Loris Malaguzzi, founder of the program in Reggio Emilia.

chapter 3

History, Ideas, and Basic Philosophy

An Interview with Lella Gandini*

Loris Malaguzzi

PART I: HISTORY

The Year 1946: The Unbelievable Beginning of a School Run by Parents

Gandini: *I would like to know about the distant roots of your group experience as well as of your own personal experience.*

Malaguzzi: The history of our approach, and of my place in it, starts 6 days after the end of the Second World War. It is the spring of 1945.

Destiny must have wanted me to be part of an extraordinary event. I hear that in a small village called Villa Cella, a few miles from the town of Reggio Emilia, people decided to build and run a school for young children. That idea seems incredible to me! I rush there on my bike and I discover that it is all quite true. I find women intent upon salvaging and washing pieces of brick. The people had gotten together and had decided that the money to begin the con-

* Translated by Lella Gandini

struction would come from the sale of an abandoned war tank, a few trucks, and some horses left behind by the retreating Germans.

"The rest will come," they say to me.

"I am a teacher," I say.

"Good," they say, "If that is true, come work with us."

It all seemed unbelievable: the idea, the school, the inventory consisting of a tank, a few trucks, and horses. They explain everything to me: "We will build the school on our own, working at night and on Sundays. The land has been donated by a farmer; the bricks and beams will be salvaged from bombed houses; the sand will come from the river; the work will be volunteered by all of us."

"And the money to run the school?"

A moment of embarrassment and then they say, "We will find it." Women, men, young people—all farmers and workers, all special people who had survived a hundred war horrors—are dead serious.

Within 8 months the school and our friendship had set down roots. What happened at Villa Cella was but the first spark. Other schools were opened on the outskirts and in the poorest sections of town, all created and run by parents. Finding support for the school, in a devastated town, rich only in mourning and poverty, would be a long and difficult ordeal, and would require sacrifices and solidarity now unthinkable. When seven more were added in the poor areas surrounding the city to the "school of the tank" at Villa Cella, started by women with the help of the National Liberation Committee (CLN), we understood that the phenomenon was irreversible. Some of the schools would not survive. Most of them, however, would display enough rage and strength to survive for almost 20 years.

Finally, after 7 years of teaching in a middle school, I decided to leave my job. The work with the children had been rewarding, but the state-run school continued to pursue its own course, sticking to its stupid and intolerable indifference toward children, its opportunistic and obsequious attention toward authority, and its self-serving cleverness, pushing prepackaged knowledge. I went to Rome to study psychology at the National Center for Research (CNR). When I returned to Reggio Emilia I started, for the municipality, a town-sponsored mental health center for children with difficulties in school. At this time I began living two parallel lives, one in the morning at the center and the other in the afternoon and evening in the small, parent-run schools.

The teachers in these small schools had exceptionally high motivation. They were very different from one another, for they had been trained in various Catholic or other private schools, but their thoughts were ample and greedy, and their energy boundless. I joined up with these teachers and started to work with the children, teaching them as we ourselves were learning. Soon we became aware that many of them were in poor health and undernourished. We also learned how alien the standard Italian language was to them, as their families had for generations spoken a local dialect. We asked the parents to help us,

FIGURE 3.1. A group of children and teachers from the Villa Cella School, 1950.

but finding ways for all of us to cooperate effectively turned out to be a most demanding task—not for a lack of determination but rather a lack of experience. We were breaking traditional patterns.

When we started to work with these courageous parents, we felt both enthusiasm and fear. We knew perfectly well how weak and unprepared we were. We took stock of our resources—not a difficult task. More difficult was the task of increasing those resources. And even more difficult was to predict how we would use them with the children. We were able to imagine the great challenge, but we did not yet know our own capabilities nor those of the children. We informed the mothers that we, just as the children, had much to learn. A simple, liberating thought came to our aid, namely that things about children and for children are only learned from children. We knew how this was true and at the same time not true. But we needed that assertion and guiding principle; it gave us strength and turned out to be an essential part of our collective wisdom. It was a preparation for 1963, the year in which the first municipal schools came to life.

The Year 1963: The First City-Run School for Young Children

Gandini: *Will you recall that event?*

Malaguzzi: It was a school with two classrooms, large enough for 60 children, and we gave it the name of Robinson to recall the adventures of Defoe's hero. You will have heard how the birth of the first school in 1963 established an important landmark. For the first time in Italy, the people affirmed the right to establish a secular school for young children: a rightful and necessary break in the monopoly the Catholic church had hitherto exercised over children's early education. It was a necessary change in a society that was renewing itself, changing deeply, and in which citizens and families were increasingly asking for social services and schools for their children. They wanted schools of a new kind: of better quality, free from charitable tendencies, not merely custodial, and not discriminatory in any way.

It was a decisive achievement, although the school was housed in a small wooden building assigned to us by the authorities. Indeed, it was difficult to find enough children to participate because of the novelty of a city-run school. Three years later, one evening it burned down. We all ran there, even the mayor, and there we stood watching until only ashes remained. Yet 1 year later, the school was rebuilt in brick and concrete. We were now involved in a serious endeavor. From these early roots of civic determination and passion, widening to become part of the public consciousness, are the happenings and stories that I am now narrating to you.

We received the first expert group of teachers from the parent-run schools. Responsibilities were clear in our minds; many eyes, not all friendly, were watching us. We had to make as few errors as possible; we had to find our cultural identity quickly, make ourselves known, and win trust and respect. I remember that, after a few months, the need to make ourselves known became so strong that we planned a most successful activity. Once a week we would transport the school to town. Literally, we would pack ourselves, the children, and our tools into a truck and we would teach school and show exhibits in the open air, in the square, in public parks, or under the colonnade of the municipal theater. The children were happy. The people saw; they were surprised and they asked questions.

We knew that the new situation required continuity but also many breaks with the past. The experiences of the past we sought to preserve were the human warmth and reciprocal help, the sense of doing a job that revealed—through the children and their families—unknown motivation and resources, and an awareness of the values of each project and each choice for use in putting together entirely different activities. We wanted to recognize the right of each child to be a protagonist and the need to sustain each child's spontaneous curiosity at a high level. We had to preserve our decision to learn from children, from events, and from families to the full extent of our professional limits, and to maintain a readiness to change points of view so as never to have too many certainties.

It was a feverish time, a time of adaptation, of continuous adjustment of ideas, of selection of projects, and of attempts. Those projects and attempts were expected to produce a great deal and to do well; they were supposed to respond to the combined expectations of children and families and to reflect our competences, which were still in the making. I remember that we really got involved in a project based on Robinson Crusoe. The plan was for all of us together, including the children, to reconstruct the story, the character, and the adventures of our hero. We worked on reading and retelling the story; we used our memory as well as our skills at drawing, painting, clay, and woodworking. We rebuilt the ship, the sea, the island, the cave, and the tools. It was a long and spectacular reconstruction.

The following year, experts by now, we went on to work on a similar reconstruction of the story of Pinocchio. Then a few years later we changed gears. I had been at the Rousseau Institute and at the Ecole des Petits (School for Young Children) of Piaget in Geneva. Because we were inspired by Piaget, we opted to work with numbers, mathematics, and perception. We were then, and still are, convinced that it is not an imposition on children or an artificial exercise to work with numbers, quantity, classification, dimensions, forms, measurement, transformation, orientation, conservation and change, or speed and space, because these explorations belong spontaneously to the everyday experiences of living, playing, negotiating, thinking, and speaking by children. This was an absolutely new challenge in Italy, and our initiative rewarded us. It marked the beginning of an experimental phase that gained breadth from examining different psychological theories and looking at different theoretical sources and research coming from outside our country.

But in reflecting on that experience, a time during which we were proceeding without clear points of reference, we should also recall our excesses, the incongruity of our expectations, and the weaknesses of our critical and self-critical processes. We were aware that many things in the city, in the country, in politics, in customs, and in terms of needs and expectations were changing. In 1954 the Italian public started watching television. Migrations from the South to the North began, with the consequent abandonment of the countryside. With new work possibilities, women were developing aspirations and demands that were breaking with tradition. The baby boom modified everything, particularly the role and the aims of schools for young children, and led to a powerful, growing demand for social services. Furthermore, the request to place young sons and daughters in preschools was developing into a mass phenomenon.

From all this emerged the need to produce new ideas and to experiment with new educational strategies, in part because the municipal government was increasingly determined to institute more schools to satisfy the emerging needs of children and families. Women's groups, teachers, parents, citizens' councils, and school committees were starting to work with the municipality to support and contribute to that development.

After much pressure and battles by the people, in 1967 all the parent-run schools came under the administration of the municipality of Reggio Emilia. We had fought for 8 years, from 1960 to 1968. As part of the larger political struggle all over Italy for publicly supported schools for young children as the entitlement of every child aged 3 to 6, we had debated the right of the state and the municipalities to establish such schools. In the national parliament confrontation, the secular forces were victorious over the side arguing for Catholic education. Our city was at the forefront: In 1968 there were 12 classes for young children run by the municipality. There would be 24 in 1970, 34 in 1972, 43 in 1973, 54 in 1974, and 58 in 1980, located in 22 different school buildings.

Today, (in 1990) when in Italy 88% of the children between ages 3 and 6 have acquired the right to go to school, and parents choose between three types of institutions—national, municipal, and private—it seems appropriate to remember those remote events, humble yet powerful, that took place in the countryside and on the urban periphery; events from which those in the city drew inspiration in order to develop an exemplary policy in favor of the child and the family.

The Year 1976: A Hard Year–A Good Year

Gandini: *You said that the education of young children was a virtual monopoly of the Catholic church; how did Catholic people react to a lay school?*

Malaguzzi: Already, since 1970, the scenario had changed. Schools and social services had become inescapable national issues and the cultural debated around them had become more enlivened and at the same time more civil. I remember that it had not been that way when in 1963 we had organized an Italian-Czech seminar on the subject of play. It had not been that way when in 1968 we sponsored a symposium on the relationship among psychiatry, psychology, and education—considered a dangerous, or unknown, combination at the time—nor, for that matter, when later we organized a meeting among biologists, neurologists, psychologists, and experts in education to discuss children's graphic expression. The latter meeting, because of its attention to biology and neurology, brought on us the accusation of having placed too much emphasis on materialism.

Our experience had brought us a long way and had become a reference point for educators in many areas of the country. This was especially true for young teachers who were discovering a profession that up to then had been monopolized by nuns. Around 1965 our schools had gained two fabulous friends. The first was Gianni Rodari, a poet, writer of widely translated stories for children who dedicated his most famous book, *Grammatica della Fantastica* (*The Grammar of Fantasy*, 1973), to our city and its children. The second was Bruno Ciari, the most lucid, passionate, and acute intelligence in the field of childhood education. They were indeed stupendous friendships. In 1971, with notable daring, we organized a national meeting for teachers only. We expected 200 participants, but 900 showed up. It was dramatic and exalting, but at the same time it was an event that allowed us to publish the first work on the subject of early education, *Esperienze per Una Nuova Scuola dell'Infanzia (Experiences for a New School for Young*

Children, Malaguzzi, 1971a). After a few months we published another work, *La Gestione Sociale nella Scuola dell'Infanzia (Community-based Management in the Preprimary School,* Malaguzzi, 1971b). Those two works contained everything that we had put together with the teachers of Reggio Emilia and Modena (where I was also a consultant) with regard to our ideas and experiences.

In 1972 the whole City Council, including the Catholic minority, voted in favor of the rules and regulations that we had drafted to govern the schools for young children. After years of polemics, or simply lack of acknowledgment, this event marked the legitimization of 10 years of laborious effort. We celebrated in every school.

In 1975, I was invited to be the keynote speaker at another meeting, organized this time by the regional government of Emilia Romagna, on the rights of children. It could not have come at a better time. I had just returned from a visit to the Institut Rousseau and the Ecole des Petits in Geneva and was inspired with admiration for the Piagetian views and with the plans, mentioned earlier, that we would soon start to implement.

The year 1976 was a hard, unexpected year. In the month of November the government speaker for the Catholic establishment, through the government-sponsored radio network, began a defamatory campaign against the city-run schools for young children and especially against our schools. They were attacked as a model of education that was corrupting the children ad as a model of a policy of harassment against private, religious schools. After 7 days of this campaign, we felt that we had to react. My decision was to suspend the regular planning activities of teachers and invite the local clergy to come to an open debate inside our schools. This public discussion lasted the better part of 5 months. As time went by, the harsh opposition became more civil, tempered, and honest; as ideas began to emerge, a reciprocal understanding began to take shape. At the end of this adventure we were left exhausted, with the sense that the anguish had dissipated, and I believe this sense of relief was shared by everyone on both sides. What remained was a feeling of enrichment and humanity.

Reflecting on this event in historical perspective, we can see that this ugly affair arose from the deep uneasiness felt by some Church officials over the loss of their monopoly on education. They were simultaneously being confronted with a decrease in the number of men and women choosing religious vocations, resulting in the increased need for secular teachers and a consequent increased cost of running their schools. Furthermore, the Italian Constitution forbade the use of federal funds to support religious schools; therefore, the Church was attempting to obtain financial support from local government (later this would be granted).

Still another factor, in my view, explaining the attack on our schools was the rapid growth of the cultural influence of our experience. Our work, the seminars, the meetings, and the publications had all contributed to a national recognition of our city-run schools. State schools for young children also existed, alongside the municipal ones, but their growth was slow and too controlled by the central government. Thus, our program was shining a spotlight on the limitations of the religious schools, which were, with a few exceptions, incapable of going beyond the old and outdated custodial approach to education.

One of the consequences was that a government agency called the National Teaching Center established ties with our group and invited me to participate in their meetings. These ties still endure. Another result was that an important publishing company entrusted me with the direction of a new journal, *Zerosei* (*Zero to Six*, 1976–1984), and later *Bambini* (*Children*, 1985–present), addressed to educators of young children. I am still involved in this enterprise.

In the end, that painful confrontation of 1976 and its favorable conclusion made us stronger and more aware of what we had built, as well as more eager to go on with it. In the 1980s we went ahead with our first flight abroad toward Sweden with the first edition of our exhibit, "When the Eye Jumps Over the Wall," and the beginning of other flights that would take us traveling around the world.

A Professional and Life Choice

Gandini: *It seem that you made a choice to dedicate your life to the education and care of young children. When did you make this life choice?*

Malaguzzi: I could just avoid answering, as other have done before, by saying that when you don't ask me I know, but when you ask me, I do not know the answer anymore. There are some choices that you know are coming upon you only when they are just about to explode. But there are other choices that insinuate themselves into you and become apparent with a kind of obstinate lightness, that seem to have slowly grown within you during the happenings of your life because of a mixing of molecules and thoughts. It must have happened this latter way. But also World War II, or any war, in its tragic absurdity might have been the kind of experience that pushes a person toward the job of educating, as a way to start anew and live and work for the future. This desire strikes a person, as the war finally ends and the symbols of life reappear with a violence equal to that of the time of destruction.

I do not know for sure. But I think that is where to look for a beginning. Right after the war I felt a pact, an alliance, with children, adults, veterans from prison camps, partisans of the Resistance, and the sufferers of a devastated world. Yet all that suffering was pushed away by a day in spring, when ideas and feelings turned toward the future, seemed so much stronger than those that called one to halt and focus on the present. It seemed that difficulties did not exist, and that obstacles were no longer insurmountable.

It was a powerful experience emerging out of a thick web of emotions and from a complex matrix of knowledge and values promising new creativity of which I was only becoming aware. Since those days I have often reassessed my position, and yet I have always remained in my niche. I have never regretted my choices or what I gave up for them.

Gandini: *What are your feelings, and how do you view your experiences when you recall the history of your program?*

Malaguzzi: Dear Lella, you have to agree that seeing an army tank, six horses, and three trucks generating a school for young children is extraordinary. The fact that the school still exists and continues to function well is the minimum that one could expect from such beginnings. Furthermore, its valuable history confirms that a new educational experience can emerge from the least expected circumstances.

If we continue to review those extraordinary origins, it is because we are still trying to understand the intuitions, the ideas, and the feelings that were there at the start and that have accompanied us ever since. These correspond to what John Dewey called, "the foundation of the mind," or Lev Vygotsky considered, "the loan of consciousness." Such concepts we have always kept in mind, especially in moments when we have had to make difficult decisions or overcome obstacles. Indeed, the first philosophy learned from these extraordinary events, in the wake of such a war, was to give a human, dignified, *civil* meaning to existence, to be able to make choices with clarity of mind and purpose, and to yearn for the future of mankind.

FIGURE 3.2. Loris Malaguzzi speaking at the University of Massachusetts in Amherst on the occasion of the opening of the exhibit The Hundred Languages of Children. Lella Gandini is the translator.

But the same events granted us something else right away, to which we have always tried to remain faithful. This something came out of requests made by mothers and fathers, whose lives and concerns were focused on their children. They asked for nothing less than that this school, which they had built with their own hands, be a different kind of school, a school that could educate their children in a different way from before. It was the women especially who expressed this desire. The equation was simple: If the children had legitimate rights, then they also should have opportunities to develop their intelligence and to be made ready for the success that would not, and should not, escape them. These were the parents' thoughts, expressing a universal aspiration, a declaration against the betrayal of children's potential, and a warning that children first of all had to be taken seriously and believed in. These three concepts could have fitted perfectly in any good book on education. And they suited us just fine. The ideas coming from parents were shared by others who understood their deep implications. And if our endeavor has endured for many years, it has been because of this collective wisdom.

PART II: PHILOSOPHY

The Sources of Our Inspiration

Gandini: *What theories and schools of thought do you think influenced the formulation of your approach?*

Malaguzzi: When somebody asks us how we got started, where we came from, what the sources of our inspiration are, and so on, we cannot help but recite a long list of names. And when we tell about our humble and at the same time extraordinary origins, and we try to explain that from those origins we have extracted theoretical principles that still support our work, we notice much interest and not a little incredulity. It is curious (but not unjustified) how resilient is the belief that educational ideas and practices can derive only from official models or established theories.

We must, however, state right away that we also emerged out of a complex cultural background. We are immersed in history, surrounded by doctrines, politics, economic forces, scientific change, and human dramas; there is always in progress a difficult negotiation for survival. For this reason we have had to struggle and occasionally correct and modify our direction, but so far destiny has spared us from shameful compromise or betrayal. It is important for pedagogy not to be the prisoner of too much certainty, but instead to be aware of both the relativity of its powers and the difficulties of translating its ideals into practice. Piaget already warned us that the errors and ills of pedagogy come from a lack of balance between scientific data and social application.

Preparing ourselves was difficult. We looked for readings; we traveled to capture ideas and suggestions from the few but precious innovative experiences of other cities; we organized seminars with friends and the most vigorous and innovative figures on the national education scene; we attempted experiments; we started exchanges with Swiss and French colleagues. The first of these groups (Swiss) gravitated around the area of active education and Piagetian tendencies, and the second (French) invented a very strange school: Every 3 years this French school would move to a new location where the reconstruction of old, abandoned farmhouses would be the basis of the educational work with the children. So it was that we proceeded, and gradually things began to come together in a coherent pattern.

The Education of Children in the 1960s

Gandini: *We know that in the 1960s there emerged in Italy a new consciousness regarding the education of young children. What was the cultural scenario that accompanied it?*

Malaguzzi: In the 1960s, issues surrounding schools for young children were at the center of fiery political debates. The need for them was undeniable, but the main debate was whether schools should exist as a social service. More substantive pedagogical considerations remained on the back burner. In reality, on the entire subject of education, Italy was far behind. For 20 years under Fascism, the study of the social sciences had been suppressed and European and American theories and experiences excluded. That kind of isolation was disappearing in the 1960s. The works of John Dewey, Henri Wallon, Edward Chaparède, Ovide Decroly, Anton Makarenko, Lev Vygotsky, and later also Erik Erikson and Urie Bronfenbrenner were becoming known. Furthermore, we were reading *The New Education* by Pierre Bovet and Adolfe Ferrière and learning about the teaching techniques of Celestine Freinet in France, the progressive educational experiment of the Dalton School in New York, and the research of Piaget and colleagues in Geneva.

This literature, with its strong messages, guided our choices; and our determination to continue gave impetus to the flow of our experiences. We avoided the paralysis that had stalled left political theorists for more than a decade in a debate regarding the relationship between content and method in education. For us that debate was meaningless because it did not take into account differences that were part of our society and ignored the fact that active education involves an inherent alliance between content and method. Also strengthening our belief in active education was our awareness of the pluralism of the families, children, and teachers becoming ever more involved in our joint project. This awareness was making us more respectful of different political positions. We were becoming more free of intolerance and prejudice.

Looking back it seems to me that this choice toward respect gave strength to our autonomy as we elaborated our educational project, and helped us resist many contrasting pressures.

The Italian tradition relied on Rosa Agazzi and Maria Montessori, two important figures from the beginning of the century. Montessori was first praised and then relegated to the sidelines by the Fascist regime because of her scientific approach to pedagogy. Agazzi was adopted as a model because her pedagogy was closer to the view of the child in Catholicism. I still believe that the writings of Montessori and Agazzi should be meditated on in order to move beyond them.

Meanwhile, in practice, the Roman Catholic church had almost a monopoly on preschool education, concentrating its efforts on helping needy children and offering custodial services rather than responding to the social and cultural changes. The typical classroom contained 40 to 50 children, entrusted to one nun with no teaching degree and no salary. The situation speaks for itself through the numbers: In 1960, only about one third of young children were in preschool where they were taught by 22,917 teachers, of whom 20,330 were nuns.

More About the Sources of Inspiration

Gandini: *You have mentioned a first wave of sources that influenced you. Can you tell us more about the ideas that have been important to you?*

Malaguzzi: In the 1970s we listened to a second wave of scholars, including psychologists Wilfred Carr, David Shaffer, Kenneth Kaye, Jerome Kagan, Howard Gardner, and philosopher David Hawkins, and theoreticians Serge Moscovici, Charles Morris, Gregory Bateson, Heinz Von Foerster, and Francisco Varela, plus those who work in the field of dynamic neuroscience. The network of the sources of our inspiration spans several generations and reflects the choices and selections that we have made over time. From these sources we have received ideas both long-lasting, and not-so-long-lasting topics for discussion, reasons to find connections, discordances with cultural changes, occasions for debating, and stimuli to confirm and expand on practices and values. And, overall, we have gained a sense of the versatility of theory and research.

But talk about education (including the education of young children) cannot be confined to its literature. Such talk, which is also political, must continuously address major social changes and transformations in the economy, sciences, arts, and human relationships and customs. All of these larger forces influence how human beings—even young children—"read" and deal with the realities of life. They determine the emergence, on both general and local level, of new methods of educational content and practice, as well as new problems and soul-searching questions.

In Search of an Educational Approach for the Youngest Children

Gandini: *In Italy, group care of very young children (4 months to 3 years of age) in a col-*

FIGURE 3.3. A place where to hide or to be with a friend in the Infant–Toddler Center, Arcobaleno.

lective environment has developed in a very successful way. How did it begin in Reggio Emilia?

Malaguzzi: In Reggio Emilia, the first infant–toddler center (*asilo nido*) for children under 3 years of age came to life 1 year before the promulgation of the 1971 national law instituting this type of service. This law was a victory for Italian women after 10 years of struggle. The new institution was an attempt to meet the joint needs of women, choosing both motherhood and work, and children, growing up in the nuclear family.

Proponents of infant–toddler centers had to deal with the polemic raised by the rediscovered writings of John Bowlby and Rene Spitz, who right after World War II studied the damage resulting from the separation of the mother–child pair. Furthermore, they had to address the resistance of the Catholic world, which feared risks and pathologies in a breakdown of the family. It was a very delicate question. Our experience with children 3 to 6 years of age was a useful point of reference, but at the same time not a complete answer. Rather than thinking in terms of custodial care, we argued that their education demanded professional expertise, strategies of care, and environments that were appropriate and unique to their developmental level.

We had many fears, and they were reasonable ones. The fears, however, helped us; we worked cautiously with the very young teachers and with the parents themselves. Parents and teachers learned to handle with great care the children's transition from a focused attachment on parents and home to a shared attachment that included the adults and environment of the infant–toddler center.

It all went much better than expected. We had the good fortune to be able to plan the environment of the first center with an excellent architect. The children understood sooner than we had expected that their adventure in life could flow between two agreeable and comfortable places—home and the center. In both they could express their previously overlooked desire to be and mature with peers and to find in them points of reference, understanding, surprises, affective ties, and merriment that could dispel shadows and uneasiness.

For us, the children, and the families, there now opened up the possibility of a very long and continuous period of living together, from the infant–toddler center through preprimary school; that is, 5 or 6 years of reciprocal trust and work. This time, we discovered, was a precious resource, capable of making synergistic potentials flow among educators, children, and families.

Today, in my city about 30% of eligible children are served by our municipal infant–toddler centers, and about 10–20% more would be if there were space. What have we learned from this experience? Twenty years of work have convinced us that even the youngest children are social beings. They are predisposed; they possess from birth a readiness to make significant ties with other caretakers besides their parents (who do not thereby lose their special responsibilities and prerogatives).

The obvious benefit that the children obtain from interactive play with peers is a most reassuring aspect of the group experience, the potential of which has wide implications not yet appreciated. In consequence, we agree with the American psychologists (such as Ellen Hock, Urie Bronfenbrenner) that it is not so important whether the mother chooses the role of homemaker or working mother, but rather that she feels fulfillment and satisfaction with her choice and receives support from her family, the child care center, and at least minimally, the surrounding culture. The quality of the relationship between parent and child becomes more important than the sheer quantity of time they spend together.

PART III: BASIC PRINCIPLES

The Structural Combination of Educational Choices and Organization

Gandini: *What kind of organization helped you to realize the innovative ideas in your schools for young children?*

Malaguzzi: We think of a school for young children as an integral living organism, as a place of shared lives and relationships among many adults and very many children. We think of school as a sort of construction in motion, continuously adjusting itself. Certainly we have to adjust our system from time to time while the organism travels on its life course, just as those pirate ships were once compelled to repair their sails all the while keeping on their course at sea.

It has also always been important to us that our living system of schooling expands toward the world of the families, with their right to know and to participate. And then it expands toward the city, with its own life, its own patterns of development, its own institutions, as we have asked the city to adopt the children as bearers and beneficiaries of their own specific rights.

Is It Possible to Create an Amiable School?

Gandini: *A visit to your schools always gives a sense of discovery and serenity. What are the ingredients that create such an atmosphere and level of positive tension?*

Malaguzzi: I believe that our schools show the attempt that has been made to integrate the educational program with the organization of work and the environment so as to allow for maximum movement, interdependence, and interaction. The school is an inexhaustible and dynamic organism: It has its difficulties, controversies, joys, and capacities to handle external disturbances. What counts is that there be an agreement about what direction the school should go, and that all forms of artifice and hypocrisy be kept at bay. Our objective, which we always will pursue, is to create an amiable environment, where children, families, and teachers feel at ease.

FIGURE 3.4. Glass walls between the Atelier and the piazza at Diana School.

To start with, then, there is the environment. There is the entrance hall, which informs and documents, and which anticipates the form and organization of the school. This leads into the dining hall, with the kitchen well in view. The entrance hall leads into the central space, or *piazza,* the place of encounters, friendships, games, and other activities that complete those of the classrooms. The classrooms and utility rooms are placed at a distance from but connected with the central area. Each classroom is divided into two contiguous rooms, picking up one of the very few practical suggestions by Piaget. His idea was to allow children either to be with teachers or stay alone; but we use the two spaces in many ways. In addition to the classrooms, we have established the *atelier,* the school studio and laboratory, as a place for manipulating or experimenting with separate or combined visual languages, either in isolation or in combination with the verbal ones. We have also the *mini-ateliers* next to each classroom, which allow for extended project work. We have a room for music and an archive, where we have placed many useful objects both large and small, and noncommercial, made by teachers and parents. Throughout the school the walls are used as spaces for both temporary and permanent exhibits of what the children and teachers have created: Our walls speak and document.

The teachers work in co-teaching pairs in each classroom, and they plan with other colleagues and the families. All the staff members of the school meet once a week to discuss and broaden their ideas, and they participate together in in-service training. We have a team of *pedagogisti* to facilitate interpersonal connection and to consider both the overall ideas and the details. The families meet by themselves or with the teachers, either in individual meetings, group meetings, or whole school meetings. Families have formed an Advisory Council for each school that meets two or three times a month. The city, the countryside, and the nearby mountains serve as additional teaching sites.

Thus, we have put together a mechanism combining places, roles, and functions that have their own timing, but that can be interchanged with one another in order to generate ideas and actions. All this works within a network of cooperation and interactions that produces for the adults, but above all for the children, a feeling of belonging in a world that is alive, welcoming, and authentic.

For an Education Based on Interrelationships

Gandini: *How do you create and sustain interaction, relationships, and cooperation among all parties connected with the schools?*

Malaguzzi: In our system we know it is essential to focus on children and be child centered, but we do not feel that is enough. We also consider teachers and families as central to the education of children. We therefore choose to place all three components at the center of our interest.

Our goal is to build an amiable school, where children, teachers, and families feel at home. Such a school requires careful thinking and planning con-

FIGURE 3.5. A structure built by parents and teachers, lined with mirrors, invites children to interact and play with their images.

cerning procedures, motivations, and interests. It must embody ways of getting along together, of intensifying relationships among the three central protagonists, of assuring complete attention to the problems of education, and of activating participation and research. These are the most effective tools for all those concerned—children, teachers, and parents—to become more united and aware of each other's contributions. They are the most effective tools to use in order to feel good about cooperating and to produce, in harmony, a higher level of results.

Anyone who starts a program thinks about actions that will transform existing situations into new, desired ones. In our approach, then, in order to proceed, we make plans and reflections connected with the cognitive, affective, and symbolic realms; we refine communication skills; we are very active in exploring and creating along with many participants, while remaining open to change. In this manner, while all the goals are shared, still the most valuable aspect is interpersonal satisfaction.

Even when the structure we have in mind (the centrality of children, teachers, and families) reveals flaws and difficulties, and the participation shows different levels of intensity, the stimulating atmosphere of the school provides a sense of positive receptiveness to all concerned. That happens because the school invites an exchange of ideas; it has an open and democratic style, and thereby it tends to open minds.

The aspects of isolation, indifference, and violence that are more and more a part of contemporary social life are so contrary to our approach that they make us even more determined to proceed. The families feel the same way; the alienating aspects of modern life become a reason to be even more eager and open to our offerings.

All this contributes to structure an education based on relationship and participation. On the practical level, we must continuously maintain and reinvent our network of communication and encounters. We have meetings with families to discuss curriculum. We ask for their cooperation in organizing activities, setting up the space, and preparing the welcoming of new children. We distribute to each child the telephone numbers and addresses of all the other children and their teachers. We encourage visits, including snacks among the children at their homes, and visits to parents' workplaces. We organize with parents excursions, for example, to swimming pools and gymnasiums. We work with parents in building furnishings and toys. We meet with them to discuss our projects and our research, and we meet to organize dinners and celebrations in the school.

This type of approach with parents reveals much about our philosophy and basic values. These include the interactive and constructivist aspects, the intensity of relationships, the spirit of cooperation, and individual and collective effort in doing research. We appreciate different contexts, pay careful attention to individual cognitive activity within social interactions, and establish affective ties. As we learn two-way processes of communication, we acquire a wider awareness of political choices regarding infancy, encourage mutual adaptation among children and adults, and promote growth of adult educational competencies. We have truly left behind a vision of the child as egocentric, focused only on cognition and physical objects, and whose feelings and affectivity are underestimated and belittled.

Relationships and Learning

Gandini: *In what particular way do you see children's learning take place within the context of the rich relationships that you describe?*

Malaguzzi: In my view, relationships and learning coincide within an active process of education. They come together through the expectations and skills of children, the professional competence of adults, and more generally,

FIGURE 3.6. A discussion about weight of different objects.

the educational process.

We must embody in our practice, therefore, reflections on a delicate and decisive point: *What children learn does not follow as an automatic result from what is taught. Rather, it is in large part due to the children's own doing as a consequence of their activities and our resources.*

It is necessary to think about the knowledge and skills that children construct independently of and prior to schooling. This knowledge base does not belong to the "prehistory" mentioned by Vygotsky (as if it were a separate experience), but to the children's social development in process. In any context, children do not wait to pose questions to themselves and form strategies of thought, or principles, or feelings. Always and everywhere children take an active role in the construction and acquisition of learning and understanding. To learn is a satisfying experience, but also, as the psychologist Nelson Goodman tells us, to understand is to experience desire, drama, and conquest.

So it is that in many situations, especially when one sets up challenges, children show us they know how to walk along the path to understanding. Once children are helped to perceive themselves as authors or inventors, once they are helped to discover the pleasure of inquiry, their motivation and interest explode. They come to expect discrepancies and surprises. As educators, we have to recognize their tension, partly because, with a minimum of introspection, we find the same within ourselves (unless the vital appeal of novelty and puzzlement has faded or died). The age of childhood, more than the ages that follow, is characterized by such expectations. To disappoint the children deprives them of possibilities that no exhortation can arouse in later years.

Yet, in so praising the child, we do not intend to return to the naïveté of the 1970s, when discovery of the child's active role in structuring events and the two-way causality in child-adult interaction resulted in a strange devaluation of the role of the adult. Nor do we wish to overvalue the child's control of this interaction. In reality, the two-way direction of interaction is a principle hard to miss. We imagine the interaction as a ping-pong match. (Do you remember the badminton games between two boys, splendidly recounted by the great Gestalt psychologist, Max Wertheimer, in *Productive Thinking* (1945).) For the game to continue, the skills of the adult and child need appropriate adjustments that allow the growth through learning of the skills of the child.

All of these considerations remind us that the way we get along with children influences what motivates them and what they learn. Their environment must be set up so as to interface the cognitive realm with the realms of relationship and affectivity. so also there should be connection between development and learning, between the different symbolic languages, between thought and action, and between individual and interpersonal autonomies. Value should be placed on contexts, communicative processes, and the construction of a wide network of reciprocal exchanges among children and between children and adults.

Yet, what is most central to success is to adhere to a clear and open theoretical conception that guarantees coherence in our choices, practical applications, and continuing professional growth.

The Widening of Communication Networks

Gandini: *You have described in great detail the importance of relationships in your approach. But is your approach based only on relationships?*

Malaguzzi: No, of course not. Relationship is the primary connecting dimension of our system, however, understood not merely as a warm, protective envelope, but rather as a dynamic conjunction of forces and elements interacting toward a common purpose. The strength of our system lies in the ways we make explicit and then intensify the necessary conditions for relations and interaction. We seek to support those social exchanges that better ensure the flow of expectations, conflicts, cooperations, choices, and the explicit unfolding of problems tied to the cognitive, affective, and expressive realms.

Among the goals of our approach is to reinforce each child's sense of identity through a recognition that comes from peers and adults, so much so that each one would feel enough sense of belonging and self-confidence to participate in the activities of the school. In this way we promote in children the widening of communication networks and mastery and appreciation of language in all its levels and contextual uses. As a result, children discover how communication enhances the autonomy of the individual and the peer group. The group forms a special entity tied together through exchange and conversation, reliant on its own ways of thinking, communicating, and acting.

The approach based on relationship best reveals how a classroom is composed of independent individuals as well as subgroups and alliances with different affinities and skills. The communicative landscape becomes variegated; we notice children who communicate less than others. The teachers, participant observers, respond to what they see by asking questions, initiating face-to-face exchanges, redirecting activities, and modifying the way or the intensity of their interaction with particular children. Small group activities, involving two to four children, are modules of maximum desirability and communicative efficacy. They are the type of classroom organization most favorable to education based on relationship. They facilitate fruitful conflicts, investigations, and activities connected to what each child has previously said and self-regulatory accommodations.

It might help to look at this in systemic terms. The system of relationship in our schools is simultaneously real and symbolic. In this system each person has a formal role relationship with the others. Adult and child roles are complementary: They ask questions of one another, they listen, and they answer.

As a result of these relationships, the children in our schools have the unusual privilege of learning through their communications and concrete experiences. I'm saying that the system of relationships has in and of itself a virtually autonomous capacity to educate. It is not just some kind of giant security blanket (the "transitional object" of D.W. Winnicott). Nor is it some kind of flying carpet that takes the children to magic places. Rather, it is a permanent living presence always on the scene, required all the more when progress becomes difficult.

What Is Needed to Make an Alliance Succeed

Gandini: *One of the many questions that comes up when talking about your program is how you succeed in enlisting and maintaining the participation of families at such a high level.*

Malaguzzi: That is one of the first questions we are usually asked. Let me answer without reference to philosophy, sociology, and ethics. Family participation requires many things, but most of all it demands of teachers a multitude of adjustments. Teachers must possess a habit of questioning their certainties, a growth of sensitivity, awareness, and availability, the assuming of a critical style of research and continually updated knowledge of children, an enriched evaluation of parental roles, and skills to talk, listen, and learn from parents.

Responding to all of these demands requires from teachers a constant questioning of their teaching. Teachers must leave behind an isolated, silent mode of working that leaves no traces. Instead, they must discover ways to communicate and document the children's evolving experiences at school. They must

FIGURE 3.7. At the end of the school year parents, children, and teachers celebrate with outside games.

prepare a steady flow of quality information targeted to parents but appreciated also by children and teachers. This flow of documentation, we believe, introduces parents to a quality of knowing that tangibly changes their expectations. They reexamine their assumptions about their parenting roles and their views about the experiences their children are living and take a new and more inquisitive approach toward the whole school experience.

With regard to the children, the flow of documentation creates a second, and equally pleasing, scenario. They become even more curious, interested, and confident as they contemplate the meaning of what they have achieved. They learn that their parents feel at home in the school, at ease with the teachers, and informed about what has happened and is about to happen. We know we have built a solid friendship when children readily accept one of their parents saying, "This evening I am going to school to talk with the teachers," or "I am going to the meeting of the Advisory Council," or when parents help prepare school excursions and celebrations.

Finally, it is important for parents and children to realize how much work teachers do together. They must see how often teachers meet to discuss, sometimes peacefully and other times more loudly. They must see how teachers cooperate on research projects and other initiatives, how they document their work with patience and care; how skillfully they wield their cameras and videocameras; with what kindness they hide their worries, join children's play, and take responsibility. All of this represents for the children a range of models that make a deep impression. They see a world where people truly help one another.

PART IV: TEACHERS

The Collegial Work of Teachers

Gandini: *In your schools there seems to be no hierarchy among teachers. Is this really the case?*

Malaguzzi: Co-teaching, and in a more general sense, collegial work, represents for us a deliberate break from the traditional professional and cultural solitude and isolation of teachers. This isolation has been rationalized in the name of academic freedom, yet wrongly understood. Its results, certainly, have been to impoverish and desiccate teachers' potential and resources and make it difficult or impossible for them to achieve quality.

I remember, however, that the archetype, one teacher per classroom, was so strongly rooted when we began our work that our proposal of co-teaching pairs, which should have been seen as a welcome liberation from excessive stress, did not at first find ready acceptance among teachers. The ones who did accept it, however, soon discovered the evident advantages, and this cleared up the uncertainty. The work in pairs, and then among pairs, produced tremendous advantages, both educationally and psychologically, for adults as well as for children. Furthermore, the co-teaching pairs constituted the first building block of the bridge that was taking us toward community-based management and partnership with parents.

Community-based management has always been an important part of our history and supporting beam of our work. At times, it has been a decisive force for revitalization, unification, or cultural education. At other times it has played a key mediating role with the town administration and political institutions. It has always been essential in strengthening our position.

One regret that has remained constant over the years—shared also by the children—has been our inability to offer a significant number of male teachers. Until a few years ago, Italian law forbade males to teach preprimary children—an immensely stupid law that we openly transgressed, ignoring the warnings and reprimands from the Ministry of Education. Now this prohibition has been lifted, yet other reasons still make it difficult to hire male teachers in the schools for young children. To make matters worse, in Italy as in several other European countries, today there are fewer women choosing to become teachers of young children. Those who do, tend to leave this type of job more easily for something else. The reasons for this phenomenon are many and should be studied carefully. But the results are clear in terms of the costs paid by children, in loss of dignity for schools, teachers, and the entire culture.

The Questionable Training of Teachers

Gandini: *Tell me about the training of the teachers of young children.*

Malaguzzi: The preparation of teachers to work with young children is, I believe, a sort of legally sanctioned farce, really unspeakable. It is, and has been, dominated by the Roman Catholic church. Since 1923, the Italian government has run only six preparatory schools for preprimary teachers—all located in small, country towns with the naive, idealistic belief that the purest source of teachers of young children would be adolescent girls untouched by the moral disorders of the city.

In 1960, there were 129 preparatory schools for preprimary teachers under private Catholic auspices with 21,621 students, versus the six state schools with only 2,531 students. Today the same proportions hold true. All of these schools are at the secondary school level but are less rigorous than the regular secondary schools that train teachers for the elementary level. They do not, and never have had, a common program of studies; indeed, the only thing they have in common is the final examination. The training lasts but 3 years. A student can enroll after finishing middle school and, therefore, obtain a diploma at age 17. The preparation is founded on nothing, in terms of either a liberal arts foundation or appropriate professional studies. There is in the works a major reform that would include a university preparation for teachers of young children, but achieving that reform will be difficult.

Even in Reggio Emilia, our teachers come out of these preparatory secondary schools. Therefore, you can see why their professional formation and development must take place while on the job working with the children.

Formation and Reformation of Teachers

Gandini: *How do you now go about supporting teacher development in your schools?*

Malaguzzi: We have no alternatives but in-service training. As the intelligence becomes stronger through use, so does the teacher's role, knowledge,

FIGURE 3.8. One of the teachers' regular meetings to plan and discuss their work.

profession, and competence become stronger through direct application. Teachers—like children and everyone else—feel the need to grow in their competences; they want to transform experiences into thoughts, thoughts into reflections, and reflections into new thoughts and new actions. They also feel a need to make predictions, to try things out, and then interpret them. The act of interpretation is most important. Teachers must learn to interpret ongoing processes rather than wait to evaluate results. In the same way, their role as educators must include understanding children as producers, not as consumers. They must learn to teach nothing to children except what children can learn by themselves. And furthermore, they must be aware of the perceptions the children form of the adults and their actions. In order to enter into relationships with the children that are at the same time productive, amiable, and exciting, teachers must be aware of the risk in expressing judgments too quickly. They must enter the time frame of the children, whose interests emerge only in the course of activity or negotiations arising from that activity. They must realize how listening to children is both necessary and expedient. They must know that activities should be as numerous as the keys of a piano, and that all call forth infinite acts of intelligence when children are offered a wide variety of options to chose from. Furthermore, teachers must be aware that practice cannot be separated from objectives or values and that professional growth comes partly through individual effort, but in a much richer way through discussion with colleagues, parents, and experts. Finally, they need to know that it is possible to engage in the challenge of longitudinal observations and small research projects concerning the development or experiences of children. Indeed, education without research or innovation is education without interest.

Already this is no small task! However, it is not possible even to begin if teachers do not have a basic knowledge about different content areas of teaching in order to transform this knowledge into 100 languages and 100 dialogues with children. We have at present limited means to prepare teachers as we would like, but we try to look within ourselves and find inspiration from the things we do.

The *Atelier* as a Place of Provocation

Gandini: *How did the idea and the establishment of the* atelier *work into your educational project?*

Malaguzzi: I will not hide from you how much hope we invested in the introduction of the *atelier*. We knew it would be impossible to ask for anything more. Yet, if we could have done so we would have gone further still by creating a new type of school typology with a new school made entirely of laboratories similar to the *atelier*. We would have constructed a new type of school made of spaces where the hands of children could be active for "messing about" (in the sense that David Hawkins was going to tell us better, later). With no possibility of boredom, hands and minds would engage each other with great, liberating merriment in the way ordained by biology and evolution.

Although we did not come close to achieving those impossible ideals, still the *atelier* has always repaid us. It has, as desired, proved to be subversive—generating complexity and new tools for thought. It has allowed rich combinations and creative possibilities among the different (symbolic) languages of children. The *atelier* has protected us not only from the long-winded speeches and didactic theories of our time (just about the only preparation received by young teachers!), but also from the behavioristic beliefs of the surrounding culture, reducing the human mind to some kind of "container" to be filled.

The *atelier* has met other needs as well. One of the most urgent problems was how to achieve effective communication with the parents. We wanted to always keep them informed about the goings-on in the schools, and at the same time establish a system of communication that would document the work being done with the children. We wanted to show parents how the children thought and expressed themselves, what they produced and invented with their hands and their intelligence, how they played and joked with one another, how they discussed hypotheses, how their logic functioned. We wanted the parents to see that their children had richer resources and more skills than generally realized. We wanted the parents to understand how much value we placed in their children. In return, then, we felt it would be fair to ask parents to help us and be on our side.

The *atelier*, a space rich in materials, tools, and people with professional competences, has contributed much to our work on documentation. This work has strongly informed—little by little—our way of being with children. It has also, in a rather beautiful way, obliged us to refine our methods of observation and recording so that the processes of children's learning became the basis of our dialogue with parents. Finally, our work in the *atelier* has provided us with archives that are now a treasure trove of children's work and teachers' knowledge and research. Let me emphasize, however, that the *atelier* was never intended to be a sort of secluded, privileged space, as if there and only there the languages of expressive art could be produced.

It was, instead, a place where children's different languages could be explored by them and studied by us in a favorable and peaceful atmosphere. We and they could experiment with alternative modalities, techniques, instruments, and materials; explore themes chose by children or suggested by us; perhaps work on a large fresco in a group; perhaps prepare a poster where one makes a concise statement through words and illustrations; perhaps even master small projects on a reduced scale, stealing their skills from architects! What was important was to help the children find their own styles of exchanging with friends both their talents and their discoveries.

But the *atelier* was most of all a place for research, and we expect that it will continue and increase. We have studied everything, from the affinities and oppositions of different forms and colors, to the complex aims of narrative and argumentation; from the transition of expressing images in symbols to decoding them; from the way children have been contaminated by exposure to mass media, to gender differences in symbolic and expressive preferences. We have always found it a privilege to be able to encounter the fascinating multiple games that can be played with images: turning a poppy into a spot, a light, a bird in flight, a lighted ghost, a handful of red petals within a field of green and yellow wheat. So positive and confirming were our experiences that they eventually led us to expand the use of the *atelier* into the centers for the youngest children in the infant–toddler centers.

Genesis and Meanings of Creativity

Gandini: *Creative behavior and creative production by children has been an elusive theme, about which pages and pages have been written. What is your own view on the subject?*

Malaguzzi: We were all very weak and unprepared in the 1950s when the theme of creativity, just landed from the United States, crossed our path. I remember the eagerness with which we read the theories of J.P. Guilford and Paul Torrance. I also remember how later on those theories could be reread and reinterpreted through the perspectives of Bruner, Piaget, and the Cognitivists, the neo-Freudians, Kurt Lewin, the last of the Gestalt psychologists, and the humanistic psychologists Carl Rogers and Abraham Maslow.

It was a difficult but exciting period; we felt that those proposals had great vigor and potential. The work on creativity seemed disruptive to many (almost too many) things; for example, the philosophical dimension of man and life and the productivity of thought. These proposals went so far as to suggest complicity with the unconscious, chance and the emotions with feelings, and so on. Yet, despite their brilliant attractiveness, we have to say frankly that after many years of work, the progress of our own experience, plus our observation and study of children and adults, have suggested to us much caution and reflection.

As we have chosen to work with children we can say that they are the best evaluators and the most sensitive judges of the values and usefulness of creativity. This comes about because they have the privilege of not being excessively attached to their own ideas, which they construct and reinvent continuously. They are apt to explore, make discoveries, change their points of view, and fall in love with forms and meanings that transform themselves.

Therefore, as we do not consider creativity sacred, we do not consider it as extraordinary but rather as likely to emerge from daily experience. This view is now shared by many. We can sum up our beliefs as follows:

1. Creativity should not be considered a separate mental faculty but a characteristic of our way of thinking, knowing, and making choices.

FIGURE 3.9. "A leaf can become...." Drawings by children of the Diana School.

2. Creativity seems to emerge from multiple experiences, coupled with a well-supported development of personal resources, including a sense of freedom to venture beyond the known.
3. Creativity seems to express itself through cognitive, affective, and imaginative processes. These come together and support the skills for predicting and arriving at unexpected solutions.
4. The most favorable situation for creativity seems to be interpersonal exchange, with negotiation of conflicts and comparison of ideas and actions being the decisive elements.

5. Creativity seems to find its power when adults are less tied to prescriptive teaching methods, but instead become observers and interpreters of problematic situations.
6. Creativity seems to be favored or disfavored according to the expectations of teachers, schools, families, and communities as well as society at large, according to the ways children perceive those expectations.
7. Creativity becomes more visible when adults try to be more attentive to the cognitive processes of children than to the results they achieve in various fields of doing and understanding.
8. The more teachers are convinced that intellectual and expressive activities have both multiplying and unifying possibilities, the more creativity favors friendly exchanges with imagination and fantasy.
9. Creativity requires that the *school of knowing* finds connections with *the school of expressing,* opening the doors (this is our slogan) to the hundred languages of children.

Starting with these ideas, we have been trying to understand how they should be revised, yet without letting the myths of spontaneity, which often accompany the myths of creativity, mislead us. We are convinced that between basic intellectual capacities and creativity, a theme preferred by American research, there is not opposition but rather complementarity. The spirit of play can pervade also the formation and construction of thought.

Often when people come to us and observe our children, they ask us which magic spell we have used. We answer that their surprise equals our surprise. Creativity? It is always difficult to notice when it is dressed in everyday clothing and has the ability to appear and disappear suddenly. Our task, regarding creativity, is to help children climb their own mountains, as high as possible. No one can do more. We are restrained by our awareness that people's expectations about creativity should not weigh on the school. An excessive widening of its functions and powers would give to the school an exclusive role that it cannot have.

PART V: IMAGES OF CHILDHOOD

Sweeping Childhood Under the Rug

Gandini: *The predicament of childhood today is the subject of much writing. What are your views on this?*

Malaguzzi: The dramatic contradictions that characterize the education of children are constantly on my mind. I am speaking about what we know of children versus what we do not know, as well as what we know but fail to do with them and for them. But the problem is wider still, for it involves the human race and the waste of its intelligence and humanity. I think David Hawkins says it best: "In its organization, in its choices, in its ways to come into relation with learning and knowledge, the educational system badly represents the nature and the potential of human capability" (personal communication; also see Hawkins, 1966).

All people—and I mean scholars, researchers, and teachers, who in any place have set themselves to study children seriously—have ended up by discovering not so much the limits and weaknesses of children but rather their surprising and extraordinary strengths and capabilities linked with an inexhaustible need for expression and realization.

But the results of those learned inquiries, describing new aspects of development and opening endless possibilities for practical application and ethical and philosophical consideration, have not been sufficiently seized on by educators. Instead, during this delay, metaphors and images reemerge portraying childhood in one of two extreme ways: as blank, powerless, and entirely shaped by adults; or on the other hand, as autonomously capable of gaining control of the adult world. We have not correctly legitimized a culture of childhood, and the consequences are seen in all our social, economic, and political choices and investments. It is a typical, frightening example of offense and betrayal of human resources.

Specific instances are clearly visible in Europe and the rest of the Western World. We see budgetary cuts, lack of policy and planning, a general lowering of prestige for those who teach or study children, with consequent loss of young people from the profession and the growth of child abuse. We can speak of all of this bad news for children without even mentioning the disasters of war and epidemics that still ravage our planet and conscience.

It is a painful story. John Dewey confronted this same situation earlier in the century and was inspired to urge a method of education combining pragmatic philosophy, new psychological knowledge, and—on the teaching side—mastery of content with inquiring, creative experiences for children. He envisioned all this, also seeking a new relationship between educational and sociocultural research. This last aspect, I believe, is part of the unfinished business of the democratic process, but represents the genuine cultural achievement that childhood and coming generations have a right to expect. Dewey said that human institutions ought to be judged by their educational influence, and by the measure of their capacity to extend the knowledge and competence of man.

I know all this could take place in such a moment as the present, when science, history, and the public conscience appear unanimous in recognizing the child as endowed with the virtues, resources, and intrinsic rights that we already mentioned. But a child so endowed paradoxically explodes in the hands of his creators; such a child becomes too overwhelming for philosophy, science, education, and political economy. The incapacity of societies to respond to such a child would seem to cast doubt on the nobility of our motives regarding children.

Others, too, have sometimes masked their true interests, perhaps even from themselves. Queen Elizabeth (Horace Walpole tells us in his *Anecdotes of Painting,* 1762–1771) was a great collector, yet there is no proof that she admired or loved the art of painting. What is absolutely certain is that she loved, with passion, the paintings that portrayed herself!

The Differences Among Children

Gandini: *One aspect that the visitors to your schools find puzzling is how you can respond to children's different capabilities and needs when you give such importance to social relationships and group work.*

Malaguzzi: We certainly recognize differences in the makeup of children along with differences that can be reduced or widened by the favorable or unfavorable influences of the environment. But children have—this is my conviction—a common gift, namely, the potential and competencies that we have already described. We hold this to be true for children who are born in any culture in any place on our planet. Yet, recognizing the universality of children's potential opens ups new questions with which so far we in Reggio Emilia have had little familiarity, but which the multicultural events of our time press on us with urgency.

I would be very cautious concerning differences in cognitive style and strategies. People are too quick to attribute them to one season of life, especially when looking at infants, whose minds undergo many rapid reorganizations and changes in development. The styles we observe are an objective fact about individuals. Beyond that, however, they also reflect the historical and cultural context.

The wider the range of possibilities we offer children, the more intense will be their motivations and the richer their experiences. We must widen the range of topics and goals, the types of situations we offer and their degree of structure, the kinds and combinations of resources and materials, and the possible interactions with things, peers, and adults. Moreover, widening the range of possibilities for children also has consequences for others. It requires teachers to be more attentive and aware, and makes them more capable of observing and interpreting children gestures and speech. Teachers thereby become more responsive to children's feedback, take more control over their own expressive feedback to children (correcting excessive monotony or excitement), and make their interventions with children more personal. All of this will make it easier for teachers to pause and make self-evaluations.

The more we distance ourselves from quick and temporary solutions, from responding to individual differences in a hurried way, the wider will be the range of hypotheses open to us. The more we resist the temptation to classify children, the more capable we become to change our plans and make available different activities. This does not eliminate the responsibility or usefulness of noting differences among children. Let us take them into account, let us keep an eye on them. But let us always exercise caution and learn to observe and evaluate better without assigning levels or grades. Let me add that in reading the specialized literature on evaluation, I have not found the factor of time to be treated correctly. Ferdinando Pessoa (1986) says that the measure of the clock is false. It is certainly false concerning the time of children—for situations in which true teaching and learning take place, for the subjective experience of childhood. One has to respect the time of maturation; of development; of the tools of doing and understanding; of the full, slow, extravagant, lucid, and ever-changing emergence of children's capacities; it is a measure of cultural and biological wisdom.

If nature has commanded that of all the animals, infancy shall last longest in human beings—infinitely long, says Tolstoy—it is because nature knows how many rivers there are to cross and paths to retrace. Nature provides time for mistakes to be corrected (by both children and adults), for prejudices to be overcome, and for children to catch their breath and restore their images of themselves, peers, parents, teachers, and the world. If today we find ourselves in an era in which the time and rhythm of machines and profits dominate those of human beings, then we want to know where psychology, education, and culture stand.

FIGURE 3.10. A small group of children share ideas and discoveries at the computer.

PART VI: THEORIES OF LEARNING

The Construction of Meanings

Gandini: *One debate in education that seems never to be settled concerns the role of the adult in children's learning. What are your thoughts about this?*

Malaguzzi: I would not want to minimize the determining role of adults in providing children with semantic structures/systems of meaning that allow minds to communicate. But at the same time, I would like to emphasize children's own participation: They are autonomously capable of making meaning from their daily life experiences through mental acts involving planning, coordination of ideas, and abstraction. Remember, meanings are never static, univocal, or final; they are always generative of other meanings. The central act of adults, therefore, is to activate, especially indirectly, the meaning-making competencies of children as a basis of all learning. They must try to capture the right moments, and then find the right approaches, for bringing together, into a fruitful dialogue, their meanings and interpretations with those of the children.

Our Piaget

Gandini: *You have mentioned Piaget's influence on your work, and at the same time you have mentioned that your views differ from his on various points. Can you tell us more about this influence and the differences?*

Malaguzzi: We maintain intact our sense of gratitude toward Piaget. If Jean Jacques Rousseau invented a revolutionary conception of childhood without ever dealing with children, Piaget was the first to give them an identity based on a close analysis of their development by observing and talking to children over extended periods of time.

Howard Gardner describes Piaget as the first to take children seriously; David Hawkins describes him as the one who dramatized children splendidly; while Jerome Bruner credits Piaget with demonstrating that those internal principles of logic guiding children are the same principles as those that guide scientists in their inquiries. In fact, in Reggio we know that children can use creativity as a tool for inquiring, ordering, and even transgressing the given schemes of meaning (which Piaget attributed also to the very young in the last years of his life). They can also use creativity as a tool for their own progress in the worlds of necessity and possibility.

With a simple-minded greed, we educators have tried too often to extract from Piaget's psychology things that he did not consider at all usable in education. He would wonder what use teachers could possibly have for his theories of stages, conservation of matter, and so on. In fact, the richest potentiality of Piagetian thought lies in the domain of epistemology, as seen in his major opus, *The Biology of Knowledge* (1971, the University of Chicago Press). Nevertheless, many suggestions can be taken directly or indirectly from his works to reflect and elaborate on the meaning of education.

Barbel Inhelder, Piaget's most devoted disciple, told friends after the death of the Maestro: "Write freely about his work, make corrections, try to render his thought more specific; still, it will not be easy for you to overturn the underlying structure of his ingenious theories." We in Reggio have followed her advice. Our interest in him increased once we understood that his concern was with epistemology, and that his main goal was to trace the genesis of universal invariant structures. Piaget sacrificed many things to that audacious research; yet he also managed to open other paths of research, such as the study of moral judgment, that he did not pursue, as if a fever was burning in him to simultaneously explore many directions. Some of these paths he later rediscovered after they have been casually abandoned.

Now we can see clearly how Piaget's constructivism isolates the child. As a result we look critically at these aspects: the undervaluation of the adult's role in promoting cognitive development; the marginal attention to social interaction and to memory (as opposed to inference); the distance interposed between thought and language (Vygotsky criticized this, and Piaget, 1962, responded); the lock-step linearity of development in constructivism; the way that cognitive, affective, and moral development are treated as separate, parallel tracks; the overemphasis on structured stages, egocentrism, and classificatory skills; the lack of recognition for partial competencies; the overwhelming importance to logicomathematical thought; and the overuse of paradigms from the biological and physical sciences. After making all of these criticisms, however, we must go on to note that many constructivists today have turned their attention to the role of social interaction in cognitive development.

The Dilemma of Learning and Teaching

Gandini: *Learning and teaching do not always go together, but in your program you have found ways to help children construct their learning. How did you balance this equation?*

Malaguzzi: After all we have said about children, we have to discuss more fully the role that children assume in the construction of self and knowledge, and the help they get in these matters from adults. It is obvious that between learning and teaching, we honor the first. It is not that we ostracize teaching, but that we declare, "Stand aside for a while and leave room for learning, observe carefully what children do, and then, if you have understood well, perhaps teaching will be different from before."

Piaget (1974) warned us that a decision must be made about whether to teach schemes and structures directly or to present the child with rich problem-solving situations in which the active child learns from them in the course of exploration. The objective of education is to increase possibilities for the child to invent and discover. Words should not be used as a shortcut to knowledge. Like Piaget, we agree that the aim of teaching is to provide conditions for learning.

Sometimes discussions about education treat teaching and learning as almost synonymous. In reality, the conditions and goals of the one who teaches are not identical to the conditions and goals of the one who learns. If teaching is monodirectional and rigidly structured according to some "science," it becomes intolerable, prejudicial, and damaging to the dignity of both teacher and learner.

But even where teachers assume themselves to be democratic, their behavior still too often is dominated by undemocratic teaching strategies. These include directives, ritualized procedures, systems of evaluation (which Benjamin Bloom believed should be properly guiding models of education), and rigid cognitivistic curriculum packages, complete with readymade scripts and reinforcement contingencies. All of these strategies provide a professional justification for waste and suffering, and at the same time create the illusion of an impressive system that reassures adults at an unthinking level. Official adoption is easy. By the time the shortcomings of such a package or system do emerge, it is already too late and the damage is done.

To conclude, learning is the key factor on which a new way of teaching should be based, becoming a complementary resource to the child and offering multiple options, suggestive ideas, and sources of support. Learning and teaching should not stand on opposite banks and just watch the river flow by; instead, they should embark together on a journey down the water. Through an active, reciprocal exchange, teaching can strengthen learning how to learn.

Our Vygotsky

Gandini: *You have mentioned the importance of the teacher's being able to capture the delicate moment in which the child is ready to take a step toward learning. Could you elaborate on that?*

Malaguzzi: At this point the intervention of Vygotsky, our own Vygotsky, becomes indispensable for clarifying this and other points raised in the previous paragraphs. Vygotsky reminds us how thought and language are operative together to form ideas and to make a plan for action, and then for executing, controlling, describing, and discussing that action. This is a precious insight for education.

But on penetrating the adult–child relationship, and thus returning to the theme of teaching and learning, the Russian psychologist (1978) tells us about the advantages of the *zone of proximal development;* that is, the distance between the levels of capacities expressed by children and their levels of potential development, attainable with the help of adults or more advanced contemporaries.

The matter is somewhat ambiguous. Can one give competence to someone who does not have it? The very suggestion sees to readmit the old ghosts of teaching that we tried to chase away. But we can dispel any risk of returning to traditional teaching by holding to our principle of *circularity* (a term not seen in

Vygotsky's writings). Put more simply, we seek a situation in which the child is about to see what the adult already sees. The gap is small between what each one sees, the task of closing it appears feasible, and the child's skills and disposition create an expectation and readiness to make the jump. In such a situation, the adult can and must loan to the children his judgment and knowledge. But it is a loan with a condition, namely, that the child will repay.

It is useless to assert that the readiness of children is too hard to observe. It can indeed be seen! We need to be prepared to see it, for we tend to notice only those things that we expect. but also we should not be in a hurry. We tend all too often today to become slaves of the clock, an instrument that falsifies the natural and subjective time of children and adults.

Vygotsky's suggestion maintains its value and legitimates broad interventions by teachers. For our part in Reggio, Vygotsky's approach is in tune with the way we see the dilemma of teaching and learning and the ecological way one can reach knowledge.

PART VII: FROM THEORY TO PRACTICE

A Profession That Does Not Think Small

Gandini: *How have you gone about putting into practice the many ideas and inspirations that you have either generated or encountered?*

Malaguzzi: The effect of theories can be inspiring and onerous at the same time. This is especially so when it is time to roll up our sleeves and proceed with educational practice. The first fear is to lose the capacity or the ability to connect the theories with the objective problems of daily work, which in turn are generally complicated by administrative, legal, or cultural realities.

But there are further fears, such as those of getting lost in a blind empiricism that can lead to a break with the connections to the necessary theoretical, ideal, and ethical principles; being troubled by the challenge of new theories and approaches that can bring into question your own training and choices; and, last but not least, missing out on the promise that the schools provide as best as possible for all the children as well as meet the expectations and needs of their families. These fears are unavoidable because in our task we cannot be satisfied with approximate results and because our choice was to set up a school with a critical and reforming function. We did not want to be only perfunctory caretakers.

Our theories come from different fields and we meditate on them as well as on the events that take place in our very hands. But a unifying theory of education that sums up all the phenomena of educating does not (and never will) exist. However, we do indeed have a solid core in our approach in Reggio Emilia that comes directly from the theories and experiences of active education and finds realization in particular images of the child, teacher, school, fam-

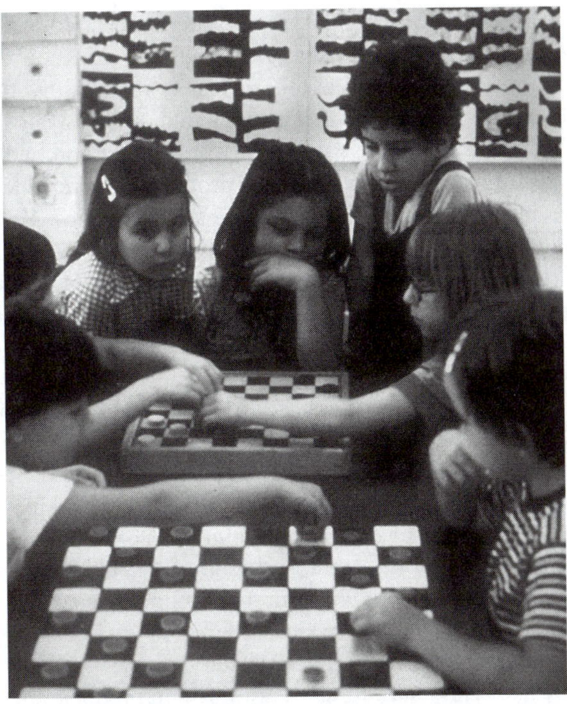

FIGURE 3.11. Five-year-old children taking their time playing checkers.

ily, and community. Together these produce a culture and society that connect, actively and creatively, both individual and social growth.

And still Ferrière, Dewey, Vygotsky, Bruner, Piaget, Bronfenbrenner, and Hawkins are very much present for us, along with the latest suggestions from Kaye on the tutorial role of the adult, Shaffer on the relationship between language and social interaction, Serge Moscovici and Gabriel Mugny on the genesis of representation and the importance of the interpersonal cognitive constructions, and Gardner on the forms of intelligence and open minds. In the same way we look to the sociolinguistic work on how adults and children jointly construct contexts of meaning, as well as to cognitive research founded on constructivist, symbolic interactionist, and social constructivist perspectives. Altogether, this literature counteracts the behaviorist theories that reduce the creative and protagonistic force of human action to simple, unreadable behavior.

The Success of a Theory Comes Out in the Practice

Gandini: *But how, concretely, do all these theories connect with what goes on in the schools?*

Malaguzzi: It is well known how we all proceed as if we had one or more theories. The same happens for teachers: Whether they know it or not they think and act according to personal theories. The point is how those personal theories are connected with the education of children, with relationships within the school, and with the organization of work. In general, when colleagues work closely together and share common problems, this facilitates the alignment of behaviors and a modification of personal theories. We have always tried to encourage this.

When we start speaking about the theory and practice of education, we can go on and on. I agree with Wilfred Carr (1986) when he says that it is good to avoid discussing theories too much because the risk is to deprive them of their practical aspect. In truth, a theory is legitimate only if it deals with problems that emerge from the practice of education and that can be solved by educators. The task of theory is to help teachers understand better the nature of their problems. This way practice becomes a necessary means for the success of theory. In this vein, taking this thought even further, David Hawkins has observed, "The knowledge of practitioners is meaningfully deeper than any found in the thought of many academic researchers; therefore, the teacher must be treated not as an object of study but as an interpreter of educational phenomena" (personal communication; also see Hawkins, 1966).

This validation of the practical work of the teacher is the only rich "textbook" on which we can count to aid us in developing our educational reflections. Moreover, the work of the teachers, when not abandoned to itself, when not left without the support of institutions and alliances with colleagues and families, is capable not only of producing daily educational experiences, but is also capable of becoming subject and object of critical scrutiny.

Getting From Research to Action

Gandini: *You said that teachers should also be researchers. How do you promote this?*

Malaguzzi: To learn and relearn together with the children is our line of work. We proceed in such a way that the children are not shaped by experience, but are the ones who give shape to it. There are two ways in which we can look into children's learning processes and find clues for supporting them: One is the way children enter into an activity and develop their strategies of thought and action; the other is the way in which the objects involved are transformed. Adults and children go about their learning differently: They use different procedures, honor different principles, make different conjectures, and follow different footprints.

Our teachers do research either on their own or with their colleagues to produce strategies that favor children's work or can be utilized by them. They go from research into action (and vice versa). When all the teachers in the school are in agreement, the projects, strategies, and styles of work become intertwined and the school becomes a truly different school. Some of our teachers proceed in this research with more intentionality and better methods than others; the records and documentaries that result from their endeavors are significant beyond the immediate needs for action and become common objects of study, at times with so much substance as to become of interest to a wider audience. As a result, these teachers feel, and help others to feel, more motivation to grow and attain a much higher level of professionalism. In the process, our teachers realize that they must avoid the temptation of expecting children to give them back what they already know, but that instead they must retain the same sense of wonder that children live through in their discoveries.

This whole approach causes children to be better known by their teachers. Therefore, they feel more open to challenge, more able to work with their peers in unusual situations, and more persistent because they realize that what they have in mind can be tried out. Children know that when pursuing their goals, they can make their own choices, and that is both freeing and revitalizing. It is, indeed, what we had promised the children, their families, and ourselves.

Our way of working makes possible the choice among different modes of interaction. Small groups of children work simultaneously and can be found all around the school setting, organized so as to facilitate social, cognitive, verbal, and symbolic constructions. Our children in fact have many choices: They have places where they can be alone, in a small number, in a large group, with the teachers or without them in the *atelier*, in the *mini-atelier* in the large *piazza*, or, if the weather is good, in the outside courtyard, rich with small and large play structures. But the choice to work in a small group, where they explore together, pleases both them and us. Because of that, the classroom is transformed into one large space with market stalls, each one with its own children and its own projects and activities. This arrangement permits good observations and organically developing research about cooperative learning as well as about the bartering and marketing of ideas.

We like this arrangement of our school. We live in the tradition of a city, with its squares and porticoes, which provide an irreplaceable model for meetings, negotiations, and dialogues of various human encounters; moreover, the central square of our city transforms itself twice a week into the hundred stalls of the market. This market has the same function as the *forum*, of which Bruner (1986) wrote, and whose echo resounds in our schools.

No Planning, Much Reconnaissance

Gandini: *People often ask what kind of curricular planning, if any, you have in Reggio Emilia.*

Malaguzzi: No, our schools have not had, nor do they have, a planned curriculum with units and subunits (lesson plans), as the behaviorists would like. These would push our schools toward teaching without learning; we would humiliate the schools and the children by entrusting them to forms, dittos, and handbooks of which publishers are generous distributors.

Instead, every year each school delineates a series of related projects, some short range and some long. These themes serve as the main structural supports, but then it is up to the children, the course of events, and the teachers to determine whether the building turns out to be a hut on stilts or an apartment house or whatever.

But, of course, infant–toddler and preprimary teachers do not start off each school year at square one. They have standing behind them a patrimony of talent, knowledge, experiments, research, documentation, and examples showing successes and failures. The teachers follow the children, not plans. The goals are important and will not be lost from sight, but more important are the why and the how of reaching them.

Reconnaissance is a strong word in our vocabulary. Our schools start off with a reconnaissance flight over all the human, environmental, technical, and cultural resources. Then more reconnaissance missions will be made to get a full overview of the situation: within and among schools, to families and advisory councils, to the pedagogical team, and to the town administration and elected officials. Also, teachers do reconnaissance trips through workshops, seminars, and meetings with experts in various fields.

What educators acquire by discussing, proposing, and launching new ideas is not only a set of professional tools, but also a work ethic that gives more value to being part of a group and to having interpersonal solidarity, while at the same time strengthening intellectual autonomy. The support resulting from an *itinerant reconnaissance education* gives us great strength and help. Its task is to startle and push us along new roads. There is not a better evaluation of our work than this.

If the Curricula Are Found in the Children

Gandini: *Children are the ones who shape their school experience rather than being shaped by them. How does this principle influence your choices about what experiences to offer to children?*

Malaguzzi: If the school for young children has to be preparatory and provide continuity with the elementary school, then we as educators are already prisoners of a model that ends up as a funnel. I think, moreover, that the funnel is a detestable object, and it is not much appreciated by children either. Its purpose is to narrow down what is big into what is small. This choking device is against nature. If you put it upside down, it serves no purpose.

Suffice it to say that the school for young children has to respond to the children: It should be a giant rodeo where they learn how to ride 100 horses, real or imaginary. How to approach a horse, how to stroke it, and how to stay close to it are all aspects of an art that can be learned. If there are rules, children will

FIGURE 3.12. The children activities supported by teachers.

learn them. If they fall off, they will get back on. If special skills are called for, they will watch their more expert contemporaries carefully, and they will even discuss the problem or ask to borrow the adults' experience.

It is true that we do not have planning and curricula. It is not true that we rely on improvisation, which is an enviable skill. We do not rely on chance either, because we are convinced that what we do not yet know can to some extent be anticipated. What we do know is that to be with children is to work one third with certainty and two thirds with uncertainty and the new. The one third that is certain makes us understand and try to understand. We want to study whether learning has its own flux, time, and place; how learning can be organized and encouraged; how situations favorable to learning can be prepared; which skills and cognitive schemes are worth bolstering; how to advance words, graphics, logical thought, body language, symbolic languages, fantasy, narrative, and argumentation; how to play; how to pretend; how friendships form and dissipate; how individual and group identities develop; and how differences and similarities emerge.

All this wisdom does not compensate for what we do not know. But not knowing is the condition that makes us continue to search; in this regard we are in the same situation as the children. We can be sure that the children are ready to help us. They can help by offering us ideas, suggestions, problems, questions, clues, and paths to follow; and the more they trust us and see us as a resource, the more they give us help. All these offerings, merged with what we ourselves bring to the situation, make a handsome capital of resources.

In the last few years we have undertaken many experiments: how children 5 years old approach the computer; the differences between graphics by boys and girls; the symbolic meanings of drawings; the constructive capacities of logical-organizational thought (which led to a documentary now revisited with George Forman); the acquisition of reading and writing in a communicative context; the forms of thought used in learning about measurement and numbers; cooperative learning through play (in collaboration with Carolyn Edwards, Lella Gandini, and John Nimmo); and the behavior of infants aged 2 in partially structured situations. The results of these studies guide us in the formulation of flexible projects. But there is another reason for experimenting and documenting, namely the necessity to reveal in full light the image of a competent child. This, in turn, bolsters our position against detractors and the mystification of official programs and practices.

In our documentaries, archives, and exhibits, which now tour the world, there is the entire story. It is a history of grown-ups, projects, curricula that are emerging, but above all, it is about the children.

PART VIII: PERTINENT EXPECTATIONS[1]

What Makes a Good Project

Gandini: *Many teachers also ask about the outstanding project work of children in Reggio Emilia. In your view, Loris, what elements contribute to making a "good" project?*

Malaguzzi: We use projects because relying on the capacities and resources of children expresses our philosophical view. Either a school is capable of continually transforming itself in response to children or the school becomes something that goes around and around, remaining in the same spot.

In trying to make a good project, one has to have, above all, a pertinent expectation, shaped in advance, an expectation also felt by the children. This expectation helps the adults in terms of their attentiveness, choices, methods of intervention, and what they do concerning the relationships among participants.

Gandini: *Could you speak about the choice of projects to undertake? Are they often based on something that is already part of their ongoing experience?*

Malaguzzi: Yes. Sometimes we pursue something that already belongs to them, but other times we follow something new. The teachers need only to observe and listen to the children, as they continuously suggest to us what interests them, and what they would like to explore in a deeper way. It is good when the adults' own interests coincide with those of the children, so they can move easily to support children's motivation and pleasure.

A good project has a few essential elements. First it must produce or trigger an initial motivation, to warm up the children. Each project has a sort of prologue phase, in which information and ideas are offered and shared within the group. These will be used later to help the children to expand their intentions along with the adults' intentions, suggesting a final objective.

---

[1] This portion of the interview took place in April 1992, while Lella Gandini with George Forman observed and participated in the project, "The Amusement Park for Birds." Loris Malaguzzi liked the interview very much but did not edit the transcription as he had done for the other interviews.

Gandini: *A discussion at the beginning, to gather the memories, thoughts, and desires of the children, is a very effective way to start.*

Malaguzzi: Yes, because it helps the adults to make predictions and hypotheses about what could happen next. Some of these expectations will not come to pass, but others will come alive during the journey taken with the children in the course of the project. And it is not only the adults who form expectations and hypotheses; those of children—who can use their capacities to make predictions—are also needed to organize the work. The strong motivation with which the children embark will help them to feel comfortable as they go down many different paths, abandoning some, trying others. To this task they will bring different kinds of intelligences and attitudes and produce an extraordinary blooming of ideas, and also (through their negotiation) a convergence in which ideas become sharper and more selected. They feel free to do so because they are not afraid of mistakes or of demolishing their own ideas. The project's objective serves as a permanent beacon that is always present. It gives the children enormous energy, because they know where they must arrive.

All through the project, adults should intervene as little as possible. Instead they should set up situations, and make many choices that facilitate the work of children. The adults have to continually revisit what has been happening, discuss the findings among themselves, and use what they learn to decide how and how much to enter into the action to keep the children's motivation high.

There are many scientific theories about motivation, but I think teachers can learn a great deal about it by working with children. Some children enter the game right away, and do not need warming up. Others warm up during the first activities. Others warm up only when something challenges their ideas within the great market of exchanges.

From Discussion to Graphic Representation

Gandini: *The prologue of discussion among children is often followed by having them do a graphic representation; that in turn is followed by another discussion, and so on. How do you see one mode of expression influencing the other, and vice versa?*

Malaguzzi: The verbal discussion is certainly the coordinating fulcrum of negotiations within the group—I mean here the small group—and it makes working together possible. Those children who are weaker in their language abilities may have some difficulty entering this great game in an active way, and therefore, we have to be very attentive to them. We must also be attentive to blocks on communication due to children's feelings, as for example, when one child feels he or she does not belong with the others in the group.

Words are powerful because they are not only the couriers of ideas, but also allow for their negotiation and transformation. The question of transferring words into graphic representation is not simple because it involves making strong selections. In moving past the flood of spoken words, the children have to say no to many thoughts to which they might be emotionally attached. Sometimes they will need to pause in order to clarify ideas before putting them down on paper and making them visible to others.

Putting ideas into the form of graphic representation allows the children to understand that their actions can communicate. This is an extraordinary discovery because it helps them realize that in order to communicate, their graphic must be understandable to others. In our view, graphic representation is a tool of communication much simpler and clearer than words.

Gandini: *I like very much what you are saying, which explains why children feel a need to put their thoughts on paper. I saw your teachers often use this process as a basis for next conversations with the children, asking them to explain what they drew and why; or they ask them to do the same but with friends in a pair or a group.*

Malaguzzi: This is a procedure that we always follow. When children are asked to proceed this way, they and the observing adults are able to revisit what has been happening. The adults should become scribes for the children and take notes that capture the details of what the children say and do. They can use the notes to talk again with the children and tell them, "Today you have done this work, and you arrived here. Tomorrow morning this is where we will start."

Gandini: *Could you tell us more about the power of graphic expression?*

Malaguzzi: The use of graphic expression comes from the need to bring clarity. There is also the fact that the child intuitively becomes aware about what this new code can produce from now on. As they go from one symbolic language to another, the children find that each transformation generates something new. This complicates the situation and advances them. As they construct their ideas, they also construct the symbols and a plurality of codes. Therefore, when they draw, they are not only making a graphic intervention, but they are selecting ideas and getting rid of excessive, superfluous, or misleading ones. They have to reestablish and clarify the frames or contours of the problem. With each step, the child goes farther and higher, as a spaceship with several stages, each pushing the rocket deeper into space.

Another reason that children like to pass through graphic expression is that they feel it as something that consolidates solidarity of thought, of action, of perspectives with other children. I could say that graphic expression serves more as a tie that favors collaborative capacities, so that the game of learning among children does not end and rather allows for discoveries to continue, to follow one after another.

Gandini: *Clearly you think it is valuable when children go back and forth between representational means or different symbolic languages. Does going from one symbolic system to another help the children to communicate? Is it satisfying to them and to others around them?*

Malaguzzi: Here we ought to agree on a definition of symbol, because, in general, when we say *symbol,* everyone has a different interpretation and the meaning becomes vague. To me, a symbol is a word or image that stands for something else. I think this can be our working definition; it is the nucleus that selects and holds secondary aspects. Symbols have profound relations with emotions, feelings, with many things that cannot be quantified through observation.

Gandini: *And when we speak of symbolic language?*

Malaguzzi: Because we are speaking of schools, we are referring to the ways in which symbols are used by children to acquire culture, grow, and communicate. I do not want to limit the domain of symbolic languages only to reading, writing, and numbers. Symbols are used as well by musicians, storytellers, and others.

Gandini: *When you speak of different languages used by children, you say that children rewrite concepts using different means. They rewrite both their emotions and/or what they have perceived intellectually. Therefore, their growth of knowledge is served by making several passages from one symbolic language to another.*

Malaguzzi: Symbols can be said to be bearers of culture for a person. Another question is how the child learns to detach from the common spoken language in order to connect it with the symbolic one. Through symbols the child learns an economical means of expression. The child learns a way to keep the concepts at hand ready to be transferred to another situation or context. Children have an amazing ability to relate to several symbolic languages at the same time. Children are able to watch television, play with a doll or train, leaf through a book, go away from the room, come back, and still reconstruct what was going on with extraordinary logic and precision.

FIGURE 3.13. Exploring measurement in the school yard.

To Be in a Group Is a Situation of Great Privilege

Gandini: *Thinking about cooperation among children, what does it mean for a small group to work together?*

Malaguzzi: In such a time as this, with society and culture as they are, the fact of young children being capable of being together for several years and working closely together is like an emergency life raft. Their relationships are really something new and different from the close relationships that are inside the family, or the usual peer relationships in traditional schools. These new cooperative relationships among young children have not yet been sufficiently studied in terms of their educational potential. They offer children the opportunity to realize that their ideas are different and not coinciding with the ideas of others, and therefore they discover that they hold their own ideas and unique point of view.

The children realize that the world is multiple and that other children can be discovered through a negotiation of ideas. Instead of interacting only through feelings and a sense of friendship, they discover how satisfying it is to exchange ideas and thereby transform their environment.

However, the differences in development should not be too great. There ought to be a right distance that is capable of producing the exchanges and the negations but at the same time not producing excessive disequilibrium. Therefore it is better, as we have learned through experiences that have been made in many places, that children be discrepant in developmental level but that their differences not be too much.

Children come to realize that through negotiations, their clashes with others can be muted. Children are willing to change their ideas, especially if the pressure to do so comes from peers rather than adults. As they work and play together, sometimes there are moments when their goal really is to establish a good relationship. They find pleasure in being in a group. Even when they disagree, they may keep it to themselves.

Gandini: *You are saying that young children can realize that others hold different points of view, even delay until an appropriate moment the act of expressing and confronting these differences?*

Malaguzzi: When we see young children cooperating, we notice a sort of ethic: they do everything they can to keep the situation stable and ongoing. Some children have more advanced capacities than do others. When one such child makes a suggestion or proposal, the others accept it more willingly than if it had come up from an adult. Many of them learn the relativity of their own point of view and how to represent their ideas in a delicate way. They say, "I think," or "In my view," or "I do not know if my ideas are right for everybody."

Of course, conflicts also exist. Clashes of principles and ideas can be very rich, but do not necessarily need to be expressed through a direct confrontation. Sometimes children feel the disparity of their views but hold back, to maintain the harmony of the group functioning. Later, the contrasting point of view can emerge. Cognitive conflicts are not to be expressed always through confrontation, but may be resolved through an act of love, a peaceful, serene act of acceptance. Sociable emotions have a strong role to play in this complex development.

All of this helps explain why it is so important to record and transcribe the conversations of children. Adults should train themselves to become more sensitive to the layers of meaning in these recorded texts. To find clarity and dispel the fog yields a great deal of information about the thoughts of children. Through careful interpretation, one learns that children continually attempt to draw connections among things and thereby grow and learn.

Therefore, for children to be in a group is a situation of great privilege, as if inside a great, transformative laboratory.

CONCLUSION

Gandini: *We are at the end of our conversation; you have offered much food for thought but not spoiled our appetite for learning more. We are eager to have other opportunities for exchanges with you and the wonderfully competent and warm people who work side*

FIGURE 3.14. Loris Malaguzzi with children and teacher Sheyla Meadow at the kindergarten of Crow Island School in Winnetka, Illinois.

by side with you. The host of bright and hopeful ideas and experiences you have been bringing to children in Reggio Emilia now travels far beyond the confines of your city.

Malaguzzi: This experience and my account of it have no leave-taking. My words instead carry a greeting to our American friends who, like us, are interested in helping children hold their heads high, our friends moreover toward whom we are culturally indebted.

If at the end any message is still needed, it is a message of reflection. I do not know how adult the world of adults really is. I know that the rich, adult world hides many things, whereas the poor one knows neither how nor what to hide. One of the things that it hides with the most rigor and callousness is the condition of children. I will refrain from detailing the data about death and desperation. I know that my account is a luxury; it is a privilege because the children of whom I speak live in the rich world.

But also in this world, deception continues; at times cynical and violent, at times more subtle and sophisticated, laced with hypocrisy and illiberal theories. Deception infiltrates even the institutions of early education. The continuing motivation for our work has been in fact an attempt to oppose, albeit with modest means, this deception and to liberate hopes for a new human culture of childhood. It is a motive that finds its origin in a powerful nostalgia for the future and for mankind.

And now, if you will indulge a weakness on my part, I propose a toast to Benjamin, the youngest child of Howard Gardner and Ellen Winner. Gardner (1989) tells of his trip to China in his book, *To Open Minds,* which I have just finished reading, and not without emotion. Why Benjamin? Because with the key that he earnestly tries to insert in a lock, he can in a way stand for all the children of whom we have been talking. Let us come closer, observe his action, and join in his adventure. It is his, and our, hope.

REFERENCES

Bruner, J. (1986). *Actual minds, possible worlds.* Cambridge, MA: Harvard University Press.

Carr W. (1986). *Becoming critical: Education, knowledge, and action research.* Philadelphia, PA: Falmer Press.

Gardner, H. (1989). *To open minds: Chinese clues to the dilemma of contemporary education.* New York: Basic Books.

Hawkins, D. (1966). Learning the unteachable. In L. Shulman & E. Keislar (Eds.), *Learning by discovery: A critical appraisal.* Chicago: Rand McNally.

Malaguzzi, L. (1971a). *Esperienza per una nuova scuola dell 'infanzia.* [Experiences toward a new school for young children]. Rome: Editori Riuniti.

Malaguzzi, L. (1971b). *La gestione sociale nella scuola dell 'infanzia.* [Community-based management in the school for young children]. Rome: Editori Riuniti.

Pessoa, F. (1986). *Il libro dell'inquietudine.* [The book of inquietudine]. Milan, Italy: Fertrinelli.

Piaget, J. (1962). *Comments on Vygotsky's critical remarks.* Cambridge, MA: MIT Press.

Piaget, J. (1971). *Biology and knowledge.* Chicago: The University of Chicago Press.

Rodari, G. (1973). *Grammatica della fantasia.* Torino, Italy: Einaudi. Translated 1966 as *The Grammar of Fantasy,* Teachers and Writers Collaborative, New York.

Vygotsky, L.S. (1978) *Mind in society: The development of higher psychological processes.* Cambridge, MA: Harvard University Press.

Wertheimer, M. (1945). *Productive thinking.* New York: Harper and Row.

Sergio Spaggiari, director of education in Reggio Emilia.

chapter 4

The Community–Teacher Partnership in the Governance of the Schools

An Interview with Lella Gandini*

Sergio Spaggiari

This is how the children at the Michelangelo School see the Advisory Council:

"It is a committee where people ask questions."
"Somebody asks a question and somebody else answers."
"They make long speeches, like this...Blah...Blah...Blah."
"I think it is a kind of Parliament."
"Yes, yes a Parliament!"

Gandini: *One of the most difficult organizational concepts to understand in the educational approach for young children at Reggio Emilia is that of "social" (or community) participation. Could you describe how this concept came into being?*

Spaggiari: It is a long story. Let me begin by emphasizing that from the 1970s on, the idea of community participation in education has had official backing. It has been viewed as a means of fostering innovation, protecting educational institutions against the dangers of excessive bureaucracy, and stimulat-

* Translated by Victoria Poletto and Lella Gandini

ing cooperation between educators and parents. This participation has evolved into two different forms: first, through the system of community-based management (what we call *gestione sociale*) in the infant–toddler centers and preprimary schools run by the city; and second, through committees in the public schools, with wide representation at every level—primary, middle, and secondary. I am going to speak about the first.

Community-based participation in infant–toddler centers and preprimary schools goes back a long way. We can trace its roots back to the extraordinary educational experiences that developed immediately after the Liberation of Italy in 1945 in certain regions of Italy (Emilia Romagna and Tuscany), thanks to the initiative and participation of women's groups, ex-resistance fighters (ex-partisans), unions, and cooperatives—all directly involved in promoting educational and welfare services. These initiatives embraced people across the social spectrum and from the very beginning emphasized the values of cooperation and involvement.

The first examples of this involvement were the "school-city" committees that were specifically formed to democratically administer schools for young children, and involved both the people who were connected with the school and those peripheral to it. These organizations were created with the specific purpose of "inventing" a school that would involve parents, teachers, citizens, and neighborhood groups not only in the running of the school but also in defending the rights of children.

Furthermore, although the most active and vibrant models of participation were begun by municipal administrations led by political progressives and leftists, we should point out that there is also a clear link between these models and traditional Catholic support for the role of the family and the community, as evidenced through the extended network of parochial preschools.

Gandini: *What exactly is the role of community-based management, and how was it developed and formalized?*

Spaggiari: In 1971, the idea of participation was finally formalized with the passage of national laws governing infant–toddler centers. This concept was one that had gradually evolved over several decades, and finally led to the legal formalization of community-based management. It was in large part the concrete realization of the sustaining slogans of many union and political battles dating back to earlier times. The demand was for the national government to provide public funding, the regional governments to take care of overall planning, and the municipal governments to be responsible for community-based management.

Therefore, in order for the experience of participation to remain valid and vital and not be left to the whims and fancies of the moment, it must be guided by clear and thoughtful pedagogical considerations. Such guidance comes from the municipal administration and the continuity of experience provided to the children and families by the system of infant–toddler centers and preprimary schools.

In the last 15 years, in our country, this experience of community-based management has been consolidated both in infant–toddler centers and preprimary schools. It now encompasses, in both its organizational and educational form, all the processes of participation, democracy, collective responsibility, problem solving, and decision making–processes all integral to an education

TABLE 4.1. The Network of Educational Services of the Reggio Emilia Municipal Administration.

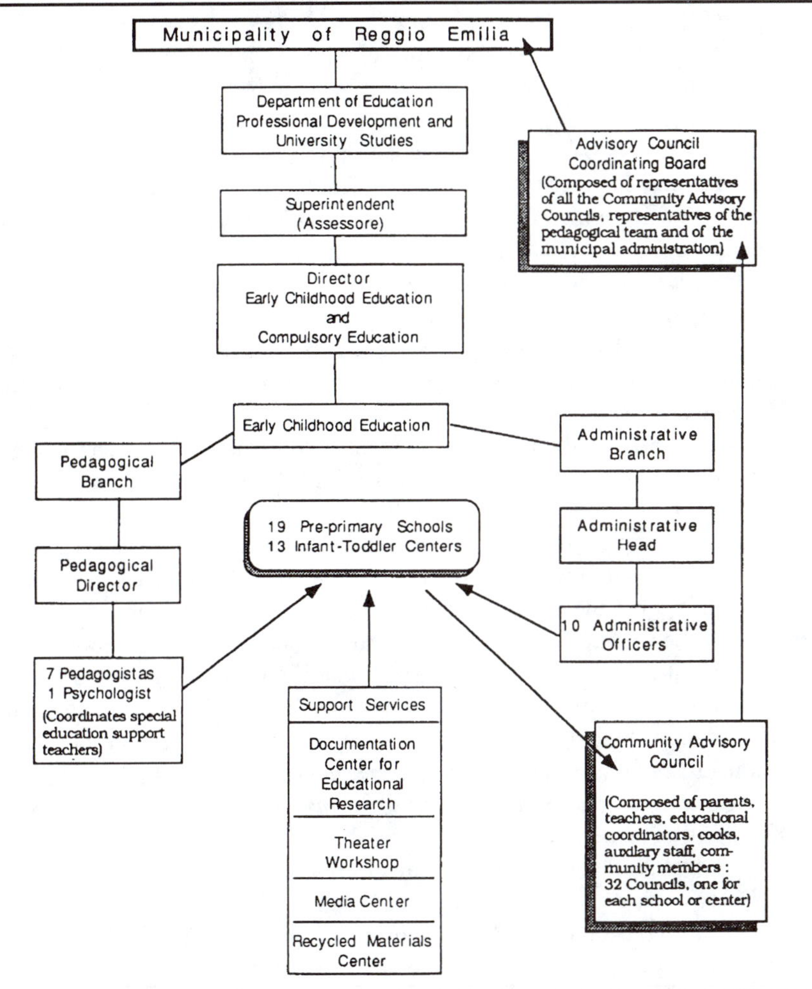

Source: "An Historical Outline, Data and Information" February, 1996 p. 34. Published by the Municipality of Reggio Emilia, Department of Education. Translated and adapted by Lella Gandini. Reprinted by permission.

institution. Community-based management embodies the theoretical and practical synthesis of the interrelationships forged among children, families, service providers, and society at large.

The experience of community-based management has shown its true worth in its ability to adapt to new cultural and social situations such as the influx of newcomers and the recent tendency of parents to view the world in individual rather than political or ideological terms.

Gandini: *How does the idea of community-based management fit in with your overall educational approach in Reggio?*

Spaggiari: At this point the goals of community-based management are an integral part of the content and methods of our educational approach. They are central to the educational experience in the infant–toddler centers and preprimary schools here in Reggio Emilia.

The community-based management in these centers and schools seeks to promote strong interaction and communication among educators, children, parents, and community. Community-based management enhances the worth of an educational approach that has its origins and objectives in the principles of communication and solidarity. The participation of the families is just as essential as is the participation of children and educators.

Obviously, such a "three-party" system is part of the community at large, which in turn becomes the fourth component, having its own particular influence and worth.

In short, community-based management is not so much a system of governing as it is a philosophical ideal permeating all aspects of the entire educational experience.

Seen in this context, participation in general, and community-based management in particular, are central to the educational experience; that is, you cannot separate them from the choices of content and method in the infant–toddler centers and in the preprimary schools. They carry equal importance and weight in the individual growth of all children, particularly in this age group. The years between birth and 6 must be seen as a precious resource of human potential, in which a forward-looking society must be prepared to invest responsibly.

Gandini: *In the last 10 years in Italy there has been a drop in the birth rate, which has brought with it a change in the structure of young families. What effect has this phenomenon had on participation?*

Spaggiari: As a consequence of this drop in the birth rate, today's child is perceived as a rare and precious object. However, in an aging society like ours, a child is also considered a disruptive presence, almost an intruder, in a world not in tune with the child's needs and rights. For these very reasons, the education of children in this age group presents a most difficult and complex task. The enormous responsibilities of this task cannot be undertaken single-handedly by either the family or the school.

There is a much stronger awareness on the part of parents today that the job of educating a child involves much support and solidarity, much sharing of ideas, many encounters, a plurality of view, and above all different competencies. It is precisely because families with only one child feel isolated that they will take the initial step toward meeting and working with others. The types of groups support that come from participation and community-based management provide a response to the psychological needs of such families. They facilitate a dialogue between the parent and the child, between educators and parents, between groups of educators and different families, and eventually extending to involve the whole community. The idea of seeking solutions collectively, as is done in many municipal education programs in Italy, is contrary to the popular notion that families tend to see problems in narrow, private terms.

Gandini: *What are the duties of the Advisory Council in community-based management?*

Spaggiari: In light of the already mentioned changes, the role of the Advisory Council has evolved over time. Besides continuing to support the needs of the city, the main role of the Advisory Council has shifted from administrative concerns (e.g., enrollment, fees) and political choices (e.g., new centers) to expressly addressing the needs of families and educators. The Advisory Council has therefore become the initiator and main vehicle of participation in all its complex aspects.

Gandini: *Who serves on the Advisory Council?*

Spaggiari: Every 2 years the parents, educators, and townspeople elect representatives to the Advisory Council from among themselves for each infant–toddler center and preprimary school. There are 32 such schools in the town of Reggio Emilia and consequently there are 32 Advisory Councils. Two or three representatives from each Advisory Council are elected to sit on the Municipal Board on Infant–Toddler and Preprimary Education, together with the Administrative Director of Early Education (myself), the team of *pedagogisti*, and the elected city official in charge of education (the *Assessore*), and the Mayor.

In recent years, 75% of the parents have voted in the elections for the Advisory Councils. And many have served. For example, in 1993–1996, out of 2,550 families using our municipal early childhood services, 554 parents were elected; that means that one out of five families participated in the running of the infant–toddler centers and preprimary schools.

The Advisory Council in a preprimary school with an enrollment of 75 children might be composed of 19 parents, 13 educators, and 7 townspeople. Within each Advisory Council, a group of volunteers takes care of administration: They draw up agendas and emergency plans, they process parental concerns and proposals, and so on. Other members serve on different committees with specific objectives. For example, they study and implement strategies to maximize parental participation; they organize meetings on special subjects

FIGURE 4.1. Parents and teachers voting to elect representatives to the Advisory Council of the Diana School.

such as children's sleep problems or the need to repaint the dining hall of a school; they consider activities to facilitate the transition between the infant–toddler center and preprimary school, or between preprimary and primary school; and so on. They also coordinate work sessions, monitor implementation, and assess the results of the work done.

This shift in the role of the Advisory Council over the last few years has proved to be particularly effective within the framework of the individual classes in each school.

Gandini: *In what specific ways do infant–toddler centers and preprimary schools involve parents?*

Spaggiari: First of all, because discussion and decision making are done collectively within each school, parents are highly involved. In addition, by widening the field of participation, the educators who participate in community-based management include all types of adults working in the schools—teachers, cooks, aides—all of whom must share the responsibility that stems from being part of a community of educators. The ideas and skills that the families bring to the school and, even more importantly, the exchange of ideas between parents and teachers, favors the development of a new way of educating, and helps teachers to view the participation of families not as a threat but as an intrinsic element of collegiality and as the integration of different wisdoms.

In order to achieve this, it is necessary, long before a child ever comes to school, to provide children, parents, and teachers with many different opportunities for interaction, as Loris Malaguzzi has suggested (Chapter 3). Carlina Rinaldi (1985) has listed and described the main opportunities for participation once the school year has begun:

1. *Meetings at the individual classroom level.* Classroom teachers meet with the parents to discuss such things as the happenings within that particular group of children, the pedagogical and practical directions of the group, examples of activities that have taken place (through slides, displays of work, etc.), and the assessment of the educational experiences. Preferably, these meetings should take place in the evening or at a time that is convenient for the majority of families. The agenda should be agreed on and parents notified well in advance. This type of meeting should be repeated at least five or six times a year.
2. *Small group meetings.* Teachers meet with a small group of parents from their class. The limited number of participants allows for a closer and more personalized discussion of the needs and problems of specific families and particular children. It is useful for the teacher to hold such meetings until all the families have participated at least once during the year.
3. *Individual parent–teacher conferences.* These are usually requested by a family or suggested by the educators and can either deal with specific problems related to a particular family or child or offer the opportunity for in-depth discussion regarding the development of the personality of the child.
4. *Meetings around a theme.* These meetings are initiated and conducted by parents and educators and are open to all those connected with the center or the school who are interested in discussing or widening their knowledge of a specific subject. Such themes might include the role of the father, children's fears, and so on. The topic in question is debated and analyzed by all the people present, thus providing everybody with the opportunity to exchange ideas and points of view.
5. *Encounters with an expert.* These encounters take the form of a lecture or round table discussion and might involve many schools. They are tailored to increase everybody's knowledge of problems or issues of common interest, for example, fairy tales, children's sexuality, books for young children, children's diet, and so on.
6. *Work sessions.* These are opportunities to contribute in a concrete way to the improvement of the school. Parents and teachers come together to build furnishings and equipment, rearrange the educational space, improve the schoolyard, and maintain classroom materials.
7. *Labs.* In these "learning by doing" meetings, parents and teachers acquire techniques with a strong educational potential, such as working with paper

(origami), making puppets, working with the shadow theater, using photographic equipment, and so on. One such example is "the cooking practicum" where the cook and parents of new children together prepare dishes on the menu that may be hitherto unfamiliar to them.

8. *Holidays and celebrations.* These are group activities where children, parents, grandparents, friends, and townspeople come together. Sometimes they involve the whole school, sometimes just a particular class. Examples of celebrated events include children's birthdays, a grandparent's visit, the end of the year, seasonal occurrences, and so on.
9. *Other meeting possibilities.* Trips into town, picnics, excursions, short holidays at the seaside or in the mountains, and staying in city-owned hostels are possibilities. One special event is "a day at the school" when a parent spends the whole day with his or her child's class. Other activities involve small groups visiting each others' homes, or the whole group spending some time in a specific place, for example, the gym, swimming pool, main city square, or the market.

Gandini: *Over these last few years, what has changed in terms of parent participation?*

Spaggiari: To put it very succinctly, what has changed most of all are the reasons and the motives that stimulate parents to participate. In other words, this is a time when the ideologies and grand ideals of the past are in a state of crisis. These ideologies and ideals, together with the trust and conviction that they engendered, have long been the main spring of people's social and public commitment. However, it is clear that nowadays people participate and become involved, even in the field of education, not so much out of idealistic fervor or political conviction, but rather out of a desire to seek opportunities for personal growth or for their children's growth, for meaningful experiences and to both give and receive enrichment and help.

At the root of this, there is a strong call for meaningful reasons for participation, which is linked closely, not just superficially, to a growing desire on the part of people to meet and interact with others, to emerge out of solitude and anonymity, and to experience new feelings of solidarity and reciprocity.

FIGURE 4.2. "Meeting of the Advisory Council." Drawing by children of the Michelangelo School.

Gandini: *Looking toward the future, what are the focal points around which the thoughts and actions of this spirit of participation and shared experience will revolve?*

Spaggiari: There are three key concepts here. The first is subjectivity. There is no doubt that modern society is increasingly examining the growing demand for subjectivity that seems to be manifesting itself in people's attitudes. Whatever its origins, neo-individualism masks a strong desire to affirm one's identity and to have one's personal rights respected. The gamble that we must now face regards precisely this: the possibility of reconciling, and not placing at odds, the needs, rights, and desires of the individual with those of the group. In fact, we can see that the kinds of participation and cooperation that give the best results are those that accommodate and welcome many different personal contributions. This is precisely so because it is the individual who participates and it is the individual who must find a reason for his or her participation. Today moreover, consideration of each individual identity is an essential condition for making participation worthwhile. Any activity that involves participation and cooperation, in order for it to attract others and be worthwhile, must be pleasurable, useful, and meaningful for the individual, rather than based on the notion that one can cooperate only by sacrificing one's individuality.

The understanding of the social nature of man and of the child, which for a long time has underlined our educational practices, must now guide us even more in this project for participation because it helps us to understand that a human being is primarily an individual in relationship to other individuals, never separate or apart from them, and that being alone and in isolation is by no means a natural state for man.

How far the educational experience in the infant and early childhood centers will be a shared and co-authored experience with parents will depend on how well the opportunities created for socialization and exchange will be able to respond to personal expectations and to value individual contributions.

What's more, there are definite ways in which our institutions for young children become distinct and unique places. We have noticed that the process of community-based management manifests itself in different ways in each school in terms of style and procedures, at times in extremely different ways. These differences that give each school its particular stamp demonstrate that the reality of each separate governing process is the result of independent decisions and solutions. Furthermore, it shows that community-based management, as we have understood and interpreted it, defies attempts at homogenization and uniformity, and prefers instead, through a relationship of close interdependency, to adhere to the particular characteristics of the school and neighborhood, and therefore of the people who are part of it.

Gandini: *And the second concept?*

Spaggiari: Parenting. There is no doubt that today the role of a parent has changed dramatically. In general, you do not become a parent accidentally, as used to happen; the birth of a child is usually thought out, desired, and planned. The decision to have a child is something that is carefully considered in the light of several very important familiar variables: economic situation, living arrangements, stability of the couple, job security, guaranteed help, and so on. In general, therefore, a couple decides to have a child when they are sure of being able to offer that child the very best. All this places on the shoulders of the parents a high degree of responsibility and expectations. There is the awareness that the advent of a child will greatly modify the life of the couple, and that being the parent, especially the parent of small children, will constitute a special experience, sometimes a unique experience that can be tiring, full of worries, but above all, full of educational responsibilities and duties toward the child.

Nowadays there is the widespread belief that a child's early years are particularly important in the future shaping of that person, that they are almost decisive in terms of his or her positive development. This conviction leads parents to invest much of their time and resources precisely in these early years.. But today parents are in the paradoxical situation of feeling and being highly responsible for an onerous educational burden for which, not only are they unprepared, but for which they have no points of reference or help. The educational know-how of the grandparents is no longer viable and the general advice offered by manuals for parents usually is of little use because it does not take into account the uniqueness and the particular nature of individual circumstances. This growing preoccupation with the quality of the child's educational experience has undoubtedly induced many parents to become involved in the infant–toddler centers and preprimary schools, in the belief that by doing so they can be closer to their children and be better prepared to handle educational choices, but also out of the conviction that they will enrich their own capabilities as parents. Against this background, the local school becomes the privileged seat of encounter and social exchange, the natural place where staff, parents, and children contribute on a daily basis to an educational community built on the premises of dialogue and cooperation.

In our own small way, in the infant–toddler centers and preprimary schools of our town, through the educational and participatory experience that views the presence of parents not as intrusive and interfering but as indispensable and necessary, the need for family has become a cultural and political undertaking in order to respect and support the duties and the identity of the family as an institution. However, families vary greatly in both size and make up. Our shared experience must therefore be open and flexible in order to respond to the expectations and demands not only of the average family, but also of families that are on the margin of society, or even beyond the margin. A public school is a school for everyone, a school where nobody should feel left out or alienated, in particular the most needy, the weakest, or the most different. We must therefore pursue these same goals through shared management.

Gandini: *And the third key concept?*

Spaggiari: Communication. In a community of people that is built on an evergrowing web of social interaction and a network of exchange, communication itself becomes the primary connector of the entire fabric of participation, the unifying agent that binds the most diverse and distant elements of this multiform and complex social system that we call a center or school for young children. Already, years ago when Loris Malaguzzi, with such thoughtful insight, developed the theory of "the pedagogy of communication," he endorsed the importance of the methods of communication and he adopted them as the basis for the design and implementation of the early childhood educational program for our city.

Meaningful and effective communication is now consciously perceived as a way of determining and measuring the quality of social and educational experiences. Today, however, there is an urgent need to reach a deeper understanding and a clearer definition of the strategies for putting into practice this "pedagogy of communication." We are well aware of the positive psychological implications of intense and sensitive communication that focuses on the personalizing of human relationships, the sense of belonging and of identity, the refinement of a common dialogue, and the feelings of attachment

FIGURE 4.3. An historic meeting at the Model Early Learning Center in May 1993; from left to right: Carolyn Edwards, Lilian Katz, Rebecca New, Lella Gandini, Baji Rankin, Carlina Rinaldi, Sergio Spaggiari, Sandra Piccinini, Tiziana Filippini, Amelia Gambetti, and Loris Malaguzzi.

and reassurance. But we have also realized that a program that seeks to create an integrated system of communication must directly involve all the aspects of the infant–toddler centers and preprimary schools. Among the factors that serve to determine the quality of the communication is the interaction of staff and parents, the collective decision making, the organization of the work and of the workplace, the planning of the calendar, the relationship between the administration and the children, the educational program and the use of materials, the interaction between the school and the community, and the timing and the organization of the meetings with families. At this level, we are still learning from our errors. In a world where communication has become the profession of many (newspapers, television, advertising, etc.), we are probably mere dilettantes. In our society that is bombarded with information, perhaps we, too, run the risk of abusing and misusing the techniques of communication.

Gandini: *How could we sum up some of the reasons favoring the participation of parents?*

Spaggiari:

1. The education of young children is of major importance and is of concern to all. It can be limited neither just to the home nor just to the school. It occurs in many places and no one place can claim to be all-encompassing or exclusive. Each environment must be aware of the partial and incomplete role it plays and must therefore seek to collaborate and be integrated with the others.
2. A child is biologically predisposed to relating to others and of being the major actor in the playing out of his or her life. For this reason, the infant–toddler centers and preprimary schools are educational communities, places not so much where one educates but where one is educated, a place where the interested parties (children, teachers, and parents) are at the same time both teachers and learners.
3. There is no doubt that families have a primary and unique function in the education of their children and have great responsibilities toward them. Families, however, cannot be left to themselves. They need a network of shared responsibility and solidarity that is of benefit and support to them.
4. There can be no doubt that the education of a child is of great importance and this predisposes the parent to being concerned and getting involved. School, which by its very nature is an environment for exchange and involvement, cannot ignore this predisposition. (The participation of parents is therefore, by its very nature, one of the fundamental premises of the educational experience, if the school views it as essential and not as an accessory or an option.)
5. The participation and active involvement of the parent in the school is perceived and appreciated by the child who can derive from it a sense of

security besides seeing it as a model and incentive for his or her own personal growth.

6. Children are not private property. Nobody, not even parents, can claim "ownership" over them. The presence and involvement in the schools of families of different cultural and social origins should offer possibilities for dialogue and encounters, thereby offering the child the possibility to grow up amongst a plurality of contributions and values.
7. A shared education sets in motion processes—neither easy nor short term—that promote a new culture of the teaching profession. The contribution of ideas, expectations, and abilities offered by families to the schools help the teachers to perceive the link with families as something that enriches rather than interferes, thereby affirming the primary values of collegiality and the integration of knowledge. Even with the best prepared teachers and in the richest situations, there are areas that can only be realized through sharing and interactive choices.
8. The school that interacts with the families and with the surrounding community works toward relating the problems of education and instruction to those of health, sport, free time, and the mass media, bringing together environments and realities too often deliberately isolated and kept separate, thereby promoting a new style of political commitment that favors childhood.
9. In schools, as in society, at a time when the peace of the world is under threat, talking together, spending time and working together, sharing the responsibilities and work, all these things have a meaningful place amongst the highest, most universal values of love for life and peace. Today educating for a culture of peace is an important idea that can also spring forth and grow powerful, without fanfare, through participation in the day-to-day life of the school.

Gandini: *So, to conclude, could you summarize what you think are the key requirements for sustaining a successful program of participation?*

Spaggiari: Yes, the cardinal elements that support a rich network of meetings include these two things: (1) a diversity of activities that meet the various interests, needs, and aspirations of different families; and (2) a focus on the classroom unit as the natural place of encounter for those who are interested in the educational experience of the school, and the starting point to becoming involved in the wider life of the community. Within this diversified context, the Advisory Council takes on a new and wider significance. it can be seen as the driving force behind participation, making possible those infinite ways of coming together presented here. In an educational experience that is truly shared, choices and decisions have to be made with the widest possible consensus, and with a deep respect for a plurality of ideas and viewpoints.

REFERENCES

Rinaldi, C. (1985). *L'elaborazione communitaria del progetto educativo.* [The community design of the over-all educational project]. In R. Vianello (Ed.), *Stare con i bambini: Il sapere degli educatori.* [To be with children: The knowledge of educators], (pp. 176–188). Bergamo, Italy: Juvenilia.

Carlina Rinaldi,
director of the schools for young children and the infant–toddler centers and scientific consultant of Reggio Children.

chapter 5

Projected Curriculum Constructed Through Documentation—*Progettazione*

An Interview with Lella Gandini

Carlina Rinaldi

In recent years, educators in Italy have been involved in a debate about planning curriculum and activities with children under 6 years of age. Two contrasting points of view have been put forward. The first defines planning as a method of work that establishes in advance general educational objectives along with specific objectives for each activity. The second defines planning as a method of work in which the teachers lay out general educational objectives, but do not formulate the specific goals for each project or each activity in advance. Instead they formulate hypotheses of what could happen on the basis of their knowledge of the children and of previous experiences. Along with these hypotheses, they formulate objectives that are flexible and adapted to the needs and interests of the children. These interests and needs include those expressed by children at any time during the project as well as those the teachers infer and bring out as the work proceeds. A great deal of time and attention is given to this projection. It is repeated at many different points, both among teachers and with the children, in order to inform their future choices and decisions.

Carlina Rinaldi, who for more than 20 years worked side by side with the late Loris Malaguzzi, is now the pedagogical director of the infant–toddler centers and preprimary schools of Reggio Emilia. She has participated in this

Italian debate over curriculum planning, and along with her colleagues in Reggio Emilia, has championed and helped to construct and formulate the second type of planning, which we call *progettazione,* the Italian term used by Reggio Emilia educators for all flexible planning—whether done by teachers, parents, or administrators—concerning any aspect of the life of the school and its connections with the community. In this interview, Rinaldi describes the ample basis of this planning and how it serves as the conceptual basis for work with children.

Gandini: *Could you describe to me your basic principles in working with young children in your infant–toddler centers and preprimary schools?*

Rinaldi: First of all, I want to state that our experience and the processes connected with it have been shared not only with the children and teachers, but also with the families. Everything has been accomplished within the context of a city that was and is still able to plan ahead, but most importantly has been able to provide a coherent direction for schools, making occasionally difficult choices that involve both quantity and quality as an inseparable pair. Our schools, therefore, are not "experimental" schools. They are, rather, part of a public system that has strived to combine the child's welfare and the social needs of families with the fundamental human rights of the child. This approach brings together the concept of social services with the concept of education, as we do not see these two as antithetical. In fact, schooling for us is a system of relations and communications embedded in the wider social system. Certainly one of our basic principles involves participation, in the broadest sense of the word. To feel a sense of belonging, to be part of a larger endeavor, to share meanings—these are the rights of everyone involved in the educational process, whether teachers, children, or parents. In our schools, the active participation of the families and collegiality among staff and children working in groups are essential.

One point among many appears to us fundamental and basic: the image of the child. The cornerstone of our experience, based on practice, theory, and research, is the image of the child as rich in resources, strong, and competent. The emphasis is placed on seeing the children as unique individuals with rights rather than simply needs. They have potential, plasticity, openness, the desire to grow, curiosity, a sense of wonder, and the desire to relate to other people and to communicate. Their need and desire to communicate and interact with others emerge at birth and are essential elements for survival and identification with the species. This probably explains why children are so eager to express themselves within the context of a plurality of symbolic languages, and why children are also very open to exchanges and reciprocity as deeds and acts of love that they not only want to receive but also want to offer. These form the basis of their ability to experience authentic growth, dependent on the elements just listed, as well as on conflict and error.

All of these potentials are expressed and achieved first and foremost within a group learning context. This fact has involved us in a continuous search for an educational approach that breaks rank with traditional education "of the individual." We embrace an approach based on adults listening rather than speaking, where doubt and amazement are welcome factors along with scientific inquiry and the deductive method of the detective. It is an approach in which the importance of the unexpected and the possible are recognized, an approach in which there is no such thing as wasted time, but in which teachers know how to give children all the time they need. It is an approach that protects originality, subjectivity, and differences without creating isolation of the individual and offers to children the possibility of confronting stimulating situations and problems as members of small peer groups. This approach requests that adults—both teachers and parents—offer themselves as resource people to whom the children can (and want to) turn. The task of these resource people is not simply to satisfy needs or answer questions, but instead to help children discover their own answers and, more importantly still, to help them ask themselves good questions.

Gandini: *You have described your educational experience as containing these strong elements of social interaction and at the same time as being constructivist. In fact, you have described the child as "a social constructivist." Could you tell me more about these concepts?*

Rinaldi: The emphasis of our educational approach is placed not so much on the child in an abstract sense, but on each child in relation to other children, teachers, parents, his or her own history, and the societal and cultural surroundings. Relationships, communications, and interactions sustain our educational approach in its complexity; they are powerful terms characterized by two important elements: action and group socialization. We consider them to be fundamental structuring elements toward the construction of each child's identity.

It is our belief that all knowledge emerges in the process of self and social construction. Therefore, the teacher must establish a personal relationship with each child and ground this relationship in the social system of the school. Children, in turn, do not just passively endure their experience, but also become active agents in their own socialization and knowledge building with peers. Their action can be understood as more than responses to the social environment; they can also be considered as mental constructions developed by the child through social interaction. Obviously, there is a strong cause and effect relationship between social and cognitive development, a sort of spiral that is sustained by cognitive conflict that modifies both the cognitive and the social system.

Conflicts and the recognition of differences are essential, in our view. Conflict transforms the relationships a child has with peers—opposition, negotiation, listening to the other's point of view and deciding whether or not to adopt it, and reformulating an initial premise—are part of the processes of assimilation

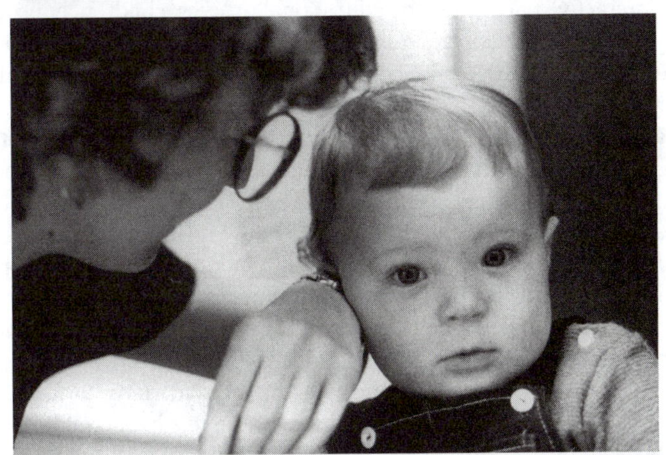

and accommodation into the group. We see these dynamics, until a short time ago considered only as part of the socialization process, also to be substantially cognitive procedures; and they are an essential element of democracy.

Now you can see the issues in their full richness but also in their complexity. The adults' difficulty is to initiate and nurture situations that stimulate this kind of learning process, where conflict and negotiation appear as the driving forces for growth. *Progettazione* allows for this social constructivist process to develop.

Gandini: *I see how this attitude on the part of educators can make your interventions with the children rewarding and stimulating. Could you describe some aspects of the work of teachers as they plan together a curriculum that is open and adaptable to the evolving ideas and explorations of children?*

Rinaldi: In our work, we speak of teacher planning, understood in the sense of preparation and organization of space, materials, thoughts, situations, and occasions for learning. These involve communication among all three protagonists and interactive partners of the educational process: children, educators, and families. The educational institution is, in fact, a system of communication and interaction among the three protagonists, integrated into the larger social system.

To carry out its primary task, then, the school must sustain the children's total welfare, as well as the welfare of parents and teachers. The system of relationships is so highly integrated that the well-being of each of the three protagonists depends on the well-being of the others. There must be mutual awareness of rights, needs, and pleasures and the attention to the quantity and quality of social occasions that create a system of permanent relations. The full participation of families is thus an integral part of the educational experience. Indeed, we consider the family to be a pedagogical unit that cannot be separated from the school.

Given this great, interactive system, it can be understood why the potential of children is stunted when the endpoint of their learning is formulated in advance. Instead, at the initiation of a project, the teachers could get together and proceed in terms of *progettazione*; that is, discuss fully all the possible ways that the project could be anticipated to evolve, considering the likely ideas, hypotheses, and choices of children and the directions they may take. By so doing, they prepare themselves for all the subsequent stages of the project, while leaving ample space for changes, for the unexpected, and for moments of stasis and digression. Because our planning is ongoing, it is impossible to separate what the teacher does beforehand from what actually takes place as the children's work on the project progresses.

Gandini: *Planning without preconceived objectives is connected, therefore, to the relationships between teachers, children, and the social network. The goal is to allow the child to make choices, communicate those choices, and receive feedback from others.*

Rinaldi: Yes, and I would like to clarify another important issue that I feel deserves special attention. This concerns the role of the teacher. The challenge for the teacher is to be present without being intrusive, in order to best sustain cognitive and social dynamics while they are in progress. At times, the adult must foster productive conflict by challenging the responses of one or several children. At other times, the adult must step in to revive a situation where children are losing interest because the cognitive map that is being constructed is either beyond or beneath the child's present capabilities. The teacher always remains an attentive observer, and beyond that, a researcher. The teacher's observations and transcribed tapes are taken to colleagues for group reflection. The documentation stimulates the teacher's self-reflection and produces discussion and debate among the group of colleagues. Such comparisons of ideas among colleagues are as important as those that take place among the children. The group discussions serve to modify, at times radically, the teacher's thoughts and hypotheses about the children and interactions with them.

Gandini: *I think we have covered the basis on which you have developed your curriculum. Could you now address this concept more specifically?*

Rinaldi: Certainly. An important aim of our schools is to sustain the social learning process and to help children learn how to learn, with the essential contributions of others. Because we believe that the construction of knowledge is a subjective process that proceeds in a spiraling rather than linear or stagelike way, it is clear that our *progettazione* must involve multiple actions, voices, times, and places. Children sometimes work with teachers, and sometimes without them; projects are sometimes short, and sometimes long. The curriculum is at once defined and undefined, structured and unstructured, based more on flexible strategies than rigid plans. There are no preconstituted paths, and consequently no set timetables or tests. Instead, relying on strategies means predicting and activating sequences that are based not only on our initial hypotheses but also on the work as it develops and unfolds. I like to use the metaphor of taking a journey, where one finds the way using a compass rather than taking a train with its fixed routes and schedules.

Gandini: *Could you elaborate on the connection between theory and practice?*

Rinaldi: Teachers work every day in a concrete context with children and parents. If we give credit to the potential of children, we must also give credit to the potential of adults. The search for meaning strongly connects children and teachers, even while their roles and responsibilities are distinct. The traditional relationship of theory and practice, which makes practice the derivative of theory, must be redefined. Theory and practice must become reciprocal and complementary, with practice even allowed some possibility of precedence.

Admitting this may seem upsetting and unacceptable to some. We would seem to be renouncing the rule of reason and the ability to determine action on the basis of logic. But we consider that within an organization such as a school, logical reasoning is most needed for inferring connections and causal relations between events that have taken place, not for deducing what is the theoretically correct action to take. When theory takes over, when it controls and commands what teachers may do and think, then teachers no longer have the duty to reflect, reason, and create for themselves. Excessive emphasis on theory can prevent teachers from being protagonists in the educational process and from exercising their rightful responsibilities. Thus, while we affirm the inseparability of theory and practice, we propose an open theory that is nourished through practice made visible, examined, interpreted, and discussed using the documentation that we produce. Documentation, then, does not mean a final report, a collection of documents in a portfolio that merely helps in term of memory, evaluation, or creating an archive. It is instead a procedure that is part of *progettazione,* and that sustains the educational process (teaching) in the dialogue with the learning processes of the children. Documentation is a point of strength that makes timely and visible the interweaving of actions of the adults and of the children; it improves the quality of communication and interaction. It is in fact a process of reciprocal learning. Documentation makes it possible for teachers to sustain the children's learning while they also learn (to teach) from the children's own learning.

Gandini: *The process of documentation that teachers in Reggio Emilia have developed is a powerful educational tool. While working with children, the teachers–supported by the pedagogical coordinators* (pedagogisti) *and the families–use documentation as a aid to communication and professional development. Documentation provides the connection between the various parts of the system that you have presented to us, and I consider it to be an educational breakthrough of great interest. Could you explain your use of documentation in more detail?*

Rinaldi: We must keep in mind that the work of teachers (or better, the group of teachers working together) involves constant discussion and making of hypotheses and predictions about the ongoing work with the children. This dynamic activity is closely linked to the other aspects of the teacher's work involving documentation–namely listening, observing, gathering documents, and interpreting them.

We have always maintained that children have their own questions and theories, and that they negotiate their theories with others. Our duty as teachers is to listen to the children, just as we ask them to listen to one another. Listening means giving value to others, being open to them and what they have to say. Listening legitimizes the other person's point of view, thereby enriching both listener and speaker. What teachers are asked to do is to create contexts where such listening can take place.

Listening is thus a general metaphor for all the processes of observation and documentation. Observation involves much more than simply perceiving reality, but also constructing, interpreting, and revisiting it. Because our observations are necessarily partial, it is essential that we leave interpretable traces of them. We use written notes, observation charts, diaries, and other narrative forms, as well as audiotapes, photographs, slides, and videotapes. These allow us to make visible the process of children's learning, the ways to construct knowledge, the emotional and relational aspects; in fact, all the facets that contribute to leave traces of a competent observation. However, it is important to note that all these documents provide partial findings and subjective interpretations, and they are biased by the tools employed. In turn, they must be reinterpreted and discussed with others, in particular, with colleagues.

Documentation is a procedure that supports the educational processes and it is supported by the dynamic exchanges related to learning. Documentation is the process of reciprocal learning. Through documentation we leave traces that make it possible to share the ways children learn, and through documentation we can preserve the most interesting and advanced moments of teachers' professional growth. It is a process in which teachers generate hypotheses and interpretations of theories that can modify the initial, more general theories. Documentation makes it possible to create knowledge not only for teachers but also for researchers and scholars. Jerome Bruner, visiting the infant–toddler centers and preprimary schools of Reggio Emilia, remarked that they were a true university.

Gandini: *This exchange with colleagues,* pedagogista, *and families becomes an occasion for the professional growth of teachers.*

Rinaldi: Indeed, it is in these shared moments of comparison of ideas and discussion (which are not always easy) that interpretive theories and hypotheses are generated. Those advance not only the knowledge of the group but also the more general theories of reference. Here again theory comes into relationship with practice.

We are aware that the medium we choose for documenting the experience observed—in other words, for making it visible and sharable—contains limitations and sources of bias that can be favorable only when multiple documents, media, and interpretations are placed side by side. Because this procedure enables discussion and the comparison of ideas, it permits us to analyze and formulate hypotheses and predictions, and thus consolidate our thinking.

This is how we produce slide documentaries, videos, books, and other written and photographic documentation that contribute to make the walls and spaces of the infant–toddler centers and preprimary schools for young children so interesting. The panels displayed on the walls, and the slides and videos become occasions for intense daily communication and reflections. They support the memory and the interactions for children, teachers, and parents—true mirrors of our knowledge in which we see our own ideas and images reflected; mirrors in which we can also find other and different images with which to engage in a dialogue.

Gandini: *Clearly, documentation influences the quality of relationships among and between teachers, children, and parents. How do you see the specific ways it helps each of these groups?*

Rinaldi: Documentation offers the teacher a unique opportunity to listen again, see again, and therefore revisit individually and with others the events and processes in which he or she was co-protagonist, directly or indirectly. This revisiting with colleagues helps create common meanings and values. Moreover, because planning involves, above all, making hypotheses and predictions (or "projections") about contexts, materials, tools and instruments, opportunities pertinent to the learning process at hand and the children's desires, documentation becomes the heart of each specific project and the place for true professional training of teachers.

With regard to children, documentation offers an opportunity for revisiting, reflecting, and interpreting. It provides occasion for self-organization and group organization of knowledge. Documentation supports the children's memory, offering them the opportunity to retrace their own processes, to find confirmation or negation, and to self-correct. Documentation allows for children to make comparisons with others and hear comparisons by others. In a sense, it invites self-evaluation and group evaluation, conflict of ideas, and discussion. It is important to remember that this takes place in a very supportive environment, created by the spirit of collaboration that is fostered all along in the daily life and experiences in the schools.

Documentation provides an extraordinary opportunity for parents, as it gives them the possibility to know not only what their child is doing, but also how and why, to see not only the products but also the processes. Therefore, parents become aware of the meaning that the child gives to what he or she does, and the shared meanings that children have with other children. It is an opportunity for parents to see that part of the life of their child that often is invisible. Furthermore, documentation offers the possibility for parents to share their awareness, to value discussion and exchanges with the teachers and among their group, helping them to become aware of their role and identity as parents.

Sharing documentation is in fact making visible the culture of childhood both inside and outside the school to become a participant in a true act of exchange and democracy.

Gandini: *You point to the need for citizens to know about the rich culture of childhood and its right to flourish and be sustained through advocacy and political engagement. A powerful use of documentation is to communicate the unfolding story of a particular infant–toddler center or preprimary school. Such particular narratives can be integrated to construct the collective history of institutions for young children in the whole community.*

Rinaldi: The school is not isolated from society but an integral part of it. The school has both the right and the duty to make this culture of childhood visible to the society as a whole, in order to provoke exchange and discussion. Sharing documentation is a true act of democratic participation. Indeed, this thought was one of the most extraordinary and forward-looking insights of Loris Malaguzzi, and part of the vision behind the exhibition *The Hundred Languages of Children*.

Gandini: *Could you give us an example of* progettezione *and tell us about a specific project?*

Rinaldi: A project, which we view as a sort of adventure and research, can start through a suggestion from an adult, a child's idea, or from an event such as a snowfall or something else unexpected. But every project is based on the attention of the educators to what the children say and do, as well as what they do not say and do not do. The adults must allow enough time for the thinking and actions of children to develop.

An example of one of the projects is called "The Crowd" (a project carried out at the Scuola Diana, documented by Vea Vecchi, overseen by Loris Malaguzzi). It began at the end of a school year in a classroom of 4- and 5-year-olds. The teachers, in preparation for the long summer vacation ahead, discussed with the children the idea of saving memories and fragments of their upcoming experiences during the holidays. Although the summer marks an interruption of the school year, our commitment to the children remains in force and we try to find ways to keep their interest in learning alive during the vacation months. So the teachers discuss ideas with children and also propose them to parents. In this case, each family agreed to take along to their vacation sites a box with small compartments in which their child could save treasures, be it a shell from the beach or a tiny rock from the mountains or a leaf of grass. Every fragment and every piece collected would become a memento of an experience imbued with a sense of discovery and emotion.

In the fall, therefore, when the children returned to school, the teachers were ready to revive those memories with questions such as: "What did your eyes see?" "What did your ears hear?" and so on. The teachers expected to hear stories about days spent at the beach or hiking, and to learn about the sight of boats, waves, and sunsets, but instead the children in this classroom brought a very different perspective. Because the children could express themselves vividly, and because the teachers could ask the right questions, an adventure in learning began quite unexpectedly. What happened was this: A little boy, Gabriele, sharing his experience said, "Sometimes we went to the pier. We walked through a narrow long street, called 'the gut,' where one store is next to another, and where in the evening it is full of people. There are people who go up, and people who walk down. You cannot see anything, you can only see a crowd of legs, arms, and heads."

The teachers immediately caught the word *crowd,* and asked other children what it meant to them. By doing so, they launched an adventure in learning, a project. The word *crowd* turned out to be fantastically rich, almost explosive, in the meanings it contained for these children. The teachers immediately apprehended an unusual excitement and potential in this word. Here is what some of the children said:

Stefano: "It's a bag full of people all crowded in."
Nicola: "It's a bunch of people all attached and close to one another."
Luca: "There are people who jump on you and push you."
Clara: "It's like a congested place when it is a holiday."

Giorgia: "There are lots of people who are going to see a soccer game... who are going to see the game, really they are all boys."

Ivano: "It's a bunch of people all bunched up together just like when they go to pay taxes."

After the group discussion, the teachers asked the children to draw their thoughts and words about the crowd. However, looking at the children's drawings, they observed that the level of representation in their drawings was discrepant from the level of their verbal descriptions. The project was put on hold for a couple of days, during which time the teachers asked themselves what was going on. How could they help the children to integrate their different symbolic languages? How could they make the children become aware of their own process of learning? So the teachers waited for a couple of days and then gave the children a chance to listen to their earlier comments (which had been taped and transcribed, so they could be read aloud, while they looked at the drawings and commented on each others' work).

The teachers now noticed a further growth in the children's vocabulary as they expanded on their stories, and the images prepared in a second set of drawings became more elaborate and detailed. For example, Teresa, thinking back on her memory of the "crowd," said, "It goes left, right, forward, and when they forget something, they go back." But Teresa then confronted a puzzle: She noticed that her statements did not match her drawing, for the figures on her paper were all facing the same way (outward toward the viewer). She seemed uncomfortable, and then before all her friends, came up with a marvelous explanation: She said that in the drawing she had shown only a piece of crowd with people who did not forget anything, and that is why they were all walking forward. Federico also had a problem with his drawing because in it everyone faced forward except the dog, which was in profile. He admitted he was only able to draw dogs this way. Ivano expressed concern about his drawing, saying that if people kept walking forward, as he had drawn them, they would smash against the wall.

At this point, there was a unanimous desire expressed by the children to learn more about how to draw people from rear and profile. The teachers' role was to sustain and support this process. They asked one girl, Elisa, to stand in the middle of the room surrounded by small groups of children placed at different vantage points where they could observe her, describe her body and position, and draw her from four angles: front, back, right, and left. Through this process, the children learned a great deal about the difficult concept of point of view. One child concluded: "We put ourselves in a square, and Elisa has four sides just like us."

The teachers also wanted to take the children outside the school—a typical step in our project work. Children and teacher went to the center of town where they observed and photographed people coming and going in the busy streets.

Children mingled with the people, becoming, once again, "the crowd." A few days later, the slides of that day were projected on the classroom wall, and the children enjoyed those images, moving through their reflections. Then they made more drawings, and Teresa proudly came up with a picture of herself, her boyfriend, and a dog, all in profile! At this point, the teacher suggested to the children cutting out the figures to add, as in a collage, to their earlier drawings. This evoked many questions: "Can we put together in a crowd people undressed for the beach and people dressed up for the promenade?" "Can we put together people of different size?" In this latter instance, children remembered that they had used the photocopy machine to reduce drawings and they decided they should now use it again to make people bigger or smaller so they could look "normal." The teachers also encouraged the children to use the cutout figures for puppet play, dramatization, and shadow play. They also sculpted figures from clay. Finally, the children concluded their exploration with a collective project in which they superimposed many of their figures in a box to create "a crowd" just as Teresa had said, "that goes left, right, forward and when they forget something, they go back."

Looking at this one example of the extraordinary capacity of children, it will be understandable how in my work with children, I have come to the conclusion that it is very important to have the capacity to grow with them. We reinvent and reeducate ourselves along with the children. Not only does our knowledge organize theirs, but also the children's ways of being and dealing with reality likewise influence what we know, feel, and do.

Tiziana Filippini, *pedagogista*

chapter 6

The Role of the *Pedagogista*

An Interview with Lella Gandini*

Tiziana Filippini
in collaboration with Simona Bonilauri

Gandini: *We would like to hear, from your own perspective and experience, how the role of the* pedogogista *has taken shape. How is it a supporting part of the Reggio Emilia system?*

Filippini: Although I've been a *pedagogista* since about 1978, I find it difficult to answer your question. My work and role are the result of a long process of personal and collective study and reflection. Furthermore, in our system in Reggio, we define our professional roles in relation to one another; each role draws from and at the same time contributes to the shape of the overall educational project. The role of *pedagogista* can only be defined starting at the image of the child—consequently, our images of the teacher, school, and family—and in turn contributes to those very images. You can see how all of our definitions and conceptualizations are interdependent. Thus, although there are *pedagogisti* in other city systems in Italy, I feel that my work here is grounded in our unique context and educational experience.

In Italy, the profession of *pedagogista* emerged during the 1970s, when a few municipalities (such as Bologna, Modena, Parma, and Pistoia, among others) began to open their own systems of first preprimary and then infant-toddler edu-

*Translated by Lella Gandini and Carolyn Edwards.

cation and care. This process spread throughout Italy, although slowly and unevenly; as a result, *pedagogisti* were found first and most commonly in northern Italy, with somewhat different definitions of their duties in the various locales.

In addition to the philosophical, educational, and ethical choices, there are organizational needs influencing the professional role of the *pedagogista* in Reggio Emilia. First, we must guarantee the coherence and consistency across time of the quality of the municipal educational program serving children under 6 years of age. Second, we must integrate and coordinate the administrative, technical, pedagogical, social, and political components of our system. We have an official, the *assessore*, appointed directly by the mayor, as the head of all public education serving children from infancy through secondary school. Under the *assessore* there are other appointed officials, including a Director of Early Childhood Education (for many years Loris Malaguzzi, but presently Sergio Spaggiari) and a Director of the Pedagogical Team (at present Carlina Rinaldi). These two directors coordinate a staff of nine, including seven *pedagogisti*, a coordinator of special education, and a curriculum specialist in theater.

Gandini: *Can you tell us more about how the role of* pedagogista *is based on a certain image of the child?*

Filippini: Our image of the child has evolved out of our collective experience and a continually reexamined understanding of educational philosophy and psychological theory. For us, each child is unique and the protagonist of his or her own growth. We also note that children desire to gain knowledge, have much capacity for curiosity and amazement, and yearn to create ties with oth-

FIGURE 6.1. Meeting of the pedagogical team.

ers and to communicate. Children are so open to exchange and reciprocity. From early in life they negotiate with the social and physical world—with everything the culture brings to them. Starting from this idea, we have tried to create the school as a system in which everything is connected. The *pedagogista* is included in this system of relations. The functions of the *pedagogista* in Reggio Emilia are multiple. I cannot interact with just one part of the system and leave the rest aside, because that would injure the system.

Gandini: *How do the* pedagogisti *work together within the pedagogical team, serving as support to each other and to the system?*

Filippini: The only way to respond appropriately, considering the premises and expectations that we have presented so far, is to work collegially—both within the pedagogical team, and also within the teams of educators in each center and school. All seven *pedagogisti* meet once a week with the directors to discuss policy and problems related to the whole network of our early childhood institutions. We engage in a continuous exchange of information regarding what is happening within the schools, new advances in theory and practice, and political developments. We must all seek to be flexible, sensitive, open, and able to anticipate change—in the same way as is expected of teachers and staff in our system.

We on the pedagogical team see ourselves as constantly transforming and growing professionally, through exchange with others. We are constantly striving for clarity and openness, one to another, and seeking to be forces for integration. In our work we deal with city administrators and employees of many kinds (elected officials, civil service employees, and representatives of cultural and scientific groups) whose suggestions must be pulled together. Furthermore, we must support and integrate the various aspects of the experience of young children (e.g., the curriculum areas) that traditional thinking would divide into separate compartments.

Because all of the *pedagogisti* must be active at different levels of the system, our competence must be multifaceted. For example, we work with colleagues in the political and administrative branches of city government, contributing to their executive, managerial functions. Another very important part of our responsibilities is the ongoing professional development and in-service training of teachers and staff. Each individual *pedagogista* is responsible for a certain number of infant–toddler centers and preprimary schools, and each also has other specific responsibilities within the system. For example, I am assigned to two preprimary schools and one infant–toddler center, and I am the coordinator of our Center for Documentation and Research in the Infant–Toddler Centers and Preprimary Schools. Another *pedagogista* works with two or three preprimary schools and two infant–toddler centers, and is liaison to the state (federally run) preprimary schools in our city. Another *pedagogista* has the charge of keeping abreast of new communication technologies; and so on.

In my work at the schools, I interact with all the adults to help sustain and implement the philosophy of our system. Many of the things I do involve issues of basic organization, the "backbone" of the system conceived as an organism. Just to give a few examples, I deal with issues of scheduling, staff assignments and responsibilities, workloads, and shifts. I deal with issues about the physical environment; for example, reflecting on needs and goals with parents and teachers and then sharing these reflections with an architect who is designing building renovations or with parents and teachers who are building new equipment. The definition and the realization of our overall educational project requires not only the elaboration of hypotheses and maintainance of values, but also the capacity to create alliances and solidarity through the organization of work, time, and space.

Gandini: *What are some of the particular things you do to support the work of teachers?*

Filippini: Social constructivism and interactionism are theoretical frameworks that guide our work with both adults and children. It is the responsibility of the *pedagogista* to work with teachers in identifying new themes and experiences for continuous professional development and in-service training. This is an important and delicate task because of the insufficient basic preparation of many of our teachers. But we believe that the highest level of teaching is best achieved through real work experience, supported by continuous reflection and enrichment. Teachers in our system each do about 190 hours a year of work outside the classroom, including 107 hours of in-service training; 43 hours of meetings with parents and committees (part of our community-based management; see Spaggiari, Chapter 4); and about 40 hours for other seminars, workshops, school parties, celebrations, and so on. The *pedagogista* works to promote within each self and among teachers an attitude of "learning to learn" (as John Dewey called it), an openness to change, and a willingness to discuss opposing points of view.

We work to favor discussion. People offer their ideas, and likewise should also take advantage of the ideas of others. The value of such a strategy comes gradually to be appreciated, even if it takes time. The *pedagogista* becomes part of the overall educational project of each institution and facilitates dialogue and reflection about general and specific educational issues.

Then, of course, I work closely with teachers at my particular schools regarding all sorts of educational issues and problems concerning children, where my ultimate goal is always to promote teachers' autonomy rather than take over their problems and solve them for them. Particularly for the infant–toddler centers, we are convinced that an essential precondition for effective teaching is the creation of an especially close teacher–parent relationship. Through professional development and in-service training that focuses on the processes and strategies of communication, we try to support in teachers and staff the competence to activate exchanges with parents, as well as among parents, and willingness to listen to others' points of view. These are necessary skills of a well-rounded professional.

FIGURE 6.2. In-service training involves teachers of several schools working together guided by the *pedagogista.*

Certainly, for the *pedagogista,* the art of working and sharing with other adults—be they teachers or colleagues—demands a long apprenticeship. It is not easy, but it leads the way to full professional and personal development. Our task, collaborating with teachers, is to analyze and interpret the rights and needs of each child and family, and then use this knowledge in our work with children. Equally important is to elaborate better relationships between parents and teachers and set up meetings in which everyone gets to know one another and the curriculum projects underway can be explored and created together. Educational continuity between the school and home is a dialectic process, based on talking and listening. Naturally, problems arise. No single model or method can earn a permanent seal of approval, because things always change.

In general, we seek to construct meaningful alliances with parents around important issues in education and suggest ways of being together. We recognize and signal how appreciated parental presence is in the schools and centers. What we hope to gain through parental participation in advisory councils and the system of community-based management has evolved and changed over time. Today, with so many parents suffering the stress and malaise of contemporary life, we think that this participation can help promote a new community ethic based on sharing experiences and ways of being. Parent participation serves educational, political, and public policy goals.

Finally, the *pedagogista* must be available to support teachers in their daily relationships with individual families. I must be receptive to everyone's expectations, needs, requests, suggestions, delicate concerns, and occasionally stressful relationships. For example, in one of my infant–toddler centers, there is this situation. A teacher has just called me to say that one little child, aged 2½, who has just started school, is suffering very much. She frequently cries to go home. I asked the teacher what they know about the family and learned that the parents work outside the city, so that during the week the child stays with her grandparents. So I wondered whether shortening the time that the child stays in the afternoon might not be beneficial. Consequently, I will go to the school and observe the little child. And I will, together with the teachers, meet with the parents to work out what might be the cause for the behavior and what might be the solution.

Gandini: *The approaches to professional development and in-service training are at the heart of the role of* pedagogista *in Reggio Emilia. Can you elaborate on this complex topic?*

Filippini: The *pedagogisti* are deeply involved in the overall educational experience taking place within each infant–toddler center and preprimary school. They support the relationships there and promote the value of exchange and discussion.

Observing and documenting are processes that invite a regular reconnaissance by teachers together with a *pedagogista.* The teachers experience a steady growth of skills related to *progettezione* (as Carlina Rinaldi, Chapter 5, describes). To us, this work together seems the most effective and long-lasting means to increased professionalism; it allows teachers to gain information and knowledge, become researchers, learn about both theory and practice, and thereby move from seeing themselves as transmitters of knowledge to creators of it. Self-reflection, discussion, and shared elaboration of meaning are difficult processes and a constant challenge to us; they stand in opposition to the straight-jacketing practice of predetermined lesson plans, and are most in tune with current thinking about adult and child learning.

The opportunities for professional development and in-service training are included in the work schedule in ways respectful of individual needs and preferences as to time and modality. For example, given the complexity of their roles, teachers need a variety of meetings addressing educational theory, teaching techniques, and sound social relations and communication. We help teachers to improve their skills of observing and listening to children, documenting projects, and conducting their own research. During the course of the year, there will be some separate meetings for infant–toddler center versus preprimary school teachers—for instance, meetings dealing with issues of child development and guidance—and then also there will be joint meetings. There will be workshops devoted to the acquisition of technical skills; for example, the design and preparation of posters to document project work and explain the school organization and functioning to parents and visitors. An outside expert might be invited to give a lecture on some topic of new interest. Also, we make it possible for adults to participate in open discussions or forums dealing with contemporary scientific and cultural debates; we always hold such a series every March and April, open to parents, teachers, and the citizens of the city.

Gandini: *You mentioned to me that one strong, central concept about the role of the* pedagogista *connects all the basic elements of your approach.*

Filippini: Yes. Let me begin here with a quote from the American psychologist, Jerome Bruner:

> [A] culture is as much a *forum* for negotiating and renegotiating meaning and for explicating action as it is a set of rules or specifications for action.... It is the forum aspect of a culture that gives its participants a role in constantly making and remaking the culture—an *active* role as participants rather than as performing spectators.... It follows from this view of culture as a forum that induction into the culture through education, if it is to prepare the young for life as lived, should also partake of the spirit of a forum, of negotiation, of the recreating of meaning. (Bruner, 1986, p. 123)

This quotation, which talks about the continual creation and re-creation of culture, is closely connected to our way of working. With our children in the infant–toddler centers and preprimary schools, we try to realize an education that is transfused, just as Bruner said, with the spirit of negotiation and shared construction of meanings. A culture of the school based on negotiation requires educators to be active participants. We cannot approach our own learning and growth passively, as if going to a university lecture to take in received wisdom on educational theory and from that shape our practice. That would be to take a hierarchical, unidirectional approach, contrary to our entire philosophy and concept of *progettazione*. Instead, we reflect on our practice—a reflection that moves toward theory—or start from a theoretical assumption and compare it to what we have seen in practice, to redefine its meaning. As we discuss and share reflections, we create culture. We consider what has happened and search for its interpretation; we negotiate to construct a collective understanding. Without these reciprocal relationships and processes of sharing, each one of us would remain isolated within his or her own perspective and our system would remain fragmented. In my view, working to create a shared culture of education within the pedagogical team and the schools is basic to all the other elements of the *pedagogista*'s role.

Gandini: *As I come regularly over the years to Reggio Emilia, I always notice things to be evolving and changing. I think such change results from your continuous reflection on work in progress. Thus, it becomes impossible to pin down and exactly describe your system, because it is always undergoing adjustment and dynamic transformation. That growth and change are consciously desired and sought for gives your work the valuable sense of being continuous research in progress.*

Filippini: This way of working lets us welcome and incorporate newcomers—children, families, and personnel—as well as allowing longtime participants to sustain an active, operative renewal. Like digging down deeply into meaning, it is a way to learn further, even for people who know a great deal. New perspectives offer new knowledge and let us see what is familiar and obvious from a different slant, even discover something fresh in it. Sometimes you have done something 20 times but it is not until the 21st time that you discover its deep meaning—even when you already possess the correct words to describe it but without really penetrating inside them.

The shared construction of meaning, I believe, is the unifying theme of our work. Without this theme, the role of the *pedagogista* reduces to a fragmentary list, a succession of interventions, actions, gestures, and encounters in multiple settings at multiple levels—a truly schizophrenic picture. Instead, if you think of this theme of creating a unified culture of education, then you can see at once the interrelationships among all the parts. This general connecting thread winds through each specific situation we face, whether a problem of professional development, school environment, organization, interpersonal relationships, or whatever else. Each situation has its specific aspects, all the while connected with the whole, and each requires one to bring a general and common perspective to every aspect of our work.

To offer an example, when I go to meet with a brand new teacher at one of my schools, I will not want to tell her she has to do a certain thing in a certain way. I will not need to hear that she has performed any supposedly necessary behaviors, such as playing ball with the infants. Rather, what is important is that we understand each other, reflect together, and construct common understandings together. Only such a process as this makes sense to her and me, the children, and the families.

What I mean is this—if I may stay with the example of playing ball (which, by the way, can be a very valuable experience, and involves one of the world's most common toys)—what would be interesting and important would be to reflect together with this young educator: "Did you ask yourself what is a ball?" "Of

FIGURE 6.3. Work session of the *pedagogista* with the pair of teachers of one classroom.

course, it is a round object that comes in different sizes, and can be bounced and rolled." But, then, what does this ball represent for this child? What kind of relationship could emerge through the interaction of the ball (with its identity) and the child (with his or hers)? Why should the teacher support such an interaction? Because it is very familiar to the child from what happens at home, and you want to offer continuity? That might seem a justification, but what if somebody else observed that because ball is what the child mainly plays at home, you should offer something new at school? Maybe you will decide to offer the child the ball, but find a way to immediately enrich and extend this activity.

Gandini: *Giving new teachers this reflective way of observing children and making choices is a bit like offering them the key to a box full of surprises within the familiar landscape of daily experience.*

Filippini: Yes, certainly. In this case, we must think about the ball's identity, bring that next to the child's identity, and see what relationships can be derived. You have to question what you know and activate your curiosity. You come to realize how many more possibilities there are beyond what you thought. Just as children need to construct their own knowledge, exercise their skills, and become aware of their learning, so the very same is true for adults. But it is a process that takes time and cannot be hurried. The challenge is to approach your involvement in each event, with your full intelligence and reflective powers operating on multiple levels of abstraction. You must be mindful that every way of defining a problem exists in relation to all the others. The goal is to try to think about all the connections, holistically, not breaking down and separating each aspect.

From all that I have said, it should be clear that, in my role as *pedagogista*, I must be part of many situations at once, on different levels of the system. Because this is a physical impossibility, I find I can and must depend on my relationships with teachers. They bring me up to date about many aspects; through their eyes I observe the children—what was seen and not seen. They tell about the differences they have noticed between the children of today and those of years past. They fill me in on how they perceived events that I could not be there to witness. Therefore, it is essential, to my work as well as theirs, that they become ever more skillful in observing, drawing conclusions, and reflecting. The understandings we collectively gain, in turn, help us to provide learning environments that contain appropriate materials and opportunities to support children in small groups and *progettazione.* This is the "knot" we face everyday. And it is on these principles that we plan for professional development, examine our own individual growth, and look for complexity in working with children. The basic principles make us ever aware of why each of our centers and schools is unique in terms of its strengths, resources, problems, and solutions; they also allow us to take advantage of these differences.

Gandini: *Discussion among people from different schools must be an important source of new ideas in your system. This reminds me of documentation and its potential*

FIGURE 6.4. Tiziana Filippini with Loris Malaguzzi, Carolyn Edwards, and George Forman during the visit at the University of Massachusetts in Amherst, on the occasion of the inauguration of the exhibit *The Hundred Languages of Children.*

to communicate at many levels and to many different audiences, and the need to continuously refine our instruments of communication to make them most effective.

Filippini: Of course, otherwise we would exhaust our resources. Conversation among people in different schools acts like a giant mirror, reflecting the choices we have made.

You can see that the *pedagogista*, as a member of the pedagogical team, has the complex and multifaceted task of promoting cultural and social growth of systems for young children. This is accomplished in a variety of ways, always acting as a resource and reference point for all sorts of initiatives and always acting as a link between people and groups, creating a network of resources to build a citywide platform of early childhood education. It is a difficult but energizing role, because it must be constructed as we go along, and because of our way of working as a guiding team interfacing with other teams and groups. That is the way our whole educational experience builds itself inside a systemic outlook.

Let me conclude with a thought from Loris Malaguzzi that captures for me the charge of humanity and the tension of a wider perspective that he always succeeded in transmitting to us:

> Each one of us who works in education has learned in the field that many things can be gathered from the cultural patrimony, many from theories and experiences, many from literature, the arts, economics, and science and technology. But

many things are also born of intuition, taste, ethics, and value choices, of reasons and opportunities that in part we control and in part are suggested by our own craft in living. Nevertheless, within this constellation of things, balancing between stable and unstable theories and practices, necessary, possible, and even accidental; and between oscillations, disequilibria, and even adversities of social policies, there remains space and freedom to use our own intelligence, passion, and creativity. (Malaguzzi, 1995, back cover)

REFERENCES

Bruner, J. (1986). *Actual minds, possible worlds.* Cambridge, MA: Harvard University Press.

Malaguzzi, L. (1995). *I cento linguaggi dei bambini.* [The hundred languages of children]. In C. Edwards, L. Gandini, & G. Forman (Eds.). Bergamo, Italy: Edizioni Junior.

Vea Vecchi,
atelierista of Diana School

chapter 7

The Role of the *Atelierista*

An Interview with Lella Gandini*

Vea Vecchi

Gandini: *What are the reasons that made you abandon the work you were doing in the middle school and come to work in the* atelier *of the preprimary schools in Reggio Emilia?*

Vecchi: It is very easy to say negative things about the way art education is treated in middle schools in Italy. It is truly marginal there. What attracted me to the preprimary schools in Reggio was, first, the use of visual languages as a construction of thoughts and feelings within a holistic education, and second, the fact that the *atelier* becomes a cultural vehicle for teacher development. This was declared to me by Loris Malaguzzi over 30 years ago, at the very first meeting we had.

Gandini: *The role of atelierista was new and original in Reggio Emilia; it does not exist in other systems in Italy. Has it measured up to your expectations?*

Vecchi: Twenty five years of work are a clear answer. They have shaped my identity as a person and a woman. The visual language, as interpreted—and constantly reinterpreted—within the wide philosophical perspective of the Reggio approach, provides the possibility to be involved in an ongoing process of communication and confrontation with people of different professional and social

* Translated by Lella Gandini.

FIGURE 7.1. Children working in the *atelier*.

backgrounds. This has naturally affected my own personal and professional identity and offered me a way to examine and validate my daily work in an authentic way.

Gandini: *Do you think that your training in art school was too narrow—for example, with not enough broad background in the liberal arts, too much focus on technical skills—for such a specific job as being an* atelierista *with young children?*

Vecchi: The art school certainly had old-fashioned methods. But so had the school that formed the other teachers in the classrooms. The artistic training at least gave me an approach to teaching that wasn't overly structured—perhaps freer and with more potential for irony, humor, or pleasure. All in all, I think my artistic training produced a certain freedom of thought that has adapted itself very well to the different styles and attitudes of mind an *atelierista* must take on.

Gandini: *How could you define the place of the* atelier *in such a complex organization as the preprimary school?*

Vecchi: The *atelier* serves two functions. First, it provides a place for children to become masters of all kinds of techniques, such as painting, drawing, and working in clay—all the symbolic languages. Second, it assists the adults in understanding processes of how children learn. It helps teachers understand how children invent autonomous vehicles of expressive freedom, cognitive freedom, symbolic freedom, and paths to communication. The *atelier* has an important, provocative, and disturbing effect on old-fashioned teaching ideas. Loris Malaguzzi (Chapter 3) has talked about this and expressed our views.

I'm not sure that we have always lived up to the expectations held for us, but I am at least convinced that having the *atelier* in every preprimary school has made a deep impact on the emerging educational identity of our system. Certainly, the *atelier* itself has changed with the passing of time, although the basic philosophy has remained the same. And, of course, the personality and style of each atelierista makes each *atelier* a different place.

I will try to tell you about the place and significance of the *atelier* in the school where I have worked. In the beginning I read a great deal of literature on children's drawings, about which I then knew almost nothing. At the same time, I talked constantly with teachers, parents, and *pedagogisti*, trying to give them deeper appreciation of what they saw as purely aesthetic activities. At the same time I know that I had prejudgments about art, and I was still virtually blind and deaf when it came to understanding children's drawings and three dimensional work. What I didn't realize was that gaining this understanding would be my ongoing quest from then on.

Working together, guiding the children in their projects, teachers and I have repeatedly found ourselves face to face—as if looking in a mirror—learning from one another, and together learning from the children. This way we were trying to create paths to a new educational approach, one certainly not tried before, where the visual language was interpreted and connected to other languages, all thereby gaining in meaning.

The other important function of the *atelier* was to provide a workshop for documentation. Documentation was seen then as a democratic possibility to inform the public of the contents of the schools. Already within 6 months after I began to work at the Diana School, we opened the school to the citizens with an exhibit of children's work.This work aroused much surprise and even some scandalized reaction, because among the themes displayed were a few usually censored for children, such as love and the nativity of Jesus.

I believe that few schools compare to the ones in Reggio Emilia in the amount of documentation prepared in the form of panels, slides, and now also small books and video tapes—materials to use with the children and families, as well as with teachers for in-service training. For example in recently reorganizing our Diana archives, we have realized that we have accumulated over 200 different sets of large panels (70 x 100 centimeters) presenting projects or experiences with children. Indeed, over time, our work in Reggio Emilia has tended to involve more and more research, visual education, and documentation. The educational work with children and the documentation have become more and more interconnected and mutually supportive.

Recently our interests have also shifted more and more toward analysis of the processes of learning and the interconnections among children's different ideas, activities, and representations. All of this documentation—the written descriptions, transcriptions of children's words, photographs, and now the videotapes—becomes an indispensable source of materials that we use everyday to be able to "read" and reflect critically, both individually and collectively, on the experience we are living, the project we are exploring. This allows us to construct theories and hypotheses that are not arbitrary and artificially imposed on the children.

Yet this method of work takes much time and is never easy. And we know that we still have much to learn. The camera, tape recorder, slide projector, typewriter, videocamera, computer, and photocopying machine are instruments absolutely indispensable for recording, understanding, debating among ourselves, and finally preparing appropriate documents of our experience.

The roles of the teacher and *atelierista* that emerge from these considerations are certainly different from how they were conceived years ago when I first came here. They require many competencies, including the capacity to reflect critically, different from what was emphasized before. Yet I am absolutely certain that the presence of the *atelierista* made possible many of the best projects

FIGURE 7.2. "Little girl telling a story." Clay drawing.

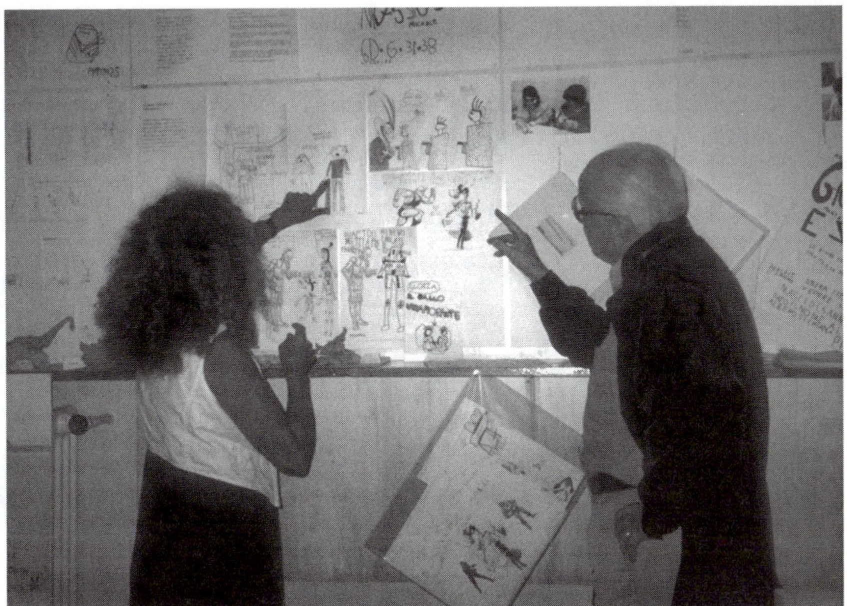

FIGURE 7.3. Vea Vecchi discusses documentation with Loris Malaguzzi.

in all of our schools. The environment of the *atelier* becomes a center of culture, where through the years the processes and tools have been modified. The relationship between the *atelierista* and teachers has grown and deepened, affecting in turn the professional relationship between teachers and children.

What has remained constant through time in my work is the way in which I work simultaneously with teachers and children, as well as the way in which I work directly with teachers. I am convinced that it is essential to construct with teachers a broad base of cultural knowledge, reflected in all of the details of our schools. This work requires immense time and effort.

Gandini: *I wonder whether through your long experience you have modified your views and theories or your relationship with the children and teachers. Have you discovered new visual and symbolic languages of children?*

Vecchi: Besides what I have said before, I can highlight a few things. I can say, first, that I have discovered how creativity is part of the makeup of every individual, and how the "reading" of reality is a subjective and cooperative production, and this is a creative act. Second, I have found it essential to have a high esteem for boys and girls, for men and women, in order to relate to them with genuine interest and curiosity. In the daily exchanges that I have with the children and adults, what has grown palpably is what I gain from them. I wish, although I am not sure, this will also increase what I give back to them. Third,

FIGURE 7.4. Making hypotheses about the placement of her own shadow.

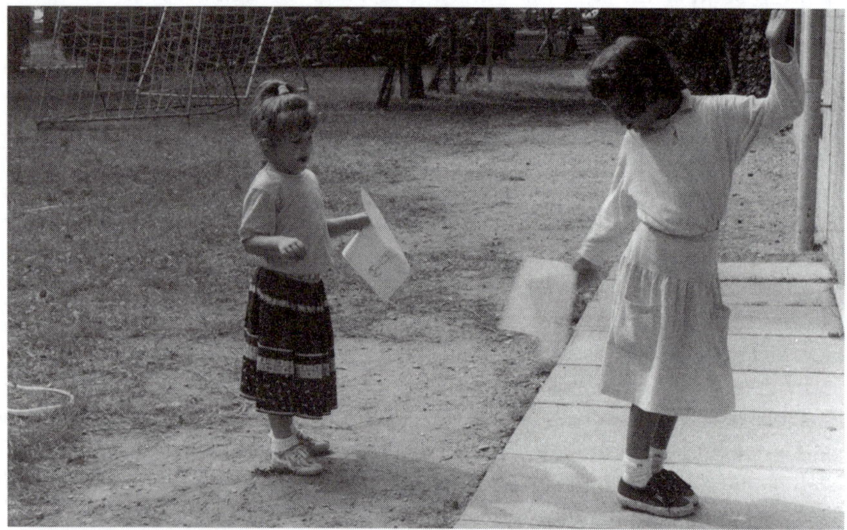

FIGURE 7.5. Exploring the shadows.

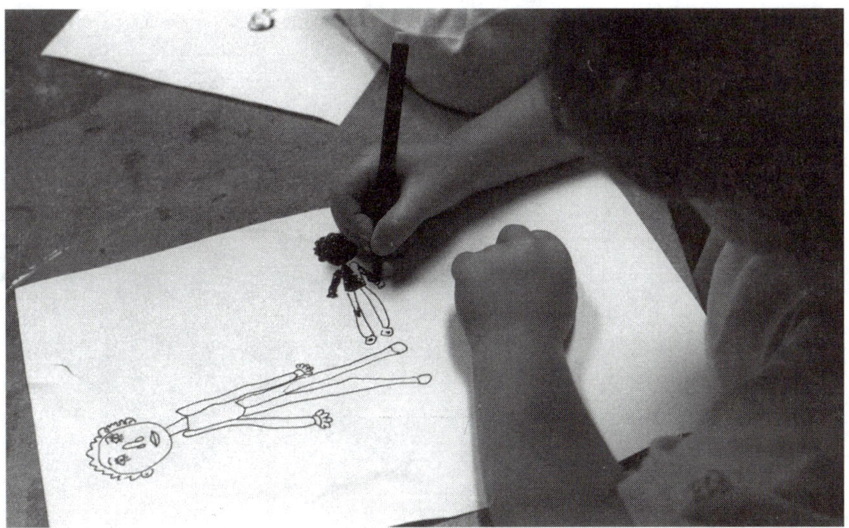

FIGURE 7.6. Revising her drawing based on new findings.

I realize that we have widened a great deal our field of interpretations, both of the processes and the results of our work. Fourth, the field of visual languages used by the children has also widened. As a consequence, in our work we are following new paths, different from the usual and the traditional. For example, we are trying to understand the feminine and masculine ways of representing reality. Fifth, I realize more and more the importance of the work done among the peer groups of children. We spend a great deal of energy in thinking about, and providing, instruments and strategies to support this way of working as a vital act of learning and a path toward social competence and maturity. We do continuously combine educational theories and our empirical research, filtered through our own, never fully adequate, professional lenses. In the school in which I work we are all women. We are curious about the world that little by little we are discovering, the world of children constructing their theories. At times we think that the relationship with the children reawakens in us a sense of our own childhood, creating feelings of tenderness, curiosity, play, and true pleasure.

Gandini: *Much of what the children do in your schools is so beautiful. Is this art? Is there an art of children?*

Vecchi: The way one should examine what children do is very different from evaluating adult artwork. It happens very often that some of the children's products are so original that one wants to compare them with the work of

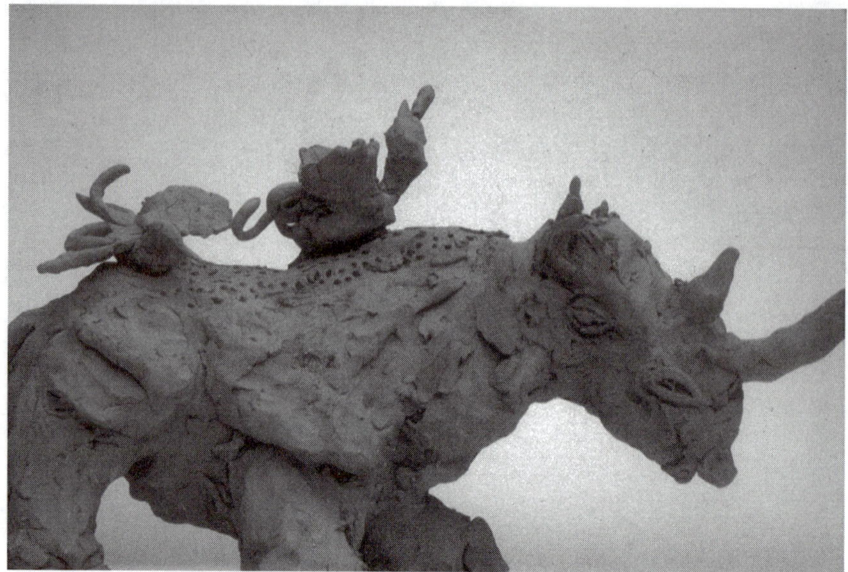

FIGURE 7.7. Rhinoceros (clay sculpture).

famous artists. But that kind of comparison becomes dangerous and fraught with ambiguity, especially if one tries to make comparisons consistently. It leads to false conclusions, such as that the behavior of children unfolds innately, or that the product is more important than the process. To make comparisons that go beyond a simple and playful resemblance shows how little one understands either children or artists.

On the other hand, I think that artistic discoveries—conceptual breakthroughs made by artists—should circulate among the adults in our schools, because we can learn from them. For example, the way that artists have solved problems of representing light, combining colors, and creating a sense of volume are all very interesting and help us explore new paths with children.

Gandini: *What advice could you give, after so many years of work, to teachers who work with young children?*

Vecchi: I hesitate to give advice. Our research is really an adventure, often exciting and diverting, and how can I give advice about going on an adventure? This pleasure and amusement is taken up by the children in their self-directed process of learning; I wish this would happen more because it works so well. And it should be shared by the teachers.

Gandini: *Tell me more about how you work on a daily basis with teachers.*

Vecchi: We meet several times a day. Every morning I do a tour of each classroom. I am particularly interested in what is happening at the beginning of the day, both with regard to the larger ongoing projects and to the smaller, independent activities. Teachers and I briefly talk about how to introduce certain things to the children and what to anticipate, and then what to do about them. Sometimes I also suggest the use of particular materials. Often, in the middle of the morning, I do another circuit, being sure to go where something of particular interest might be happening. Or sometimes, a teacher comes to ask advice or to get me to come and visit. Then, at the end of every morning I find at least 15 minutes to consult with each teacher. And often, we gather as a group for discussion. An important part of my role is to ensure the circulation of ideas among teachers. I am really their constant consultant. Because my training is different from theirs, I can help them see the visual possibilities of themes and projects that are not apparent to them. I may even intervene directly with the children to create possibilities that have not occurred to others. For example, once I noticed that the sun, shining behind one of the trees outside the window, cast a shadow of the leaves onto the glass. I taped a sheet of translucent white paper onto the glass. As children came in that morning, they exclaimed with surprise and pleasure at the sight of the shadow of leaves on the paper. Many things followed. The children even came to use the shadow as a clock. One said, "It's time to go to lunch. Look at the design on the paper!"

Certainly, I closely follow all of our major and longer term projects. I always find most interesting and wonderful the project on which we are currently working, because it seems to me that with each project we advance and learn a little more, and thereby we work better with the children. For example, we have found that shadows offer extraordinary educational possibilities. This theme, described in our book, *Tutto Ha Un' Ombra Meno Le Formiche (Everything Has a Shadow Except Ants)*,[1] involves an integration of acts of visual representation with scientific hypothesis testing. It goes far beyond the emphasis on aesthetic expression and perceptual exploration with which I began my work over 25 years ago.

---

[1] Published by the Comune di Reggio Emilia, 1990.

Drawing by
5-year-old children

chapter 8

The Voice of Parents

An Interview with Lella Gandini*

Gianna Fontanesi
Miller Gialdini
Monica Soncini

Observing in the schools of Reggio Emilia, listening on many occasions to the thoughtful presentations by the educators, and reading their reflections in the first edition, have made us aware of the critical role of parents as protagonists alongside their children and the teachers. Therefore, we wanted to include their own thoughts and voices in this new edition, and asked for their help in understanding the layers of parental experience and following their journeys toward heartfelt and competent participation. In the interview that follows, they offer us their views on the experience of co-constructing the educational experience and forging a deep, committed, reciprocal alliance with educators and children.

The three parents, interviewed in June 1995, are Monica Soncini, Miller Gialdini, and Gianna Fontanesi. Each one of them has participated in a significant way in the life of La Villetta School and each was willing to speak about his or her personal experience. The day before this interview, I had observed parents and teachers being together during the fantastic celebration called *La Festa dell'Acqua* ("Water Party"), marking the end of the school year. This celebration

* Translated by Lella Gandini and Carolyn Edwards.

included food, surprises, a clown, and special games for the children to do with parents. Several parents, including two of those I was to meet for the interview, stayed late helping to put things back in order.

All three of the parents interviewed had long-term experience with the municipal centers and schools of Reggio Emilia. Two (one mother and one father) had gone through the experience of having their children (two children each) first attend the Arcobaleno infant–toddler center, and then go on to La Villetta preprimary school. (This mother is the one with the little girl "in love," as recounted in the book, *Tenderness*; see Additional Resources, at the end of this volume). The third parent, a mother, had herself been a child in La Villetta. Teachers and parents of La Villetta School recently held a reunion, inviting all those who had been children at the school in 1970. At this reunion, people spoke about what they remembered of their experience and they formed a little committee to conduct a survey in order to find out how long after leaving the school people had remained friends and also about what kinds of school and work people had gone on to.

A more formal study, based on questionnaires and interviews, was conducted in 1987–1988 with former parents and children of Diana School, about their memories.[1] The former children (all born between 1970 and 1972) reported memories of a school that was stimulating, friendly, and happy. Their parents likewise made positive comments about the teachers and the school atmosphere. In response to open-ended questions asking them to compare their memories of participating at the elementary versus preprimary school, they pointed out their strong sense of difference between the two systems. The sense of familiarity that they had felt at Diana School contrasted sharply with the professional distance of teachers they experienced at the elementary school. They stated that discussions with teachers at Diana were highly mutual and focused on children's growth and on events connected with all aspects of children, whereas at the elementary school, the communication was mainly one way and focused on the academic profile of children.

Gandini: *I saw two of you yesterday evening, staying well after eight o'clock.*

Mr. Gialdini: We are always the same four or five parents who are here until the very end. We are always the last to leave any celebration. Among parents as well as children there is a sense of affection and attachment. We like the climate of serenity in the school.

I came to this system of schools in 1987 with my first son, and then 3 years later with my second boy. This is my last year, and then I will have both my children at the elementary school.

Gandini: *When did you first bring your oldest child to the infant–toddler center?*

Mr. Gialdini: He was 5 months old. He was very young, but I can give you

[1] Scuola Comunale Diana, 1988: *Ricerca sui percorsi dell'utenza quindici anni dopo* [Follow-up research on clients after 15 years].

a very subjective, personal reflection on that. We were completely outside the reality of these schools and did not know very much about them, but when we entered the school it seemed unbelievable.

We had little experience as parents and no support. My mother lives in Reggio Emilia but is very old and ill, and my mother-in-law lives far away, so we completely leaned on the institution. We were at risk of not getting a place because the waiting list was so long, but we were lucky. We began to leave our child at the infant–toddler center while we went to work, and we learned to be close to the child in a new way. For me, as I observed the kind of attention that was given to our child, there was a message that we parents, in turn, should become more attentive to the teachers and to what they were indirectly indicating to us.

Mrs. Fontanesi: It seems that they help us to *discover* our children.

Mr. Gialdini: Exactly. The kind of attention given the children at the infant–toddler center was just the beginning of something that has continued in a coherent way. In fact, there has been a continuous growth, both from the point of view of the child's learning and from our point of view as parents. Because of this attention to our child, we became involved immediately, and we came to look at our child's education as involving our participation. What they do is useful for us, but they also need us.

Mrs. Fontanesi: Yes, both the infant–toddler centers and the preprimary schools live on our participation.

Mr. Gialdini: I also want to say something regarding myself as a parent, beyond being a client and consumer of services. We offer our participation, yet I, for one, had much to learn about how to approach and be with my child, because I had no role models. My father, poor man, did not even have time to talk to us.

Gandini: *Among your generation, a new role for fathers has already been accepted, has it not?*

Mr. Gialdini [He is about 40 years old]: Oh yes, for my part that is absolutely true! [To the two mothers] I don't know about the case for you mothers.

Mrs. Fontanesi: Yes, we are speaking about fathers, but I think these changes reflect general changes in society. As new parents, we had to learn to read the signals our children gave us, and we learned that by bringing them to the infant–toddler center.

Mr. Gialdini: At one series of meetings at the center, we discussed being a father and being a mother—the common experiences of parenting—and by sharing and comparing our experiences, we would understand them better.[2] We stayed at some of these meetings until midnight, and we would even go on after the coordinator had left. Later on, we organized meetings with other parents that continued through the winter and following spring.

---

[2] Some of these meetings were held in 1994 in connection with an extensive study by the European Economic Community of parents' needs and perceptions of child care (see Chapter 1, this volume). Both Mr. Gialdini and Mrs. Fontanesi participated in these EEC meetings.

FIGURE 8.1. Interview with the parents at La Villetta School.

Gandini: *You said before that with the infant–toddler center, you offered your participation, and you also received back from the school. Now, if we turn to your experiences of the preprimary school, could all three of you comment on the reciprocity of this exchange?*

Mr. Gialdini: For my part, it has been a continuation of what happened before. But now you also learn about new curriculum and teaching aspects, because your child needs attention and help. When you come to pick him up at the school, it is not like a parking lot where you only ask if he is okay, but you really participate in what the children have been doing. The children feel at home there at school, as at their own home, and we are curious and interested about what has been happening at the school.

Mrs. Fontanesi: I have to say that in the beginning, with my first child, I would ask the teachers, "Did he eat? Did he drink? Was he okay?" And as you know, there is a display panel in the infant–toddler center providing notes about what each child ate, so I was very rigid, and controlled about how many check marks there were in the food columns everdyay. The teachers, with sweetness and kindness, would calmly explain to me that time was needed, that one should go step by step, and that I should understand that the child's relationship with food was one part of the child as a person. As a result, I learned gradually; they were not forcing me or pushing me.

The kind of exchanges that you can have with your own parents, with your women friends, with your female colleagues at the office, are all useful, but they are just small fragments. What you receive from the infant–toddler center and the preprimary school helps you understand that you are part of an overall educational project, and that you can participate even when the children are at home. For example, you may become ready to participate in the community-based management and advisory councils. Even preparing for a celebration like the one yesterday involves a thousand details requiring discussion and work, and they are all connected with the general project, the overall educational project: the care of the children.

Mr. Gialdini: All those problems that growing children give us ("Does he eat? Does he not eat? Does he wake up during the night?"), when you participate with other parents and educators, you come to realize that such problems are all part of growth.

Mrs. Soncini: You know, when you listen to the children, it sometimes seems that they are speaking about things that are much too advanced for their age. But they show us that they have learned how to discuss this way because of the stimulation received at school. For example, once when we went for an excursion, one child took a toy from another. My son took the toy and gave it back to the first child, saying, "Do not cry. This is your toy." This seems a small incident, but it is important because it shows what it means to negotiate. That is what the teachers explain to us: Children find solutions.

Mr. Gialdini: I want to go back and say something more about the parent meetings. Over the last 8 or 10 years, one can see a great deal of growth. Yet there are still families where everything is delegated to the mother. I talked with some friends in that situation, and they asked me, "How can you participate so much at home and at the center?"

Mrs. Fontanesi: At home, I talk all the time with my husband about participation. We realize that like most men he has only the one role model of his own father. For women it is different. The mother's role seems to have always been understood to relate to all the caretaking functions, whatever they might be, just as Laura Balbo found.[3]

Gandini: *To support the father, you have to work together to invent a new role for him to participate in the home. And the same thing applies to a new role for the father at the infant–toddler centers and preprimary schools.*

Mrs. Fontanesi: It is true, in fact, you construct that new role. Actually, I would have to say the same for mothers. You construct, day by day. You know, many times I have asked the teachers, "Tell me, how should I behave, how should I do it? They have never told me, but they have helped me to find the answers by myself, through my own reflections. I feel so positive about my experience, that I think I will continue to participate even when my children are no longer in preprimary school.

---

[3] Laura Balbo, an Italian sociologist, conducted research that showed the strong role of women in Italian families as mediators between needs and services. The women's efforts actually serve to help the "welfare state" to function. See Balbo (1976).

Gandini: *How did you feel about the very intimate exchange and trust between your daughter and the teacher that is recounted in the* Tenderness *book?*

Mrs. Fontanesi: I had thought I was very possessively attached to her. But I learned through this experience that I felt enriched as a mother to see my child have other attachments. You know, I knew all about her relationship with the teacher. My child had been there with her a long time.

Gandini: *Therefore, it may be more of a surprise to us readers that a child could be so trusting toward a teacher.*

Mrs. Fontanesi: I knew about many things in the book for a long time. I could easily imagine that she would say many of those words. But the fact that she spoke to the teacher was very positive. Their relationship was always close like that. In fact, today—as my daughter graduates—she is saying that she wants to come back and visit the school next year.

Gandini [Turning to Mrs. Soncini]: *One thing that I heard yesterday was that your son, who is usually afraid and protests about going in the shower, was running happily under the sprays of water at the celebration!*

Mrs. Soncini: In fact, I was surprised, too. Taking a shower is a problem for him because he hates to get soap in his eyes, and I still have to use a visor with him. He prefers to just use the bathtub. But here it is different, together with the other children. It was too beautiful! Well, of course, he was doing something that usually we adults do not allow.

Gandini: *I would like to use this example to ask what you think about how the expe-*

FIGURE 8.2. Interview with the parents at La Villetta School.

rience of being with other children helps children to grow and do new things.

Mrs. Soncini: Well, when we started coming to school, all the other children had problems about separation, but Mattia [who is 3 years old] never cried. In fact, on Saturdays and Sundays, he could not accept that he was not going to school. It is the same with your daughter [to Mrs. Fontanesi]. I know that it is going to be a problem when the school closes for the summer. I'll have to explain that the teachers need some rest.

Gandini: *I want to put to all three of you a question that people in the United States always ask us. When the children leave primary school, how is their transition to elementary school? What has been your experience, as parents?*

Mrs. Fontanesi: I think that the teachers here have been able to give the children enthusiasm and curiosity, and these qualities help the children to encounter new things. I know the children recognize the new school to be different, but I think I would be failing in my roles as parent and educator if my child were to say, "I don't want to go to elementary school. I want to return to preprimary school." As a parent, I must be able to support my child's enthusiasm for a new situation, even though it is hard for me to find the new school to be stimulating. But I have to go on and help my child find some interesting aspects.

Once again it has been the teachers here at the preprimary school who have helped me understand that I have to support the transition, to try not to create a conflict with the previous experience. There are even things that create continuity. For example, it was very positive for my child when they started to work on the Italian language in elementary school, and they collected stories from the children. That was very positive because of the experience my child had here at the preprimary school.

Mr. Gialdini: My son does everything with great desire to learn and discover. He confronts the elementary experience with curiosity and interest. What went on in preprimary school has become internalized as a personal trait. And I agree with Gianna Fontanesi, that you can and must support that.

I want to add something else, however. These children have learned to create relationships with others. I think that knowing how to be with others and do things with them is the most important and meaningful thing that the school has given our children.

Mrs. Fontanesi: Yes, but it depends also on the children's personality; our children are sociable. However, I think that in preprimary school, it is guaranteed and certain that everyone will have companions and friends; this is positive for all children.

Gandini (to Mrs. Soncini): *You yourself were once a child at this school, La Villetta. You could make observations that might interest these other parents. Do you remember what they have described? For example, what was said about going to elementary school and having the curiosity and desire to discover, is that something you experienced? If so, how long did it last?*

Mrs. Soncini: I think it is something that remains with you forever.

As I am very shy, it was also important for me to be able to enter into relationships with others. I don't know about elementary school; I think there I did use what I had learned [in the social sense]. And I have always worked in situations where relationships are important. Now I work with senior citizens, which might seem different, but is really based on the same principle.

I also want to say that when I returned to this school as a parent, I was very happy because I found things I remembered. Of course, the school has changed, but the old portion of the building has remained. We only had that old part, and

FIGURE 8.3. Drawings of parents by children of Diana school

it was very beautiful. And in the playground, just as I remember, there were June bugs and a turtle.

Gandini: *You had not been back to visit before you came for the first time as a parent?*

Mrs. Soncini: Well, I live around here and often pass the front of La Villetta. I see the playground roundabout and pioneer wagon that were here before, and these have for me a charm I will never forget. And I remember my special symbol that I chose with my teacher. I still have some of my clay creations and other things that I keep because they hold very strong memories.

Gandini: *What about the other children who were with you and went on to the elementary school with you? When did you lose track of each other?*

Mrs. Soncini: I guess it was by the end of elementary school. I don't think of it as losing track, because there were not too many children at the elementary school. And it is true that you always need others; you need relationships in everyday life.

Gandini: *How did you feel when you met again, at the reunion for children who had started school in 1970?*

Mrs. Soncini: When we met, I looked at them and remembered each and every one of them! Even at yesterday's celebration, I met a woman who was with me and now also has her child at La Villetta. I asked, "Are you Marina?" and she said, "Yes," and said my name, too. It was very beautiful to meet her again.

Gandini: *The fact that you have your child here must give you particular feelings.*

Mrs. Soncini: Oh yes, and it also makes it interesting for my son. Other children ask, "Is it true that your mother was a child here?" And he answers, "Yes, my mommy came here. Now she is a grownup. But she was a child like me, and I will grow up." My son always needs to remind himself that he will grow up, perhaps because he is smaller than other children.

Mrs. Fontanesi: Let me tell you how much this school means to me. We had the experience of first not getting into the infant–toddler center near my home. But finally a place was found for my child at Arcobaleno, which is far from my home. Yet when it came time to decide on a preprimary school, I will tell you the sincere truth, I only went to look at schools where Carlina Rinaldi was *pedagogista* [as she was at Arcobaleno]. When I had questions, she was the one who helped me find answers within myself. When my second child came along, I again did all I could to send him to Arcobaleno and La Villetta.

Gandini: *Thanks to all three of you for your thoughts. I am sure that those who read this interview will learn much from your personal accounts and reflections of your own and your children's participation in the Reggio Emilia schools.*

REFERENCES

Balbo, L. (1976). *Stato di famiglia: Bisogni privato collettivo.* [Family status: Private collective needs]. Milan, Italy: Esta Libri.

part III

Reflections on the Interplay of Theory and Practice

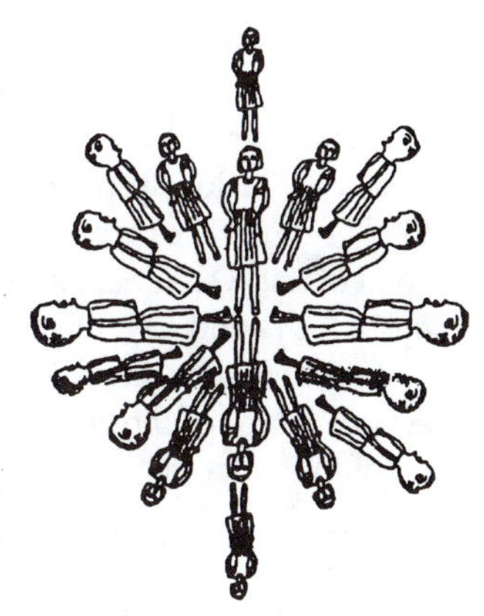

The mirror kaleidoscope, drawing of 5-year-old children to help the incoming 3-year-olds to orient themselves at Diana School.

chapter 9

Educational and Caring Spaces

Lella Gandini

In the entryway of the Diana School, a poster containing the words of 5-year-olds proclaims *the rights of children:*

> Children have the right to have friends, otherwise they do not grow up too well.
>
> Children have the right to live in peace.
>
> To live in peace means to be well, to live together, to live with things that interest us, to have friends, to think about flying, to dream.
>
> If a child does not know, she has the right to make mistakes. It works because after she sees the problem and the mistakes she made, then she knows.
>
> We've got to have rights, or else we'll be sad. (Diana School, 1990)

This is an engaging way for a school to greet parents and visitors.

Next to the poster are photographs of each team of two teachers (those who teach the 3-, 4-, and 5-year-old children) then photos of the *atelierista,* the cook, and the auxiliary staff members, along with their names and welcoming smiles. On the same wall are posted schedules of events: teacher training sessions, meetings with parents of each age group, meetings of the whole school, meetings with other schools, field trips, and celebrations.

All these messages are addressed to parents and visitors, but the children are also part of this welcome, for on the opposite wall there are photographs of small groups of boys and girls engaged in activities. Below, at the children's eye level, are self-portraits and small, square mirrors that open up like book covers. They reflect the image of the children as they enter but they also allow for trying out a host of funny faces if one feels like it.

SPACE AS AN ESSENTIAL ELEMENT OF THE EDUCATIONAL APPROACH

A visitor to any institution for young children tends to size up the messages that the space gives about the quality of care and about the educational choices that form the basis of the program. We all tend to notice the environment and "read" its messages or meanings on the basis of personal experience and the knowledge we have acquired about child development; all that also shapes our own ideas about childhood. We can, though, improve our ability to analyze deeper layers of meaning if we observe the extent to which everyone involved is at ease and how everyone uses the space itself. We then can learn more about the value and meaning of the relationship among the children and adults who spend time there.

Already in the entryway of this school we are aware of the value given to communication and openness of information. We learn right away that two teachers work together in each classroom and that every member of the staff is considered important. We also learn that, besides the words of the children and what they express through other symbolic languages, their photographs are important from the prominent way they are displayed. We also realize that these messages are addressed not only to the school's many visitors but also the parents, who morning and afternoon enter the school. Moving from the entryway, we find the spacious central area bathed in light, inviting us to explore and become involved.

Educators in Reggio Emilia have evolved through the years a philosophy based on partnership among children, teachers, parents, educational advisors, and the community. They succeeded, along with many teachers in other regions of Italy, after many years of effort and political action, in obtaining public funding for early education and local support for their program. Early in the development of their educational program, the participants in this collaboration appreciated the educational significance of space and invested a great deal of their energy into thinking and planning about it.

Furthermore, in the last 10 years, the educators in Reggio Emilia have given particular attention to the social constructivist theory of learning and have continued to develop the organization of space in their schools by considering this theoretical perspective in novel ways. The structures, choice of materials, and attractive ways in which educators set them up for the children become an open invitation to explore. Everything is thoughtfully chosen and placed with the intention to create communication, as well as exchanges among people and interactions between people and things in a network of possible connections and constructions. The constant reflection about the daily practice with the children, in light of this theory and in light of what the teachers learn in the process, brings the teachers to be observers of and participants with the children engaged in project work. The teachers pick up the children's interests and their ideas, share and discuss them among colleagues, and then return them to the children themselves, engaging them in dialogue and offering tools, materials, and strategies connected with the organization of space to extend those ideas, to combine them, or to transform them. The children see the adults as a support also in the way they organize and use the space, and they see them interested in and open to discovering and learning along with them. At the same time the wider system of organization (i.e., the cooperating system of the whole school staff, the *pedagogisti,* parents, and community) sustains teachers, directly and indirectly, in and around the environment of the school, and makes it possible for them to work at this high level of engagement.

Educators in the United States are well aware of the importance of the environment. This is evident, for example, in their imaginative use of outdoor spaces, a marvelous American resource not so readily available to, or so easily tapped by, Italian teachers, who work in a highly urbanized environment. However, American teachers have always contended with funding limitations and thus have been forced to make compromises with regard to indoor space. The unfortunate result, as seen in many day care centers and schools for young children, has been a set of discouraging physical conditions, especially the lack of natural light and of uncluttered space.

This is a time in the history of education of young children in the United States when many educators are engaged in making their voices heard by the public and by national and local governments, in favor of the rightful needs of children and of the people who care for them.

In this regard the guidelines compiled in 1992 at the meeting on Architecture and Education in Racine, Wisconsin, are relevant. These guidelines call for a school environment that gives a sense of well-being to children, educators, and families, and at the same time favors learning and exploration. Instead of the traditional boxlike classroom, schools of the future should be specifically designed as hospitable environments for the new styles of learning and organizing schools that are taking hold around the country. Considering that learning now means individual and small groups of students posing questions and generating information from multiple sources, and recommunicating it to others, teachers, no longer lecturers, now serve as keen observers of learning and of their own teaching. Their task is to foster students' thinking as mentors and coaches in the learning process. For the same reasons, classrooms will be like studios; there will be an array of spaces of various sizes, including central gathering spaces for the school community; there will be workspace for cooperative learning for groups of different sizes; and there will be quiet, private areas where students can think and work independently or in one-on-one sessions with teacher, mentor, or fellow student. With this new way of teaching, there will be need to accommodate a full range of social services. Above all, the new schools need to be child- and family-friendly institutions where all feel welcome and have a sense of belonging (Report of the Second National Invitational Conference on Architecture & Education, 1992).

THE ARCHITECTURALLY PLANNED SPACE AND THE EXTENDED SPACE AROUND THE SCHOOL, THE CITY, AND BEYOND

Once the basic philosophy and choices of their educational program were in place, Reggio Emilia educators planned and worked out the structure and arrangement of space. Following the idea that the education of young children is a community-based concern and responsibility, children's centers ideally had to be integral parts of the urban plan. Moreover, rather than occupy marginal space in a neighborhood, they had to be placed in full view of the public, where the life of children and teachers would be a visible point of reference for the community. The presence of the school in the neighborhood itself is a pronouncement about respect for the rights of children and families.

For each building, whether built completely anew or modified from an existing one, pedagogical coordinators, teachers, and parents met to plan with the architects. The people who were going to work and live there for so many hours had to be participants in every choice: A wall that was too high or the lack of a partition could modify the possibility or the quality of interaction in an educational approach where partnership and interaction are paramount. In fact, as Tiziana Filippini pointed out, educators in Reggio Emilia speak of space as a "container" that favors social interaction, exploration, and learning, but they also see space as having educational "content," that is, as containing educational messages and being charged with stimuli toward interactive experience and constructive learning (Filippini, 1990). Therefore, the structure of interior spaces tends to evolve along with everything else about the educational program in Reggio Emilia.

Loris Malaguzzi, in an interview together with Vea Vecchi in 1992 about the space in the Diana school, said:

> In 1970 we were processing many things that we had not yet worked out fully. Some to be sure were in place already: the transparency of the walls, the flood of light, the continuity between inside and outside. We already had the *piazza* but it was not until we lived in it that it aquired its full significance. The *piazza* does more than extend the classrooms for it encourages many different encounters and activ-

> ities, and we assign still other purposes to it. For us it represents the main square of the Italian city, a space where people meet, speak to one another, discuss and engage in politics, conduct business, do street theater, and stage protests. The *piazza* is a place of continuous passage, where the quality of exchange becomes more intense, whether among children or adults. The more they meet, the more ideas circulate among adults and children. We might say that the *piazza* is a place where ideas arrive and depart.

At this point Vea Vecchi remarked that traditional schools also have large central spaces, and the issue is not having space but how it is used.

Malaguzzi: That's right. These large spaces are used for recess, for "recreation," because between 10:00 and 10:30 there is supposed to be a break, yet in truth there are neither objects nor structures, not even any purpose, except for the hypocritical and ignorant one of handing the children a space so that they can do what they want for half an hour!

Vea Vecchi: It was precisely this that I wanted to point out. If we call that central space a "piazza" it means that we have a theory about its use. Spaces could look more or less alike but if they are part of a culture and subject to some pedagogical reflection about their use, their significance changes completely. The objects and structures found here, in the space of the Diana School, allow purposefully for a variety of encounters.

Loris Malaguzzi: The *piazza* is also a passage. In part it is structured by the objects in it, but there are also the children, and it allows them to flow through,

FIGURE 9.1. The central space (piazza) of Diana School.

to walk, or to linger as they wish. It is also necessary to keep in mind how influential the environment is with regard to the affective, cognitive, and linguistic acquisitions. The environment becomes part of the individual so that any response to a request we make of the children or to a request children make of adults is facilitated or obstructed by the environment and its characteristics. In general, what architects ask is: "How many children do you have? Twenty, thirty? The place for the desks?" Already we know that they are thinking of a school where learning takes place sitting down. For a school where children stand up and where they learn moving around, their way of measuring is useless. We have to consider that each child is an organic unit who needs personal space for action and movement in his or her own personal way, and we have to reflect on that; we cannot use the tape measure.

Vea Vecchi: An architect and a pedagogical coordinator *(pedagogista)* could also build a beautiful school, but then if the teachers who go to work there neither reflect on nor prepare to deepen their understanding about what is the meaning of living in a space, nothing happens. One has to return to the initial ideas that determined choices about the space. For example, to inhabit the space according to philosophical choices that respect children transforms mere hygiene into genuine care and transforms interaction with objects into communication. Without a philosophical basis that gives meaning to the educational experience to be lived in a space, the identity of the space will not emerge; in fact the risk is to try to live an experience disconnected from the space. Often one walks into a well-built building that is used for a school for young children and one sees many things done to that space that run against its own important positive features creating a dissonance and fragmentation. (Malaguzzi & Vecchi, interview, 1992)

The teachers also value what is special about the spaces that surround their schools, considering them extended classroom space. Part of their curriculum involves taking children to explore neighborhoods and landmarks in the city. One example of the extension of the school is a project undertaken for many months by La Villetta School, during which children went out to explore how the city is transformed during rainstorms. This project brought the children and teachers to explore first the reality of the city without rain, taking photographs in both familiar and less familiar places, and then making hypotheses about how the rain would change them. Because that year the seasonal rains were so late to arrive, the children had weeks to prepare the tools and equipment they thought would help them observe, collect, measure, photograph, and record everything about the rain. In the meantime, the children's expectations grew tremendously. Every day the teachers and children went up to the school roof terrace to gaze hopefully at the sky, gaining much knowledge about cloud formations and wind direction.

When a good rainstorm finally arrived, the experience was feverish and exhilarating. The children noticed how people changed their speed and posture

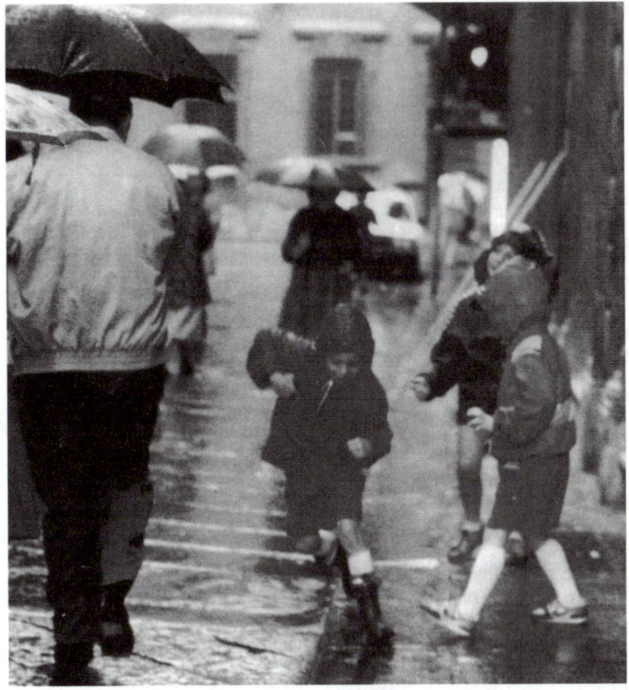

FIGURE 9.2. Children are enjoying their city under the rainstorm.

in walking, how the shining reflections and the splash from the puddles changed the streets, how the sound of the raindrops differed depending on whether it was falling on the pavement, the hoods of cars, or the leaves of trees. Then, after experiencing the rainstorm, and following the customary procedure in Reggio Emilia, the children became engaged in representing many of its aspects. This, in turn, led to further questions, hypotheses, and explorations that the teacher and the *atelierista* thoroughly documented. The whole exploration eventually was recorded in "The City and the Rain" segment of the "Hundred Languages of Children" Exhibit, and serves to tell us of the many ways in which the familiar space of the city can become the stage for and subject of activities and constructive explorations (REGGIO CHILDREN, S.r.l., 1987, 1996).

THE WELCOMING SPACE AS A REFLECTION OF LAYERS OF CULTURE

When one enters the schools for young children in Reggio Emilia, as in the example we saw at the outset, one immediately senses a welcoming feeling, an atmosphere of discovery and serenity. Moreover, one gains an overall impression of richness in the quality and types of the activities of children, as well as of high professional standards and care on the part of adults. These impressions come from the way the environment is thoughtfully organized, and especially from seeing how children, teachers, and families move about in the schools. Yet, how does all of this come about? Loris Malaguzzi (interview, June, 1990) said:

> To be sure our schools are the most visible object of our work. I believe they give multiple perceptions and messages. They have decades of experience behind them, and have known three generations of teachers. Each infant–toddler center and each preprimary school has its own past and evolution, its own layers of experience, and its own peculiar mix of styles and cultural levels. There has never been, on our part, any desire to make them all alike.

The space in many ways reflects the culture of the people who create it and, on careful examination, reveals even distinct layers of this cultural influence. First of all, there is in these schools a great attention to the beauty and harmony of design. This is evident in the functional and pleasing furnishings, often invented and built by teachers and parents together. It is also evident in the colors of the walls, the sunlight streaming through large windows, the healthy green plants, and many other details such as careful upkeep of the space. This special care for the appearance of the environment and the methodical care for the living space of the home, along with the design of spaces that favor social interaction, are essential elements of Italian culture.

Built into the organization of the environment for activities and routines are features that favor cooperation, a concept with strong social and political value in the Emilia Romagna region, where a century-old organization of producers' and consumers' cooperatives is still thriving. Further regional touches can be heard in the language, seen in some of the materials and implements available, and in the typical food that the cooks prepare fresh each day, much to the children's delight. The culture of the city can also be detected in the documentation on the walls about outings and activities that involve city landmarks and people. One example is the famous visit to the stone lion, who sits forever waiting for the children in the market square of the city.

The next layer is the culture of the school, of each particular school. The school itself, through each and every person that directly and indirectly participates in its life, constructs a culture, starting from the particular story of how the building was chosen, designed, and built, going on to the experience that each child and each family brings from home and the way the participation of parents in the life of the school is manifested. All this contributes to the construction of a distinct culture along with the sharing of special events and daily rituals. In Reggio Emilia it is considered particularly meaningful that the environment of the school, besides being welcoming, shows the traces of those children who spend so many hours in those rooms for a cycle of 3 years. There are individual and group histories carefully documented, and there is a daily weaving of routines that are meaningful stepping stones in the life of all involved. All these contribute to the creation of symbols and metaphors that are elaborated and constructed together and become part of the common discourse.

Materials brought into the school by children and families contribute to creating a particular culture. Some are natural materials, such as displays of pine cones, shells, or pebbles arranged by size, shape, or color. There are transparent boxes that contain treasures collected during a special excursion or simply exploring the garden surrounding the school. There are implements and objects brought from home, from the kitchen or the sewing box or even the toolbox. These objects and materials are brought to the school by the children but the parents themselves help place them inside the transparent bags that go back and forth, creating a connection between life at school and life at home.

Furthermore, the action of the children contributes to mold the space in a specific way. The history of children who were there before creates special characteristics, but the adults have great flexibility and interest in continuous renewal . The environment mirrors the new relationships that bring new ideas and continue to nourish the life of the school. It is a common practice on the part of educators to adapt and change the space to respond to the different needs of incoming children every year. The space therefore also reflects the changes and evolution of thought and reflections on the part of educators.

All this contributes to render each school different and to create a specific culture. The creative soultions, the care of the environment, the attention to details, and the reflection of the reality brought in by children and families are common elements in this system, and they leave distinct traces in each school.

SPACE AND TIME

> An environment is a living, changing system. More than the physical space, it includes the way time is strucutured and the roles we are expected to play. It conditions how we feel, think, and behave; and it dramatically affects the quality of our lives. The environment either works for us or against us as we conduct our lives. (Greenman, 1988, p.5)

When one observes children and adults in the schools of Reggio Emilia, one perceives that there is a particular connection between time and space and that the environment truly works. The consideration of the children's own needs and rhythms shapes the arrangement of space and the physical environment, and in turn, the time at disposal allows for the use and enjoyment, at a child's pace, of such carefully thought-out space. In fact, the way time is thought of in the Reggio Emilia approach is influenced by at least three major factors. First of all, their experience has extended over 30 years since the first municipal school was established, and that in turn was based on the parent-run schools established immediately after World War II. Therefore, what we see in the arrangement of spaces is based on many changes and much learning through a long experience. As a consequence, educators do not push to obtain immediate results.

Second, parents and their children establish a long-standing rapport with the program, because many start sending their sons and daughters to the infant–toddler center before age 1. When they are 3 years old the children transfer to the municipal preprimary schools, which take them on between the ages of 3 and 6 years. The system provides for teachers to be with the same children from the beginning to the end of each school cycle. The relationships that are established during this long stay of the same groups of children, parents, and teachers shape the space, which in turn, becomes a familiar niche for them. Because there is no separation at the end of each year, and thus no period of adjustment to new relationships, there is less pressure to reach certain goals, to finish the year's work with a clean break or start each year with a clean slate.

Third, the public programs for young children in Italy are not divided between education and day care. These programs do differ but only because they cater to children of different ages; they are all supposed to provide both care and education. The programs are considered social services, with flexible schedules. Although most of the children stay in the municipal centers between 8:30 a.m. and 4:00 p.m., there are parents who need to leave their children as early as 7:30 a.m. to as late as 6:20 p.m., and still others prefer to pick up the children right after lunch, at 12:30 or 1:00 p.m. Most of the children, in fact, spend many hours in group living. Accordingly, the educators provide a leisurely social setting for their meals; a quiet, protected environment for their naps; and for their activities several areas with a great deal of interesting and engaging proposals that are carried out at a generally unhurried pace, creating a sense of security, self-esteem, and the possibility to work problems through. Loris Malaguzzi commented, "One has to respect the time of maturation, of development, of the tools of doing and understanding, of the full, slow, extravagant, lucid and ever-changing emergence of children's capacities; it is a measure of cultural and biological wisdom" (Malaguzzi, Chapter 3, this volume).

SOCIAL SPACE, ACTIVE SPACE, AND A SPACE FOR HANDS AND MIND

For the educators in Reggio Emilia, social exchange is seen as essential in learning. Through shared activity, communication, cooperation, and even conflict, children co-construct their knowledge of the world, using one child's idea to develop another's, or to explore a path yet unexplored. Because social development is seen as an intrinsic part of cognitive development, the space is planned and set up to facilitate encounters, interactions, and exchanges among children. The space has to guarantee the well-being of each child and of the group as a whole. At the same time the space is set up to favor relationships and interactions of teachers, staff, and parents among themselves and with children. For example, adults can meet, work in small or large groups, discuss problems, and eat together inside the school. The well-being of the adults who work in the schools and the trust of parents, who entrust their children to the school before going about their activities, are essential for the educational project to work. As stated by Loris Malaguzzi (interview, June, 1990):

> We have tried always to help and maintain strong ties between work and research, a healthy cooperation with the school staff and with the families, an unfailing faith in the potential and capacities of children, and lastly, a ready willingness to think about and discuss what we do.

In the Diana School (see Figure 9.3) the classrooms for the children aged 3, 4, and 5 years of age open toward the large common space designated by the same term used for a city square *(piazza)*. The other interior spaces open toward this *piazza,* or common space. The classrooms are subdivided in two or three spaces because the teachers are convinced that smaller spaces can offer opportunities for children to work well in small groups, to listen and be listened to, and therefore to communicate. This arrangement also gives teachers the opportunity to set up situations that invite constructive exploration and action.

Vea Vecchi commented about the importance of reevaluating the space periodically:

> There are things that could be modified in our space; even the building materials used are not so appropriate anymore. They should be rethought with some good, forward-looking planning on our part. What continues to work well are the trans-

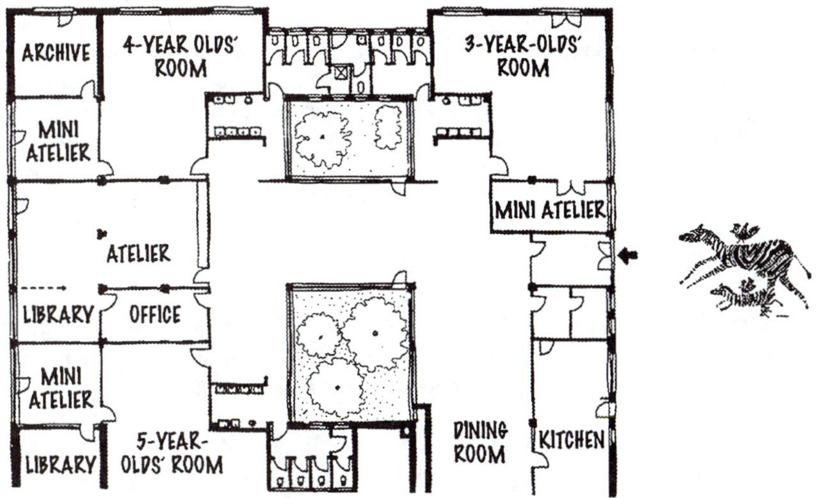

FIGURE 9.3. Map of Diana School.

> parent walls, the large *piazza,* the single level, and the subdivision of each classroom into three spaces, which permits the children to work in small groups. The concept of the large central space together with satellite spaces dates from 1976 when we formed work groups to analyze the times and the ways that space was used in six schools. We divided the day into time periods, and for each of these we observed how children, teachers, staff members, and parents moved. We tried to judge the quality of the various displacements and the identity that the different places assumed, especially in terms of how these fostered communication. Then we discussed the results among educators and with the Advisory Council, where parents, teachers, and citizens work together. The discussions were very full because our very way of working was at issue. The decision to add or make available more room in all the schools brought about significant changes, in particular the division of each classroom into three spaces, of which one is a *mini-atelier.* (Malaguzzi & Vecchi, interview, 1992)

Among the other interior spaces that open toward the *piazza* of the Diana School, there is the large *atelier,* a library with space for computers, an archive, and a storage room. The *atelier,* a workshop, or studio, used by all children and adults in the school is described by Loris Malaguzzi in this way:

> The *atelier* was included in each school as part of our wider educational project for young children and it became part of each infant–toddler center starting in 1970. The work in the *atelier* is seen as integrated and combined with the entire didactic approach. The intent was to react to the marginal place assigned generally to visual and expressive education. We also wanted to react to an education based on words and meaningless rituals and give possibilities to a child seen as rich in resources, and interests to a child interactive and constructivist. We wanted to create possibilities to refine taste and aesthetic sensibility, to observe and find theories about children starting from scribbles and going forward. We also wanted to try out tools, materials, and techniques. We wanted to support creative and logical paths the children would choose to explore. The *atelier,* in our approach, is an additional space within the school where to explore with our hands and our minds, where to refine our sight through the practice of the visual arts, where to work on projects connected with the activities planned in the classroom, where to explore and combine new and well-known tools, techniques, and materials. (Malaguzzi, 1988, p. 27)

The teacher in charge of the *atelier,* the *atelierista,* has training in art education, is co-organizer of children's and teachers' experience, and serves as editor and designer of the documentation of the work done in the school. Each age group has a classroom (a large room) and next to it a *mini-atelier.* Again Loris Malaguzzi commented about this decentralized workshop:

> Years ago the space had exploded with the growth of ideas. Technology had brought into the *atelier* the camera, the taperecorder, the VCR, the photocopy machine, the computer, and more. Our toolbox had become larger. We had to decentralize the *atelier* in smaller spaces. We had to build archives in the schools

> and in the Municipal administration; furthermore, we instituted a Documentation Center. (Malaguzzi, 1988, p. 29)

Continuing our visit to a school, we would see that the kitchen, dining room, wash room with sinks for washing or water play, and bathrooms are all laid out in efficient and pleasant ways. None is considered marginal space; for example, the mirrors in the washrooms and bathrooms are cut in different shapes to inspire the children to look in a playful way at their image. The ceilings are used as host to many different types of aerial sculptures or beautiful mobiles, all made with transparent, colored, and unusual material, built by children and set up by teachers. There are glass walls to create a continuity between interior gardens and outside gardens; they contribute much natural light and give occasion for playing with transparencies and reflections. Glass walls also separate working spaces to create a communal feeling. However, if one desires to be or work alone or chat with one friend, there are various options, such as the space of the *mini-ateliers* or other comfortable small enclosures to which one can retire and spend time.

The organization of the day and of the active space shows the attention to individual childrenas well as to the group of children. Every morning around 9:00, when all the children have arrived at school, each classroom has a meeting. In some schools the meeting space is on a sort of bleachers. Then, once the children have chosen from among the activities available or to continue with one of the projects in progress, they will find the necessary materials and tools set up on tables, light tables, and easels, or placed in convenient spaces. They will be able to find everything else they need on well-organized open shelves, stocked with recycled and other materials. Those materials have been previously selected and neatly placed in transparent containers with the help of teachers.

The arrangement and the use of space for activities, for constructive exploration of materials, or for work on projects and themes is critical. Loris Malaguzzi said:

> What actually goes on in the schools is a basic test for all of us. The continuous activity is the most important thing for us and represents that which can contribute the most to keeping fresh (a term dear to Dewey) our interest and the continuous mobility of our thought and action. I believe that our schools show the attempt that has been made to integrate the educational project with the plan for the organization of work and the architectural and functional setting, so as to allow for maximum movement, interdependence, and interaction. (Malaguzzi, interview, June 1990)

One of the images that Malaguzzi used to make a point about setting up the space for stimulating and meaningful centers of activity, is that of "market stalls" where customers look for the wares that interest them, make selections, and engage in lively interactions.

FIGURE 9.4. Communication between two rooms in the Infant–toddler Center Arcobaleno.

SPACE APPROPRIATE FOR DIFFERENT AGES AND LEVELS OF DEVELOPMENT

In the infant–toddler centers, the attention given to the physical environment has a particular quality that reminds one of the need that the youngest children have for closeness and nurturing exchanges. Right at the entrance, comfortable wicker chairs invite parents to take time to pause with their infants, meet with one another, or converse with the teachers. There are rooms covered with carpets and pillows where children can crawl safely or else snuggle up with a teacher to look at a picture book or listen to a story. There is a large space with equipment appropriate for movement. But there is also an *atelier* where the children explore with paint, markers, flour, clay, and much more. The glass partitions are used especially in the infant–toddler centers, where children tend to feel a greater sense of separation. There, glass walls are used to allow one to see into the kitchen and into the room where the children's clothes are changed, or to look back and forth between the rooms where children of different age groups play.

Similarly, in the preprimary schools, in the classroom of the youngest group, more space is left for play with unstructured materials such as blocks, Legos, toy animals, and recycled materials. The area covered with rugs is larger, to allow the children to play on the floor. Furthermore, the housekeeping space is wide and rich with small replicas of pottery and glassware commonly found at home, jars of pasta of different sizes, and beans of different colors. Entering the *mini-atelier*, one might notice, in late autumn, that the children are exploring the properties of three materials: clay, paper, and wire. They spend several weeks on each of these materials. In later months, teachers and children will return to these materials to use their higher level of skills and understanding. Through the year, as they acquire more self-assurance, these children carry out many explorations and projects also in the main *atelier*.

SPACE THAT DOCUMENTS

According to Loris Malaguzzi, "The walls of our preprimary schools speak and document. The walls are used as spaces for temporary and permanent exhibits of what the children and the adults make come to life" (Chapter 3, this volume).

One of the aspects of space that strikes visitors is indeed the quantity and quality of the children's own work exhibited all around the schools. In fact this is one of the ways in which children and teachers contribute to shaping the space of their school and to constructing the culture of a particular school. They do it through the mediation of the *atelierista,* who with the teachers selects and prepares the displays with great care. Most of the time these displays include the teachers' reflections, and next to the children's work, photographs that tell about the process, plus a description of the various steps and evolution of the activity or project. These descriptions are meaningfully completed with the transcription of the children's own remarks and conversation (often tape recorded) that went along with this particular experience. Therefore, the displays, besides being well-designed and contributing to the general pleasantness of the space, provide documentation about specific activities, the educational approach, and the steps of its process.

The process of documentation itself, which is done collaboratively through observation, collecting a variety of documents, and interpreting them, gives teachers the possibility to make informed curricular choices, to assess the process and the results of the children's activities. In fact documentation contributes notably to their professional growth. Of course it also makes the children aware of the regard adults have of their work. Finally, to document the educational process is a way to make parents, colleagues, and visitors aware of the children's potential, their developing capacities, and what goes on in the school.

Malaguzzi commented about documentation:

> Today we would need other kinds of space. It is clear that where there is an image of the child as being active and productive, the form, the distribution, the size,and the organization of space has to take that into account. One thing is a school that speaks; another a school that is silent. If it is a school that speaks we

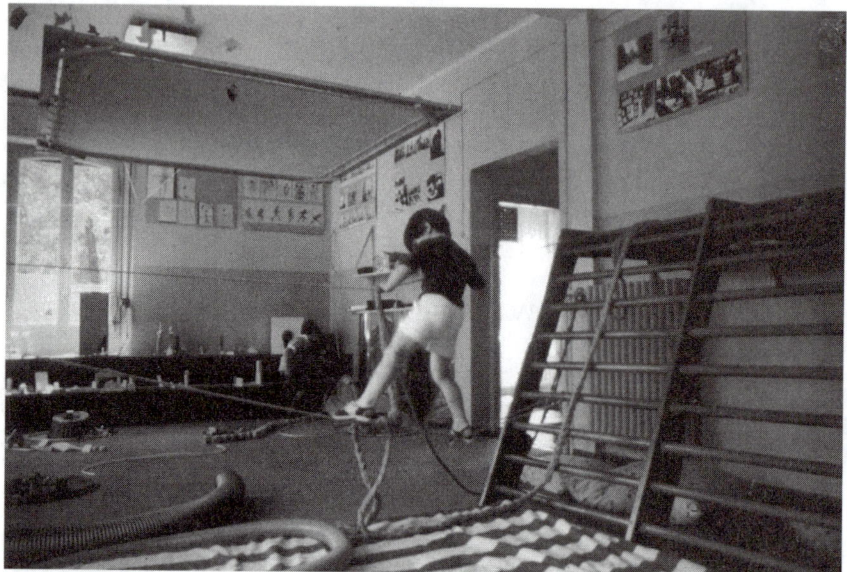

FIGURE 9.5. The 4-year-olds room at Villetta School.

have to consider and help it to speak. We should create a space that includes the documentation where parents can tarry or take time. I would like to set up a specific space, with comfortable armchairs, where the parents can pause and receive a flow of messages, that will be continuously transformed. We should organize a place where parents, visitors, and teachers have dialogues and exchange thoughts and ideas. It is not casual that an archive has become a notable element of our work. The archive has resulted from our own need to document. But if one documents, for whom does one document? I document only if I have an organization that includes the family; otherwise the messages bounce away. What I want to say is that the archive and the documentation change completely the professional stature of each person who is within the school. This complete change comes about because if one must document, not only must one record, but also make predictions; that is, think carefully about what to document and why that particular thing and not another. Our school of course has to be physically attached to the earth, but, as an image, it has to be a ship in movement. This means that parents will always be on board with us to see different landscapes, transformations, phenomena, and so on; that is what one sees when one follows the children's interests. Parents have to have an idea of a school in motion, because the children move around all the time and not only physically; for their minds and social exchanges are in continuous motion, just as their language is. We need to become able to have this open vision of the school. (Malaguzzi & Vecchi, interview, 1992)

A SPACE THAT TEACHES

The environment is seen here as educating the child; in fact it is considered as "the third educator" along with the team of two teachers.

In order to act as an educator for the child, the environment has to be flexible: it must undergo frequent modification by the children and the teachers in order to remain up-to-date and responsive to their needs to be protagonists in constructing their knowledge. All the things that surround the people in the school and that they use—the objects, the materials, and the structures—are seen not as passive elements but on the contrary as elements that condition and are conditioned by the actions of children and adults who are active in it. In the words of Loris Malaguzzi (personal communication, 1984):

> We value space because of its power to organize, promote pleasant relationships among people of different ages, create a handsome environment, provide changes, promote choices and activity, and its potential for sparking all kinds of social, affective, and cognitive learning. All of this contributes to a sense of well-being and security in children. We also think as it has been said that the space has to be a sort of aquarium that mirrors the ideas, values, attitudes, and cultures of the people who live within it.

The schools in Reggio Emilia thus could not be just anywhere, and no one of them could serve as an exact model to be copied literally elsewhere. Yet they have common features that merit consideration in schools everywhere. Each school's particular configuration of the garden, walls, tall windows, and handsome furniture declares: This is a place where adults have thought about the quality of environment. Each school is full of light, variety, and a certain kind of joy. In addition, each school shows how teachers, parents, and children, working and playing together, have created a unique space: a space that reflects their personal lives, the history of their schools, the many layers of culture, and a nexus of well-thought-out choices.

REFERENCES

Diana School. (1990). *In viaggio coi diritti dei bambini.* [A journey into the rights of children]. Booklet published by the school and republished by REGGIO CHILDREN S.r.l. (1995). Distributed by Reggio Children USA, Washington, DC.

Filippini, T. (1990, November). Introduction to the Reggio approach. Paper presented at the annual conference of the National Association for the Education of Young Children, Washington, DC.

Greenman, J. (1988). *Caring spaces, learning spaces: Children's environments that work.* Redmond, WA: Exchange Press.

Malaguzzi, L. (1988, December). *Se l'atelier e'dentro una storia lunga e ad un progetto educativo* [If the *Atelier* is part of a long history and an educational program]. *Bambini,* pp. 26–31.

REGGIO CHILDREN, S.r.l. (1987, 1996). *I cento linguaggi dei bambini.* [The hundred languages of children: Narrative of the possible]. Distributed by Reggio Children USA, Washington, DC.

Report of the Second National Invitational Conference on Architecture & Education. (1992, May). The Prairie School and Wingspread, Racine, WI.

Portrait by 5-year-old from Pablo Neruda School.

chapter 10

Partner, Nurturer, and Guide: The Role of the Teacher

Carolyn Edwards

In Reggio Emilia, the teacher's role in assisting learning is a subject of central and abiding interest and concern. Over the past 30 years, teachers and administrators have discussed and considered the responsibilities, goals, difficulties, and opportunities faced by the teachers in their public child care system. They have evolved together a shared discourse, a coherent way of thinking and talking about the role of the teacher inside and outside the classroom, based—as are all aspects of their organization, environmental design, pedagogy, and curriculum—on an explicit philosophy about the nature of the child as learner. This language of education serves to organize and bring together all of the participants in the Reggio Emilia system into one community.

This chapter describes the view in Reggio Emilia of the teacher's role. The chapter draws from videotaped observations in one preprimary school, the Diana School, and recorded discussions and interviews with teachers and administrators conducted since 1983 and described in Edwards, Gandini, and Nimmo (1992, 1994, in preparation). Quotations from formal interviews, group discussions, and observations (collected, transcribed, and translated by Gandini and Edwards) are used throughout this chapter to illustrate the concepts and convey the distinctive meanings, the particular ways of packaging ideas and communicating with others, that we encountered in Reggio Emilia.

DEFINITIONS OF THE TEACHER'S ROLE IN REGGIO EMILIA

What is the role of the teacher in the early childhood classroom? When answering this question, a good place to begin is to analyze and list the different important dimensions, such as: (a) promoting children's learning in cognitive, social, physical, and affective domains; (b) managing the classroom; (c) preparing the environment; (d) providing nurturance and guidance; (e) communicating with important constituencies (parents, colleagues, administrators, the public); and (f) seeking professional growth. These same aspects are seen in the work of teachers in Reggio Emilia, and in addition, two other components are seen as essential: (g) engaging in political activism to defend the cause of public early education; and (h) conducting systematic research on daily classroom work for purposes of curriculum planning, teacher development, and professional dissemination.

Yet, although Reggio Emilia teachers face a similar list of challenges and responsibilities as American teachers, nevertheless, when asked to define the role of the teacher, they never begin in an analytic style and list the components of the teacher's work. Instead, they begin holistically, and speak of an idealized image—or more precisely—idealized pair of images: teacher and child. The adult role of teacher belongs with a complementary image of the child as learner. If adults can agree on how they shall look on the schoolchild's nature, rights, and capacities, then they can also come to agree on what kind of teacher is needed to educate and provide for this child.

How to define this learning child? The educators in Reggio Emilia say that young children are powerful, active, competent *protagonists* of their own growth: actors in their shared history, participants in society and culture, with the right (and obligation) to speak from their own perspective, and to act with others on the basis of their own particular experience and level of consciousness. All children seek identity, individuality, completion, and satisfaction through dialogue, interaction, and negotiation with others. Their contexts for action are the ceaselessly changing, intersecting worlds of classroom, community, and culture, with adults nearby to serve as partners, resources, and guides.

This intrinsically social view of children—as protagonists with unique personal, historical, and cultural identities—involves parallel expectations and possibilities for adults. Teachers are likewise protagonists—participants with children and parents in singular moments of time and history.

> The definition of the teacher's professional identity is thus not seen in abstract terms, but in context, in relation to her colleagues, to the parents, and above all, to the children; but also in relation to her own identity and her personal and cultural background and experience. (Rinaldi, 1995; quoted in Rabitti, 1995, p. 4)

Thus, a definition of the teacher's role can never be accepted once and for all, but instead constantly undergoes revision—as circumstances, parents, and children change, the dynamics of their concerns and exchanges shift, and as more comes to be understood about the fundamental processes of teaching and learning. Questions about what teachers can and should do can never be finally answered, but rather must keep returning to the original problem: What kind of teachers are needed by our children—those real individuals in the classrooms of today?

LISTENING TO CHILDREN

Tiziana Filippini (1990), speaking about the child in Reggio Emilia and what the teacher should do to promote the intellectual life of children, put the action of "listening" at the heart of the teacher's role. The teacher must not merely think about children as strong and competent, but must act in such a way as to persuade children that they deeply share this image (Rabitti, 1995). "Listening" means being fully attentive to the children, and at the same time, taking responsibility for recording and documenting what is observed and then using it as a basis for decision making shared with children and parents. "Listening" means seeking to follow and enter into the active learning that is taking place. As Filippini stated:

> Sometimes the adult works right inside a group of children and sometimes works just around the group, so he has many roles. The role of the adult is above all one of listening, observing, and understanding the strategy that children use in a learning situation. The teacher has, for us, a role as *dispenser of occasions*; and it is very important for us that the child should feel the teacher to be, not a judge, but a resource to whom he can go when he needs to borrow a gesture, a word. According to Vygotsky, if the child has gone from point **a** to point **b** and is getting very close to **c**, sometimes to reach **c**, he needs to borrow assistance from the adult at that very special moment. We feel that the teacher must be involved within the child's exploring procedure, if the teacher wants to understand how to be the organizer and provoker of occasions, on the one hand, and co-actor in discoveries, on the other. And our expectations of the child must be very flexible and varied. We must be able to be amazed and to enjoy, like the children often do. We must be able to catch the ball that the children throw us, and toss it back to them in a way that makes the children want to continue the game with us, developing, perhaps, other games as we go along. (Filippini, 1990)

Thus, the teacher needs to enter into a kind of intellectual dialogue with the group of children and join in their excitement and curiosity. Although learning is a serious matter, the teacher must approach it in a spirit of playfulness as well as respect. The metaphor of "catching the ball that the children throw us," is a favorite one in Reggio Emilia. They like to use the metaphor of the children and teacher participating in a game of ping-pong. What they have in mind, though, is not a fast-paced championship-level game among adults, but rather, a game where child novices are trying to play, assisted and supported by an adult expert.

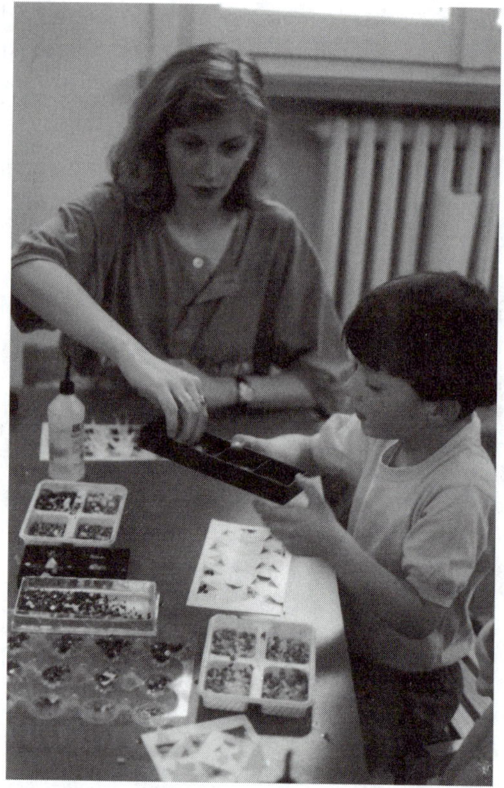

FIGURE 10.1. Teacher working as partner of a child.

The adult is trying to help keep the game going. Sometimes he or she steps in to return the ball, or puts the ball back in play, or coaches children on technique, or fixes or adjusts the materials, or even calls a break and rests or feeds the children. All of these supportive adult interventions are based on keying in to the rhythm of the game and modeling an attitude of attention and care. The teacher seeks to extend the children's stamina and attention span, increase their range of techniques and strategies, enhance their concentration and effort, and still allow them to fully experience pleasure and joy in the game.

SPIRALING LEARNING AND SHARED CONTROL

Thus, the teacher's role centers on provoking occasions of discovery through a kind of alert, inspired listening and stimulation of children's dialogue, co-action, and co-construction of knowledge. As in the United States, such optimal teaching is understood to be a complex, delicate, multifaceted task, involving many levels and calling for much expertise and continuous self-examination.

Carlina Rinaldi once sought to explain what is involved in the teacher's role. In an interview with Lella Gandini, she highlighted how a teacher's work should be grounded in political beliefs and advocacy. This perspective is rooted in her own political philosophy, a leftist progressivism and idealism common among people in her city and region of Italy. Rinaldi is proud of the ancient heritage of her region—rooted in an agrarian culture and tradition of large cooperating farm households—of relying on communal rather than individualistic enterprise (Hellman, 1987; Putnam, 1993). She believes that citizens have a moral obligation to invest public resources in children's welfare and to enter into continuous and permanent knowledge creation with children, in order for her city, and society in general, to progress and improve human well-being.

Rinaldi also made clear that the teacher's role must be imagined in terms that are holistic and circular, not segmented and linear. Such a circularity—or better, *spiraling*—is seen in reciprocal connections among the three protagonists (educators, children, and parents) as well as the temporal dimension. The actions that teachers do are not expected to take place in a set order, or once only, but instead to repeat in continuous cycles of revisiting and rerepresentation. Such a way of thinking about time is typical of agrarian Italian culture, such as in the countryside surrounding Reggio Emilia.

> Agrarian cultures tend to perceive time as a cyclical alternation of paired opposites in accordance with the regular passing and return of the seasons, of occasions for commemoration, of life and death. In rural Italy this cyclical perception is aptly expressed in the wheel-of-time image. (Bell, 1979, p. 34)

The Reggio teacher thus assesses what is happening with children within a cycle of days taking place within larger cycles (weeks, months, even years). Such a spiraling, rather than linear, way of thinking and proceeding is characteristic of Reggio educators—whether they are weaving together theory and practice; describing the course of child learning and development; narrating the story of a particular curriculum project; or, as here, thinking about pedagogical roles.

Rinaldi went on to talk about the shared control between teachers and children. For example, the teacher leads the learning of a group of children by searching for individuals' ideas to use to frame group action. Sometimes this involves leading group meetings and seeking to stimulate a "spark"—writing down what the children say, then reading back their comments, searching with them for insights that will motivate further questions and group activity. At other times, it involves the teacher sitting and listening, noticing provocative or insightful comments, then repeating or clarifying them to help the children sustain their talk or activity. Loris Malaguzzi stressed the importance of keying in exactly to what children say in dialogue, so that the teacher can pick up an idea and return it to the group—and thereby make their discussion and action more significant. This is vital when children seem unable to proceed. Their work may have lost all momentum, or their interest diminished. The teacher can help the children uncover their own insights or questions, perhaps expressed in a tentative or partial way—not fully clear to themselves or the group as a whole. The teacher, noticing and appreciating the idea's potential to restimulate the whole group, steps in to restate the idea in clearer and more emphatic language, and thereby makes the insight operative for the children, a kind of intellectual spark for further talk and action:

> In this way the play of participation and the play of communication really take place. Of course, communication may take place without your assistance, but it would be important not to miss such a situation. (Vea Vecchi, Group Discussion, June 15, 1990, Diana School)

And at yet other times, especially at the end of a morning's activity, the teacher is needed to help the children search for an idea—especially one that emerges from an intellectual discussion or dispute between children—and then shaping it into a hypothesis that should be tested, an empirical comparison that should be made, or a representation that should be attempted, as the basis for another day's activity by the group. Examining the question, hypothesis, or argument of one child thus becomes part of an ongoing process of raising and answering questions for all. With the help of the teacher, the question or observation of one child leads others to explore territory never encountered, perhaps never even suspected. This is genuine "co-action" of children.

As a project gets underway, teachers reflect, explore, study, research, and plan

FIGURE 10.2. Teachers' meeting at lunch.

together possible ways to elaborate and extend the theme by means of materials, activities, visits, use of tools, and so on. These ideas are then taken back to the classroom and investigated. The teachers have for decades worked in co-teaching pairs in each classroom. The co-teaching organization is considered difficult, because the two adults must coadapt and accommodate constantly, but nevertheless it is powerful because it requires each adult to become used to peer collaboration, acquire a value for the social nature of intellectual growth, and become more able to help children (and parents) as they undertake joint learning and decision making.

Teachers communicate with parents about the project theme and encourage them to become involved in the activities of their child through finding necessary materials, working with teachers on the physical environment, offering supplementary books, and so on. In this way, parents are provoked to revise their image of their child and understand childhood in a more rich and complex way.

The teaching team works closely with other adults (at times the *atelierista*, at times the *pedagogista*), to plan and document the project. This happens in different ways in different schools, but in general, documentation involves handwritten notes as well as audio recordings and transcriptions of children's dialogue and group discussions, print and slide photographs or videotapes of key moments and activities, and collection of products and constructions made by children.

Throughout the project, the teachers act as the group's "memory" and discuss with children the results of the documentation. This systematically allows children to revisit their own and others' feelings, perceptions, observations, and reflections, and then reconstruct and reinterpret them in deeper ways. In reliving earlier moments via photography and tape recording, children are deeply reinforced and validated for their efforts and provided a boost to memory that is critical at their young age.

The teacher sometimes works inside the group of children and at other times outside, around the group. From this vantage point, the teacher observes and selectively documents the children's words, actions, interests, experiences, and activities. The teacher also observes and documents her own words and actions. Such observations are needed to interpret what is happening with the children and to make predictions and projections about how to go forward; on this basis, the teacher intervenes, joins with the children in their experiences and activity, and facilitates or provokes the next occasions for learning—always in negotiation with the children and on the basis of agreement with them.

The teachers constantly pay close attention to the children's activity. They believe that when children work on a project of interest to them, they will naturally encounter problems and questions they will want to investigate. The teachers' role is to help children discover their own problems and questions. At that point, moreover, they will not offer ready solutions, but instead help children to focus on a problem or difficulty and formulate hypotheses. Their goal is not so much to facilitate learning in the sense of making it smooth or easy, but rather to stimulate it by making problems more complex, involving, and arousing. They

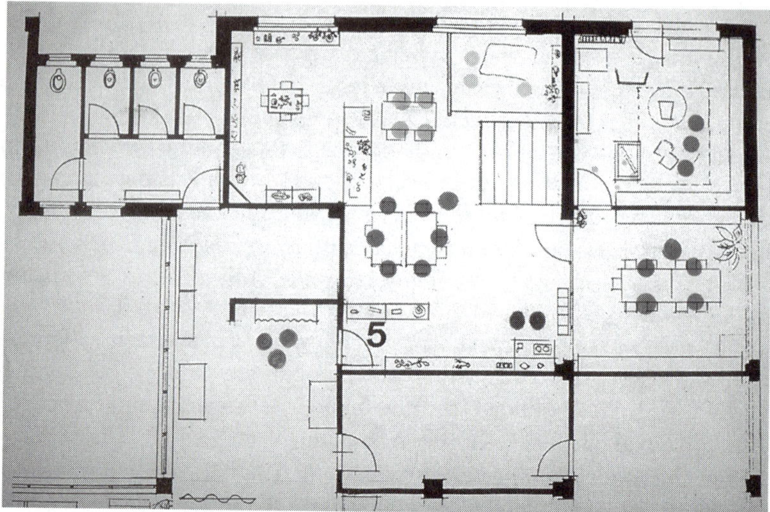

FIGURE 10.3. Map of the 5-year-olds room at Diana School during the morning activities. The dots indicate where children and teachers might be positioned one day. One teacher works closely with a group of 4, and another floats among all the others (but is with a group of 5 at present).

ask the children what they need in order to do experiments—even when they realize that a particular approach or hypothesis is not "correct." They serve as the children's partners, sustaining the children and offering assistance, resources, and strategies to get unstuck when encountering difficulties. Often teachers encourage children to continue with something, or ask them to complete or add to something that they are doing. They prefer not to leave children always working on their own, but try instead to cooperate with the children's goals.

While working with a group of children, each teacher takes notes, including descriptions of her own words and actions. The notes should be taken in ways that are understandable to others and able to be communicated because they will always be discussed with others. Discussions take place at different levels involving different sized groups, ranging from discussions with a few others (co-teacher, *atelierista, pedigogista*), to meetings of the entire school staff, to workshops designated for particular types of teachers, to large assemblies of teachers from the whole municipality. Such discussions are integral not only to curriculum planning but also to teacher professional development (Rabitti, 1995). Analytic and critical activities are vital to the development of the individual teacher and, ultimately, the Reggio Emilia system as a whole. Systematic documentation allows each teacher to become a producer of research; that is, someone who generates new ideas about curriculum and learning, rather than being merely a consumer of certainty and tradition.

THE SPECIAL DIFFICULTIES OF THE TEACHER'S ROLE*

Educators in Reggio Emilia do not consider the teacher's role to be an easy one, with black-and-white answers guiding what teachers should do. They do possess, however, the confidence and sense of security that their approach to teaching, developed collectively over the past 30 years in Reggio Emilia, is the way they *should* be working. As teacher Laura Rubizzi put it, "It is a way of working not only valid but also right" (interview, November 11, 1989). Her colleague at the Diana School, Paola Strozzi, said, "We are part of a project that is based on the co-action of children, and on the sureness that this is a good way of learning" (interview, June 14, 1990).

Finding Challenging, Satisfying Problems

The day-to-day work, nonetheless, involves constant challenge and decision making because of the use of emergent curriculum or *progettazione.* One difficult task for the teachers is to help children find problems that are big enough and hard enough to engage their best energies and thinking over time. The dinosaur project documented by Rankin (Chapter 12) is an example of such a challenging project. Rankin makes clear, however, that sometimes teachers steer away from a project that does not seem to be going anywhere.

Identifying "Knots"

Not only must the larger project contain meaty problems, but even a daily work session should ideally contain sticking points, or "knots." Just as a knot (whorl) in woodgrain impedes a saw cutting through, and just as a knot (tangle) in thread stops the action of a needle sewing, any problem that stops the children and blocks their action is a kind of cognitive knot. It might be caused by a conflict of wills or lack of information or skills to proceed. Such "knots" should be thought of as more than negative moments of confusion and frustration, however. Rather, they are moments of cognitive disequilibrium, containing positive possibilities for regrouping, hypothesis testing, and intellectual comparison of ideas. They can produce interactions that are constructive not only for socializing but also for constructing new knowledge. The teacher's task is to notice those knots and help bring them to center stage for further attention—launching points for future activities.

Deciding When to Intervene

A third aspect of the teacher's role that Reggio teachers experience as difficult is knowing how and when to intervene, because this depends on a moment-by-

* Interview by Lella Gandini

FIGURE 10.4. Children and teachers discussing a project.

moment analysis of the children's thinking. As teachers Magda Bondavalli and Marina Mori stated:

> With regard to difficulties [in teaching], we see them continuously. The way we suggest to children things that they might do, leaves things always open. This is a way to be with them through readjusting continuously. There is nothing that is definite or absolute. We try all the time to interpret, through their gestures, words, and actions, how they are living through an experience; and then we go on from there. It's really difficult! (interview, June 14, 1990).

Also in the United States, teachers worry about how much and when to intervene and how to support problem solving without providing the solution (Edwards, 1986). As Malaguzzi (1987) wrote, children are "dangerously on the brink between presence that they want and repression that they don't want" (p. 17). Thus, the teacher should not intervene too much and yet does not want to let a valuable teaching moment go by. Vea Vecchi expressed this eloquently:

> But you are always afraid that you are going to miss that hot moment. It's really a balancing act. I believe in intervention, yet personally I tend to wait because I have noticed that children often resolve the problem on their own, and not always in the way that I would have told them to! Children often find solutions that I would never

> have seen. But sometimes waiting means missing the moment. So it's a decision that you have to make very quickly. (group discussion, October 18, 1990, Diana School)

What they were describing is a genuine commitment to *progettazione* (Rinaldi, Chapter 5, this volume), not a subtle manipulation of the project theme so that it will end up in a certain place. The teachers honestly do not know where the group will end up. Although this openness adds a dimension of difficulty to their work, it also makes it more exciting. As Laura Rubizzi put it:

> I work in a state of uncertainty because I do not know where the children will arrive to, but it is a fabulous experience! (interview, November 11, 1989) [I]t is as if we are starting off together on a voyage. It could be short; it could be long. But there is an eagerness in doing it together. (group discussion, October 18, 1990, Diana School)

Moreover, beyond being exciting, their way of working has the added advantage of the built-in support structures. The teacher is not expected to figure out all by herself what she should be doing. She always works in collaboration with other adults, as Magda Bondavalli and Marina Mori attest, "It's really the way to be in this school, where we compare notes continuously, and we talk to one another all the time" (interview, June 14, 1990). Such conferring takes place on an almost daily basis, in short meetings between teacher and co-teacher, teacher and *atelierista*, and informal discussions between teachers of different classrooms at lunchtime. Teachers believe that by discussing openly, they offer models of cooperation and participation to the children and parents and promote an atmosphere of open and frank communication. More formal and extended analysis occurs during staff meetings of one's own school or some larger group meeting involving administrators, teachers from other schools, and perhaps even outside visitors or lecturers.

A METHOD OF EXTENDED MUTUAL CRITICISM AND SELF-EXAMINATION

It is important to note that analysis and feedback in Reggio Emilia involves both support and criticism. In contrast to a system in which concern for hurt feelings or ownership of ideas prevents extended examination and argumentation, in Reggio Emilia intellectual conflict is considered pleasurable for both adults and children. As Paola Strozzi said, "I am convinced that there is some kind of pleasure in trying to agree about how to do things" (interview, June 14, 1990). The point of a discussion is not just to air diverse points of view, but instead to go on until it is clear that everyone has learned something and moved somewhere in his or her thinking. A discussion should go on until a solution or next step becomes apparent; then, tension dissipates and a new, shared understanding provides the basis for future joint activity or effort.

Certainly, teachers and staff offer one another emotional support and encouragement as well as concrete suggestions and advice. In addition, however, a method of extended mutual criticism and self-examination is very much accepted. Our research team participated in several such meetings at the Diana School, each several hours long and involving teachers, auxiliary staff, cooks, *atelierista*, *pedagogista*, and Malaguzzi. At the first meeting, Loris Malaguzzi explained the benefits of collectively looking at a videotape, obtaining a range of interpretations ("circle of ideas"), and then working toward a common understanding or point of view. Teacher Laura Rubizzi then presented her edited videotape showing three 4-year-old boys working together to make a dinosaur of clay. She talked about what questions she asked herself after reviewing the session, suggesting what aspects of teaching were most on her mind and challenging for her: Did she miss an occasion when she should perhaps have gotten the boys to discuss together? Did she miss an important "knot" in the session, by failing to notice how one child tried to make a neck for the animal, but then dropped the problem unsolved? Finally, what should she have done to help the children gain more technical knowledge about how to stabilize three-dimensional clay structures?

At the second meeting, teacher Paola Strozzi presented an edited videotape of an activity in which four 3-year-olds had their second encounter with a new material. Paola explained to us how she presented the material (wire) to the children, what questions she asked them, and how she returned insights of individual children to the group. Her presentation was followed by a lengthy critique that addressed her pedagogical decisions. Had she overly "led" the children in creating verbal images about their constructions? Had she offered them an adequate range of materials, so that they could compare and analyze the properties of wire? The next day, the wire activity was repeated with a greater choice of wire thicknesses to study whether this change would lead to more experimentation and hypotheses by children.

On the third occasion, teacher Marina Castagnetti presented an edited videotape and behavioral analysis of a session involving two 5-year-old boys trying to draw a castle on a large piece of paper, using a Logo turtle activated by computer. She had created a behavior code and visually represented their whole interaction in a chart. Her presentation also led to lengthy discussion. Had the children been adequately prepared to solve the problem? Could they handle the computer commands? Did they need a set of rulers near at hand to stimulate ideas of measurement? Were they left too long to flounder on their own without the teacher's assistance? Did Marina let a "hot moment" go by, or "abandon" the children too long? Did the children's frequent language of joining ("Let's do this," "Let's try this," "Let's see," "We must," etc.) indicate productive collaboration or increasing desperation? Marina eventually asked, "As a teacher, what was I supposed to do that I didn't do?" but she was never offered a definitive right answer. The point of the discussion, evidently, was to think critically about difficult questions, not reach closure.

FIGURE 10.5. The pair of teachers meeting with the *atelierista* at Diana School.

In all three cases, our research team was impressed by the depth of discussion and lack of defensiveness by teachers. At the end of the last one, we summarized our reactions and commented on their rigorous method of critical reflection. Loris Malaguzzi, with demonstrable affection for Marina, said, "Yes, we always have to have two pockets to reach into, one for satisfaction and one for dissatisfaction" (group discussion, October 16, 1991).

Intellectual conflict is understood as the engine of all growth in Reggio. Therefore, teachers seek to bring out, rather than suppress, conflicts of viewpoints between children. Similarly, among themselves they readily accept disagreement and expect extended discussion and constructive criticism; this is seen as the best way to advance. The teachers' pleasure in teamwork and acceptance of disagreement provides a model for children and parents.

EXAMPLES OF TEACHER BEHAVIOR

To give a fuller picture and provide concrete examples of the abstract principles presented here, we offer four short observation records drawn from videotapes taken at the Diana School in 1988 and 1990. They illustrate different kinds of teacher behavior commonly seen in the Reggio Emilia preprimary schools.

The Teacher Gets Children Started

In this episode (May 24, 1988, videotape taken by research team), teacher Giulia Notari acts as "dispenser of occasions" in helping children make the transition from morning group meeting to their first activity. Notice her flexibility and nurturance in meeting the needs of one little girl who is not ready to enter into a focused activity.

> It is 9:23 a.m. in the 3-year-old classroom, and morning meeting has just ended. During this meeting, teacher Giulia Notari has told the whole class about the morning's activities, all of which concern the theme of springtime that they are currently pursuing. Then her co-teacher, Paola Strozzi, departs with eight children to work with clay in the school's central *piazza.* Giulia supervises the remaining 12 or so children. She moves around the classroom encouraging children to settle into an activity, and she spends a few moments with each small group in turn, getting them started. For instance, at one table she introduces a group of four children to the materials set there, "Feel it, this paper is different from other paper."
>
> "It is cold," a child says.
>
> "It is cold," she agrees. "It is cold. And here is another paper that is still different. And look, here are markers, chalks, and craypas, all yellow."
>
> As she moves from one table to the next, Giulia sees children not yet involved and asks, "Do you want to work with the green colors in the little *atelier*? Or do you want to cut with scissors and use glue?"
>
> She comes to a small table, where two children sit facing sheets of white paper and little baskets full of leaves, grass, and flowers picked earlier that morning. Giulia says, "Do you see what is here? Little bits of green that you found. And flowers that you picked. You can place them on the paper as you like. If one piece of paper is not enough, you can place a second right next to it. Okay?" (Giulia explains later that the activity communicates the importance and pleasure of exploration and helps the children become accustomed to collage). As Giulia moves off, the two children proceed happily, chatting with each other. "Do you want this?" "I've taken that kind, too." "Look how pretty this is." "Take your time" (this is obviously an imitation of something the teacher sometimes says). At 9:26, Giulia returns to look and admire their work, saying, "I like it very much. You can use extra sheets of paper. If you want something, tell me."
>
> At 9:28 she enters a small room that is an annex to the classroom. Two girls are seated at a table there. One is drawing with markers. Giulia Notari gives this first girl more drawing materials, then goes to the second one.
>
> "Well, then, shall we look for the work you have already started? Let's see where it is." She takes a folder out of a drawer and begins leafing slowly through it, saying "Which one is yours? Which one? Which one? Which one?" The child looks despondent and does not answer. They eventually locate the child's drawing, then Giulia says, "What does this need? Do you need some more black marker to continue? Do you want to work on another drawing? Do you want another paper to go work with the glue? Would you like to go and play? Love, what do you want to do?" The despondent child does not answer any of her questions. Finally the teacher simply crouches down, kisses her, and talks with her gently. Then she takes

down some picture books from a high shelf and puts away the drawing. Another child appears in the doorway looking for help, and Giulia says, "I'm coming, sweetheart." She leaves the little girl wiping away her tears and looking through a book. As she goes by, she stops to praise the drawing of the first little girl.

The Teacher Provides Instruction in Tool Use and Technique

It is now 9:34 on the same morning (May 24, 1988), in the large shared space (*piazza*) where co-teacher Paola Notari is working with eight 3-year-olds and large mounds of artists' modeling clay. She provides the children instruction in the correct use of the materials and tools as part of the process of facilitating, supporting, and encouraging. When asked about this, she says she tries to provide the help and advice that is needed for children to accomplish their own artistic and representational goals and not be defeated by the materials. For example, she knows that if children roll out the clay too thin, then it breaks during firing and children are upset.

The children are seated around a long rectangular table, while Paola stands and moves among them. In front of each is a large wooden tablet on which to work the clay. Paola is preparing each child a flat slab of clay: She tears off a hunk of clay, rolls it out thin with a rolling pin, cuts off the sides to make a neat square, then gives it out. She is using a knife to cut the clay and says, "This tool we can use to cut the clay when it is nice and thick."

The children have many cutting and rolling tools nearby. They are working on the problem of "representing movement, on a surface." With a knife, they can cut out a piece of the clay, then fold it up and over to give a sense of motion on the surface of the slab. (She explains later that some of the children don't actually succeed in getting any sense of movement into theirs. But Paola doesn't interfere and insist on her idea of movement. Because all are very involved in what they are doing, she does not impose her ideas on them. However, she does instruct them on matters of technique—showing them how to roll and cut the clay and use the tools.) At 9:34 Paola Notari is seen using a spatula to give a newly rolled slab of clay to a child. "Do you need this?" she asks. She tells another, "You are pressing too much. If you press too much, we will not be able to pick it up, and then we will not be able to fire it in the kiln. Don't press too hard." Then another child turns to her, "Is this all right?"

"Yes, yes," Paola replies, "That's fine. If you want another slab of clay, I can prepare one for you."

She observes a little disagreement between two children. One wants the pastry cutter that the other has been using. That child protests, "This is mine. I had it before."

"But they are all the same," says Paola, pointing out more cutters. "They really are all the same." She moves closer and the first child shows her that in fact the desired cutter makes a different kind of track in the clay than the others. So she revises her opinion, "Oh, I see. Well, if you look in the tool box, there you will find another, precisely like this one." The child goes off happily to look.

She begins to prepare a slab of clay for one of the girls, and while doing so, looks up at the child opposite her. "What are you doing?" she asks. The boy shows, and Paola says, "That's nice."

Finishing the new slab, she takes it over to the girl needing it. Seeing her first piece, Paola comments, "Look at that marvel! Now you have to think about what else you want to do. You could put the same marks in it [the new slab] you did before. Or you could place these pieces folded, or standing up." She demonstrates, using little strips of clay. The little girl has in her hand a pastry cutter, which she moves over the slab without saying anything. Paola continues, "You only want to cut with this little wheel, don't you? It does make very beautiful marks."

Paola goes to the opposite side of the table where a very small child seems to be having difficulties. She asks him, "May I clean it up for you?" Her hand smoothes down his slab, using slip. She explains to him, "This is sort of like an eraser. And now I will show you how to use this tool [a cutter]. You can make a thin strip, like this, and fold it or pick it up." She shows him to lift one end of the strip. Then she puts the cutter into his hand and standing behind him, guides him in the use of both his hands. "With this hand, hold the clay. Now with this other hand, push very hard. More. This way. Okay? Now you can do it."

At 9:41 she asks all the children at large, "Do you want more clay? I can go get it."

"Also I!" "Also I!" shout all the children.

"Okay," Paola says, "I'm going to get some more." She goes out of the room for a few minutes, leaving the children alone for a few moments. The observation continues in the same way when she returns.

The Teacher Turns a Dispute Into a Hypothesis to Test

It is 9:12 on a morning late in May (1990, videotape taken by research team), and teacher Laura Rubizzi sits with six 5-year-old children at a table in a small room off the *atelier*. Her group is involved in a project to prepare an "instruction booklet" about their school to send to the homes of those small children who will be entering the Diana School next fall. The group of three boys and three girls has decided, among other things, to include in the welcome booklet some directions for how to find the way to the *atelier*.

But how to communicate those directions? In a discussion that had taken place on the previous day, one girl, Giulia, had proposed that because little children cannot read, the group should instead draw them a picture. But Silvio then asserted that little children speak differently than big ones do, so they should write their instructions in "scribbles" to speak the language of 3-year-olds. The others strongly disagreed! A scribble picture would be no good!

Laura had made a constructive suggestion, that the children draw both kinds of pictures and see which one worked better. So at the end of their time yesterday, the children had prepared two pictures. Silvio drew his scribble diagram, and Giulia drew a picture of a child playing on the video machine in this small room next to the *atelier*. To test which picture communicated better, the group of six proposed to enter the classroom of the smallest children in the Diana School and ask them, "Which picture do you prefer? Which do you understand?" Cristina, another of the girls, noted that they should show the picture to a group of children containing an equal number of boys and girls, because the girls would understand Giulia's picture better, whereas the boys would understand Silvio's.

Thus, at 9:18 we see the six 5-year-olds standing with Laura Rubizzi at the head of the circle where are seated all of the children in the 3-year-old classroom, along with their teachers, Paola Strozzi and Giulia Notari. Notice how the teachers cooperate to highlight the interesting problem to resolve through comparison of ideas, and how Laura, without heightening or calling attention to possibilities of hurt feelings, nevertheless offers Silvio nurturance at a potentially sensitive moment.

> Laura tells the expectant 3-year-olds, "We have a big, big problem." The child, Giulia, begins to explain how they need to find out what pictures work best with 3-year-olds; Laura takes over and standing close to Giulia, looking at her, echoes and inserts points to make the explanation clearer. Then teacher Giulia Notari, looking around at the faces of her 3-year-old group, speaks as if for them, again repeating the main points. As she finishes, voices are heard all around the circle as the 3-year-olds chime in their initial opinions.
>
> Teacher Laura takes her six 5-year-olds into a huddle to work out a game plan for how to proceed next. Then, with her help, they get ready: Silvio and Giulia stand at the head of the children's circle, excitedly holding their pictures. Laura says that the 3-year-olds will come up, study the two pictures, decide which communicates best, then stand behind the boy or girl holding that picture. To the side of Silvio and Giulia, at right angles to the circle, stand the remaining 5-year-olds; their job will be to decide which line of children turns out to be longest.
>
> Giulia Notari selects, one by one, individual 3-year-olds to go up. One boy goes forward, studies the pictures, points to Silvio's, then with the teacher's help takes his place behind Silvio. Another boy comes up, points to Giulia's picture, then returns to his seat, although his teacher tells him to go stand behind her. The next child to go up also points to Giulia's picture and does then correctly go to stand behind Giulia. Now the system is working. Another boy goes to stand behind Silvio; then the next four children select Giulia's picture and take their places behind her.
>
> At this point, teacher Laura, decides the case has been made and she should intervene. "Very good," she states, then looking at her little group of judges, "Children of the group! This is the line of those who select the scribble drawing, and this is the line of those who select the other drawing. According to you, which line is longer?" The group points decisively to Giulia's line. "This one!" they say.
>
> It is now 9:26. Laura bends over and speaks directly to Silvio alone. Then she straightens up and says, "Okay! Thank you very much! We'll return to our room," and off they go.
>
> As the 5-year-olds take their seats and begin to discuss drawing a map of their school for the booklet, everyone, including Silvio, seems equally cheerful and involved.

The Teacher Encourages Children to Solve Their Own Disputes

It is just before lunchtime (Spring 1990, videotape taken by staff of the Diana School), and two 5-year-old boys, Daniele and Christian, are setting the tables for their class. In this school, children of each succeeding age are given more responsibility in preparing the table for lunch. The 5-year-olds take turns at deciding who is to sit where. The Diana School teachers believe that their system of letting a few children each day set the table and decide on the seating arrangement works better and is more in line with their philosophy than either having a fixed seating order (controlled by the teachers) or allowing free choice for everyone at the moment of seating themselves.

> Daniele and Christian lay out the tablecloths, plates, and silverware, and decide where everyone is to sit by placing their individual napkins (each in a little envelope with the name sewn on). As they work, another boy comes in and asks to be seated near a certain boy. The tablesetters agree, and he leaves. Then a girl, Elisa, comes in and asks, "With whom did you put me?" Daniele answers, "Look for yourself." She says, "Well, Daniele, don't you want to tell me where you put me?"
>
> In the meanwhile other children have come in. It is difficult to follow exactly what they say, as they are struggling with the caps on the mineral water bottles. This distracts Daniele and Christian from Elisa's request. Eventually Daniele says, showing her one of the napkin envelopes, "Is this yours?" She replies, "Yes."

FIGURE 10.6. Teachers at la Villetta School discussing the work of children.

Christian comments, "Near Michele." This obviously displeases Elisa, who protests, "And I don't like it."

The teacher, Giulia, enters, and observes the dispute. Daniele asks Elisa, "You don't want to stay near Michele?" She says, "NO! Finally, you do understand!"

Giulia glances toward the second teacher, who is silently videotaping the scene, and makes a decision not to intervene. "Find an agreement among yourselves," she tells the children, "Elisa, find an agreement with them." She returns to the next room. Christian seeks to find out with whom Elisa wants to sit, then explains to her that she must sit where they placed her. She cries out, "All right!" and leaves, mad, stamping her feet, and slamming the door. Christian runs after her, calling her name, and bringing her back into the classroom. He asks twice, "Do you want to sit near Maria Giulia?" She remains angry. "Do what you like!" she shouts. (Later, in discussing this situation, teacher Giulia Notari stated that she thought it appropriate to minimize this situation and let the children take care of it themselves. Elisa often has such reactions, she noted, and it was not really a very painful situation for her.)

CONCLUSIONS

The role of the preprimary teacher in Reggio Emilia shows many similarities to the role as commonly conceived in the United States. In both settings, goals are set high—as ideals that are expected to be difficult to attain and sustain in practice. In both, early childhood education involves complex interaction with multiple constituencies (children, parents, colleagues, government, the public) and stimulating children's learning and development through the design of optimal school organization, physical environments, curriculum, and pedagogy. In Reggio Emilia, however, the preprimary teacher always works with a coteacher. As a pair, these two relate to the other teachers, auxilliary staff, and the *atelierista* in their school, and moreover, receive support from a *pedagogista,* who works with several schools, as well as the central city administration. In their interaction with children, Reggio Emilia teachers seek to promote children's well-being and encourage learning in all domains (cognitive, physical-motor, social, and affective), at the same time taking advantage of key moments to instruct children in ever more sophisticated use of tools and materials needed to express themselves in the multiple symbolic and artistic media. From their own point of view, the teachers' classroom work centers on "provoking occasions" of genuine intellectual growth by one or more children: especially, listening to the words of children and then offering them back to the group to restimulate and extend their discussion and joint activity. Such a method of teaching they consider important, complex, and delicate, constantly evolving and changing, and a matter of collective effort and concern. Their tendency to engage with colleagues in extended mutual criticism and self-examination of their teaching behavior seems to notably distinguish the educators of Reggio Emilia. Just as they see children as learning best through communication, conflict, and coaction, they also see themselves as learning in this way. They see the work and development of teachers as a public activity taking place within the shared life of the school, community, and culture; they place a strong value on themselves communicating and interacting within and outside the school. Striving to fulfill these ideals is demanding, they well know, but rewarding and sustaining as well, and vital to the progress of society and human well-being.

REFERENCES

Bell, R.M. (1979). *Fate and honor, family and village: Demographic and cultural change in rural Italy since 1800.* Chicago: University of Chicago Press.

Edwards, C.P. (1986). *Promoting social and moral development in young children: Creative approaches for the classroom.* New York: Teachers College Press.

Edwards, C.P., Gandini, L., & Nimmo, J. (1992). Favorire l'apprendimento cooperativo nella prima infanzia: Concettualizzazioni contrastanti da parte degli insegnanti in due comunitá. *Rassegna di Psicologia, 9*(3), 65–90. Republished in 1994 as Promoting collaborative learning in the early childhood classroom: Teachers' contrasting conceptualizations in two communities. In L.G. Katz & B. Cesarone (Eds.), *Reflections on the Reggio Emilia Approach: Perspectives from ERIC/EECE: A Monograph Series,* (No. 6, pp. 81–104). Urbana, IL: ERIC Clearinghouse on Elementary and Early Childhood Education.

Edwards, C.P., Gandini, L., & Nimmo, J. (in preparation). *Children and teachers together: Collaborative learning and community building in the early childhood classroom.* Baltimore, Maryland: Paul Brookes Publishing.

Filippini, T. (1990, November). *The Reggio Emilia approach.* Paper presented at the annual meeting of the National Association for the Education of Young Children, Washington, DC.

Hellman, J.A. (1987). *Journeys among women: Feminism in five Italian cities.* New York: Oxford University Press.

Malaguzzi, L. (1987). In REGGIO CHILDREN, S.r.l. (1987, 1996). *I cento linguaggi dei bambini.* [The hundred languages of children: Narrative of the possible]. Distributed by Reggio Children USA, Washington, DC.

Putnam, R.D. (1993). *Making democracy work: Civic traditions in modern Italy.* Princeton, NJ: Princeton University Press.

Rabitti, G. (1995, November). *Interpretations and reflections on the role of the teacher in the schools of Reggio Emilia, Italy.* Paper presented at the annual meeting of the National Association for the Education of Young Children, Washington, DC.

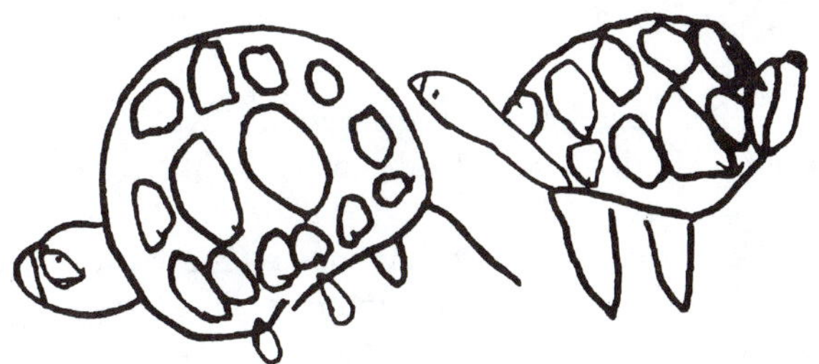

Drawing by 4-year-old children at Neruda School.

chapter 11

Children With "Special Rights" in the Preprimary Schools and Infant–Toddler Centers of Reggio Emilia

Cathleen Smith

This chapter is adapted from an interview conducted by Cathleen Smith with Ivana Soncini, the *psychologist-pedagogista* specializing in special education for the municipal early childhood system of Reggio Emilia. Tiziana Filippini, *pedagogista* for the Diana School, served as translator and added her perspectives. Observations of a child by Sharon Palsha (early childhood special education researcher and in-service trainer at the Frank Porter Graham Child Development Center at the University of North Carolina at Chapel Hill) have been woven in; Sharon is a colleague who was on a later delegation. Cathleen Smith has visited Reggio Emilia on four occasions; her most recent trip was made possible by a Rosemary Dybwad Memorial International Fellowship.[1]

INTRODUCTION

Italy has long been recognized as a leader in the general movement for integration and inclusion of individuals with mental and physical disabilities. Since the

[1] I would like to thank Carolyn Edwards, Mary Louise Hemmeter, Sharon Palsha, Kathryn Ruthenbeck, and Diane Strangis for comments on earlier drafts of this chapter; and Stephania Ramacciato for translating the comments at the chapter end of Carlo Vacconi.

mid-1970s, international organizations have pointed to Italian education for children with disabilities as the most inclusive of all the countries of Europe (Berrigan, 1994–1995).

This movement for integration and inclusion started in the 1960s when institutions for the disabled and the mentally ill were closed down, and health services were reorganized into decentralized units for each region. The deinstitutionalization movement created a parallel movement within education against segregation of students with disabilities.

In 1971, the Italian Parliament passed the first law concerning education for children with disabilities, and established the right to a desegregated education of children in public schools. This law and a subsequent law in 1977 are directed to the entitlement of children aged 6 to 14 to an inclusive education, unless a child's disabilities are so severe as to make it impossible to function in a regular class. However, health and education authorities have also recognized the need for early intervention, and many regions have programs serving children aged 6 months to 6 years (Cecchini and McCleary, 1985; McCleary, 1985; Robins, 1985). In 1995 a new law stated that infants with disabilities, from 0 to 3 years of age, had guaranteed placement in the infant–toddler centers.

According to the 1971 law, a child with disabilities is defined as one with persistent difficulties in mastering skills and behaviors specific to the chronological age; the definition includes children diagnosed as having Down syndrome, cerebral palsy, mental retardation (IQ less than 60), aphasia, childhood psychosis, severe language disabilities, and severe learning problems. Deafness and blindness were included in following years. The local health service is the responsible agency for the diagnosis. The assessment usually is based on observations conducted in a variety of settings, neurological and psychological evaluations, and standardized testing where applicable. The local health service remains continually involved over the years, teaming with the child, family, and teachers. The same people usually remain on the team over long periods of time, providing continuity of service to the child, family, and school, and aiding in transition across different levels of schooling. A holistic approach to the child is stressed, and for the most part, psychotropic drugs for behavior management and strict behaviorism are not well accepted (Mallory & New, 1994; McCleary, 1985).

In 1977 and 1992, further national laws specified strategies for implementing integration in the public schools. A maximum of two children with disabilities may be integrated into any one class, and integrated classes are limited to 20 pupils. Teachers of integrated classes may receive the additional assistance of a support teacher; the support teacher works with the child, the regular teacher, and the class as a whole, in order to achieve integration. No specific help is mandated for children with mild learning or behavior disorders. In practice, however, teachers and health service team members are aware of children below the norm and provide them with special attention without the disadvantages of labeling (McCleary, 1985). Teachers of integrated classes are mandated to have 40 hours

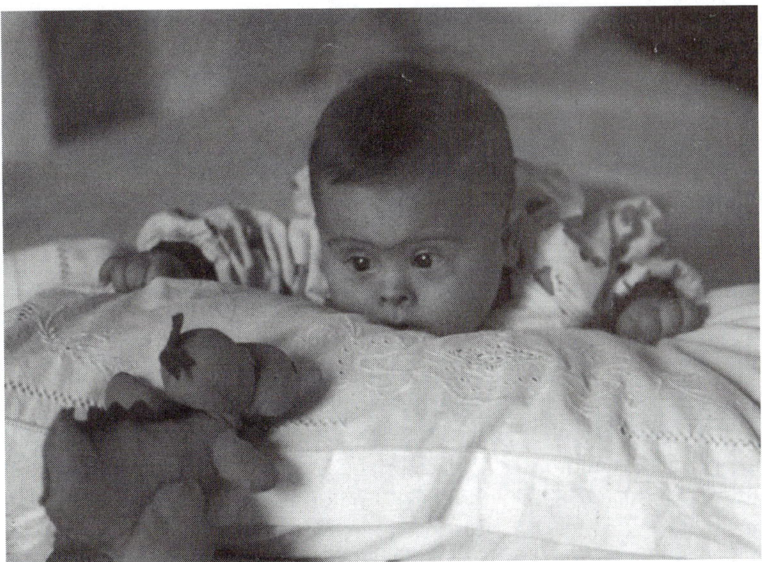

FIGURE 11.1. An infant: all infants have special needs and special rights.

of in-service education, which is often used to give training in inclusive practices.

The Italian system of education for young children with disabilities is a downward extension of the integration model for the compulsory school years (Cecchini & McCleary, 1985). In the beginning, socialization was the main goal of integration. The philosophy has progressed from physical integration to full inclusion, with the child included and made a part of the class, with the objective to develop the potentials for learning, communication, and social relations (law of 1992).

Smith: *Five years ago on my initial visit to the Diana School, I remember asking Tiziana Filippini, "Do the municipal preprimary schools and infant–toddler programs accept children with special needs?" Tiziana looked surprised and replied, "Yes, of course. They have first priority for admission. We consider them to be children with special rights!"*

At that point I became very interested in learning more about your policies and practices concerning children with disabilities. Ivana, you are the pedagogista *specializing in supporting children with disabilities. Can you tell us about special education for young children in Reggio Emilia?*

Soncini: Inclusion began to occur in the preprimary schools in Reggio Emilia even before it was decreed by the 1971 national law. The integration experience is very carefully planned and carried out in all of our municipal infant–toddler and preprimary schools. Children with physical and emotional needs and single parents are always given top priority for admission, even though there are waiting lists. Children are placed with agemates, and only one child with special needs is placed in any class. Usually, and following the judgment of the *psychologist-pedagogista* and teachers, an extra teacher is provided in the class, as a supplementary teacher for the whole group. Such a staffing pattern avoids what Swedish special educator Agneta Hellstrom called the *bodyguard model,* in which an aide (often with little experience and training) becomes the special worker assigned to the child who needs extra support. Bodyguard staffing, it is felt, leads to an unhealthy two-way dependency between the child and the worker.

The practice of placing only one child with special rights into a class group prevents a situation that adds too many adults to the classroom, undermining the formation of the children's community. Furthermore, it avoids overstressing the teachers, and helps all of the parents feel comfortable about the amount of teacher attention their child receives.

The parents of children with special rights pay for their children's attendance according to the same sliding scale as all other families, and their children can attend the extended day program until 6:00 p.m., just like other children do when both of the parents work outside the home.

Smith: *Can you describe your professional role with regard to the children with special rights?*

Soncini: I am the *psychologist-pedagogista* responsible for all of the children with disabilities who are enrolled in the municipal preprimary schools and infant–toddler centers of Reggio Emilia. As such, I am a regular member of the pedagogical team that meets regularly with the system director, Sergio Spaggiari, and the director of the pedagogical team, Carlina Rinaldi. My particular role is to coordinate between the early childhood system and the various members of the health department and social service and community health agencies who deliver medical and therapeutic services to the children at our schools and centers. For example, I often deal with psychiatrists, neurologists, psychologists, speech therapists, physical therapists, and physicians; we hold regular meetings several times a year to coordinate our work.

I am the key person for receiving referrals, meeting families, helping parents of a child with disabilities to select an infant–toddler center or preprimary school, identifying any special equipment needed, reassuring the parents of other children at the first general parent meeting of the school year, and supporting all of the teachers and school staff as they receive necessary in-service training. I support and assist the teachers and classroom staff in planning improvements to the classroom environment, furnishings, resources, and curriculum materials. I sometimes need to teach them routines for any specific care that must be given in a prescribed way. I often suggest activities and materials that will help the child get along in the classroom, for example, high-contrast paint colors are appreciated by children with visual impairments. I help staff figure out how to relate to each family. If the child in question has not had much group experience, I help the teachers to devise activities that might encourage social interaction with other children.

Later, as graduation time for the child approaches, I hold meetings with the relevant staff of the elementary school and after-school program, to ensure that the child's transition into other systems goes as smoothly as possible. In general, we believe that meetings between parents, teachers, therapists, and municipal officials help promote accessibility for children with disabilities into their whole urban environment, and also encourage parents to become concerned with the issues their child will be confronting in the future as a young adult.

Smith: *How do you support and work with the parents of children who have special rights?*

Soncini: All children in Reggio schools have a long gradual entry *(inserimento).* This period may be even longer for the child with special rights, in order to ease the separation process and to attend closely to attachment. For example, in one case of a child with autism, the parent and child visited the center for an entire year before the child formally began to attend the program.

We do a number of things to orient the new child and family, and pay particular attention to sleeping and eating patterns. In our meetings with the parents, we seek to alleviate any possible fears they may have about their child starting school. Our relationship with the parents has to be very carefully planned and thought out. Building a positive relationship is the most important part of our preliminary work: All arrangements are made with the comfort of both the child and the family as top priorities. Parents report that when we ask them so many questions about their child, we give them confidence that we understand everything basic about their child's needs and requirements, their likes and dislikes. This is especially comforting to them when their child is an infant, and they may already be feeling guilty or reluctant to leave the child with anyone else. Also, the question-asking process provides a kind of modeling to the parents, and encourages them to make their own inquiries about their child.

The viewpoints of parents are very important, and must be publicly aired and documented. A few years ago we held a forum of parents, educators, and officials who met over several months to discuss the inclusion of children with disabilities in the full life of the city of Reggio Emilia, including the preprimary schools. You can read about it in our publication (*Coordinamento pedagogico didattico nidi e scuole comunali dell'infanzia,* 1993).

Once the child is settled in, we try to help parents find some projects to help with, so that they can feel that they are contributing to the well-being of their child and the other children. We want the child with special rights to become part of the classroom routines, and for their parents to see their child in a more positive and capable way and to watch the child participating with others in exciting and interesting projects. Our hope is to avoid negative comparisons and to pay attention to the particular gifts and contributions of each individual. We like the parents of children with special rights to spend time at the center so they can see how their children are making friends; and we also encourage a network among parents of special children. It is good for these parents to find mutual support and to see other viewpoints.

Smith: *How do you go about planning the child's educational program?*

Soncini: Work with a child who has special rights is considered to be a "didactic project" collectively undertaken by myself, the child's classroom teachers, and the *pedagogista* of the school or center. This means that like all our work with children, we begin with observation and documentation. Observation and documentation are always fundamental, but they are of particular benefit with regard to children with special rights.

What we do is this. After a rather long period of initial observation and documentation, we jointly compose what we call a *declaration of intent.* This is a written agreement between the school and the health authorities to ensure collaboration. The declaration includes statements about the methods and materials we will probably use, as well as any ideas about how the work might be carried out. The declaration is *not* a formalized, binding document, which staff would have to follow without flexibility. In fact, as we get to know the child better, the teachers are expected to continually revise, reinterpret, and refine the child's program, under the supervision of the school *pedagogista* and myself. The point of the plan is not to focus only on the child's disabilities but also on his or her tremendous capabilities. It is important for us to offer many rich possibilities and have high expectations. Our work is to help the child find the way, and we do this through motivation and interest.

Another process of documentation that is standard practice for all our children is very important for children with special rights. Each child in an infant-toddler center or preprimary school has an ongoing binder of photographs, written observations, anecdotal records of significant events, and samples of the child's work. Educators take a great deal of time and effort to keep these records current and reflective of what is happening with the child. The documentation is more than a report. It is a reflection of the collaboration among professionals, family, and educators to support the child's progress. The documentation is always available to the family; in fact, the completed set of binders is taken by the family at the end of the child's multiyear experience in the school.

Smith: *Please explain about the processes of training and support for the classroom teachers and other personnel in the schools who will work on a daily basis with the children.*

Soncini: There is no specific training for staff who will work with children who have special rights. In fact, as mentioned earlier, if an extra teacher is needed, that person will be generally considered to be a teacher for all the children. For example, Stella, a child attending the Diana School, needed a particular relationship with one adult for a considerable time because of the seriousness of her attachment needs. The general principle is that if there is any particular information about working with a specific child, I share it with all staff at the center including the cooks and the cleaners. Then all the staff will feel comfortable and competent, so the child will be welcome everywhere, in other classes, in the kitchen, on the playground, and so on.

My major way of providing teachers with in-service training is based on methods of self-observation and self-analysis. When I go to a center and see some practice occurring that does not seem to be in the best interest of the child, I videotape the situation. Later on, at a staff meeting, I encourage the teachers to reflect on what they see themselves doing in the videotape. I especially get them to focus on how the child is reacting. Then I ask all the staff to talk about what they have noticed, and people's various insights are compared. From there, we will reelaborate the new insights that have emerged. Thus, we co-construct and problem solve together.

For example, in one case a child who was not mobile seemed to be spending too much time seated at a table. After viewing my tape, the teachers saw how this situation was isolating for him. They considered ways that they could move activities to the floor where he and his peers could become more engaged with each other. In such cases, the teachers take a lot of time to figure out just what activities interest the child. Then they can base group work and projects on things that highlight the child's experiences and assets.

Smith: *I know that in Reggio Emilia, children are viewed as powerful and as having rights. As you have already mentioned in your remarks, children with special needs are given special rights such as being put in the first place on waiting lists and provided with supports as needed. How does your general image of the child affect how you see a child with disabilities?*

Soncini: Our basic theoretical approach is to value differences and to bring out as much potential as we can. Each of us is different; this is considered positive. We acknowledge that a handicap brings with it a difference, but that it is just one of many differences. As we recognize our differences, we develop knowledge of who we are and who others are. What are the things that are unique? What are the things that are the same? Through coming to terms with conflicting ideas, a person attains a sort of equilibrium about who he or she is in terms of similarities and differences. We gradually synthesize our own identity. There are many ways to look at ourselves in order to construct our own images.

With the children this becomes our educational approach. As the children describe themselves and discuss the differences, they build their concepts of themselves and others. As a child, at times you declare who you are and what you are like. But other children will also tell you who you are. They discuss it, argue about it. We believe that in this way, the child develops a cognitive sense of, and true knowledge about, differences, and constructs a self-concept based on knowing oneself and others.

This is all built on relationships with others. It gives the children a picture of themselves in association with others. This leads to more authentic relationships with their peers, as well as with adults. In working with children who have special rights, it is important to identify who should be their key adults and children: the people who can spend the most time with them and form motivating and sustaining relationships. In these ways, we can help them build relationships, especially when they are new to the program. We also want to help them see themselves in relation to their parents and families.

Much of the work in the classrooms with all the children is done in small groups. This kind of grouping helps the children with special rights to enjoy what they are doing and want to repeat it. Our goal is for the children to want to come to school and for them to develop a sense of autonomy.

Smith: *Your centers have so many mirrors. For example, at the Diana School, there is a huge, walk-in pyramid (or kaleidoscope) of mirrors in the* piazza, *mirrors in the dress-up area, mirrors at child eye-level lining the entryway, lots of tabletop mirrors, a paradoxical series of mirrors in the bathroom, a funhouse distorting mirror, and even tiny mirrors embedded in the cement walls outside the school.*

I must tell you, this has proven illuminating and personally moving for me. I have a condition that causes curvature of the spine. It was not actually until a few months after my first visit to Reggio Emilia that I became conscious of the "importance of looking at

FIGURE 11.2. Looking outside, greeting her parents coming to pick her up at her school.

yourself" (to quote your name for one of the major project themes in the Exhibit, "The Hundred Languages of Children"), in terms of what it has to do with the self-image of persons with physical differences. Late one night, I was alone in a hotel room in Seattle, Washington, and I began to think about reflected images. As the sun rose, I took some photographs of my own bare hunched back glowing in the mirror. It was a cathartic moment, and it motivated me to write to Loris Malaguzzi and activated my quest to discover and articulate what goes on for children with "special rights" in Reggio Emilia.

Can you discuss your view of the purpose of all these mirrors, in terms of self-image, especially for the children who look different?

Soncini: Mirrors are one way that children construct their own identities. We always use the mirrors in a social context and as part of play, not in a specific therapeutic or contrived way. Mirrors can provide insights on living with yourself and who you are!

For the children, especially when they dress up in costume, mirrors give the chance to experiment. Children seem to start little games when they enter a new role or character, but they remain in control and can come in and go out at will. Mirrors are a way for the children to get to know themselves and can be very powerful when they begin to experiment with their ideas about themselves, about new roles or behaviors for themselves.

Some children with special rights do not find it very easy to look at themselves in the mirror. They may not accept their own image and it should not be forced on them. But the teacher must be alert, because suddenly children who have not been using the mirror will discover their own reflection. These children may be surprised and delighted and even stop playing to observe themselves more carefully. The teacher should certainly notice this. We have observed that when children begin playing with their own images, they experiment and make faces and study their own expressions. Perhaps this is a way of gaining power and controlling their image, how they look. When they become playful with images, they often like to start using the funhouse distorting mirrors, but this should always be determined by the child. And they should always have the chance to return to the regular mirror to confirm their actual image. At other times the mirror allows children with physical disabilities the opportunity to watch and observe others without having to move. This can be significant, especially for children who cannot walk. Sometimes they like to observe others in the mirror without the other child realizing it.

Smith: *It seems to me that all of the things you have said could apply equally well to all of the children, even if they are especially important for the children with special rights. Can you comment on the way that children relate to their classmates with disabilities?*

Soncini: We observe that the children are aware of differences, but a difference is not a reason to leave someone out. We find the children very clever in discovering their own ways to give more chances—more opportunities and possibilities. They try very hard to figure out ways to include the child who is disabled. We believe that our philosophy of emphasis on collaboration instead of individual achievement helps. Children are continually negotiating between their individual pride in achievement and their efforts as part of a group.

We firmly hold as a primary value the right of all children to find and organize their own strategy for developing and reaching knowledge. Every single person comes into the world with some abilities and competencies. Our obligation is to figure out ways to encourage that development. We always remind ourselves, especially with regard to young children, that we cannot determine or know their potential. Indeed, a breakthrough may be just around the corner! We do not want to limit what may appear or happen later.

Smith: *This could fit in with your general reluctance in the preprimary schools and infant–toddler centers to use standardized tests, evaluation instruments, and check lists.*

Soncini: We try to go beyond the medical diagnosis, beyond the description of deficits, to look at how the disability affects the whole child. We are always searching for clues to the child's own preferred strategies for learning. Here is where what we call the "hundred languages of children" comes in. We are always looking for an alternate way that the child might learn. The more varied possibilities and options, the more likely you will find the most effective way for the child to learn. Through creative planning, the teacher provides more possibility for the child to succeed.

Filippini: Teachers need to do a lot of imaginative planning. The thing is that if you plan really interesting and exciting activities, the other children will want to join in, too. Everybody can participate in the projects. There is always something to do that is at the child's level, that has meaning for that child. My daughter is in elementary school now, but she still talks about exciting projects she did at the Diana School that involved all levels of children. We do not emphasize the final product but instead participation in the process.

Persons who only see the spectacular products of children, such as those in the exhibit, the "Hundred Languages of Children," may not realize that those documentations are only an exquisite sample of the things that are happening continually in Reggio schools. And the children are not always engaged in such high-power productions. They spend much of their time in quiet and noisy activities that provide the soil in which to nurture the special projects. These ongoing daily activities provide an opportunity for all the children to experiment and explore.

Smith: *Can you discuss how you work with the children on the issue of expressing their feelings?*

Soncini: We take a lot of care with all of the children's feelings. Especially for children who have special rights, we have to give them credit for their feelings and pay attention to ways for them to learn to express themselves. Sometimes people get so focused on cognitive skills that they miss the children's feelings. Feelings are important for everyone; and kindness and sensitivity to others need to be supported in all the children.

Sometimes we see a child with special needs who seems to be depressed. This may be a result of depression in the family; for example, a parent's sadness about the condition of the child. We might decide to try to refer the parent for some support or therapy. Especially for a child with a chronic condition, when the family finally comes to terms with the situation, the enormity of it may seem overwhelming.

Filippini: Do you see that little girl? (A child is sauntering by, stopping to twirl several patterned targets that are mounted on the wall). When Lucia[2] came here last year she was diagnosed as psychotic. She had many horrendous tantrums and her behavior was really difficult to manage. The health department provided us with a psychologist to help us make plans for her. Our *psychologist-pedagogista*, Ivana, worked with the parents and the staff, and we also used an extra classroom teacher for the first few months. Now Lucia gets along quite well at school, although her home life is rather tough.

Smith: *As I have observed Lucia throughout the day today, it appears to me that some of her behaviors might be labeled as "autistic" in Canada or the United States.*

Filippini: Perhaps so, but we have found ways to handle those behaviors casually and effectively. The staff at the Diana School are now very pleased with the extent to which Lucia participates in the program with her friends and is able to express her feelings effectively. We are reluctant to focus on symptoms, causes, and labels, and we believe that our principles of working with children with special rights and needs actually contribute to increased positive experiences for all the children.

Smith: *When I was here several years ago, I saw a little girl with cerebral palsy named Antonella at the Diana School. How is Antonella doing now, do you know?*

Filippini: Antonella spent 3 years with us at the Diana School. We learned a lot from her about how gaining skill in one activity can help the child master another activity. For example, Antonella had very little small-muscle control, but as we observed her interests, we noticed that she liked to work with computers and with clay. Through ongoing months of working with clay, she began to understand spatial relationships: up, down, right, and left. This helped her recognize and learn the shapes of letters—a key step in learning to read and write. She also needed some assistance getting around the school and going to the washroom. This was handled by the teachers, after planning meetings with Ivana and me. Antonella is a rather quiet little girl, but the other children enjoyed taking her outside and giving her exciting rides around the playground. Now she is doing very well at elementary school. She uses her computer to communicate and for her school work.

Smith: *Stella is another child with special rights who is presently attending the Diana School. Would you tell us about her?*

Filippini: Stella came to the Diana School 2 years ago when she was 3 years old. The teachers knew her family well because her older sister had recently

---

[2] All children's names are pseudonyms.

come through Diana. Stella was totally cared for at home by her family for her first 3 years. Her mother gave up her job, and her father took on extra work so the mother could stay at home. The parents were a bit ambivalent to bring Stella to school because they were not sure whether anyone else would know how to care for her needs. The mother was particularly protective.

When the health officials began discussing with the family whether Stella should come to school, the mother called Ivana Soncini often to ask more and more questions. She wanted to be reassured that if Stella were unhappy, she could be taken out of the school. Because there is such a long waiting list for the school, this was a legitimate concern.

Smith: *What were your earliest experiences with Stella when she began to come to the Diana School?*

Soncini: We knew that Stella's parents were not convinced that going to school was a good idea for her. In fact, we ourselves were not quite sure how it would go. We tried to be very open when answering the parents' questions, but we also wanted to give them confidence that we would know what to do.

Stella's mother told us, "I don't know what she will do at school because at home she sleeps all morning." We explained that we would not force Stella to stay awake, although we would try to see if we could help her to be more alert. Actually, ever since Stella has started coming to the Diana School, she has never slept through any morning she is here.

So from these first encounters and experiences, Stella's family began to realize that she has more potential than they had previously known. Indeed, in this particular case, the family had never accepted their doctor's diagnosis. They seemed to be thinking that Stella would just wake up one day and be like all the other children. They had been at odds continually with the health authorities concerning Stella's medical diagnosis.

As part of our philosophy in all of our schools, we declare that as the educators, we want to form our own knowledge of the child. We want to see the child from our own point of view and to observe the child among other children; we distinguish our professional role from that of the medical system. Through many meetings with the family, we ask the parents lots of questions about how they are with their child and find out what they do, what the child does, every little detail.

We wanted to make it clear to Stella's parents that we were interested in how they felt about their child. What we did not want to happen was for us to become another system for them to confront. We wanted to know from them what their expectations were. As we learned more and more about their ideas, we formed the hypothesis that the family was waiting for a miracle to transform Stella, but that at the same time, they were not interacting very frequently or intensively with her.

We concluded that we needed to co-construct with Stella's family a common point of view; together we would develop shared ideas about how to proceed and handle things. However, because we at the school were more equipped than the family to formulate proposals for her program, we had to develop some hypotheses and plans. Everything we did last year was toward those goals.

Our first goal was to activate her attention. She seemed not always to be wide awake. The second was for her to form some special or particular relationships; so we selected Giulia, one of our oldest and most experienced teachers, now partly retired, to come serve as her key relationship.

At first, Stella tired very easily. She was not really so disabled, but she did not use her body very much. Perhaps, we thought, she did not yet know how. We thought maybe she could learn how to direct and control her body better. Also, she never showed changes in her facial expression.

We decided that we had to create a context in which to meet and respond to any tiny attempts she made. We organized the necessary circumstances of her day, beginning with establishing stability and regularity. At first she was with only the teacher, Giulia, who just spoke quietly with her and then later brought her into the classroom to greet the others. Stella did not like noise and so it was avoided. We began with her in a quiet space with only one other child present. Giulia, her teacher, sat right in front of Stella and tried different ways of communicating with her, all the modes of stimulation—auditory, tactile, visual, verbal. When talking with her, Giulia continually described what was going on around her, both on the physical and emotional levels. We felt we had to try to help Stella get a sense of meaning about what was going on around her, and we wanted her to make an effort to do something. We wanted her to identify expectations, learn what to do, and understand and predict what will happen at different moments. We wanted to stimulate her intentionality.

This patient process of waiting, watching, and responding eventually was successful. By the middle of the school year, Stella was engaging in water play in the bathroom with small groups of children. She still loves to play in water, but then, what child doesn't! Then she progressed to sand play, and we noticed that as her interest in play was becoming stronger, her attention span was growing longer. She began to join the others during meeting time, and she began to enjoy singing and play at the light table.

This year, she has begun to stand. The erect posture enables her to be much more alert and awake, although she still shows some problems focusing and paying attention.

At home, her family has observed that she is more attentive. They have recently decided to go see another doctor, a specialist. It seems that they are now coming to accept that Stella does have a special problem.

Smith: *Sharon, you are a special educator who had the opportunity to observe Stella during the visit of your delegation to the Diana School. When you observed Stella, how did you see her included?*

Palsha: I first noticed Stella, a frail child with cerebral palsy, on my entry into the Diana School. I had come with my delegation for a tour of the school. Stella was sitting in a young woman's lap, on a bench in the *piazza*. The woman was stroking the child, as a mother would touch her most precious possession. And so I thought to myself that that was what I was witnessing—a mother who had come to drop off her child and was taking a few extra moments before going off. Or else, I thought, perhaps this was a mother and child who had come to see the Diana School with the idea of applying to the school in future.

I proceeded with the rest of my delegation into the *atelier* to receive a brief overview given by Vea Vecchi (the *atelierista*). Half an hour later, we were given free time to individually observe in the classrooms. Vea, in her remarks, had informed us that there was a child with "special rights" in the 4-year-olds' classroom. Could this be the little girl with cerebral palsy? But where had she gone? She was no longer in the *piazza* or the classrooms.

As I was the lone special educator in my delegation, my colleagues knew of my interests and came immediately to take me to see a child with special needs, in the 3-year-olds' classroom. I wondered why Vea had not mentioned this child as well. I went with them and found an energetic 3-year-old boy playing enthusiastically with his friends. He was missing the lower portion of his right arm, and had short digits extending where usually there would be the elbow. I thought that in North America, this boy certainly would have been identified as a child with a disability. However, in fact, we could see that he was having no trouble keeping up with his classmates and needed no special accommodations. Evidently, in Reggio Emilia, this boy was not considered to be a child with special rights.

I continued to search for Stella. I rounded the corner to the 4-year-olds' bathroom, and there sat Stella in a small wooden chair with a tray on the front holding a tub of water and toys. She was the center of activity, surrounded by four classmates, all splashing, blowing bubbles, and giggling with delight. The woman who had been sitting with her earlier was also there, and I realized that she was the teacher, not the mother. Right now, this teacher was interacting with all five children.

Soon the classroom doors were opened, and all the mobile children ran outside for outdoor playtime. The teacher moved Stella over in front of one of the many mirrors inside the school. She took a brightly colored scarf and draped it around Stella's shoulders, and then began to brush Stella's hair. This interaction had a very positive tone, but I wondered if Stella was to be excluded from playing outdoors. A few minutes later, however, the teacher placed Stella into a stroller and moved with her toward the exit. As they went through the door, two of Stella's classmates met them. One gave the teacher her bouquet of yellow flowers, and the other little girl placed her bouquet on Stella's lap. Then these young friends put their hands together on the handle of the stroller and moved with Stella and the teacher to the sandtable.

There the teacher took Stella out of the stroller and leaned her against the table. She positioned herself behind Stella to provide extra support. Children were busily engaged in building a sand castle. All the children were hard at work, filling buckets, packing down the sand, then upturning the buckets to build the castle. Everyone became so busy that a few seconds passed before anyone noticed that Stella had lost head-control and had sunk face down into her sand castle. Slowly, she pulled her head upright. She was covered in sand, but a bright smile lit up her face. Her classmates giggled, and one child ran to get a towel while the teacher gently brushed the sand away. Everyone enjoyed a happy laugh, and then building commenced in earnest again.

In sum, despite the fact that Stella is nonverbal and nonambulatory, during my observation she was fully included in the morning's activities. I saw her as another of the strong, competent, resourceful children attending Diana School—a child with full rights to a quality early childhood program that involves deep and satisfying personal relationships with teachers and friends. I saw no special equipment being used, no cumbersome wheelchairs or positioning chairs that set up physical barriers to interaction. Instead, Stella was included along with the others in a natural way that illustrated perfectly for me what Loris Malaguzzi said should always be the teacher's goal: to create an amiable school.

Smith: I want to end with some thoughts of a parent, Carlo Vacconi, published as the concluding section of a municipal report (*Coordinamento pedagogico didattico nidi e scuole comunali dell'infanzia*, 1993). The report documents a major civic forum that brought together for many months a group of parents, teachers, support staff, administrators, and municipal officials, to discuss and debate the inclusion of children with disabilities in the city of Reggio Emilia from the preprimary schools through adulthood.

For Mr. Vacconi (pp. 32–41), the report "represents a sort of reflection on those things with which the family with a disabled child must live, and the context in which the workers find themselves." He feels the problems are urgent: although institutions have ample time to "think, reflect, program, redefine, restructure, *etcetera, etcetera*, the families do not have all this time." There is still too big a gap between ideals and realities; the system "is organized to guarantee its own survival. Tomorrow it will be organized to guarantee the best service to the citizen… to the family of the disabled child."

Several things must be reflected on:

> The first is the acceptance of the disabled child on the part of the family. This involves a very long process that begins from birth and continues until the handicap, the disability, becomes a part of family life, so that without drama, the family can seek happiness like everyone. This positive approach cannot come about if the community, the city, constantly poses obstacles. There are obstacles of many kinds, but there is one in particular—leaving the family alone. The family that symbolically locks itself inside the home represents a defeat for all of us, for the entire city.

He goes on to point out that in terms of integration, there is a big gap between principles and their application. "We have thought about elastic institutions, able to model themselves according to the various needs of the citizens. Is it a dream? A utopia? Without dreams and utopias, the 'new' is never invented. And in this field, there is a great need to invent." Finally, his third reflection concerns the necessity for the various services to communicate with each other. "It is necessary to have the courage to break the rules of the past," he concludes. "The family demands an active and recognized role in the health and most of all, the education of their child."

REFERENCES

Coordinamento pedagogico didattico nidi e scuole comunali dell'infanzia [Pedagogical team, infant–toddler center, and preprimary municipal schools]. (1993). *Quaderni Reggiani: I bambini disabili.* Reggio Emilia, Italy: Assessorato Istruzione del Comune di Reggio Emilia.

Berrigan, C. (1994–1995). *Schools in Italy: A national policy made actual.* Syracuse, NY: Syracuse University, Center on Human Policy.

Cecchini, M., & McCleary, I.D. (1985, Summer). Preschool handicapped in Italy: A research-based developmental model. *Journal of the Division for Early Childhood,* 254–265.

Mallory, B.L., & New, R.S. (1994). Social constructivist theory and principles of inclusion: Challenges for early childhood special education. *The Journal of Special Education, 28*(3), 322–337.

McCleary, I.D. (1985, Summer). Overview, Italy. *Journal of the Division for Early Childhood,* 203.

Robins, K. (1985, Summer). Italian preschool education and integration of handicapped children: A response to Cecchini and McCleary. *Journal of the Division for Early Childhood,* 266–271.

Dinosaur,
Anna Frank School

chapter 12

Curriculum Development in Reggio Emilia: A Long-Term Curriculum Project About Dinosaurs

Baji Rankin

Paolo (5;8):	Dinosaurs are enormous....
Federico (6;0):	It's almost as if we would crush an ant.
Paolo:	And dinosaurs would crush us!

This exchange between Paolo and Federico is one fragment of many conversations that took place during a project about dinosaurs in a Reggio Emilia preschool. This chapter describes the unfolding of this project, which took place over 4 months (44 separate sessions) from mid-February through June, 1990. A group of 5- and 6-year-old children in the Anna Frank School for 3- to 6-year-olds took part in the project, guided by their *atelierista*, Roberta Badodi. My own role evolved gradually from observer to participant, as I documented the experience for Roberta and myself on audio-tape, slides, and videotape. Roberta would use the documentation in her work with children, teachers, parents, and the community. I would use it for better understanding the Reggio approach and then communicating to United States audiences (Rankin, 1992, 1996).

I lived in Reggio Emilia for most of one school year, a 9-month period from October, 1989, through June, 1990. Living in Reggio for such an extended period of time allowed me to observe and participate in the project as well as in the surrounding system of social relationships in the Anna Frank School, the municipal early childhood system, and the city.

HOW IT BEGAN

I first heard of Reggio Emilia in 1982 while conducting my Certificate of Advanced Graduate Studies (CASS) thesis in Italy on policy concerning early childhood education. Struck by the profound philosophy, aesthetical environments, spirit of reciprocity, tolerance of conflict, and integration of theory and practice, I carried my interest forward over the next 7 years of work and study in the United States, leading finally to a decision in 1989 to return to Reggio and do my doctoral dissertation on curriculum development.

My first several months of exploratory investigation led to a decision to study the course of one single project. Supported by the Reggio administration, I began work with Roberta Badodi in mid-February. She was just about to begin a new project with children and graciously accepted my presence, along with all of my questions, comments, cameras, and tape- and video-recorders, and even invited my active participation. She received my questions and comments as a welcome stimulus to her own professional growth.

A similar openness was apparent in all of the educators with whom I worked in Reggio Emilia, an example of their guiding philosophy of reciprocity, or circularity, put into action. Carlina Rinaldi, *pedagogista* at Anna Frank, was a particularly strong model of this attitude. And in varied ways, all of the teachers and staff demonstrated interest in learning from me—someone with a cultural background and set of experiences different from their own—just as they seek to learn from all visitors to their schools.

What, then, can educators in the United States learn from my report on the unfolding of a project in Reggio Emilia, when our cultures, systems of education, and political realities are so different? Many people in the United States, first learning of the Reggio Emilia approach, ask both large and small questions. How does the Reggio approach differ from progressive education and open education, two movements that have been a prominent part of our experience in the United States? How does the Reggio approach compare to the concepts behind "developmentally appropriate practice," as defined by standards of the National Association for the Education of Young Children? How does *progettazione* in Reggio (see Rinaldi, Chapter 5, this volume) compare to what U.S. educators seek to implement in "the project approach?" More specifically, what is the role of the teacher in guiding children's learning; how much does she lead them and structure their activity? All of these questions are considered in depth in this book. This chapter, however, is the only one to provide empirical observations of the actual unfolding over time of a particular project; my goal is to provide the kind of information that readers can use to better come to their own conclusions regarding these important questions.

The dinosaur project, like any other in Reggio, had its own unique momentum and sequence of events. It could never be exactly duplicated in Reggio Emilia or any other place. Roberta made numerous decisions based on the particular group of children with whom she was working, their preferences and capabilities, and the daily features of the situation. Therefore, this report should not be thought of as providing a model to copy, but rather a description of process that illustrates principles that can be applied in other situations, especially the principle of *reciprocity,* which involves mutual guidance of the educational process by teacher and learner and responsiveness in circular paths of communication, caring, and control (see Malaguzzi, Chapter 3). A metaphor used by educators in Reggio Emilia to describe this sense of reciprocity is that of a ball being tossed (see Edwards, Chapter 10). As Tiziana Filippini said in her 1990 speech to the National Association for the Education of Young Children:

> Our expectations of the child must be very flexible and varied. We must be able to be amazed and to enjoy—like the children often do. We must be able to catch the ball that the children throw us, and toss it back to them in a way that makes the children want to continue the game with us, developing, perhaps, other games as we go along.

The adults involved in the dinosaur project sought to toss the ball in just such a way.

THE UNFOLDING OF THE PROJECT

The Initiating Context

In Italy, just as in the United States, images of dinosaurs abound. Children participate in a culture of dinosaurs through books, movies, television, and toys. Often they are fascinated and excited, as well as worried or frightened, by the images they see of those dinosaurs most immense, powerful, and aggressive.

Children in Reggio Emilia, just as in other places, like to bring things from home to school. At the Anna Frank School, beginning in fall of 1989, teachers of the 5- to 6-year-olds noticed that many children were bringing dinosaur toys to school. The children's play sometimes spontaneously turned to dinosaurs. The teachers took note, valuing the interest in dinosaurs as an opportunity to understand more about the children. In keeping with the principle of reciprocity, teachers decided to begin a journey together with the children and study dinosaurs in depth.

As is the customary practice in Reggio Emilia, a group of children, rather than the whole classroom, conducted this project. Educators in Reggio (see Malaguzzi, Chapter 3, and Rinaldi, Chapter 5) believe that small group work activates the most intense learning and exchange of ideas; when coupled with systematic rotation (so that every child participates in at least one such experience a year), interaction between the project group and the whole class at key points (so that knowledge and insights are shared), and collaboration between adults—parents, teachers, *atelierista*, and *pedagogoista* (to deal with the complexities and problems that arise and jointly benefit from all that is learned). In the case of the dinosaur project, the adults decided to work with the children who were most interested in dinosaurs. These children represented the spectrum of the class in terms of cognitve and linguistic maturity, and they were about equally divided between boys and girls.

Another customary practice in Reggio Emilia is that before the children actually gather to begin the project, the adults involved meet to discuss various possibilities, hypotheses, and potential directions that the project might take. This is important, Carlina Rinaldi pointed out in a meeting with Roberta and myself on April 20, 1990:

> If adults have thought of 1,000 hypotheses, then it is easy to accept the fact that there can be 1,001 or 2,000 hypotheses. The unknown is easier to accept and adults are more open to new ideas when they have generated many potentialities themselves. The problem comes from having only one hypothesis which then draws all the attention of the adult.

Accordingly, before opening the project with the children, Roberta and Carlina brainstormed many possibilities and potential directions. They also formulated some "provocatory" questions for Roberta to use in a first discussion with children, to open the project and assess their initial level of knowledge about dinosaurs' evolution, physical characteristics, behavior, and living habits. The adults had caught the idea of dinosaur study from the children, and now they wanted to return it to them in a way that would generate observations, questions, suggestions, hypotheses, and set the initial direction of the project work.

Continual collaboration among adults throughout this project is critical to its progress. In this case the primary adults involved were the *atelierista*, Roberta, who works exclusively in the Anna Frank School; the *pedagogista*, Carlina, who works with adults in several preprimary schools and infant-toddler centers, and myself. (In many other projects, classroom teachers take leading roles as well; e.g., see The Long Jump Project, described by Forman & Fyfe in Chapter 13, this volume). Accordingly, we three met to talk and plan together through a variety of means. We held formal scheduled meetings together, we made frequent phone calls to Carlina during many phases of the project, and we held informal conversations whenever Carlina came to the school for other purposes. Roberta and I conferred continually—before, during and after activity times. Roberta held frequent discussions with the two lead teachers of the 5- to 6-year-old classroom to inform and involve them in events.

The Beginning

The initial phase is an essential part of any project: The aim is to open up and to assess the children's knowledge and interests concerning the subject. The adults want to help children to set up a context in which the children can find their own questions and problems to explore. The goal is to help each individual and the group as a whole advance the construction and co-construction of knowledge. Thus, instead of only responding to those questions that adults think they will find interesting, the children are involved right from the start in defining questions to be explored.

The initial phase also involves establishing the community of the small group. Emphasis is placed on learning as a group and developing a sense of "we." Reggio Emilia educators use the phrase, *"Io chi siamo"* ("I am who we are") to express the idea that it is within this shared space of "we" that each child can offer his or her best thinking, leading to a rich and fertile group exchange and stimulating something new and unexpected, impossible for any one person to create alone. The teacher's role in this process is to galvanize each child to participate and to grow, as much as he or she can, within the context of the group investigation. This is done within a framework of seeing that the project belongs to the group: each child is a part, an essential part, but only a part. The reality of "we," which the Reggio educators believe is inside each child from birth, is valued and encouraged in all of the activities of school life. In this sense the actual theme or content of the project is nota as important as the process of children thinking, feeling, working, and progressing together with others.

At the beginning of the dinosaur project, then, about half the 5- to 6-year-old class gathered in the *atelier* of the Anna Frank School for the first time. Roberta, establishing the sense of *"Io chi siamo,"* explained to the children that they would be working on dinosaurs for awhile. She encouraged all of them to do their best and pointed out that they had a special opportunity to work together. She first initiated a graphic (pictorial) and then a verbal investigation. The children began to draw dinosaurs, any way they liked, around a large square table. They talked together as they drew and asked each other questions about their drawings and other things. Good ideas spread contagiously around the table. Several times a child changed his or her drawing because of comments or questions from a friend. "Oh, that's not a dinosaur. Dinosaurs have four legs!"

After the children finished their drawings, Roberta spoke individually with each child about his or her drawings. Then she gathered the children together for a group discussion and asked a series of open-ended questions, encouraging discussion among the children. Where did dinosaurs live? What did they eat? How did they take care of their babies? How were the babies born? Are dinosaurs living now? What are the differences between male and female dinosaurs? These questions, growing in part out of the children's earlier play and comments, and in part out of the questions compiled by the adults, evoked a great deal of interest and response.

The ideas discussed by the children became the catalysts for later activities and conversations that adults gave back to the children on later occasions. The game was expanding. This critical process was facilitated (as is typical in Reggio Emilia) by tape recording all of the major conversations related to the project. The tapes were transcribed by Roberta at home and typed up by parent volunteers, so that we adults could study and reflect on what the children had said and not said, what issues aroused greatest interest, how children interacted, and so on. (But note, in different schools and on different occasions, the process of transcription and typing will be done by various people).

The boys in the dinosaur group—three in particular—started with a great deal of knowledge that informed the others. Here is an excerpt from the discussion:

Federico: There aren't any more dinosaurs... because among all the animals that were already born, the dinosaurs already existed; therefore the dinosaurs were already of two species....

Francesca: But all the dinosaurs are dead. They killed and buried them.

Michele: No! They didn't bury them! They died themselves.

Fabio: In fact, it's not true [they were killed] because who could have killed the dinosaurs? Primitive people were there after the dinosaurs, not at all when there were dinosaurs. Cartoons show that when there were dinosaurs there were primitive people, but really there weren't primitive people when there were dinosaurs. The primitive people existed after the dinosaurs.

Federico: Men came when dinosaurs were dead.

Fabio: When there were dinosaurs, there were all the little animals that were all small insects when the dinosaurs disappeared. They became big and they became the monkeys and all the other animals... but not at all the elephants that there are now.

Francesca's statement that "they buried dinosaurs" was resoundly defeated by the three boys, who had more information and confidence than she did on this topic. They also had agreement among themselves. This is an example of cognitive conflict where one position dominates.

The pictorial investigation revealed intriguing differences in ways of thinking between boys and girls. The educators in Reggio have noticed that boys and girls often approach situations differently. They are interested to learn more about those differences. Here the boys' knowledge was more accurate. Several boys indicated which dinosaurs were female by drawing baby dinosaurs inside the mother's belly. The girls, on the other hand, represented female dinosaurs by using decorations such as long hair, and by drawing baby dinosaurs close to the mother.

The next day, a Thursday, the second day of the investigation, neither the discussions nor the drawings were as rich or extended as the first day. Afterward, the adults decided to wait a few days before continuing, to assess whether the children were genuinely interested enough to go ahead with a long-term project. Such a project requires a deep sense of inquiry on the children's part to sustain the effort.

However, another possible cause of the second day's lowered energy could have been the approach of the adults. Reactivating a group, maintaining the inquiry between one day and the next, is a very important and delicate matter. We had chosen to introduce the topic the second day in much the same way as we had on the first. But perhaps it would have been more effective to focus on one or two of the themes that had been of greatest interest to children on the first day, for example, the time period in which dinosaurs lived, their size, their origin and disappearance, or the differences between females and males. In any case, when we met with the children the following Monday, their interest was high once more, when we offered them clay to use in constructing dinosaurs.

These initial investigations revealed the children's many interests in the dinosaur topic. In part these reflected the questions that Roberta had raised with them; however, the attention children showed to certain questions and the exchanges that ensued, demonstrated their genuine curiosity as well as their capacities to construct knowledge collaboratively.

The adults used the children's tape-recorded conversations throughout the project in many ways. They referred to specific conversations as they spoke with children. They used quotations in speaking with the parents. They enlarged written quotes as parts of displays for the school as a whole. The thoughts of the children were highly valued, and everyone knew it—children, teachers, and parents. As Roberta put it (in a formal delegation to a Swedish delegation on May 9, 1991):

> A determining contribution to children's construction of knowledge, we believe, is the involvement of the adult, not only because the adult legitimizes children's knowledge and curiosity, but also because the adult values and addresses children's investigations with supports and suggestions."

The Need for More Information

It was clear that the group needed more information. The following day, Roberta initiated a discussion asking them where they could get more information about dinosaurs. This set off an explosion of excitement as children remembered possible sources: television, movies, stores, magazines, newpapers, books from home and library, older brothers, sisters, and other relatives: "My grandfather knows about dinosaurs!" "My sister!" "My brother!" "My uncle!" "My cousin, because he goes to school."

The children went to the local library the next day and found many books. They studied the books at the library and brought many back to school. These became long-term residents of the *atelier* (the work site for the project), enabling the children to browse or to refer to the books for specific information. Children enjoyed books individually and in small groups. They compared their own drawings to the drawings in the books. When they formulated a question, they often retrieved a book to help them clarify what they were asking about.

The children invited friends and relatives to school to share information. The task of writing a letter of invitation to friends and relatives generated much enthusiasm. The letter was composed by the whole dinosaur group, each child offering ideas while Roberta acted as scribe, reiterating, every once in a while, the purpose of the letter. Then, taking turns, two children at a time wrote out the final draft, copying Roberta's model, while others addressed envelopes, drew accompanying drawings, and made posters about the coming events. The visitors, arriving over the next few weeks, were enthusiastically received. They included two older siblings, graduates of the Anna Frank School, bearing impressive notebooks and full of zeal from their third-grade study of dinosaurs; a father; a grandmother; and an expert from a local nature society. The children prepared questions ahead of each visitor, so that each child had specific questions to ask. These discussions were very rich for all participants, especially for the particular children whose relatives came.

During this period, children were also constructing dinosaurs out of clay, painting them with tempera and water color, and drawing with chalk. Differences re-emerged in how girls and boys used clay. Just as in the earlier case with the drawings, the girls used more decorations, embellishments, and tiny details, than did the boys. A group of four boys built a large clay dinosaur, and this collective activity produced talk about making a really big dinosaur. Children then engaged in shadow play before images of dinosaurs projected onto the wall. In this way they had the opportunity to directly experience the large dimensions of dinosaurs.

How to Make a Big Dinosaur

At this point, many topics were of interest to the group, including the size and physical dimensions of dinosaurs, their origin and disappearance, their daily habits, differences between male and female dinosaurs, and how baby dinosaurs were raised. However, one theme kept recurring—that of size and dimension.

To follow up on this theme, Roberta asked the children what they could do to build a really big dinosaur. The discussion was lively: there were many ideas and many different suggestions about materials and techniques to use. In the midst of this discussion, an important point emerged: the necessity of deciding what kind of dinosaur to build.

Francesco: Well, the thing to think about is what dinosaur to make… which dinosaur!

Roberta: It's true. We know many dinosaurs and maybe the first thing to do is to understand which one we want to make. Why is that important to you, Francesco?

Francesco: Because if not, we'll make all different things of each different dinosaur!

Giulia: First we need to decide about what dinosaur to make. We need to say, "Let's do this dinosaur! Let's do this dinosaur."

After much debate, the children eventually decided to take a vote. *Tyrannosaurus Rex* won in a close victory over *Stegosaurus.* With more discussion the next day about what kinds of materials to use and how to use them, the children set themselves to work, spontaneously dividing themselves into smaller groups to do the work. Four girls came together to form one group, and four boys another. Once more, different patterns were seen in how boys and girls proceeded.

Girls. The girls quickly chose one book to look through, easily selected one *Tyrannosaurus Rex* to make together, and soon began looking for construction materials. They headed first toward small materials that they could use for dec-

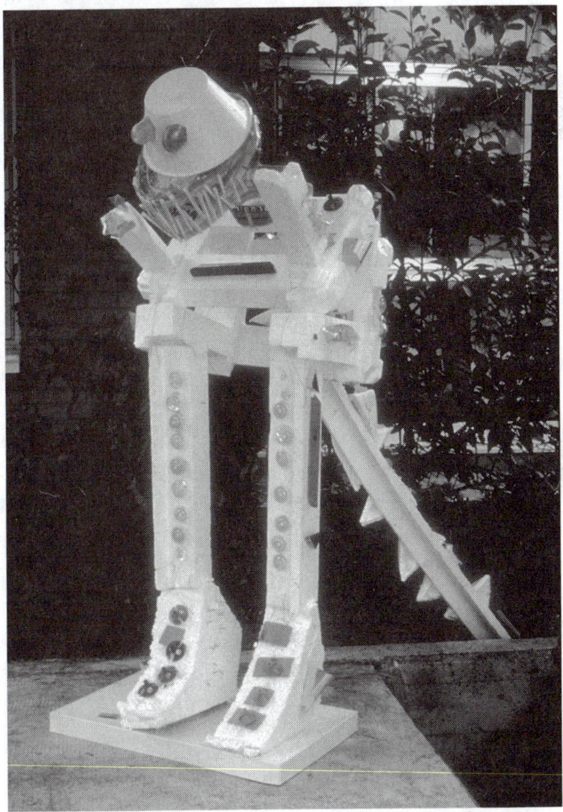

FIGURE 12.1. Four girls collaborated on building a Tyrannosaurus Rex out of Styrofoam–decorating it in style.

orating the dinosaur. It was only after Roberta talked with them that they began to think about and seek larger material for the structure of the body. Roberta brought in a ladder and encouraged them to use it to search for bigger materials higher up on the shelves of the *atelier.*

The girls chose styrofoam as their medium. This material turned out to be rather easy to work with as it was easy to handle and the shape and size of the styrofoam pieces suggested to them different parts of the dinosaur. They had to ask for Roberta's help only at specific times; she did some things they were unable to do, such as attaching pieces of foam in a stable way with a piece of wire. A satisfying, three-dimensional, approximately 4-foot high, highly decorated *Tyrannosaurus Rex* resulted, along with a stronger friendship among these particular girls.

Boys. The four boys, in contrast, had a more difficult time. To start with, each

FIGURE 12.2. Four boys chose wire and metal for their dinosaur. The toughness of the material made the construction very difficult–but satisfying in the long run.

chose a different book and it took them a much longer time than the girls to choose which image to use as a model. Then they chose wire and metal as their construction material. Perhaps the hardness of the wire suggested to them the roughness and sharpness of *Tyrannosaurus Rex*. In any case, it was a very difficult material to use. They had to ask for Roberta's help during most of the stages of construction, and their work went quite slowly. Whereas the girls had seemed oblivious to other people in the room, the boys were highly distracted and at times discouraged by seeing the girls' dinosaur taking rapid form. The boys had to return over the next several days to finish their work. However, in the end, their dinosaur was also very satisfying to them.

Measuring and Drawing A Life-Size Dinosaur

As the adults read and re-read the texts of the children's conversations and searched for a next direction in which to move, they noticed how the theme of size and dimension kept recurring. They decided to challenge the children to draw a dinosaur life-size and find some way to hang it, so it could be seen actually standing upright on its feet. I must admit, as a participant in these discussions, that I found this proposal preposterous. How could the children do such a difficult thing? But then I gradually became more and more excited. Would the children want to do it? Could they do it? I knew that they would have to be highly motivated to get through the difficulties.

Roberta and I marked the transcribed texts so that she would be able to remind the children of what they had said in previous sessions about the size of dinosaurs. Roberta gathered six children, those who remained the most curious and active in their participation up to this point. We decided that six children—three girls and three boys—would make a good group to confront the challenge of making a life-size dinosaur. Although educators in Reggio Emilia have found that five or fewer is ideal in order to maximize the cognitive learning processes in the group, we wanted a fairly large group and a balance of girls and boys.

Roberta's suggestion was met with great enthusiasm; it stimulated a productive and multi-faceted discussion and led naturally to the proposal to make a life-size drawing. Notice her active role in guiding and shaping, but not controlling, the discussion:

Roberta: Rereading all the things that you said, there's one thing that came to our minds that you could understand better. It has to do with the real measurments of dinosaurs, the real measurements. We've talked many times and you've said many things, but, in fact, no one has talked exactly about the real measurments of dinosaurs, no one's talked about that really.

Federico: In fact, we have it in there, the "thing-a-ma-jig" of dinosaurs. (Federico is referring to a poster of dinosaurs in the classroom that a child brought to school. It shows the height of a dinosaur in relation to the height of a man.) "Only that if there is a dinosaur as high as that, then, yeah, he could be high!" (Federico shakes his head; his eyes open wide; and he smiles as if in amazement, imagining how high that would be.)

Roberta listens carefully and then asks: "What are you talking about? What's over there?"

Federico: That is, we have a big poster of dinosaurs. There is a big *Tyrannosaurus Rex* behind and a small man in front.
Roberta: Oh.
Giulia: We can also look in the books and take a meter and make it as big as it really was.
Roberta: Certainly, in fact, it's true what Giulia said.
Federico: I think the legs are as high as the ceiling.
Roberta: Of all dinosaurs or of some?
Tommi: No, of the *Tyrannosaurus Rex*, maybe. (He looks up to the ceiling.)
Federico: Of some. (Tommi and Federico continue talking between themselves.)
Roberta: Well, Giulia has already mentioned something important. If we look for a drawing of a dinosaur as big as... (Roberta pauses.)
Giulia: As this picture.
Roberta: As a real one, eh?

(The three boys talk among themselves, very quickly.)

Federico: Maybe we'll need a piece of paper as big as this table.
Roberta: Or maybe much larger.
Federico: It has to be big and long.
Fabio: Or you could copy a dinosaur that we made ourselves, that we built.

This animated conversation continued in many directions, concerning the probable size of the drawing, where they could work, what kind of dinosaur to draw. There turned out to be no need to re-read texts from previous conversations. The children exploded with interest and amazement at the proposal. The difficulties faced seemed to be the most fascinating aspects to the children.

They went to the books and started looking for an image of a dinosaur to use. They gravitated to a simple line drawing of a *Diplodacus* placed in a rectangle clearly blocked off in 3-meter units of height. The represented animal was 27 by 9 meters in size (about 81 by 27 feet). Next to it there was the figure of a standing man (2-meters tall), drawn to provide a sense of the dinosaur's gigantic size.

The first problem the children wanted to tackle was to see how big 27 meters was. They were familiar with meter-sticks and took the two of them from the *atelier* out into the courtyard. But there first problem was that they had only two meter-sticks, when they wanted 27. The idea of using one meter stick 27 times did not occur to them. Instead, they went in search of 25 more sticks, but were only able to discover one more in another classroom.

At this point the children were stuck. What could they do? Roberta suggest-

FIGURE 12.3. After finding the three meter sticks in the school insufficient to measure the length of 27 meters, the children return to the *atelier* to find other objects they could use. They discover several plastic rods which Roberta measures: they are one meter long!

ed going back into the *atelier* to look for other measuring material. There on the shelves the children found a bunch of long plastic rods for hanging posters! The children and Roberta verified that they were each 1 meter long. The children counted the rods and found more than enough. The investigation could continue! By suggesting that the children return to search for other materials, Roberta enabled the investigation to go on. Her intervention—not the only possible one she could have made—supported the children in their quest for a solution but did not impose upon them an adult one.

Trying to lay out 27 of these rods in the courtyard made it evident that the courtyard was too small. An idea, suggested earlier by one child, came up now again: Use the sports field in front of the school. There was clearly enough space there. The next problem became that of laying the rods in straight lines and forming the huge rectangle.

After trials, errors, and corrections, three sides of the rectangle were measured out: 27 rods by 9 rods by 9 rods. On the fourth side, however, another problem arose: There were not, after all, enough plastic rods to complete the rectangle. Two of the children went back to the school in search of other objects and arrived several minutes later, victoriously, with a roll of toilet paper! The rectangle could now be completed.

FIGURE 12.4. Running out of plastic rods, two children return to the school in search of other objects they can use to close the rectangle. They return victoriously with a roll of toilet paper.

Sitting down on the grass, looking at what they had done, was satisfying to the children. However, it was also clear to them that there was a long way to go. Elena said, “Let’s try it on a small piece of paper, how it should be done. Then we’ll make it bigger.” Everyone agreed the next step should be on smaller paper.

The Girls. Before starting to work the following day, Roberta telephoned Carlina. Because two of the boys were sick, it made sense to Roberta and me to go ahead with the three girls first and then work with the boys another day. Carlina agreed, and suggested offering the girls a choice of papers to use—unlined, lined, and blocked. This choice of papers was a key element for them because, without them realizing, it forced them to render their hypotheses more concrete and therefore more public and accessible. Roberta’s role was then to permit the children’s problem-solving abilities to flourish in whatever ways the children chose.

Given the choice of three kinds of paper, two girls chose graph paper and one chose the unlined paper. The two using graph paper began to draw, whereas the third focused on telling stories. After much trial and error, and through interaction with Roberta, the girls got the idea to search the shelves of the *atelier* for objects that came in large amounts of at least 27. By placing these objects on the paper, they would be able to re-create the rectangle they had made outside, but this time on paper in a smaller scale. At this point, all three girls started to use graph paper. They experimented with various materials. After several attempts, one girl succeeded with 27 small rectangular blocks that she placed along one edge of her paper. Then she made the other three sides with the same blocks. The other two girls came to watch and ended up collaborating by counting out the 27 squares on the graph paper, then 9, 9, and 27 to make the rectangle.

The girls then became interested in the horizontal lines seen in the reference book to indicate 3-meter units of height. Using the squares on their graph paper, in one case, and the small rectangular blocks in the other, they counted off 3- and then 6-measures and were able to draw on their papers the two horizontal lines that marked the height. This was a tremendous accomplishment this particular morning for these three girls.

The Boys. When the boys had their turn, the importance of choice of paper was dramatic. Federico immediately chose graph paper and began to count off 27 squares. He obviously had some kind of understanding that graph paper would be most suitable. Tommi, on the other hand, chose blank paper and began making dots, 27 of them in a rough row. He then made 27 more dots, in a row parallel to this first row but higher up on his paper, and when he finished he was very surprised to see that the bottom line was longer than the top one.

At this point Tommi was curious, eager, and a little upset. Something was not working right.

The role of the teacher in this kind of moment is important. Roberta could have made some comment or asked a question, but instead she chose to pause. Federico stepped in:

> *Federico:* It's because, I think, here you made them closer together. Try and count them....

Tommi re-counts his dots.

> *Federico:* Yeah, here you made them too close because look here, they are all messed up here, and look how they are here. (He compares the top and bottom lines). Maybe you were in too much of a hurry.

Although this incident has similarities to a traditional Piagetian conservation of length task, it arose spontaneously out of the children's on-going work. As a result, the two children were very motivated to solve this problem. Tommi was clearly a boy in the process of establishing conservation of length. While he was counting the 27 dots, he demonstrated that he knew counting to be a way to establish equivalence of length. However, on completing the counting, the obvious discrepancy between the length of the two lines confused him. He did not yet understand how the counted number of units only applies when the units are of equal length. Federico, whose concept of conservation of length was clearly established, was able to articulate the relationship of distance between dots and overall length. He was easily able to coordinate two relationships and explain it to Tommi.

After Federico's comments, Tommi appeared indecisive and stuck. Roberta suggested he could change paper if he wanted to, and he jumped at the chance: His enthusiasm was evident as he stood up to get a new piece of paper. He selected a piece of unlined paper. While Federico and Roberta went back to their respective works, Tommi pondered. He looked at Federico working on his graph paper; he looked at the three choices of paper in front of him; slowly he put the blank paper back, chose graph paper, and began counting the squares.

Roberta's intervention, a quiet suggestion, was just enough to get Tommi started again on his exploration. In the words of Loris Malaguzzi (founding director of the Reggio Emilia municipal preschool system), in a taped interview with me on June 21:

> The teacher must intervene as little as possible but in a way that's sufficient to start the exchange again or to reassure the children. Therefore, interventions must be measured, not overbearing, not subverting what the children are doing. Rather it is a kind of taking the child by the hand, always letting the children stand on their own two feet. (Malaguzzi, 1990, p. 5).

It was not so much Federico's intellectual capacity that made the difference in this situation, but rather the reciprocity between Tommi and Federico, in grappling together over what they knew and did not know. Tommi came to appre-

FIGURE 12.5. This drawing was chosen by the children to use in drawing the life-size dinosaur. By creating a grid on graph paper, the children were able to figure the length of various body parts.

ciate the benefit of the evenly spaced marks provided by the graph paper, and Federico developed his capacity to express himself about these ideas.

The two boys then glued in a cut-out shape of the dinosaur, 27 × 9 centimeters long, that fit into the 27 × 9 square rectangle on the graph paper. They were interested in how long the body parts of the dinosaur were, and by counting squares they could figure it out. “Let’s pretend that one square stands for one meter,” said Federico. They counted squares to find out how long each body part was and then made verticle lines on their drawing, marking out how long the tail was, the body, the neck and the head.

The Group of Six Back Together. The next day, the boys and girls presented to each other and to Fabio, who had been out of school for a few days, what they had done. They asked questions about what the others had done. It was not at all a smooth discussion; there was excitement, disbelief, and incomplete understanding. (For more information see Rankin, 1996.) Giulia summed it up quite well with her comment, “I think the drawings of both the girls and the boys are needed!”

Each child made his or her own plan, using photocopies of 27 × 9 centimeter dinosaurs. The drawings were then taken outside to use while redrawing the rectangle in the sports field—much easier this time although still difficult—and beginning to think about how to draw the dinosaur inside of it. Tommi and Federico suggested laying out the verticle lines, so they could mark out the length of the body parts as they had done on their papers.

FIGURE 12.6. The grid previously done on paper is now reconstructed in the field. The outline of the back of the dinosaur appears.

Giulia suggested putting on the horizontal lines that the girls had drawn on their papers, confirming what she had said earlier that the drawings of both the girls and the boys were necessary. With this grid of horizontal and verticle lines now in place, it was possible to mark the outline of the back of the dinosaur, connecting crucial points on the grid with a rope. The back of the dinosaur was visible; the dinosaur was taking shape.

An interesting point about this morning is the timing of the activities. The discussion among the six children had started at around 9:30 in the morning, and when lunchtime arrived, at noon, the children were still in the midst of working in the field. Roberta told the children to go in for lunch and said that they could come back right afterward if they wanted to. Everyone did. Working after lunch represented a departure from the usual schedule, but it is done from time to time. It was seen as acceptable because the children were in the midst of a problem. In fact, several times during the project, children even worked through nap time.

Completion of the Life-Size Dinosaur

The group of six children went through several other transitions before the actual drawing of the life-size *Diplodacus*, including having to change the dinosaur's dimensions when it was discovered that they could no longer use the sports field. Instead, the children had to draw a 13 × 6 meter Diplodacus to fit into the court-

FIGURE 12.7. How many children do you think can fit in the tail of the dinosaur?

yard behind the school. The problem changed from one of defining the space based on the dimensions of the dinosaur to that of fitting the dinosaur into the defined space.

A few days later, the children went out in the courtyard with new drawings. The group was now able to construct a 13 × 6 meter rectangle, the grid of horizontal and verticle lines, the top line of the dinosaur's body, and finally the rest of the body. (For more details, see Rankin, 1992, 1996.)

The hardest work was now done. Over the next few days painting the dinosaur on a huge piece of plastic drew the participation of most of the children in the 5-year old class. It attracted the attention of all the children and teachers in the school who came to watch the progress of this dinosaur in their backyard.

CONCLUDING PHASE

The children in the dinosaur group were interested in sharing what they had learned and done with the rest of the children in the school. Roberta, like other educators in Reggio, values this kind of exchange and had, indeed, talked about it with children right from the beginning. As she explained later (in her May 1991, lecture): "The re-reading of the experience was important: children identified the steps that they decided were most meaningful. They were able to transfer knowledge that they just acquired."

Organizing the information to present to classmates clarifies and consolidates the knowledge the children gain from their work. Moreover, it allows adults to evaluate that work and the children's progress.

The children in the dinosaur group prepared an exhibit for the rest of the school, laying out the activities they had done and the steps they had gone through. The preparation of the exhibit was significant. They chose drawings and sculptures; they made invitations and posters, they thought of ways to present their experience to their classmates. The other children were excited to come to the exhibit and seemed to enjoy it; however, I judged the children of the dinosaur group to enjoy it the most, as they explained with animation the course of their adventures.

An inaugural festival was also planned for one Friday afternoon at pick-up time. The adults had arranged for the dinosaur to be raised to its feet by a set of pulleys attached to the high fence around one part of the sports field. This generated much excitement and represented a culminating moment for the project—especially for the children among the dinosaur group—as they beheld their creation rising to its feet.

A final meeting of the dinosaur group came as a result of a letter they had written to the city mayor, asking for a permanent place to hang the dinosaur (it was too big to stay in the school). The children met with the mayor, who commended them on their work and said he would do his best to find a place to hang the dinosaur.

FIGURE 12.8. At the inauguration of the painting, the dinosaur stands on its own feet!

SUMMARY

We have seen one example of a project unfolding in a preschool in Reggio Emilia. Like any other experience, its development was unpredictable and emergent. It unfolded as a particular group of adults and children interacted, setting in motion a unique dynamic.

Even though there is not, and can not be, one right way a project should go, nevertheless, there are some general guidelines and principles that are worthwhile to review. First, establish and maintain reciprocity as a central operating principle, with emphasis on developing a sense of "we." Second, start the project with a graphic and verbal exploration. Third, base the development of the project on the questions, comments, and interests of the children involved.

Fourth, provide ample time for children to come up with their own questions and their own solutions. Finally, bring the knowledge and experience of the children back to other children in the school. Share the experience of the project with other adults.

How many of these proposals are relevant here in the United States? While every reader will have to answer that for himself or herself, here are my thoughts. It seems that in the United States, many teachers value such things as observing and listening to children as a basis for planning; having children work in small groups; emphasizing both cognitive and social growth of children; and encouraging children's active involvement in meaningful activities where they have power to make decisions. Thus, there are many similarities between the Reggio Emilia approach and developmentally appropriate practice as understood in the United States. What seems most different from early education in the United States is the fact that in Reggio Emilia there exists an operative network of 35 public schools for 0- to 6-year-olds. The leaders of this public system work together with teachers and parents to promote and stimulate growth and enact their shared principles of reciprocity, communication, and interaction. The network of relationships validates and supports development in a cohesive diretion.

How can we learn from this in the United States? We can build on what we are doing right now in a more collaborative way. Interested people can find one another and share what is happening in their classrooms. We can observe, tape record, analyze, and document the work of children and then exchange our documentations of projects and experiences with others. Besides providing delight and sustaining enthusiasm, this sharing will help us take our work to a higher level. With a greater sense of "we," we can begin to construct a better world together, a world where the needs and rights of children are placed where they properly belong, at center stage.

AFTERWORD, 1997

Since I left Reggio Emilia in 1990, I have had 6 years to reflect upon my experience, including a year in which I was a classroom teacher working with 5- and 6-year-olds in New Mexico. This time and these experiences have deepened even further my respect for the work of children, educators, and families in the municipal preprimary schools of Reggio Emilia. I have become even more aware of the necessary base of experience that the participants bring to their joint project work.

In the Dinosaur Project, for example, the children's previous experiences provided them with high expectations for their work on the project. They came to it with the anticipation that something wonderful could happen if they made the proper effort. On the first day, they were so excited and also so focused that they were able to draw and talk together for 3 hours about their initial conceptions and questions concerning dinosaurs. With Roberta's support, they demonstrated the social and cognitive skills to represent their ideas, as well as to listen to one another and accomodate to their thoughts and actions. Roberta demonstrated the complementary skills of knowing how to frame the conversation so that individual children listened to others who spoke. Readiness and expectations were high as the project was undertaken.

In my teaching last year, I did not find that the children had those same expectations and preparedness for project work, perhaps because they did not have prior experiences of watching others or themselves being deeply involved in long-term projects. Furthermore, I, as the teacher, had not yet built up the experience of guiding the development of long-term projects. While I am convinced that U.S. teachers and children can develop the skills necessary for high-quality project work, I realize this takes time as well as thought, effort, and collaboration on the part of educators, children, and families.

How can we in the United States and other countries work to help ourselves and the children to develop the needed skills? How can we fine-tune the observational and listening skills of ourselves and the children? What kinds of teacher provocations and interventions will help galvanize and mobilize children? Can we jump-start projects so that children will experience the joys of this work? Where can we find the time and the strength to talk with our colleagues about children's behavior and thinking, and about our own thinking and teaching?

Because the Dinosaur Project was built on the children's and teachers' prior experiences of project work and on the strong beliefs that guide all the processes and facets of their work, it demonstrates how key principles of the Reggio Emilia approach can be translated into practice. Reggio principles and pedagogy developed over long years—years that we do not need to repeat if we can learn from their experience. But in our classroom work with children who are less experienced in project work, we must start at the same place that Reggio educators do when children first enter their programs: with small groups of children exploring the grammars of different materials and working on short-term projects.

Even such explorations and short-term projects require keen observation by teachers, as well as the time and space to discuss these observations with colleagues. In small group work organized around short-term projects, children can develop the skills of expressing themselves and listening to others. They can develop the abilities to represent and communicate their ideas in different kinds of materials, such as paper, clay, paint, and markers. And teachers can advance their capacities for listening deeply to the words of children. Short-term projects contain within them all the seeds for long-term projects to eventually flourish.

REFERENCES

Filippini, T. (1990, November). *The Reggio Emilia approach.* Paper presented at the annual meeting of the National Association for the Education of Young Children, Washington, DC.

Rankin, B. (1985). An analysis of some aspects of schools and services for 0–6-year-olds in Italy with particular attention to Lombardy and Emilia Romagna. Unpublished CAGS thesis, Wheelock College, Boston, Massachusetts.

Rankin, B. (1992, May-June). Inviting children's creativity: A story of Reggio Emilia, Italy. *Child Care Information Exchange,* 85, 30–35.

Rankin, B. (1996). Collaboration as the basis of early childhood curriculum: A case study from Reggio Emilia, Italy. Unpublished EdD dissertation, Boston University, Boston, Massachusetts.

Drawing by a 5-year-old child at la Villetta School.

chapter 13

Negotiated Learning Through Design, Documentation, and Discourse

George Forman*
Brenda Fyfe

Reflective practice of teaching must stand on a well defined theory of knowledge. Otherwise, we know not where to go. One needs a definitiuon of knowledge as a standard for effective teaching. The theory of knowledge to which we subscribe is constructivist, more precisely social constructivism as found in Doise, Mugny and Perret-Clemont (1975) and co-constructivist as found in Berger and Luckmann (1966), Tudge and Winterhoff (1993), Vygotsky (1934, 1986), and Wertsch (1985). This theory holds that knowledge is gradually constructed by people becoming each other's student, by taking a reflective stance toward each other's constructs, and by honoring the power of each other's initial perspective for negotiating a better understanding of subject matter (see Jankowicz, 1995; and Palincsar & Brown, 1984). The theory further holds that knowledge is never verifiable through listening or by observation alone, but rather it gains clarity through a negotiated analysis of the communication process itself. This analysis necessarily contains tacit knowledge that is inferential and not literally "in the data" (Piaget, 1978; von Glaserfeld, 1995).

Once this premise is accepted, our educational practice changes radically from a study of facts to a study of how we study and how we move from facts to meaning. The education of children now lies in helping them study their ways of making meaning, their negotiations with each other in a context of symbolization (Gardner, 1983), communication (Tharp & Gallimore, 1988), narrative, and metaphor (Bruner, 1990).

The principles of this epistemology lead to practice similar to what we have observed in Reggio Emilia, a practice that we prefer to call *negotiated learning.* This term *negotiated* captures the centrality of the social, co-constructivist principles just mentioned. The teachers seek to uncover the children's beliefs about the topics to be investigated. Their study goes beyond simply identifying the children's interest. Their analysis reveals the reasons behind the children's interest, the source of their current knowledge, and their level of articulation about its detail. Children are encouraged to talk about what they know before they begin their projects. At a metalinguistic level, the children talk about how they represent what they know. In this co-constructivist curriculum, the teachers form a community of learners with the children and with the parents and other teachers (see Rinaldi, 1996). They discuss the social and symbolic processes by which meanings are negotiated toward some level of shared understanding.

The curriculum is not child centered or teacher directed. The curriculum is child originated and teacher framed. The children discuss many interests, for example, what amusement rides would small birds enjoy. These interests are reframed into slightly more general concepts considered important by professional teachers, from the previous example, say, the relation between anatomy and machine (see Forman & Gandini, 1994). Then specific follow-up activities are proposed and negotiated with the children and at the more general level, with the parents (see Fyfe & Forman, 1996).

We specify three components that define negotiated learning as a dynamic system of causes, effects, and countereffects. These components are *design, documentation,* and *discourse.* In general, these three components create a system such that academic skills are engaged within the context of meaningful problem solving and communication to others. For example, when teachers document children's work and use this documentation as part of their instruction with the children, the net result is a change in the image of their role as teacher, a change from teaching children to studying children, and by studying children, learning with children (see Rinaldi, 1996). Asking children to design their future work changes the way they talk about their work. Their talk becomes the discourse of prediction and explanation.

THREE COMPONENTS OF NEGOTIATED LEARNING

Design refers to any activity in which children make records of their plans or intended solutions. A drawing can be a design if it is drawn with an intent to guide the construction of the items drawn, or to guide a sequence of steps. For example, children at the Eighth of March School in Reggio Emilia drew the steps in a "Drop the Handkerchief" game so that children unfamiliar with the game could learn the rules by reading the drawings. Children at La Villetta School in Reggio Emilia drew fountains and amusement rides, knowing that these drawings would be used to guide the actual construction and layout of these amusements in their outdoor playground. Designs can be in many media; a clay fountain to guide the construction of one made from pipe and hose, a wire figure to portray the movements of a dance to be learned by others. Because the design will be revisited later to guide another activity, the design must be crafted in order to be read. Thereby, design refers to the function of a record to communicate and not simply to the record itself. The educational value of design flows from the special attitude of the designer, an attitude of producer and communicator (Dunn & Larsen, 1990; Kafai & Harel, 1991).

Discourse connotes a deep desire to understand each others' words. Discourse is more than talking. Discourse connotes a more reflective study of what is being said, a struggle to understand, where speakers constructively confront each other, experience conflict, and seek footing in a constant shift of perspectives. In effect, discourse is an analysis of communication, a metalinguistic process where meaning is questioned in the name of growth and understanding (Gee, 1990; Stubbs, 1983). Discourse is the voice we use for schooling and learning (Goodman, 1992). Design and documentation serve to focus, maintain, and improve the discourse during the negotiated process of learning.

Documentation refers to any activity that renders a performance record with sufficient detail to help others understand the behavior recorded. Thus, a single drawing by a child would not be considered documentation, but an edited videotape of the child creating a drawing or a set of redrawn portions to plot the development of the final drawing would be considered documentation. The intent of documentation is to explain, not merely to display. Documentation may or may not be publicly displayed, such as panels of photographs and text placed on the classroom walls. Documentation may be filed in a portfolio and later browsed as a collection. Strictly speaking, documentation is not a form of assessment of individual progress, but rather a form of explaining, to the constituents of the school, the depth of the children's learning and the educational rationale of activities. Documentation is central to negotiated learning and much of what this chapter discusses deals with the relation between documentation and the two other components; design and discourse.

The foregoing comments contain a distinction between design and documentation. Design seeks to instruct and documentation seeks to explain. Design is prospective and documentation is retrospective. Both are more than the physical record. Thus we use the word *documentation* instead of document, and *design* instead of designs in order to put into relief the pedagogical function of these symbolic acts.

A Diagram for all Relations

To ease our discussion of this pedagogical system, we have provided Figure 13.1. This diagram contains all three action components and all four constituents. We have deliberately made the connection rather loose among the four constituents and the three action components. Otherwise the diagram would look like a tangle and cease to be useful. We describe specific relations in the text of the chapter.

These three components—design, documentation, and discourse—form a system of relations that are everywhere reciprocal. Design can be used to improve documentation; for example, the children's drawn designs can be placed within the wall panels. Documentation can be used to improve discourse by serving as a database for reflective teaching. Discourse can be documented and then used to improve a second design session. We use the activity flow among these components as a scheme to organize the segments of this chapter. (Please note that, as we describe the interrelation among these three components, we venture into

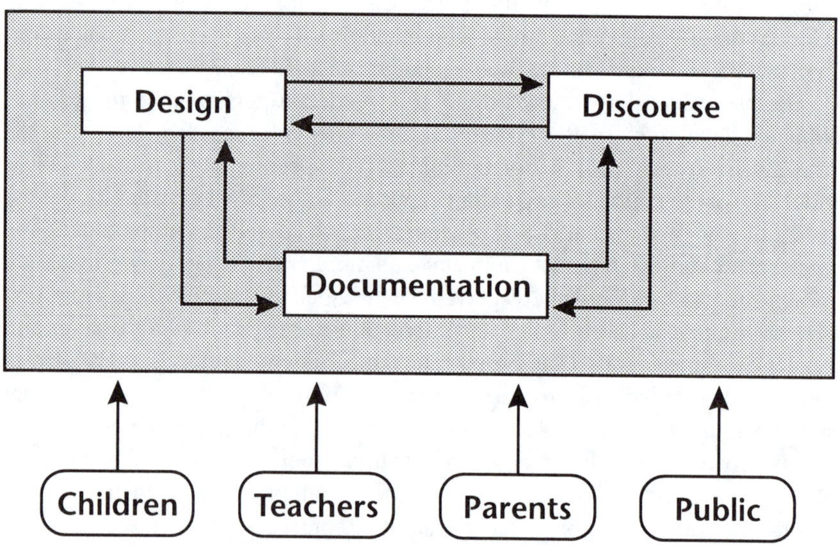

FIGURE 13.1. Components of negotiated learning.

some suggestions for practice that have not necessarily been seen in Reggio or anywhere else.)

These components serve a variety of constituents: children, teachers, parents, and the general public. Consider documentation. Selected records of the children's thoughts certainly serve the children as they revisit their own ideas to deepen and broaden the application of their concepts. Documentation helps teachers plan follow-up activities, it helps parents who want to extend the child's study into the home, and it serves the general public, who must decide on the level of support for the education program.

These relations to constituents are not simple or one way. Constituents often work together around a component to improve another component. Teachers and children together engage in a design activity and this improves their level of discourse when they study their designs. The design sessions are also documented. Teachers and children revisit these documents and that in turn improves discourse further.

Traffic Within the Diagram

A useful theory not only specifies the components of a system, but also makes propositions about traffic among those components. A theory tells us what to expect when one path is taken rather than another. In reference to the flow chart in Figure 13.1, here are some paths that exemplify the use of documentation to enhance discourse:

> Four children draw their plans for a Moon village (design). Then they use their drawings to explain the buildings to peers who ask them to clarify (design affects discourse). The teachers use an audiotape of these explanations to study assumptions children have about conditions on the Moon (discourse affects documentation).

PASSAGES TOWARD GREATER UNDERSTANDING

This diagram can illustrate principles of negotiated learning. We present these principles as a set of passages, from an initial understanding of a teaching practice to a more comprehensive understanding. We begin with the passage from description to design, which is a passage from a narrow view of representation as record to a broader view of representation as a recommendation for action.

From Description to Design

As we mentioned briefly, design has an instructive intent that is beyond mere description. This difference applies to many media, not just drawing. But for illustration's sake, let us consider the passage from drawing an object to using a drawing as a design. A drawing may be judged good if its referent can be recognized by another person. Granted, a realistic drawing can improve discourse, because it serves as a common referent, but such a drawing remains no more than a picture of something else.

A design, on the other hand, is made in order to build something or instruct someone on how to do something. The designer needs to capture action in the marks and needs to help a new reader discern these implied actions. Somehow the "reader" must translate the marks on the paper into a set of acts in order to accomplish some desired result. For example, a drawing used to build a toy wooden boat might be drawn with less detail regarding the texture of the wood and more detail for the manner in which the parts are articulated. The interface between two parts carries more information for building the boat than does the texture detail. The design also includes marks that carry a message of action and sequence that is more than a static record of the features of a stationary object. Arrows, numbers, and a row of progressive drawings are some common techniques of representing actions. This shift from visual analysis of detail to the representation of a set of procedures is a fundamental shift in science and education (Piaget, 1970). This same shift underlies the high-level use of representations in negotiated learning. Furthermore, the child's desire to explain how something should be done implies an audience that vicariously participates in the co-construction of knowledge (Vygotsky, 1934/1986; Wertsch, 1985) The dual emphasis on procedural knowledge and communication defines the interface between Piaget and Vygotsky in negotiated learning.

Here is an example of the description to design passage. A group of children were interested in the huge sunflowers outside their window. There were absolutely amazed that the blossom head contained so many seeds. The teacher thought that this prolific blossom should be preserved in the children's memory somehow, so she suggested that the children make their own rendering of this blossom using paper and colored pencils. The drawings were beautifully done, with great attention to the individual seeds in the center of huge flower. The teacher and children agreed that the drawing activity had sensitized them to details that they would not have noticed had they not taken pains to draw these details on paper.

On second thought, we decided that this flower drawing activity was too limited. We asked the children why they were amazed about the seeds in the flower head. They told us that they remembered the seed that they had placed in the ground 6 weeks ago, and now the flower has seeds in the blossom that look just like the one they planted. So we asked them to draw pictures that showed how these seeds were produced, that is, draw what they cannot see, draw what they thought were the steps that took place inside the sunflower to produce the seeds. In essence, we were asking them to design a seed factory.

The drawings were diverse, clever, and revealing. The children did not give as much attention to the graphic realism of their drawing, but rather became more interested in communicating their ideas about the procedures that yielded seeds in the flower's head. One child drew a set of drawings that portrayed the original seed advancing from the ground, inside the strawlike stalk of the sunflower, the same seed popping out of the blossom in the last picture! Through these designs of seed growth, the teacher found many more opportunities to engage the children's minds about their theories than were possible with the descriptive drawings of the sunflower *per se.*

From Display to Documentation

The passage from display to documentation travels the path from informing to educating and thereby changes the teacher's perspective from observing children to studying children. Museums, particularly science museums, are places to find examples of both displays that inform and documentation that educates. Take as an example a frequently found exhibit, a row of silhouettes that show the changing profile of the human skull over the last 100,000 years. The display of these silhouettes is not itself documentation of an evolutionary process. The panel merely displays the evolution, informs us of its occurrence. Documentation, on the other hand, would make an explicit attempt to walk us through an explanation.

For example, we could add a caption to this row of skull silhouettes: "As humans evolved, the thickness of the brow ridge decreased and the cranial capacity increased, indicating a decrease in a defensive structure and an increase in brain size." Now the row of silhouettes exemplify an interesting principle and can be studied for features that exemplify similar principles. What might the reduction of jaw length mean? Good documentation provokes study of the graphics because the text helps frame the graphics as examples of something more general than the features themselves.

When applied to negotiated learning, displays should be converted to documentation by adding interpretation and explanation to the graphics. A set of photographs pasted to posterboard showing a trip to the farm is a display. A set of photographs captioned with the children's words would still be a display. The panels need commentary to qualify as documentation.

Imagine this set of photographs with a display of the children's words. One child, looking at 12 piglets suckling on the same sow, says, "Do all the piglets get enough to eat?" Elsewhere on the panel an account is printed about how this child's concern grew into a study of sows and piglets, then cow and calves, then family size of the children in the class. The panel exemplifies how a small project grew from a real concern. Documentation invites inquiry about the children's thinking and invites predictions about effective teaching. A panel with only pictures and the children's words would not be enough. The teacher's commentary is necessary to frame the data as examples of something more general, some principle that can be applied in new contexts. Display invites pleasure and satisfaction, but is not deliberately designed to provoke hypotheses. Documentation is a research report used to enhance discourse rather than a record of a past event.

This brings us to a difference between documentation in negotiated learning and portfolios that are becoming more popular in American schools (Glazer & Brown, 1993; Tierney, 1991). Portfolios are touted as a more authentic form of assessment, primarily because portfolios are the actual artifacts that children produce as they work, which can include drawings, diagrams, math sheets, photographs, and even videotapes that when studied chronologically and in all their qualitative detail, present a unique path of progress for each child.

Documentation, as we mean it here, is more focused on children than on a child. Even when a child is featured in documentation, the intent is to have the viewer treat this child as a representative child. The documentation presents the spirit of the school, the pedagogical principles at work, which may include Shawn as the protagonist here and Rane as the protagonist there. Beware that the interest of the featured child's parent could be inversely related to the interest of the other parents. The other parents need a message to which everyone can relate.

Documentation tries to raise questions about children's thinking and teaching strategies rather than to mark the progress of all individual children. Documentation should always be defined in the context of at least the other two components, design and discourse. Technically, documentation is not an attempt to evaluate the effectiveness of teaching for all the children. The viewer is asked to assume that what one sees in the documentation of four children has happened at other times with all the children. Documentation presents the wisdom of the teachers who write the explanations and provocations, but documentation, by itself, is not a systematic evaluation of instruction. These two objectives, evaluation and documentation, should be kept separate.

From Talking to Discourse

We talk almost all the time. Sometimes we listen to our own words and to the words of others in order to understand more deeply. It is this attitude toward talking, as an intelligent pattern worthy of study, that defines the discourse of schooling (Forman & McPhail, 1993; Isaacs, 1930; Palincsar & Brown, 1984).

Take for example the following conversation from several children:

Erica: Look, my legs are long, but I am not split all the way up
John: Yeah, but your hand is split into five fingers.
Tim: Yeah, think about your hair, it is really split.
Erica: No, that's not how hair works.

We could transcribe and read this conversation as a team of teachers. We might list what the children were talking about; for example, legs, growth, what has been split, and what has not been split. But to truly understand the children's talking, we should treat it as discourse, an intelligent pattern of thoughts that is worthy of study. We do this by asking, "What are the reasons the child might have for making their claims?" Could it be that Erica saw her long legs as an indication of a process that was still operative, like rails splitting from a whole log? How does John's comment build on Erica's? Was he looking for other body parts that could have been whole, then split? Was Tim simply making a quantitative extension from five fingers to many hairs, which provoked Erica to disagree? The two children might together establish category boundaries between things that are differentiated by splitting from a larger mass and things that are multitudinous and tiny from the beginning, like the hair. The procedures used to create a form help to explain the meaning of the form.

Treating talk as discourse causes teachers to look for theories, assumptions, false premises, misapplications, clever analogies, ambiguities, and differences in communicative intent, all of which are pieces to be negotiated into shared meaning by the group. Discourse analysis carries over into teachers talking to teachers, to parents, to the public, and all possible relations portrayed at the bottom of Figure 13.1. Discourse also changes as it is affected by design and documentation, and of course, discourse changes design and documentation. As we study the children's designs, hear them explain their plans, and revisit our documentation of these projects, we begin to speak differently about our subject matter, the children. We speak of them as exemplifications of growth, development, and power. Furthermore, as we take explicit note of how we speak differently we become conscious of our own professional development. Instead of saying, "the children seem to enjoy the activity," we say, "the children enjoy watching the birds without being noticed." These are not trivial or jargon differences in discourse. They bespeak fundamental shifts in levels of analysis and understanding (see Solisken, Wilson, & Willette, 1993).

From Remembering to Revisiting

Teachers of young children can serve as a memory, a record of an experience that can be revisited. This function can be served by writing down what the children say and then reading these words back to the child on a later day when the children are trying to extend their understanding of something. Or the teacher can show the children photographs of the experience and ask them to use the photographs to help them remember what they were doing and thinking during that experience.

There is a difference between remembering what one did and revisiting the experience. For remembering, the children are content with a simple listing of what they did: "We saw a pig. We rode the tractor. We looked down into the deep silo." But revisiting is more than remembering. Revisiting is just that, a return to a place of significance for the purpose of reestablishing friendly relations and establishing new relations, like going to one's hometown after a long absence. As a visitor, you now look on the experience as an outsider. You no longer reside in the experience, but you seek to establish a new meaning and new feelings from that experience. You are a bit more detached, as a nonresident, but no less eager to be there. The past is reconstructed from the new perspectives of the present. You look for patterns to create meaning and for connections that were not obvious while you were resident in the experience.

"I remember you said that the man on the tractor made it turn by stopping one of the big wheels. Let's remember what you were thinking and try to figure out what you meant," the teacher begins as she invites the children to revisit their field trip to the farm. In regards to an experiment with shadows, "Here is a photograph of your jumping in the sunlight. Tell me what you were thinking just as you were in midair over your shadow." Here the teacher is asking two girls to confront their question about whether one's shadow is always attached to one's feet. Note that the teacher does not say, "Look at the photograph and tell me if your feet are attached to your shadow." The focus is on memories about the children's thinking, not photographic evidence of an answer.

The initial question might be to recall a thought or an observation, but the teacher carefully chooses memories that will draw the children into conversations about something that was unresolved or an incomplete action. It is the intent of revisiting to take children further and not simply list the places they have been. The photograph should be treated as a door to enter a world of possible events, not as a window that pictures a single time and place (Forman, 1995).

From Symbol to Language to Languages

As we ask children to represent their thoughts, it is important to understand the concepts of a symbol and a language. We have often heard the phrase from Reggio Emilia, "100 languages of children." What does this mean? It could refer to the 100 different ways children can use their native language to express their general attitude toward something. Or, more literally, it could mean that there are 100 different symbol systems that qualify as protolanguages that children could use if the classroom culture would allow it (see Gardner, 1983). For example, several children choose to use gesture to retell the story of a lion capturing a gazelle; others use music and others use drawings. We need some clarity on this often-used phrase.

The first meaning of languages can best be translated as *voice* as in "he speaks with the voice of authority." Children have a hundred such voices. We also know that *voice* is central to revelations about gender differences in communication styles (Tannen, 1982, 1989). Although the concept of voice is important, it is probably not the meaning implied in the phrase "100 languages of children." Let us look more closely at the second meaning, different symbol systems.

A language is more than a set of symbols. A language contains rules of combining these symbols to convey meaning. Thus, a panel where each child's photograph contains a little animal stamp to stand for that child's identity is not a language. But a child's stamp followed by an arrow and another child's stamp could mean, "Amy likes Zoe." A simple syntax is born, and with it a new language for children to invent and explore relations. Likewise, a clay figure of a runner is a symbol, but is not itself a language. However, when 12 children make different clay figures in order to tell the other children how to play "Drop the Handkerchief," these clay figures become the elements in a proto language. Tree leaves can be arranged on posterboard in rows, but this is not a language of leaves because it tells us nothing. However, if the children tried to arrange the leaves to show the presence of a strong wind or a weak wind, then the relation among the leaves would constitute a proto syntax and the whole enterprise would engage the children to think about the language of leaves and what the leaves can tell us. These various media, when combined to tell a story, form the 100 languages.

In summary, we need to move children beyond the level of making symbols into the level of inventing language and from the stance of using only the native spoken language to the use of many different symbol systems: leaves, gestures, rubber stamps, clay, and so on. It is the nature of the relation among the symbols that converts the medium into a message; and it is the presence of an intended message that motivates children to negotiate shared meanings and to co-construct knowledge.

From Listening to Hearing

We can give ourselves time to listen to children. We can say that our classroom is child centered. We can transcribe the children's conversations and affirm the importance of their words. We may listen, but what do we hear?

To foster negotiated learning it is essential for teachers to listen with the third ear, to hear the implied meanings of children's words. Take the case of Hattie, who was upset with a teacher, Tom, who was wearing over his face a life-size photographic mask of Lisa, another teacher. Hattie said to Tom, "You can't do that, that's Lisa's name" (Forman & Kuschner, 1986, p. 216). We can listen to Hattie's exact words and we can print them on a panel that documents the encounter, but what is the deeper structure of Hattie's complaint? What have we heard her say?

Hattie, like other 4-year-olds, probably has some difficulty distinguishing between words that refer to *objects* and words that refer to *words.* The word *Lisa* refers to, at a minimum, the unique face, an object; but the word *name* refers to the spoken word we use to identify that unique face. Hattie treats all words as symbols that refer to objects, so it makes sense to her to say *name* when *face*

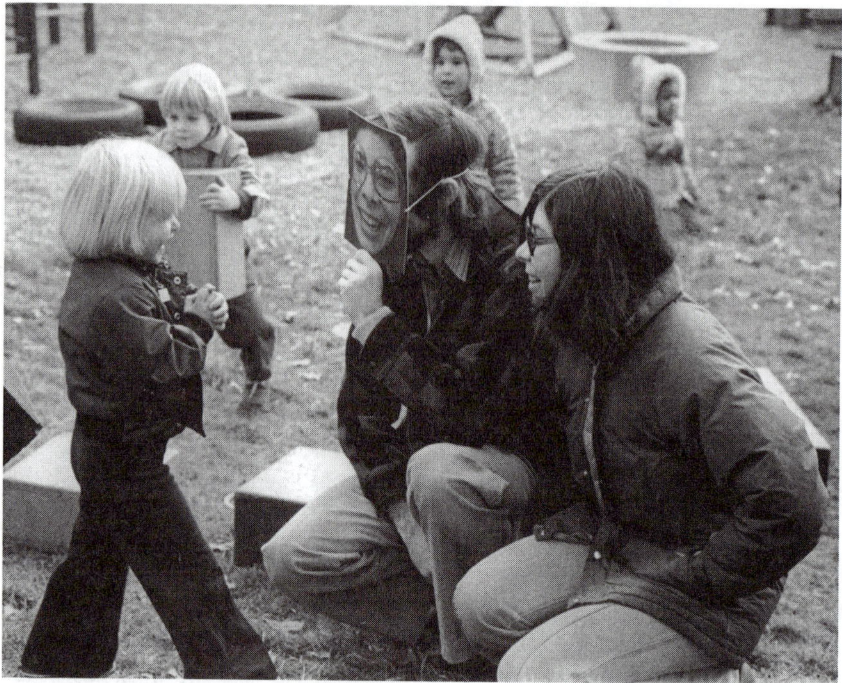

FIGURE 13.2. Hattie says to Tom, "You can't do that, that's Lisa's name."

would be better, albeit the removable face is psychologically somewhere between the concept *name* and *face*. Nevertheless, the idea that the word *name* refers to another word (*Lisa*) is a bit beyond the ken of the average 4-year-old. So we listen to Hattie's exact words, but our third ear hears the struggle she is having with the more difficult forms of reference. From this understanding we are in a better position to negotiate and scaffold her progress.

From Understanding to Provocations

Continuing the example of Hattie, what might we do with this understanding? Granted, teachers who foster negotiated learning become researchers, but they must translate their study of children into a design for education. Do we simply ask Hattie, "What do you mean?" Do we ask Hattie, "Why did you say 'name' instead of 'face'?" Asking such direct questions would be like asking an infant why she repeatedly throws her cup from the high chair. We have to design encounters that cause children to engage the differences between these concepts, symbols for things versus symbols for words.

The photographic masks were one such encounter, albeit, an unplanned

The Intelligence of a Puddle (Diana School)

Comments by George Forman

When rain leaves a puddle, thanks to the good fortune of there being a hole in the ground and a little sunshine, children are full of joy. If the adults do not place limits and instead play the game, the puddle of water then can become for the children an entire universe to observe. (Malaguzzi, 1987)

Photo 1: The children are filled with anticipation. The rain has stopped. They don their boots to run outside and step into the puddle. As they approach the puddle they observe their own reflection. At this particular moment one girl can see only the upper torso of her body. The partial reflection of the whole body is rather curious to the children.

Photo 2: The children step gently. They notice both the changes in the water and the reflections. "The water is lazy, but when we walk in it, it makes little waves. They get bigger and bigger." the child herself is the epicenter of the intriguing event. Another child says, "Hey, I can see myself." A third joins in, "Me too!" The first says, "But the colors are all dirty!" sensitive to how the agitated dirt affects this new mirror.

Photo 3: One child leans over, "Help, we are under water." "I can touch the top of the tree (reflection) because this is another world, a world of water." Another says, "It is like entering in the reflection and living under water," acknowledging the liquid state of an image that can be entered.

Photo 4: A teacher places a mirror on the ground. One child remembers the muddy water: "Hey, now the colors are right!" A girl pushes up on her hands on the mirror, "Help, I am falling into a world without end." Perhaps the reflection of the blue sky makes the mirror on the ground look like an infinite continuation of the world above. A hole through the earth.

Photo 5: Now children make paper cut outs to stand around the mirror. The cut outs have details drawn on their surface as if the children realize, unlike shadows, these details will be reproduced in the reflections.

Photo 6: They place their cut outs around the mirror. A child remarks, "When you are close to a puddle, you see everything, but if you are far away, you see less and less." Another counters, "But if I put my head down close, I see also the trees that are far away." Which could mean that you don't see less and less, you just see things other than yourself.

Photo 7: The children continue their study of reflections by drawing a puddle on blank paper and placing their cut outs around the drawing. But now they have to construct the reflections, since there is no mirror. This progression from real puddle to mirror to drawing is well conceived.

Photo 8: A teacher offers the children a flashlight to make it possible for them to explore shadows as well as reflections. Contrasts help the children understand what a reflection is not, as well as what it is.

Photo 9: Notice the drawings include both figures with detail inside the contour lines and reflections—gray figures with no details inside the shadows. Also, notice that the projected angles of puddle figures are true to their source cut outs and appropriately show partial bodies.

Photo 10: The girl with the flashlight (Photo 8) has drawn a figure of herself and decides to study her reflection in the mirror in order to improve her drawing. She stands on the mirror. "Look, I can see my underpants." She raises her left leg and notices how it appears in the mirror, showing the under side of her leg.

Photo 11: She deliberately bends the left leg forward on her paper cut out figure. Then she carefully draws the reflection of the bottom of her leg, impressed that the mirror lets one see the underside of things. In these ways, using these props, the children are able to make their thoughts visible so that they can ask even better questions about the relations of light, space, and point of view.

Photo 12: The young girl has clearly drawn shadows and reflections. Recall how she cast a shadow with a flashlight (Photo 7) as a way to explore the invarients of a shadow. You will see in the final conversation that the children gradually construct the invariants of shadows and reflections. Shadows are always dark while reflections capture the color, albeit sometimes dull from muddy water. Shadows are always attached to your feet, but your reflection is sometimes not attached to your feet (partial reflection of the body) when you are not standing directly adjacent to the edge of the puddle or the mirror.

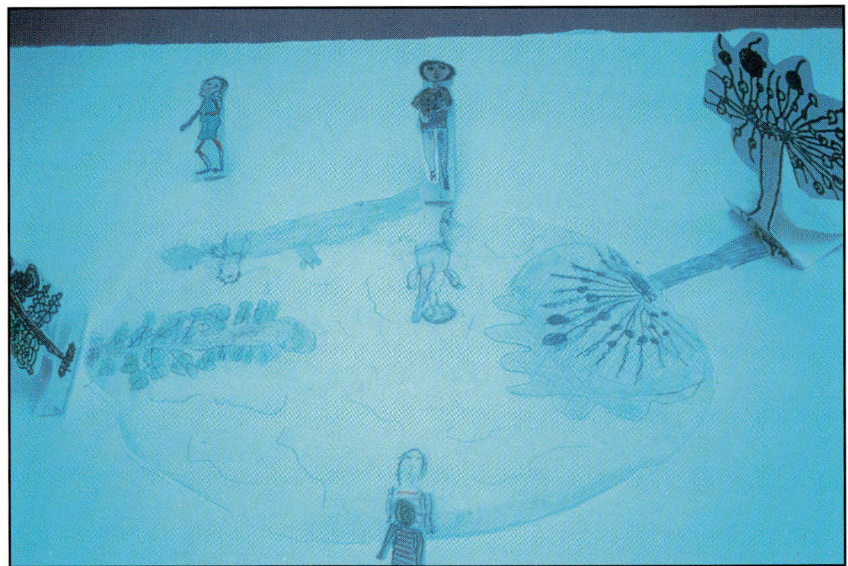

Photo 13: The children have constructed reflections and shadows in their drawings and made a composite drawing of figures around a single puddle. they reveal their knowledge of projected angles, details, and scope. The drawings allow the children to make explicit, and thereby to consolidate, their understanding. The children represent the partial reflections that result when the figures are positioned away from the puddle's rim. Their composite shadows show how the puddle presents the front of a cut out figure which has its back to the point of view. But in one case a child paid more attention to copying the features exactly than to capturing the correct orientation of the profile. The reflection has a profile facing in an orientation opposite to that of the paper cut out. Even this concept will come in time as the children use these clever props to negotiate their understandings with each other.

The children summarize their findings:

"The shadow is there when the sun is out. But can you see the reflection then also?"

"When the sun is out, the reflection looks faded. The light fades everything."

"No, you are wrong. The reflection is not close to you; it is deep and it has colors. Instead, it is the shadow that is near you and has no colors but is always dark."

encounter. We support negotiated learning by extending these fortuitous discoveries into a variety of contexts. Ideally teachers will meet as a team and discuss Hattie's comments, look in their documentation for other episodes where children are dealing with this transition to word–word relations, and plan ways to provoke the children to reflect on these different types of symbols. It could be that the teachers and children will revisit the photographic mask game, where Lisa wore Tom's photograph and Tom wore Lisa's photograph mask. Together with the children a new game could be planned. Perhaps the children want to place their own photograph mask over their best friend's face, or place a printed sign "chair" on the table and a sign "table" on the chair. If the children invent this game of inverting the markers for identity, they may be provoked to think, for the first time, about the range of referents that words can have, and eventually that the word *name* refers to a word, not an object.

From Encounters to Projects

When possible, learning encounters should be expanded to projects. Projects have a longer duration, have more contexts that provoke a given set of concepts, have a community atmosphere to them, involve more children as they progress, and progress to more complex concepts as they run their course. Projects also have some central theme in which children have an emotional investment. This is one of the most important differences between learning encounters and projects.

In a curriculum based on negotiated learning, teachers and children get excited about what they are doing. They do things that are big and wonderful and often rather ambitious, like building an amusement park for the birds that visit their playground or holding an Olympic-style long jump contest for the entire school. But these projects can emerge from an episode such as the learning encounter between Hattie and the photographic mask.

In a class meeting the children and teachers decide that pictures placed in the wrong place, like Lisa's photograph on Tom's head, can be confusing, but pictures placed in the correct place can be helpful. By degrees and in the course of several meetings, the teachers and children decide to study pictures they see outside. One child mentions the pictures he sees on the road, such as the picture of children playing that is a warning for cars to be alert. The children decide to add pictures all over their classroom and playground that will inform people about what to do, what to watch out for, ground rules, and so forth.

A variation of this project was actually done at The Eighth of March school in Reggio Emilia. Eventually the children invented an entire fantasy about a dragon, snakes in a pit, and a princess held captive in a tower, requiring road signs for all rescuing knights. The medieval adventure of this project motivated the children to invent these symbols, while not in the least diminishing their high-level thinking about how symbols convey meaning. In fact, these children invented the convention that any pictures drawn inside a triangle meant "danger" and any picture drawn inside a circle was a directional pointer.

From Assessment to Study

Assessment, that follows from negotiated learning, involves the ongoing study of children. This study enables teachers to plan a responsive curriculum that supports individual and group development. It is not done to compare children, to determine placement or inclusion into programs, or to label or grade. It is done in order to understand children—their schema, feelings, interests, dispositions, and capabilities. This knowledge makes it possible for teachers to plan learning experiences that are meaningful and yet challenging to children.

Assessment of this nature is not focused on what children cannot do, but rather on what they can do, independently, with assistance, and in different kinds of social contexts. It is a dynamic and flexible process. It does not aim to freeze the child in time in order to quantify achievement or development through a score, rating, or grade. It is a living, contextualized process that aims to understand children within ever-changing life experiences and situations. Documentation, as we have described it, is at the heart of this kind of assessment.

Much attention has been given in recent years to promoting democracy in the classroom, to developing a sense of community in schools, and to cooperative learning, but we seem to assess the effects of these kinds of strategies on only the individual. Our work with parents, in like manner, is solely focused on their own child, not the group. Sometimes we present what the child can do in group situations, but generally these are cases where the child's behavior within a group is extracted in order to characterize the individual child, not the group.

The educators in Reggio Emilia study and assess the development of the individual, but also the development of the group, the development of a community of learners, a community of caring people. They celebrate how children learn from and with each other. By presenting documentation on the work of the group, and relating particular children's progress to the development of the group, teachers, parents, and children focus on the social dynamics of learning. Through negotiated learning, educators collaborate to develop a social consciousness about the rights of all young children.

From Parent Involvement to Intellectual Partnership

Many teachers view parent involvement as parent education. This could mean that the teacher's job is to share her expert knowledge with parents. From this standpoint, teachers might consider organizing documentation panels in order to give information to parents about their children's learning. If teachers operate on this assumption about the teacher's role in relationship to parents, documentation is likely to be used as a one-way communication. Parents are not seen as designers, nor are they invited to engage in discourse with teachers. Parents may be encouraged to ask questions about documentation, but not to debate or supplement. Parents are expected to look to the teacher as a source of information.

On the other hand, if we apply the principles of negotiated learning to our work with parents, documentation of children's experiences can be used by teachers to support interactive communication, to provide a focus for discourse between teachers and parents. The observations teachers have documented through photography, audiotaping, anecdotal records, note taking, videos, or collections of children's work can be shared and explained, and then serve as a base for further inquiry, discussion, and analysis. Just as teachers share such documentation with each other in order to gain multiple perspectives that lead to new insights into children's thinking, they can do so with parents. Parents offer different kinds of insights. They have knowledge of children outside the classroom. Their observations, combined with the teachers' observations, can lead to an even deeper understanding of children's thoughts, feelings, and dispositions. By engaging in such discourse, parents and teacher may be able to negotiate an understanding of the learning documented. They become study partners. Designs for future learning experiences naturally flow from this kind of study.

Teachers invite parents, whenever possible, to think with them not only about how to support children's learning, but also about how to best communicate with other parents. If panels or other forms of documentation are to be read by parents, what better way to test the readability than to invite a representative parent to consult in the process.

Records of parent involvement can promote partnership with families. It is important to keep records of any form of parent involvement (e.g., parent–teacher committee meetings, parent–teacher conferences, parent participation in contributing and organizing materials for the classroom). Records might take the form of photographs, written descriptions of events, minutes of meetings, videotapes of family celebrations or field trips, or written records of parent questions or comments. These records are then converted to documentation by revisiting them with parents in order to understand the parents' role in negotiated learning. Such records can provide a common reference for discourse, a common memory of experiences or accomplishments that otherwise may have been forgotten or remembered differently. This conversion of records to documentation paradoxically can generate richer experiences in the future, much as reading last year's journal about a trip will enrich this year's trip. If the journal is not revisited, the current trip stands to yield only the same discoveries forgotten from the first one, or even worse, the failure to generalize our subtle insights to new experiences. Our subtle insights are most easily forgotten and require the support of documentation to yield growth from experience.

Documentation of parent involvement can be organized and displayed in the form of panels that invite the viewer to recognize the many and diverse opportunities for parents to become intellectual partners in curriculum support. The display, again, becomes more than an accounting of parent involvement if it includes notes about the process, purpose, and value of the involvement. Quotes or questions from parents can be added to panels in order to communicate parent perspectives on the experience. We have even displayed photographs of parents looking at classroom panels with their children. Such moments, captured and displayed, give a visible presence to parental involvement in the study of their children's work and give a clear message of the partnership among teacher, child, and parent and the essential and tangible form of this trilogy. Photographs of parents looking at panels about projects express the *study of study* that defines the discourse that supports negotiated learning.

Parent involvement documentation can be organized and disseminated in many other forms, such as newsletters, phone messages, binders of information, videotapes, and so on. The form of documentation should suit the population for whom it is targeted. Take the example of a class where parents bring their children to school or frequent the classroom regularly. In this case, wall panels very well may be an efficient means of communication. On the other hand, in a program where parents seldom visit the school or frequent it only occasionally, other forms of documentation may be more effective in communicating and affirming parent involvement. A newsletter or minutes of parent meetings could be sent home. A lending library of videotapes or multimedia of parent involvement inside or outside the classroom might be made available. A combination of these forms of documentation may be even better, because children, teachers, and visitors to the schools are also audiences for parent involvement documentation panels. If teachers wish to use any of these records to develop partnerships, they need to be designed in ways that invite response and dialogue.

From Cooperation to Co-Construction

The components of design, documentation, and discourse have the power to transform teacher–teacher relations and to move the teaching team from routine cooperation to a truly generative co-construction of new knowledge. In the first case, team members can cooperate by staying within a defined role, by acknowledging each member's area of expertise, and by providing material and psychological support for each other. But these features of cooperation may not lead to growth through co-construction where each team member is seen both as a learner and a teacher, where each team member feels comfortable about making suggestions regarding another member's work. The dynamics of negotiation involve the creative use of confrontation and conflict.

Collective reflection and analysis of documentation at planning meetings leads to more coordinated planning in which teaching teams make better decisions about how to organize themselves and their time, to share their work, yet differentiate it in order to best support the diverse needs of children within small group projects, individualized activity, or larger group learning experiences.

Another aspect of organization that supports collaboration among teachers is the documentation of team discussions and planning. In negotiated learning, teacher planning is complex and time consuming. It involves the collective study of the words and work of children and then planning for possible experiences that connect with or challenge children's current schema. When such study and planning for possibilities has been done, the team must then agree to strategies for presenting the plans to children so that they will want to participate. Teachers must determine the roles that one or more team members will play in regard to facilitating small group activities, while another monitors the activity of the rest of the children. They must plan strategies and time for documenting ongoing observations of learning; they must determine who will have responsibility for organizing appropriate documentation tools (e.g., camera, camcorder, tape recorder, paper and pen) and who will use them, they must schedule time to analyze the ongoing documentation that is collected and to involve parents through documentation and discourse. As the project evolves they need to examine ways to use documentation (e.g., photographs, slides, videotape, transcripts of children's dialogues, and children's drawings, writing, paintings, constructions) to sustain children's interests and involvement in the project (see Fyfe, Cadwell & Phillips, Chapter 22, this volume).

Minutes preserve the collective memory of the group about these teacher agreements and remind each member of the team about how they will coordinate their work. Without documentation of this sort, complete team efforts can easily fall apart. It is relatively easy to simply divide work among teachers in a preset and fixed curriculum, but to coordinate the flow of work to support negotiated learning, teachers must engage in self-reflective planning. Such planning, organization, and co-construction of purposes and possibilities enables teachers to function efficiently and flexibly in ways that are responsive to children.

From Co-Construction to Advocacy and Community Support

Just as it does with other constituents, documentation can give educators and the public a common platform for discourse about what goes on in schools. It gives to the public something tangible, visible, and accessible. If done well, it invites dialogue among educators, parents, and public. It can provide better facts to discuss in order to address long-held beliefs. Take the case of 4-foot rope lengths, placed as loose strands on the classroom floor. These rope strands are used in many preprimary schools in Reggio as a play material. The legal-minded public often has the initial reaction that ropes are too dangerous as a free play material for young children. But actual photographs and videos of how children use the 4-foot spans of rope as pretend fire hoses, as a two-way telephone line, as a line to guide block building on the floor, as a pulley rope when looped around a table leg, and even as a game in a supervised tug of war, would dispel the fear that braided cotton rope is a dangerous material.

Too often we use sweeping generalizations when we attempt to change public opinion about our schools. We loudly make claims such as:

- Children learn best in small groups!
- Children need hands-on materials to help them learn!
- Teachers need more time for planning and reflection!
- The environment is the third teacher!
- Children need meaningful projects, not drill on skills!

We may even back up these positions with evidence from research. We may be very articulate in communicating these positions and needs for resources and occasionally succeed in swaying votes on a particular school referendum. However, such accomplishments are often short-lived. Public opinion can easily change when someone or some group speaks louder and stronger.

If we apply the principles of co-construction to our efforts in gaining community support, we are less inclined to proclaim to the community and more inclined to engage community members in discourse about educational issues. We often feel that the community is not interested in the details of our work, so we present the sweeping "should" and "ought" to gain their support. But our assumption that community members feel too distant from our class projects assures that they will remain so. We have learned from Reggio Emilia that documentation can be a powerful tool for engaging the public in reflective discourse (Rinaldi, 1996). Documentation panels make visible the work of the schools and the capacities of children. Real examples of documented learning offer the public a more particular kind of knowledge that empowers and provokes them to reflect, question, and rethink or reconstruct the image of the child and the rights of children to quality education.

When the children of Reggio Emilia interview the farmer about the process of harvesting the grapes or ask the street worker about the city's underground drainage system, they and their teachers are giving community members first-hand experience with the kinds of active learning processes that are characteristic of good schools. The documentation of these community-based activities can be returned to the community members as small booklets; for example, booklets sent to the Audubon Society volunteers who helped hang the bird houses, to the public works people who helped add a new water supply. These documents build personal bonds and meaningful connections between children and adults in the community. These smaller documents often increase attendance to open house events at the schools, which in turn provide opportunities for discourse among educators, parents, and community members.

Educators begin to ask community members for intellectual contributions, not just manual or monetary ones. They treat the community as a "fund of knowledge" for children (Moll, 1990). This kind of treatment is an expression of respect, and a way to build connections through shared experience leading to shared conceptions of being and sense of belonging. It strengthens the "we" identity of a community that cares about each other and helps each other learn and live more productive lives. These are the ingredients of effective advocacy.

We have to be careful not to assume that any contact with the community will engender support for the schools, or that such contact is an inherent good. The community members involved, let's say in a class project, need to hear good questions from the children, need to sense that the teaching staff have prepared children for the field trip, and need to learn how the experience will be used in the classroom in the future weeks. No one likes to feel that they have provided only a diversion for children, an outing to the fire station, an emotional high that is isolated from true educational objectives, a trip to a celebrated place leaving with only a plastic fire hat as a memory.

Once again, this is where the combined components of design, documentation, and discourse can assure more generative encounters with community members. Children, before meeting the community members, will discuss their expectations in group meetings. They will design a purpose, a set of questions, and a reason for making the trip. They may even draw what they expect to see and then take these drawings with them as hypotheses to check out. They will bring a camera and an audio recorder to document the experience, which in turn will indicate to the community members the seriousness of the trip for the children. They may bring their sketch pads in some cases. As was mentioned, the children will also share these records with the community members later when they create a documentation for public viewing. This cycle from designing the purpose of the experience to documenting the experience to engaging the community in discourse during and after the experience are essential components needed to create an informed advocacy and community support.

SUMMARY OF THE DESIGN, DOCUMENTATION, DISCOURSE SYSTEM

To summarize how these three components affect each other, we follow the traffic of a classroom activity using Figure 13.1. Let us say that a group of children want to enter a checker tournament with another school in the town. Two children know how to play checkers fairly well, but they do not know how to explain their skill to others. The class decides to take notes on how these two children play. These notes are written in a notation system that the children invented *(documentation)*. These notes are then summarized and organized into a guide for more novice children *(design from documentation)*. The expert players use the guide to walk the more novice players through a variety of board set-ups. The novice and expert discuss the rationale contained in the notes *(discourse from design)*. The teacher videotapes the lessons *(documentation from design)* so that the students can revisit these lessons. The children discuss how effective the lessons were and how well the checkers strategies worked *(discourse from documentation)*.

The parents study the documentation and marvel not only at how well the children play checkers but also at how well they can explain their expertise to others and how well the novice players explain what they need in order to understand. The parents listen to each other as they study the documentary video *(discourse from documentation)* and make plans for how they will help the children learn other board strategies *(design from discourse)*. These plans are brought before the children for discussion *(discourse from design)*.

Documents of the design meetings by the parents and the lessons from the more expert children are revisited by the teachers *(discourse from documentation and from design)*. The teachers create panels using video prints and printed words from the documented activities. The teachers add their own commentary to these panels explaining what the children, teachers, and parents learned from these experiences *(documentation from discourse)*. Then new parents and the general public come to the school to read these panels. The panels become the focus of a discussion for continuing the co-constructive thrust of the school *(discourse from documentation;* then *design from discourse)*.

In these various ways, the community of the school produces the following:

- Drawings function as design.
- Descriptions transform into documentation.
- Talking elevates to discourse.
- Remembering supports revisiting.
- Symbols combine into languages.
- Listening includes hearing.
- Understanding leads to provocations.
- Encounters expand to projects.
- Assessment is replaced by study.
- Parent involvement develops into intellectual partnership.

And what could be dismissed as only a beautiful example of cooperation becomes a generative case of co-construction, generative with the special consequence of creating an informed public who will advocate for the continued success of the school program.

REFERENCES

Berger, P., & Luckmann, T. (1966). *The social construction of reality.* New York: Irvington.

Bruner, J. (1990). *Acts of meaning.* Cambridge, MA: Harvard University Press.

Doise, W., Mugny, G., & Perret-Clemont, A.N. (1975). Social interaction and the development of cognitive operations. *European Journal of Social Psychology, 5,* 367–383.

Dunn, S., & Larsen, R. (1990). *Design technology.* New York: Falmer Press.

Forman, E.A., & McPhail, J. (1993). Vygotskian perspective on children's collaborative problem solving activities. In E.A. Forman, N. Minick, & C.A. Stone (Eds). *Contexts for learning,* (pp. 213–229). New York: Oxford University Press.

Forman, G. (1995). Constructivism and the project approach. In C. Fosnot (Ed.), *Constructivism: Theory, perspectives, and practice* (pp. 172–181). New York: Teachers College Press.

Forman, G., & Gandini, L. (1994). *An amusement park for birds* [VHS 90-minute video]. Amherst, MA: Performanetics.

Forman, G., & Kuschner, D. (1986). *The child's construction of knowledge,* Washington, DC: NAEYC Publications.

Fyfe, B., & Forman, G. (1996). The negotiated curriculum. *Innovations in Early Education: The International Reggio Exchange, 3*(4), 4–7.

Gardner, H. (1983). *Frames of mind: The theory of multiple intelligences.* New York: Basic Books.

Gee, J. (1990). *Social linguistics and literacies: Ideology in discourses.* New York: Falmer Press.

Glazer, S.M., & Brown, C.S. (1993). *Portfolios and beyond.* Norwood, MA: Christopher Gordon.

Goodman, K. (1992, September). Why whole language is today's agenda in education. *Language Arts,* 69, 354–363.

Isaacs, S. (1930). *Intellectual growth in young children, with an appendix on children's "why" questions by Nathan Isaacs.* London: Routledge & Kegan Paul.

Jankowicz, A.D. (1995). Negotiating shared meanings, A discourse in two voices. *The Journal of Constructivist Psychology, 8*(2), 341–348.

Kafai, Y., & Harel, I. (1991). Learning through design and teaching. In I. Harel & S. Papert (Eds.), *Constructionism* (pp. 85–110). Norwood, NJ: Ablex.

Moll, L. (1990). Creating zones of possibilities: Combining social contexts for instruction. In L. Moll (Ed.), *Vygotsky and education* (pp. 319–348). Cambridge, UK: Cambridge University Press.

Palincsar, A.S., & Brown, A.L. (1984). Reciprocal teaching. *Cognition and Instruction, 1,* 117–175.

Piaget, J. (1970). *Science of education and the psychology of the child.* Grossman: New York.

Piaget, J. (1978). *The development of thought: Equilibration of cognitive structures.* London: Blackwell.

Rinaldi, C. (1996). Malaguzzi and the teachers. *Innovations in Early Education: The International Reggio Exchange, 3*(4), 1–3.

Solisken, J., Wilson, J., & Willette, J. (1993, Fall). Interweaving stories: Creating a multicultural classroom through school/home/university collaboration. *Democracy and Education,* 16–21.

Stubbs, M. (1983). *Discourse analysis: The sociolinguistic analysis of natural language.* Chicago:

The University of Chicago Press.

Tannen, D. (1982). Ethnic style in male–female conversation. In J.J. Gumperz (Ed.), *Language and social identity* (pp. 114–122). Cambridge, UK: Cambridge University Press.

Tannen, D. (1989). *Talking voices: Repetition, dialogue, and imagery in conversational discourse.* New York: Cambridge University Press.

Tharp, R.G., & Gallimore, R. (1988). *Rousing minds to life: Teaching, learning, and schooling in social context.* Cambridge, MA: Harvard University Press.

Tierney, R. (1991). *Portfolio assessment in the reading-writing classroom.* Norwood, MA: Christopher Gordon.

Tudge, J., & Winterhoff, P.A. (1993). Vygotsky, Piaget, and Bandura: Perspectives on the relations between the social world and cognitive development. *Human Development, 36,* 61–81.

von Glaserfeld, E. (1995). *Radical constructivism: A way of knowing and learning.* London: Falmer.

Vygotsky, L.S. (1986). *Thought and language* (A. Kozulin, Trans.). Cambridge, MA: MIT Press. (Original work published 1934).

Wertsch, J.V. (Ed.). (1985). *Culture, communication, and cognition.* Cambridge, UK: Cambridge University Press.

Wood, D., Bruner, J., & Ross, G. (1976). The role of tutoring in problem solving, *Journal of Child Psychology and Psychiatry, 17,* 89–100.

Drawing by children of the Reggio Emilia schools.

chapter 14

Theory and Praxis in Reggio Emilia: They Know What They Are Doing, and Why

Rebecca S. New

There is much to marvel about within the infant–toddler centers and preprimary schools of Reggio Emilia, as their growing international acclaim attests. Yet the enthralling beauty of the classrooms, the awe-inspiring quality of the children's work, and the compelling appeal of Reggio Emilia's more visible practices may also blind outsiders to the ideological underpinnings of this long-term collaborative endeavor. Many have noted the affinity between Reggio Emilia's philosophy of early care and education and that which has characterized past and present interpretations of high-quality early childhood programs in the United States (Barden, 1993; Bredekamp, 1993; New, 1990). Yet even as some rush to assign trademark status to its name, this Italian community serves as a source of perturbation in the field; and close inspection of their practices provides challenges to American assumptions of what is normative, feasible, desirable, and appropriate (New, 1993b). The stance that motivates this chapter is that there is more to be gained by understanding Reggio Emilian interpretations of early childhood education, both ideological and practical, than will be accomplished by direct emulation of their practices (New, 1997). Such an understanding has the potential not only to increase our appreciation of "the Reggio Emilia approach," but may contribute to the development of a more coherent vision for our own work as well.

To that end, the primary purpose of this chapter is to examine contributions from Reggio Emilia to a sociocultural theory of knowledge construction. A related aim draws on Reggio Emilia's interpretation of teachers as researchers to demonstrate the utility of such a theory to inform pedagogical practice, thereby reconceptualizing the relationship between theory and praxis as it is currently characterized in the field of early education. The chapter concludes by considering the example of Reggio Emilia as it illustrates the inextricable relationship between theories of human development and the penumbra of values, beliefs, and goals of the surrounding sociocultural context.

The discussion begins by briefly considering Reggio Emilia's entry into the broader context of a contemporary paradigm shift in American pedagogical thought.

REGGIO EMILIA: A PEBBLE IN THE POND

Over the course of the last decade, many in the field of U.S. early childhood education have been involved in three related enterprises: debating the concept and content of professional guidelines for the determination of developmentally appropriate practices (Bredekamp, 1987, 1993; Kessler & Swadener, 1992; Mallory & New, 1994a); evaluating constructivism as a point of reference for sound early educational practice (Berk & Winsler, 1995; DeVries & Kohlberg, 1987; Mallory & New, 1994b); and becoming increasingly familiar with and enamored of "the Reggio Emilia approach," to the point that there are now Reggio Emilia support networks and dedicated online discussion groups. The fortuitous timing of Reggio Emilia's entrance into U.S. educational discourse has contributed to its significant role in contemporary discussions of each of the two related issues. In particular, Reggio Emilia has served as a major point of reference in the evaluation of guidelines for developmentally appropriate practice. First used to highlight the ethnocentricism in the initial position statement (New, 1993b), examples from Reggio Emilia are now interspersed throughout the revised edition to support principles of developmentally appropriate practice (Bredekamp & Copple, 1997). This chapter continues the discussion, this time taking advantage of our increased conceptual knowledge of Reggio Emilia to join the constructivist debates that are characterizing professional discourse and activity in the broader field of education.

CONSTRUCTIVIST THEORY: VARIATIONS ON A THEME

There is now a burgeoning body of educational literature on constructivist theories, each claiming hegemony with respect to its particular emphases and interpretations, all sharing the belief that knowledge is constructed by the learner rather than being transmitted to the learner. Many have join the chorus in making "the case for constructivist classrooms" (Brooks & Brooks, 1993) finding common cause in the dramatic contrast between this now generally accepted premise of knowledge construction and the more traditional "minimic" views of teaching and learning that have characterized U.S. education for much of this century. In spite of continued declarations that "constructivism is not a theory about teaching" (Brooks & Brooks, 1993, p. vii), the constructivist paradigm now serves as the basis for school reform efforts across the U.S., including the movement to inclusive special education (Harris & Graham, 1994). Indicative of the powerful pull of this ideological shift, some view the constructivist movement as tantamount to a new religion (Phillips, 1994); still others would agree that the paradigmatic shift toward constructivism falls within the tradition of a major scientific revolution (Kuhn, 1962/1970). Notwithstanding the strength of the general constructivist stance, the differences among "the many faces of constructivism" are significant enough to warrant extensive deliberation and analysis (Phillips, 1995; also see Cobb, 1994a, 1994b, 1995; Prawat & Floden, 1994). In response to concerns of conceptual ambiguity and amid heightened interest in the general theoretical constructs, recent constructivist analyses have sought to delineate major differences among the various constructivist propositions as well as to establish empirical bases for supporting major arguments. For many in on the discussion, the debate boils down to the "issue of whether social and cultural processes have primacy over individual processes, or vice versa" (Cobb, 1994b, p. 13). For still others, the issue is not one of either/or; it is a better understanding of the roles and natures of both the individual and the social processes (Driver & Scott, 1995).

These positions are echoed within the field of early childhood education, where traditional interpretations of constructivism have retained a focus on the child's endogenous cognitive processes, making little distinction, for example, between such sources of knowledge as educational toys and "a talkative parent" (G. Forman, personal communication, 1995). Other interpretations place somewhat greater emphasis on the social processes of children's learning, particularly as social interactions contribute to cognitive disequilibrium. Many of these same interpretations, however, continue to rely primarily on a Piagetian framework, emphasizing the internal mechanisms of assimilation and accommodation over socially constructed meaning (e.g., DeVries & Zan, 1994; Kamii, 1995).

Winds From New Directions

Of growing interest to the field of early childhood education, and of relevance to this and other discussions on constructivism, is a third body of literature that is the result of efforts in the adjacent fields of anthropology, cognitive psychology, sociolinguistics, child development, and sociology. The focus of attention from this multidisciplinary audience is directed to the socially and culturally situated nature of mental activity. Drawing heavily on the work of Vygotsky and neo-Vygotskian "activity theorists" such as Lave, Cole, Bruner, Rogoff, and Wertsch, recent scholarship in this area has led to a reassessment of the interface between cognition and its sociocultural context. Research in culturally diverse settings has further contributed to an expanding conceptual and empirical knowledge base on children's interpretive and collective processes of knowledge construction as resulting from their active and guided participation in sociocultural routines (Corsaro & Miller, 1992; Rogoff, 1990; Rogoff, Mistry, Goncu, & Mosier, 1993). When coupled with the emerging field of cultural psychology, this body of work contributes to a radical positioning on the constructivist continuum, such that the individual and the culture are viewed as inextricable, and neither can be adequately examined or understood in isolation from each other (Rogoff, Radziszewska, & Masiello, 1995).

There is little argument that much remains to be understood about the internal mechanisms of knowledge construction by children and adults irrespective of their diverse sociocultural contexts. At the same time, it is now increasingly evident that an exclusively narrow focus on the individual at the expense of the social can explain, at best, only a small part of the complex and compelling story of human learning and development. For the duration of this chapter, the label *social constructivism* is used to describe the epistemological and philosophical position that mental activity is bound to its social context (Wertsch, 1991). The use of this term precludes any meaningful distinction between the constructivist and sociocultural perspectives.

Among those educators who share such a social constructivist perspective, the discussion frequently centers on two pressing issues: the dynamic features of the transactional and negotiated relationship between individuals and the sociocultural context; and the theory's usefulness in influencing educational enterprises. Reggio Emilia has much to contribute to this discussion, including provocative interpretations of social constructivist theory itself and well-documented linkages between the theory and related instructional practices. The hypothetical question regarding the feasibility of a social constructivist pedagogy has been framed by Reggio Emilians as an epistemological course of action [defined, by Webster's (1994) dictionary, as an investigation into the "origins, nature, methods, and limits of human endeavor" (p. 480)]. Throughout their years of working together, Reggio Emilia classroom teachers, *pedagogisti,* and Loris Malaguzzi himself have focused on the processes and potentials of children's learning, the symbolic meanings assigned to that knowledge, and the ways in which adults might use such knowledge in children's best interests.

The following sections of this chapter consider select examples of common Reggio Emilia practices as they illuminate and expand on three concepts essential to most contemporary interpretations of a social constructivist paradigm:

(a) the sociocultural context, (b) sociocognitive conflict, and (c) the zone of proximal development. Each section begins with a brief review of current understandings of the theoretical concept at hand, so as to situate the example of Reggio Emilia within the contemporary discourse.

The Sociocultural Context: *Io Chi Siamo* [I Am Who We Are]

Anthropologists have long studied the intricacies of relationships and routines that characterize particular social groupings and their influence on children's learning and development, beginning with the work of Margaret Mead (1928) and continuing in the tradition of the Six Cultures study orchestrated by John and Beatrice Whiting (Whiting & Whiting, 1975). B. Whiting's (1980) work on culture as a "provider of settings" extends our understanding of the significance of the sociocultural context on children's behavioral options and developmental opportunities. Children's prosocial skills and cooperative abilities, for example, as well as their more antagonistic behaviors have been found to be a function of "the company they keep" (Whiting & Edwards, 1988). The role of the sociocultural context in mediating adult belief systems and patterns of child care is also now well documented in the cross-cultural literature on parenting and, to a lesser extent, in comparative studies of early education.

Findings from cross-cultural studies on child development, parental behavior, and early education, in combination with the previously cited work by activity theorists and cultural psychologists, support a view of human development-in-context. Research in this tradition has led to an understanding and characterization of the relationship between cultural contexts and social activities as dynamic, negotiated, and mutually influenced rather than static and unilateral (Corsaro & Miller, 1992; Goodnow, Miller, & Kessel, 1995). Put yet another way, children and adults are now understood to coexist in a social world full of culturally defined meanings and significance, and contribute to their own development through their participation in everyday cultural events (Bruner, 1985; Rogoff, 1990). This view lends credence to a more holistic conception of children and adults that includes recognition of their membership in a particular sociocultural context represented by the family, the community, and the larger society—each with its own set of interdependent characteristics (New, 1993a).

The Developmental Niche. Reggio Emilia represents a unique sociocultural context that draws on centuries of tradition and history associated with the larger Italian culture as well as that at the local and regional levels (New, 1993a). In particular, the values assigned to social responsibility for children and the benefits of collaborative relationships in Reggio Emilia may also be found in both regional and national traditions. Their collaborative model of early childhood education—known to the rest of the world as "the Reggio Emilia approach"— reflects and contributes to cultural values and principles of the larger Italian setting.

Rogoff's interpretation of knowledge construction within such a situated context such as Reggio Emilia is that it takes place through the child's apprenticeship to the rites, rituals, and routines as well as possibilities inherent within a family, a classroom, a society (Rogoff, 1990). Super and Harkness (1986; Harkness & Super, 1983) further elaborated on the environmental features supporting and defining such an apprenticeship, identifying the physical and social environment, patterns of social interaction, and ideology of the adults as codeterminants of the structuring, aims, and interpretation of children's development.

The guiding metaphor for the preprimary schools of Reggio Emilia is that of schooling as a "system of relationships" (Edwards, Gandini, & Forman, 1993). Reggio Emilian teachers consciously orchestrate the tacit and visible dimensions of the sociocultural context that are within their control, thereby maximizing the possibilities of this culturally sanctioned relational premise on children's learning and development. Examples of what constitutes the culture of schooling in Reggio Emilia may be found in organizational features, the physical environment, curriculum content, and pedagogy, as well as the more mundane daily rituals and routines—each contributing to the nurturing of select culturally valued tools, knowledge, and understandings.

The physical characteristics of any school environment reveal much about how children are regarded and the value assigned to the processes of teaching and learning that characterize the setting. The Reggio Emilia school environments are noteworthy not only because they are aesthetically and intellectual-

FIGURE 14.1. The three protagonists, child, parent, and teacher, are here in the environment that enriches their relationship. Diana School.

ly stimulating, but because they convey a respect for the interests, rights, needs, and capacities of those who use that space (Gandini,1984/1990). The provision of stimulating and provocative displays of objects, whether a careful arrangement of seashells or the positioning of a mirrored surface, serves to educate children's attention to design, detail, or difference; and to contribute to the development of an alert and active response to the world. The frequent display of collective efforts, such as the woven bags of leaves collected on a walk outside, whereby each child can identify his or her contribution to the collaborative product, heightens the child's awareness of self as a member of and contributor to the larger group.

Organization features also serve to promote children's development in Reggio Emilia in ways that are consistent with the values held by the school and the surrounding community. The practice of placing children within the same class group for 3 years promotes the development of strong and enduring relationships among children, families, and teachers; and contributes to a sense of community within the larger school setting. Children also benefit directly when teachers utilize their knowledge of children's home and family lives to inform and enliven their group discussions. The lack of hierarchical status among members of the teaching staff and the active partnership role with parents combine to provide children with a culturally congruent model of adult cooperation and

FIGURE 14.2. Putting on bibs becomes an opportunity for stories about children's family life.

collaboration. Numerous other practical arrangements capitalize on the environment's capacity to provoke children's natural interest in each other. Central arrangements of dress-up clothes, the enticing and playful nature of bathrooms, and the frequent use of windows rather than walls to separate classrooms all serve the purpose of inviting children to acknowledge, observe, and interact with one another.

Pedagogical characteristics, including the use of long-term projects within the general framework of *progettazione* as well as short-term small group activities, provide not only opportunity but the necessity for communicative skills and patterns of discourse that reflect school goals and cultural norms. To that end, children are encouraged to observe, contrast, and confront as well as to negotiate their understandings. An appreciation and need for multiple points of view develops through activities that encourage children to rely on one another's knowledge or competences, as when several children are invited to draw an object from diverse perspectives, thereby necessitating a joining of the perspectives at such time that a more complete image is required. Skills at communication and collaboration are developed through activities that utilize a variety of media to represent common experiences as well as through those that require children to identify common goals and strategies by which to achieve those goals. We now have access to several fine examples of this pedagogical approach, including *The Long Jump* and *The Amusement Park for the Birds* (see Resource List at the end of this volume).

The environment's ability to mirror and nourish the school's regional goals and social dimensions is also readily apparent in the documentation of collaborative projects where multiple points of view are represented. Documentation provides children with feedback about their work, and serves as a "springboard" from which they can continue in their pursuit of an idea or the representation of an experience, often in a partnership with other children. As teachers view each other's efforts, they are encouraged to collaborate in the exchange of ideas and materials. Such thoughtful evidence of children's schoolwork also engages parents in discussions of children's school lives in a way that is conducive to further involvement. And the public display of information about the school organization itself—what Vecchi (1993) described as "a democratic possibility to inform the public" (p. 121)—serves to acknowledge the full complement of people essential to making a school successful, and in the process invites parents to join in those collective efforts. Through their use of simple and elaborate forms of documentation, Reggio Emilia's school environments reiterate the collective cultural values previously identified, even as they also contribute a historical perspective to children's development.

The cumulative effect of the messages conveyed to and about children reinforces the Reggio Emilia image of the child as capable, competent, and possessing of rights—including the right to active membership and nurturing relationships within the school community. The principle of schooling built on relationships is much more than a pleasing slogan; it is a commitment that runs like a thread throughout the entirety of their discourse and their efforts, contributing to that "seamless" quality of home–school–community connections observed by visitors to Reggio Emilia (Gardner, 1993). The philosophical congruity of the Reggio Emilia approach, "in which everything is connected" (Filippini, 1993, p. 117) is one of the key features that distinguishes their efforts from those of other high-quality early childhood programs in the world. The sociocultural context that supports and has resulted from this collaborative endeavor provides what would be, to many, an optimal educational context in which children's membership is acknowledged and support is provided for their growth and development "consistently and reciprocally over time" by all of those who claim to be members of the community. In Reggio Emilia, parents, teachers, and other citizens have strived for years to develop and maintain such a learning and living environment, utilizing their material and human resources to maximize the salience of selective traditions and values drawn from the larger sociocultural context.

Yet, as Spaggiari (1994) noted, children are not mere recipients of a "prepackaged culture." Through the processes of exchange that characterize the social relationships in this setting, children not only benefit from the sociocultural context within which they are embedded, but contribute to it as well. The expression *Io chi siamo* captures this reciprocal relationship between the child and the larger

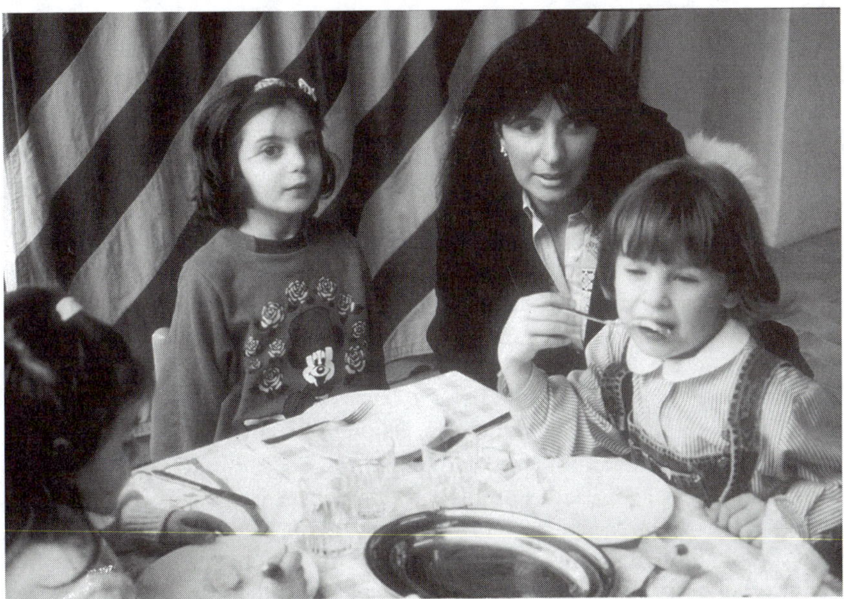

FIGURE 14.3. Even though most parents are employed they know that they can be part of the daily life of the school.

(school) community, and challenges any unilateral interpretation of the role of the sociocultural context in children's learning and development. The contributions of children's ways of thinking about complex and enduring social issues such as war, friendship, gender relations—all shared vis-à-vis documentation efforts—are evident in the quality and content of adult discourse at the larger community level. The value placed on children's contributions to the affective and intellectual tone of the community is also apparent in the significance assigned to the role of social relations and social activity in that learning and development.

Children as Peers, Playmates, and Provocateurs

Vygotsky's expansion of a Piagetian-based constructivist theory rests heavily on his thesis of the interplay between social and developmental processes (Vygotsky, 1978). He attached primary significance to the social dimensions of knowledge construction, described as a "genetic law" of relations among people underlying "all higher functions and their relationships" (Vygotsky, 1960/1981, p. 163). Contemporary interpretations of this premise are that children depend not only on the broadly described sociocultural context within which they live, but also on the more discrete social exchanges that take place among and between individuals in that setting (Bruner, 1990; Wertsch, 1985). What it actually means to "negotiate" or socially construct meanings within this context, and what aspects of knowledge are negotiable, however, are less well understood (Prawat & Floden, 1994).

Cognitive psychologists are among those who have attempted to better understand the role of social relations in cognitive development, and have delineated a number of social influences on knowledge construction, including the "mere presence of others" (Levine & Resnick, 1993, p. 588). Additional contributing factors to cognition include social roles, positions, and identities as sources of influence on qualities of mental representations and subsequent cognitive change. Research on these and other social bases of cognition has led to the conceptualization of "cognition as collaboration" (p. 599), supporting the Vygotskian notion that higher forms of mental activity derived from sociocultural contexts "are shared by members of those contexts" (Berk & Winsler, 1995, p. 12).

Collaborative cognition is not an immediate outcome of social exchanges, however. Sociocognitive conflict—and the desired conflict reduction—plays a major role in both Piagetian and Vygotskian interpretations of cognitive development. Whereas there is a "paucity of empirical findings" (Rizzo, 1992, p. 94) concerning the role of conflict on the development of children's social relationships, there is an impressive body of research supporting the premise that conflict within those relationships contributes to cognition. Such sociocognitive conflicts have frequently been observed as children collaboratively co-construct their understandings of "the meanings and rules of serious life" (Rogoff, 1990, p. 186). There is also a related body of empirical literature testifying to children's abilities to negotiate understandings of shared social knowledge (Corsaro, 1985; Corsaro & Eder, 1990). Even very young children, otherwise labeled egocentric, have been observed to generate and debate this social knowledge, including the establishment of "markers of affiliation" (whether a particular toy, item of clothing, or style of communicating) to connote their joint membership in the peer culture (Fernie, Kantor, & Whaley, 1995; Kantor, Elgas, & Fernie, 1993). Vygotsky cited the adaptive function of such socially shared cognition given that the processes of knowledge construction are more likely to generate exchanges of differing views, which, in turn, are reorganized to a "higher plane of thinking" (Berk & Winsler, 1995, p. 12).

Reggio Emilia extends our interpretation of the frequencies and qualities of these social exchanges. In particular, the work being done in Reggio Emilia sheds new light on the value of sociocognitive conflict to children's development. Reggio Emilia's educators have not only acknowledged this knowledge-generating process, but have focused on increasing opportunities for children to experience various, conflicting, and sometimes confusing perspectives. Thus they create "disturbances" in the physical environment, and they support children's predisposition to challenge one another's views, all the while providing

FIGURE 14.4. Working with clay, the child is getting support from a friend, the wire structure, and the teacher who understands the timing and amount of assistance necessary for helping the child achieve his goal.

opportunities for them to revisit, revise, and review their theories and their hypotheses. Contrary to a recently made distinction between negotiation as a form of compromise versus negotiation as a strategy to "skillfully overcome obstacles" (Prawat, 1989; Prawat & Floden, 1994), Reggio Emilia teachers utilize children's multiple points of view even as they create needs for children to negotiate shared understandings. The successful outcomes of this Reggio Emilia strategy—as represented in such large-scale group projects as the creation of a life-size dinosaur or a schoolwide athletic event—illustrate the benefits noted in research on the contributions of diverse perspectives (including a single minority position) on group decision making. Consistently, such research has found that the ultimate position reached by a group with multiple positions represents more deliberate thought and negotiation than is typically the case in a group without conflict (Levine & Resnick, 1993).

Children, of course, are not the only sources of cognitive stimulation in the Reggio Emilia environments. Adults, too, provide "guidance, support, direction, challenge, and impetus" to learn, through a process Rogoff (1990) described as guided participation. This concept emphasizes the mutual roles played by the learner and a more skilled adult or peer and describes the interpersonal transactions that take place during social interactions. Whether teachers or children are the "more capable others," the process is characterized by a gradual internalization of shared knowledge, with an increasing ability on the part of the child to move from other-regulated to self-regulated activity (Brown & Ferrara, 1985). The success of this process is dependent on the extent to which the assistance provided is within the appropriate range of interest and possibility.

Zone of Proximal Development as Opportunity and Optimism

Vygotsky's general genetic law of cultural development, in which he described the emergence of new capacities first during the processes of collaboration, led him to identify the "region in which this transfer of ability" takes place (Vygotsky, 1978). First identified as a counterpoint to the assessment of "fossilized" knowledge, Vygotsky's zone of proximal development concept has been considered among the most significant of social constructivist concepts for educational settings. Described as "the dynamic zone of sensitivity" (Berk & Winsler, 1995, p. 26) in which learning and cognitive development take place, the zone of proximal development was considered by Vygotsky a "tool" for educators "through which the internal course of development can be understood" (Garrison, 1995, p. 726; Vygotsky, 1978, p. 87).

Practically speaking, the "tool of the zone" may be applied to issues of curriculum as well as assessment. Children are viewed as capable of benefiting from problems that initially require the assistance of others, and appropriate assessment processes attempt to tap into this dynamic process. In turn, acknowledgment of the zone of proximal development places new demands on the role of the teacher. Principles of developmentally appropriate practice can no longer rely on knowledge of children's current developmental status to make curricular decisions. Rather, teachers must remain alert to the child's ever expanding reach, and stay one step ahead (Berk & Winsler, 1995). Of equal significance in terms of social constructivist theory is the degree of influence that the child has in responding to learning opportunities within his or her "zone." Rogoff elaborated on this view of the individual through her use of the term *participatory appropriation* to describe the highly subjective and selective process by which a learner constructs new understandings as a result of participating in a task or group activity. A growing body of research supports this premise that children now not only make choices about what to learn, but how and from whom (Stone, 1993). The Kamehameha Elementary Education Project (KEEP) is one exemplar of an educational system that has successfully demonstrated the characteristics and consequences of adult efforts to respond to children's potential competencies and "rouse minds to life" in culturally appropriate ways (Tharp & Gallimore, 1988/1991). Reggio Emilia is another.

In Reggio Emilia, teachers' conceptions of children's zone of proximal development therefore assume a major role in their curriculum decisions. Although others have acknowledged the philosophical nature of young children's thinking (Matthews, 1994), teachers in Reggio Emilia routinely elicit children's opinions and then develop projects around such existential topics as death, aging, love, and war. Teachers' responses to children's fears and misunderstandings around gender roles, for example, acknowledge a belief in children's rights and *abilities* to deal with such issues. As U.S. scholars continue to reassess and clarify Piagetian interpretations of developmental constraints on children's learning (Metz, 1995), Reggio Emilia teachers place no such preconceived limits on children's capacities to deal with abstract concepts. Rather, teachers encourage children to debate, hypothesize, and test the merits of their beliefs, whether it is with regard to a special handicap for girls in "The Long Jump" project or the proposition put forth by a group of 3-year-olds that gender identity is a function of clothing. The Reggio Emilia interpretation of teacher as provocateur, one who "complicates" the child's already complex thinking process, expands the notion of operating within the child's zone of proximal development. Indeed, such a reconceptulization suggests that the teacher may actually participate in stretching the limits of such a "zone" through the presentation of challenges that require more active engagement and social negotiations. Such curriculum projects are especially successful when Reggio Emilia teachers capitalize on their knowledge of young children to build on the transactional relationship between affect and intellect.

In many ways, Vygotsky's view of children's enhanced capacities within the zone of proximal development is akin to Reggio Emilia's image of the child. In each case, children are viewed as capable of doing more than they are typically permitted. There are differences, however, in the Vygotskian and Reggio Emilian interpretations of the conditions most capable of eliciting the child's potential

FIGURE 14.5. By working together, these children build competence through a shared, collaborative experience.

capacities. For Vygotsky (1978), play was the ultimate setting within which the zone of proximal development might be revealed, a context in which the child is "a head taller than himself" (p. 102). For Reggio Emilians, play is highly valued for its ability to promote development, but no more so than the complex and long-term projects in which children and teachers become engaged.

As noted previously, one of the results of participating in sociocultural activities with more capable others is the gradual ability on the part of the one identified as learner to assume more of the responsibility and initiative in directing attention, taking actions, and developing new goals. In Reggio Emilian classrooms, this process occurs within and between children as teachers utilize various forms of documentation, including audio and video recordings, transcriptions of conversations, photographs, and examples of work to inspire children to revisit their old ideas and understandings. As children (individually and collectively) are provoked to reflect on former conceptions, they are then in a position to critique those understandings and challenged to create new hypotheses. In this sense they become their own and one another's more capable peers. The child, along with peers and adults, is a protagonist in his or her own development.

The Reggio Emilia interpretation of the zone of proximal development, reflected in their image of the child as "rich in potential, strong, powerful, competent, and most of all, connected to adults and other children" (Malaguzzi, 1993, p. 10), builds on the valuing of social relations that characterize the larger sociocultural context, and as such, serves as a self- fulfilling prophecy. As this and previous sections have suggested, Reggio Emilia has much to contribute to current discourse regarding both the concepts and the potentials of a social constructivist theory of learning and development. Equally significant is Reggio Emilia's illumination of the contributions of practices to the articulation of theory.

TEACHING AS REFLECTIVE PRAXIS

Key elements of the personal, political, philosophical, and theoretical roots grounding the efforts of Reggio Emilia have been described on numerous occasions by our Italian colleagues, and may be found elsewhere in this volume. Reggio Emilia's collective efforts over the past three decades have resulted in a pedagogical system bearing the touch of a wide array of philosophers, researchers, and epistemologists, many of whom are well-known within the U.S. educational community (e.g., Dewey, Bronfenbrenner, Bruner, Gardner, Hawkins, Piaget, and Vygotsky), as well as lesser known (at least to American audiences) European philosophers and theoreticians such as Foucault, Wallon, Varela, and Rodari. Malaguzzi and others in Reggio Emilia have graciously acknowledged, on numerous occasions, these contributions to Reggio Emilia's knowledge base.

It is insufficient, however, to ascribe credit for Reggio Emilia's accomplishments solely to their selective synthesis of the empirically and philosophically based positions espoused by other contemporary scholars. Rather, under Malaguzzi's visionary leadership, educators in Reggio Emilia have strived to "continuously combine [others'] educational theories and our empirical research" (Vecchi, 1993, p. 123) in the quest to articulate a philosophical framework congruent with their evolving pedagogical practice. Until his untimely death several years ago, Malaguzzi remained emphatic about the importance of this shared construction and testing of knowledge, proclaiming that educational ideas and improved practice derived much-needed sustenance from their own social discourse as well as from "official models or established theories" (1993, p. 51).

Thus, in Reggio Emilia, theory and practice are bound together by the binding power of their ongoing research that characterizes teachers' roles and permeates their daily routines. Teacher interpretations of their roles are similar to that of collaborative action researchers in the U.S., as they observe and interact with children, exchange concerns and understandings with parents and other community members, and join other teachers in their ongoing inquiry into children's abilities and potentials (New, 1991). Throughout, teachers shift their focus back and forth between what they know and what they are learning about children as a group and as individuals, and what they can gather from families and the larger community that is of relevance to their educational pursuits.

The socially mediated construction of knowledge is perhaps the most distinctive of Reggio Emilia's interpretation of teacher as learner and researcher. Teachers in Reggio Emilia are encouraged to think about their work within the context of a stable and supportive network of parents and professionals, some of whom have worked together on collaborative projects for more than two decades. The provision for teachers of such a "community of inquirers" (Killion & Todnem, 1991), seen as vital to teacher development yet uncommon within the U.S., is central to Reggio Emilia's practice.

This view of teacher as simultaneous theoretician, researcher, and practitioner belies traditional distinctions between those in the applied and academic communities of our profession, and contrasts dramatically with the more typical professional development and curriculum practices in the U.S., where teachers struggle to comprehend and then put into action someone else's epistemology. It is no wonder, then, that misconstruals abound regarding the full meaning and implications of contemporary theories of learning and development. Piaget's stage theory of cognitive development, translated into slogans such as "hands-on learning" remains for many overly ambiguous and hence inadequate to guide teacher decision making (Forman & Fosnot, 1982)—a problem that might have been avoided had teachers had a hand in coming up with the slogan as a symbol of their own experiences with children.

Reggio Emilia's three decades of researching their teaching forecast the premises now put forward by contemporary writers on teacher development and reflective practice. Many now echo Reggio Emilia's practices in advocating for teachers to assign value, interpret responses, and generate hypotheses regarding their work (Drummond, 1994), all the while emphasizing the need teachers have for "activity, reflection, and discourse" (Fosnot, 1996, p. 206). Few, however, are engaged in the struggle to "connect what has often been divided" (Cochran-Smyth & Lytle, 1993, p. xi) to the extent portrayed by Reggio Emilian teachers. At the same time, the working image of Reggio Emilia supports findings by Cuffaro (1994) and others writing on teacher reflections who point to the inadequacy of theory alone in influencing practice. Contemporary research on successful schools within the U.S. notes the potential of the school culture itself to function as a source of support for teachers as well as child development. Such research consistently notes the need on the part of teachers to confront alternative frameworks as a means of modifying the "teacher dominion" associated with traditional schooling (Wien, 1995). Reggio Emilia's efforts support all of these premises, and especially the principle that teachers need many of the same conditions necessary for children, including multiple opportunities to hypothesize, experiment, evaluate, reflect, and share their understandings with others (New, 1992).

The Reggio Emilia approach to teacher research demonstrates the potentials for adults as well as children when the act of teaching is interpreted and supported as "inherently interwoven with the process of learning" (Fosnot, 1989,

p. 112); and when teachers, too, can make choices about what to learn, when, and from whom. Teaching and the accompanying research efforts are designed, in Reggio Emilia, to illuminate children's potentials rather than their problems, their strengths rather than their weaknesses, their rights rather than their needs. Similarly, teacher research and associated professional development activities build on the assumptions that teachers are competent observers and capable decision makers in the educational enterprise. As is the case, then, with other features of their pedagogy, teacher research in Reggio Emilia reflects the sociocultural context, functioning as a form of "cultural practice" that serves "both to represent values and to shape them" (Smagorinsky, 1995, p. 199). Thus this analysis comes full circle, as the qualities of the school environment combine to promote culturally valued attributes of adult as well as child development.

CONCLUSION

Two needs have converged in this chapter: one for a better understanding of the ideological bases of Reggio Emilia's work with young children—a need of growing importance, given the rapidly expanding number of teachers, schools, and entire districts that align themselves with the Reggio Emilia approach. The second goal was twofold: to contribute to a more complete conceptualization of social constructivist theory, and to illuminate the pedagogical possibilities inherent within a theory that has, itself, been constructed as a result of the application of its own principles.

The work of Reggio Emilia provides a strong counterargument to the dual proposition that the sociocultural perspective is limited solely to its ability to inform us "of the conditions for the possibility of learning," whereas the more "pure constructivist focus" allows for greater understandings of "what students learn and the processes by which they do so" (Cobb, 1994, p. 13). Numerous examples may be drawn from Reggio Emilia practice to put to rest the notion that the *what* of children's learning and "the processes by which they do so" could be considered independent of the sociocultural context.

Reggio Emilia eliminates the need to express fidelity to only one or the other of a constructivist or sociocultural point of view; their work informs their joint perspectives and makes visible the pedagogical implications as well. Reggio Emilian educators' skill at making explicit not only the details of their practice but also the ideological interpretations are well demonstrated in this volume, their constant documentation, and the collaborative video productions (with George Forman and Lella Gandini). Their clarity about and commitment to the ongoing dialogical approach to their ideology and their pedagogy also belies the traditionally held view of theory as the mover and maker of practice. The interdependent nature of the two dimensions of pedagogy (thought and action) is acknowledged by Malaguzzi (1993), who noted that, "In truth, a theory is legitimate only if it deals with problems that emerge from the practice of education and that can be solved by educators" (p. 82). There is a message here for U.S. educators, borrowed from lessons learned in the 1970s when teachers attempted to become "Plowden teachers," implementing pedagogical practices without a concomitant commitment to theroy testing and development (Drummond, 1994).

Before coming to a conclusion of this discussion, there is another dimension to Reggio Emilia's theory of learning and development that should also be acknowledged, if only briefly. Theories of learning and development are products of social and political forces as well as experience and experimentation. Granted, the particular interpretation of social constructivist theory that has been described in this chapter is resonant in a number of ways to positions expressed in contemporary literature, both empirical and philosophical. Yet there is a political side to the Reggio Emilia ideology that is also consistent with emerging views of the politics of curriculum theory, and offers at least partial explanation for the lack of traditional research in that Italian community.

American educators have been perplexed at the lack of empirically derived data with which to validate Reggio Emilia's practices, and yet Reggio Emilians are persistent in their refusal to participate in this positivist tradition that has played such a strong role in determining U.S. educational policies and practices. Rather, the reliance, in Reggio Emilia, on teacher reflection and documentation of their work with young children as their primary means of research and evaluation, falls within the tradition of qualitative research—a tradition that has often been criticized for its socio-political orientation. This characterization, in Italy, would be viewed as advantageous rather than detrimental to the summative evaluation of a community's early childhood program.

The context of Reggio Emilia's theoretical and practical work is the Italian culture—and particularly, the region of Emilia Romagna—a setting in which the values of collaboration and interdependence and the social and legal status assigned to children and their families are well established (New, 1993a). Yet Reggio Emilia is much more than a polished image of Italy's more worthwhile traditions. Reggio Emilia's mindfulness of the choices made provides vivid testimony to the role of personal as well as cultural values, and the power of ideal images as conveyed by a charismatic leader such as Malaguzzi. As such, the totality of the Reggio Emilia experience represents much more than could be adequately represented by any one theory of learning or instruction, as Malaguzzi (1993) himself acknowledged. Rather, the successes of Reggio Emilia provide testimony to the importance of a "continued vigilence" regarding the necessary linkage between theory building and ethical principles, and the futility of trying to separate theory from their political agendas (Malaguzzi, 1993). All of what is visible in Reggio Emilia, as well as the somewhat hidden supportive elements, is in response to the collective desire to present a more positive and compelling image of children than is currently held in contemporary society, with the aim of generating "hopes for a new human culture of childhood"

(Malaguzzi, 1993, p. 88). The success of Reggio Emilia in convincing themselves and others of the possibility of such a "new human culture" reveals the possibilities of theory, passion (Greene, 1986), and practice; their efforts also help us to understand the conditions by which teaching assumes the more philosophical and political congruence implied by the term *praxis* (Friere, 1977/1995).

The Greek term for theory also means "to behold." The power of Reggio Emilia's projected image of the child cannot be underestimated, nor should we dismiss the power of the related discourse that is now being heard around the world. The more we consider Reggio Emilia's work and accomplishments, the more some are convinced that such a transformation in schools, teaching, and

FIGURE 14.6. This possible, every-day occurrence is rich with shared meaning that has been socially constructed by teacher, parent, and child.

learning, is possible in our own settings as well. Dewey (1925/1981) understood the potential of such socially constructed knowledge when he noted that "to understand...is to anticipate" (p. 141), thereby encapsulating his promise of societal reform through education. For Reggio Emilians, the collective and social construction of knowledge is a right of citizenship (children's as well as adults') as well as an explanation of the processes of and conditions in which optimal learning can take place. And it is this potential—of the work of Reggio Emilia to influence the learning and living possibilities in other cultural settings—that provokes one last expansion of a social constructivist concept within this chapter.

Dewey (1916/1980) observed that "education will vary with the quality of life which prevails in a group" (p. 87) This profoundly simple insight has recently been described as analogous to the zone of proximal development, such that the "quality of participation in the communal life of the zone" (Garrison, 1995, p. 729) ought to have a direct bearing on learning and developmental outcomes. A second metaphorical interpretation of the zone of proximal development describes its simultaneous qualities of being "constrained by development but simultaneously serving as its cutting edge, actively directing the course that development takes" (Moshman, 1982, p. 375). Together, these images of the zone of proximal development have direct implications for how we might envision and plan for our own futures, as well as the role that Reggio Emilia might play in this endeavor.

Reggio Emilia can be considered as representing the cutting edge within the zone of proximal development of the community of early childhood educators. In contrasting ourselves with the image put forth by Reggio Emilia, we have become more keenly aware of our limitations as well as our possibilities. It has been noted that "one's anticipations about what will be found in the environment [tend to] bear fruit" (Prawat & Floden, 1994, p. 46). To assure that our anticipations become more optimistic, however, requires that we direct more of our effort into imagining the possibilities within our own deficit-oriented society. The example of Reggio Emilia, combined with the metaphor of community as a zone of proximal development, requires us to welcome the diversity within our pluralistic society, to acknowledge the real competencies and circumstances of the children on whose behalf we work, and to invite the families of the children in our care to contribute their educational aims and objectives to the educational discourse. Such an undertaking will inevitably acquaint us with the social and political realities of children's lives and require us to seriously debate the role of schooling in our contemporary and tumultuous society. Such a perspective on education, one that includes the active participation of all citizens within a particular sociocultural context, expands our views of social constructivist theory, illustrates the principles of the Reggio Emilia approach, and provokes us to reconceptualize our roles as educators. The results of such efforts will be more likely to illuminate Reggio Emilia's imagined "new culture of childhood" than all of the light tables in the world.

REFERENCES

Barden, M. (1993). A backward look: From Reggio Emilia to progressive education. In C. Edwards, L. Gandini, & G. Forman (Eds.), *The hundred languages of children: The Reggio Emilia approach to early childhood education* (pp. 283–295).

Berk, L., & Winsler, A. (1995). *Scaffolding children's learning: Vygotsky and early childhood education.* Washington, DC: NAEYC.

Bredekamp, S. (1987). *Developmentally appropriate practice in programs serving children from birth through age 8.* Washington, DC: NAEYC.

Bredekamp, S. (1993). Reflections on Reggio Emilia. *Young children, 49*(1), 13–17.

Bredekamp, S., & Copple, C. (Eds.). (1997). *Developmentally appropriate practice in early childhood programs* (rev. ed). Washington, DC: NAEYC.

Brooks, J.G., & Brooks, M.G. (1993). *The case for constructivist classrooms.* Alexandria, VA: Association for Supervision and Curriculum Development.

Brown, A., & Ferrara, R. (1985). Diagnosing zones of proximinal development. In J.V. Wertsch (Ed.), *Culture, communication, and cognition: Vygotskian perspectives* (pp. 273–305). New York: Cambridge University Press.

Bruner, J. (1985). Vygotsky: A historical and conceptual perspective. In J.V. Wertsch (Ed.), *Culture, communication, and cognition: Vygotskian perspectives* (pp. 21–34). New York: Cambridge University Press.

Bruner, J. (1990). *Acts of meaning.* Cambridge, MA: Harvard University Press.

Cobb, P. (1994a). Constructivism in mathematics and science education. *Educational Researcher, 23*(7), 4.

Cobb, P. (1994b). Where is the mind? Constructivist and sociocultural perspecives on mathematical development. *Educational Researcher, 23*(7), 13–20.

Cobb, P. (1995). Continuing the conversation: A response to Smith. *Educational Researcher, 24*(7), 27–28.

Cochran-Smith, M., & Lytle, S.L. (Eds.). (1993). *Inside/outside: teacher research and knowledge.* New York: Teachers College Press.

Corsaro, W. (1985). *Friendship and peer culture in the early years.* Norwood, NJ: Ablex.

Corsaro, W. A. & Eder, D. (1990). Children's peer cultures. *Annual Review of Sociology, 16,* 197–220.

Corsaro, W.A., & P. Miller, (Eds.). (1992). *Interpretive approaches to children's socialization.* (New Directions for Child Development, No 58). San Francisco: Jossey-Bass.

Cuffaro, H. (1994). *Experimenting with the world: John Dewey and the early childhood classroom.* New York: Teachers College Press.

DeVries, R., & Kohlberg, L. (1987). *Constructivist early education: Overview and comparison with other programs.* Washington, DC: NAEYC.

DeVries, R., & Zan, B. (1994). *Moral classrooms, moral children: Creating a constructivist atmosphere in early education.* New York: Teachers College Press.

Dewey, J. (1980). Democracy and education. In J.A. Boydston (Ed.), *John Dewey: The middle works, 1899–1924, Vol. 9* (pp. 221–229). Carbondale & Edwardsville, IL: Southern Illinois University Press. (Original work published 1916).

Dewey, J. (1981). Experience and nature. In J.A. Boydston (Ed.), *John Dewey: The later works, 1925–1953, Vol. 1* (pp. 87–101). Carbondale & Edwardsville, IL: Southern Illinois University Press. (Original work published 1925).

Driver, R., & Scott, P. (1995). Mind in communication: A response to Erick Smith. *Educational Researcher, 24*(7), 27–28.

Drummond, M.J. (1994). *Learning to see: Assessment through observation.* York, ME: Stenhouse Publishers.

Duckworth, E. (1987). *The having of wonderful ideas.* Cambridge, MA: Harvard University Press.

Edwards, C., Gandini, L., & Forman, G. (Eds.). (1993). *The hundred languages of children: The Reggio Emilia approach to early education.* Norwood, NJ: Ablex.

Eisner, E.W. (1994). *Cognition and curriculum reconsidered* (2nd ed.). New York: Teachers College Press.

Fernie, D., Kantor, R., & Whaley, K. (1995). Learning from classroom ethnographies: Same places, different times. In A. Hatch (Ed.), *Qualitative research in early childhood settings.* (pp. 155–172). Westport, CT: Praeger.

Filippini, T., (1993). The role of the *pedagogista.* In C. Edwards, L. Gandini, & G. Forman (Eds.), *The hundred languages of children: the Reggio Emilia approach to early childhood education* (pp. 113–118). Norwood, NJ: Ablex.

Forman, E., Minick, N., & Stone, C.A. (Eds.). (1993). *Contexts for learning: Sociocultural dynamics in children's development.* Oxford, UK: Oxford University Press.

Forman, G., & Fosnot, C. (1982). The use of Piaget's constructivism in early childhood education programs. In B. Spodek (Ed.), *Handbook of research in early childhood education* (pp. 185–214). New York: MacMillan.

Fosnot, C.T. (1989). *Enquiring teachers, enquiring learners: A constructivist approach for teaching.* New York: Teachers College Press.

Fosnot, C.T. (Ed.). (1996). *Constructivism: Theory, perspectives, and practice.* New York: Teachers College Press.

Friere, P. (1995). *Pedagogy of the oppressed.* New York: Seabury Press. (Original work published 1977).

Gandini, L. (1990). Not just anywhere: Making child care centers into "particular" places. *Exchange, 78,* 5–9. (Original work published 1984).

Gardner, H. (1993). Foreward: Complementary perspectives on Reggio Emilia. In C. Edwards, L. Gandini, & G. Forman (Eds.), *The hundred languages of children: the Reggio Emilia approach to early childhood education* (pp. ix–xiii). Norwood, NJ: Ablex.

Garrison, J. (1995). Deweyan pragmatism and the epistemology of contemporary social constructivism. *American Educational Research Journal, 32*(4), 716–740.

Goodnow, J.J., Miller, P.J., & Kessel, F. (Eds.). (1995). *Cultural practices as contexts for development.* (New Directions for Child Development, No. 67), San Francisco: Josey-Bass.

Greene, M. (1986). Perspectives and imperatives: Reflection and passion in teaching. *Journal of Curriculum and Supervision, 2*(1), 14–19.

Harkness, S., & Super, C. (1983). The cultural construction of child development: A framework for the socialization of affect. *Ethos, 11*(4), 18–23.

Harris, K.R., & Graham, S. (1994). Constructivism: Principles, paradigms, and integration. *Journal of Special Education, 28*(3), 233–247.

Kamii, C. (1995). *Young children continue to reinvent arithmetic: Grade 3.* New York: Teachers College Press.

Kantor, R., Elgas, P., & Fernie, D. (1993). Cultural knowledge and social competence within a preschool peer culture group. *Early Childhood Research Quarterly, 8,* 125–147.

Kessler, S., & Swadener, B.B. (Eds.). (1992). *Reconceptualizing the early childhood curriculum: Beginning the dialogue.* New York: Teachers College Press.

Killion, J.P., & Todnem, G.R. (1991). A process for personal theory building. *Educational Leadership, 48*(6), 14–16.

Kuhn, T. (1970). *The structure of scientific revolutions* (2nd ed.). Chicago: University of Chicago Press. (Original work published 1962).

Levine, J.M., & Resnick, L.B. (1993). Social foundations of cognition. *Annual Review of Psychology, 44,* 585-612.

Malaguzzi, L. (1993). History, ideas, and basic philosophy. In C. Edwards, L. Gandini, & G. Forman (Eds.), *The hundred languages of children: the Reggio Emilia approach to early childhood education* (pp. 41-89). Norwood, NJ: Ablex.

Mallory, B., & New, R. (Eds.). (1994a). *Diversity and developmentally appropriate practices: Challenges for early childhood education.* New York: Teachers College Press.

Mallory, B., & New, R. (1994b). Social constructivist theory and principles of inclusion: Challenges for early childhood special education. *Journal of Special Education, 28*(3), 322–337.

Matthews, G.B. (1994). *The philosophy of childhood.* Cambridge, MA: Harvard University Press.

Mead, M. (1928). *Coming of age in Samoa.* New York: William Morrow.

Metz, K.E. (1995). Reassessment of developmental constraints on children's science instruction. *Review of Educational Research, 65*(2), 93–127.

Moshman, D. (1982). Exogenous, endogenous, and dialectical constructivism. *Developmental Review, 2,* 371–384.

New, R. (1990). Excellent early education: A town in Italy has it. *Young Children, 45*(6), 4–10.

New, R. (1991). Early childhood teacher education in Italy: Reggio Emilia's master plan for "master" teachers. *Journal of Early Childhood Teacher Education, 12.1*(37), 3.

New, R. (1992). The integrated early childhood curriculum: New interpretations based on research and practice. In C. Seefeldt (Ed.), *Review of research in early childhood education* (rev. ed., pp. 286–322) New York: Teachers College Press.

New, R. (1993a). Italy. In M. Cochran (Ed.), *International handbook on child care policies and programs.* (pp. 291–311). Westport, CT: Greenwood Press.

New, R. (1993b). Cultural variations on developmentally appropriate practice: Challenges to theory and practice. In C. Edwards, L. Gandini, & G. Forman (Eds.), *The hundred languages of children: the Reggio Emilia approach to early childhood education* (pp. 215–231). Norwood, NJ: Ablex.

New, R. (1994). Culture, child development, and DAP: An expanded role of teachers as collaborative researchers. In B. Mallory & R. New (Eds.), *Diversity and developmentally appropriate practices: Challenges for early childhood education* (pp. 65–83). New York: Teachers College Press.

New, R. (1997). Next steps in teaching "The Reggio Way": Advocating for a new image of the child. In J. Hendrick (Ed.), *First steps in teaching the Reggio way,* (pp. 224–233). Columbus, OH: Merrill.

Phillips, D.C. (1995). The good, the bad, and the ugly: The many faces of constructivism. *Educational Researcher, 24*(7), 5–12.

Prawat, R.S. (1993). The value of ideas: Problems versus possibilities in learning. *Educational Researcher, 20*(2), 3–10.

Prawat, R.S., & Floden, R.E. (1994). Philosophical perspectives on constructivist views of learning. *Educational Psychologist, 29*(1), 37–48.

Rizzo, T.A. (1992). The role of conflict in children's friendship development. In W.A. Corsaro & P.J. Miller (Eds.), *Interpretive approaches to children's socialization.* (New Directions for Child Development No. 58), 93–111. San Francisco: Josey-Bass.

Rogoff, B. (1990). *Apprenticeship in thinking: Cognitive development in social context.* New York: Oxford University Press.

Rogoff, B., Mistry, J., Goncu, A., & Mosier, C. (1993). Guided participation in cultural activity by toddlers and caregivers. *Monograph of the Society for Research in Child Development, 58*(8).

Rogoff, B., Radziszewska, B., & Masiello, T. (1995). Analysis of developmental processes in sociocultural activity. In L. Martin, K. Nelson, & E. Tobach (Eds.), *Cultural psychology and activity theory* (pp. 125–149). Cambridge, UK: Cambridge University Press.

Smagorinsky, P. (1995). The social construction of data: Methodological problems of investigating learning in the zone of proximal development. *Review of Educational Research, 65*(3), 191–212.

Smith, E. (1995). Where is the mind? Knowing and knowledge in Cobb's constructivist and sociocultural perspectives. *Educational Researcher, 24*(7), 23–24.

Spaggiari, S. (1994, September). *History and philosophy of Reggio Emilia.* Paper presented at Reaching Potentials: The Challenge of Reggio Emilia Conference, University of Melbourne, Melbourne, Australia.

Stone, C. A. (1993). What's missing in the metaphor of scaffolding? In E. Forman, N. Minick, & C. Addison Stone (Eds.). *Contexts for learning: Sociocultural cynamics in children's development* (pp. 169–183). Oxford, UK: Oxford University Press.

Super, C., & Harkness, S. (1986). The developmental niche: A conceptualization at the interface of child and culture. *International Journal of Behavioral Development, 9,* 545–569.

Tharp, R.G., & Gallimore, R. (1991). *Rousing minds to life: Teaching, learning, and schooling in social context.* Cambridge, UK: Cambridge University Press. (Original work published 1988).

Vecchi, V. (1993). the role of the *atelierista.* In C. Edwards, L. Gandini, & G. Forman (Eds.), *The hundred languages of children: The Reggio Emilia approach to early childhood education* (pp. 119–127). Norwood, NJ: Ablex.

Vygotsky, L.S. (1978). *Mind in society.* Cambridge, MA: Harvard University Press.

Webster's encyclopedic unabridged dictionary of the English language (1994). New York: Gramercy Books.

Wertsch, J.V. (Ed.). (1985). *Culture, communication and cognition: Vygotskian perspectives.* Cambridge, UK: Cambridge University Press.

Wertsch, J.V. (1991). *Voices of the mind: A sociocultural approach to mediated action.* Cambridge, MA: Harvard University Press.

Whiting, B. (1980). Culture and social behavior: A model for the development of social behavior. *Ethos, 8,* 95–116.

Whiting, B., & Edwards, C.P. (1988). *Children of different worlds: the formation of social behavior.* Cambridge, MA: Harvard university Press.

Whiting, B., & Whiting, J. (1975). Children of six cultures: A psychocultural analysis. Cambridge, MA: Harvard University Press.

Wien, C.A. (1995). *Developmentally appropriate practice in "real life": Stories of teacher practical knowledge.* New York: Teachers College Press.

"Zebra." Drawing by 5-year-old child at Diana School.

chapter 15

Poppies and the Dance of World Making

Paul Kaufman*

SCENE ONE: FELLINI WOULD APPROVE

The warm, honeyed breath of the Italian spring hangs in the air. A line of children moves quietly into the poppy field. Parting the long grasses—like Moses and the Israelites—they make their way through a blazing sea of red. "You may pick a few flowers," says the *atelierista,* a handsome woman with Botticellian hair and a 35mm camera.

A boy holds a poppy up to the sunlight, scrutinizes it with obvious discernment, and blows at it. "This is better than ice cream," he murmurs. In the sweetest of primeval rituals, two girls groom each other.

"Let me try to put the flower in your hair," one says. She inserts the stem of the poppy delicately into her friend's hair and pats it approvingly. The other girl responds in a soft, husky voice, "I want to make a cross of flowers in your hair."

Eeeeee! Shrieks and squeals. A zebra has entered the far end of the field: Some of the children have spotted it. Head vigorously bobbing up and down, a bouquet of poppies clenched in its foam rubber mouth, its stark black and white formal attire clashes deliciously with the country reds and greens. A boy shouts:

"It's the Diana School zebra and *I* know *who* it is!" The children hurry across the field to greet the beast and the teacher's aides crazy enough to bob and sweat under the zebra's skin.

SCENE TWO: "AH… NO… AND PLEASE PASS THE ACQUA MINERALE."

Flashback. In the lunchroom of a Reggio Emilia school several days earlier, founder Loris Malaguzzi and staff eat with the American television crew. The Americans want to capture the essence of the Reggio Emilia approach to early education for a new television series on creativity. The Italians are polite but appropriately cautious. There is much cross-talk among them about possible arrangements.

"We'd like to shoot the poppy project."

"But you're here for only five days. There are a number of stages. It will take much more time than you have, to show the whole process."

"But, we don't have a lot of time! Believe me, we wish we had more."

"Yes, but first the children do individual drawings. Then, they begin to work with each other. Finally, the whole group creates a work."

As he listens and savors the delicate pasta, the American producer recalls that his old school lunchroom in San Diego was never like this. He drifts. He becomes momentarily disoriented and imagines he sees an evanescent shape release itself from the corporeal Malaguzzi, who is listening intently to a discussion about just what should be put on television. An apparition of Malaguzzi himself rises from the table and, wine glass in hand, wanders over to the American. The spirit lays a translucent paw on the producer's shoulder. "Look here, my friend, you Americans come over here a lot these days. Especially the scholars—oh, they're some bunch—a few of them have made a cottage industry of studying us—but now also the media has discovered Reggio Emilia. After you leave, there's another television crew heading in. One day we'll be in *Newsweek*. Ehhh… "The phantom takes a sip of wine. "Here's my point: Nothing changes back there. You come. You look. You go back. You come, you look…"

The producer snaps back to reality. Malaguzzi is arguing with the teachers.

"The zebra should come into the poppy field," he says. It will be a surprise."

"Ah… No… Malaguzzi!" a teacher demurs with a dramatic flourish of her hands. "The zebra is *not* part of the project. It will only distract the children." Malaguzzi will not back down. "The children need surprises." She pleads. "But Malaguzzi, the children will get too excited."

Someone asks for the *acqua minerale*. Eating and talking and eating and talking, the producer relaxes into the feeling of being part of a big, loving, quarrelsome family to which he has belonged all of his life.

SCENE THREE: SHOOTING AT DIANA SCHOOL

The video crew's director of photography shoulders the heavy video camera. She needs to frame Malaguzzi better as he walks through the schoolroom, pointing to the artwork done by the children. The producer back-peddles awkwardly to stay out of the shot but still maintain eye contact with Malaguzzi. They converse in French. The sound engineer, grappling with a swaying fish-pole microphone, scuttles about like Quasimodo on a bad day. Malaguzzi pauses before a collage. "This is the final part of a project exploring one word only. The word is 'crowd.' As you can see, the crowd is made up of children, of old people… of adults, of little dogs, of smells, of sounds. It's a very complex picture. Here, what children are doing is taking apart the word 'crowd' and drawing out all of its separate meanings."

The children's drawing shows a woman walking in one direction, while a man walks in another. A mother pushes her child along in a stroller. A dog is held by the collar. "The problem is this: to give a visual meaning to a word as complex and explosive as 'crowd' can be. Children have the ability to put many images in their minds. One image can even become a crowd of images and a crowd of images can create a *dialogue* between children. This dialogue is not only a means of conveying something. It is also the child's way of inventing new directions, of enlarging the possibilities of speech, of enriching one another," says Malaguzzi. Malaguzzi pauses, his eyes shining with the light of informed passion. "*I believe there is no possibility of existing without relationship. Relationship is a necessity of life.* From birth, children are in continuous relationships. They have this need, this desire, to master interaction: to be protagonist one time, to be listener another time. And then, to be a protagonist again. For children, dialogue opens this game of playing different parts. Children have the great fortune to know how to pull thoughts and meanings from one another's voices. They can speak in images that are close but also images that are remote. To adults, these images may appear out of focus, but they are always close to the sensitivity of children."

SCENE FOUR: THE CHILDREN PAINT

The former denizens of the poppy field now sprawl on the floor together, painting a large fresco. The poppies and their friends—grasshoppers, frogs, dragonflies—appear in a startling aesthetic that is simultaneously primitive and sophisticated. Flamboyant creatures, expressions of newly awakened little phenomenologies, meld into a vernal dreamscape. As the children paint, they negotiate. "What's this *thing* doing inside the poppy?" asks one girl of another. *"Ma!"* she responds with a gasp of exasperation: "It's a joke!" "Ohhh… " says the other with the smile of a 6-year-old going on thirtysomething. Malaguzzi comes over

FIGURE 15.1. Detail from "Summer Fresco" mural painted by 5-year-old children at Diana School.

to where the children are working and observes, "It's not just the images that come from the hands and imagination of the children that count, but also the fruit of the harmony of all their ideas. To place the colors, to find the right balance in a symphony of colors, means for the child to become the extraordinary instrument of an orchestra."

SCENE FIVE: WRAP AND BANQUET

The Americans are wrapping up production. Cables are coiled and light stands are trundled away. The crew is especially careful not to leave a mess, even searching for the wads of used gaffer tape that hide under tables and behind desks. On the last night, the school staff and the Americans have dinner together at a country inn. The Americans toast the Italians. The Italians toast the Americans. The producer embraces Malaguzzi. Malaguzzi embraces the producer, *"Caro amico."* If there is a dry eye in the house, it belongs to the waiter.

Back at the hotel, the Americans are depressed about leaving Reggio Emilia. Their next stop is an innovative factory in Sweden. A colleague who has gone ahead reports by telephone that Sweden is cold and expensive and, besides, she isn't sure how good the story is. The producer is assailed by dark fantasies. The Swedish plant is a chill, gloomy cavern in which a few bearded giants in coveralls move about, occasionally clanking their wrenches. He tries to interview them about creativity, but all they will talk about is why Swedes love to visit sunny Italy.

The producer repairs with a beer to an outdoor table facing onto the grand *piazza*. It is evening and he watches the men of Reggio Emilia gather as they have gathered for centuries... to talk. They stand in little groups just as their fathers and grandfathers before them stood. He wonders what they are discussing. Politics, no doubt. The producer longs to belong in such a ritual, this communion through communication. He recalls Malaguzzi's words: *"I believe there is no possibility of existing without relationship. Relationship is a necessity of life."*

A field of poppies, a *piazza* of people—it is all the same. The children dance their dance of world making and the old men also dance. The bells of a nearby church sound and the producer recalls the faces of the children.

"Little saviors of Interpretation," he muses. God knows we need them.

part IV

The Extension of the Reggio Emilia Approach Into American Classrooms

If...*

Pamela Houk

If I can
    ask my own questions,
    try out my ideas,
    experience what's around me,
    share what I find;

If I have
    plenty of time for
    my special pace,
    a nourishing space,
    things to transform;

If you'll be
    my patient friend,
    trusted guide,
    fellow investigator,
    partner in learning;

Then I will
    explore the world,
    discover my voice,
    and tell you what I know
    in a hundred languages.

---

* This poem, first used as an introduction to *The Hundred Languages of Children* Exhibit at the Dayton Art Institute, was meant to alert viewers to aspects of the Reggio Emilia experience as well as to the dialogues of the children printed on many panels. It was written by Pamela Houk with valuable suggestions from Lella Gandini and the late Loris Malaguzzi.

The stone lion,
drawing by 5-year-old child,
La Villetta School.

chapter 16

The Child in Community: Constraints From the Early Childhood Lore*

John Nimmo

ANOTHER WAY OF SEEING THE CHILD?

As a teacher, I have learned repeatedly that my understanding of young children is limited by my own experience and knowledge, and that I need to always be open to new truths, new perspectives on children's capabilities, and most of all, new protagonists or people who stimulate change. The preprimary educators in Reggio Emilia have been, of late, important protagonists for me in terms of changing the possibilities I see for young children to be active and contributing members of communities. In this chapter I show the limiting power of preconceptions about young children's potential for community participation, and examine some constraints that exist in my own culturally based set of rules and expectations about what young children are able to do.

The Reggio Emilia early childhood educators speak over and over of their belief that the environments and curriculum of a school begin with an image of

* A version of this chapter was presented as a keynote address at the conference, "The Challenge of Reggio Emilia: Realizing the Potential of Children," September 27, 1994, University of Melbourne, Melbourne, Australia.

the child. What are our expectations of the young child? How does the child learn and develop? Where does the child's identity come from? What are the child's goals, needs, desires, and rights? The answers we hold (often unconsciously) are a reflection of our values, our aspirations for the next generation, our beliefs about child development, and more generally, our cultural perspective. This image becomes a lens through which we view and interpret the child and decide how we will respond as teachers and parents.

What is regarded as best practice among early childhood professionals in the United States is also based on an image of the child. Although educators' views are diverse and constantly changing over time, there is at any point in time a predominant view, reflected in the leading textbooks and the publications of the major professional organizations, which I refer to as "The Early Childhood Lore." A close look shows how deeply this common professional perspective (reflected recently, for example, in the body of principles called "Developmentally Appropriate Practice;" Bredekamp, 1987) is grounded in Anglo-American cultural meaning systems, in which self-reliance, self-actualization, and the pursuit of personal freedom and equality are highly valued (Bellah, Madsen, Sullivan, Swidler, & Tipton, 1985; Bowman & Stott, 1994; Stewart & Bennett, 1991; Williams, 1994). The lens of individualism has led the profession to focus on how young children attain autonomy, individualism, and uniqueness in their learning, development, and interpersonal relations.

To intensify matters, there is a frequent perception among early childhood educators that young children are primarily "egocentric," focused on the self, and limited in ability to relate to and care about the concerns of others (Goffin, 1987; Hill & Reed, 1990). Although this focus on the individual and concern for the developmental limitations of young children have helped shape many innovative approaches to early education, they have also allowed many in the profession to set aside or downplay much accumulated knowledge and research about very young children's prosocial, intersubjective, and empathic capacities, and to reject as "developmentally inappropriate" the contrasting cultural assumptions and wisdom valuing "interdependence" as opposed to "independence," stemming principally from communities of color in North America (Mallory & New, 1994; Williams, 1994).

By validating a particular view of the potential of young children, the early childhood profession has fostered a discontinuity between preschool programs and the goals of many families and their communities (Phillips, 1994). One strategy for ensuring the success of all children in a pluralistic society would be to stretch the vision of childhood that guides its social institutions.

THE IMAGE OF THE CHILD AS A SOCIAL ACTOR

Tiziana Filippini, *pedagogista* in Reggio Emilia, offers in Chapter 6 (this volume) an image that affirms the child's role as a "protagonist of his or her own growth" but also emphasizes children's yearning from the very earliest years for relationships and the need to negotiate "with everything the culture brings them."

The idea of schools as a system of relationships in Reggio Emilia is captured in a phrase that is used in the Emilia Romagna region of Italy and is reflective of its socialist traditions: *Io chi siamo* (Rankin, Chapter 12, this volume). Like so many of the terms used by these teachers, this phrase can only be roughly translated into English because it hints at an unfamiliar cultural concept. *Io chi siamo*, "I am who we are," refers to the possibility of reaching beyond the individual through mutual exchange with others.

This shared conception of education can be characterized as a true community, a place where collaboration, caring, and conflict between adults and children go hand in hand. This sense of community becomes the envelope around the important interactions that occur within each classroom and school. In Reggio Emilia, the assumption is that children from their very beginnings are active contributors to the life of a community.

By community, I am not referring to the pseudocommunities that some politicians love to talk about. Nor is community simply the physical proximity that occurs for every group. Gatto (1992) offered a description of what I mean by community:

> A community is a place in which people face each other over time in all their human variety, good parts, bad parts, and all the rest. Such places promote the highest quality of life possible, lives of engagement and participation. (p. 56)

SOME CONSTRAINTS ON COMMUNITY PARTICIPATION

The experience of Reggio Emilia offers us a way to make changes in our own teacher lore concerning the child's role in community, because it challenges images of the child prevalent in many early education settings. These images not only guide, but also *constrain*, views of what is possible with young children. I discuss six constraints, concerning the following issues: *ownership*, *conflict*, *emotions*, *identity*, *public life*, and *history*. Each constraint works against young children's active participation in a caring and truly dynamic learning community. The central ideas that I propose, drawn from teacher interviews and classroom observations in the United States and Italy, will be examined more fully in a forthcoming book by Carolyn Edwards, Lella Gandini, and myself (in preparation).

The ideas to be discussed have for me grown out of these interviews and observations, but it is important to recognize that already in North America there exist many programs likewise challenging the predominant preconceptions about child development (Hale, 1994; Ladson-Billings, 1994; Williams & Gaetano, 1985). My hope is that this analysis will provide a further occasion to challenge prevailing assumptions, and also for many readers, a recognition that their culturally based views of childhood—treated by the mainstream profession as marginal to The Early Childhood Lore—are indeed worthy of great respect and required for a new professional view of young children's capacity to contribute to community.

Constraint 1: Do We Create Boundaries Around Children's Work and Ideas by Designating Individual Ownership?

The individualistic lens of Anglo-American culture, as reflected in early childhood teaching, is evident in adults' active protection of the individual child's ownership of her or his work. This is particularly the case when it concerns children's artistic work. With the exception of some group creations such as collages or murals, artwork is seen as strictly "belonging" to the individual who created it.

Here is an example from my dissertation observations in the United States (Nimmo, 1992). A 4-year-old boy is happily constructing a wooden car under the guidance of his teacher. The teacher, having noted that the preschooler has his own ideas about where the wheels should go, pulls back from insisting on her procedure for completing the car. Nearby, a slightly older, more skilled peer looks on, awaiting his turn at the activity. Full of ideas and a desire to participate, unable to hold back any longer, he moves to hammer a wheel on the side of the car and thereby initiate a possible solution. At this point, the teacher intervenes, telling the older boy he must ask if this is all right with the builder of the car. Later the teacher explained her intervention as a matter of ownership:

> Because it was Jacob's car and we try to communicate to the kids that they need to be respectful of other kid's property and… it was Jacob's car and so Jacob could control what happened to it. (Nimmo, 1992, p. 139)

We also showed the video clip of this event to a large group of educators in Reggio Emilia. Whereas some teachers from Reggio recognized the teacher's desire to protect the child's project and that this action was a mark of "respect" for the child, others seemed uneasy with the teacher's intervention. One teacher from the Diana School offered this advice to the teacher: "Have more confidence in the resources of the children to help each other" (Nimmo, 1992, p. 139).

Certainly, the teachers in Reggio Emilia recognize the need of individual children to pursue ideas without interruption, and children do complete many pieces of work that will bear their name alone. Children's work is collected and archived over the course of their entire 3 years at the center. Then they each take home a huge bag of their creations—a virtual history of their time at the center—at the graduation celebration. What is different here is that the focus or value is not on ownership, but rather on the sharing of perspectives.

On a visit to the preschools in Reggio Emilia, one can commonly observe

FIGURE 16.1. Children planning and working together on a paper construction of a city, La Villetta School.

one child commenting on, or even working on, another child's drawing, painting, or other representation. This kind of movement across the boundaries (at least those created in my mind) between one child's work and another's, was striking to me and not familiar in my experience, but it was clearly woven into the fabric of these schools.

Consider this event I observed at the Diana School. A young child is at work at an easel drawing the image of a flower she sees in a vase nearby. A peer watches her intently for some time, and then reaches forward, takes another brush from a pot, and carefully adds to the painting. The other child is clearly not happy about the intervention, but the painting is neither hurriedly destroyed, nor does a teacher come to her rescue. I am not suggesting that teachers should invite children to impose themselves on other's work, only making the point that in Reggio Emilia, individual ownership is lower in the priority of values than the goal for representation to be a means to communication—a symbolic language for exchange of ideas between and among children and adults. Representation is more than the expressive act of an individual; it is, instead, an invitation to interact.

Constraint 2: In Our Desire to Help Children Get Along With Each Other, Do We See Conflict as Something Only to Be Avoided?

In early childhood education as I have experienced it, there is a great desire for children to be able to "get along with each other." Helping children learn to cooperate, share, and take turns is viewed by parents, as well as teachers, as one of the most important goals and benefits of group settings. Indeed, I would agree with these goals and purposes. But one problem arises: Too much stress on niceness can lead to avoidance of any conflict. *Conflict* refers here not to abiding

FIGURE 16.2. The children encounter the stone lyon and represent the experience with many languages.

anger, antipathy, violence, and hatred, but rather the differing of perspectives and the possibility of co-constructing a shared understanding.

Often, when teachers engage in problem solving and conflict resolution with children, they support the individuals in expressing their ideas and feelings ("I'm mad," "I wanted that"), but then do not proceed to help children really negotiate. This behavior, I suspect, reflects teachers' concern that they will squash one child at the expense of another if they favor a negotiation process where, yes, some individual ideas will get lost or changed, to emerge as new ideas that reflect collaboration.

The work in Reggio Emilia asks us to view intellectual conflict as a social event—even an enjoyable process. Paola Strozzi, one of the Reggio teachers, commented that young children spend a great deal of time discussing how a game will proceed, with their interest not subsiding until they have decided: "I am convinced that there is some kind of pleasure in trying to agree about how to do things" (Teacher interview, June 14, 1990). The question that arises for the teacher is whether the children are allowed sufficient freedom and opportunity to negotiate—even to argue—within the structure of the curriculum. Conflict within the envelope of a caring community is a source of growth.

To understand conflict as an opportunity for intellectual exchange and the building of community cohesion, teachers themselves must feel at home with such experiences. In Reggio Emilia, our research team sat in on some lengthy discussions involving all the teachers, custodial staff, the cook, and the *pedagogista* and *atelierista* of the Diana School (described in Edwards, Chapter 10, this volume). These were occasions for frank, often tense discussion about issues of genuine concern to everyone. The intent was not simply to share ideas but to resolve issues, learn something, and move to new levels of understanding. Tension and disequilibrium were not expected to be resolved internally, each person by himself or herself, but rather in and through interaction.

Constraint 3: Do We Limit Children's Emotions in Our Desire to Protect Children and Ourselves?

Part of the uneasiness many teachers experience in relation to conflict has to do with the strong emotions—anger—it arouses; and the same may be true in the face of other emotions, too: sadness and even joy. Teachers (particularly those with an Anglo-American cultural orientation) seem to believe that the best reason for children to express strong emotions is as a therapeutic outlet, certainly not as an act of communication integral to learning. Yet, if we are seeking to support true community, we should remember that emotions are a binding force; they add depth and breadth to the humanity of a program. Our programs ought to include collective events creating shared, intense emotions—excitement, surprise, laughter, and even, at times, sadness and anger. Moments when something scary or unpleasant gives way to relief or triumph are times when community is built, because they are occasions that become part of the shared memory and vocabulary of the group.

In Reggio Emilia, the teachers talk about using "provocations" in their long-term project work, to initiate a virtual outpouring of ideas, images, questions, and emotions. In the videotape, "The Portrait of a Lion" (see Additional Resources at the end of this volume), we see a number of provocations: teachers, dressed in a life-sized animal costume that symbolizes the Diana School, arriving at lunch to greet the children; children taken on to a "meeting" with a familiar lion statue in the town square; and slide photos of this statue as well as wild lions projected in the classroom so the children can frolic and play with the color and line dancing on their bodies. Some American teachers viewing "The Portrait of the Lion" are taken aback by these provocations and the intensity of the Reggio children's emotions. Yet as the project progresses, these shared emotions become a kind of fuel for the children's learning, and their energy is harnessed and focused as they make sense of their shared experiences—together.

Constraint 4: Do We Honor Individual Differences by Keeping Them Invisible?

A dilemma faced by many early childhood teachers concerns how to recognize children's individuality and uniqueness without at the same time fueling social comparison and competition. Teachers are concerned that children's fragile self-image and self-esteem may suffer if strengths and weaknesses are made too public, and so they focus children's attention away from differences toward the idea that "we are all the same."

There is, however, another way to view individual differences that supports the building of a connected community, and that derives from the philosophy of John Dewey (Greenberg, 1992). We saw this philosophy in action both in Reggio Emilia and a school in Amherst, Massachusetts. Children are viewed as "resources" to each others' learning. An awareness of each others' profile of strengths, weaknesses, interests, and dislikes is important public knowledge for the community. Individual children are appreciated for being able to make different kinds of special contributions, as "experts" of different sorts. They are simultaneously allowed to benefit from and depend on the expertise of others. Thus, useful expertise is acknowledged within a wide definition of valuable skills, competencies, and resources, from being good at coloring with crayons, to being able to run fast, to having older friends who can use the encyclopedia. As an example, in one of the preschool classrooms that I studied for my dissertation research (Nimmo, 1992), there was a little girl recognized by everyone in her class as being the "class dinosaur," whenever acting out stories narrated by children (in Vivian Paley style):

> Today, for instance, I had a bus that fell off the railroad tracks and turned into a

> dinosaur and that was the end of the story. Then the girl said, "But no, I can't do that because I want Simone to be a dinosaur too!" So, okay, it has to be two dinosaurs, because she already knew that she was going to be one of the dinosaurs. So she actually planned ahead. She knew Simone would volunteer because whenever there is a dinosaur in any story it's always Simone—she's our classroom dinosaur! (teacher interview in Nimmo, 1992, p. 162)

In Reggio Emilia the use of the many symbolic languages of young children and the avid pursuit of children's questions allows for a truly wide definition of valued resources. The use of multiple languages (e.g., gesture, movement, clay) gives children many entry points for offering and negotiating their ideas. Through the process of representation, children make their ideas (and misconceptions) explicit and the focus of communication.

In this volume, Carolyn Edwards (Chapter 10) tells the story of a small group of 5-year-olds in Reggio Emilia discussing with their teacher what information to include in an "instruction booklet" they are preparing for the new families coming to the school next fall. Two 5-year-olds disagree on what kind of school map would be best to include; and so, after much discussion and with the help of their teacher, they decide to take two sample alternatives down to the 3-year-olds' classroom to get those children's advice on which map best serves the purpose of communication. A clear preference is expressed by the 3-year-olds as to which type of map they like best, and with the sensitive support of the teacher, the project proceeds.

Many educators would perceive a great risk in supporting this kind of feedback on children's work, for fear that a child's self-esteem could be at risk (in this case, the child whose map suggestion was not taken). Within the culture of Reggio Emilia, though, this kind of act does not come as a hurtful judgment, but rather as another opportunity to share perspectives in a long journey of clarifying ideas and establishing the kinds of resources that exist amongst peers. If one child is having trouble figuring out how to work with a wire tool, someone else can assist her. At the same time, she can offer her knowledge of snakes to the friend trying to make one with clay, or draw a human figure in order to help the class conceptualize this problem. These exchanges do not enhance competition (where one person's gain is another's loss), but are, instead, a quite *public* way of recognizing individual differences within the context of a group—an approach supportive of the sense of community that is being built.

In Reggio Emilia, Tiziana Filippini talked about the detailed and intimate knowledge that children establish over the course of 3 years, where they remain with the same two teachers and virtually the same group of 25 peers:

> It is, in fact, with regard to everybody that they have a cognitive map that is very rich and elaborate, and as a consequence a strategy of behavior that is very individualized. (group interview, October, 1990)

This cognitive map facilitates collaborative learning because children are able to adjust their strategies of communication for each of their peers.

Attempts to dissuade children from noticing each other's differences are not likely to be successful. Young children begin to engage actively in social comparison during the late preschool years (Chafel, 1987). They begin to notice differences between themselves and others and seek to understand what these differences mean. Toward the end of the preschool years, dominance hierarchies and "pecking orders" begin to emerge in children's unsupervised play all around the world (Whiting & Edwards, 1988). For the children, these behaviors have a deeper purpose than simply getting to know one another; they have to do with the development of self-identity. For example, Debbie LeeKeenan and I led a project at the University of Massachusetts with 2- and 3-year-olds, called "Looking at Each Other." This project grew out of the toddlers' emerging interest in each other and included a series of activities by which children could construct a clearer self-image, including body image (LeeKeenan & Nimmo, 1993).

When Loris Malaguzzi talked about the effect of group size on children's project work, he said that a group of two can be very desirable (Rankin, 1990). His concern was with enabling the exchange of ideas, *not* with separation. Malaguzzi said:

> [P]erhaps a group of two would be a relationship to support strongly, because it means putting the child in front of the other; it means helping a child reach or gain a self-identity that is different from what he had before. (Rankin, 1990, p. 1)

Malaguzzi believed that a child's self-identity is constructed out of relationships formed with people and things in the environment: without the group, the child could not find or develop any identity. In contrast, in the United States and Australia, The Early Childhood Lore seems to be based on highlighting and celebrating the uniqueness of each child's identity as a means toward making each child feel secure; this approach seems to suggest that identity is prior to group life and is a characteristic of the child apart from others.

Laura Rubizzi, a teacher in Reggio Emilia, integrates a recognition of the individual with a more connected sense of identity in her discussion of children's participation in group conversations:

> Every group conversation is important. Yet I think that every child must understand and know his limits. The self must exist. I want for every child to be an individual. The children must know and appreciate each child for who he is: an exchange, a give and take. (Teacher interview, November 11, 1989)

This more connected or social view of identity is also reflected in the Reggio educators' talk about favoring the *circulation* of ideas among children and adults in order to promote flexibility rather than rigidity in thinking: Ideas do not simply reside in the individual in isolation.

FIGURE 16.3. Children involve the community with an invitation/map for a soccer match they are organizing in the school.

Constraint 5: Do We View the Young Child as Living Only in Nests Composed of Family and Friends and Hidden From Public Life?

Early education programs in the United States and in my home country of Australia are known for their focus on the family. Teachers recognize that their work with young children is dependent on a relationship of cooperation with children's lives in the home environment. Home visits, regular parent conferences, and opening the doors of preschool programs to parent and guardian participation have been notable features of quality programs in these countries. Certainly, there is an urgent need to work toward a more reciprocal relationship with parents (see Chapter 8, this volume), and to recognize and respond to differences in each family's cultural goals. But it is the young child's "protection" from a much wider world of contacts that is particularly challenged by the work in Reggio Emilia.

Concerned with issues of separation and attachment, The Early Childhood Lore has limited the child's world to immediate peers, the classroom, and family. In some ways, children are viewed as fragile and self-centered, only aware of those people and places in the most immediate environments. Programs may have ventured into themes on "community helpers," such as firefighters and police officers, but have not taken children on more complex explorations of how they are part of and contribute to the surrounding neighborhood.

A more connected identity for young children raises the possibility that young children should be active participants in the wider arena of neighborhood and city contacts. In-depth projects in Reggio Emilia, whether it is curiosity about the workings of pipes under the city roads or the annual grape harvest, are grounded in a recognition of children's need to understand their relationship to the community. Children are invited to talk with city and farm workers about what they are doing. Field trips focus on incursions into the life of the surrounding streets and countryside rather than museums, zoos, and packaged entertainment. When a project is in process, teachers spread news of the children's work in the local newspaper. When it is time for celebration of a completed project, it is likely that the Mayor or other community members will be invited (see Rankin, Chapter 12, this volume).

For some cultural groups in the United States, it is hard to imagine separating children from community life as a way to protect them and there are existing programs that incorporate this view into curriculum design. For instance, the Alerta Approach (Williams & Gaetano, 1985) asks teachers to closely observe the local community so that resources can be identified and used in the program and material and curriculum can be developed in a truly responsive way. A step further, the antibias curriculum (Derman-Sparks & the ABC Task Force, 1989) encourages teachers to support children to be "activists" in creating social change beyond the classroom in ways that are relevant to children's understanding of bias and fairness (Pelo, 1996).

Bringing children into the public sphere celebrates their potential to contribute and lets them feel the pulse of their future lives. Although "The Week of the Young Child" has been a time to make the public aware of the lives of children in group care in this country, I would suggest that children's participation in and contribution to public life needs to be a part of their daily life.

Constraint 6: Do We View the Young Child as Living Only in the Present?

Just as with the sense of children's lived space, the image that saturates The Early Childhood Lore is also bound by, defined by, a sense of time limited to the short-term present (see Phillips & Bredekamp, Chapter 23, this volume). Yet, commitment, attachment, and identification with a community are long-term processes. John Dewey (1916), who has been a source of inspiration for progressive educators in both Italy and the United States, believed that over time, people engaged in repeated and varied experiences to learn more about each other, build common interests, and commit energy based on awareness of a shared future. Community stretches beyond a static life in the present to include a complex interaction of memories of the past, events in the present, and hopes for the future. The sociologist Robert Bellah and his colleagues (1985) wrote:

> Communities... have a history—in an important sense they are constituted by their past—and for this reason we can speak of a real community as a "community of memory," one that does not forget that past, a community that is involved in retelling its story, its constitutive narrative. (p. 153)

The image of the child in Reggio Emilia is one that places the child within the context of history—both personal, lived history, and the heritage of one's culture and society. Malaguzzi (1992) made this point eloquently on one of his visits to the United States:

> We have to think in the plural—the children, the people. Each of us contains many people. I contain many people, you contain many. Children are big bowls of *minestrones* [vegetable soup]—they contain lots of pieces of history and are a continuous reconstruction of that history. (p. 10)

Educators in Reggio Emilia talk frequently about the importance of "continuity" in children's lives, and use many practices that support this notion. For one thing, children spend 3 years in the company of the same teacher and the same group of children. For another, documentation provides a concrete memory of adults' and children's lives together (see Rinaldi, Chapter 5, and Forman & Fyfe, Chapter 13, this volume). The walls of the classrooms and school are literally drenched with the signs of past and ongoing activity; each panel offers an opportunity to retell a story. Unlike end products (which Vea Vecchi, 1994, referred to as only the "witness" to an event), documentation panels allow for a reenactment. For a final example, ritual and celebration are used to mark the passage of time in a way accessible to children. For instance, a zebra has become the special symbol of the Diana School. Many years ago, it was painted on the walls of the dining room, partly because of its design elements and potential to provoke projects. From time to time, teachers do such things as cover the Zebra,

FIGURE 16.4. Children with farmers during the harvesting of grapes. Children worked along with them and asked them many questions. (From the exhibit, The hundred languages of children)

in order that it can emerge as a three-dimensional creature (a life-sized puppet acted out by teachers), for special occasions. Children greeting this Zebra with a joyous response can be seen in the videotape, "To Make a Portrait of a Lion," and in "The Summer Fresco" portion of The Hundred Languages of Children Exhibit. Over the years, the older children (the veterans) have informed the younger children (the novices) of the many adventures of the Zebra and the likelihood of more to come.

All of these practices help to ensure that the past is kept alive for a classroom community—a source of identity and inspiration, rather than a restriction on change and innovation.

CHANGE: WHERE TO BEGIN?

In this chapter I have presented some of the ways in which the approach in Reggio Emilia might challenge early childhood educators to reexamine the mainstream assumptions about the potential of young children to participate in and contribute to a rich community life. And yet, in Reggio Emilia a system of education has developed over time that tells its own unique stories about people and places. How could this approach offer useful ideas or answers to what is happening in our American classrooms? Teachers must co-construct the answer with the children and families of their classrooms because together they are the keepers of the history, geography, and culture of their communities (Jones & Nimmo, 1994). Any possible adaptation of intriguing or inspiring ideas from Reggio Emilia must begin with a close look at their own situation; each preschool, kindergarten, and day care center is "not just anywhere" but "a very particular place" (Gandini, 1984, p. 20).

My own encounter with the experience of Reggio Emilia has provoked me to reconsider what I am doing and brought down a deluge of questions, rather than answers, to stretch my thinking about how I work with both young and adult learners. These are the questions I have come to believe are most important to consider:

1. What is your image of the young child?
2. How do you define and balance individual and collective "ownership" of ideas and products in the classroom?
3. How do you view the role of conflict and strong emotions in your classroom?
4. How do you celebrate the child's identity within the context of a group?
5. How do you connect the child to the ever widening circles of neighborhood and public life?
6. How can your child's sense of self reach beyond the present to include both the past and future?

In answering these questions we must begin with ourselves and the community of learners of which we are a part. This is not always easy. For instance, I myself do not feel that I really know how best to contribute to my community, collaborate genuinely with colleagues, and move through conflicts with a certainty that we will all arrive at a place of better understanding. These understandings are not in my bones, because they have been missing from my cultural experience and education. Yet, in building communities with young children, we educators must begin by trying our best to model collaboration and community at the adult level.

Many will need to develop new skills and dispositions as they place themselves in unfamiliar cultural territory. As an Australian with an Anglo-European heritage, I also need to remind myself that the individualistic lens that has so influenced The Early Childhood Lore is not the worldview assumed by everyone in this profession or country. Many cultural groups different from my own have always placed greater emphasis on the binding and affirming values of family and community interdependency. [For instance, just as the Italian educators refer to the phrase *Io chi siamo*, in African-American cultural heritage, there exists a parallel concept of interdependence and mutual aid referred to as "I am because we are" (Warfield-Coppock, 1994).] Although the early childhood profession has always shared a strong commitment to the rights of children and families, we still need to learn better ways to listen closely to all voices and learn from their collective wisdom.

The educators of Reggio Emilia, too, are eager to learn. In particular, Loris Malaguzzi talked often of his desire to learn from North American teachers about the complexities of multiculturalism as Italian society becomes more ethnically diverse. I believe that teacher Paola Strozzi reflected this sense of openness in the following words about entering investigations with children:

> The point is that we are entering a world of views, and it is very important for us to say that there is not only one truth, because the truth can always be falsified. It is important to be able to explore a world full of surprises. Also with a sense of wonder and pleasure. (Interview, June 14, 1990)

For me, it is a sad comment on the long journey ahead for this country in truly embracing multiculturalism, that it was international experience of a European program that provoked widespread recognition of multiple views of childhood, when all the time, here at home, many diverse communities and programs have struggled to be heard and supported in the mainstream.

The exchange of perspectives enables us to discover a more complex truth about the potential of children; it allows us to go beyond the false dichotomies, the either–or's, that we so often set up between care and education, similarity and difference, individual and group, past and present, product and process. If we can begin to complicate and transcend these false dichotomies, we will surely be better able to play our role in realizing the potential of all children.

REFERENCES

Bellah, R.N., Madsen, R., Sullivan, W.W., Swidler, A., & Tipton, S.M. (1985). *Habits of the heart: Individualism and commitment in American life.* Berkeley: University of California Press.

Bowman, B.T., & Stott, F.M. (1994). Understanding development in a cultural context. In B.L. Mallory & R.S. New (Eds.), *Diversity and developmentally appropriate practices* (pp. 119–134). New York: Teachers College Press.

Bredekamp, S. (Ed.) (1987). *Developmentally appropriate practice in early childhood programs serving children from birth through age 8.* (revised edition). Washington, DC: NAEYC.

Chafel, J.A. (1987). Social comparisons by young children in preschool: Naturalistic illustrations and teaching implications. *Journal of Research in Childhood Education, 2*(2), 97–107.

Derman-Sparks, L., & the ABC Taskforce. (1989). *Anti-bias curriculum: Tools for empowering young children.* Washington, DC: National Association for the Education of Young Children.

Dewey, J. (1916). *Democracy and education: An introduction to the philosophy of education.* New York: Macmillan.

Gandini, L. (1984, Summer). Not just anywhere: Making child care centers into "particular" places. *Beginnings,* 17–20.

Gatto, J.T. (1992). *Dumbing us down: The hidden curriculum of compulsory schooling.* Philadelphia: New Society Publishers.

Goffin, S.G. (1987). Cooperative behaviors: They need our support. *Young Children, 42*(2), 75–81.

Greenberg, P. (1992). Why not academic preschool? Part 2. Autocracy or democracy in the classroom. *Young Children, 47*(3), 54–64.

Hale, J.E. (1994). *Unbank the fire: Visions for the education of young children.* Baltimore, MD: Johns Hopkins University.

Hill, T., & Reed, K. (1990). Promoting social competence at preschool: The implementation of a co-operative games program. *Australian Journal of Early Childhood, 14*(4), 25–31.

Jones, E., & Nimmo, J. (1994). *Emergent curriculum.* Washington, DC: NAEYC.

Ladson-Billings, G. (1994). *The dreamkeepers: Successful teachers of African-American children.* San Francisco, CA: Jossey-Bass.

LeeKeenan, D., & Nimmo, J. (1993). Connections: Using the project approach with 2- and 3-year-olds in a university laboratory school. In C. Edwards, L. Gandini, & G. Forman (Eds.), *The hundred languages of children: The Reggio Emilia approach to early childhood education* (pp. 251–267). Norwood, NJ: Ablex.

Malaguzzi, L. (1992, November). *Question and answer session with Loris Malaguzzi, founder, preschools of Reggio Emilia.* The National Learning Center, Washington, DC.

Mallory, B.L., & New, R.S. (Eds.), (1994). *Diversity and developmentally appropriate practices.* New York: Teachers College Press.

Nimmo, J.W. (1992). The meaning of classroom community: Shared images of early childhood teachers. *Dissertation Abstracts International, 53,* 10A. (University Microfilms No. 93-05876).

Pelo, A. (1996). Our school's not fair: A story about emergent curriculum. In D. Curtis & M. Carter (Eds.), *Reflecting children's lives: A handbook for planning child-centered curriculum* (pp. 100–106). Saint Paul, MN: Redleaf Press.

Phillips, C.B. (1994). The movement of African-American children through sociocultural contexts: A case of conflict resolution. In B.L. Mallory & R.S. New (Eds.), *Diversity and developmentally appropriate practices* (pp. 137–154). New York: Teachers College Press.

Rankin, B. (1990, June). *Interaction: The importance of interaction among children and of work in small groups* (Unpublished interview with Loris Malaguzzi). Reggio Emilia, Italy.

Stewart, E.C., & Bennett, M.J. (1991). *American cultural patterns: A cross-cultural perspective.* Yarmouth, ME: Intercultural Press.

Vecchi, V. (1994, June). *The uses of clay (Informal title).* Unpublished presentation at the symposium of the National Learning Center, Washington, DC.

Warfield-Coppock, N. (1994). The rites of passage: Extending education into the African-American community. In M.J. Shujaa (Ed.), *Too much schooling, too little education: A paradox of Black life in White societies.* (pp. 377–393). Trenton, NJ: Africa World Press.

Whiting, B.B., & Edwards, C.P. (1988). *Children of different worlds: The formation of social behavior.* Cambridge, MA: Harvard University Press.

Williams, L.R. (1994). Developmentally appropriate practice and cultural values. In B.L. Mallory & R.S. New (Eds.). *Diversity and developmentally appropriate practices.* (pp. 155–165). New York: Teachers College Press.

Williams, L.R., & Gaetano, Y. (1985). *Alerta: A multicultural, bilingual approach to teaching young children.* Menlo Park, CA: Addison-Wesley.

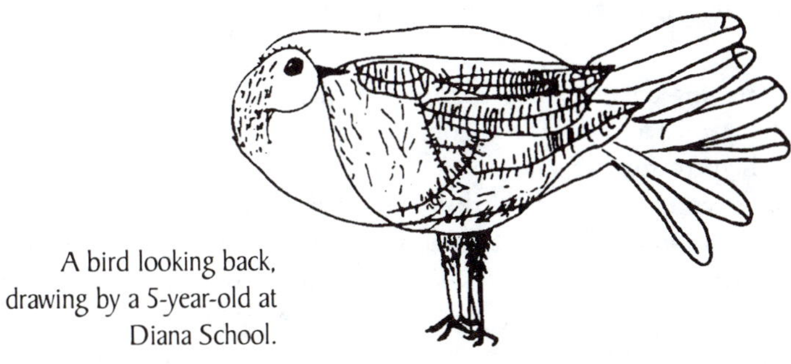
A bird looking back, drawing by a 5-year-old at Diana School.

chapter 17

Existing Frameworks and New Ideas From Our Reggio Emilia Experience: Learning at a Lab School With 2- to 4-Year-Old Children

Rebecca Kantor
Kimberlee L. Whaley

INTRODUCTION

In 1991, the early childhood staff of the A. Sophie Rogers Lab School at The Ohio State University had the occasion to take the first of what would be several trips to visit the classrooms of Reggio Emilia. As a Lab School, we were used to being visited by others who are interested in our work, searching for "educational possibilities" (Fernie & Kantor, 1994) for their own settings, or seeking professional renewal. An advertisement to join a study tour to see the acclaimed programs in Reggio Emilia afforded us the opportunity to become the visitors—an opportunity we readily took for the same reasons people visit our programs. Even more fortuitous was the chance to visit these programs as an entire staff, including our teachers and directors from the two mixed-age classrooms that comprise our school, one serving infants and toddlers from 6 weeks through 3 years of age, and the other serving preschoolers from 3 to 5 years of age. As is the case for all who have had the privilege of visiting in Reggio, we were awed and inspired by the incredible work of the children, their teachers, and their families.

In this chapter, we share our experiences as visitors and how we have changed as a result of our contact with the programs in Reggio Emilia in order to help readers create their own framework for looking at the approach. For some, coming as close as they can to an accurate reproduction of the outstanding work in the Reggio Emilia programs is a goal (and a worthy one; e.g., The Model Early Learning Center). For others like us, exploring new educational possibilities through existing frameworks is a different worthy goal. This process of examining our practices and exploring what we have learned from our Italian colleagues is demonstrated through two curricular examples—one from the preschool and one from the infant–toddler room in our Lab School.

Classrooms as Cultures: A Sociocultural Perspective

As interpretive researchers with an ethnographic orientation, we believe that every educator brings an implicit, personal frame of reference on a visit to another's program. This personal framework, constructed over time out of one's experiences, one's own and others' orienting theories (e.g., theories of child development), one's curriculum philosophy, and so forth, strongly influences what the observer is able to see and how he or she makes sense of what he or she sees. In similar fashion, ethnographers use their orienting theories as they enter a setting and collect data in order to understand the life-world constructed there; however, ethnographers are self-conscious about this frame of reference. Empirical researchers might see this as a form of bias and seek to reduce or control this bias; ethnographers consider the information a "resource" to guide and understand their own interpretations (Olesen, 1992). An explicit goal for the ethnographer is to reveal these existing frameworks as part of the research process. Eisner (1991), in his discussion of qualitative methodology, characterized the researcher as a "connoisseur" who uses an "enlightened eye" to interpret information collected. Further, to suggest that researchers can rid themselves of this background is not viewed as realistic: "We cannot rid ourselves of the cultural self we bring with us into the field any more than we can disown the eyes, ears and skin through which we take in our intuitive perceptions about the new and strange world we have entered" (Scheper-Hughes, 1992, p. 28). Thus, as interpretive researchers, we entered our experiences in Reggio with our views of child development, learning, and curriculum, as well as our existing program philosophy firmly entrenched in our thinking.

The central concept of our ethnographic (or alternatively, sociocultural) perspective is *culture,* the notion that a group of people (including the children and adult members of a classroom) in prolonged interaction within a particular setting will construct a patterned way of conducting life together. This "mini-society" (Goodenough, 1971) includes norms and expectations, rights and obligations, and roles and relationships for its members across each and every context of the classroom, including planned curricular events and informal interactions. A classroom's group life becomes patterned over time as routines and rituals develop, events recur, norms become established, and a common set of expectations and a common language develop for "doing" life (Fernie, Kantor, Klein, Meyer, & Elgas, 1988; Green & Wallat, 1981; Spradley, 1980; Whaley & Rubenstein, 1994). Thus, as ethnographers of educational settings, we held the orienting expectation that our groups' constructed cultures, our ways of doing life and constructing curriculum together would be different from the *specific* and distinctive cultural patterns (rituals, routines, norms, etc.) that are locally constructed in Reggio's classrooms (and further embedded in their wider layers of culture; i.e., in the community of Reggio Emilia and in the broader Italian culture). Further, we held the belief that a new approach is not something that you can "learn how to do," but rather is something that must be incorporated into existing classroom cultures. This process as we experienced it following our return from Reggio is demonstrated in the two examples of curriculum offered in the following, one from the preschool and one from the infant–toddler room.

THE PRESCHOOL CLASSROOM: THE "CITY PROJECT"

In the preschool, the general philosophical "tone" of the curriculum has always been similar to the tone we sensed in the Italian programs. Like our Reggio colleagues, we are grounded in constructivist theories of development (Piaget, 1932/1965) and learning (Vygotsky, 1978), and Deweyian perspectives on classroom and curriculum (Dewey, 1966). Over the past 10 years, however, we have been struggling to find the language within our existing constructivist frameworks to better capture and make visible the more social aspects of a curriculum—what happens "between the heads" as opposed to "within the heads" of the children and teachers as they engage in curricular experience. Our search has led us to the theoretical framework of *social constructionism* (Gergen, 1985; Rizzo, Corsaro, & Bates, 1992), which for us captures what the Reggio educators describe as *progettazione* (see Rinaldi, Chapter 5, this volume). A passage from the foreword to our school curriculum document, first articulated in 1986, illustrates this search:

> We truly believe that our curriculum is the result of a negotiated process—teachers and children construct and negotiate the curriculum together.... Thus, we can only share with the reader some beginning ideas, basic guidelines, examples, anecdotes, and ways to choose activities, experiences and materials that match our curricular framework. From there the children take over, take the curriculum content in unforeseen, unpredictable directions which the sensitive, skillful teacher must go along with, carefully guiding, facilitating, probing and exploring.... In our program, the teachers value the children's ideas above their own or those of the manufacturer of materials. Thus, the motto of our program is "Working from the Ideas of Children. (Kantor & Elgas, 1986, pp. 1–2)

The focus on socially constructed inquiry described in this quotation also characterizes our "small group" curriculum, a daily curricular practice that provides the setting for project explorations with the children in our lab school. The development of this small group curriculum also predates our first exposure to the ideas of the Reggio educators; in fact, we had been developing this small group curriculum over the 10 years prior to our trip. For the teachers in the Lab School, the small group curriculum began as an "educational possibility" (Fernie & Kantor, 1994), as there was little suggestion within the child development literature of the time that egocentric 3-year-olds could engage in collaborative group activity. In fact, accepted theory and research pointed in the opposite direction (Parten, 1932; Piaget, 1932/1965). Yet, we firmly believed that to nurture children's cooperation and collaborative abilities within small group formats would serve children well in this classroom, in later schooling, and in life beyond the classroom.

Small group is a daily event in our preschool, and therefore, it has its own regular cultural pattern for how it is accomplished. The classroom group of 20 is divided into two smaller groups of 10 each based on age and experience. Generally one group is younger (about 3) and less experienced in group work, and one is older (about 4) and more experienced in collaboration. Each group is stable and ongoing, led consistently by the same teacher with an established routine and a set of norms for where to meet and how to interact with one another.

For the younger group, the teachers' goals prior to our visit were described as a developmental progression: First, the small group of 10 must "become" a group, and then they are able to engage in collaborative projects. In the early part of their time together, the teacher typically presents diverse, open-ended materials to provide a vehicle for each child to explore his or her own ideas within a group context. As children do so, the teachers make public comments about each student's ideas, asks students to describe to each other what they are doing, and works alongside them modeling group membership. In this incipient togetherness, the focus is on experiencing the group, and on learning how to share space, materials, and ideas. Over time, the teacher facilitates the children's continuing progress as a group: She helps them to choose a name for their group through a democratic process, suggests and creates group displays of their individual art products, and uses conversation to help children become aware of one another and their responsibilities to the emerging group, as well as their individual rights within it.

Eventually, the children's guided progress enables them to engage in collaborative activity and, in turn, to participate successfully in new and more socially involved curricular formats. Over time, initial group projects such as murals and group wood constructions become the result and focus of collaborative inquiry (but, prior to our delegation to Italy, these projects were simpler in scope and lasted only a few days at a time).

This development of inquiry within the small group was conceived to be a social construction to which teachers and students make distinctive contributions. As just described, the teacher used talk and social action to help children first become a group, and then to act like one. Although the teachers in this setting had activities and goals in mind as starting points for the small group activities, they primarily followed the lead of the children, which often took the group in new and unanticipated directions. For example, a teacher once brought in a variety of construction materials (e.g., toilet paper rolls, cardboard, industrial junk, wood) with the idea that the group might want to build a "city." But, after her deliberately neutral introduction of the materials ("I thought we could use these to build something today"), the children worked together to build a "Teenage Mutant Ninja Turtle" sewer, following their intense interest at that time in superhero characters on television.

For many years, the teachers in the Lab School worked in this way to develop this educational possibility guided primarily by their intuitions. Eventually however, we felt the need for a more formal and systematic description of what we were doing. Within a comprehensive classroom ethnography conducted by Kantor and Fernie (Fernie et. al., 1988), the lead teacher of the 3-year-old group conducted a year-long systematic analysis of the development of her group's interactions (Williams, 1988). This detailing of the socially constructed learning of group social action raised the possibility of doing small group work with very young children from an intuitive educational possibility to an informed and documented curricular format.

Our prior history with an existing framework for constructing projects with young children made us very eager to see the work of the Italians. Yet, we were unprepared for what we saw in the Reggio classrooms. The aspects of project work we found most startling were the level of involvement of the participants, the complexity and scope of the projects, and that with teacher support, children's interests could sustain them for weeks, months, or even a year. We had clearly underestimated children's abilities; we were constrained by our existing theoretical frameworks. We returned from Italy eager to rethink our own project explorations with our children in the Lab School.

We debated for a long time over whether to alter our standard practice of organized small group time in favor of the more flexible practice in Reggio of working in groups whose composition changed across projects, sometimes changing the teachers, sometimes the children. We decided to stay with our own format, on the hunch that our children, raised in an individualistic society, might need a more predictable format to learn about collaboration, in contrast to Reggio children who grow up in a highly collectivist city and region of Italy. Or perhaps we simply preferred a familiar practice that we had spent so many years developing.

In any case, starting modestly and developing over time, we have accomplished many exciting projects since our experience in Italy within our small groups format. We cannot describe the whole journey here, but have chosen one example—called the "city project" to highlight certain aspects of project work that are particularly salient to us, as well as the process of incorporating new ideas into existing frameworks. We try to show how our own program history led us in certain directions, perhaps different from those the Italians pursue but meaningful to us.

The City Project

The city project accomplished by the 4- and 5-year-old group and their teachers emerged in the way we understand many projects to emerge within the Reggio schools—that is, it spontaneously grew out of the children's group experience and their interests. In brief, the children had been interested in a recycled collection of hard, cardboard cylinders (used for winding photographic paper). For several weeks during group time (the first time we ever worked on the same idea for so many days) the children painted these cylinders, stacked them, explored their shape, glued other material on them, and created a large pile of them (this growing quantity was its own fascination). One day, two of the children used string to tie several of them together and called them "creatures." These creatures became the focus of elaborate dramatic play over the next few days as the children took their creatures for a walk, to the dentist, and off to school. Lisa, their teacher, suggested that they might build a town for these creatures, trying to capitalize on their pretense of "places to take the creatures."

The children were very enthusiastic about this idea and launched a project that took 8 months to conclude. The project could be described in terms of the many cognitive "knots," as the Italians call them, that sustained the group over time: issues of design (how to construct the city they imagined in their collective mind's eye); issues of scale (they wanted their buildings to be big, bigger than themselves, but later figured out how they could show the buildings as big if they could instead make small representations of people and cars); issues related to building materials and their physical properties (where to get concrete and cement; then becoming more realistic and deciding how to create a city using the recycled materials at their disposal); and, issues related to mapping the city (e.g., how to place roads and sidewalks for the cars and creatures to use).

But, in keeping with our own central questions and frame of reference, we adults most wanted to document the group sociocultural processes rather than to explore these cognitive issues. How could we best help the children stay focused on their goals and learn to be accountable to one another within such an extended group project? How could we incorporate long-term investigation into this group's cultural patterns for group interaction? What new roles would the teacher take in such an extended process? We did not believe that social action is unrelated to cognitive process, but rather that an analytic strategy of foregrounding social processes was the best way to answer such questions.

We already knew from our ethnographic research how to recognize "group development" and document change over time in the children's ability to function as a whole rather than a side-by-side collection of individuals, but we were now focused on new social processes we had never explored before. Over the course of the project, we explored *group cycles of social attention* (L. Gandini, personal communication, November, 1994) and introduced new cultural elements into this group event.

Cycles of Social Attention

Having agreed to the start of a city project, the children felt eager to build. Anticipating a more extended process, their teacher Lisa took the risk of interrupting the group's momentum to interject the idea of "planning." During this initial cycle of social attention, she introduced the children to the experience of brainstorming, the collecting and recording of everyone's ideas. To support this process, Lisa brought in magazines with pictures to represent the children's ideas alongside the print they could not yet decode. Surprisingly, the children showed great interest in these magazines and wanted to browse through them to cut out pictures that showed their ideas for the city. What resulted from this cycle of attention was a huge compendium of "city ideas" stapled together as a resource guide for the construction process. Eventually the children had to resolve the issue that they would not be able to try out every idea in their compendium, but they impressed themselves with the sheer number of possibilities they had created. The compendium was displayed as part of the ongoing documentation of the project, and the children referred to it frequently.

After the brainstorming phase, the teacher now judged the group ready to build. Once the children came to accept that they could not use concrete and cement, they still needed help realizing that a city could be built out of recycled materials. In this "representational development" phase, the children spent a period of time exploring materials and trying them out. They experimented with cartons, styrofoam, wood, plastic containers, and small and large boxes, and they held lively discussions about "cities" and how they should look.

At this point, Lisa intervened again to suggest that they do "research" to get some ideas for their project. The group first explored the local campus area to look at the buildings and the layout of the streets, but soon decided they wanted skyscrapers in their city. With the help of the husband of one of the school staff members, they made a trip downtown to a seventh-floor office in a Columbus skyscraper. As they looked out the windows and made sketches, they noticed many new things. For example, they observed the elevated walkways that connected one building to another and they decided to place these in their city (which they did accomplish). They discussed the roads and how the buses looked from above as they passed by below.

Throughout this research cycle, the notion of investigation itself became meaningful to the children, including the idea of extending their knowledge by using local resources. At a later point in the project, the children themselves suggested the need for more research when they were stuck on a construction problem. This discussion, held at the end of the project, illustrates their increased awareness of the need for research.

Elise: We just went downtown and we got some research done and that helped us make flags and skyscrapers…
Nico: …and parking garages.
Lisa: What about the walkways? How did we know how to make the walkways?
Max: I discovered them.
Lisa: You discovered them? Tell us about that, Max.
Max: I made it by thinking it would be a bridge but it turned out to be a walkway with a roof.
Lisa: Talk about research… was research important for this project?
Max: YEES! So we can make this city *really* happen.

Working in Pairs: A Step Toward Group Ventures

During the course of the project, the teaching staff talked about the Italians' suggestion that smaller group sizes benefit collaboration (we remembered them saying that they did not work in groups larger than five). We decided to try pairing children within the group of 10 around common interests. This proved to be a very fruitful decision. In twosomes, the children learned to accommodate each other, and to support each other through difficult moments over the course of the most extended and elaborate work they had ever engaged in together. For example, Danielle and Maxwell blended their respective interests to create a "Jurassic Park/Princess Castle," with dinosaurs living on the first floor and the princesses on the third floor.

2-D or 3-D: Learning How to Have and Resolve Conflict

At one point in the project, the children and Lisa drew a map to help them know where their city parts would be placed in relation to one another. Surprisingly, some of the children felt that the map could be the city itself. Other children disagreed and wanted to stay with the plan to construct a city. A strong conflict ensued with much heated discussion. Lisa reminded the children that they had started with the goal of making a place for the creatures to go in. She asked if this would be possible with the map. Lisa, by serving as historian and memory, was able to keep the group focused on their goals and to facilitate conflict resolution. Over the 8 months, the group continued to grow in their ability to sustain strong disagreement and reach resolution.

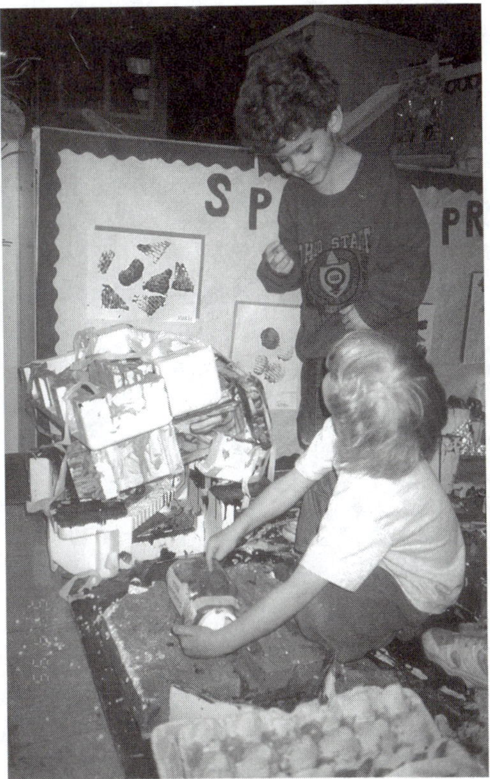

FIGURE 17.1. Working in pairs on the city project the children learned to accomodate one another.

John David: We started out and we painted and painted and painted and then we didn't forget about it. And we painted parking lots. And I said, no Andrew said, "This is a street." And, I said, "No, it's a parking lot" and Andrew said, "It's too big for a parking lot. Parking lots are small." But, I said, "Parking lots can be big or small and then you already painted a street. But, I painted a parking lot where we didn't paint streets. It's because it is just too big a space to paint all the roads."

New Teacher Roles and Interventions

When we first visited in Reggio, we were struck by what at times seemed a very active role for teachers during children's activity (e.g., showing a child how to mold clay in a certain way) and, at times a very uninvolved role (e.g., sitting at a distance taking research notes while children worked). The first kind of role

FIGURE 17.2. John works to place roadways in the city.

seemed dissonant from our own Piagetian training to keep "hands off" during children's exploratory play (so as to allow the children to construct their own knowledge). The second kind of role disagreed with our training to enter and support children's social and thematic play.

Over time, however, we came to understand the purpose of the Reggio teachers' interventions (see Edwards, Chapter 10, this volume). The interventions are careful and specific—designed to facilitate children's thinking, to "provoke" them to go further in their thinking, or to give them the facility they need with a medium such as clay to use it successfully as a language to explore and express knowledge. Rather than constraining children, the teachers are seeking to open up the possibilities for them, just as a maestro helps students learn to play an instrument, but does not make the music for them.

Besides experimenting with this new, more active role for the teacher, we have also tried to provoke children to go further with their efforts than we once would have. Prior to our exposure to Reggio, we did not challenge children's efforts, believing this to be the way to show ourselves to be child centered and supportive. Now, instead, we sometimes help children remember their goals and gently encourage them to go further. For example, in the city project, Samantha decided to create a hospital and started building with her partner, Nick. Although they could verbalize their plans, they had a great deal of trouble using materials to represent them. They did not understand how to make a stable base, and their hospital kept tumbling over. With Lisa's encouragement to stick with their goals and solicit help from their peers, Sam and Nick finally succeeded. What most encouraged Lisa was the children's pride when they finished:

> *Sam:* We first started making creatures and started to work on the building and it was hard to make a hospital, but we got it finished.
>
> *Lisa:* How did you do that? It was really hard to make the hospital, remember that?
>
> *Sam:* Yea.
>
> *Lisa:* What helped? … Did it help that I asked you to keep working on it and keep thinking about it so that you made it work out?
>
> *Sam:* Yea. So Nico brought his school over so I could look what he was doing.

Finally, we have learned how critically important it is to document all of these processes through slides, pictures, and audiotapes. We "heard" our Italian mentors tell us that documentation is key; but, admittedly, it was the last piece we explored as we tried ideas in our own classroom. It was the most difficult piece to incorporate into our day. Even the mechanical aspects of keeping a camera and tape recorder available seemed overwhelming at first, but our motivation increased once we realized how much insight we gained from listening to children's words and reviewing our notes. Documentation allows the teacher to be careful and effective while intervening.

FIGURE 17.3. The final city.

Documentation also helped in other important ways. Three months into the project, we arrived at our summer transition time when half the children graduate to go on to kindergarten and a new group enters into the program. This transition put the city project on hold for several months and we thought it was permanently finished. However, Lisa decided to use slides with the group to revisit the course of the project and see if the children would become reengaged. The review reactivated the project and served to bring the new children into it. Later, when the entire project was over, we invited the parents to a final celebration where we used the slides to share the complexities of the project. The children were able to verbalize much about the experience with the support of the slides. We have a new appreciation for the teacher roles of historian and documenter that we believe the Italians suggested to us.

THE INFANT–TODDLER CLASSROOM

Whereas we were able to see the immediate links between the project work we had seen in Reggio Emilia and our own practice in the preschool, it took us a little longer to find connections for the infants and toddlers. In many ways, the practices we observed in Reggio were so similar to our own that it seemed difficult at first to determine how to best use what we had seen. The educators in Reggio had communicated more about their work with older children, and the preschool children's work has more obvious products to examine. The younger children's investigations, in contrast, seem more process oriented and more difficult to observe. So, when we first returned from Italy, the infant–toddler staff focused on redesigning their environment while they discussed and considered what they had learned.

Following the advice of the Italians to consider our implicit images of young children, our discussions focused on our existing philosophy. The infant–toddler program of our Lab School, like the preschool, has generated curriculum based on the work of Vygotsky (1978) and Piaget (1932/1965) since its inception 7 years ago. In addition, we have drawn heavily from the work of Gerber (1991), consider the terms *care* and *educate* to be synonymous in our infant–toddler classroom, and trust the children to communicate their needs and interests. We view infants and toddlers as competent individuals worthy of our respect. In reflecting on our own philosophy as well as what we had seen while in Reggio Emilia, we realized that there were several "points of contact" between the implicit theories underlying our respective programs.

Point of Contact: Curriculum and Materials

The first point of contact we conceptualized centered around the use of a wide variety of materials in the Reggio infant–toddler classrooms, materials that support the view of infants and toddlers as competent in their ability to interact with things in their world. A typical day in our infant–toddler classroom has always included a variety of activities from which children can choose. Among these opportunities are teacher-planned sensory, creative, and play experiences, as well as the spontaneous play ideas and interests that arise from the children themselves during the day, all available as options for participation. Painting, collage, clay, and water have always been a vital part of our program for even the youngest babies, even though we have occasionally been criticized by visitors who have considered such activities unsafe or unsanitary. Yet, although our infant–toddler program had challenged American standards in terms of material exploration opportunities, our trip to Italy showed us that we had only begun to imagine the possibilities.

In particular, we were introduced to the ideas that each medium (paint, collage, etc.) can be conceptualized as a language to be mastered, as well as the importance of extending time to allow children to more fully explore these media and understand the physical world around them. We also realized that knowledge gained in the infant–toddler room about individual materials and the use of these materials could later be translated into the preschool as children worked with the now-familiar materials to participate in projects such as the construction of the city.

Other parts of our thinking about curriculum and materials were challenged by our visit to Reggio as well. Using Gerber's (1991) ideas of being responsive to babies as a guiding framework for curriculum, we are responsive to their ideas as we plan. Thus, our curriculum also differs from the norm for infant–toddler care in this country because it emerges from the ideas and actions of the children; plans come from careful observation of the children rather than being drawn from a predetermined curriculum book. Our visits to Reggio classrooms both validated and extended our thinking about curriculum planning. We began to reconsider our adult role in the planning. Specifically by adding in our adult ideas we could create "horizontal" learning experiences for our babies and toddlers; that is, extended explorations of a single material in diverse ways. Thus, within the framework of our existing curriculum, we considered how extended explorations of materials could be combined with our use of an emergent curriculum in the classroom. Further, although we had considered (and encouraged) the possibility of individual children being involved in a project for an extended time period, we had not considered the possibility that children could engage in an extended *group* exploration of an idea, particularly in a group of babies and toddlers.

Point of Contact: Relationships

The Italians' emphasis on relationships provided us with another point of contact between our program and what we saw during our visits. Our own major focus has always been on social development and interactions. We have always believed in and encouraged children's first relationships as toddlers, recognizing them as more complex and mature than traditionally described by researchers, and as being vital to the children and their development. This is not to say that we have ignored the cognitive aspects of development, but rather that we believe that cognitive development occurs as a result of social interaction with others in the environment (Vygotsky, 1978). Our strong intuitions about the nature and importance of these relationships among the youngest children led to a longitudinal, qualitative study documenting these friendships (Whaley & Rubenstein, 1994). In this work, we revealed the strength and complexity of these earliest friendships, showing them to be a vital part of a young child's daily life in a child care setting.

The interest in relationships in the programs of Reggio was in part reflected in their emphasis on continuity of the groups found in the classrooms. The homogeneous-age classrooms of Reggio keep children and teachers together for 3 years; in contrast, we create continuity through a mixed-age setting, where children from birth through age 3 spend their days together. Thus, in trying to incorporate some of the ideas we brought back from Reggio, we had to find ways that respected and acknowledged the wide range of developmental stages present in our classroom.

We have tried numerous ideas since returning; however, we offer the following discussion of one extended experience in the classroom, the "gluing project," to serve as an example of how we have integrated our learning and thinking into our existing practice in the infant–toddler room. The project also represents an example of how we have come to balance the needs and interests of both infants and toddlers within an extended exploration of a material, in this case glue.

The Gluing Project: Exploring a Material

The gluing project began spontaneously when the teachers carefully observed the children and their skill (or lack of it) in using glue during collage. Watching the teachers of Reggio had given us the freedom to feel we could sometimes simply sit in the classroom and observe rather than participate in all parts of the children's activity. This allowed us to do more careful observation of their interests and skills. During this planned collage activity the teachers took notes and used tape recorders to carefully document what the children were telling us about their interests by means of both their verbal language and their "activity language." During a weekly staff meeting held soon after this experience (as well as after several other collage opportunities), a discussion arose about the children's interest in the *properties* of the glue itself, rather than about what they could do with the glue. As many of the children were older infants and young toddlers, we had a number of children who did not yet seem to understand the properties of glue. This idea of material exploration for its own sake was a new one for us, drawn from our observations in Reggio. Previously, we had viewed activities as wholes (collage) rather than as the sum of their parts (paper + glue + materials).

In addition, we did not have a long-range view of how experiences in the infant–toddler classroom could relate to what they would do later in the preschool classroom. Thinking about various media as languages gave us a new frame for thinking about continuity between programs. We had previously thought of activities such as collage as whole experiences, but we had not thought of them as languages with distinct components to be mastered. Also, our understanding of verbal language development in young children stimulated our thinking about this issue. As infants and toddlers learn spoken language, they first learn sounds, then words, finally stringing these words together to communicate more and more meaning. Likewise, if we thought about collage as the language, it began to make sense to us that children should also learn the component parts first—the glue, the tools, the materials—before moving toward combining them into longer "phrases" (collage). Thus, the idea of separating out the components of an experience such as collage construction was a new one for our teachers. By thinking about this part language and its parts, we began to see how we could focus on the individual media and build competence with its component materials.

As we mentioned, one concern we had as we began exploring projects centered around the fact that we have a mixed-age group of children in our class-

FIGURE 17.4. Infant–Toddlers engaged in the gluing project, explore how glue works.

room. At this particular time, although we had a majority of children who were quite inexperienced with glue, we also had several children who were quite competent and experienced in making rather elaborate collages. Following the conversation at the staff meeting and remembering the Italians' practice of systematically observing children's action, we decided to simply offer the glue and observe both the older and younger children to determine how we could make the experience appropriate for all ages. Thus, we began the project by simply offering glue to the children on a covered space to allow for exploration of the material. We were surprised to see that not only were the inexperienced children constructing physical knowledge about the properties of glue (i.e,. dipping their fingers in it, tasting and rubbing it on their bodies) but the older, more experienced children who had never had this opportunity to focus on glue as a material were also exploring the physical properties of the glue at a higher level (i.e., noticing the stickiness of it and how it could be peeled off when dry).

This first experience with exploring the glue began by covering the table with brown paper, but we soon moved to offering a variety of background materials for exploring the wet glue as it dried on differing textures and colors. These backgrounds included black squares of cardboard, bumpy textured paper, brown paper bags, and other bases. During this time, children explored the properties of glue, both wet and dry. They made dots with glue on their fingers, drew shapes and lines, covered their hands and bodies with glue, and dripped it onto the background materials. After several opportunities to explore the glue

FIGURE 17.5. Trying out brushes with the glue.

alone, teachers introduced tools to the exploration process. Paintbrushes, sticks, and Q-tips were offered to help children further their knowledge of the properties of glue. Finally, in this initial stage of exploring the properties of glue, we offered the children glue sticks.

This phase of the project highlights other ways our thinking changed as a result of visiting Reggio. We reexamined our ideas about how much variety is necessary and desirable. In our experience, teacher training programs, activity books, and published curricula typically stress the need to present children with a wide, ever-changing variety of experiences; these resources often suggest ways to elicit specific developmental behaviors in babies and toddlers. The classrooms of Reggio opened our minds to the idea that a single material could be presented and explored across an extended period of time, allowing children to deepen their understanding of the material and its properties (horizontal learning). They challenged us to think about new strategies to present materials to children in ways that would extend their learning.

Making Connections: Mixing Materials

Once the children began to lose interest in the basic exploration of glue, we decided to challenge them to move closer to an understanding of how glue and materials could work together. In this phase, we offered the children bowls of white glue and bowls of powder paint to mix with it. Mixing was an idea familiar to the children, as we had presented mixing opportunities on numerous occasions. Children mixed the powder paint into the glue and discovered that it changed color. Over several days, they were offered different background materials and tools to experiment with the colored glue.

At this point in the project we arrived at a crossroads of sorts, a point where the staff could not agree on where to go next. Half of the staff felt the children were ready to have materials introduced to construct, whereas the other half felt the children were still busy exploring the glue itself. A careful discussion and review of observations revealed that the older toddlers did appear to be ready to move to the next place, whereas the babies and younger toddlers seemed to be still in the early exploration stage. We were not, however, convinced that even the older children really understood the connection between the glue and creating a collage with materials. In order to compromise, materials were introduced into the glue itself to suggest the idea that glue can be an adhesive. On different days, sequins, glitter, and beads were put into the glue, and children experimented with backgrounds and tools. To further challenge their thinking, and to meet the needs of the older toddlers, an extra bowl of glitter was offered on one occasion. Ayanna tried dumping some of this glitter onto the paper without first putting glue on. When she lifted the paper and all the glitter fell off, teachers took the opportunity to help her, as well as the others at the table, to make the connection between the glue and the collage.

From Glue to Collage

Finally, these same materials (glitter, sequins, or beads) were presented to the children in small containers on the table next to the containers of glue. Taking the children to the next step, we now presented collage materials in a more traditional way, separated from the glue. This allowed those toddlers who were ready to move to constructing collage to use the glue as an adhesive, while the babies could continue to explore the glue in combination with the materials by dumping them into the glue and continuing their mixing explorations. Transcripts of conversations reveal that the topic moved from being centered around the glue and its properties to the materials and how they worked in combination with the glue. This was our signal that we were ready to return to the traditional way of presenting collage opportunities by offering a variety of materials in the middle of the table to be applied to various backgrounds. Now, as we watched our children constructing collages, we found the older children to be more thoughtful about how they used materials rather than impulsively and randomly putting them on the paper.

New Teacher Roles and Interventions

Just as in the preschool, in the infant–toddler room we were stimulated to think about the power of documentation throughout this project. We had always used documentation through portfolios and displays of the children's work, but we had not considered documenting processes such as interactions between children or their development as they participated in experiences. We had never used photographs and audiotapes to inform curriculum planning and provide us with a form of memory for the history of our classroom. Throughout the gluing project, we took photographs, recorded conversations, made drawings and notes, and mounted these on display boards as the project progressed. This documentation served as an aid in planning for the teachers, as memory for the children, and as information for the parents, who showed new interest in what was happening in our classroom during the project.

We have been astonished by how different our insight into the children's interests has been when we take a systematic look at their thoughts and behaviors than when we were relying on memory alone. Further, although our focus remains on social interaction between children in our setting, we have now moved this focus into the curriculum, viewing these experiences as opportunities for extended interaction, opportunities for the children to guide each others' participation, and places for us to guide participation for them.

Discussion

Our experience visiting the programs in Reggio Emilia put us in a role that seems very reminiscent of the one described by the Italians for their own students—that is, we were provoked by what we saw and heard there to further explore our own understandings (of children and good practices) just as their children are provoked by their teachers to explore their understandings of the world further. Our process began with revealing to ourselves the implicit theories (our words) we held, a starting point that the educators in Reggio Emilia also suggest but describe in terms of revealing the "images" we hold of the child. This is a first step that we would argue is critical for all who hope to engage in a change process.

The hurdle we faced was how to get started, how to make personal meaning out of what was shared in Reggio, knowing that we had not brought home a prescription for "doing" the Reggio approach. In addition, we did not want to transform our programs in such a way that they would lose their own character.

In the Lab School, through such projects as the Gluing and City Projects (and many others), new routines had to be constructed (e.g., planning and brainstorming), new language had to be created by the group (e.g., project, research), new roles had to be constructed for teachers (e.g., documenter/historian, researcher, observer) and for children (e.g., collaborator, researcher), new rituals had to be experienced (e.g., heated discussion), and so on. In other words, the norms and expectations for both our small group work and our emergent curriculum planning were reconstructed to anticipate and support long-term project work and media exploration with all the elements just listed. This did not happen all at once, but slowly with early project initiatives reaching more modest conclusions than eventual ones.

As we have already described, in both the infant–toddler room and the preschool, we believe the group cultures that existed and framed the social construction of curriculum were highly compatible with those we interpreted as characterizing the classrooms in Italy. But, what would the process look like in the case of very discrepant practices? We opened this chapter with the stated intention that in telling our story we might help others create a framework for looking at the work in Reggio Emilia. We realize that there will be as many different starting points as there are classrooms coming into contact with Reggio ideas. We suggest that viewing one's classroom in group culture terms can serve as a framework; we believe every classroom has such a culture (with attendant norms and expectations, routines and events, rituals and language, roles and relationships). Just how distant that culture is from the ones constructed in the Reggio classrooms must be assessed and recognized so that strategies can be created for incorporating new ideas that may not follow naturally from the existing cultural patterns and for redefining those patterns.

For example, if a classroom of children and teachers do not have the expectation of collaborative curriculum in any form (following from a more individualistic image of the child as egocentric, etc.), then a teacher might begin to introduce informal contexts for simple collaborations between and among children to "warm up" to more involved projects. If documentation is seen as a valuable routine, then a teacher may have to examine his or her list of regular routines and replace one or more of them with processes of documentation. If a classroom's material resources do not support the use of media as languages to clarify and express concepts, the new ones may have to be introduced to children along with a set of classroom norms to guide their productive (and even appropriate) use with the expectation that it will take time before their competence with these materials grows.

We would argue that a classroom's culture must be considered and that when innovation fails, it is often because this culture has not been considered. In other words, new formats cannot be simply inserted into ongoing practice or substituted for existing formats. Although the educators in Reggio did not share our language for viewing classrooms as cultures in this way, they seemed to be encouraging something similar. When attendees on the study tour asked to understand how projects were accomplished, our hosts would assert that first, all the ideas that support project work must be understood, for example the nature of relationships, the importance of community, the competence with materials and languages, the expectation of collaboration, the various roles taken up by adults, and so forth. The projects, they let us know, follow from everything else; they are not separate.

FINAL THOUGHTS

Our learning from Reggio has been a multilayered process. On our first visit to the Reggio programs we, like many others, were overwhelmed by the aesthetic quality of the classroom environments and by the final products created by the children in the context of project work. It was not until the second visit that we could look beyond the now familiar environments and products to see the teachers' role in guiding and documenting the projects. Even today, each time we "revisit" the Reggio programs through our reading or by attending workshops in this country, we move to a new level of understanding. Like the toddlers in the gluing project, we have had to master component parts in order to understand the whole. The more we understand and incorporate into our existing framework, the more we are able to see and understand the next time we encounter the ideas of our Reggio colleagues.

REFERENCES

Dewey, J. (1966). *Democracy and education.* New York: Free Press.

Eisner, E. (1991). *The enlightened eye: Qualitative inquiry and the enhancement of educational practice.* New York: Macmillan.

Fernie, D., & Kantor, R. (1994). Viewed through a prism: The multifaceted enterprise of early childhood in higher education. In S. Goffin & D. Day (Eds.), *New perspectives in early childhood teacher education: Bringing practitioners into the debate.* (pp. 156–166). New York; Teachers College Press.

Fernie, D., Kantor, R., Klein, M., Meyer, L., & Elgas, P. (1988). Becoming ethnographers and becoming students in the preschool. *Journal of Research in Childhood Education, 3*(2), 132–141.

Gerber, M. (1991). *A manual for parents and professionals.* Silver Lake, CA: RIE Publications.

Gergen, K. (1985). The social constructionist movement in modern psychology. *American Psychologist, 40,* 266–275.

Goodenough, W.H. (1971). *Culture, language and society.* Menlo Park, CA: Cummings.

Green, J., & Wallat, C. (1981). *Ethnography and language in educational settings.* Norwood, NJ: Ablex.

Kantor, R., & Elgas, P. (1986). Unpublished document from the A. Sophie Rogers Laboratory for Child and Family Studies, The Ohio State University, Columbus.

Olesen, V. (1992). *Re-writing ethnography, re-writing ourselves: Whose text is it?* Paper presented at the Qualitative Analysis Conference, Carleton University, Ottawa, Canada.

Parten, M. (1932). Social participation among preschool children. *Journal of Abnormal Psychology, 27,* 243–269.

Piaget, J. (1965). *The moral judgment of the child.* New York: Free Press. (Original work published 1932)

Rizzo, T., Corsaro, W., & Bates, J. (1992). Ethnographic methods and interpretive analysis: Expanding the methodological options of psychologists. *Developmental Review, 12,* 101–123.

Scheper-Hughes, N. (1992). *Death without weeping: The violence of everyday life in Brazil.* Berkeley: University of California Press.

Spradley, J.P. (1980). *The ethnographic interview.* New York: Holt, Rinehart & Winston.

Vygotsky, L.S. (1978). *Mind in society: The development of higher psychological processes.* Cambridge, MA: Harvard University Press.

Whaley, K., & Rubenstein, T.S. (1994). How toddlers "do" friendship: A descriptive analysis of naturally occurring friendships in a group child care setting. *Journal of Social and Personal Relationships, 11* (3), 383–400.

Williams, D. (1988). *The complexities of small group process for beginning preschoolers.* Unpublished master's thesis, The Ohio State University, Columbus.

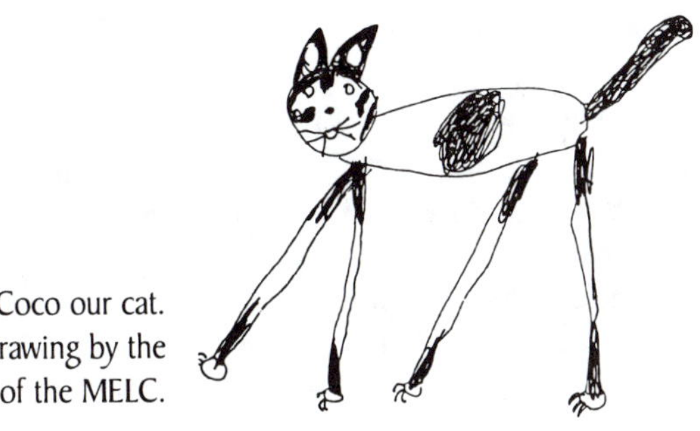

Coco our cat.
Drawing by the
children of the MELC.

chapter 18

Bridge to Another Culture: The Journey of the Model Early Learning Center

Ann W. Lewin*
With contributions from Genet Astatke, Jennifer Azzariti, Wendy Baldwin, Deborah Barley, Amelia Gambetti, and Sonya Shoptaugh

INTRODUCTION

During the last 10 years, as the preprimary schools of Reggio Emilia, Italy, have became increasingly well-known in the United States, questions about their relevance to American education have taken on more and more urgency. Yes, these schools are beautiful, but what do they have to say about early childhood practice here? Can the approaches used in prosperous, culturally homogeneous Reggio Emilia transfer to our culturally diverse contexts? In particular, can they be effective with American inner-city children, the victims of poverty and many forms of ever-increasing environmental abuse?

In 1983, the Secretary of Education, Ted Bell, issued a major report called *A Nation at Risk.* The report succinctly summarized facts that were becoming widely recognized, that American education, which could be considered good or at least adequate for about 20% of students, was nevertheless failing the other 80%. Especially for children in poverty, the failure was abysmal. Whatever indices were used—international economic comparisons, academic test scores, school drop-out rates, or frequencies of teenage substance abuse, crime, and suicide—American education was in trouble. As a result of this and other high-profile reports, American interest in education soared. Exemplars of excellent educational practice held increasing fascination, and by 1993, over 2,000 American educators had visited the preprimary schools of Reggio Emilia.

Coincident with the national concern to describe American education came an increasing number of experiments to transform education. These ranged from state and local systemwide reforms of public education, to individual parental experiments with home schooling, from broad national coalitions of exemplary schools, to an outcropping of single experiments by independent educators. The Model Early Learning Center in Washington, DC was one such independent effort.

The Model Early Learning Center

This school, serving 36 children aged 3 to 5 years old, was established in 1990 by The National Learning Center (TNLC), a not-for-profit educational organization, in collaboration with the District of Columbia Public Schools, Washington, DC (DCPS), which uses the school as a research and demonstration center. The Model Early Learning Center (MELC) is located in the rambling complex of buildings that houses TNLC, in the very heart of downtown Washington. Within sight of the great Capitol Dome, the MELC is found in the part of the city that most visitors to the nation's capital try to avoid. Yet, they know from daily exposure to newspapers, television, and other media that the children who grow up in areas such as these are witnessing not the American dream, but the American nightmare.

The Model Early Learning Center is in the largest of The National Learning Center buildings, which also houses the most visible of the programs, the Capital Children's Museum. The MELC is on the fifth floor of the Museum building and enjoys a grand expanse of space, including a mix of large and small rooms, nooks, dormers, closets, and hallways. The children attend full time (a full 6-hour school day), and function together as one group, with complete access to the entire environment at all times. There are no divisions of spaces into rooms for older children versus younger children, and no division of children into age-based groups.

The selection of children to attend MELC is the responsibility of DCPS, which has designated the neighborhoods of eight nearby elementary schools as the population from which children will be drawn for the MELC. These eight schools meet federal poverty guidelines and contain Head Start Programs for preschool children. The MELC actually receives the overflow from those Head

Start programs, and DCPS certifies the families' eligibility. Children are admitted to the MELC once DCPS has certified that they live within the boundaries of the designated schools, that their birthdays fall on dates that meet public school requirements for entrance, and that their families meet the free-lunch guidelines. Preference is given to siblings, because of the MELC's strong emphasis on family participation. An attempt is made to maintain roughly equal numbers of children in the three age groups (3, 4, 5), and equal numbers of girls and boys. Otherwise, children are admitted on a first-come, first-served basis.

Five teachers work with the 36 children. Initially, they held distinct roles (two co-head teachers, studio teacher, assistant teacher, and teacher's aide). However, 6 months after beginning to adapt the Reggio Emilia approach, the teachers decided to drop these titles because the distinct functions of their different jobs had become blurred through their collaboration. They had evolved from functioning as a hierarchy to working as coequals.

The purpose of the MELC, besides serving the children and families in the school, is to develop new practices that can advance the field of early childhood education (Lewin, 1994). In doing this, the MELC draws on theories and other practices that it believes offer the soundest basis for promoting young children's development. At the MELC, a unique synthesis of theories and practices has evolved, apparent in the design of the environment, the materials and curriculum, the staff collaboration, the program of parent participation, the display panels documenting student work, and the robust projects in which young students engage. All of these facets are documented in the products and publications of The National Learning Center (see References).

Although the MELC is a young program and its practices are still emerging, its philosophy began to take strong shape and became visible in the children's work by the end of the third year of operation, June 1993. By that time, the school had devised basic operating procedures. More important, it had developed guidance strategies for promoting behaviors in the children that enabled them to begin to become self-directing, self-disciplined, able to make choices, and to engage in projects for sustained periods of time. These procedures and early steps in program development were the essential first steps without which the school could not have gone on to adapt and incorporate the Reggio Emilia approach.

Educational Theories for the Model Early Learning Center

Three educational theories have been fundamental to the work at the MELC. The first is constructivist theory, first proposed by Jean Piaget and recognized today as one piece of Piaget's legacy supported by empirical research. This theory says that people construct their own knowledge from direct interactions with the environment, interactions that form the basis for what Resnick (1985) called *situated cognition.* According to Resnick, learning and thinking are not a set of skills in our head but are emergent activities in a particular situation. That is, as we move from situation to situation, through our interactions with people, objects, symbols, and ideas, we construct a way of thinking that works for that situation. The stability is biographical; what we have are not skills so much as a set of adaptive responses for getting started in a new environment. The more suited the past environment, the more quickly a person moves into a new environment.

A second theory undergirding the MELC is social constructivist theory, first proposed by Russian psychologist Lev Vygotsky. This theory proposes that the multiple, complex, and subtle interchanges with other people are the substances from which we co-construct intelligence. Social constructivism is fundamental to the philosophy and practices of the early childhood programs of Reggio Emilia (see New, Chapter 14, this volume). It has also been applied to educational practice by Reuven Feuerstein (1979, 1980) in his theory of *mediated learning experience,* now utilized worldwide with numerous and diverse populations.

According to the theory of mediated learning experience, direct experience is not enough for learning to occur. Rather, direct experience must be mediated to bring to a child's consciousness the meaning, intent, purpose and transcendent purpose, and other aspects of the experience. Approaches based on this theory include activities to help children build awareness of their own thought processes, internalize processes for planning, act with precision, make comparisons and connections, focus attention selectively, and perform other essential cognitive processes.

A third theory underlying the MELC is the theory of *multiple intelligences* proposed by Gardner (1993). This theory says that we have seven domains of intelligence (logical-mathematical, linguistic, musical, kinesthetic, spatial, interpersonal, and intrapersonal), that our learning profiles differ significantly from one another, and that educators should try to achieve heterogeneous, not homogeneous, results from pupils. Gardner proposed that by age 5, children have developed robust theories in all domains of intelligence about how the world works. Teachers should help children gradually bring those theories into closer correspondence with experts' understanding of the world.

From Theory to Practice

Besides the three theories just described, two robust approaches to early childhood practice have been key in the development of the MELC. From Montessori practice (Chattin-McNichols, 1992), the MELC has taken concepts of the prepared environment, self-initiated and self-paced activity, and respect for people and things in the environment. From the Reggio Emilia approach, the MELC has taken such fundamental practices as extensive documentation of children's words, interests, and actions; encouragement of self-expression in a wide range of symbolic media; project-based learning; a role for teachers as researchers and collaborators with children; and listening closely to children, and using their representations and self-expressions as a window into their minds, literally as a picture of what they are thinking. Undergirding all of these practices is a deep belief in the robust intelligence of very young children.

VOICES FROM THE MODEL EARLY LEARNING CENTER

The story of the Model Early Learning Center now shifts to the protagonists, who speak in their own words: founder/director, consulting master teacher, classroom teachers, and parents.

Founder and Director, Ann Lewin

Between 1964 and 1976, long before founding the Model Early Learning Center, I had founded or been involved with several schools and school systems. Sheer frustration drove me out of that work. Schools, I came to believe, were not only impervious to change but at best only benign. I felt that the chances of schools actually helping children were slim. The spate of critiques on school practice—over 40 such studies appeared in the 1980s—only reinforced my opinion.

At the same time, between 1976 and 1989, I met or read the works of a number of people whose theories and practices held potential for deep change in educational practice. The combination of my own frustrating early experiences as change agent and the emergence of sound theories of learning led me to want to try again to transform school practices, and so in December 1989, the Model Early Learning Center opened.

The goal of creating a transformed education for young children was strengthened by my first visit, in March 1992, to the preprimary schools of Reggio Emilia, Italy. This visit left me with no doubt about the direction the Model Early Learning Center would take. The school would adapt, as much as possible, the philosophy and practices of the Reggio Emilia schools. But how to do so was still not completely clear.

In July 1992, I went, together with the MELC's newly promoted co-head teachers (Wendy Baldwin and Sonya Shoptaugh), to a 3-day workshop on the Reggio Emilia approach, held at Mount Ida College in Newton, Massachusetts. There, we heard a *pedagogista*, *atelierista*, and teacher from Reggio Emilia describe the philosophy and practices underlying their schools. We sat on the grass and talked; we met at meals and talked; endlessly we talked about how we would apply the ideas being presented at the workshop.

Then the two teachers left for vacation, and I spent the rest of the summer redesigning the physical environment of the MELC. Beginning with the storeroom and continuing into every corner of the school, I commandeered the time of TNLC maintenance and exhibit-construction staff for the work of rebuilding.

By chance, in the spring of 1992, TNLC had been the recipient of a generous grant of $5,000 cash, or $10,000 in goods, in celebration of the opening of a new retail outlet, The Container Store. Using most of that $10,000 to acquire containers, hanging systems, and shelving units; soliciting advice of arts educator, Pamela Houk, in the layout of the studio; drawing on my own 15-year experience as designer of exhibits for the Capital Children's Museum; and inspired by the space and environments in the Reggio Emilia schools, I readied a new MELC for staff and children to return to in the fall of 1992.

Major changes included the construction and outfitting of a communication center that included mailboxes for each child and a table complete with every manner of paper, writing implement, and tool for measuring, fastening, punching, gluing, and erasing; several light tables; a reordered storeroom; a new kitchen (real but scaled in size for the young child); a train area with storage, mirrors, and a suggestive miniature mural; an expanded block area; a dress-up closet; a soundproof music room; a library and book-sharing area; a built-in slide-viewing area; a new dining room, a studio where children could experiment with "wet" materials, such as clay, paint, glue, and water; and a lab where they could experiment with "dry" materials, such as leaves, shells, rocks, and a host of other items; two new sinks, long and low, with special gooseneck faucets; shelves; storage; equipment; materials; and supplies (Environment, Project, and Learning to Use Materials, Slide Sets; 1993 MELC). It was the end of August 1992. The environment was finally ready for a new phase of the educational program.

On the teachers' return, we embarked on an effort to try to adapt the Reggio Emilia approach. First, we restudied the Reggio Emilia schools using slides that I had taken or acquired. The set of slides touched on many subjects: documentary panels, environments designed with attention to every detail, teaching practices sensitive to the difference between interference and intervention, collaborative work among teachers and children, respect and trust by teachers for children, the work of teachers as researchers, and the work of children on projects that can last for months or even from one school year into the next. My slide presentation summarized the best understanding I had at that time of the Reggio Emilia experience. Each slide became the subject of extended study and discussion; for most of the week before the children returned, the teachers and I discussed how to proceed.

Then the children came, and tentatively the teachers began. By the end of the fall, many children were working in small groups on projects that included studying the movement of Coco (the school cat), discovering the trains at Union Station next door, exploring a variety of ways to use paint, making complex block structures, and becoming friends by exchanging messages with one another through the mailboxes. Calm prevailed, the children were engaged and productive, and the teachers were at peace. We were pleased with where we had gone, but we did not understand how to go farther and deeper.

In November 1992, I returned to Reggio Emilia to plan The National Learning Center's upcoming first symposium on the Municipal Schools of Reggio Emilia, carrying with me a list of questions that the teachers felt urgently needed response. It included the following: How do you decide what projects to do? How do you select children for projects? How do you add children to projects? How do you keep children from fighting over who gets to do what with whom? How long do projects last anyway?

I returned with an outline for the symposium but with no answers to the questions. Instead, the unsatisfying response I brought back—the same response to every question—was, "It depends."

By early spring 1993, I knew that we had to have help. Fortunately, that help was at hand in the person of Amelia Gambetti. Amelia had retired at the end of the 1991–1992 school year from her teaching position at La Villetta School in Reggio Emilia. During the 1991–1992 school year she was working as Visiting Faculty at the University of Massachusetts, Amherst, as a facilitator of student teachers at the Human Development Laboratory School, at the invitation of George Forman, Professor of Education.

For 20 of the 25 years she worked in the Reggio Emilia schools, Amelia Gambetti had taught at La Villetta School, working over long periods of time with the same staff and families. Instead of biding time in the classroom, waiting to be promoted to an administrative position or to move from education to business, she had considered her work in the classroom to be of the highest calling. Amelia Gambetti began work in the Reggio Emilia preprimary schools at the age of 19, and, as she says, the ways of those schools are "part of her skin." Projects she carried out with her colleagues at La Villetta ("Portrait of a Lion," "City in the Rain," "The Field," "Amusement Park for the Birds") are gaining international repute as the Reggio Emilia experiences become better and better known. The memories of these projects are preserved in many forms of documentation including videotape, photographs, texts, and examples of the children's work. In my view, they reflect the kind of education that every young child should have: an education in which the environment is beautiful; the life of the town is integrated in the work of the school; nature, aesthetics, and history intertwine; and children and adults collaborate. As a reflection of Amelia Gambetti, these projects reveal a woman of great passion, able to accommodate her personal desires to group processes and skilled at helping children to stretch themselves beyond current levels of comfort to higher levels.

The questing side of Amelia's nature led her to the United States. Curious about this huge nation because of the American delegations who had arrived at her school with such strange questions, she finally decided she had to come see for herself. She posed herself the challenge of working in our country. She set for herself the task of trying to adapt, in an American school, the practices she had used for 25 years in Italy. During the 1992–1993 school year, she initiated this work at the Human Development Laboratory School, a teacher-training setting under the School of Education at the University of Massachusetts (Gandini, 1994). When I asked her to consider coming next to the MELC, she accepted; she was already committed to working in the United States, and she was eager for the next challenge. She provided just the assistance the Model Early Learning Center then needed.

Amelia first spent a weekend with us in April 1993. Although we would not articulate it until later that spring, both Amelia and I realized we had a common agenda. I needed someone with long and deep experience in the Reggio Emilia approach, and Amelia needed receptive soil in which to try to plant her experiences. By the end of the 1992–1993 school year, and after a second weekend at the MELC, Amelia agreed to spend the fall semester of 1993–1994 in Washington, DC. As it turned out, Amelia also came for the spring semester, and for both fall and spring semesters of 1994–1995.

Amelia arrived in mid-September 1993. The teachers welcomed her back eagerly, the environment gleamed with promise, and I gave her free reign to work in the MELC in whatever way she deemed best. The previous year, I had met twice weekly with the staff; now I agreed to have dinner with Amelia once a week and to be available in whatever ways Amelia needed to support her effort with the MELC teachers, children, and parents. I felt immense relief that at last the staff would have the guidance they needed. Amelia felt immense relief to be in an open, accepting culture. "They were so available," Amelia has often remarked of the MELC staff. I remember Amelia's protesting that she was not up to such a big challenge. Amelia remembers my assuring her that she was.

FIGURE 18.1. The wide, central space of the school.

FIGURE 18.2. The studio where children, the studio teacher, and the other teachers explore many languages.

Teachers, Genet Astatke, Jennifer Azzariti, Wendy Baldwin, Deborah Barley, and Sonya Shoptaugh[1]

Ann Lewin went to visit Reggio Emilia in 1992 and came back with the mission of implementing these ideas directly in the MELC setting. Her first attempt at creating an innovative school was to rework the entire environment. When we returned in the fall for the 1992–1993 school year, there were entirely new structures for the school and all new materials. It is important to understand that Ann Lewin made a committed decision to support these ideas to the fullest extent. She did this by providing structure, organization, money, and most importantly by acting as a mentor.

Two years earlier, Ann had sent a memo to the staff saying that we should pay close attention to the ideas of Reggio Emilia because of its importance to the field of education. At that time, Sonya wrote a memo back, asking, "WHO is Reggio Emilia?" This is how unfamiliar we were with the approach. Ann then sent us articles by Rebecca New and Lella Gandini about the environment [Editor's note: see Additional Resources]. We were also fortunate that the

---

[1] Several of the quoted contributions of the teachers and Amelia Gambetti are drawn from two long interviews published in *Innovations in Early Education: The International Reggio Exchange,* Vol. *2*(4), and Vol. *3*(1). We thank the Merrill–Palmer Institute for permission to use these interviews.

"Hundred Languages of Children" exhibit was on display in the Capital Children's Museum, allowing us immediate access to examples of project work and to the video, "A Portrait of a Lion." The samples of children's work and the video overwhelmed us with their richness, with the beauty of the environments, but most importantly, with the sophistication of the children's thinking.

After we began to be familiar enough with the philosophy of Reggio Emilia and Ann gave us more information, we decided to meet once or twice a week to discuss what we thought were exciting and inspiring ideas. Although the information was captivating, the approach felt distant. We weren't quite sure that this would ever work for us because we were in an environment that we assumed didn't like change. But, after much consideration and Ann's continuing dialogue, we found these ideas too important to ignore. Ann came to the realization that we would have to get some help directly from the Reggio teachers themselves. With Ann's drive and initiative, she found a person to give us that help, Amelia Gambetti. Ann played the critical role of connecting us with Amelia, at first at conferences and then for two long weekends, and finally for a 6-month consultation. This turned into a close, collegial long-term relationship.

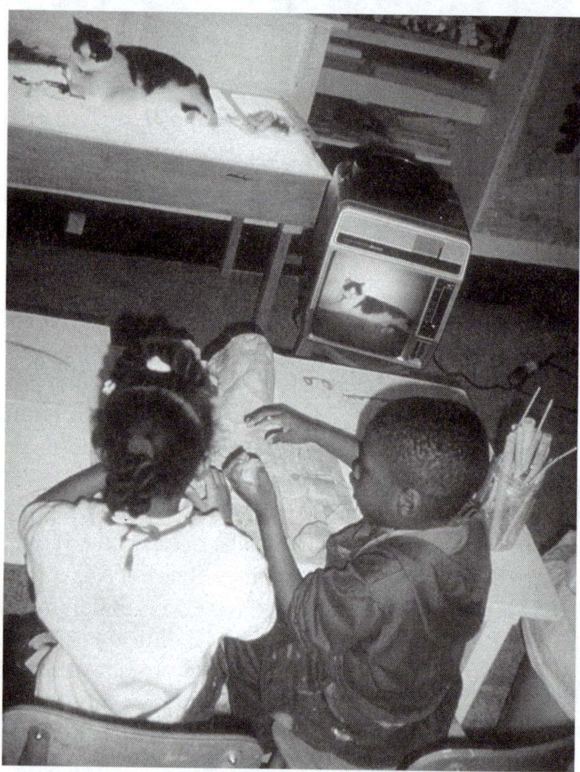

FIGURE 18.3. Coco inspires work in clay.

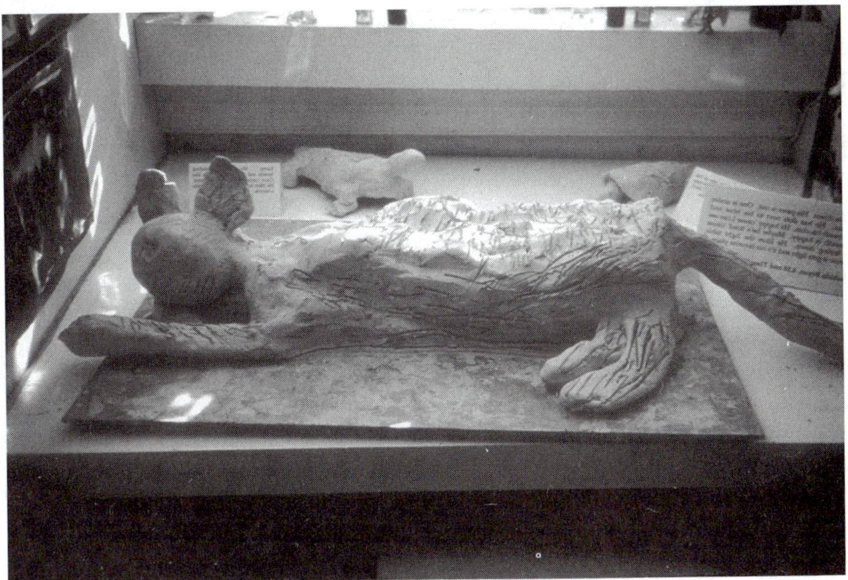

FIGURE 18.4. Coco in clay sits on the window-sill.

Master Consulting Teacher, Amelia Gambetti

We wanted to be a team and to use the differences among us as a resource for us all. We knew that the only way to make a connection with the Reggio Emilia approach was by working together. From the beginning, we tried to create an atmosphere of confidence. When I tried to communicate with the teachers, I wanted to let them know that I was also there in order to understand more and to know more. Only through this new knowledge would I have a chance to help the teachers grow. I knew that if I could add to my own knowledge, I could help them. I could include what I learned about the context of the school and about their personalities.

I asked to observe for 1 week to 10 days in the fall of 1993. Like a shadow, I followed everyone everywhere and took many notes. The staff did their part by accepting this immediately. Together we understood that I was not there to criticize or evaluate, but to understand. The director, Ann Lewin, gave me complete freedom to act in the school. It was a big message of trust. I was a little concerned about the amount of responsibility, but totally grateful to Ann because she showed her strong belief in what I could do. I was asking the teachers to give me the same confidence. We liked each other and we understood each other immediately. The staff gave me their total trust.

During the first period of my observations, I asked the teachers to organize a list of questions for me. I asked them to write down what they wanted to know about my experiences, what they demanded of me, and what they expected from me. After only 10 days we began our first staff meeting together and immediately we had something to share: my observations and the teacher's questions. Through my observations and their questions, we began to understand better who we were, where each of us was coming from, where we wanted to go, and why. We worked toward understanding the things that we wanted to do and the motivation behind our choices. We understood that it was essential in the daily functioning of the school that everyone know about everyone else. We needed to understand each others' ongoing projects, activities, and initiatives so that we could combine our ideas and could organize and understand them together.

Everyone took on responsibility for writing down observations of the children and for keeping notes. This was crucial because we had to organize our ideas as the basis for experiences with the children and we had to share our observations in order to raise our level of knowledge and awareness. We needed the strength of everyone's collaboration, cooperation, and availability. It was imperative for each team member to understand the importance of exchanging ideas, sharing, and negotiating. It is easier to say "Yes," and then do what you want to do, than to say "No," and explain the motivation behind the "no" and together reach agreement.

One of the qualities we had to develop was our availability to show our vulnerabilities. We needed to be able to talk honestly about who we were, who we are, and what we were doing. We needed to discuss our confusions and our mistakes so that we could learn together through each other's experiences, as well as our own. We started to listen to each other, which meant that we had to express our opinions, and through our opinions we confronted the problems of negotiating.

Ann Lewin

A major breakthrough during Amelia's first weeks in the Model Early Learning Center was the realization of how to hold conversations with children; conversations will not happen unless time is set aside for them. The teachers saw that time for conversations is at least as important—maybe more so—than any other activity; in conversations are found the embryos of projects.

The embryos of projects are also found in hypotheses. In the early weeks of the 1993–1994 school year, the staff was going through a process of learning how to organize and emphasize the hundreds of threads that are spun every minute in the rich lives of preschool children. Fleeting questions, ephemeral ideas, wisps of poetry, huge questions, and mathematical expressions are the stuff of a young child's mind. But only in a listening environment are these fleeting expressions captured, nurtured, and developed. Only in an environment that is prepared to hear children's questions and that knows how to hold on to those questions will powerful projects emerge.

Amelia helped the staff learn to listen, and then to listen more closely. Together, they made a list of ongoing projects and experiences, like an inventory. But there was a problem: How could they organize this huge inventory? The instrument they came up with was a hypothetical organization—a supposition—of what could occur in the coming week or coming month: what *might* happen. Together, they divided the week into days; then, they tried to figure out how to proceed. They devised a form, a sort of calendar of the days of the week, on which to write the hypothetical times *when* hypothetical activities might take place, *who* might do them, and *where.* Why were these considered hypothetical? Because, if you follow the actual flow of teachers and children, something different might happen than what you expected. So, you have to be flexible. And the form, the hypothetical organization, by the end of each week looked like a road map drawn by a crazy man who walked a jaggedly bizarre path in bold streaks of color. Arrows everywhere, the visible traces of conversation, conjecture, collaboration, and evolution; a picture of the big changes that occur in the thoughts and the doings of 36 children and the five adults who all day picked up the threads in the conversations and set them into a warp so that a tapestry of cohesive activity emerges.

FIGURE 18.5. Children work in the studio to prepare a mobile.

FIGURE 18.6. The teachers have placed a videocamera that can be helpful with the observation.

Teachers

Day after day, Amelia shared with us her previous experiences in Reggio Emilia. It was important for her to revisit her own teaching. By doing so, she was able to support us in our new adventure. Eventually, after much time, thought, and energy, we began to see the connection between philosophy and practice. We believed in the underlying tenets of the Reggio Emilia approach: recognizing children's full potential, working in collaborative groups, the importance of time and the physical space, the role of the teacher as researcher, the use of the studio and the role of the studio teacher *(atelierista),* the expression of children through more than a hundred languages, documentation, revisiting, and parent involvement. Significantly, we did not face these issues one by one, but at the same time, one element supported by and inextricable from the other ones.

We proceeded in small steps. The consideration of the child and the child's potential helped us begin to establish a new style of communication with families. We started by communicating our projects and experiences through documentation that became more detailed day by day. We learned to see documentation not just as a product, but as something that always evolves. Everything that we did needed time and organization. The importance of working as a team became clearer as the projects evolved and as our observations improved. Our improved observation deepened our relationships with the children, and a new kind of awareness blossomed that had not existed before.

Amelia Gambetti

One of our primary objectives was to make the school and the children visible to the families in ways they had not been in the previous years; we wanted to make everything that we were doing visible and to help the parents understand *why.*

We documented the projects with the children, so that the presence of the children became increasingly evident everywhere. All this stimulated the families' interest, raised their curiosity, and increased their desire to know and their ability to ask for more.

The more this happened, the more families began to see themselves as an essential and competent component in the life of the school. They began to feel that they really counted, and to recognize that they had not only responsibilities but also rights.

It was, and still is, not an easy process. It requires extraordinary openness and effort on both parts. It means learning self-esteem, trust, how to collaborate, to believe in what you are doing and in its importance for the well-being not only of the children, but also of the families and of the teachers.

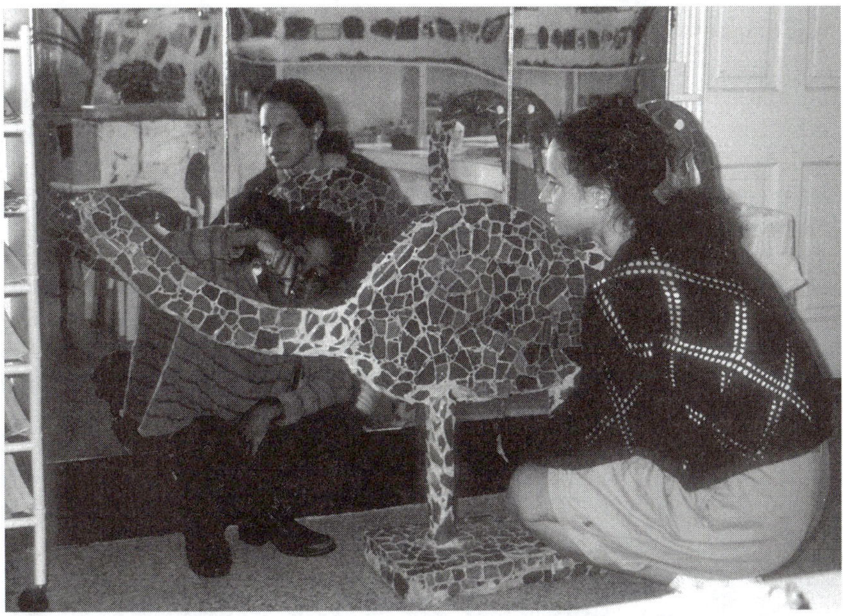

FIGURE 18.7. This child likes very much the sculpture made by an artist.

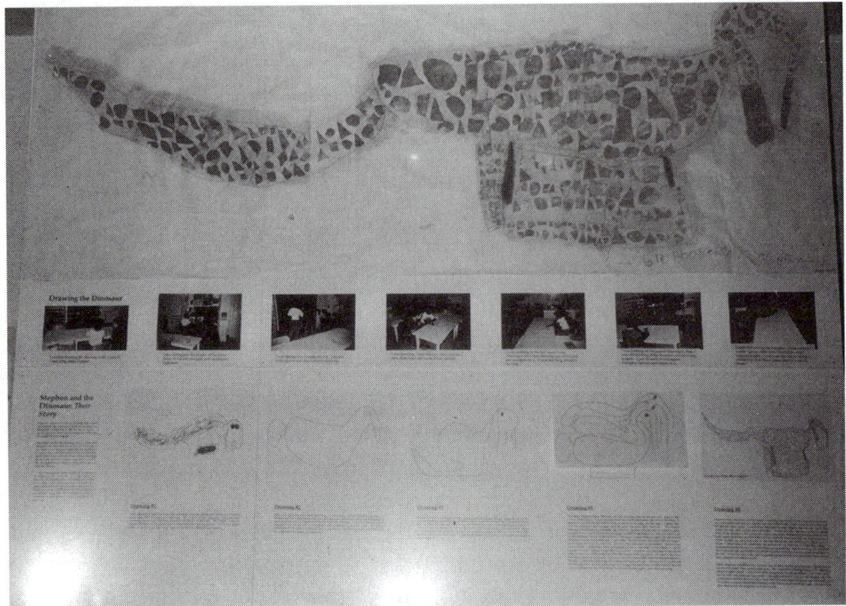

FIGURE 18.8. The documentation shows the process of how the child represents the sculpture and the observation of the teachers.

Ann Lewin

The questions evolved. Now the teachers wanted to know, "How do projects flow? How do we get the children into groups? How are children provoked into thinking? Among all the possibilities for projects, why would you choose to do one project and not another? *Why* is one project better than another?" They learned through their own, at first faltering but surer and surer explorations. They learned with Amelia's voice ringing in their ears, "You think you have listened to the children well enough? Why did you proceed in *this* way? What is the purpose of your action? What is your motivation? Ask yourself as many questions as you can so that you understand the choices you have made." The teachers gradually came to understand why the children's expressive products were not merely "artwork."

Teachers

At the beginning of our work with Amelia, she helped us to understand ourselves and our use of time as well as the meaning of time in the school. Through Amelia's observation, we discovered that the children were eating lunch at an incredibly rapid rate. We realized how much we disliked the transition from Group Assembly (the time when children come together to share, discuss, organize themselves, and summarize what they have done that day) to use of the bathroom to nap. We clocked it at a total of 12 minutes! We also discovered that lunch time was so rushed that children did not talk to each other. There was a lot of movement and chaos with children and adults up and down. We realized *how much* we disliked our rushed lunch.

So, we reorganized the entire procedure in order to give new significance to a time of day that had been such a struggle. We began to value the dining room as its own environment as well as the time we spent there together. Our discovery about lunch time and our use of transitions was very significant. As a result we began to examine time, to converse with children more slowly, to give ourselves time to explore materials, the space, and the environment. Often, time and educators expectations don't combine very well. Research shows that the average time a teacher waits for an answer is 4 seconds!

We maintained a regular time for lunch, breakfast, and nap, but we reorganized the rest of the day to allow for the development of different projects. It is important to mention that the children were part of each of these decisions. We kept a written inventory of ongoing experiences, summaries, and predictions for the next week or two in connection with different projects. We wanted a flexible organization that was ready to be modified in case something came up. We increased our awareness of how we were organized by writing it down. We tried to connect the entire day and our times of action. Even now this requires a lot of effort and detailed organization, but our awareness gives us another vision of the use and the value of time.

Time with parents is also different. We wanted to have families involved in the program because they are an important presence in the education of children. We analyzed our previous experiences and found that we had a problem with communication. We did not let parents know enough about their child's experiences and what was happening in our program. We realized that we wanted parents not only to know everything that was going on in the school, but also to understand what led to our actions and what motivated our choices. We sent many different flyers home in order to maintain a living communication system. We included parents in our projects, asking for participation. We called them "researchers at home." As a result of these efforts, many parents participated extensively. We had many different kinds of meetings in which we explained our ongoing projects. We had celebrations, parties, field trips, and working meetings for building or preparing materials; all were done collaboratively.

Our ongoing projects were documented on panels that gave parents strong messages about experiences in the school. As more of the teachers' and children's work became visible, parents began to ask us questions. We collected these questions in order to understand the origins of the children's ideas and the parents' concerns. Sometimes the parents would bring us children's questions that turned into problems to be solved. Parents could revisit what we were doing through the panels or in folders that contained their children's work. This made all the difference in their interest. It facilitated and increased their curiosity and their confidence in us and the school. The well-being of their children became evident to them. Children began to talk even more about what they were doing at school and at home. The parents could find the presence of their children and themselves everywhere in the school.

Amelia Gambetti

Right from the start, we identified strategies for information exchange as an initial way to approach the families. The parents and the family unit were sent newsletters that contained children's words and drawings, because we wanted first and foremost to give them a sense of their children's potential. Then an Advisory Committee was formed, consisting of five parents and two teachers. Each member had the same level of importance in organizing, promoting, supporting, and publicizing various initiatives in process. We also held frequent meetings with the families, in which we explained what we were doing at school; we used the children's dialogues, slides, and photographs to help parents understand the origins of the projects and the various experiences taking place in the school.

Our parents—many of them living at the margins of "mainstream" society—have found a place for themselves in the school and have been helped to construct a powerful image of their children.

FIGURE 18.9. The communication center is set up to invite children to prepare messages.

FIGURE 18.10. The mailboxes are used by children, teachers, and parents.

Ann Lewin

By year's end, the teachers had learned to slow down, listen to the children, hold conversations with them, and hear the children's own hypotheses. They had learned to involve parents in the life of the school and to let them play a role. They had succeeded in pursuing projects in great depth, working in groups, distinguishing hypotheses with most potential, becoming observers and researchers, and recording the experiences of children and parents. They could document the evolution of the projects, make panels that accurately captured the story line of a project, and use the documentation as part of a self-reflective process both for individuals and the group as a whole. They could collaborate and work as coequals. They could develop and explore the "hundred languages" of children. The results were apparent everywhere, especially when looking at the parents.

The growth in parent participation was evident in several ways. The rich documentation affected the parents who took great pleasure in seeing the pictures of their children engrossed in a wide variety of activities, concentrated, happy, and learning. The many transcriptions of children's dialogue helped the parents to value their children more. Parents studied the documentation intensely and asked many questions about it. They sent things from home for the projects. Given the parents' preoccupation with many huge problems in their lives, the extent of their involvement in the school was really amazing.

In the course of the 1993–1994 school year, there were more than 44 occasions for parents to join the teachers and children, including meetings, planning sessions, festivals, outings, work parties, celebrations, holidays, birthdays, field trips, and presentations. By the end of the school year, every parent, as well as extended family members, had attended one or even several of the events. The school offered parents a way to meet one another, to know each other better. Not only had the children become friends, but their families had done so, as well.

Teachers

In May, 1995, we conducted exit interviews with all of our departing parents.[2] One question we asked concerned what experiences had been most successful for them in terms of learning more about what goes on at MELC and becoming part of the school, and another concerned whether the panels and other documentation had helped them to understand the development of their children. Their answers were very interesting because it was clear that although all aspects of the parent involvement program had been effective and appreciated, for each family there had been different highlights and different memories most important to them. The parents' own words best describe how they felt about their experiences.

Parents

Ahmed's Mother. Parent meetings were what helped me the most. Real wonderful meetings! I appreciated that you talked in detail about the children. The meetings were not based on [making] decisions, but on what the children were doing. Because I know what the children were doing, I felt I could go ahead and know what *I* should do. Every day I can see the panels, but sometimes I can't get a chance to read the walls. The meetings really helped to know what to look at, and what to pay attention to. I've never been bored. The meetings were always very interesting.

---

[2] Carolyn Edwards and Ruth Ann Crum of the University of Kentucky suggested questions for the exit interviews, which were conducted with all nine exiting families. Carolyn prepared the selection of excerpts. The children's names have been changed to protect confidentiality.

Kiesha's Mother. My mother had a crisis last year (surgery), and so I couldn't participate and be as active as I would have liked. I relied on the messages for my information—for my understanding of the school and the teachers. I appreciated how you put down the children's dialogues word for word as the children said them. [Picking up one of the conversations given her and waving it above her head] And I'm going to bring this with me to Kiesha's school [next year] and show them how you *listened* to my child and wrote down *exactly* what she said. I don't think it is right to consider "proper" English as what must be spoken or taught all of the time. As long as they get the point across, who cares? Maybe it's because you can't understand them, not because they can't communicate. You want to change the way I hear this at home? I resent that. Let the children speak their language. I'm going to *read* this to them.

Daniel's Mother. I read the journal on the parent board every day. This is the best way for me to know what is going on. The documentation was very helpful too, in order to know what was happening in the school over a span of time. This summer, we plan to continue using the library.

Georgie's Grandmother. I wasn't the family member who came most frequently; Georgie's aunt and great grandmother came to most things. Georgie's great grandmother [who recently passed away] thoroughly enjoyed all of the events, and spoke of them often. I did come to the Octoberfest last year. During this celebration, I had the chance to meet all of the children that Georgie talked about at home so much.... This is not a place where you just drop your child off. You can see what children are involved in, through the pictures around, and you can see children enjoying themselves in what they are doing.

Cindy's Grandmother. I thoroughly enjoyed the book sharing program. I like the books, sending books home every day. Sometimes I read them, sometimes Sam, sometimes her grandfather. Her father buys her books, too. This routine of sending books home helped me to become part of the school, and it was valuable for Cindy's learning. Also, the researches that were done at home let me have input into my granddaughter's education. Both Sam and I helped Cindy do the research.... [As to the documentation] I like the panels. I think this is very nice. It lit up the school by putting all the stuff on the wall. I love it! It brightens everything up, and it helped to understand what was going on.

Karen's Mother. Over the 3 years, I enjoyed the field trips the most. I especially like the field trips to the arboretum. I feel these experiences opened up the children more, and encouraged them to talk more, and to ask more questions. A lot of parents came on the field trips, and so I got to know them better, and the other children, too. Also, I got to bring my youngest son on the trips, and this was a great opportunity for him.

Renee's Mother. I did not enjoy the field trips most! Everything but the field trips! But from Renee's perspective, she'd say the field trips.... As for having input into the school, I input a whole lot, you know that! I must have asked about 500 questions over the 3 years. I was new at the motherhood game, but

I'm doing it. Whatever I asked, you all took care of it. [As to the panels and documentation] It's good. It reminds the children of what they've done, and it helps the parents, too. They must help the visitors to see what you do. Maybe the DC Council members should come here and see them!

Alicia's Mother. I liked the big parent meetings, because it was good to hear what the other parents had to say, and this was a good way for everyone to voice their opinions. The celebrations were fine, but sometimes the eating part got out of hand! Alicia shared a lot with the family, and when there was home researches the whole family participated in the project that she brought home. Sometimes it seemed the family liked the project even more than Alicia did! She made it her business that everyone in the house knew what was going on in the school.... The panels helped me a lot in understanding the projects. What I like is that it was so clear. The words and the pictures explain everything. One of the children will explain to you, and help you understand the panels, because they know what they have done. I like the comments under the pictures. I especially like the birthday panel, because it had all the children's names and birthdays on it.

William's Mother. Parent meetings were most helpful for me. All of them were helpful. They let me know what is going on. The papers were helpful also.... William learned a lot. Taking the books home was nice.... The panels helped me understand more about what is going on in the school. The parent board is especially helpful. It's a great way to communicate.

Amelia Gambetti

All this took place in a school in Washington, DC, so far from Reggio Emilia, but so near to those of us who believe that people of different cultures can be bound by shared human values.

Ann Lewin

In September 1994, REGGIO CHILDREN S.r.l. awarded a certificate of accreditation to the Model Early Learning Center. This was a courageous step for a new organization, and a huge responsibility for a school young in its practice of the Reggio Emilia approach.[3] So, the challenges will go on.

As for me, in the winter of 1995, I moved away from Washington, DC, after serving as founder/director of The National Learning Center for 20 years. Particular people come together at different times and interact with each other and with the forces present in their era. Loris Malaguzzi rode his bicycle to the

---

[3] This certification expired December 1996. REGGIO CHILDREN S.r.l. no longer has a special collaboration with MELC but remains convinced that the experience that took place from September 1993 to December 1996 has a value that cannot be diminished and remains an example of highest quality work and commitment by educators, children, and parents.

outskirts of Reggio Emilia just after World War II to see for himself the school that a few mothers had made for their children. He stayed the rest of his life and left a legacy of 32 schools that celebrated their 30th birthday shortly before his death in January 1994. Amelia Gambetti and I joined hands for over two years on the fifth floor of a children's museum across the railroad tracks in northeast Washington, DC. What will be left as the result of our union could hold some answers to the clamor of questions from Americans about how to adapt the practices of the Reggio Emilia preschools for early education.

If you had not taken part in such a journey it would be easy to mistake the Reggio Emilia approach as merely an arts-based approach. Or, you could dismiss Reggio Emilia merely as a place where, because the teachers value drawing, of course the children draw. But, as the MELC teachers have come to understand, what happened at the school was much more than art, much more than the mere reflection of what teachers valued. Our experience could have taken place in many classrooms, but we were fortunate that it happened in ours. Together we built a bridge between two cultures—the culture of a small town in northern Italy, and a large inner city in the United States. It was an awesome challenge and stands as an inspiration to anyone who believes in the power of a young child's mind.

REFERENCES

A Nation at risk. (1983). Washington, DC: Report of the National Commission on Excellence in Education.

Chattin-McNichols, J. (1992). *The Montessori controversy.* Albany, NY: Delmar Publishers.

Environment, projects, and learning to use materials. Three sets of 40 slides each, illustrating the adaptation of the Reggio Emilia approach at the Model Early Learning Center in Washington, DC. Available from Education Products, The Model Early Learning Center, 800 Third Street NE, Washington, DC 20002.

Feuerstein, R. (1979). *The dynamic assessment of retarded performers: The learning potential assessment device, theory, instruments, and techniques.* Baltimore, MD: University Park Press.

Feuerstein, R. (1980). *Instrumental enrichment: An intervention program for cognitive modifiability.* Baltimore, MD: University Park Press.

Gandini, L. (1994, March). What can we learn from Reggio Emilia: An Italian-American collaboration. An interview with Amelia Gambetti and Mary Beth Radke. *Child Care Information Exchange,* pp. 62–66.

Gardner, H. (1993). *Frames of mind: The theory of multiple intelligences,* (2nd ed.). New York: Basic Books.

Lewin, A.W. (Ed.). (1994). *Model Early Learning Center history and practices.* Washington, DC: The National Learning Center.

Resnick, L.B. (1985). *Comprehending and learning: Implications for a cognitive theory of instruction.* Pittsburg, PA: Learning Research and Development Center.

To build a bridge in clay. (1994). Available from Education Products, The Model Early Learning Center, 800 Third Street NE, Washington, DC 20002.

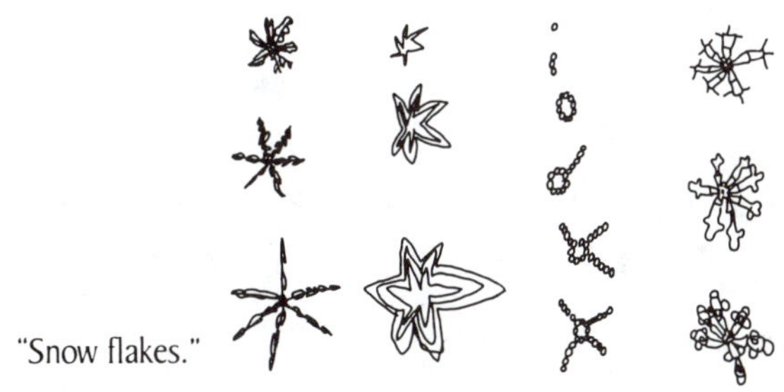
"Snow flakes."

chapter 19

The City in the Snow: Applying the Multisymbolic Approach in Massachusetts

George Forman, Joan Langley, Moonja Oh, Lynda Wrisley

ORIGINS OF THE PROJECT

Ties With Reggio Emilia

In Fall 1988, four classroom teachers at the Marks Meadow Elementary School, a public school in Amherst, decided to initiate a long-term project based on our understanding of the multisymbolic approach used in Reggio Emilia. Several of the education faculty at the University of Massachusetts visited the Reggio preschools and we were shortly to host a visit from three of the Reggio educators. Marks Meadow became a type of sister school during this period, with several exchange visits.

This first of two projects completed at Marks Meadow was based closely on a project completed in Reggio Emilia called, "The City in the Rain." This project is well documented in the traveling exhibit, "The Hundred Languages of Children." Basically, the City in the Rain was a study of how the city and the people in the city change when it rains. The project began in a manner that has become standard in Reggio Emilia, a type of verbal outpouring of children's ideas: From where does the rain come? How does the rain sound as it hits different surfaces? What in the city is built because of the rain? How is rain harnessed for good uses?

Then, as the children waited for the first rain, they drew their ideas on large poster paper. Some drew their theories of the rain's source: "The devil makes it rain," said one 5-year-old. Another insisted that "the rain is made by big machines in the sky, and the rain goes into the clouds, and when the clouds are too full the rain falls out." These drawings were the children's initial theories about the rain cycle and they served as a platform from which to discuss and expand the children's understanding (see Forman, 1989).

The project in Reggio Emilia continued for many weeks, including such activities as making audiotapes of the rain sounds on different surfaces and then making a graphic rendering of these sounds, going into the city filled with questions that had been raised from the classroom discussions and drawings, drawing machines that could make rain, drawing a system of water works that brings the rain water from the sky to the ground to pipes to homes, using a sequence of photographs that show a changing sky and then drawing these changes on paper, drawing a city before and during a rainfall, and drawing many more examples of multisymbolic learning.

Adaptation of the Project for Amherst

The teachers at Marks Meadow Elementary School were quite attracted to the basic idea of using nature as a theme. Our New England version was The City in the Snow. The snow season was near and we discussed how to modify the Reggio project on rain into a project on snow for children from 5 to 7 years old. The four classes involved were as follows: the young fives, Lynda Wrisley's kindergarten class; another kindergarten class taught by Cindy Weinberg; a group of 6-year-olds taught by Sharon Edwards; and a class of 7-year-olds taught by Joan Langley. Collectively these four classes occupied what at Marks Meadow is called the Early Learning Center. The classes had between 19 and 22 students per class. The head teacher typically had an aide or intern. The documentation team consisted of George Forman and Moonja Oh. The six of us met for several hours each Wednesday to plan the project and to study the documentations. The project lasted several months.

Note that the age range extends to 7 and even some 8-year-olds by the project's end. At no time did we feel that the instructional activities were too elementary for these children. In fact, this chapter comments on how the multisymbolic approach is suitable for all ages. Furthermore, unlike the small group of four used in the Long Jump project, the City in the Snow project more typically was carried out as a series of full-class activities.

SEQUENCE OF ACTIVITIES

Consistent with the method of running projects in Reggio Emilia, this City in the Snow project blended planned objectives with emergent objectives, the latter derived from discoveries the teachers made during the course of the project. For the sake of discussion, the actual sequence as it evolved is laid out here in advance. These segments are indexed so the reader will have an easy guide for the actual chronological order of events.

1.0 *Verbal Outpouring:* Children discuss the recollections of snowfall, how it changes the playground, how it affects walking, what you can do in the snow, and how the city handles huge quantities of snow. These class discussions occurred for several weeks before an appreciable snowfall.

2.0 *Initial Drawings of Snow Scenes:* Children drew scenes of skiers, houses covered with snow, even children falling through ice into a pond. These pictures were also included in further discussions.

3.0 *Simulated Snowfall:* We realized that a major concept of this project was the relation between form and function, for example, whether the form of a particular roof functions as an efficient shelter from snow. Therefore, we decided to use a symbolic version of falling snow by sifting baking flour onto a miniature city of wooden blocks. This medium simulates rather closely what would happen in a real snowfall, the upper edges coated with "snow," the covered areas shielded. We also were using our time well as we waited for the first snowfall, which was, not surprisingly, later than usual.

4.0 *Mural of the City:* During this snowless period, Cindy Weinberg's class made a wall-size cityscape without painting in the snow. The cityscape, filled with office buildings, pet shops, fire trucks, and school buses, mostly cut out from construction paper and pasted to the wall-length bulletin board, remained without snow for several weeks. The children thought about how they would add the thick white paint to represent the results of a snow storm. This they did. Other classes did this same activity on a smaller scale.

5.0 *Field Experience of First Snow:* It snowed in early January 1989. The children went into the snow filled with questions raised from the earlier activities.

6.0 *Second Drawing of the Snowfall:* After the simulated snowfall and actual field experience, the children once again made drawings of snow on the city. These new drawings showed more concern with the exact placement of the snow on edges and protruding surfaces.

7.0 *Drawing Sounds of the Snow:* The children became interested in the silence of the snow and also the special sounds of walking, running, and shoveling the snow. These sounds were audiorecorded and the children tried their hand at making graphic representations of these three sounds.

8.0 *Drawing Individual Snowflakes.* From observations with microscopes [*5.0*], and by looking at enlarged photographs of snowflakes at the beginning of this segment [*8,0*], the children became interested in the beauty of the snowflake. So the children set about drawing individual snowflakes.

They used a variety of media, including white chalk on black paper, bits of colored paper, beans, macaroni, and parquetry blocks.

9.0 *Watching a Video on the Growth of a Snowflake:* By coincidence, we had a 3-minute videotape available that showed the growth of a snowflake in time-lapse photography. The children watched this video clip several times, knowing that they would then draw what they were watching.

10.0 *Drawing the Growth of a Snowflake:* The children were given long pieces of paper and asked to divide the paper into four panels. Then the children set about drawing their understanding of how a snowflake grows from Time 1 to Time 4.

11.0 *Drawing How Water Changes to Ice:* The work of the physical structure of snow led to discussions on the difference between ice crystals and snow crystals. After an introductory period of verbal discussions and writing attribute lists, the children froze water, checking its progress every hour. They finished by drawing this transformation across three time frames.

12.0 *Drawing Clouds and Machines That Make Snow:* Some of the children during [*11.0*] believed that the melted snow would be retransformed into snowflakes in the freezer. So all of the classes discussed how snow is made, both naturally and artificially. Some children drew snow-making clouds, whereas others decided to invent their own snow-making machines. These drawings were some of the most interesting in the project because they revealed the children's theories about the water-to-snow process.

CYCLES OF SYMBOLIZATION

The team at Marks Meadow used the concept of cycles of symbolization as a guide to enhance the reflectivity of children as they drew and cycled back to redraw their current assumptions, ideas, and theories. The children were using symbolization, not only to represent what they already know, but also to reflect and question what it is they say they know. They, in essence, rerepresent their knowledge in order to improve its coherence. The drawing, in this sense, is done in order to learn, instead of in order to communicate what is known.

Cycle One: Verbal Outpouring

It is appropriate that teachers start out children with their most fluent symbol system, talking [*1.0*]. The ideas flow without being encumbered by the demands of technical skills. Five- to seven-year-olds already know how to talk. What they do not yet do well, however, is know how to reflect on their words, to debug their logic, or to check the evidence. This is where the subsequent cycles and symbol and systems come into play.

Cycle Two: Initial Drawings and Further Discussion

These initial drawings are determined partly by the verbal outpouring and partly by the continuation of ideas that unfold as the children draw. It is the combined source of these ideas that make drawing powerful. The children talk about snowfall and they get new ideas from what they see emerging on their paper. One can hope that these two sources will create small discrepancies. Discrepancies are the engine behind questioning and subsequent problem solving.

Look for the moment at Figure 19.1. The child has drawn deep snow on the ground and on the roof of the house, but no snow on the top of the car. The snowless car resulted from a habit of drawing. The child usually draws cars like

FIGURE 19.1a. Child from New England recalls snow.

FIGURE 19.1b. Child from Africa imagines snow.

this, so that is how it ends up in her drawing. But in the group discussion that follows, inconsistencies such as these are noted. The child artist now explains the discrepancy away by saying that the car just arrived in front of the house. We should not dismiss this as rationalizing a mistake. In fact, the child has probably thought for the first time that the snowless car could be a clever way to figure out how long a car has been parked someplace else.

Other discrepancies were noted between the two drawings (see the differences between Figures 19.1a and 19.1b). The child who drew the thatched hut (Figure 19.1b) was from Africa and had never seen snow. In his drawing, snow was not well distinguished from rain. The children discussed these differences and the child from Africa was filled with excitement and was eager to discover just what real snow does to the objects outside.

Cycle Three: Simulation

The drawings and verbal discussions by now had convinced the children that snowfall was more complicated than they had first thought. The drawings, in particular, move the children into a closer analysis of the dynamics of falling snow: where it will land, where it will stay. But because we had no snow, we had no means to confirm our guesses. Thus, the third cycle was included to give the children some physical confirmation of their theories.

Before the teacher sifted the flour onto the miniature city of wooden blocks,

FIGURE 19.2. Flour is sifted over miniature village.

FIGURE 19.3. The car, once removed, shows where the snow did not fall.

the children predicted where they thought the "snow" would fall, where it would stick, and where it would not fall. One kindergartner said, in reference to a curved roof, "It will land on the top of the curvey part, but it will not stay here (pointing to the more vertical part of the curving roof)." Another child offered her opinion that the snow would not get under the toy car.

The teacher, Lynda Wrisley in this case, then sifted the flour evenly over the entire miniature village as the children watched intently (Figure 19.2). This predict-then-observe strategy of teaching enhanced their interest and maximized the opportunity for an observation to be more than an interesting occurrence, but also relevant evidence for a hypothesis.

Children were pleased with their correct predictions (see Figure 19.3) and pleasantly surprised at the unexpected. One boy said, in reference to a tiny ridge of flour on the skyward point of a triangular block, "I did not think that it would land there!" More than one child commented that two identical triangles had noticeably different amounts of snow on their skyward facets. Through some guided discovery they learned that this difference was caused by differences in grain textures between the two wooden blocks; one was smooth and the other rough.

Thus, the simulation cycle adds physical confirmation to the guesses and theories defined in the two previous cycles. Now the children are even better prepared for the actual snowfall that is certain to arrive, soon, we hoped. In one class,

Cindy Weinberg's kindergarten class, the children did yet another activity before the snow actually came—a large mural across the entire back wall of the room.

Cycle Four: Using the Drawing as the Referent

The children in Cindy Weinberg's class spent several days filling up a huge mural with drawings and paper cutouts of houses, cars, trucks, people, trees, streets, and buildings [*4.0*]. Then they waited and thought about this drawing as the place where the snow would one day fall. Thus, the drawing itself was the referent, the "real object" so to speak. After a week of looking at the completed cityscape, they now returned with white paint to add the snow. Yet, unlike the flour sifted on wooden blocks, the drawing would not give the children physical confirmation. Knowing that they could do anything, because the medium allows it, caused the children to talk even more about how to add the white paint. One might rightly assume that by contrasting simulation with drawing, children would be more reflective when drawing how they think the system behaves. That is, the simulation confirms that the system is not capricious or fanciful, and the freedom to say anything in drawing places more responsibility on thinking to figure out what would really happen. With the simulation alone, children might have a tendency to say, "I don't know," and just wait for the teacher to sift the flour. Thus, it is useful to have both these cycles: simulation and drawing as referent.

Figure 19.4 shows how one child added white paint (snow) to a house. The

FIGURE 19.4. Snow envelopes the house on all sides.

white paint enveloped the entire house, including the vertical walls, instead of resting only on the upper surfaces of the house. Perhaps we should have cycled again through the simulation to generate discussion about differences in their predictions in the simulation and their drawings in the fourth cycle. As you will see, the field trip, perhaps in combination with the simulation, did sensitize children to the functional differences in vertical and horizontal surfaces. Notice, however, that this child had been sensitized to an in-between case, the slanted roof. She had drawn some snow on the roof, itself drawn in perspective. We felt that this awareness, that the roof has a horizontal "footprint" to the open sky, was a major breakthrough for several children.

Cycle Five: The Experience

Finally the snow arrived. The children were primed to seek answers to questions raised in the verbal outpouring [*1.0*], during their initial drawings [*2.0*], during the simulation with flour [*3.0*], and as they added white paint to the mural [*4.0*]. They went out into the snow to inspect the fall of the snow on the seesaw, the way the snow slowed you down on the slide, and the crystal structure of an individual flake frozen on the fabric of the teacher's coat.

We would like to caution ourselves and others about the use of the word *experience.* Not all experiences are equally educational. Once again we draw on the distinction between the occurrence of an event and an event that serves as evidence for a theory, answer to a question, or satisfaction of curiosity. The prior cycles of symbolization make the field experience more a case of evidence than the less reflective case of an occurrence. In fact, it is the *hands-off* activities that make the *hands-on* activities more educational.

Cycle Six: The Postexperience Drawings

What we said about the importance of representations prior to the field experience can also be said for representations subsequent to the field experience. Granted, the children make discoveries in the field, but their excitement and physical movements make it difficult for them to synthesize their discoveries at some higher level. During this postexperience round of drawings [*6.0*] the children learned that their discoveries are shared (or debated), and they then tried to represent the revisions of their knowledge.

As shown in Figure 19.5 it becomes clear that the same children who drew the cityscape mural are no longer placing snow along the vertical walls of the buildings. They are also aware that the snow will fall on any edge that is at least as wide as an individual snowflake. This attention to dynamics of falling snow, as a powdery medium coming to rest on horizontal edges, broadened and deepened the children's interest and curiosity and led to activities [*7.0*] through [*12.0*].

FIGURE 19.5. Emphasis on the lay of the snow.

Cycle Seven: Broadening

Instead of asking what happens when the snow makes contact with objects, they began to ask what happens when an object comes into contact with the snow. For example, what sound does a shovel make when removing snow? The teachers decided to help children think about these object-to-snow questions by *drawing* these sounds.

The teachers brought in audiotapes of several such sounds; the children discussed what they might be; all agreed and then they tried to make graphic representations of these sounds. Making a visual representation (picture) of a nonvisual experience (sound) is called *cross-modal representation.* The graphic rendering of sounds encourages the child to think in more creative ways about sound. This is true because the cross-modal representation has few clichés and because the activity is clearly metaphorical. In addition, the children listen to the sounds through their eyes and thereby hear different aspects of sounds, such as intervals of silence, continuous tones, and other attributes that have spatial analogies. Children often listen to the less formal and more content-based attributes when they are preparing to give a verbal description. That is, the cross-modal graphic picks up attributes of continuity and discontinuity as shown in Figure 19.6, whereas the verbal description will orient the child to the source of the noise or other noises that are similar, for example, "snow shoveling sounds like sanding wood." Thus, the cross-modal representation has a metasymbolic cast, compared to the verbal account.

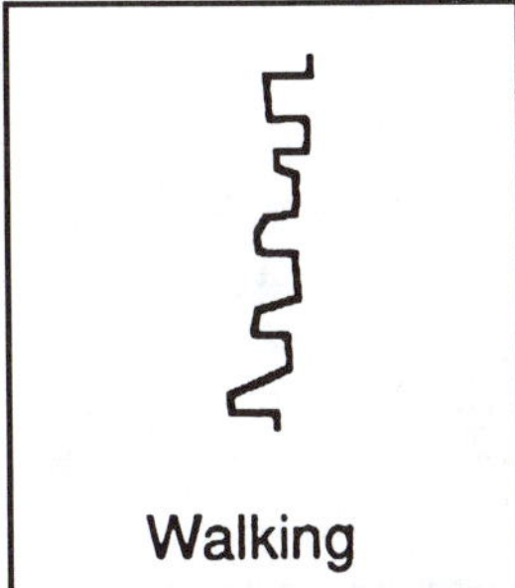

FIGURE 19.6. One child's rendering of snow sounds.

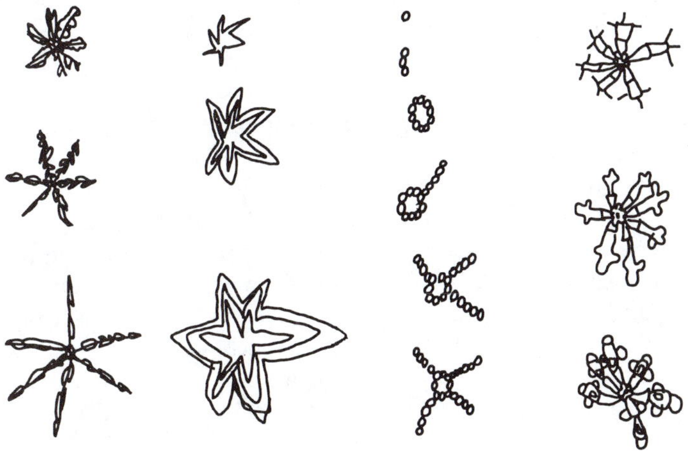

FIGURE 19.7. Four versions of a growing snowflake.

Cycle Eight: Deepening

The children had already made many comments about the snow as a medium of particles. This naturally led to activities that focused on the particle level of snow, the individual snowflake. Activities [*8.0*], [*9.0*], and [*10.0*] dealt with the look and growth of the individual snowflake. These three activities represent a type of spiral with the cycles of symbolization because the children are using representation, experience and rerepresentation within this special topic: the growth of a crystalline structure. The spiral is a recapitulation of this cycle sequence, but is at the same time an advance because these activities deepen the children's worldview of the snow.

The children laid out their rendering of snowflakes [*8.0*], watched a time-lapse video [*9.0*] of a growing snowflake, and then rendered these stages of growth themselves [*10.0*]. Figure 19.7 shows four theories of growth from four different children, all who had watched the same time-lapse video. Note that these four children, from left to right, view growth as a process of (a) enlarging, (b) layering, (c) adding unit elements, and finally (d) growth by differentiation of parts.

This spiral of cycles impressed on us that even the best video presentation [*9.0*] does not give the facts away. The children still have to reconstruct these facts into a set of relations that make sense to the children themselves. Drawing their theories on paper helps each child see the other child's thoughts and to rework one's own thoughts during the small group discussions. The video without the cycle of representations would let these diverse theories remain unexpressed and thereby provide no constructive conflict among the students. The video alone could also encourage mental passivity and the acceptance of superficiality that comes when children are not asked to communicate their thinking to others.

Final Cycles: More Broadening and Deepening

The activities that followed, and they could have been continued indefinitely, continued to broaden and deepen the children's interest and understanding. The children both drew the ice-to-water transformation and performed empirical experiments [*11.0*]. The children made drawings of clouds and snow-making machines [*12.0*], and they observed these systems outdoors and on area ski slopes. The snow-making machines were quite fascinating, and actually led to our next annual project, simple machines, carried out the following year.

WHAT THE TEAM LEARNED

Resources for Success

Our own reflection on this project continues. The project team learned a number of important principles. Broadly speaking, we learned that the multisymbolic project approach, at least the version that we have presented here, can be implemented into the curriculum of an American classroom. It should be noted, however, that even though this school system provided time for all teachers to plan and reflect, much of this special planning for the City in the Snow was done by teachers during their spare time. We are still working to give teachers more resources for this form of project teaching. Documentation of the children's thinking and subsequent interpretation is primary for the success of this approach. In addition to this appreciation for documentation, we did develop a set of important instructional principles.

Representation and Rerepresentation

It is important to have children cycle back through a first draft of a representation after they have had practical or simulated experience. The rerepresentation, as part of our cycle of symbolization, helps the child consolidate knowledge or improve the definition of their misconceptions. Both objectives are laudable.

Using Ready-Made Symbols as Catalysts

The teacher can serve as a resource to help the child enter the system under study. The photographs of the snowflakes and the videotape of how the snowflake forms were ready-made symbols. These ready-made symbols are complex. Therefore, the reproduction of these symbols requires high-level thinking about the referent and referent processes.

The teacher does not directly teach drawing by focusing on graphic details. Rather, the teacher asks the children to reflect on the meaning of these ready-made symbols in order for the children to reinvent the geometric rules of structure or the dynamics of particles forming clusters. The ready-made symbols serve as a frame, a delimitation of the system. The ready-made symbols are hints at latent patterns, patterns that could be interesting to know. But a pattern needs to be constructed by the child to be known. Patterns do not exist in the ready-made symbol. Patterns exist in the cognitive order the child brings to the stimulus array. The drawing presents a window to this cognitive order for both the child himself or herself, for the teacher, and for other children to whom the child is communicating.

Open Media Versus Simulation

Instruction is a two-phase process: the phase of generating questions followed by a phase of testing questions. If teachers only use graphic art to stimulate the imagination, the instructional value of art has been truncated. Thus, we came to value media that have consequences: media that are not so open-ended that anything can happen. This is why we shifted to sifting and why we used the videotape of the growing snowflake.

Representations as a Platform for Asking Questions

Once drawn, the graphic representation becomes a platform on which the children and the teacher can play out their interpretations. The finesse comes in how to affirm the child's thinking, while at the same time challenging the child to think more deeply (see Forman, 1989).

Let us take the case of a child who drew an elegant but superfluous snow-making machine, a machine that made snow from an ample supply of existing snow

FIGURE 19.8. Snow on, melted, frozen, and chopped.

(Figure 19.8). The machine would suck in the snow, melt it, chop it up, and spit out the "snow" (the chopped ice). The proper platform for instruction in this case is to deal with the child at his level. We would question the child from the higher perspective about machines in general. We would not immediately tell the child to consider work as the production of something finished from something raw. We would ask the child to give a verbal rendering of the process *as drawn*, hoping to hear him describe both the nature of the snow that comes in and the nature of the snow that goes out. From his own reflections on his own verbal descriptions, he might well become aware that he has invented a snow-moving machine, not a snow-making machine. The illogicality of the snow-in/snow-out redundancy would be one level higher and attained further on; and the fact that chopped ice is not really snow could also eventually come to his consciousness. These broader questions about purpose and exact products often came into consciousness during small group discussions among four to five children.

Building on Intuitive Knowledge

This is a difficult principle to implement, because it presupposes that teachers have sufficient time to learn what their students know and have time to continually update the transition from intuitive to more objective knowledge structures. But this City in the Snow project made it perfectly clear that knowing what the children believe is essential for a successful project.

Building on the child's intuitive knowledge is important for two reasons. One is motivation. When children have some intuitive theories about a process, it means they are interested in the subject matter. They have gone beyond an attitude of "that's just the way it is." It validates the source of these initial theories to use them as departure points for instruction and this, in turn, heightens the children's motivation.

The other reason for building on the children's intuitive knowledge concerns continuity of instruction. Much has been written about the value of developmental education, but unfortunately these guidelines have been taken too literally. The child's development has to be gauged by general stages rather than by phases of domain-specific learning. This project, this chapter, and indeed this book speak more to the use of domain-specific phases of understanding a content system. For example, look once again at the various theories of snowflake growth. The theory of growth as a simple case of getting larger is more elementary than a theory that notes the changing location of a unit element. The project approach, combined with documentation of children's thinking, helps each teacher become knowledgeable about the developmental phases within a content domain. We can let the general stages take care of themselves.

Shifting From Static Patterns to Dynamic Systems

As is consistent with existing literature on early learning (see Forman & Hill, 1984), teaching children to ask good questions requires that they be presented with rich problem-solving environments. A rich problem-solving environment is more causal than descriptive. Children try to figure out how something happens rather than try to describe how something looks. While close inspection may be an initial step toward understanding, it should not be isolated from the search for cause.

This shift from static patterns to dynamic systems can be a change in the mental attitude one has as they study patterns. Pattern has typically been described with static attributes (symmetrical, planar, linear, differentiated, homogeneous). But the study of dynamic patterns, that is, the relationship of form to function, presents the child with a rich problem-solving environment. Questions, such as what if this pattern were changed by this cause, become relevant for the first time: What if the water molecules were square instead of V-shaped; how then would snowflakes grow?

The Necessity for Careful Documentation

Documentation and time to study the documentation are essential for a successful project. This is perhaps the first priority in Reggio Emilia, with great emphasis placed on the time to study the documentation. The project team, as a plea to improve education in general, recommend that all schools find ways to provide "documentarians" for classroom teachers. If done properly, good documentation can serve all masters simultaneously, from individual assessment, to curriculum planning, to instructional accountability.

The Necessity for Long-Term Projects

We were impressed with our own commitment to continue this theme for a long period. In retrospect, we realized that the theme was always changing in its specific form. The children did not feel they were continually rehashing the same concept. The long-term nature of this project was our long-term discussion of how earlier activities specifically related to current activities, how they related in terms specific to content, for example, how snowfall relates to snowflakes, how snowflakes relate to ice, and how refrigerator relates to snow cloud or snow machine. We needed a long time, several months, to carry this project through. Had we rushed ourselves we would not have been able to use the emergent objectives as they happened because we would not have had the reflection and planning time needed to define these emergent objectives. And to make a project from only one objective is to miss a great opportunity to help children construct whole systems from subsystems.

REFERENCES

Forman, G. (1989). Helping children ask good questions. In B. Neugenbauer (Ed.), *The wonder of it: Exploring how the world works* (pp. 21-25). Redmond, WA: Exchange Press, Inc.

Forman, G., & Hill, F. (1984). *Constructive play: Applying Piaget in the preschool.* Menlo Park, CA: Addison-Wesley.

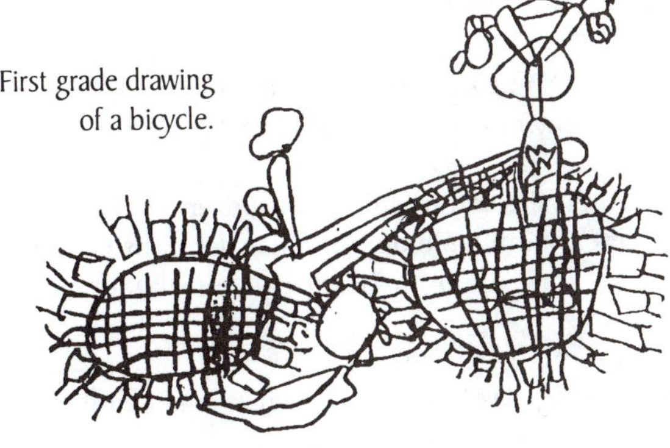
First grade drawing of a bicycle.

chapter 20

Looking in the Mirror: A Reflection of Reggio Practice in Winnetka

Eva Tarini
Lynn White

INTRODUCTION

We have had formal contact with Reggio for a number of years. Eva first saw the exhibit, "The 100 Languages of Children," in Boston in 1989. She attended a Reggio Seminar in Detroit in October 1991, where she met Carlina Rinaldi and was compelled to inquire about possible internships. In February 1992 she went on a delegation to visit the schools in Reggio Emilia. In May 1992, she was accepted as an intern in the Reggio schools for the 1992–1993 school year. Lynn's first contact with Reggio was on a delegation in May 1991. She was struck by the philosophical underpinnings of the Reggio approach because it felt so closely connected to her own work with children as well as the philosophy of the Winnetka schools. In order to explore and understand Reggio principles more fully, she continued studying Reggio ideas. This included attending seminars led by educators from Reggio Emilia, ongoing discussions with colleagues at her school, and collaborations with those she met in Reggio. Both Lynn and Eva have been trying to incorporate Reggio principles in their own teaching for the past several years.

The Winnetka philosophy has historically been based around the child, who is at the center of our thinking. Thus, the teachers place a great deal of emphasis on:

- Observing and listening to children.
- Offering multiple opportunities for construction of knowledge.
- Providing opportunities to solve problems and interact with materials and others.
- Integrating curricula.
- Keeping class sizes small with some flexibility in our schedules.
- Collaborating with colleagues.

There are a number of key Reggio principles that we have found to be very important in our work with young children. They affect us in a spiraling and deepening sort of way. We were initially impressed with the precision Reggio educators used when discussing their work with children. In listening to their descriptions, we noted points that piqued our curiosity or challenged our thinking. As we moved back to our classrooms with this new set of lenses, we began to see new dimensions in children's learning processes and new opportunities for redefining our role as teachers. The Reggio principles began to make more sense as we saw evidence of them in our interactions with children. This heightened awareness caused us to think in a more purposeful way about these ideas and to be more deliberate in including them in our teaching. Some of these key principles are in the following sections.

KEY PRINCIPLES

Time

One of the most important organizational elements is that of time. In Reggio's municipal preschools, children are afforded a great deal of time to explore both long-term projects and typical, everyday preschool activities. Children are both expected and encouraged to spend long periods of time concentrating, whether it be on a painting, in the dramatic play corner, or during a conversation. Being able to work at something for a long time is highly valued because it indicates a deeper level of involvement and hopefully of understanding. Teachers are very observant and respectful of children's time, giving them the time they need to process information, to come to a new level of understanding, and to construct new knowledge. In thinking about our own treatment of time, we wanted to slow down the pace of our busy day in order to provide opportunities for our children to explore topics in even greater depth than had traditionally been true. We worked hard to find blocks of time in our schedules that would allow for long, uninterrupted work times. We wanted to be able to explore themes, big or small, in the long term, allowing children to return to something over and over again in order to master it in their own way. This could mean, for example, working on a project such as shadows over the course of several months in an effort to grapple with some of the "problems" inherent in the nature of shadows. Or it could mean a continual availability of paints for color mixing over the course of the year as an opportunity to slowly internalize both the nature of and joy in mixing colors.

Use of Small Groups

Another element that struck us has to do with the frequent use of small groups when working with children. Reggio educators believe that children co-construct knowledge and that the small group is the ideal situation for children to do so. We have been fascinated to see in our own work with children how a small group situation affords them greater opportunities for purposeful thinking. In a small group, it is easier for children to pay attention to one another, to reflect on each others' thoughts, to have an opportunity to express themselves, and to repeat this cycle. It is also easier for the adult to hear the children, to help children explain themselves, to keep the conversation on track, to encourage children to listen to one another, and to think about what is being said. This said, we realize that it is a luxury to be able to work uninterrupted with a small group of children. In Winnetka, we are fortunate to work with an assistant, and this allows us to spend time alone with a limited number of children in order to explore a topic in a way that would otherwise be difficult.

We also believe that the work done in small groups should be shared with the larger group. In some cases it is extremely important to have a private conversation with a group of children or to allow them to work without the distractions of the rest of the class. However, there are times when it can be useful for the group as a whole to have the opportunity to observe a small group working on a special project. This can be accomplished by strategically placing a small group in a location where they can be viewed by the entire group. It can be equally important to have a small group report back to the larger group about a conversation they have had or a project they are working on. We have found that periodically providing for "reporting back" is more instructional than merely reporting to the group at the very end of a project. Periodic reporting can allow participants to once again verbalize their thoughts, giving them another opportunity to explain what they have been doing. It also provides an opportunity for a greater number of viewpoints or ideas to be shared because the circle of contact with the projects is widened. Children not involved in the project inevitably have comments to make or ideas to suggest.

Role of the Adult

Our contact with Reggio educators has caused us to reevaluate the role of the adult in the classroom. We believe that simply providing materials and then managing the group is not sufficient in helping children extend their thinking. Instead, working alongside children for long periods of time helps us all arrive at deeper and richer understandings. We have found that a stronger presence can be very important in helping children to focus for longer periods of time, in helping them rise to new challenges, and in helping them express themselves in ways that are more creative, more communicative, and more thoughtful.

Documentation

We believe that documenting children's work through note-taking, photography, audiotaping, and videotaping is an essential component of *progettazione.* In part, it can provide teachers with the opportunity again to hear or see a conversation or a work time that occurred in the classroom. This can help us to decide where to go next with a project or can provide us with the possibility of gaining a greater understanding of what and how children think. Having the occasion to listen to children in a variety of ways (both in the moment and after it) can be an important tool in better understanding both children and ourselves as teachers. We have also come to realize that we must carefully choose what and how we document as the method will inevitably affect our level of involvement with children as they work.

BICYCLE PRESENTATION
EVA TARINI

I started the 1994–1995 school year with the intention of providing various expressive opportunities for my class. I wanted to choose some activities that would go beyond some of the simpler "art" activities I had typically set out for my first graders before I went to Reggio Emilia. By "go beyond," I meant several things. First, in choosing activities, I wanted them to involve some type of challenge so that the children would get away from a sort of repetitive use of familiar materials (another opportunity, say, to use watercolors or tempera paints in the same old way). The challenge would involve either some specific direction or instruction from me, or an invitation to participate in an unfamiliar activity. Second, I wanted the activities to challenge me as a teacher. I wanted to force myself to be more involved during the process and I wanted to see if by being present, I could also support the children in attempting more difficult tasks. I wanted to see if I could push them to do more than just a first try and to "go beyond" their usual experience, perhaps surprising themselves with the complexity of their final product, or their enjoyment of a new process and of the challenge itself.

One of the main reasons I wanted to challenge myself as a teacher has to do with what Reggio educators believe about the way children learn and about the adult's role in this process. Reggio educators would say that it is not always sufficient to put materials, even provocative ones, on a table and expect that children are going to make cognitive leaps on their own. Surely this does occur at times, and free exploration is an integral part of any program (as is the case in all Reggio classrooms), but constructed situations are also important. Educators in Reggio believe that carefully constructing and posing problems or challenges to young children is important in helping them push their thinking. When I was in Italy I was struck by how specific the educators in Reggio can be about exactly how those interactions might look and how they might be structured. It is important to remember that these teachers also maintain a delicate balance between providing structured challenges and allowing the children expressive freedom and the opportunity to explore (Tarini, 1997).

Educators in Reggio stress that materials, projects, and activities must pose problems to the children and that children need to confront these problems as a group, a small group, in order to solve them. When I say *problem,* I am first of all translating directly and somewhat incorrectly from Italian. They use the word *problematica* to mean something like a challenge. A *problematica* should be a situation, a task, which in some way stimulates cognitive conflict, or a push in thinking. Second, I am using the term *problem* in the broadest sense of the word. A problem might simply be the first contact with a new material and the discoveries that come from working with it (a material like clay, or wire, or craypas). A problem might involve pushing one's observational skills, but with very familiar materials, say pencil and paper. A problem might have to do with representing graphically an idea or a theory that has been previously discussed.

Reggio educators believe that the adult's role here is very important. The adult is a facilitator, keeping the problem present, keeping the children focused, acting as a memory, helping the children share techniques with one another, or perhaps proposing a new problem. Although children are seen as skillful in using these materials, it is thought that they can use guidance to become even more skillful, and thus better able to express or represent what they know or what they observe. So the adult's role as facilitator also involves helping children to expand and refine their skills in working with various materials. I think it is important to note that this type of guidance is not to be interpreted as telling children what to do, but rather as scaffolding their development of skills toward a greater facility with the material. Children do not need to reinvent the wheel of techniques when it comes to working with various materials—at the moment a child needs a skill, a technique, or specific information, an adult can tell him or her how something might work better, or why something has to be done in a certain way.

So, last fall, one of the challenges I provided involved pushing the children's powers of observation using a familiar object and paper and pencil. I borrowed a bicycle from a fifth grader and chose five children who I thought would benefit from such a provocation, but who would be able to rise to the challenge without becoming too frustrated. I purposely set them up in the middle of the classroom, instead of in a more protected spot, because I wanted the other children to see what was going on. I put three girls next to one another and two boys across from the girls. I gave them very simple directions: I told them I wanted them to try to draw the bicycle, to do their very best, but that I certainly did not expect it to look exactly like the bike in front of them. I asked them to take their time and to look very carefully at the bicycle. I was quite surprised at what a nice job these children did. I did not talk to them much as they worked. I was trying to photograph the process, which prevented me from being able to communicate with them as they drew. Nevertheless, they did beautiful work. The detail they used was quite intricate and one can even see the effect that the subtle change in perspective had on their drawings.

A few months after this drawing challenge, I was fortunate to be able to present this experience at the 1994 NAEYC Conference in Atlanta. I spoke with some of the Reggio educators after my presentation, and we talked about the importance of embedding, when possible, these challenges within a broader exploration of a topic, in order to put the activity into a more meaningful context. This gives the children an opportunity to express their thoughts and to push their thinking to a deeper level. It provides them a richer experience because so much more is involved and because they have participated in the decision making. They therefore better understand why they are doing certain activities. For the

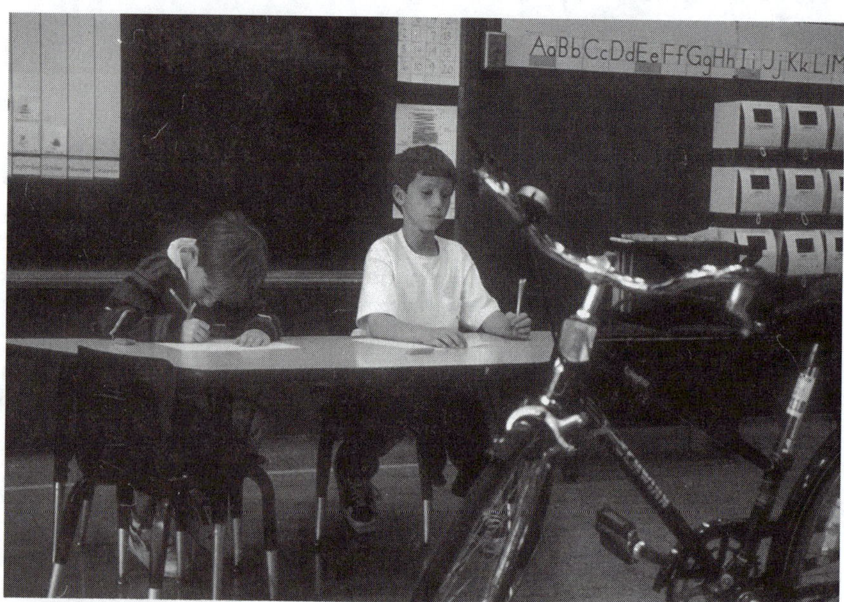

FIGURE 20.1. Children drawing a bicycle.

teacher, it provides an opportunity to research what children know about something, and to see how they are able to put into words, perhaps for the first time, something they have experience with, and then transfer their verbal expressions to other symbolic languages, such as drawing or working with clay or wire.

As a result of this conversation, I carried out a small project on bicycles with four girls this past spring. I chose these four because I thought they would have a lot to say, would be thoughtful and able to listen to the others and to reflect on what they were saying. I also thought they would enjoy being out of the room doing something special.

For my first conversation, I was interested in finding out what fundamental information they had about bicycles, but I was also curious to see what *they* would most want to talk about. I had some basic questions planned ahead of time, some things I wanted to know in case they did not come up spontaneously. However, I started out with a very general question that would give them the opportunity to discuss what *they* thought was important about bicycles. It turned out that they wanted to describe their bikes, the color, the seats, the accessories, and how they got them. They also wanted to discuss how difficult it was to learn to ride a bike, and how it made them feel when they were finally able to do so independently. They were wonderfully articulate, listened to one another, and commented on each other's observations:

T: Tell me about riding your bikes.

Kelsey: When I think of my bike, it seems like I'm riding a horse because it has the speed and when I'm holding onto the handlebars it seems like I'm holding the reins. And I just like it because when I learned how to ride it, the second morning I just started riding back and forth, back and forth, back and forth, and I did that for a long time.

T: Do you think it's hard to learn how to ride a bike?

Kelsey: Yeah, because every time I got balanced I fell down.

Julia: Kelsey taught me how to ride a two-wheeler bike.

T: Tell me about teaching her to ride a two-wheeler.

Kelsey: Well, first, she had training wheels when she came over to my house one day and I said, "Julia, do you want to learn how to ride without training wheels?" I let her ride my little bike and I said, "Julia, you have to hold onto the handlebars and you have to go up and down." I think she fell down about 6 times, maybe less, but she was *really good* at starting. I was holding onto the handlebars and I said, "First you have to get the *feeling* of it," and then I holded on and she started pumping and I said, "I'll run up with you and I'll give you a push," and then when she did, I think she couldn't control herself, but I don't think she fell down.

Jane: My mom taught me how to ride a bike. I remember she was holding onto the back of the seat, but it didn't feel like it because she was barely holding onto it, so I was really just riding it by myself. Our neighbor, he taught me a trick. It was, when you start off, have one foot on the pedal and the other on the ground and push with the foot on the ground and then put your other foot on, the one that was on the ground and it worked!

Sarah: My dad, what he did to help my sister ride, my sister was holding onto the handlebars and moving her feet, but my dad was pushing her the whole way. She made the pedals move, but he was pushing her.

T: What do you think is the hardest part of learning how to ride a bike?

Kelsey: The hardest part is to balance, 'cause every time, you don't get up on it soon enough and you just tip over, and once you get on it, you start balancing and you just tip over because you're not pedaling fast enough. You're like, "Wow, I got on the bike and I'm balancing!" And you just tip over.

Sarah: I think it's hard to stay balanced too, but there's another thing that's hard. It's hard to get started because sometimes when you push on the pedal it goes around and you lose the pedal. See, if you put both feet on the pedals you'll fall off the bike. You have to keep one foot on the ground, push on the pedal and then quickly put that other foot on the pedal and keep on riding.

Julia: It's sort of hard to me, the part when you get on the bike, because sometimes when learners are just learning how to ride a bike, they try to get on right away and they think that they're gonna right away get it but it doesn't happen that way. It takes a couple days to do it and sometimes people don't know that.

T: What does it feel like when you're riding really well or very fast?

Julia: It feels really good, like when it's been the winter and you really have not been thinking about your bike, but you know that you're going to try to ride really well. I didn't really think about my bike, but now I tried and now I'm getting really good at riding my bike and I'm getting the feeling of it, like I'm not going to fall off and I really don't feel that I'm going to fall as much as I did when I first started to ride.

Sarah: It feels like you're speeding on the sidewalk.

Kelsey: Sort of like a horse. If you see someone ride a bike when you're just starting, you think it's really easy, but when you try it, like Jesse was saying, you're a little disappointed because that person can do it and you can't. But when you *can,* you just feel a little bit...*proud.*

I want to comment briefly on using a conversation as a tool for teacher reflection. I first began taping and transcribing conversations with children when I was in Italy. I was shocked at a couple of things: first of all, that I talked so much. I discovered that practically every other comment was mine. I could see that I really wanted to gain greater understanding of some puzzling statements those children made, which is why I asked so many questions, but I decided that it was important to give the children the opportunity to talk to one another without so many teacher interruptions. I am much happier with my presence in this first bicycle conversation. I feel that I guided the conversation, gave it some boundaries, and asked questions when I needed clarification or when I wanted to change the direction of the conversation a bit. But I am glad the girls had the opportunity to play off one another as well, and that would not have happened in the same way had I interfered more frequently. Another feature that I think is inherent in recording and transcribing children's conversations is the opportunity it gives the teacher to hear a conversation again. It really makes it possible to *hear* differently because my role is changed. During the conversation, I need to be very attentive to what they are saying, constantly deciding when to let the conversation take its course, when to intervene to clarify something, or when to change the direction of the discussion. The energy it takes to do all this makes me pay attention in a certain way. When I am listening to the tape later on, I no longer have a job to perform, except for listening carefully—so I have the opportunity to listen with new ears. I probably hear things I completely missed the first time. I may come to better understand a comment that was initially puzzling to me or I may form new questions to further explore their thinking. In my experience, I always am impressed by the richness of the conversation, far more so than when we are actually having the conversation. I remember Laura Rubizzi, a teacher at the Diana School, telling me that there were times that she would have a conversation with children and be disappointed with the way it went, but then she would listen to the tape of it, and hearing it again almost always changed her opinion of what transpired. I think that the nature of our jobs, that there is so much to do, to plan for, to organize, to remember, makes us somewhat distracted when we are with children—not distracted in a very obvious way, but on a very subtle level. In the back of my mind, I know that I have all the other elements of our day rumbling around in my brain. So when I listen to a tape, the depth of the children's thoughts comes through to me more clearly than the first time.

After listening to this first conversation, I thought about what step to take next. Sarah had made an interesting comment: "Your feet are only going up and down, but the pedals are going round and round." I decided I wanted to explore with the girls how the body moves when riding a bicycle, and then I wanted to give them the opportunity to ride a bike directly after the conversation so that they could compare their words to some real-life observations. On the day that I planned to do this, both Kelsey and Sarah were absent. Because I wanted there to be at least three children involved, I decided to include Diana, who had not participated in our first conversation. Jane and Julia filled her in on our previous conversation and we moved on from there.

T: I want you to think about exactly what your body does when you're riding and try to explain it.

Julia: My hands aren't moving but my legs are going in a circle sort of and I'm using the pedals to make my feet go around.

Jane: My body, it's sort of like what Julia said, it doesn't feel like your feet are going in circles when you're pedaling, but they are.

Julia: It sort of feels like they're going up and down.

Jane: Yeah, because you don't feel them going in a circle, you feel them going up and down. When I first started to ride it felt like up and down but now I know it's going in a circle; it's easy to tell because you sort of feel your foot going in an oval.

Diana: Riding a bicycle, if you want to turn you just put your hands on the handlebars and you turn the handlebars a little bit. And you have to be careful where you're going because you might run over a person by accident. What Jane said, it's sort of like an oval, but to me it feels like my feet are going up and down not like an oval.

Julia: But I feel that when I am riding my bike I feel like, what Kelsey said last time, I feel like I'm sort of riding a pony. Except I'm not as high as when I'm riding a pony, I'm lower. And *I* have the control, not the horse, *I* have the control.

Next, the group moved outdoors in order to ride Jane's bicycle.

T: We're going to take turns riding Jane's bicycle. The people who are watching have a job. Your job is to watch the person who is riding and to look at her body. Mostly watch her legs because that's what you were trying to describe before. Jane, while you're riding, if you can, concentrate a little bit on what your body feels like when you're riding.

Julia: We're gonna watch you and sort of say what you're doing.

Diana: We're going to be reporters. Right now Jane's riding the bike and we're gonna look to see what she's doing, so we know a few other things about it. Her legs go, not in a circle, but thinner, just a tiny bit thinner

Julia: It's in a oval shape.

Diana: Yeah, and sometimes she lets her feet go because that's as fast as she wants to go.

Julia: Her legs are moving in the same way as her wheels.

FIGURE 20.2. Jesse rides her bicycle with friends observing.

After Jane is finished riding, we sit together to discuss what they noticed.

T: I want to know what you saw her body doing and what you, Jane, felt your body doing.

Julia: The wheels and her feet were going in mostly the same direction and it looked like sort of an oval shape the way her legs were moving.

Diana: I think her body was sort of going a little back and forth, a little bit.

T: What do you think that has to do with?

Diana: I don't know.

T: When Diana rides, will you look for the back and forth that she's talking about, the side to side?

Jane: Whenever my legs were at sort of the top of the oval, I felt them going up and when they were at the bottom I felt them going down, and it felt sort of neat, it felt like my legs were just going up and down.

Julia: When you're riding it feels different than it really is, cause it feels like you're going up and down because you're going pretty fast. When you're going slow you can feel that you're going in an oval. When you're going fast it feels like you're going up and down.

Diana takes her turn riding the bike while both Jane and Julia watch her.

Julia: Diana just started and it's looking like her legs are going in a circle.

Jane: What I was talking about when you go up and down, it sort of looks like what she's doing right now cause you don't see her feet going in a circle and she's far away. And it's sort of neat to see that. Now we can see her better since she's away from the bushes; and like Diana said, she's going side to side a little bit.

Diana stops riding and we all stop to talk once more about our observations.

T: Remember what you said about noticing that Jane was going side to side when she was riding? Did you feel yourself going side to side when you were riding?

Diana: I felt like I was going side to side just a tiny bit.

T: Why do you think your body does that? Does it do that for a reason?

Jane: So you don't fall off as much, so you keep sort of steady on the bike. I saw Diana going side to side.

My final plan for this miniproject was to ask the girls to make a bicycle out of wire as I thought it would be an interesting challenge for them. Wire was a material they had not used in my classroom, and I expected that making a bicycle would be difficult. I also thought that this group would enjoy the challenge.

I offered them the drawings they had done previously in case they needed a reference. Initially, they did not want them. Julia even said: "I don't really need a drawing, 'cause I can imagine my bike in my head," and the others agreed. But then later on I noticed Sarah looking at her drawing to see how the wheels were connected.

FIGURE 20.3. Jesse's drawing.

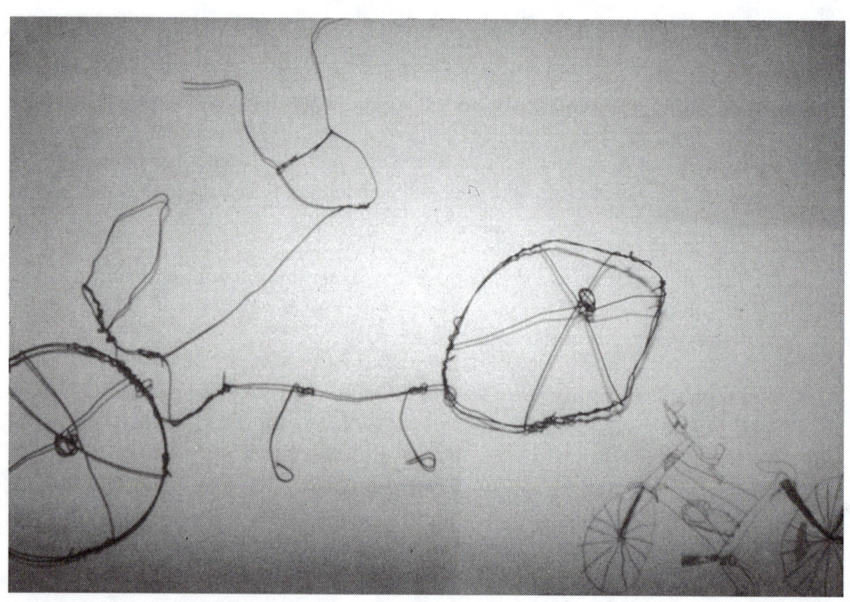

FIGURE 20.4. Jesse's drawing and wire construction.

The girls immediately decided that this task was very hard, and during this first bike-making session they complained the entire time. However, they never stopped working. They kept talking, complaining, and asking for help. They even had a sense of humor about the difficult nature of their task. Sarah announced, "Don't try this at home, kids, it's too hard," and they all took up a chorus of "Don't try this at home, kids!" Nevertheless, they quickly began to determine how much wire they wanted in order to make the various parts of a bicycle. I have to say that they *really* tried hard, because it was not until I started to help them that I realized the wire was too thick for them to manipulate easily. (Of course, I should have tested it before using it with the girls.) They could bend it into the shapes they wanted freely enough, but when it came to wrapping the ends around in order to connect pieces, they kept getting poked and it hurt.

I videotaped the second bike-making session. I use video for a variety of purposes: as a opportunity to revisit the entire experience with new eyes, much in the same way I use an audiotape; as a tool for self-evaluation as a teacher—how was I able to support the work the children did, and how might I improve?; and as a visual element during presentations to other educators. As I watch the video, I try to keep lessons I learned in Reggio present in my mind as a useful frame of reference in evaluating what takes place.

For example, there is a segment in which Jane shows Sarah how to make a hub for the spokes of the wheel. The teachers I worked with in Reggio were always very careful to help children help other children. They thought it was very important for children to "traffic" their skills, and saw the individual children as very important resources for other children. I was pleased to see that my students were willing to help one another, and that I was able to allow this connection between them (instead of being the teacher and taking charge). Another moment that I noted is a time when I tell Kelsey that we are not having a shoe-tying contest, that we are instead trying to make bicycles. Teachers in Reggio were not hesistant about reminding children to concentrate on their task at hand. They were always very attuned to individual children and paid close attention to whether or not their social chatter was impeding their concentration for the task at hand.

The girls were talking quite a bit while they were working. I was not nearly as directive as the Italians would have been. However, there are also several instances where I asked them to stop fooling around or where I simply wondered aloud if they could concentrate as well when they were talking about so many other things. Having said all that, I noticed how quickly they pick up on all sorts of conversation, from comments about their life in general to requests for help to impressions of their own work.

After having watched the video a few times, I feel that Kelsey especially needed more teacher support in making her bicycle and in staying focused. She spent the least amount of time actually working on her bicycle and the most amount talking. Although she is a very chatty, engaging child by nature, I feel that had she felt more competent, she might not have talked so much.

Another observation I would like to make has to do with how difficult it is to document these instances. It is no accident that I do not have any slides or video of the first session with wire. During that session, I quickly realized that I was trying to do too much. I had my camera, I turned on the tape recorder, I had the video camera ready, but without a tripod. I had not cut any wire ahead of time. Most importantly, I had not realized how difficult the wire would be to manipulate, nor how much help the girls would actually need. I was, therefore, unable to document effectively. Fortunately, I learned from that first experience. Simply setting up the video camera with a tripod proved to be a simple solution to getting some basic documentation. At the same time, it was hard to be present for the girls and give them the support they deserved while simultaneously trying to get some slides with my camera and some close-up shots with the video. This makes me wonder if teachers can support children effectively in undertaking difficult challenges while concurrently, and thoroughly, documenting their efforts.

The fundamental message that I take away from this experience is that there is tremendous potential within children. Giving ourselves permission to take time to listen to children and to *reflect* on their words can make it a little bit easier to structure challenging opportunities for children. With appropriate support, children illustrate to us again and again that they are capable of deep reflection, precise explanation, great interest, fervent concentration, and stunning expressive ability.

"MY DAD HAS LOTS OF PAPERS... LOTS OF FOLDERS... LOTS OF WORK TO DO"

LYNN WHITE

Each time I speak, write, or reflect on the experiences I have had with children since my 1991 trip to Reggio Emilia, I always remember the words of Loris Malaguzzi: "A child's world should be a world of the possible" (personal communication, June, 1991). I took his words to mean that children are capable of a much wider and richer variety of learning activities than we normally assume. Since hearing that phrase from Malaguzzi, I now strive to be more open to a range of possible experiences with children, experiences that in the past I might have determined to be too complicated to carry out. Even more important than my own growth, however, is that I am able to help children see the range of the possible and for them to know that they can indeed turn the possible into a reality.

As I write about a project that emerged in my classroom last year, it is my intention to convey some of the principles mentioned in the introduction to this chapter and to include my observations and reflections as a window into the thinking I do whenever I share a long-term experience with young children.

The Project

In my first-grade class of 20 students, it is common for us to agree collectively on what to construct in the block area. So, on November 1, 1993, we had a typical class meeting to discuss what to build next. During the meeting, ideas were shared, questions were raised, and in the end it was decided by vote that "Chicago and the Zoo" would be built in the block corner. I offered my assistance (as I usually do in the fall of each year) to help the students organize and record their plan. Once the plan was in the form of a diagram and initial jobs had been assigned, I moved to the edge of the block corner and began to observe. I watched a group of six children grapple with the many mathematical, scientific, and social problems that always arise in this area of the classroom. Although I have worked with this age group for 8 years, I continue to be fascinated by the creativity and resourcefulness they bring to their endeavors, as well as by the process that children go through as they negotiate the space, the materials, and each other. For this reason, I enjoy spending as much time as I can afford observing this area of the room.

The children began by constructing buildings found in the Chicago skyline. Once the Sears Tower and the John Hancock building were finally built and in the right places according to the maps, postcards, calendars, and books that we had been collecting, I heard the beginning of an interesting conversation:

John: Here's the Sears Tower. My dad has his office in the Sears Tower!

Matt: My dad's office is in the Wrigley Building. That's in our plan! It's by the river. I want to build it!

John: I've been to my dad's office millions of times. He's a lawyer. He has a candy jar in his office.

Austin: Hey! My dad's a lawyer too! I'm gonna build his building 'cause it's in Chicago. He travels a lot. He has a lot of folders, a lot of work to do. Let's build some offices too! We could use papers, tape, rulers, pencils, the tape measures!

A few other children working at a table nearby heard the conversation and joined in to talk about what their fathers did and where they worked. The conversation became intense. It was busy and purposeful, but they were listening closely to one another, each child's interest sparking another's. I could see excitement in their faces and their body language and I could hear it in their voices. Whenever this kind of enthusiasm occurs in my room, I always want to explore it more fully. I do this by meeting with them as soon as possible in order to describe to them my observations and to have them elaborate on their ideas. Exploring their enthusiasm for a certain topic is important to me for several rea-

FIGURE 20.5. Children building Chicago with blocks and recycled materials.

sons. First of all, I like to clarify my perception of the level of their interest: Is this topic as important to them as I sense that it is? Second, I feel it can be a meaningful experience to mirror back to them their feelings and excitement. I believe this communicates to them my interest in their lives, as well as giving them the opportunity to revisit or relive a recent experience. By discussing an event right after it happens, children are brought right back to that powerful moment of engagement. Because their enthusiasm and excitement are so high, they often keep on discussing and clarifying their ideas, which can bring them to a deeper and richer understanding of themselves. During these discussions, it is common for children to become infused with a certain kind of energy that propels them to want to act on or explore their ideas in greater depth.

Because their conversation was centered so strongly around their fathers' workplaces, I decided to ask them if they would like to study their fathers and their work. (I knew before I asked that each child had a father and that each father had a job at that point.) There was an overwhelmingly positive response from the entire class. Although we did briefly discuss the idea of studying both mothers and fathers, in the end the children decided to begin by studying their fathers.

That evening, I began to think of the possibilities for a project such as this. I prepared a very simple flowchart of some possible paths we might take. I did this in order to help myself prepare for the range of ideas the children might have, not to plan in advance a group of activities that I, the adult, thought the children should have. Preparing the flowchart helped to confirm for me the validity of pursuing the project "Dads and Their Work" for three reasons:

1. The topic was of great importance to the children and would require engagement with the real world as well as parental involvement in their child's learning.
2. The topic would respond to a community need—these young children needed to feel closer to their fathers by knowing and understanding more about what they did while not in their presence.
3. The children could have numerous conversations and opportunities to participate in various activities, share ideas, solve problems, and learn some new skills.

The next day I shared the previous day's events and my subsequent thoughts with a small group of teachers who were meeting to discuss Reggio-related topics. Our conversation added to my flowchart and served to expand my ideas about possible paths for this project.

Because *progettazione* unfolds over time (as opposed to being a set of predetermined experiences), I did not know the path this project would take. But I knew where I would start—with the ideas and theories of the children. Over the past few years I have been working on listening more closely to children. Listening, in its most active and attentive form, involves hearing, understanding, and assigning meaning to the words of another. By actively listening to children, I learn best how to provide learning experiences for them in which they have many opportunities for "making meaning." By encouraging children to listen to one another, I help to create an environment where "making meaning" can occur in a multitude of ways.

I prepared carefully for this first step of gathering information and I did so in a number of ways. I decided to ask the children one broad question in order to determine what basic understandings each child had of his or her father's work. I then divided the children into small groups, taking into consideration verbal expressiveness and gender. As tools for documentation, I decided to use a tape recorder (so I could listen to the conversations more than once in order to gain greater understanding of their thinking) and a camera (in order to establish a common visual memory of the experience).

Several days after our decision to study the children's fathers and their occupations, I was ready to begin gathering information. I told the class that we would be meeting in small groups in the studio (a space in our classroom) over the next few days and that it was necessary for each group to be able to work uninterrupted because I had an important question to ask each of them. I purposefully did not reveal the question ahead of time because I wanted them to be able to respond spontaneously within the small group context. This also created a sense of anticipation among the children that served to heighten their expectations and their interest.

In planning for small group work, I found myself paying closer attention to details that I previously was unaware of. This shift in my thinking is due in large part to Malaguzzi's emphasis on the importance of taking great care in preparing for any work with young children:

> The adults should set up situations in advance that facilitate the work of children. The adults must be able to listen a great deal, revisit what has happened in order to keep the children's motivations high, and know when to enter and how much. (*A Message from Malaguzzi,* 1995)

I explained to each small group that they had two jobs during our conversation: "You will either be describing something and making it as clear as you can so that other group members understand your ideas, *or* you will be listening carefully to the child who is speaking and then asking questions to better understand their ideas."

I then asked each child individually to tell us everything they knew about what their father does at work. They approached this task with a seriousness and a willingness to be as clear as they could and to understand as much as they could. Each small group spent 45 to 60 minutes in the studio with me sharing, explaining, questioning and clarifying their ideas. After each of the children had had a turn, I asked them to draw a picture of their dad at work in his office. I did this because Giovanni Piazza once said that "drawing helps to anchor their memory" (personal communication, July 1995). When I first heard this, I was intrigued by its possibilities. It is now common for me to ask my students to draw their ideas or theories after having a conversation.

These conversations took place over a span of 4 days during our choosing time. While this activity was going on in the studio, a very busy group of children began to work with empty boxes, paint, and other materials to create their dads' office buildings. The block area was filling up quickly with skyscrapers, smaller buildings, Lake Michigan, parks, the city's Christmas tree, outdoor sculptures, and trees lining Lake Shore Drive, the major thoroughfare that runs along the lake. (It took three children 45 minutes to decide how to recreate Lake Shore Drive in terms of its location, which way the cars drive, and how many lanes go each way. After using postcards and their own personal experiences as a guide, they were accurate in the end.)

FIGURE 20.6. Getting the train to go dowtown Chicago to visit the dads at work.

Each night after the small group discussions took place, I transcribed the audiotapes. Although this activity is time consuming, I find it invaluable because it gives me the opportunity to more fully understand what the children said. I made it a point to have each child's drawing of his or her dad in his office in front of me while I listened to that child's portion of the tape. This helped me to more fully understand the elements of the children's drawings. Rehearing the conversation also gave me the opportunity to reflect on the children's understandings and to think about what step to take next.

A common theme present in all the small group discussions was that although most of the children had visited their father's workplace and many of them could describe objects in the office, they all had a harder time describing their father's actual work. This led me to believe that the children's understanding of their father's work was somehow lacking in comparison to their detailed recollection of the physical space of his office. I believe this is due, in part, to the distance between the child's daily life and that of his or her father's.

From my perspective, they needed more experiences around this topic in order to gain more knowledge, but I wanted to know what they thought. In our next class meeting, I told them that our small group work had provided us with a lot of information and that I noticed that although they knew a lot about their dads, it seemed to me that there might be more things that they could find out. A few children responded by telling me they thought they knew everything about their dad, but when questioned by the children who had met with them in their small group, they were reminded about some things they did not know. At this point, they all agreed they could gather more information and we began to discuss how to proceed.

Bryan: We could do an interview.
T: What is an interview?
Rashelle: Like when people are asking you a question and you give an answer.
John: When you try to find out more about something.
Michael: It's like when we asked our buddies questions.
Kathryn: It's when you ask someone what they think or do, take a tape recorder or paper and write it down.
Rashelle: It's like when you interviewed us for our Time Capsules.
Bryan: Let's say this person wanted information about you. You have to give an interview about yourself.
Matt: It helps you know more about people.
T: How does an interview help you?
Bryan: It helps you to think.
Rashelle: It helps you to learn something you didn't know about the person before.
T: Why would you interview your dads?
John: Because you want to know more about them.
Matt: Because it's important.
Austin: You want to know more about them 'cause you don't usually see them when they're working.

Although I had already thought of the use of an interview as a next step, I was hoping that the children themselves would bring this up as a possible tool. I was gratified when they did so, because it was my goal that the children see the interview process as a useful way of gathering information. In addition, investment in a particular idea is usually deeper when it comes from a child or a group of children. Children who are involved in the decision-making process have a richer understanding of why they are carrying out a certain task because they themselves have seen the need for something and found the appropriate tool.

The class immediately decided to brainstorm a list of questions for the interview. "Would you write them down and xerox them because that would be a lot of writing for us?" someone asked. We all agreed that this was a good idea because they had come up with 22 questions. (I found a number of the questions to be interesting for various reasons, but in particular, I found the last request, #22, to be especially meaningful based on the children's classroom experiences.

It read, "Please draw a picture of yourself working.") They reminded me to leave some space after each question for the answer. As I heard that reminder, I thought of another important idea. The next day, as I read the questions aloud in class, the children drew pictures next to each of the questions so they could remember what the question was about and would not be overwhelmed by the number of words on the page. At the end of the day they brought their interviews home, planning to bring them back the following morning.

That evening, I began to reflect on a few things:

1. That during the activities related to this project, the children were able to focus for longer periods of time (45–60 minutes) than is typical for first graders at that time of year.
2. That the small group work around a purposeful topic created more opportunities to pay attention, to reflect on themselves and others, to express themselves, to formulate and/or answer questions, and to practice the skills of communication from the point of view of the speaker as well as that of the listener.
3. That communicating and understanding can be hard work, but that they are worthwhile endeavors; that they had considerable practice in communicating their ideas and then representing their knowledge in multiple ways (through verbal language, through drawing, and through construction with various materials including blocks, boxes, and recyclables).
4. That my active presence—observing, questioning, and documenting—helped them to see that I valued their thinking, that I believed in them, and that I trusted each child's individual ability to reflect.
5. That the audiotapes were key in helping me to "hear again" what was said, allowing me to know where the children were in their thinking and where to go next, in affording me the opportunity to transcribe their comments and ideas and make the transcriptions available so all of us (children, parents, and teachers) could revisit and use them again whenever they were needed.

The next morning, the children came running into the classroom with completed interviews in hand and began talking to each other and to the teachers about what they had learned. After about 20 minutes of this excited and productive bustle, we sat down to talk about what they had noticed. They noticed many things, as we imagined they would, but reported on the three things that surprised many of them the most:

1. Most, if not all, fathers have no free time at work.
2. "How can my dad be a boss and have a boss, too?"
3. Most fathers did not get a snack at work.

I realized from this conversation that each child had gathered a great deal of information about his or her father. However, I viewed the interview as just one piece of the puzzle of this emerging project. As I was listening to the children discuss what they had learned about their fathers, I was trying to decide what new experiences I could offer them that would lead them to even greater understandings of their fathers and their jobs. As Amelia Gambetti, former teacher at La Villetta School, said, "Offer a new stimulation, provocation, to make other connections."

It became clear to me that I wanted the children to go on a "purposeful" visit to their father's workplace. I felt I needed to discuss this idea with the parents before approaching the children with this plan. I had never had a parent meeting to discuss an emergent project such as this one, but I felt I needed to share what had happened so far and get some of their feedback and opinions about a possible visit. I wrote a letter home and asked that at least one parent attend the meeting. To prepare for the meeting, I put the children's drawings of their fathers' offices and the transcriptions of the small group discussions on the tables and I placed a map of downtown Chicago on a bulletin board.

The meeting had an excellent turnout. It was not until I invited them to read their child's and other children's thinking that I saw overcoats come off and fathers sit down, reading silently to themselves and aloud to each other and smiling. I told them the story of the project to date, and asked them what they thought about the idea of a visit from their child. The response was overwhelmingly positive! After plotting their workplace on the map (or on the side of the map if they did not work in Chicago proper), we made a set of organizational decisions to facilitate the visits. We chose dates in December based on the location of each father's workplace. For instance, two children had fathers with offices two blocks away from each other. Those two children would visit those two fathers with one adult (a teacher or parent who would document the visit). Each office visit was to last about 35 to 45 minutes. The entire visit, to and from school, would last one morning.

The children were thrilled the next morning! Some of them had heard about the meeting from their parents and the rest were anticipating hearing about it from me. They spontaneously congregated around the map, pointing out the exact location of their fathers' offices, as well as the proximity of one father's office to another's. After the children had all arrived, we had a class meeting in which I briefly explained what happened the night before. After the update, I asked, "Now that you know you will be visiting your father at his office, what other information do you think you will need?"

Rashelle: A map! A map! So we know how to get there!
Kinsey: Yea, my dad drives so we need a map.
John: My dad takes the train. Will I take the train too?
Dave: And sit on the top… (pause)… up the stairs?

We collectively decided that each child would travel to his or her father's office the same way his or her father traveled to work—some by train and taxi, some by train and walking, and some by car. The children planned to take home a sheet of paper in order to draw a map with their father that would explain what route he took to work and with what mode of transportation.

When asked, "What will you do on your visit?," there were many responses. The following is the final list of things to bring and to do.

To Bring to Father's Office:

- A new interview, designed by each child (although the first interview was uniform, the second interview was individually based on what each child's father did).
- Paper for sketching.
- Snack for dad.
- Zipper-locked bag to collect a business card, if any (one child had already shared her father's card and many showed curiosity about it), company stationery, if any, and something to bring back to class for sharing.
- Map.
- Money, if needed.

To Do While at the Office:

- Interview dad and write answers to questions.
- Sketch something that the child found interesting.
- Collect items to bring back.
- Give dad the snack.

From the time of our parent meeting to the first child's visit, two weeks passed. During this time, we met with newly formed small groups in order to prepare the special interviews for their fathers. These small groups were based on proximity of fathers' offices, and therefore which children would be visiting their fathers together. In preparing for their individual interviews with their fathers, the children used the following resources: their drawing of his office, the transcription of their first small group discussion, the map they drew at home with their father about how he goes to work, and the original collective interview. Also during this time, I met with parents who were willing to accompany us and to help document the visits. I knew I wanted photographs of each visit. Photographs can serve as a memory of an encounter and are also an excellent tool in helping children to revisit and therefore rethink an experience. I explained and practiced with these parents the process of documentation so that all were clear about what to photograph and why it was important.

In the end, the visits occurred in the morning on one of three chosen days in December. The children who were not visiting on any given day were in the classroom with my assistant. Those who were visiting were with me or other volunteer parents.

FIGURE 20.7. Mary's Hypotheses about her dad's office.

I was very impressed with how the visits went and with how involved the children were. They carried themselves with an exuberance and a sense of purpose that truly struck me. I believe that this is due to the fact that the children were instrumental in planning the visits. It was not an adult-directed activity. Rather, their participation was fundamental throughout the planning process and I am convinced it heightened their investment and their self-confidence.

In general, a visit played out in the following manner: Once in the lobby of his or her father's office building, the child was responsible for finding the elevators and pushing the appropriate button. After arriving at the designated floor, he or she spoke to the secretary or the receptionist and waited for his or her father. Typically, the parent and child would excitedly hug one another, and then go to his office where the child would proceed with the plan. The child carried out the interview (lasting between 10 and 25 minutes), sketched something of interest, and collected a business card, company letterhead, and an item of the father's choosing to share with the class back at school. Finally, the child presented his or her father with a snack just before leaving.

Back at school that afternoon, I once again asked the children to draw a picture of their fathers working. They then shared their experiences with the entire class. It was during these sharing times that the curiosity in business cards surfaced again. I had not originally thought about the aspect of business cards, but as Carlina Rinaldi (Chapter 5, this volume) said, "Use a compass instead of a train schedule." I was ready to be open and I decided to follow their lead and investigate business cards because the children were unusually curious about them and their use. As an important symbol of their fathers and their work, I felt it was important to pursue this path.

To facilitate this investigation, I invited Mrs. Stanley, a former parent and professional artist with experience in advertising, to come to our class and share her knowledge about business cards. The two of us led a discussion about business cards with the class. By exploring their fathers' business cards, the students were able to co-construct quite a bit of knowledge about what a business card is, what is on a business card, and how a business card is used. When our friend Mrs. Stanley brought out her portfolio of various designs, showed the students the products, and explained the process of producing business cards, they began to comment on her work:

Bryan: That's neat.
Michael: Business cards can have color? Look at that color!
Austin: Why doesn't my dad's card have color?
John: Mine doesn't either.
Kylie: My dad's business card has a little color on the letter in the corner.
Rashelle: These cards are much more boring than yours, Mrs. S.
T: Why is that?
Rashelle: There aren't any pictures to show what our dads do.
Michael: There's no color!
T: Would you like to design a business card for your dad with your own ideas?
All: Yes!

Each child was then given a sheet of paper and asked to come up with three designs. (We decided to put only their father's names and work phone number on the card because of the allotted space.) They chose their favorite of the three designs to reproduce on a card the size of an actual business card. The children measured card stock to the appropriate size for a business card. They used rulers and pencils to achieve this. They were allowed to use up to four colors in their design. Mrs. Stanley and I were amazed at the designs that were produced and the conversation that ensued. We were also impressed by the connections being made among their experiences within this project, their thinking about the cards, and the designs they invented. We had recognized their early enthusiasm as a catalyst for this work. Designing business cards was yet another opportunity to communicate and to represent their knowledge, and through this process, to come to new understandings.

It was at this point that I began to reflect on the project and all that the childrenhad gained. I began to wonder what I often wonder when a project emerges and is in process: "When should this project end? How should it end?" As I thought about these questions, I returned to an idea that seems to be prevalent in Reggio and has been quite important in my classroom in the past few years. I believe it is important and useful to have children summarize a project or an experience by communicating to others the thinking that occurred throughout

FIGURE 20.8. Mary's drawing of her dad's office after visiting him there.

and the knowledge that was gained. In fact, it is common for me to offer children multiple opportunities to share their thinking and their knowledge with others. In guiding the children in preparation for such an event, I help them to think about three things: (a) what to say, (b) how to say it, or (c) to whom to say it. This process is valuable for the children because it is essentially another opportunity for them to revisit their experience and possibly arrive at new and/or deeper levels of understanding. This preparation process is valuable to me because it enables me to see the various levels of understanding within my class as well as what individual children gained from the project.

I met with my class the next day around this issue of communication. We talked together about how best to communicate what we now knew and with whom to share this knowledge. The second part was easy for them—they wanted to share their knowledge with their parents. As they began discussing how they might share this experience, I had an idea and I suggested it to them. "Why not communicate what you know through a slide presentation on Portfolio Night?" (Portfolio Night is an evening event in which children share with their parents work that has been saved throughout the school year.) They agreed, although they had limited knowledge about slide shows. During the next two weeks, they worked very hard and learned a great deal about it.

There were six steps in this process:

1. I began by giving a 5-minute slide show of a trip I had taken. I told them at the beginning, "Let's see how much information I can communicate to you through slides and words since you were not with me on this trip." At the end of the small slide show, I asked, "What did you learn from my words and the

slides about this experience?" The children were very observant and mentioned in great detail everything they had heard throughout the slide show.

2. The children decided that they would like to create individual slide shows. They each chose five photos from their office visit that they felt would give information about their father's work and about their visit to his workplace.
3. Each child put the five photographs in order and numbered them.
4. Each child captioned all five photos on a note card and then practiced reading the cards in order.
5. The negatives from the photos were made into slides. The slides were then placed on a light box and the children ordered and numbered their slide collection.
6. They learned how to place the slides in the slide tray and practiced their presentation with their notes and projector.

The children practiced in small groups of five before presenting their slide show to the entire class. This was done to prepare them for the Portfolio Night presentation for their parents. Each child also used the photo of their father's workplace to draw a picture of the outside of the building on a precut puzzle, writing a message for the dad underneath the drawing.

I then scheduled five families for each Portfolio evening. Part of the evening's activities included the slide show, the presentation of the business card designs, and an envelope of puzzle pieces for their parents to put together. Watching the faces of the children and parents, listening to their conversations and comments, and seeing a number of fathers put the business card right into their wallets were valuable for me and validating for the children.

Project Summary

The Dads and Their Work project was started in November and continued as our main focus for 6 weeks as we created interviews and went on our visits. After the winter break, we took a week to explore business cards in greater depth. In February and March it became a focus once again as we prepared for Portfolio Night. After spring break, the children compiled all of their work from the project into a book.

Most of the documentation of the project was done with audiotapes and photos, although some videotape was also used. The documentation of the project was used (a) to interpret children's ideas and thinking processes; (b) as a memory for the children, teachers, and parents; and (c) as a guide for teachers.

Post-project experiences surfaced within 6 months of completion. One such experience occurred during the last few days of school when we were packing our room and preparing "surprises" for next year's first graders. I noticed that something was being built in the blocks. I went over to the three children who were busy at work and asked, "What are you building?" Austin replied, "These are offices, we have work to do!"

In September, the second-grade teacher approached me with a copy of her first classroom newsletter in hand. "Look," she said excitedly while pointing out an illustration. "No one can tell me your Dads Project wasn't important to these children!" She showed me a picture of a school bus arriving at our school with the Chicago skyline prominent in the background. "Two children from your class were responsible for this drawing," she explained.

Shortly after, a parent who had shared in the project with her daughter came into my room to show me an invitation. Her husband's business associates were so taken with what had transpired through the visit, they decided to institute a "Discovery Day" for children of their employees to visit their parents at work.

I realized during the fall that I had my own reflections and the children had their memories, but I had not realized the impact the project had on the parents as well. In order to collect their reflections, I wrote to each father and asked if he would put into words his thoughts about last year's experience. Some of the comments I received were:

> What parents do when they leave the house each morning to go to work is a mysterious thing for kids. Where do they go? Why? What do they do? The beauty of the "Dads" program was that it demystified this pattern in a very systematic fashion on a level that was exciting, yet understandable for the kids. For Kathryn, in particular, this was a high impact project. She still "fits" the things I tell her I am doing on any given day into her experience with the project, and I know that she is comforted by this ability to better relate to my daily work routine.
>
> Concerning my experience before, during and after, some random thoughts are: it really required very little time and effort on my part and was well worth it; the office visit created a natural moment to share some of my life with my son, something that I probably wouldn't have initiated on my own, but an experience that I'm very happy to have enjoyed; the presentation that the kids made gave me a chance to share in his school work and something that he was proud of. His presentation was certainly something I was proud of; it was an experience that I'll always remember.

Uncertainty often makes us feel uncomfortable. However, in constructing the "Dads and Their Work" project alongside the children in my class, I discovered that uncertainty is a necessary part of the process. Unlike conventionally planned themes in which a teacher predetermines a set of activities, *progettazione* by definition is based on working with children, observing and listening to children, reflecting on their understandings, and deciding what step to take next. I feel the following aspects are important when uncertainty arises:

- Trust your own instincts as a teacher
- Trust your students (they need to know you believe in them)

- Talk with your colleagues, ask them questions, and share and reflect with them

Through reflection of the project, I found powerful understandings about the families in my classroom. I believe this project gave the parents an opportunity to see how their children think and learn while the children "discovered" the work of their fathers. As the parents participated in this project, they "entered" the school in new ways. They had the opportunity to see a particular curriculum unfold, but of equal importance, they provided a fundamental contribution to the emergence of that curriculum. Because the fathers made themselves available to their children and the work they were carrying out at school, they made it possible for their children to see them in new ways. One of my goals had been to provide opportunities for the children to have a broader understanding of their fathers, but I did not recognize that it would also create an opportunity for the fathers to see themselves mirrored in the eyes of their children.

I feel that the work being done in Reggio Emilia has messages for all of us. I find that it challenges my thinking to rise to new levels of understanding in my classroom practice with children. I often remember Carlina Rinaldi's words about the role of the teacher: "Not to transmit knowledge but to discover the best way for helping children to know." I believe the more opportunities we can offer to children "to know," the more opportunity they will have "to understand."

REFERENCES

A Message from Malaguzzi (1993). Video interview by L. Malaguzzi and L. Gandini. Distributed by Reggio Children USA, Washington, DC 20005-3105.

Tarini, E. (1997). Reflections on a year in Reggio Emilia: Key concepts in rethinking and learning the Reggio way. In J. Hendrick (Ed.), *First steps in teaching the Reggio way,* (pp. 56–69). Columbus, OH: Merrill.

To dance in the sun.
The rights of children,
Diana School.

chapter 21

The Project Approach Framework for Teacher Education: A Case for Collaborative Learning and Reflective Practice

Mary Jane Moran

Educators throughout the world have had a wide range of reactions to the Reggio Emilia approach. Some teachers emulate the physical environment of classrooms visited in Reggio Emilia, or provide more diverse media for children's representations of their meaning making, or implement and document long-term projects with children. Little attention has been focused on what the Reggio Emilia approach to early education means for preservice teacher education. There is convincing research that reflection (LaBoskey, 1994; Sparks-Langer, Colton, Simmons, Pasch, & Starks, 1990; Zeichner & Liston, 1987) and collaborative learning (Oja & Smulyan, 1989) help teachers better understand their students.

Some may contend that preservice teachers are too busy simply surviving initial experiences (Fuller & Brown, 1975) and do not have the luxury of time (Katz, 1991) nor the depth and breadth of experience from which to contemplate more than the "craft" of teaching. Opportunities for engaging in reflective practice and collaboration are often reserved for graduate internships. However, it may be that preservice teachers simply have not been provided the time, opportunity, and mentoring that typifies new teachers' experiences in the preprimary schools of Reggio Emilia.

A project approach to early education provides experiences for preservice teachers to increase their level of reflectivity (Van Manen, 1977). Projects help them move away from focusing on simply surviving or attending to self-concerns and classroom management. Instead they begin to focus on collaboration and reflective practice, concerns that are more typical in the later stages of teacher education. Through project work the teacher enters the classroom thoughtfully and behaves improvisationally, yet purposefully, as he or she co-constructs knowledge with children. This dynamic process requires the teacher to consider many elements simultaneously, with no single one having more import than the other. The convergence and reconvergence of elements is a cycle that guides teacher practice as he or she supports the life of a project.

THE COURSE

The Project Approach Framework for Teacher Education (PAFTE) is incorporated into a beginning teaching methods course, divided into three phases over a 16-week semester: Orientation, Implementation, and Interpretation.

The Orientation phase is a foundation and covers the first 5 weeks. Preservice teachers (undergraduate students) are randomly placed into teaching teams and provided with opportunities to get to know one another, the children in the classroom, and the logistics of implementing projects. *Engaging Children's Minds: The Project Approach* (Katz & Chard, 1989) and *Enquiring Teachers Enquiring Learners: A Constructivist Approach for Teaching* (Fosnot, 1989) are texts that are used to provide a basic introduction to projects and constructivist teaching, and *The Hundred Languages of Children* (Edwards, Gandini, & Forman, 1993) provides a description of a learning context within which projects and constructivist teaching are described. Because teachers attend their practicum once each week and children come either 3 or 4 days per week, teachers are assigned to a teaching team of three or four teachers and teach the same group of 3-, 4-, or 5-year-old children for the semester.

Time is scheduled for teaching teams to meet in and out of class, alone and with their teacher educator. Class lectures focus on the application and guidance of projects. Teachers from previous semesters share their experiences using videotape clips and documentation panels to assist in a description of their project work. Student teachers are provided with sufficient information about implementing projects and constructivist teaching so they can begin their project during the sixth or seventh week of the semester.

During the Implementation phase, which lasts approximately 6 weeks, teaching teams implement their projects. They have already chosen a topic by closely attending to children's play, conversations, and questions. Nevertheless, they are often anxious about how to begin a project, how the lead teacher of the team should begin. Following his or her day, the lead teacher consults with the team to help prepare the second teacher, with this sequence continuing throughout the life of a project.

Preservice teachers are expected to develop both teaching skills and conceptual and theoretical understanding for guiding their practice. Coupled with videotapes and audiotapes of each teaching session, preservice teachers are provided written feedback. This constructive criticism is intended to offer personalized attention for the development of each teacher's ability to use the more technical tools of teaching and enables the teacher educator to individualize instruction. Students are rated on as many as 40 different skills and techniques ranging from "facial affect and body language" to "acknowledges when child responds to limit setting." One later stated:

> I appreciated the opportunity to receive feedback immediately following my project session. Sometimes I would read it and ask myself why did I do that? or say this? This allowed me to change my focus of my own approach.

Additionally, the teacher educator includes a narrative about whether the particular activity seemed to make sense within the context of the emergence of the project (Moran, 1997).

As preservice teachers are encouraged to audiotape, transcribe, and analyze a variety of records, they begin to leave behind their pocketbooks and notebooks and replace them with audio recorders, cameras, and bags of children's earlier representations. On a daily and weekly basis, they refer to documentation to determine the next step in the project as well as work on their individual teaching skills.

At the core of the final Interpretation phase, which lasts 3 more weeks, preservice teachers create documentation panels and present their analysis to their peers and less formally, to parents. They prepare oral presentations as they attempt to analyze what happened during the project—for both children and themselves. For example, teams often interpret ways in which they could have more successfully "hit the developmental mark," taken advantage of teachable moments, and use materials that afford children different perspectives on the concepts that they are trying to represent.

THEORETICAL FOUNDATIONS

The Project Approach Framework for Teacher Education is built on two theoretical perspectives about teaching and the teacher. These perspectives continually interface to guide teacher practice and include: the tenets of social constructivism and the image of the teacher.

Social Constructivist Teaching

Our social constructivist theory acknowledges that we value the contributions of children in the development of their own knowledge and reflects a belief that knowledge is constructed with others. These beliefs explain why we guide children's group work and why we cannot prescribe this work. Projects are implemented with groups of five or six children by teaching teams of three or four preservice teachers. Group work guided by more than one student teacher is central to the belief that children and adults socially construct knowledge and create *shared meaning* as they actively engage in activities. The co-construction of knowledge is dependent on the ability of group members to learn from one another. The strategy of pairing less experienced with more experienced learners is useful only if the members of the dyad or group are able to listen to one another, negotiate, and accept different perspectives while remaining in relation to engage in joint activities. This is true for both teaching teams and groups of children. However, it is the responsibility of the teaching team to nurture and manage the social cohesion of the group and work to ensure *intersubjectivity,* the mutual understanding that is achieved by people in communication (Berk & Winsler, 1995). It is likewise the responsibility of the teacher educator to reflect this role for the teaching teams.

Teacher as Learner, Researcher, and Collaborator

Although teachers in Reggio Emilia have been described in many ways, including provocateurs (New, 1991), protagonists (Edwards et al., 1993; Rinaldi, 1993), partners, nurturers, and guides (Edwards, Chapter 10, this volume), as well as learners and researchers (Bredekamp, 1994), preservice teachers trained within this framework are asked to create an image of themselves as learners, researchers, and collaborators. These roles are central to both the dynamic quality of their work and the use of reflective practice and collaboration. The image of self as learner means that the educator does not view himself or herself as expert dispenser of knowledge, that learning is lifelong, and constructed not only within his or her team but along with the children he or she teaches.

This ongoing learning is made possible through both the researcher and collaborator roles. Teachers who behave as researchers in this context behave as classroom ethnographers (New, 1994). Ethnographers immerse themselves within a learning context in order to gather a great variety of data. These data are at the core of teachers' reflective practice. To make sense of the variety of data, collaboration with others is critical and results in a "thick description" (Geertz, 1973) of project events, through an analysis and interpretation of dialogue, artifacts, and interaction that reflect not only the learning processes but also the sociocultural life of a classroom. This thick description is often reflected in the documentation of project work. Documentation is used by teachers not only to record the history of a project, but most importantly to guide practice (Goldhaber, Smith, & Sortino, 1997).

The teaching team is the site where different dispositions, talents, perspectives, and past experiences come together and are integrated so that the task of implementing a project is accomplished. As one preservice teacher remarked:

> We worked as a team to produce both of our panels and working together helped us combine our perspectives. We collaborated our efforts and developed combined work, rather than individual work. It helped us in where we needed to focus our attention in our presentation—our changes as a team.

Thus, as a result of engaging in collaboration in order to use data to inform teaching, previous ways of knowing and believing are often challenged, supported, and give rise to new perspectives, new knowledge, and even new beliefs. A perspective is developed that values inquiry and brainstorming followed by walking into a classroom with new provocations as determinants for becoming thoughtful and improvisational.

TEACHING STRATEGIES

Revisiting

Many of the skills and strategies we seek to instill in our preservice teachers reflect what we know to be practiced in the preprimary schools in Reggio Emilia. The practice of revisiting is one such strategy that is consistent with a social constructivist theory. This practice reflects the belief that given the opportunity to review and reflect on earlier work along with diverse ways of representing new understandings, children's co-construction of knowledge is *scaffolded* or bridged from previous to new ways of knowing. Teachers likewise engage in these practices in order to co-construct their knowledge about their own teaching. They revisit their earlier practice along with data gathered from those events and return to the classroom to rerepresent what they have learned. An aspect of revisiting is learning to view a task, representation, or practice from multiple perspectives.

Multiple Symbolization

Different media offer different affordances for representation (Forman, 1994). Allowing children opportunities to represent a single concept in a variety of media creates more meanings for the concept. This happens as children reflect on their own symbolizations. By diversifying media, teachers can help children discover multiple ways to symbolize their knowing and return to earlier symbols to gain deeper insights. These strategies support the emerging life of a project.

Documentation

Documentation is the primary way of capturing the life of a project, as we have

FIGURE 21.1. To aid discussion of the different observations collected, the tape recorder is used to preserve the reflections of the group.

seen in Reggio Emilia. Documentation can serve many purposes, but within this training approach it is most valuable as a guide for ongoing professional development. The act of gathering and using documentation requires the teacher to closely attend, reflect, and seek another's assistance on ways to analyze and interpret the intention of children's words and drawings. In this manner he or she can return to the classroom with thoughtfully prepared provocations and anticipated responses to children's inquiry.

Teachers work together to select records to include on documentation panels. This requires a second level of reflection. This reflection is more global and historical in focus and includes thinking about teaching strategies, children's change in knowing, phases of the projects, multiple ways children symbolized their meaning making, and points where teachers may have made different choices. This postproject reflection is typically a validating and rewarding experience because teams are frequently surprised and delighted at how much was accomplished. They discover shifts in knowing and behavior that they had not previously noticed. As one stated:

> If we hadn't paused to do those panels we would have left the project not realizing what happened. I mean, there was dialogue that we found as we were doing our panels that all of a sudden just jumps out at you. You know—look what happened here. We picked out dialogue that I had never heard, I had never realized was there. That was really great. The panels also helped us formulate our presentation.

Teams are given a limited time to present their analysis to the class using documentation panels, videotape clips, and verbal recall to tell the story of their project. This experience is often transformative. The decision on what to highlight in their oral presentation forces them to isolate what they considered among the most important and significant outcomes of the project. This final round of negotiating, listening to multiple perspectives, and compromising on which parts of the project to highlight is often exhaustive, intensive, and sometimes confrontational but in the end a reflection of the team's commitment to one another and the task. This postproject reflection is a culminating experience in which the "voices" of the individual teachers come together in a final pictorial and oral history of their teaching. One said:

FIGURE 21.2. Working and sharing in group the preparation of documentary panels.

> The panels were a lot of work so it gave our group a great sense of accomplishment. To put items on the panels we really needed to pull things out of the project. We needed to make a lot of decisions. The things the children learned and their process of learning jumped out when we pulled dialogue out and drawings and pictures.

From Exploration to Representational Sequence

A teacher needs to judge whether it is more meaningful to move children into an exploration phase [E] or a representational phase [R] of a project. Every project has an E-R-E-R sequence. The *exploration phase* refers to experiential and investigatory experiences by children to acquire new information. Photographs, books, conversations, artifacts, and field trips are examples of exploration experiences. Certainly books and photographs are representations, but in this context they are explored rather than produced by the children. In a *representational phase,* children produce their own representations and invent new ways of knowing. These symbols also create an opportunity for children or teachers to document changes in knowing over time. Examples of representational experiences include drawings, constructions, and dramatizations.

Teachers guide the intention of their practice by determining the phase of the project and they fluctuate back and forth between these two ways of experiencing a topic. They typically return to an exploratory phase to introduce new content, introduce new perspectives about a topic, or renew interest in a topic.

For example, in a castle project implemented with toddlers, the children lost interest in playing with their constructed castle. The teachers decided to introduce a provocation and so one day, Dragon Green and Dragon Red (finger puppets) were introduced [E]. Soon the toddlers were creating story lines and wishing for more dragons. Letters were dictated to teachers to invite more dragons [R]. As a result, there are now seven dragons occupying the castle, which will remain in the classroom to welcome the return of the toddlers next year.

The length of time and the ways through which each phase is experienced are as variable as the number of project topics one can pursue. It is possible to remain in a single phase for days or to fluctuate between the two in one day. The point is that the teacher must know the phase of the project in order to analyze the best way to prepare and lead children through the next steps of co-constructing knowledge.

During a tractor project with 4- and 5-year-olds, focus shifted from farms to tractors as a result of teachers considering the E-R-E-R sequence in the early days of the project. On their first day, teachers decided to include a story about farms, questions about whether children had been to a farm, and what children remembered seeing [E]. Children were given crayons and paper and asked to draw something they remembered from the story or a trip to a farm [R].

On the second day, the children went to the local cow barns as teachers continued to tape children's comments and questions [E]. It was clear that the most significant part of the trip was when children stood next to a huge tractor. The children experienced being dwarfed by tires taller than any of them and continued to recall the event with great enthusiasm.

The teacher for that day contacted her teammates and discussed the impact of the tractor. As a result, the team decided to pursue tractors rather than farms. Based on the many questions and comments by children about the tires, on the third day the third teacher on the team remained in an exploration phase by preparing to provoke discussion about types and sizes of tires. She organized a visit to the school parking lot to look at stroller tires, car tires, and bicycle tires. Children moved into a representational phase as they measured tires, took pictures of tires, and constructed a tire out of rubber tubing. As they handled the tubing, their attention to the treads provoked a conversation about what kind of pattern the tire would make in the mud. On the next day as tire-ness continued to be represented, children began to recall other parts of the tractor and decided to make a tractor.

The remaining 2 weeks of the project were centered primarily around tasks reflective of a representational phase as children drew pictures of tractors; studied photographs, pictures, and the videotape of their tractor visit; returned for a second visit to sketch the tractor, and negotiated parts to be included on a final tractor constructed by all the children. Children negotiated the color, types of dials, who would make the steering wheel, and how to build the headlights, warning lights, and signs typically found on tractors. This collaborative representation is typical of work that emerges late in these projects because teachers are asked to encourage children to generate a single group representation as a culminating experience.

SHIFTS TOWARD COLLABORATIVE LEARNING AND REFLECTIVE TEACHING

From Individual to Shared Meaning

Preservice teachers' ways of knowing are brought to the surface and exposed by the project framework. As a member of a teaching team, teachers are compelled to think, articulate, question, explain, and problem solve with one another. As a result, there is a move away from considering one's own viewpoint toward considering multiple perspectives of the collective, resulting in a shift from individual to shared meaning. This position often frees the teacher from a focus on producing correct answers. If there is more than one way to view a challenge, then perhaps there is more than one correct response to that challenge.

From Error to Opportunity

During team meetings, teachers are encouraged to revisit perceived failures in order to generate a variety of responses. Often teachers are encouraged to return to the classroom to rerepresent their new perspective by altering their own behavior. These rerepresentations include changing teaching strategies, altering media, and/or modifying directions. For example, a team implementing a project on castles were beginning their last week in which children were to act out a play written earlier in the project. Much time had been devoted to the story line. Yet, the preservice teachers exclaimed, "We blew it." They were referring to their inability to convince the children to act out the script. The teachers were disappointed because the play was to be a culminating event.

Once teachers discussed possible reasons why the children were reluctant, they determined the problem may have been that children were being asked to act without the teacher's "guided participation" (Rogoff, 1995). Their guided participation had reverted to directing. The children seemed concerned rather than excited and asked questions such as, "What if all the girls want to be the princess?" A decision was made that a dramatization was still a worthwhile collaborative experience, but it required a few significant changes: (a) Have two teachers co-teach, (b) dress in costumes, (c) provide new and realistic props, and (d) simply invite children to "play castle." The dramatization was a success because the script was replaced by the teachers' guided participation which surprisingly resulting in the children's recall of much of their original script. The shift was away from the view that a perceived error is a failure toward an opportunity for professional growth.

From Isolated to Collective Teaching

The project framework provides numerous opportunities and time for teachers to talk about what they believe, value, and consider worthwhile practice. For many, this is the first time they have been given the opportunity to express these opinions. As they listen and respond to one another, the role of the teacher educator changes. Once they have shared the responsibility for teaching, listening to one another's suggestions, and going into the classrooms to implement those suggestions, trust among the team members increases. The shift is away from a dependence on the teacher educator toward interdependence resulting in a shift from teaching in isolation to teaching collectively. As they actively exchange ideas, beliefs, and suggestions, there is a shift from external problem solving to internalizing strategies for solving similar problems in the future. The result is a decrease in reaction time in the classroom so that reflection-on-action moves toward reflection (and response) in-action (Schon, 1983). As a preservice teacher noted:

> By reflecting on my work, both alone and in my team, I really strengthened my awareness of how to respond to the children. These projects forced us to external-

> ize our knowledge and explain it to our classmates [and as a result of these externalizations]—made the concepts and what to do clearer for me.

This collective reflection is an important context in which "other reflection" serves as a catalyst for "self-reflection."

From Familiar to Special Words

A change in language is a telling indicator that preservice teachers have begun to internalize collaborative learning and reflective teaching. They begin to substitute words such as *provocations* for *teach them, symbolic representation* for *art, guided participation* for *direct them,* and *scaffolding* for *help them.* As one teacher revealed:

> At first, I never thought I'd be able to utilize all those teaching strategies but now I realize I really can do this. I described this process to my friend and she was amazed at the language. I find myself using the language to articulate the work that I do and it really does make a huge difference, especially to some people who refer to my class as 'baby-sitting." Now they realize they couldn't do it and it's much, much more than that.

This collective, verbal reflection is the primary means for a preservice teacher's externalization of thought processes so that those processes can be clarified, corroborated, and/or challenged. This interaction is what is meant by other reflection. The context is a relatively safe one, unlike speaking out in a large class. They recognize that the process is an exploration of the possibilities for all of them to consider and so they expect to take some shots in the dark in order to generate ideas in their attempt to hit the developmental mark. When the "hit" is made in the classroom or when there is mutual agreement about how to proceed among team members, there is often an increase in energy and commitment to the process along with a clarity about how to improve practice. When this clarity is internalized, self-reflection guides the development of each teacher's practice.

SUMMARY

The PAFTE establishes a community of learners through revisiting, documenting children's work, and other practices that we have seen in Reggio Emilia. Through these practices, preservice teachers develop a new vision of a themselves as learners, researchers, and collaborators. These practices help them to enter teaching episodes thoughtfully and to become increasingly capable of responding improvisationally. Teachers trained within such a framework view collaborative teaching and reflective practice as valuable and necessary as they make predictions, try things out, and then interpret them. They not only look to themselves but also look out to their children as they work to develop educative experiences in which co-construction of knowledge is actualized.

REFERENCES

Berk, L. E. & Winsler, A. (1995). *Scaffolding children's learning: Vygotsky and early childhood education.* Washington, DC: NAEYC.

Bredekamp, S. (1994, June). *Training of teachers in Reggio Emilia: Implications for professional development in the U.S.* Paper presented at the Reggio Emilia Study Seminar, Reggio Emilia, Italy.

Edwards, C., Gandini, L., & Forman, G. (1993). *The hundred languages of children: The Reggio Emilia approach to early childhood education.* Norwood, NJ: Ablex.

Forman, G. (1994). Different media, different languages. In L.G. Katz & B. Cesarone (Eds.), *Reflective essays on the Reggio Emilia approach,* (pp. 43–49). Urbana, IL: ERIC Clearinghouse on Elementary and Early Childhood Education.

Fosnot, C. (1989). *Enquiring teachers, enquiring learners: A constructivist approach to teaching.* New York: Teachers College Press.

Fuller, F., & Brown, O. (1975). Becoming a teacher. In K. Ryan (Ed.), *Teacher education (The Seventy-Fourth NSSE Yearbook).* Chicago: University of Chicago Press.

Geertz, C. (1973). Thick description: Toward an interpretive theory of culture. In C. Geertz, *The interpretation of cultures* (pp. 3–30). New York: Basic Books.

Goldhaber, J., Smith, D., & Sortino, S. (1997). Observing, recording, understanding: The role of documentation in early childhood teacher education. In J. Hendrick (Ed.), *First steps in teaching the Reggio way,* (pp. 198–209). Columbus, OH: Merrill.

Katz, L.G. (1991, November). *Critical commentary.* In invited symposium on "Diversity and developmentally appropriate practice: Implications for administrators and teacher educators." NAEYC Annual Conference, Denver, CO.

Katz, L.G., & Chard, S. (1989). *Engaging children's minds: The project approach.* Norwood, NJ: Ablex.

LaBoskey, V.K. (1994). *Development of reflective practice: A study of preservice teachers.* New York: teachers College Press.

Moran, M.J. (1997). Reconceptualizing early childhood teacher education: Preservice teachers as ethnographers. In J. Hendrick (Ed.), *First steps toward teaching the Reggio way,* (pp. 210–221). Englewood Cliffs, NJ: Prentice Hall.

New, R.S. (1991, Winter). Projects and provocations: Preschool curriculum ideas from Reggio Emilia. *Montessori Life,* 26–28

New, R.S. (1994). Culture, child development, and developmentally appropriate practices: Teachers as collaborative researchers. In B. Mallory, & R.S. New (Eds.), *Diversity and developmentally appropriate practices: Challenges for early childhood education.* (pp. 65–83). New York: Teachers College Press.

Oja, S.N., & Smulyan, L. (1989). *Collaborative action research: A developmental process.* London: Falmer Press.

Rinaldi, C. (1993). The emergent curriculum and social constructivism: An interview with Lella Gandini. In C. Edwards, L. Gandini, & G. Forman (Eds.), *The hundred languages of children: The Reggio Emilia approach to early childhood education.* (pp. 101–111). Norwood, NJ: Ablex.

Rogoff, B. (1990) *Apprenticeship in thinking: Cognitive development in social context.* Oxford University Press.

Schon, D.A. (1983). *The reflective practitioner.* San Francisco: Jossey-Bass.

Sparks-Langer, G.M., Simmons, J.M., Pasch, M., Colton, A., and Starko, A. (1990). Reflective pedagogical thinking: How can we promote it and measure it? *Journal of Teacher Education, 41*(4), 23–32.

Van Manen, M. (1977). Linking ways of knowing with ways of being practical. *Curriculum Inquiry, 3*, 205–228.

Zeichner, K.M. & Liston, D.P. (1987). Teaching student teachers to reflect. *Harvard Educational Review, L7*(1), 23–47.

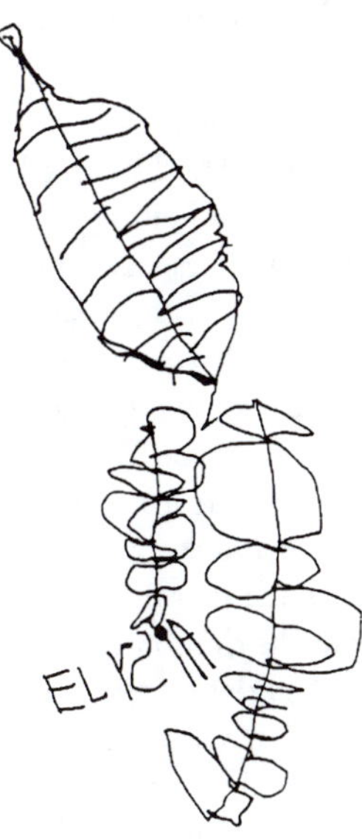

Drawing by a 4-year-old child at the College School.

chapter 22

Adapting the Reggio Emilia Approach: Becoming Reference Points for Study and Practice

Brenda Fyfe
Louise Cadwell
Jan Phillips

In the fall of 1992 a group of teachers from the St. Louis area formed a network to support their study and implementation of the principles and practices of the Reggio Emilia approach to early education. They began as a group of 20 from five different schools in the St. Louis metropolitan area. They were networked through a system of support for professional development that was funded for a 3-year period by The Danforth Foundation.

The teachers came from public and private programs, including Head Start and public school districts, in both city and county locations. The group included teachers of infants, toddlers, preschool-age children, kindergarten, and first and second grades. Prior to the start of the project, half of them had participated in week-long study tours of the Reggio Emilia schools, most had viewed and studied The Hundred Languages Exhibit when it was in St. Louis in late 1991, and all had either attended workshops or read articles about the approach. This chapter presents some of the insights and understandings that have grown out of our work with these teachers and with each other.

The three authors of this chapter codirected the project. Jan took the lead in administering the budget, scheduling, publicizing, and orchestrating events for the overall project. Louise and Brenda offered individualized and on-site consultation for teachers from all of the schools. All three authors designed and organized support services, programming, and documentation of learning across the project.

Each of us, however, played a particular role at The College School, which was the demonstration site for the network. Jan Phillips is the director of this private, independent school for preschool through eighth grade located in Webster Groves, Missouri. Louise Cadwell, an art educator who spent a year as an intern in Reggio Emilia from 1991–1992, has worked as *atelierista* with a team of early childhood teachers from The College School since the beginning of the project in 1992. Brenda Fyfe, Professor of Education from Webster University, has consulted with this team on a regular basis, in some respects, like a *pedagogista* might in Reggio Emilia.

Two years into our project, Brenda was asked to present reflections on our work at a study seminar in Reggio Emilia held in early June 1994. That paper was subsequently published in an ERIC monograph called *Reflections on the Reggio Emilia Approach* (Fyfe, 1994) and in the Italian edition of *The Hundred Languages of Children*. This chapter elaborates on that writing and draws on an additional 2 years of experience. We have chosen to begin with Brenda's explanation of the professional development system that evolved in response to our ongoing analysis of participant needs and interests. This is followed by Louise's discussion of the process of change as exemplified in a particular mini-story of her experience in collaborating as an *atelierista* with teachers, children, and parents. This story illustrates our progress in developing a strong image of the child and in projecting and facilitating ongoing experiences that are rooted in our study of children's thinking and experiences, thereby connected and continuous rather than just related and imposed. Finally, Jan draws from her personal journal to share the perspective of an administrator in supporting change and professional development of teachers. This is followed by a brief synopsis of other significant teacher insights and observations, and change in practice. The chapter ends with an explanation of our ongoing commitment to collaborate with our colleagues in St. Louis, in Reggio Emilia, and the United States.

THE PROFESSIONAL DEVELOPMENT SYSTEM

The graphic in Table 22.1 depicts the components of a professional development

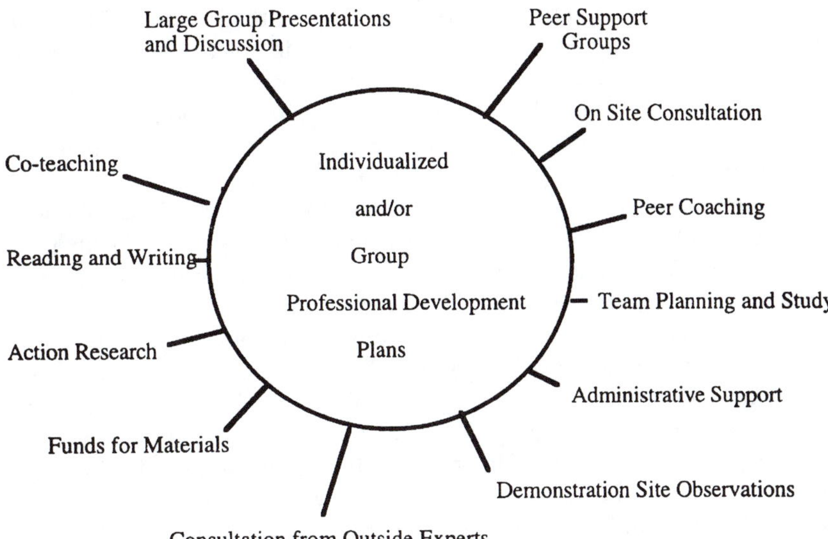

TABLE 22.1.

support system that evolved over the course of the project. When planning the project we reviewed literature on critical attributes of effective teacher development programs and ways to support change in schools (Costa, Garmston, & Lambert, 1988; Eisner, 1992; Fullan, 1990; Fullan & Miles, 1992; Fullan & Stiegelbauer, 1991; Hord, Rutherford, Hulling-Austin, & Hall, 1987); we studied the system of support for professional development established for teachers in Reggio Emilia; and we assessed the needs and interests of teachers, administrators, and parents in our project. We attempted to establish a network of relations among all of the members of our learning community.

When devising professional development opportunities, we tried to keep in mind that "effective change facilitators work with people in an adaptive and systemic way, designing interventions for clients' needs, realizing that those needs exist in particular contexts and settings" (Hord et al., 1987, p. 7). Different responses and interventions are required for different people. Our system of support grew and transformed as we responded to the needs and interests of the participants in the project. We kept abreast of these through discussions at group meetings, questionnaires, on-site consultation visits, and written professional development plans.

Individual or group professional development plans of teachers helped bring focus to their study. Teachers were strongly encouraged to collaborate, when possible, on group or partner professional development plans. Those who chose to do so had more incentive and opportunity to engage in discussion, reflection, and interpretation of their collective work. In some cases these teachers worked toward common goals in the same ways (e.g., by forming a study group to discuss shared readings). Or they may have worked in different ways to reach a common goal and then come together to share experiences, reflections, and perspectives. Even when teachers did not develop group or interdependent professional development plans, their written plans served as vehicles for communication with other teachers and administrators.

Our format for professional development plans was derived from the work of Vartuli and Fyfe (1993). It asked teachers to (a) select goals, (b) identify methods of support that could help them achieve their goals, (c) plan a portfolio of evidence or data that could be collected through the year to help analyze progress toward goals, and (d) identify resources or additional information needed. In addition to helping teachers focus and plan for professional development, these written documents informed the project's codirectors of appropriate ways to allocate resources of the grant and plan for group learning opportunities. For example, in the second year of the project, 40% of our teachers identified goals related to "learning better ways to work with parents as partners in the development, analysis, and implementation of curriculum." When Amelia Gambetti, George Forman, and Lella Gandini were invited to come to St. Louis to consult with us that year, we asked them to address this topic in their presentations.

At the beginning of the third year of our project, we worked with a local educator who asked to focus her doctoral dissertation study on our work (Entzminger, 1995). With consultation from the directors of the project, she designed a questionnaire and a set of interview questions for educators in the project. One set of questions related to the components of the support that teachers found most effective in promoting their understanding of the principles and practices of Reggio Emilia. The six highest rated components are described here with explanation of how they evolved as we continuously studied our work together.

On Site Consultation

Most teachers wanted on-the-job consultation. In the first year, Louise and Brenda scheduled regular visits to each of the centers or classrooms. Teachers utilized them in many different ways. Some wanted help in reorganizing and reconceptualizing their classroom environments; others wanted to be observed and coached in how to support the hundred languages of children. In many cases, teachers were asking us to tell them what to do differently, how to change, and where to start. Although teachers indicated satisfaction with this kind of help, the consultants observed that in some cases teachers were developing a dependency and feelings of helplessness. We also felt that some of our time was not being used productively because we had to spend part of it on-site exploring what it was that the teachers wanted in regard to consultation.

By the second year we decided that a more efficient approach and one that would engage teachers more as active partners would be to ask the teachers and administrator from each site to develop a written plan or proposal for our consultation visits. We suggested possibilities and provided a form with possible areas of focus to frame the visit. We also asked teachers to relate this plan to their professional development goals and plans for the year. Such written plans enabled the consultants to come better prepared to focus on the interests and needs of the group. It required the teaching team and administrator to collectively reflect on current knowledge and to make explicit their questions and preferred areas of focus for the consultation. It required the team to coordinate a plan that best utilized our time for individuals as well as the group. This was especially important at sites where several teachers were involved in the project.

We also learned by the third year that it was very helpful for consultants to write a short report summarizing observations, recommendations, agreements, and/or issues and problems that had been addressed during the visit. These documents could be sent back to the sites and copies distributed to each member of the team. We found that this kind of record helped all of us to remember and reflect on our work together. We were beginning to grasp one of the Reggio "fundamentals" (Gandini, 1993), that there is interdependency between collaboration and organization.

Large Group Meetings

Once a month we scheduled meetings for all members of the network. We rotated locations across the schools in the network each month so that we could visit each other's classrooms and study work in progress. The evening generally lasted 3 hours beginning with time to visit the classrooms, a social over dinner, then proceeding to a group discussion, presentation, or workshop. The group activities were planned by the project directors based on the information gleaned from our analyses of professional development plans and our ongoing observations and anecdotal records from on-site consultations. These included teacher presentations of documentation explaining projects in progress; workshops on exploring, organizing, and utilizing materials such as clay, paper, and recycled materials to help children construct knowledge; and analyses of recorded small group conversations of children to identify concepts, ideas, and interests that could be revisited or further investigated in ongoing experiences with children.

This group gathering was valued by the participants for a number of reasons. It offered them regular opportunities to discuss, share, and commiserate with teachers from other programs. This kind of exchange was a great stimulus for creative thinking about alternative ways to adopt and adapt the Reggio approach. Teachers often gave each other encouragement to persevere in the face of difficulties. It was an opportunity for teaching teams (teachers, art teacher, and their administrator) to participate in a shared experience that provided a common focus for later team discussions.

Peer Support Groups

In the second year of the project, we began to set aside 1 hour of the monthly group meetings for peer support group discussions. Originally we had anticipated that this need would be met at each of the sites through their own team meetings. However, it became clear through both the written and oral feedback that many of the teachers wanted to meet with colleagues from other schools who worked with similar age populations or in similar positions (e.g., teachers of toddlers; teachers of preschool age; kindergarten, first, and second grades; *atelieristi;* and administrators). They wanted the cross-fertilization that came from the exchange of ideas and experiences. Some admitted that it is often easier to discuss differences of opinion about teaching practices with people with whom we do not work each day.

In the beginning, we just asked each group to assign a recorder to keep minutes and to be sure to set aside time at the end of the hour to plan the agenda for the next month's meeting. This would ensure that all members could come prepared to focus on the agreed on topic or problem. The agenda for each group was announced in the minutes of the monthly meetings. This would enable anyone who could not attend to keep abreast of the activity of the support group. After the fourth or fifth meeting, some frustrations were expressed that meetings were sometimes dominated by a few and that conversations were not always focused. In response, we provided some written guidelines that

FIGURE 22.1. One of the many group discussions.

explained the roles and responsibilities of participants in discussion groups. These were discussed at the next meeting and seemed to support more productive discussion. Once again, this was a lesson in the relationship between organization and cooperation.

Demonstration Site Observations

Another change that took place in the second year of the project was the development of a demonstration site. During the first year our grant made it possible to hire Louise only half time as a consultant to teachers from the network. She was employed by The College School to teach in its preschool program the other half of the time. More funding in the second year allowed the project to employ her full time. Through the first year many teachers expressed a need to see Reggio methods modeled. We might have anticipated this, because much of the change process literature (Fullan, 1990) suggests that teachers need a clear model of implementation when an innovation is being studied. Because Louise had spent a year in Reggio observing master teachers and practicing some of their methods, many of our teachers asked her to model some of these techniques in their classrooms (i.e., facilitating conversations with children). She was able to do this to some extent, but on reflection we agreed that this was not consistent with our understanding that good teaching flows from ongoing observation of children and study of their experience. It runs counter to the premise that teachers are in the best position to support children's learning when their interactions are grounded in a long-term relationship. We decided that the best way to offer an observational learning opportunity that was consistent with these principles would be to invest more of our resources into one school that could become a demonstration site. Because Louise had already established a strong relationship with The College School teaching team, it seemed the logical choice. Here she could practice and demonstrate teaching and collaboration with children, teachers, and parents in a real context of ongoing relationships and study. At The College School we were able to build a team with two sets of coteachers who work with preschool-age children, with Louise functioning as *atelierista* and Brenda as a part-time *pedagogista.* Jan would provide the administrative support and understanding so needed during the change process, especially in this case where it was necessary to accelerate the process in order to help others.

Although the team was still clearly an early work in progress and felt uneasy about exposing limitations and, perhaps, misinterpretations of the approach, we agreed to schedule visits from teachers in our project in the second year. The conditions were that visitors would observe for an hour and then participate with Louise and one other member of the teaching team in a discussion and analysis of what was observed and how it did or did not relate to our understanding of principles and practices from Reggio Emilia. This kind of critical analysis was as beneficial for The College School team as it was for the visitors. As Fullan (1995) once said, when we are in the process of change, it may be wise to modify the old adage, "Ready, aim, fire," to "Ready, fire, aim." Sometimes we need to move more quickly into acting on our newfound knowledge and then aim our focus on an analysis of the process and results of those actions to determine how far on or off target we were and why. After all, doesn't the constructivist approach value error in the learning process?

Consultation from Outside Experts

Through the 3 years of the grant, we were fortunate to have the resources to bring Amelia Gambetti, Lella Gandini, George Forman, and Lilian Katz to consult with us. They offered group workshops and presentations as well as a few on-site consultations to some of the schools. These were a great stimulus for us to work even harder in our efforts to implement ideas from Reggio and make this work visible to outsiders. It was like preparing for company. We had invited our esteemed friends and looked forward to our time with them, but we also felt pressure to clean house and organize ourselves so that we might present our best work. These efforts to prepare for visits became a significant part of our learning process. It gave us the added stimulus to move further and press harder for change.

Over the next 2 years we were able to bring Amelia Gambetti to St. Louis to offer workshops for our network and intensive on-site observation and consultation at our demonstration site. Her on-site coaching led to deeper understanding of the fundamentals of the approach, especially the kinds of organization that support continuity and depth of learning for children, teachers, and parents.

Team Planning and Study

This approach to professional development took shape in many different ways across sites. Teachers and an administrator at one site organized weekly discussions about chapters of *The Hundred Languages of Children*. Another group from a large center held biweekly meetings for teachers and the administrator to collaborate on schoolwide projects and family involvement.

At the demonstration site, the four preschool teachers, the *atelierista* and the *pedagogista* met weekly to organize and coordinate the experiences of children, teachers, and parents. We have come to realize that we need to direct the main focus of these meetings to studying records of children's experiences (i.e., transcripts of recorded conversations; children's work—drawings, paintings, sculptures; videotapes; teachers' notes; etc.) and then discussing the organization of ongoing experiences that could be supported in the coming week(s). This provides a common platform for discourse (Forman & Fyfe, Chapter 13, this volume) that helps us stay focused and productive. Without this, it is much too easy for us to jump from one topic to the next depending on what is on the mind of each individual in the group. Another important organizing tool is a preplanned, written agenda. We try to keep minutes of each meeting and distribute them as quickly as possible so that we might preserve our collective memory of the reflections, insights, observations, and agreements about the organization of our work.

Several teams have been able to negotiate additional planning time and others have added it to the work schedule. Still others have been able to utilize parent volunteers to free them for planning periods. The issue of finding time and making efficient use of time for team planning and study is complex and continues to be a challenge (Fyfe, 1994). Teachers find the time issue most challenging when it comes to studying and organizing documentation. Amelia Gambetti suggested that we need to value "time for children" as well as "time with children." This may free us to think about ways to utilize volunteers or teacher aides to free up a teacher for a period of time during the day in order to work on the display and organization of documentation. She also suggested that we consider involving children to work with us on documentation.

THE PROCESS OF CHANGE THROUGH THE EYES OF AN *ATELIERISTA*

There are many examples of change that could be told. In this section of the chapter, we would like to take the opportunity to tell one story that grew out of our experiences with children, our experimentation with materials and the presentation of materials, and the connections that can develop between materials and children's experiences and memories.

We would like to give an example of a story about a small group of children on a wintertime walk to our "outdoor classroom"—the hillside and glade across the lane and down the hill from The College School. The first explorations of the glade began in the autumn with the changing leaves and falling acorns. The team of five teachers had recorded many conversations of the children that focused on the children's ideas about the cycles of seasons and the changes they witnessed. Based on these conversations, the teachers had projected ways of further learning. The exploration of the glade in winter was part of a long story of children's investigations of weather, seasons, and outdoor phenomena in a place that was becoming very familiar to all of us.

Snow Explorations

It had been cold and snowy for a week or more and all of the children and teachers had played outside, enjoying the white world. One morning, we invited several children from the 3- and 4-year-old and the 4- and 5-year-old classes to explore farther afield. Louise remembered a day in Reggio Emilia when she went outside with three 5-year-old girls to discover what the trees must feel like

FIGURE 22.2. Children exploring the hill near the school in the snow.

under the snow. Vea Vecchi, the *atelierista* at Diane School, suggested that we begin by talking together inside about what we thought we might discover outside. This seems to be a way of heightening curiosity and expectation for children and adults. We began our snowy day expedition in this way.

A Conversation on a Walk on a Snowy Day
The College School. January 23, 1995

Louise Cadwell, teacher, Kelly O'Neal, Alexandra Heimann, Olivia Sobelman, Robert Stupp, Jodie Schutt

(This part of the conversation occurred before going outside)

Louise: What do you think we'll find when we go outside?
Kelly: Treasures; probably diamonds!
Robert: It will be cold. Maybe we'll find a bear cave.
Jodie: There's snow outside.
Olivia: There will be food.
Louise: Like berries for the birds?
Olivia: Yeah. Can we go?
Louise: Do you think there will be snow on the trees?
Kelly: I don't know. I don't think so.

(This part of the conversation occurred outside.)

Kelly: There is snow on the bushes! And, you can see smoke coming from your mouth.
Jodie: Look at the tree. There are red berries and corn. Are they for the birds? Can we eat them?
Olivia: (Jumping) Look at what I can make in the snow!
Louise: Are you making footprints?
Robert: Me, too. Look at my prints.
Louise: Hey, what's this? (Pointing to cracks in the snow.)
Kelly: They are snowy lines walking down the hill!
Louise: What do you hear when we walk?
Jodie: Scrunch, scrunch, scrunch.
Kelly: It crunches.
Robert: Hey, look at this; a miracle! It's ice. (All the children bend down to see closely.)
Olivia: The snow on top is like sugar.

(Down in the glade, the children find sticks and begin to draw in the snow.)

Louise: Look, you're drawing lines in the snow.

(Alexandra draws a circle with lines crossing in it.)

Kelly: Look, I found more tracks.
Louise: What do you think they are?
Olivia: I think they are a bird's.
Louise: Alexandra, it looks a little like the drawing you were making with the stick.

(Several children begin to make tracks of lines in the snow. They all have drawing sticks now.)

Robert: Look, I found treasure! Here's another one!" (A cement block among frosted, snowy ivy.)
Jodie: And, look, more tracks!
Louise: What are those?
Robert: Maybe a kitty. Kitty tracks.
Louise: My toes and fingers are getting frozen. Shall we go in? Look, the sun is coming out!
Kelly: It's so sparkly. It is like diamonds.

What wonderful things and ideas to bring back from our snowy day travels—treasures, diamonds, a bear cave, snow like sugar, breath like smoke, prints in the snow, and the fun of drawing with sticks. For the children, it was a great adventure into the wild world. Bringing back little pieces of ice and the drawing sticks along with their memories was an important part of the journey. It reminds us of what Scott Russell Sanders remembers of his childhood in his essay, "News of the Wild." He tells us that whenever he returned home from a journey, even as short as a walk around the backyard, his father would ask, "What did you find?"

> And I would show him a fossil or a feather, tell him how the sun lit up the leaves of the hickory, how a skunk looked me over; I would recall for him the tastes of elderberries or the rush of wind in the white pines or the crunch of locust shells underfoot. Only in that sharing of what I had found was the journey completed, the circle closed. (Sanders, 1995, pp. 118–119)

This group remembered the day and shared it with classmates and the other teachers through looking at projected slides of themselves in the snow that Louise had taken. Using slides is another way to maintain a "strong umbilical cord" as Vea Vecchi said, between their experience outdoors and their memories and images of it. They moved into the slides, with the snow images projecting on them and danced their memories.

Later in the week, we invited children to choose materials with us that would be evocative of the snowy walk. Together we chose whites, blues, and grays from the tempera paint cart. We chose a sturdy, semitransparent roll of vellum as a background paper. We selected small pieces of lacy white doilies, and other feathery white papers from the collage drawer along with some small pieces of clear acetate and Lucite. Finally, we assembled the collection of drawing sticks they had brought in with them. All these materials could be used to represent the cold, blue day, the soft snow, the clear ice, and the fun of drawing in the snow with sticks. Five or six different children, including some who did not go on our particular walk, worked on the mural over a period of several days. They painted side by side, mostly enjoying the liquid winter colors, the feel of the "snow and ice" collage materials, and the effect of drawing in the paint with sticks as they had drawn in the snow. In the end, what the children had made was an impression of their experience in our winter surroundings that we had explored together.

What about this story is different from a story we might have told before we had studied the Reggio approach? The winter walk was part of an ongoing project on the glade—the exploration of a familiar, outdoor place, and the investigation of change and transformation throughout the year. Although spontaneous, the walk was preceded by talk and predictions about what might be discovered. The context afforded by the long story and the excitement generated by imagining what might be heighten the children's commitment to, focus on, and curiosity about the walk. Before our studies of the Reggio approach, we might not have thought these elements to be so important for young children.

A small group went on this expedition, allowing a setting in which children could explore together without the distractions of a huge group. Because the group was small, the teacher was able to focus on the children's actions and interests. The teachers involved were prepared to take notes on what children said, and to observe their wonder and curiosities outdoors. Before, a whole class of children might have played in the snow or gone out with their teacher to observe some phenomena the teacher wanted to teach them about. In this case, the teacher set the stage for discovery by facilitating discussion and prediction, and then followed, encouraged, and recorded the children's discoveries through taking notes and shooting slides.

The experience of the snowy day walk was shared with the larger group and revisited by the original group through viewing and moving in projected slides of the walk. As we experiment with the practice of the Reggio approach, it has become clear to us that we must provide ways for children to revisit, remember, and represent what they do, think, and feel if learning is to be lasting and life in school is to have real meaning.

Many materials evocative of snow and ice and the children's particular discoveries in making prints and drawing with sticks were available to choose from in the *atelier*. Teachers and children went looking for them together. A mural was made by a group of children as a shared memory of shared delights. Previously, children might have worked on individual representations with limited materials or one material. Before, an art activity with a more prescribed outcome might have been suggested.

Finally, through children's words and work and the photographs and thoughtful reflection on the part of the teachers on the value of this experience, it becomes visible as part of the story of the children and the glade and the history of life at school that is communicated to parents, visitors, and the children themselves. Before, our walk and the children's discoveries might have lingered only as a fading memory for children and teachers.

REFLECTIONS ON THE CHANGE PROCESS: JOURNAL OF AN ADMINISTRATOR

Long-term change in the direction of the Reggio approach must be systemic. It requires the support and collaboration of all the stakeholders in the system. Jan's journal reflections describe some of the challenges that she observed and experienced in regard to the team efforts of her teachers and her own participation in supporting the innovation they all embraced.

"Ten Best Schools in the World!" the article read. It supported Reggio Emilia, Italy as the best early childhood program; and they had not even visited my school! Although I was intrigued by the article, I continued to think that The College School was one of the best programs around.

The exhibit from Reggio was making the rounds and had spent a few months in St. Louis. True, to say it was impressive was an understatement. In fact, it was so good that one had to question if 3- to 6-year-old children were actually responsible for the results. The detail and observations were incredible.

We were so impressed that a group of three teachers, one parent, and I as administrator signed up for a trip to Italy and a week of intensive workshops under the tutelage of founder Loris Malaguzzi. Louise Cadwell, who was studying as an intern in the Reggio schools, served as one of our interpreters. She told us of her interest in working in American schools to adapt the approach. On our return, we were able to obtain funding that allowed Louise to come to St. Louis and begin work with us.

I am the director of a small, independent school—preschool through eighth grade. As an administrator, I have seen the agony and the ecstasy of Reggio.

I considered the Reggio approach a close fit with the philosophy of The College School. We have always used a thematically integrated, experiential approach. We are child centered. We focus on a topic (theme) and invite a variety of subjects to be explored. We use a whole language approach. We use photographs, illustrations, and journal entries to share or to reflect on the theme for the larger audience within the community who have not been a part of the experience. We use the community as our classroom. We believe that the reflection on an experience is as important as the experience itself. We are visually oriented and have student art and written work prominently displayed. We were a good match with Reggio. Our approaches could be combined. I was encouraged by our similarities.

Yet, when Louise Cadwell entered our preschool space, she was doubtful if the Reggio approach could be adapted there. To her it was dark, it lacked natural light, and it had no center garden. In fact, she felt it was unacceptable.

As an Outward Bound enthusiast, it would be easy to think that you could not do Outward Bound in Kansas—the lack of rock cliffs, the lack of ocean, the flat lands. Of course, you can do Outward Bound in Kansas by focusing on different challenges. So, how could the Reggio experience be adapted? It seemed unlikely that every school interested in the Reggio approach would be able to rebuild in order to implement this philosophy.

We engaged in a "what if" exercise. We spent time brainstorming ideas to give the space another look. We rebuilt the room in words—"Mirrors here…" "Clear glass entry into the space…" "Wall out here…" "Paint all the walls white…" "A country cupboard placed there…" "Risers for group meeting…" "Glass and panel structure to separate work areas…" "Wall for children's work and for documentation…" "Baskets as containers…" "Clear glass as containers…" "Use of reflective paper…" "Skylights in the roof…"

The Preschool space took shape slowly. The teachers and Louise discussed the rationale for each change. The entry room was transformed into a homelike space. A beautiful antique piano became the focus for performing arts. A couch and book area invited parents and children to enjoy reading together or to each other. Light tables illuminated colored tissue paper and an oak twig with acorns. A large bouquet of sunflowers graced a prominent table. The bathroom window ledge displayed glass jars with colored water. Interesting pictures hung on the walls. A wooden see-through storage shelf defined a play space and displayed materials. An antique chest containing dress-up clothes became the focus for dramatic play. A glassed area with a mirror-tiled ceiling became the *atelier.* The space was changing to meet the Reggio expectation that the environment should be the third teacher.

A grant funded by The Danforth Foundation allowed a number of teachers, art educators, and administrators from different kinds of settings in both the city and county of St. Louis to network and to share Louise as a consultant, who would work 2½ days as a consultant to other schools. Brenda Fyfe, the chair of the education department at Webster University, co-authored this grant with me. She became the *pedagogista* and facilitator of the teachers' action research. This grant was fundamental to the success of our project.

Because Louise worked in other schools as well, I hired another teacher to do lunch duty and to be the other part-time preschool teacher with Louise. Both half-time teachers would satellite around a full-time teacher in the classroom.

Teachers were both excited and apprehensive for the first day of school. We were eager for the preschool year to start. Six eager educators had been to Reggio and were ready to begin—two preschool teachers, the art specialist, a parent, our newly hired *atelierista,* and myself. I believe it is important to include the administrative role in any change. This was a great mix for a success story to follow. Perhaps that was why I was surprised by and unprepared for what took place.

The two half-time teachers met with me to ask for help with team planning time and documentation. They also asked for lunch duty release and a lunch time for all five to meet 1 day a week. To give support, I took over the daily hour of lunchroom supervision until a replacement could be hired. I suggested volunteer mothers help with the lunch and playground time so that the team of five could meet. I gave permission for my administrative assistant to type documentation.

Roles and job definitions were questioned. The task seemed overwhelming. The team of five was not meeting regularly and real collaboration was not occurring as had been anticipated. Documentation was hard and took so much time. And then we had visitors who came to see us in operation. Oh, me! High stress!

Change was taking place, albeit not without considerable tension, questioning, and uncertainty. Administrators from the other network schools confirmed similar experiences at their sites. Having a support base was helpful. The more we talked, the more we realized that change—even wanted and desired change—takes time. It took months for trust to emerge and for real collaboration to occur among the team. In the process there were many emotions, not unlike those felt in a grieving process, that needed to be recognized.

The process seemed to support the following course:

- Tension is present.
- There is a period of denial ("This isn't so hard. We can do it.").

- Then there is a period of demanding reality and pressure that creates stressful concern and questioning ("This is hard. I don't think I can do it. Why am I even trying to do it? Is it worth it?").
- Next is often a "bottoming out" ("I quit! I don't care. I'm not interested anymore. This is ridiculous to spend so much time!"). There is often a separation from the group at this point and a tendency to complain, blame, and resent.
- After this low point, there is usually a need for reassurance—and additional time and space—to decide that the task is possible.
- As portions of the task begin to take shape, more energy and hopefulness reenters ("What if we did this?" "Let's try that!"). Noteworthy here is that the group is pulling together to solve the task and to spend considerable time completing the task by being involved.
- The finished task or product gains a feeling of pride ("It was a lot of work, but isn't it wonderful" "Next time we might do more").
- There is renewed energy and a feeling of accomplishment. Individuals have a sense that "I can do anything after having lived through that!"
- Reflective time is important. It allows for down time, for analytical viewing, for recognition of learning that has occurred. It is also the beginning of the reentry into new tensions. And the process is repeated.

As we continue to grow and change, we continue to cycle through some of these stages, yet they are more familiar now and less threatening. We have a foundation now to build on.

OTHER CONSIDERATIONS AND INTERPRETATIONS OF CHANGE

Participants in our project made significant progress in their study and implementation of principles and practices from Reggio Emilia. A review of data collected from teacher journals, minutes of peer support group meetings, yearly evaluation questionnaires, interviews, and field notes from on-site consultation visits documented significant insights and changes in teaching practice. They include our ever growing image of the child that leads us to treat them as negotiators of the curriculum, rather than passive receivers of a fixed plan (Fyfe & Forman, 1996). They include our insights and achievements in developing environments,

> which promote interaction, encounters and relations, yet support focused activity and dialogue; … which promote a sense of belonging by making connections with home, community, culture and nature; … where we organize, display and present materials, not simply for the sake of aesthetics, but in order to provoke thinking about function, texture, color, transparency, thickness, pliability and other properties which influence thought and communication. (Fyfe, 1994).

Teachers continue to voice the critical importance of slowing down to listen to children (Fyfe, 1994). This means not only slowing down at the moment of conversation, but slowing down to study children's comments, graphic representations and play. Teachers have learned that such study enables them to project possible experiences, provocations or suggestions that will make sense to the children, yet challenge their thinking. It has become apparent to all that the ongoing experiences of the curriculum must be connected to the children's ideas, questions, and theories if there is to be continuity from the child's point of view.

A continuing challenge for many teachers is in learning how to support focused curiosity, conversation, debate and discussion with and among children (Cadwell & Fyfe, 1997). The study of transcribed audio tapes of teacher/child conversations has proven very helpful in developing new insights about such interactions. Video analyses and peer observations help teachers to focus on other factors affecting conversation (e.g. the organization of space, noise level, use of children's drawings or other graphic representations as a platform for group discussion, the organization of time and other activity within the environment).

Teaching teams are still struggling, but making great progress in working collaboratively to organize themselves and their work so that they can develop documentation that moves beyond telling a "story" of learning experiences to telling a "study" of learning experiences; documentation that not only presents information and interpretation, but also provokes questions that invite response from all who read it. All of us have learned that, when done well, documentation becomes the glue that makes ongoing experiences and investigations cohesive and clear to children, teachers and parents.

Teachers reflect that they are communicating more openly with parents. Documentation enables teachers to provide an organized focus for dialogue among teachers and parents, rather than just a one-way communication from teacher to parent. By taking the risk to share their thinking, their observations and their questions about teaching and learning with parents, teachers have experienced new levels of collaboration and shared ownership of the curriculum (Cadwell, Strange, & Develin, 1995).

WHAT'S NEXT?

In June of 1995 our grant expired. We had learned a great deal, but we wanted to go further, with even more intensive consultation from Reggio Emilia. Through the determined efforts and creative thinking of several participants, a plan was developed to enable us to bring Amelia Gambetti back to St. Louis for a month in the fall of 1995. She and REGGIO CHILDREN S.r.l. had agreed that she would work closely with teachers in three of the network schools during this period of time in preparation for a conference at which they would share their learning with others from the United States. These three schools are The

College School of Webster Groves; The St. Michael School in Clayton; and The Family Center, the school district of Clayton's early childhood and parent support programThe proceeds from the conference would finance our ongoing network of professional development and exchange with Reggio Emilia.

The work with Ameilia has been intensive, exhausting, and rewarding for all. As a result of the month of consultation in the fall of 1995, our first conference was a great success. Since that time the three schools, now known as "The St. Louis–Reggio Collaborative," have organized periodic "delegation days." Educators from all 50 states and several other countries have come to St. Louis to study our work. Delegations observe in the schools, dialogue with teachers, administrators and parents, and hear formal presentations of projects and other research. Amelia Gambetti has consulted several times over the past few years, each time offering new provocations that challenge our thinking and our practice.

Our plan is to continue to help ourselves and others by regularly offering delegation days when visitors can observe and critically examine our work in progress, hear the stories of our change, and participate with us in an ongoing dialogue about ways to adapt the Reggio approach. We benefit from the critique as well as the process of organizing and presenting our learning. We have learned that adults, as well as children, construct new and deeper levels of understanding when we attempt to communicate what we know to others. We have learned that it is essential to work collaboratively in the development of these presentations in order to gain the benefits of the multiple perspectives of our colleagues. This style of work demands that we develop an openness to giving and receiving direct and honest observation and critique.

The logical extension of this disposition to openness is to look at our outreach efforts as opportunities to learn. Each presentation of a project or analysis of a learning experience is a documentation of our own professional development. Since we have come to understand that documentation is a vehicle for ongoing learning and reflection and should be utilized to provoke questions and further inquiry, we must welcome response, dialogue, and debate with visitors to our schools.

The teachers in our network will continue to study together by meeting regularly to discuss issues, share practices, and study documentation of learning experiences among children and adults. We have agreed to observe in each other's classes and offer peer coaching. We continue to learn from our colleagues in Reggio by sending our teachers there periodically and bringing consultants from Reggio to work with us in St. Louis. We will use action research strategies to systematically collect and analyze documentation of our own professional development. We believe this mode of operation is consistent with the emphasis in Reggio Emilia on exchange and continuous research of learning among all the subjects of education—children, teachers, and parents.

REFERENCES

Cadwell, L., & Fyfe, B. (1997). Conversations with children. In J. Hendricks (Ed.), *First steps toward teaching the Reggio way.* (pp. 84–99). Columbus, Ohio: Merrill.

Cadwell, L., Strange, J., & Devlin, J. (1995, November). *A new understanding and practice of collaboration among teachers, parents, and children–What we are learning from Reggio Emilia.* Paper presented at the annual conference of the National Association for the Education of Young Children, Washington, DC.

Costa, A., Garmston, R., & Lambert, L. (1988). Evaluation of teaching: The cognitive development view. In S. Stanley & W.J. Popham (Eds.), *Teacher evaluation: Six prescriptions for success.* Alexandria, VA: Association for Supervision and Curriculum Development.

Eisner, E.W. (1992). Educational reform and the ecology of schooling. *Teachers College Record, 90*(4), 611–627.

Entzminger, E. (1995). Teachers perceptions of a pedagogic innovation: Barriers and mechanisms for a successful implementation. *Dissertation Abstracts International.* (UMI 9543317)

Forman, G., & Fyfe, B. (1998). Design, documentation and discourse: A theory of negotiated learning. In C. Edwards, L. Gandini, & G. Forman (Eds.), *The hundred languages of children: The Reggio Emilia approach to early childhood education (2nd edition).* Greenwich, CT: Ablex Publishing.

Fullan, M.G. (1995). Keynote address to the American Association of Colleges of Teacher Education, Washington, DC.

Fullan, M.G. (1990). Staff development, innovation, and institutional development. In B. Joyce (Ed.), *Changing school culture through staff development.* Alexandria, VA: Association for Supervision and Curriculum Development.

Fullan, M.G., & Miles, M.B. (1992). Getting reform right: What works and what doesn't. *Phi Delta Kappan, 73*(10) 745–752.

Fullan, M.G., & Steiegelbauer, S. (1991). *The new meaning of educational change* (2nd ed.). New York: Teachers College Press.

Fyfe, B. (1994). Images from the United States: Using ideas from the Reggio Emilia experience with American educators. In L. Katz & B. Cesarone (Eds.), *Reflections on the Reggio Emilia approach.* Urbana, IL: ERIC/EECE.

Fyfe, B., & Forman, G. (1996). Negotiating the curriculum through discourse, design and documentation. Innovations in early education: *The international Reggio exchange, 3*(4) 4–7.

Gandini, L. (1993, November). Fundamentals of the Reggio Emilia approach to early childhood education. *Young Children 47,* 4–8.

Hord, S., Rutherford, W., Hulling-Austin, L., & Hall, G. (1987). *Taking charge of change.* Alexandria, VA: Association for Supervision and Curriculum Development.

Sanders, R.S. (1995). *Writing from the center.* Bloomington: Indiana University Press.

Vartuli, S., & Fyfe, B. (1993, May). Teachers need developmentally appropriate practices too. *Young Children 48*(4) 36–42.

Drawing by children of
Pablo Neruda School

chapter 23

Reconsidering Early Childhood Education in the United States: Reflections From Our Encounters With Reggio Emilia

Carol Brunson Phillips
Sue Bredekamp

As administrators of nationwide systems designed to improve the quality of early childhood education in the United States, we have devoted our professional lives to exploring questions about children's development and learning. We have visited many settings for young children in connection with two credentialing programs (Child Development Associate, (CDA); and National Association for the Education of Young Children, NAEYC, center accreditation). Every opportunity, whether in the United States or elsewhere, provides us the chance to observe the ways in which institutions (and the adults in them) respond to ideas about children's development and in turn, consider new ways to create the best possible programs. Our many visits to the preprimary programs in Reggio Emilia, Italy, in addition to providing a much-needed experience of professional renewal, have profoundly influenced our thinking about practices in the United States. Primarily because of the extraordinarily rich outcomes we have observed there for children, these encounters have renewed our energies to struggle to make sense of what we are learning in relation to what we already know.

Although many insights have occurred, the most intriguing are those that result from our attempts to deal with the polar opposite reactions to the Reggio Emilia experience that we have observed among Americans. At one extreme, people feel the approach is simply an extraordinary example of good early childhood practice. At the other, people feel the approach is too teacher directed and not developmentally appropriate. Both reactions at various times have plagued our thinking. Yet, we have found that in place of aligning ourselves with one view over the other, the tension that these opposites generate has been powerful and important in forcing us to think deeply about our own societal and cultural contexts as an influence on the American reactions to Reggio. Consequently we have tried to put Reggio Emilia in front of what we, as American early educators, do and think (almost like holding up a mirror) to help us better discern our own most cherished principles and beliefs, and thus sharpen our ability to reconsider and to expand our thinking about them.

In this chapter, we discuss some of the ideas realized from this process in three early childhood issue domains: program practices, professional development, and policy; domains that, although inextricably related in the real-life context, are discussed here separately. Further, because the cross-cultural perspective seemingly illuminated our own insights, we also point out some cultural tendencies in the United States that should we attempt to adapt dimensions of the Reggio approach to improve early childhood education in the United States, would appear to mitigate against change. Thus, as covert cultural obstacles, we further suggest possible strategies for overcoming them.

EARLY CHILDHOOD PROGRAM PRACTICES: RECONSIDERATION IN LIGHT OF REGGIO EMILIA

On first encounter with the Reggio schools, many American early childhood educators sense they are observing a confirmation of our work here, feeling "Yes, we were right!" Much about the Reggio Emilia approach is congruent with traditions of progressive education in this country and with the principles of developmentally appropriate practice (Barden, 1993; Bredekamp, 1996; Edwards & Forman, 1993). This congruence is not accidental, but derives from shared philosophical underpinnings. Reggio educators readily acknowledge the influence of Dewey, Piaget, Erikson, Bronfenbrenner, Kagan, and Vygotsky, among others on their ideas (Malaguzzi, 1993b). Thus, when American educators recognize similarities between the Diana School and the Bank Street School for Children or Pacific Oaks Children's School, they should not be surprised. For the most celebrated themes and principles fundamental to early childhood practice in the United States resonate well with those manifested in the Reggio Emilia approach:

1. The study of child development as the core of practice.

2. The critical importance of teacher–child relationships.
3. Children's experiences as the basis on which curriculum is built.
4. The importance of a rich, engaging environment for promoting learning.
5. The importance of ongoing teacher development as a dynamic in creating meaningful learning experiences for children.
6. The integral role of relationships with parents in the life of the school.

These commonalities in our approaches create the foundation for our sense of *simpatico* with the Reggio educators. Yet, because disparities in specific early childhood practices have evolved, these bid us to the most intriguing places from which to begin an exchange of ideas—partly because the areas where we differ are the very ones where our own debates continue, but in part because they are also areas where the ideas and beliefs are articulated with great clarity by Reggio educators.

One such place in the domain of program practices is the school's relation to parents. Although the importance of strong relationships with parents is a foundation of early education both in Reggio Emilia and in the United States, the closeness in Reggio between parents and teachers is palpable. One sees abundant evidence of parents' presence in the schools. But further, when teachers describe parents as their partners in the education of children, what prevails is *reciprocity* in those relationships. Teachers, children, and parents are considered key protagonists in the school experience where the school itself evolves as a consequence of their interactions. Therefore, as Loris Malaguzzi often said, a teacher cannot have a relationship with a child if there is no relationship with the parents. (By corollary, if there is no relationship with parents, there is no school.)

With this concept as a backdrop for reflection, looking at the school's relation to parents in the United States a different thrust becomes evident. Although early education gives far more recognition than other levels to the importance of establishing partnerships with parents and developing relationships with families, still, widespread use of innovative methods to accomplish these partnerships continues to lag behind (Powell, 1989; 1994). The currently popular uses of parent involvement and parent education concepts seem based on the implicit assumption of the school as a static entity (a building that contains programs) into which parents come or through which they pass. Parents are the *recipients* of actions through which they become changed. In contrast, reciprocity assumes both parties to be powerful and active. Therefore, the potential for the school to change in the interaction with parents is as great as the potential for the parents to change.

To some extent, American cultural values of hierarchical authority feed separation of domains between parents and schools and increase the psychological distance between them. Further, self-reliance and independence mediate against our ability to develop close relationships with other people's children, although American parents still seem to desire a loving, caring relationship in their child care arrangements (Reisman, 1996). Some of this distance is the product of a litigious society that makes teachers afraid to touch even very young children.

Another is attributable to the growing voice for parents' rights that mitigates against teachers doing anything with or for children that is not a carefully prescribed aspect of the academic curriculum. In some ways, the American resistance to multiage or family grouping in schools is a clear rejection of the concept of developing deep relationships between parents and teachers, and thus, between children and teachers. Regardless of its origin, this tendency toward social distance between adults in the United States would make it difficult to grow the intimate relationships that we could foster by keeping children with the same teachers in the same groups for longer periods of time.

American early childhood practice still has much work to do to align itself with parents as reciprocal partners and vice versa. Some of the tension between parents and child care providers continues to be inequality of status (either the child care teacher is viewed as the professional and the parent the amateur, or the parent as the employer and the teacher, the lowly servant). To gain greater reciprocity between teachers and parents would be of enormous benefit in our vision to empower the full potential of children as an outgrowth of parents as participants in and advocates for their children's optimum development and education (Phillips, 1995).

EARLY CHILDHOOD PROFESSIONAL DEVELOPMENT: RECONSIDERATIONS IN LIGHT OF REGGIO EMILIA

In the same way that encounters with Reggio Emilia help us see salient aspects of our early childhood practices in a mirror, they have also helped us reconsider several dimensions of professional development.

One of our biggest surprises when first visiting Reggio Emilia was to discover that teachers bring minimal preservice professional preparation to their jobs there. The high level of practice we observed in addition to the highly articulate descriptions of their work offered by even very young teachers led us to presume high preservice requirements for teachers. Instead, the beginning qualification is the equivalent of one year of vocational school, not unlike the average qualification of a child care teacher in America (Whitebook, Howes, & Phillips, 1993; Whitebook, Phillips, & Howes, 1989). Obviously, the ongoing professional development of teachers in Reggio is highly effective and essential to successful implementation of the Reggio Emilia approach. It is equally important to understand if attempts to adapt the classroom practices in the United States are to be successful.

Fundamentally, teachers in Reggio Emilia are not "trained" any more than children are trained. Instead, teachers are engaged in a learning environment that supports various types of relationships—relationships with children, parents, teachers, and other staff—that in turn, support the teachers' co-construction of knowledge about children, the learning process, and the roles of the teacher. Even though it is not possible to separate the professional development of teach-

Il computer è come uno straniero
e se vuoi parlare con lui
devi parlare la sua lingua.
The computer's like a foreigner, and if you want to talk
to it you have to speak its language.
Sì ma anche il computer
deve capire come parliamo noi
e deve fare quello che vogliamo noi.
Yes, but the computer has to understand how we talk,
too, and it has to do what we want it to do.

FIGURE 23.1. Drawing by children of Diana School.

ers from the other domains of the Reggio approach, six factors are discussed here that contribute to the effectiveness of teacher training in Reggio and challenge us to reconsider how professional development is conducted in the U.S.

Shared Sense of Mission/Philosophy

The schools of Reggio Emilia are part of a system that is based on a shared set of beliefs about children, families, and learning, and reflects a well-conceptualized organization. Everyone connected with the schools, including the parents and the mayor of the city, seems to know what the schools are about and is an effective spokesperson for them. New teachers coming into the system (just as visitors to it) are presented a clear and consistent, although complex, picture of what is expected. A prospective teacher whose beliefs about children and learning were inconsistent with or fundamentally at odds with the approach would not choose to work there or would quickly be discovered. In short, a stable and explicit fundamental structure surrounds teachers and provides the security of a vibrant core mission for their daily work. Teachers are freed to add to and enhance the structure, but they do not have to invent its fundamentals.

Of course, the framework in Reggio Emilia was not always there and it did not always function at the level it does today. The conceptual integrity has been built in part through the visionary leadership provided by Loris Malaguzzi. He was the philosopher, the leader, the provocateur, the repository of history, the pusher, the prodder, and the questioner. His role cannot be explained precisely, but must be acknowledged as a dynamic in the system.

But while the contribution of Loris Malaguzzi to this interesting history is important, it is not solely responsible for sustaining the conceptual integrity of the Reggio Emilia approach and its current level of functioning in the schools. The ongoing dynamics that contribute to the way the mission permeates the environments are the result of many factors, not the least of which is leadership. Holding together the whole in a highly visible way, while simultaneously working on the separate parts, is a critical responsibility that someone must take at the level where teachers are working on their own professional growth.

Too many teachers in the United States work in programs that do not have a well conceptualized philosophy and organization; they are expected to make do without one or to make it up as they go along. This absence sometimes stems from poor interpretations of principles of good practice, such as when "developmentally appropriate practice" is taken to mean that teachers let children play aimlessly, or leave them to "develop" totally on their own (Kostelnik, 1992). At other times, it may stem from thinking lodged in the day care versus education dichotomy, where "care" is thought to be limited to children's protection and safety. In cases like these, little importance is placed on the need for a collective consciousness about the intricate nature of the relationships that exist in group care settings and the impact of them on the developing child. Culturally, we are still struggling with the value of group programs for children this age—birth to 5, and where this struggle is reflected in ambivalence toward committing to a shared mission, teachers have no trajectory for their development as early childhood professionals.

Two Co-equal Teachers in Each Classroom

The presence of two co-equal teachers in each classroom who work as colleagues over time should not be underestimated as a dynamic in professional development of teachers. Presumably in Reggio Emilia, new teachers are matched with more experienced veterans who serve as models. At the same time, however, experienced teachers also learn from the fresh perspectives of the new teacher. The concept of reciprocity that underlies relations with parents is equally striking in the way teachers are encouraged to relate to other teachers, to ensure that both parties grow and change as a result. Suggesting a wider cultural principle at work, reciprocity is what makes it safe to argue in Reggio Emilia—the consequence of conflict is not viewed as winning versus losing but as change for all involved (LeeKeenan & Nimmo, 1993).

The equal status of the teachers reinforces the value placed on reciprocal relationships and supports the ability to question and solve problems in new ways, thus becoming an essential professional development tool in the Reggio approach. Two teachers also ensures more than one perspective on every situation. Having opportunities for collaboration, problem solving, and perspective taking contributes to teachers' growth and confidence as co-constructors of curriculum with children and other teachers. Two coequal teachers also have different strengths and weaknesses, can play different roles at different times, and provide different relationships for children—almost like two parents in a family.

In the United States, the economics of two equal teachers in a child care classroom or family day care home seems an impossible barrier, and yet the potential benefits of reciprocity in the teaching team should challenge our thinking and cause us to reconsider both structure and process. This is a particularly important insight given the trend toward differentiated staffing (NAEYC, 1994), where ideal patterns are constructed with two to three staff per group of children, each with a different level of preparation and expertise. Although this constellation makes sense given the current context of training access and wages and working conditions, we might think more carefully about ways to stem what could easily become a hierarchical top-down expertise flow, resulting in a failure to nurture the kind of reciprocal exchanges that could yield a much more vibrant professional development environment.

The Role of the *Pedagogista*

The most significant teacher training strategy in Reggio Emilia resides in the dynamics that stem from the presence of the *pedagogista*. Although he or she operates much like what we might think of as a resident teacher educator, the role he or she plays is in very significant ways unlike the trainers' role as we see it in the United States. In Reggio Emilia (Filippini, Chapter 6, this volume), the *pedagogista* visits each center 1 day a week and works to create a relationship, not just with the teachers but with the children and families, and engages in problem solving with teachers in the context of actual situations. Thus although the *pedagogista* is responsible for framing practice issues in the larger conceptual context, he or she can offer suggestions or solutions that are not purely theoretical, but real to the school, the children, and the families. Moreover, the *pedagogista* brings not only a high level of expertise in theory and practice; he or she is the match that keeps the fire of the Reggio approach lit, constantly prodding teachers to explore different perspectives, to rethink situations, to revisit experiences, to be reflective—to stretch beyond wherever it is that they are at the moment.

In the United States, the use of on-site professional development personnel is common (although uneven), perhaps best systematized by Head Start, military child care, and large national child care chains, where education specialists and/or mentor teachers are employed. However, to ensure the professional development dynamics generated by the *pedagogista,* the emphases in these roles must be carefully examined, and in some cases realigned. These trainers often are not in contact either with children or their parents. Further, where external trainers are brought in to provide in-service, the challenge to establish the requisite underlying continuity looms large. In both cases, the challenge is to refocus the tendencies to supply expertise from without and to ignore the importance of supporting the capacities for reciprocity in the ongoing staff relationships. Further, the challenge remains to consider how to shift the emphasis to growing teachers' abilities to generate questions and test their own hypotheses.

Time for Staff Development

A major contributor to professional development of teachers in Reggio Emilia is time itself—the amount of time devoted to it. By working with a consistent group of children for 3 years, teachers in Reggio Emilia learn their craft from children through their firsthand exposure to the developing child over an extended age span. This provides the context for learning about child development in greater depth and breadth than any training course could imitate. Also, staying with a group of children over time makes the development of relationships possible, thereby supporting learning based on relationships (Malaguzzi, 1993a). Further, the time that is set aside each week for teachers to work together, prepare documentation, meet with parents, and so on, is an essential support structure for professional development.

These factors challenge our thinking about dimensions of time in relation to teacher development. American early childhood educators rarely think about teacher growth as a function of continuity with the developing child. Instead, in this country we devote more energy to developing teachers with age-specific special skills—a teacher who is skilled working with babies, versus the teacher who is better with the 3-year-olds. In addition, when we think about wide age range groupings, our discussions are almost always about the benefits for the child(ren) rather than for the developmental breadth of the teachers.

Much could be achieved if we think about these dimensions of time in new ways and work harder to slow ourselves down. This will likely be an uphill battle because the task is more than merely carving out more time for professional development. We must acknowledge that we are surrounded by a cultural context characterized by a basic assumption of linear time (Stewart & Bennett, 1991), where time is treated as the ultimate scarce commodity, and where efficiency must prevail above all else. The measurement of this to some extent is how quickly we can get things done, and as such, there will be continuous pressure to make things fit into delimiting time slots. For instance, the potency of the trend to quantify professional development and training as an accumulation of "clock hours," or a series of chunks of content dispatched in "modules" is extraordinary. Yet when this works against our ability to grow better and better professional development strategies, we must be slower to yield.

Documentation

The process of documenting children's learning through their project work is an invaluable tool for professional development. To document, teachers must relentlessly watch children, listen, observe, and learn from different perspectives and with various tools—the notebook, the camera, the audiotape, and the videotape. As a collaborative interaction with other teachers, the documentation process gives meaning and concrete reference to the teachers' learning process. Teachers have a record of their own ideas in historical context, and a means to revisit their own growth and change.

Documentation as done in Reggio Emilia does not have a true analogue in the United States. It is not anecdotal recording; it is not portfolio assessment. Documentation is an iteration beyond anything that has yet been done widely in the United States. And for us to marshall the power it can yield for capturing experiences in ways that amplify the processes of cognition and recognition for adult development, will require developing a new concept for most American early childhood educators.

A Philosophy of Provocation and Learning

Among the roles of the teacher in Reggio Emilia are researcher and learner. Therefore, professional development is actually part of the job description, an ongoing and continuous process, rather than a qualification for employment. Perhaps the most important prerequisite for employment as a teacher there is the disposition to go on learning. This strategy results in Reggio teachers with 25 years of experience continuing to struggle and grow as professionals. No matter how much longevity they accrue, they never believe they have all the answers.

Again, in reconsidering professional development in the United States, it is necessary to redefine the teachers' role. Some of this is already happening in teacher education with the emphasis on reflective teaching, but because American teachers tend to work in isolation, they must reflect alone. They may reflect inaccurately or they may not have a valid basis to evaluate their practice. Reflection is important, but it is not the professional development tool that co-construction is. The American system could benefit from teachers socially constructing knowledge and building relationships with other teachers.

Even this brief discussion of professional development considerations reveals that much of the high-quality practice we observe in the Reggio schools depends, in fact is built on an *infrastructure,* and these supportive policies make it possible for such practice to be sustained over time. We now turn to these elements.

FIGURE 23.2. Children encountering the computer. From the exhibit The Hundred Languages of Children.

EARLY CHILDHOOD POLICY: RECONSIDERATIONS IN LIGHT OF REGGIO EMILIA

Comparing family and child care policies between the United States and Italy is discouraging because so much that exists there is still missing here. For example, parental leave policies that guarantee salary demonstrate that in Italy, parents are clearly regarded as the most important caregivers of their children. Similarly, heavily publicly subsidized child care for working families (in elegantly equipped facilities) illustrates the value that Reggio Emilia places on children and early education. That these values and commitments are realized through nationally and municipally legislated policies that strike at the core economics of child care is important. But what is equally instructive is what they yield in terms of stable dimensions of the infrastructure that underlie the delivery of high-quality early childhood education in the Reggio schools: adequate compensation for staff, time for professional development, staffing that supports the delivery of high-quality services, and questioning quality rather than relying on regulation.

Adequate Compensation for Staff

The schools of Reggio are supported by federal and city funds that make it possible to pay salaries comparable to public school teachers (although more hours are worked by preschool teachers). Such salaries enable the schools to attract and keep teachers of high caliber.

When American early childhood educators learn about the policy infrastructure that sustains Reggio schools, some want to use it as an excuse for why such a practice could never be implemented here. However, what they fail to acknowledge is that the policy context in Italy was not always as it is today; the citizens of Reggio Emilia did not acquire (nor do they keep) their lovely schools by magic. Instead, they fought (and must continue to fight) to achieve these public policies. People organized and acted strategically to get their voices heard in the public arena, where among the most vocal and effective advocates were parents. The schools in Reggio did not begin as public schools; they began more like parent cooperatives. Their growth and development were possible because parents (private citizens) rather than just professionals alone demanded the service for children. In the United States, we continue to struggle to try and soften policies that are basically unfriendly to families or in battles that pit child care providers against families. The successful advocacy for Reggio schools is probably at least in part due to the reciprocal relationships that develop there between teachers and parents, and thus illustrates a lesson we have yet to demonstrate we fully understand: We cannot separate policy from advocacy from practice.

Time for Professional Development

Well-funded programs also support the delivery of the apprentice-type training of teachers already described. Such professional development, supported by 5 hours of paid planning time each week (although surely not enough), provides beginning teachers with the best possible field-based learning experience, in real schools with real children in collaboration with master teachers. The economics of paying teachers for 5 hours of planning time each week seems daunting for Americans, but rather than rejecting this strategy as too costly, it would be instructive to determine what is spent by school systems and Head Start on other forms of in-service training that do not as directly affect classroom practice and do not transform performance.

Staffing That Supports Delivery of High-Quality Services

The physical structure and organization of the Reggio schools and the way they are staffed are critical elements of the quality of practice. The size of the schools (75 children) is manageable; big is not better with little children, despite the trend in America toward larger centers in order to lower costs. The number of people in various capacities, two teachers per class, and judicious use of specialist positions (*pedagogista* and *atelierista*) create an organizational climate that supports collaboration. The way the staff is assigned to group constellations (where teachers stay with the same group of children for 3 years) creates an atmosphere that promotes in-depth and individualized developmentally appropriate practice, where waiting is possible and teachers do not feel pressure to cover the curriculum or get children ready for the next level of schooling.

Staffing to ensure continuity of relationships is one policy that could be easily adopted in the United States. It would not cost more for groups to stay with the same teacher, and in a transient society such as the United States, where children experience far more transitions than the children of Reggio Emilia, it does not make sense that institutions artificially impose many more changes by moving children every 6 months or every year. This policy change would require some adjustments in child care regulations but would require primarily changes in attitude; people always get alarmed about the possibility of a child's being stuck with a bad teacher for several years (unfortunately, more alarmed than over the existence of bad teachers in the first place.)

Questioning Quality Rather Than Relying on Regulation

In the United States, professionals have often relied on standard-setting as the primary vehicle for ensuring high quality in services for children. Our children's programs are regulated through licensing standards that most teachers in Reggio would find extraordinarily burdensome. In addition, our professional organizations have sought to influence program quality by setting a variety of national standards for practice, like the CDA competencies in the early 1970s and continuing in the 1980s with NAEYC standards for accreditation and guidelines for developmentally appropriate practice.

Standards are, of necessity, relatively conservative documents; they must reflect not only research and theory but also the consensus of those to whom they are applied (Bredekamp, 1993). Nevertheless, in the United States, standard-setting is seen as an essential function of professional organizations, especially in their educational and advocacy roles. Although standard-setting typically is designed to achieve the goal of improved quality, overreliance on standards can lead to standardization and thwart continuous quality improvement (Morgan, 1996).

By contrast, Reggio educators, starting with Malaguzzi, express hesitation over writing down the principles of their approach because they so highly value questioning, reflection, research, and adaptation. Justifiably, they fear that written descriptions will be taken as prescriptions, and such an outcome would be antithetical to their philosophy. The high level of practice that they have obtained in Reggio may be largely attributable to the fact that teachers there continually question, refine, and change their practices rather than codify and replicate them.

Therefore, American early childhood educators and organizations such as NAEYC face the challenge of continuing to set standards that can be used to influence practice and policy on behalf of children, while also encouraging and promoting expansion of the knowledge base through continual questioning and reflection. Standard-setting and questioning are each important professional functions, but they are not interchangeable functions. Standards are action-directed statements; they serve the vital function of protecting children from harm and promoting their welfare. However, questioning is also essential, for growth, change, and expansion of knowledge.

Although public policy differences between Reggio Emilia and communities in the United States dishearten us from thinking about adaptations in improving our work here in light of theirs, in some cases simple reconsideration of how we do business could have major effects in developing and sustaining our ideal of high-quality early childhood environments. At the same time, we should not underestimate the critical importance of infrastructure supports that only policy changes can create because practice sits atop these. Mere changes in classroom practice cannot be sustained without policy supports.

CONCLUSION

In order to ultimately achieve our practice and professional development goals, there is no question that an underlying political struggle to achieve and sustain public support (particularly to buttress the economics of child care) must continue. In the same vein though, also outside the immediate environment of program operation, another underlying struggle must continue—the struggle to be cognizant of the obstacles to change that reside in our cultural tendencies.

Perhaps no other cultural trait is so pervasive an influence in practice, professional development, and policy, as is the concept and use of time. Americans have "a tendency to equate efficiency with quality.… We're clock watchers; following the schedule takes precedence, and children are constantly interrupted by the adults in their lives" (Jones, 1995, p. 3). Throughout this chapter, we have suggested ways that American early childhood educators can reconsider our concepts of time toward the goals of giving more time for in-depth curriculum exploration; more time for staff development, collaboration, and reflection; and more time to build relationships among teachers, children, and families. To achieve these strategies would require major attitudinal shifts, or at the least continuous reinforcement, monitoring, and maintenance.

Reggio educators, and especially Loris Malaguzzi, resisted writing down lists of the elements that comprise their approach because such lists never convey the connectedness, the interrelationship among the parts that make up the whole. Once the relationship is clear, in fact, it becomes almost impossible to talk about any one element of the system without referring to all the others every time. Focusing on the whole as greater than the sum of its parts—what we call *conceptual integrity* (Bredekamp, 1993)—reflects an Italian way of viewing the world.

Obviously, conceptual integrity—the ability to see connections, to focus on the whole rather than its separate parts—is not solely a cultural phenomena. And yet, there is an American cultural tendency toward analytic thinking that tends to break concepts into pieces and treat the pieces as if they have meaning outside of their relation to the whole, or to dichotomize complex problems into simplistic, contrasting alternatives (Dixon, 1976; Tharp, 1994). Overcoming this tendency to dichotomize, divide, and separate will contribute vastly to maintaining a sense of mission between practitioners and a holistic vision of high-quality practice—the type requiring visionary leadership, but not wholly dependent on one person. The challenge for the early childhood profession then becomes growing leaders rather than technocrats, individuals with the ability to conceptualize integrated systems and inspire others to work toward achieving them.

By reconsidering elements of American early childhood practice, professional development, and policy in light of our experiences with Reggio Emilia, we do not mean to imply that there are not many aspects of early childhood education in the United States of which we are justifiably proud; there are. However, in spite of these, the early care and education system in our country is not good enough (Cost, Quality, and Child Outcomes in Child Care Study Group, 1995; Morgan et al., 1993). It is uneven, unsteady, and unreliable, in ways that could be made better through the opportunity that encounters with the Reggio approach may open up to us. But, because Americans are who we are culturally, and because our society is different from and far more complex than one town in northern Italy, the greatest risk we run is to copy, to imitate, and to try to adopt the form of the Reggio approach without the substance.

Our reconsiderations offered in this chapter are in the interest of sparking a substantive exchange, for we consider a continuing struggle in dialogue with our Italian colleagues to be a worthwhile and important professional endeavor. Yet, as we remain actively engaged and continue to struggle with both our questions and our answers, we hope the authors in this volume will engage as well with one of the new questions that this evolving exchange has raised for us: If this is truly a dialogue between the educators of Reggio and the United States—a cognitive conflict in which both parties are changed—how have the many encounters with American early childhood educators influenced practices in Reggio Emilia today?

REFERENCES

Barden, M. (1993). A backward look: From Reggio Emilia to progressive education. In C. Edwards, L. Gandini, & G. Forman (Eds.) *The hundred languages of children: The Reggio Emilia approach to early childhood education* (pp. 283–297). Norwood, NJ: Ablex.

Bredekamp, S. (1993). Reflections on Reggio Emilia. *Young Children, 49*(1), 13–17.

Bredekamp, S. (Ed.). (1996). *Developmentally appropriate practice in early childhood programs serving children from birth through age eight* (Rev. ed.). Washington, DC: NAEYC.

Cost, Quality, and Child Outcomes in Child Care Study Group. (1995). *Cost, Quality, and Child Outcomes in Child Care*. Denver, CO: Author.

Dixon, V. (1976). World views and research methodology. In L.M. King, V.J. Dixon, & W.W. Nobles (Eds.), *African philosophy: Assumptions and paradigms for research on Black persons*. Los Angeles: Charles Drew Postgraduate Medical School.

Edwards, C., & Forman, G. (1993). Conclusion: Where do we go from here? In C. Edwards, L. Gandini, & G. Forman (Eds.), *The hundred languages of children: The Reggio Emilia approach to early childhood education* (pp. 305–312). Norwood, NJ: Ablex.

Jones, E. (1995, June). *From Reggio Emilia to the United States: What are the risks in translation?* Paper presented at the annual conference of the National Institute for Early Childhood Professional Development, San Francisco, CA, June.

Kostelnik, M. (1992) Myths associated with developmentally appropriate programs. *Young Children, 47*(4), 17–23.

LeeKeenan, D., & Nimmo, J. (1993). Connections: using the project approach with 2- and 3-year-olds in a university lab school. In C. Edwards, L. Gandini, & G. Forman (Eds.), *The hundred languages of children: The Reggio Emilia approach to early childhood education* (pp. 251–267). Norwood, NJ: Ablex.

Malaguzzi, L. (1993a). For an education based on relationships. *Young Children, 49*(1), 9–12.

Malaguzzi, L. (1993b). History, ideas, and basic philosophy. In C. Edwards, L. Gandini, & G. Forman (Eds.), *The hundred languages of children: The Reggio Emilia approach to early childhood education* (pp. 41–90). Norwood, NJ: Ablex.

Morgan, G. (1996). Licensing and accreditation: How much quality is "quality"? In S. Bredekamp & B. Willer (Eds.), *NAEYC accreditation: A decade of learning and the years ahead* (pp. 129–138). Washington, DC: NAEYC.

Morgan, G., Azer, S., Costley, J., Genser, A., Goodman, I., Lombardi, J., & McGimsey, B. (1993). *Making a career of it: The state of the states report on career development in early care and education*. Boston, MA: The Center for Career Development in Early Care and Education at Wheelock College.

National Association for the Education of Young Children. (1994). A conceptual framework for early childhood professional development. In J. Johnson & J.B. McCracken (Eds.), *The early childhood career lattice: Perspectives on professional development*, pp. 4-23. Washington, DC: Author.

Phillips, C.B. (1995). Culture: A process that empowers. In P. Mangione (Ed.), *A guide to culturally sensitive care* (pp. 2–10). Sacramento: California Department of Education.

Powell, D. (1989). *Families and early childhood programs*. Washington, DC: NAEYC.

Powell, D. (1994). Parents, pluralism, and the NAEYC statement on developmentally appropriate practice. In B. Mallory & R. New (Eds.) *Diversity and developmentally appropriate practices: Challenges for early childhood educators* (pp. 166–182). New York: Teachers College Press.

Reisman, B. (1996). What do parents want? Can we create consumer demand for accredited child care programs? In S. Bredekamp & B. Willer (Eds.), *NAEYC accreditation: A decade of learning and the years ahead* (pp. 139–148). Washington, DC: NAEYC.

Stewart, E.C., & Bennett, M.J. (1991). *American cultural patterns in cross cultural perspective*. Yarmouth, ME: Intercultural Press.

Tharp, R. (1994). Intergroup differences among native Americans in socialization and child cognition: An ethnogenetic analysis. In P. Greenfield, & R. Cocking (Eds.), *Cross-cultural roots of minority child development* (pp. 87–105). Hillsdale, NJ: Erlbaum.

Whitebook, M., Howes, C., & Phillips, D. (1993). *The National Child Care Staffing Study revisited.* Oakland, CA: Child Care Employee Project.

Whitebook, M., Phillips, D., & Howes, C. (1989). *Who cares for the children? The National Child Care Staffing Study.* Oakland, CA: Child Care Employee Project.

part V
Conclusion

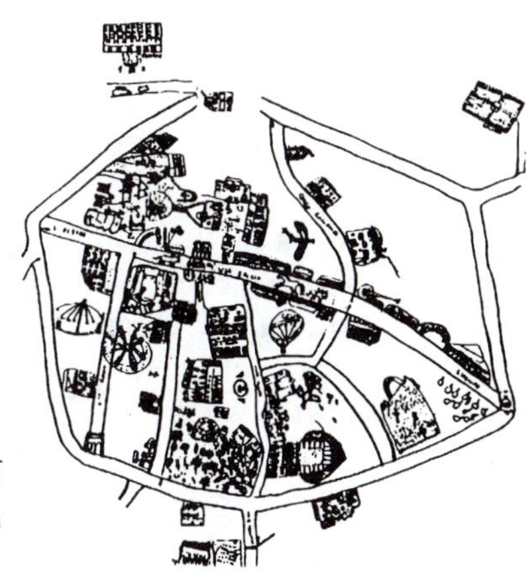

Map of the city of Reggio Emilia

chapter 24

Conclusion: Final Reflections

Carolyn Edwards
Lella Gandini
George Forman

This book has presented an introduction and overview to the Reggio Emilia approach to early childhood education. The purpose of this educational project, so say the educators in Reggio Emilia (Department of Early Education, 1984), is to produce a *reintegrated child,* capable of constructing his or her own powers of thinking through the synthesis of all the expressive, communicative, and cognitive languages. But this reintegrated child is not a solitary investigator. On the contrary: The child's senses and mind need help from others in perceiving order and change and discovering the meanings of new relations. The child is a *protagonist* and *co-constructor.*

The book, like the Reggio Emilia system itself, is the product of many collaborations. First of all, it is one result and manifestation of the ongoing and accelerating drama of dialogue and exchange between educators in Reggio Emilia and the United States. As the dialogue expands and more people enter, the questions asked become ever more complex, the conversations reverberate farther into more and different kinds of settings and situations, and the process of spread and flow of ideas takes on a life of its own. Of course (as David Hawkins reminds us in his Remarks), importing foreign models wholesale never works; each society must solve its own problems. Educational innovations can never be transplanted from one country to another without extensive translation and adaptation. However, the fact that programs cannot be transplanted intact does not mean that *cultural diffusion* (the exchange and flow of ideas and products, as it is called in anthropology) is so difficult and delicate that it rarely can be expected to occur successfully. Rather, diffusion and exchange have occurred since the dawn of human history, and take place continually, without direction or premeditation or expert control, indeed whenever human beings of different groups come into contact with one another. These processes are the very ordinary and yet also extraordinary source of endless human vitality and cultural progress. In the case of experiences and insights springing from Reggio Emilia, therefore, we can expect the ideas to flow as long as they are found to be useful to others and to help them with their own problems and issues. Certainly, cross-cultural dialogue always happens best when "cultural insiders" (those who have grown up in a place and are members of a cultural community) and "cultural outsiders" (those who have grown up elsewhere as part of a different community) talk together about the meaning of actions, words, events, and ideas (Edwards & Gandini, 1989; Whiting & Edwards, 1988). Both "insiders" and "outsiders" offer necessary perspectives—complementary interpretations—and out of that juxtaposition emerges a more complete "truth-for-now" about the meaning and significance of the Reggio Emilia approach for the American context.

Second, the book represents something we would like to encourage: the collaboration—fusion, really—between the liberal arts and the professional discipline of early childhood education. The knowledge base of the arts and humanities is too often used superficially and uninspiringly in classrooms, because teachers feel they are not well enough prepared or are "not good at" things related to art, music, history, and literature. In contrast, the program in Reggio Emilia demonstrates how teachers can, through documentation and teamwork, prepare school environments and activities that awaken in young children powers to perceive, study, and represent the beautiful and orderly worlds of nature and culture surrounding them. As a result, children, through guided exploration, play, and self-expression, are introduced in appropriate ways to the important symbols and knowledge systems of adults. Children early on gain a deep sense of their history, heritage, and cultural traditions.

Finally, the book represents a yearning toward the most hopeful kind of collaboration of all, the one between children and adults. As Murray Schwartz said, introducing the 1988 "Hundred Languages of Children" Conference at the University of Massachusetts:

> One of the things we have learned in this century from people who work with children is that play is not only a way of testing reality, but also a way of creating it. The freedom of children to play creatively changes the world! When those children grow to adulthood and teach other children ... if they can create an adult

community, then it will have a profound effect on the way that we perceive, change, and respect the real world.

So then (as we asked at the end of the first edition, and now need to reask at the end of this second edition), where *do* we go from here? The Reggio Emilia approach represents a unique combination of elements, but its basic philosophy and premises about teaching and learning are ones that most American early childhood educators have found familiar and sympathetic. In spite of the heavy American emphasis on autonomy and individualism, most of us are seeking to promote greater cooperation, community, and democratic participation, and to build on our own unique cultural strengths of openness to innovation and change and willingness to form associations and voluntary organizations to solve problems. Even though American educators might find situations in which to use sequential or behavioral approaches, we are still basically child centered and holistic. The common intellectual heritage bestowed by the great philosophers, psychologists, and educational reformers of Europe and North America ensures that the same issues resonate on both sides of the Atlantic and the same hopes and basic goals inspire many of the same kinds of continuing experimentation in early education, child care, and family support systems.

One worthwhile pursuit will be to continue to study in greater depth the work ongoing in Reggio Emilia. We have begun to understand the usual ways in which teachers work together with adminstrators, parents, citizens, and the children themselves, as described and illustrated in the chapters of this book. Nevertheless, we need more and additional studies, especially of topics relating to the infant–toddler centers; parent participation; work with children with special educational needs; methods of in-service training, professional development, and documentation; interactions between the school system and policymaking and political choices; and the processes of children's transition from home to school, from infant–toddler to preprimary school, and from preprimary school to elementary school and beyond.

Some of the questions that we Americans ask most frequently about the Reggio Emilia approach ("What happens to the children when they go on to elementary school?" "What does research say about the long-term benefits of the Reggio Emilia approach for children?"), however, may also be studied fruitfully in our own country, looking at our own programs featuring elements of the Reggio Emilia philosophy and practices. These kinds of questions turn out to be particularly American in style, because U.S. society so strongly emphasizes science and technology, the systematic application of scientific findings to daily life, and the belief that progress depends on defining problems in terms of researchable hypotheses that are supported or refuted by the data. In our own context, therefore, studies can well be designed to examine questions concerning the enduring effects of project work on children's representational capacities, curiosity, and creativity; the impact of documentation as part of teachers' professional development; the applicability of the Reggio approach to the elementary school; and the benefits of continuity of care (staying with the same teacher for longer than 1 year) on children's attachment and social development and their parents' involvement and participation.

Beyond studying the programs in Reggio Emilia, moreover, we should be looking abroad at other Italian and other international successes in education (Cochran, 1993; Lamb, Sternberg, Hwang, & Broberg, 1992; Olmstead & Weikart, 1989, 1994). The programs in Reggio Emilia fit into a larger context of progressive education and innovation with respect to Italy, Europe, and the world. Because in the present era, the peoples of Western Europe have moved out in front of North Americans with regard to social services and family policy, we should be studying their experiences as we debate whether and how publicly to finance early childhood care and education, how to design spaces and environments for infants and young children, and the different possible models for grouping children, organizing the school day and year, defining adult roles, and building decision-making structures. Likewise, our friends in Reggio Emilia are expanding their circle of interest beyond Italy; all of us need to examine ourselves and seek dialogue within the widest possible circles.

When it comes to "bringing it home," there are many possibilities. One initial issue still remains: How best to proceed in adapting and translating ideas from Reggio Emilia. Is it best to proceed by setting up demonstration schools or classrooms that embody as closely as possible all of the important central premises of the Reggio Emilia approach, that, indeed, in the ideal become places of study for others wishing to learn about the adaptation of the Reggio approach to the American context? Or, in contrast, is it more realistic and productive to proceed by seeking to incorporate one or a few strands of the approach,—or insights derived from contact with the Reggio program, into ongoing endeavors in whatever setting or level of education we happen to work? Yet, this is really a pointless debate. Both approaches can be extremely fruitful, as the juxtaposed chapters by Kantor and Whately (Chapter 17, exemplifying the second way of proceeding) and by Lewin and collaborators (Chapter 18, exemplifying the first, holistic approach), make clear. Indeed, all attempts to incorporate the ideas and approaches of others are bound to be more or less partial, and more or less fruitful depending on the commitment and the level of support and collaboration received. Even with all of the money, freedom, partnership, and resources wished for, one cannot do everything anew, or import exactly what they do in Reggio; nor would that be desirable. After all, with 19 municipal preprimary schools and 13 infant–toddler centers in Reggio Emilia—each with its own distinct individuality evolving over time—there is no single, static "it" to model on. One should rather examine these ideas and practices carefully, see how they are connected and form a meaningful system of education in Reggio, and *then* try to adapt the fundamental principles to the specific cultural and social situations at hand.

In all cases, however, the best (and most permanent) change processes are those that take place gradually, carefully, and collaboratively, with slow but steady assimilation and accommodation rather than wild and sudden lurches from one educational fashion to another. As insights and knowledge gained from the experiences of Reggio Emilia become shared by more and more Americans, we expect that the arguments about their meaning and significance will increase rather than decrease, that there will be less rather than more agreement about what constitutes the Reggio Emilia approach and exactly how it translates from theory to practice (over there and over here).

So the question, "Where do we go from here?" raises many provocative possibilities. We hope that your adventures are dense with moments of confusion and illumination, and conflict and progress.

GUIDING PRINCIPLES

Here we offer a list—certainly incomplete and oversimplified—of guiding suggestions extracted from all the previous chapters as a condensation and synthesis that may be helpful for the readers.

Beginning and Maintaining Project Work

- Think in terms of "reconnaissance" rather than "planning." Always listen to the children even after the project's theme has been decided. Negotiate changes accordingly. Be comfortable with initiating an idea as long as you have evidence that your children have expressed interest.
- Do not be concerned about the project modifying its theme. What holds a project together are the gradual transitions made by the children as their interests lead from the one interesting aspect to another. These aspects may not have a conventional relation to a central theme, but they are related in the life of the project as experienced.
- Use small groups of four to six children to work on defined aspects of the project. With more than this, the children cannot focus and thereby cannot engage their minds at the deepest level possible. Provide quiet spaces for this work. Children will assume a more reflective mode when they are in this space if it is used consistently for focused work.
- Allow themes to be both mundane and exotic. Help to make the mundane unfamiliar and the exotic familiar. This reframing is often done during the revisiting of a simple idea some days later.
- Do not shy away from themes that are large and complicated. But give the development of these themes a lot of time, perhaps several months. Appreciate how even young children can deal with complicated ideas in a way that does not eliminate the significance of the idea.

- Do not shy away from controversial or emotion-laden themes such as children's fear of crowds or being lost. School can be a supportive and neutral place to discuss such topics.
- Make the children aware that their work will be documented and displayed and that they will be asked to explain their thoughts to others. Encourage them to treat their drawings as designs for future thinking and acting.
- Prepare your mind for possible and feasible directions for a project to take. Study written transcripts of the children's preliminary discussion of the theme. Mine these transcripts for the treasures of children's words and thoughts.
- Anticipate where a project could take a natural turn toward academic content such as measuring, approximating, sending messages, going to library for resources, and so on.
- When children take these turns, comment on them in your documentary panels for parents and teachers. A documentation without interpretative commentary does not effectively explain or support professional development or create an informed public to advocate for your program.
- Document, document, document! Use documentation for in-service teacher development, parent involvement, curriculum and instructional design, and as a support for learning by the children themselves.

Representational Strategies

- When children get stuck, allow them to copy representations as a starting point. For example, when some children could not understand a common tape measure they were encouraged to "reinvent" it by first copying what they saw written on a purchased tape measure. As they copied (and miscopied) they created theories about how one reads the symbols and designed a measuring tape notation that worked.
- Let children make visible drawings of sounds, or make musical sounds of things that are visible. These are called *cross-modal representations* and they can bring new perspectives and insights to light. The mismatch between symbol and referent forces the child to be inventive.
- Stimulate a more reflective stance toward the child's work by showing them photographs and video of their activity and transcripts of their words. Use these devices to revisit thoughts, not just the physical experience. Avoid using these records as evidence. Revisit them as a context to recall a theory or idea in order to expand that theory or idea.
- Use drawing as a way to learn something about the world, in addition to a skill to be learned. That is, help children draw to learn in addition to helping them learn to draw.
- Encourage children to sketch their ideas rather than to get too concerned about how good the drawing looks. This will facilitate them using drawings as a way to figure how something works rather than how something looks.

- Use drawing as a platform to dialogue with the children and as a window on how they are thinking. Drawings often reveal ideas that the child's words do not reveal. Each medium orients the children to different aspects of the world.
- Use modern technology to help children present their ideas. For example, the photocopy machine can be used to enlarge, reduce, or to repeat the symbols that the children have made. Make constant use of the video camera. Its presence gives children a reason to adopt a more explicit form of discourse.
- Use video prints or grabbed frames to help children reflect on the reasons for a sequence in action. Photo prints from a video are well situated in the flow of action (e.g., three positions of the body in a somersault video). Allow children to capture and print the key frames.
- Encourage children to invent their own notations in order to communicate to others. These notations could be a set of drawings or a series of clay figures. Extend this principle beyond inventive spelling with our conventional alphabet.
- Use one symbolic domain (e.g., drawing) to push another (e.g., sculpting). Use one as the referent for the other. Revise the first representation after the second has been completed. This latter principle helps children to consolidate learning. An initial, incomplete representation should be understood rather than replaced.
- Appreciate the relation between the aesthetics of a representation and its symbolic stance toward the real world. Even though aesthetics deal with the formal properties of art (e.g., symmetry, contrast), these dispositions toward the art in progress can generate interesting questions about the real world (e.g., Is my face really as symmetrical as my drawing indicates?).
- Encourage children to draw the same object from different perspectives and then to discuss the reason for the differences. Debate and perspective taking are important in negotiating a meaningful consensus.
- Encourage children to consider how things work, how things change across time, and how things look that are too small for the naked eye to see or are otherwise inaccessible. In other words, encourage children to draw what they cannot see, because it is here that their most interesting ideas and theories will emerge.

Group Dynamics

- Model on the adult level the kinds of democratic participation, collaborative learning, and conflict resolution you are trying to teach to the children. Negotiate not only such things as the choice of activities, but more fundamentally, negotiate the meaning, significance, and implication of shared experiences.
- Allow children to criticize each other's work. Help them find gentle and considerate ways to do this, but allow peer criticism. Such a system will help children reflect more deeply on their own work and give them motivation to be explicit.

- Trust that the children can develop the ability to debate and stay on the topic. Their success will be facilitated by your documentation of their work as they progress. Documentation validates the work of the children. Furthermore, topic maintenance remains high when children are looking at their own photographs and their own words, not because of some basic egocentrism, but because these records have a wider context that the children remember and greater continuity with the work of the current day.
- Consider the natural interests of children at various age ranges and build on those interests. For example, as children approach 6 years of age they develop a great interest in rules and fairness. Projects can include a component on crafting the rules of the game. These units can lead to a great deal of social knowledge development.
- Be sensitive to gender differences in problem-solving styles. Be sensitive to the dominance hierarchy among children in your class. Ask for volunteers for project work. Create small groups that are comprised only of children who are interested in the work and who you think have complementary styles of working. Do not cajole a child into participating in a project that he or she has no interest in. Either find a component of the project in which this child is interested or let the child learn by observing the work of others. Often such a child will become interested in the project in time. Allow children to enter when they are ready. Defend this policy to the end !
- Have the project grow from small group work to larger group involvement, such as a classwide review, celebration, competition, or community performance. The anticipation of this final performance increases the children's interest and their desire to reflect on the details of the topic.

Teaching and Learning Strategies

- Dispense occasions that challenge children intellectually and emotionally. Be comfortable with your role as a provocateur. Teachers not only facilitate learning, they also stimulate learning by presenting a counterperspective or counterexample.
- Serve as the children's scribe. Write what they say. Display selected discussions in panels on the wall. Let children know that their thoughts are something you care about deeply. Always ask yourself, what it is that these children believe that I really care about? Be sure the answer is not "finishing things on time."
- During those times that it is clear to the children that they are doing their best thinking, hold the children accountable for how well their representations communicate. It is appropriate at these times to react with confusion if the child has not been clear.
- Provide children with representational tools that allow them to gain better purchase on what they are trying to say. Reduce the technical difficulties of

these tools when ideas are really coming. Work on technical skills in sessions that precede the more intense exploration of an idea. At these latter times it is appropriate to demonstrate for the child the correct use of a brush or implement for sculpting clay.

- Encourage children to decide among themselves which media might best carry the message and which symbols produced by various children best carry the specific meanings intended. These discussions develop metasymbolic awareness that can become a useful mental disposition.
- Revisit documentation with the children. Go beyond asking children to remember what happened. Use recall as a platform for further exploration of new ideas from the children.
- Be flexible in how you work. Question your certainties. Sometimes you will be directive, sometimes facilitative. Trust the children to cue you about the correct balance.
- Be comfortable about supporting a child-initiated experiment even when you know that it will not yield the desired result. Reframe your role as one who helps children invent methods of investigation. For children to find out that something does not work means that they have learned how to get to that point.
- Be comfortable that two children, in a heated debate, are often able to establish some limits to their intensity. Delay your intervention by one or two degrees more than your raw intuitions tell you. Sometimes the structure of a theory or position is clarified the best when children get a little agitated about a difference of opinion.
- Work in collaboration with other teachers. Discuss the meaning of transcripts and other records with other educators. Effective teaching requires a level of interpretation of performance that can come only from discourse with other professionals. Revisit records of both the children's work and your interaction with the children. Notice patterns.
- Be comfortable about telling children information, as long as you also appreciate that this information still has to be constructed and reinvented by the children who hear it. A co-constructive curriculum does not ignore the content expertise of the teacher. Rather it honors the expertise of both teacher and children who collectively attempt to negotiate shared meaning over time and deliberate effort.

REFERENCES

Cochran, M. (Ed.). (1993). *International handbook of child care policies and programs.* Westport, CT: Greenwood Press.

Department of Early Education, City of Reggio Emilia, Region of Emilia Romagna. (1984) *L'Occhio se Salta il Muro* [When the Eye Jumps Over the Wall]. Catalog of the Exhibit, "L'Occhio se Salta il Muro." Reggio Emilia, Italy: Author.

Edwards, C.P., & Gandini, L. (1989). Teachers' expectations about the timing of developmental skills: A cross-cultural study. *Young Children, 44*(4),15–19.

Lamb, M.E., Sternberg, K.J., Hwang, C.P., & Broberg, A.G. (Eds.). (1992) *Child care in context.* Hillsdale, NJ: Erlbaum.

Olmstead, P. & Weikart, D. (Eds.). (1989). *How nations serve young children: Profiles of child care and education in 14 countries.* Ypsilanti, MI: High/Scope Press.

Olmstead, P., & Weikart, D.P. (Eds.). (1994). *Families speak: Early childhood care and education in 11 countries.* Ypsilanti, MI: High/Scope Press.

Schwartz, M. (1988, December). *Introduction.* The Hundred Languages of Children Conference, University of Massachusetts, Amherst.

Whiting, B.B., & Edwards, C.P. (1988). *Children of different worlds: The formation of social behavior.* Cambridge, MA: Harvard University Press.

FIGURE 24.1. Farewell, from Pedinovela, Exhibit The Hundred Languages of Children.

Glossary of Terms Used by Educators in Reggio Emilia

Asilo Nido **Infant–Toddler Center:** Full-day program providing education and care to children aged 4 months through 3 years.

Assessore: Official, serving under the Mayor, in charge of all public education for the city.

Atelier: Workshop, or studio, furnished with a variety of resource materials, used by all the children and adults in a school.

Atelierista: Teacher trained in art education, in charge of the *atelier;* supports teachers in curriculum development and documentation.

Comune: Also called *municipio,* municipality; the city government and the building where it is located.

Consiglio di Gestione **Advisory Council on Community-Based Management:** Elected committee of parents, citizens, and educators serving a preprimary school or infant–toddler center.

Consulta di Asili Nido e delle Scuole dell' Infanzia **Municipal Board of Infant–Toddler and Preprimary Education:** Composed of representatives of the Advisory Councils; has governing authority over the early childhood system.

Direttore **Director of Early Childhood Education:** A civil service professional who oversees the whole infant–toddler and preprimary system and guarantees the quality and integrity of the educational services provided to children and families.

Educatore **Teacher:** In a preprimary school.

Gestione Sociale **Community-Based Management:** The system of governance, involving representatives of the different sectors of the local community, used in the Reggio Emilia municipal early childhood system.

Operatore **Teacher:** In an infant–toddler center.

Pedagogista **Pedagogical Coordinator:** Acts as consultant, resource person, and coordinator to several schools and centers. The team of *pedagogisti* has a pedagogical director. The team serves under the system Director, who is responsible for the preprimary schools and infant–toddler centers in the city.

Pzogettezione: Flexible planning concerning any aspect of the life of the school and in connection with the community. (See Chapter 5).

Scuola dell'Infanzia **Preprimary School:** Full-day program providing education and care to children aged 3 to 6 years of age (includes the American kindergarten year).

Additional Resources

BOOKS

Cadwell, L. (1997). *Bringing Reggio Emilia home: A narrative of practice and place.* New York: Teachers College Press.

Edwards, C.P., Gandini, L., & Forman, G. (Eds.). (1993). *The hundred languages of children: The Reggio Emilia approach to early childhood education.* Norwood, NJ: Ablex.

Hendricks, J. (1997). *First steps in teaching the Reggio way.* Columbus, OH: Merrill/Prentice-Hall.

Katz, L.G., & Cesarone, B. (Eds.). (1994). *Reflections on the Reggio Emilia approach.* (Perspectives from ERIC/EECE: A Monograph Series). Urbana IL: ERIC Clearinghouse on Elementary and Early Childhood Education. (Doc. No. DERR 9300 2007)

Lewin, A.W. (Ed.). (1994). *Model Early Learning Center history and practices.* Washington, DC: The National Learning Center, 800 Third Street NE, Washington, DC 20002.

Malaguzzi, L. (1995). *Volpino, last of the chicken thieves.* Bergamo, Italy: Edizioni Junior. Distributed by Reggio Children USA, Washington, DC 20005-3105, Phone (202) 265-9090, Fax (202) 265-9161.

REGGIO CHILDREN S.r.l. (1987). *I cento linguaggi dei bambini* [The hundred languages of children: Narrative of the possible]. Exhibit Catalog. Distributed by Reggio Children USA, Washington, DC 20005-3105, Phone (202) 265-9090, Fax (202) 265-9161.

REGGIO CHILDREN S.r.l. (1995). *Tenerezza* [Tenderness]. Distributed by Reggio Children USA, Washington, DC 20005-3105, Phone (202) 265-9090, Fax (202) 265-9161.

REGGIO CHILDREN S.r.l. (1995). *In viaggio coi diritti delle bambine e dei bambini* [A journey into the rights of children]. Distributed by Reggio Children USA, Washington, DC 20005-3105, Phone (202) 265-9090, Fax (202) 265-9161.

REGGIO CHILDREN S.r.l. (1995). *Le fontane* [The fountains]. Distributed by Reggio Children USA, Washington, DC 20005-3105, Phone (202) 265-9090, Fax (202) 265-9161.

REGGIO CHILDREN S.r.l. (1996). *I cento linguaggi dei bambini: Narative del possibile* [The hundred languages of children: Narratives of the possible]. New extended exhibit catalog. Distributed by Reggio Children USA, Washington, DC 20005-3105, Phone (202) 265-9090, Fax (202) 265-9161.

REGGIO CHILDREN S.r.l. (1996). *I piccolissimi del cinema muto* [The little ones of silent movies]. Distributed by Reggio Children USA, Washington, DC 20005-3105, Phone (202) 265-9090, Fax (202) 265-9161.

REGGIO CHILDREN S.r.l. (1997). *Scarpa e metro* [Shoe and meter]. Distributed by Reggio Children USA, Washington, DC 20005-3105, Phone (202) 265-9090, Fax (202) 265-9161.

ARTICLES AND CHAPTERS

Abramson, S., Ankerman, K., & Robinson, R. (1995). Project work with diverse students: Adapting curriculum based on the Reggio Emilia approach. *Childhood Education, 71*(4), 197–202.

Bartlett, S. (1993). Amiable space in the schools of Reggio Emilia: An interview with Lella Gandini. Includes "Children in Reggio Emilia look at their school." *Children's Environments, 10*(2), 113–129.

Benham, H. (1992). Reggio Emilia: The power and value of the child. *Scholastic Pre-K Today, 7*(2), 5.

Benham, H. (1996). Reggio: Beauty everywhere. *Scholastic Early Childhood Today, 10*(4).

Bredekamp, S. (1993). Reflections on Reggio Emilia. *Young Children, 49*(1), 13–17.

Cohen, D.L. (1992). Preschools in Italian town inspiration to U.S. educators. *Education Week, 12*(12), 1, 12, 13.

Dolci, M. (1994, July). When the wolf both is and is not a wolf: The language of puppets. *Child Care Information Exchange*, 43–46.

Edwards, C.P., Gandini, L., & Nimmo, J. (1992). *Favorire l'apprendimento cooperativo nella prima infanzia: Concettualizzazioni contrastanti da parte degli insegnanti in due comunita* [Promoting collaborative learning in the early childhood classroom: Teachers' contrasting conceptualizations in two communities]. *Rassegna di Psicologia, 9*(3), 65–90. Republished in L.G. Katz and B. Cesarone (Eds.) (1994), *Reflections on the Reggio Emilia approach* (pp. 81–104). Urbana, IL: ERIC Clearinghouse on Elementary and Early Childhood Education.

Edwards, C.P., Shallcross, D., & Maloney, J. (1991). Promoting creativity in a graduate course on creativity: Entering the time and space of the young child. *Journal of Creative Behavior, 25*(4), 304–310.

Edwards, C.P., Shallcross, D., & Maloney, J. (1996). Adults and children with hundreds of language: Using insights from Reggio Emilia in a course on creativity. In W.F. Garrett-Petts (Ed.), *Integrating visual and verbal literacies.* (pp. 19–34). Manitoba, Canada: Inkshed Publications, University of Manitoba, Winnipeg, MB, R3T 2N2.

Edwards, C.P., & Springate, K. (1993). Inviting children into project work. *Dimensions of Early Childhood, 22*(1), 9–12, 40.

Edwards, C.P., & Springate, K. (1995). The lion comes out of the stone: Promoting creative expression in young children. *Dimensions of Early Childhood, 23*(4), 24–29. Reprinted in ERIC/EECE Digest, Order #EDO-PS-95-14.

Firlick, R. (1995). *American early childhood reform: Adaptation not adoption from Reggio Emilia, Italy.* [ERIC Clearinghouse on Elementary and Early Childhood Education, Order # 022434, 805 W. Pennsylvania Ave., Urbana, Illinois 61801-4897].

Forman, G.E. (1989). Helping children ask good questions. In B. Neugebauer (Ed.), *The wonder of it: Exploring how the world works* (pp. 21–24). Redmond, WA: Exchange Press.

Forman, G.E. (1992). The constructivist perspective. In J.L. Roopnarine & J.E. Johnson (Eds.), *Approaches to early childhood education* (pp. 137–155). Columbus, OH: Merrill.

Forman, G.E. (1997). Beyond the attentive eye. *Reflections:* Winnetka. Public Schools, Winnetka, IL.

Gandini, L. (1984, Summer). Not just anywhere: Making child care centers into "particular" places. *Beginnings,* 17–20.

Gandini, L. (1992, May–June). Creativity comes dressed in everyday clothes. *Child Care Information Exchange,* 26–29.

Gandini, L. (1993). Fundamentals of the Reggio Emilia approach to early childhood education. *Young Children, 49*(1), 4–8.

Gandini, L. (1994). Celebrating children day by day: A conversation with Amelia Gambetti. *Child Care Information Exchange,* no. 100. 52–55.

Gandini, L. (1994). What can we learn from Reggio Emilia: An Italian–American collaboration: An interview with Amelia Gambetti and Mary Beth Radke. *Child Care Information Exchange,* no. 96. 62–66.

Gandini, L. (1996, March). Teachers and children together: Constructing new learning. *Child Care Information Exchange,* 43–46.

Gandini, L., & Edwards, C.P. (1988). Early childhood integration of the visual arts. *Gifted International, 5*(2), 14–18.

Gandini, L., & Gambetti, A. (1997). An inclusive system based on cooperation: The schools for young children in Reggio Emilia. *School Leadership.*

Katz, L.G. (1990). Impressions of Reggio Emilia preschools. *Young Children, 45*(6), 10–11.

Kennedy, D.K. (1996) After Reggio Emilia: May the conversation begin. *Young Children, 51*(5), 24–27.

Lane, M.S. (1993, October). Loris Malaguzzi's one hundred languages. *Scholastic Early Childhood Today.*

LeeKeenan, D., & Edwards, C.P. (1992). Using the project approach with toddlers. *Young Children, 47*(4), 31–36.

Lewin, A.W. (1992). The view from Reggio. *Hand to Hand: Youth Museums Newsletter, 6*(1), 4–6.

Malaguzzi, L. (1993). For an education based on relationship. *Young Children, 49*(1), 9–12.

Malaguzzi, L. (1994). Listening to children. *Young Children, 49*(5), 55.

Malaguzzi, L. (1994). Your image of the child: Where teaching begins. *Child Care Information Exchange,* no. 96, 52–61.

McLaughlin, M. (1995, May). Will Reggio Emilia change your child's preschool? *Working Mother,* 62–68.

Millsom, C. (1994). An inspiring example of community-supported child care: Reggio Emilia, Italy. In H. Nuba, M. Searson, & D.L. Sheiman (Eds.), *Resources for early childhood.* New York: Garland.

Neugebauer, B. (1994). Unpacking my questions and images: Personal reflections on Reggio Emilia. *Child Care Information Exchange,* 67–70.

New, R. (1990). Excellent early education: A city in Italy has it! *Young Children, 45*(6), 4–10.

New, R. (1991). Early childhood teacher education in Italy: Reggio Emilia's master plan for "master" teachers. *The Journal of Early Childhood Teacher Education, 12*(37), 3.

New, R. (1991). Projects and provocations: Preschool curriculum ideas from Reggio Emilia. *Montessori Life, 3*(1), 26–28.

New, R. (1993). Italy. In M. Cochran (Ed.), *International handbook of child care policies and programs.* (pp. 291–311). Westport, CT: Greenwood Press.

Newsweek. (1991, December 2). The 10 best schools in the world, and what we can learn from them, pp. 50–59.

Rankin, B. (1992, May–June). Inviting children's creativity: A story of Reggio Emilia, Italy. *Child Care Information Exchange,* 30–35.

Rody, M.A. (1995, January–February). A visit to Reggio Emilia. *Early Childhood News, 7*(1), 14–16.

Rosen, I. (1992). Reggio Emilia, a model in creativity. *Scholastic Pre-K Today, 7*(2).

Trepanier-Street, M. (1993). What's so new about the project approach? *Childhood Education, 70*(1), 25–28.

United States General Accounting Office. (1995, February). *Programs in Reggio Emilia considered the best in early childhood programs: Promoting the development of young children in Denmark, France, and Italy, a report.* Order #GAO-HEHS-95-45BR, US GAO, PO Box 6015, Gaithersburg, MD 20877.

DISSERTATIONS/THESES

Cadwell, L.B. (1996). *Making places, telling stories: An approach to early education inspired by the preschools of Reggio Emilia, Italy.* Doctor of Philosophy in Education, The Union Institute, Cincinnati, OH.

Rabitti, G. (1991). *Preschool in La Villeta, Reggio Emilia, Italy.* Master of Arts in Education, University of Illinois at Urbana-Champaign.

Rankin, B. (1985). *An analysis of some aspects of schools and services for 0–6-year-olds in Italy with particular attention to Lombardy and Emilia Romagna.* Certificate of Advanced Graduate Study thesis, Wheelock College, Boston, MA.

Rankin, B.M. (1996). *Collaboration as the basis of early childhood curriculum: A case study from Reggio Emilia, Italy.* Doctor of Education, Boston University, Boston, MA.

Sussna, A.G. (1995). *The educational impact on preschool teachers of an adaptation of the Reggio Emilia documentation process.* Doctor of Education, University of Massachusetts, Amherst.

Yoo, S.B. (1996). *The effects of using 35 mm photos vs. video prints on revisiting and documentation by preservice teachers.* Doctor of Education, University of Massachusetts, Amherst.

VIDEOTAPES

100 Languages of Children. (1995). By S. Lyon. Available from M.S. Lyon, 101 Lombard St., 608W, San Francisco, CA 94111, Fax: (415) 397-8211.

The Amusement Park for Birds. (1994). By G. Forman & L. Gandini. Performanetics Press, 19 The Hollow, Amherst MA 01002, Fax: (413) 253-0898.

A Message from Loris Malaguzzi. (1995). By L. Malaguzzi & L. Gandini. Distributed by Reggio Children USA, Washington, DC 20005-3105, Phone (202) 265-9090.

Childhood. (1991). Short segments on Reggio Emilia in Parts 3 (*Love's labors*) and 4 (*In the land of the giants*) of 7. Ambrose Video Publishing, 1290 Avenue of the Americas, Suite 2245, New York, NY 10104.

The Creative Spirit. (1992). Segment on Reggio Emilia in Part 2 of 4 (*Creative beginnings*). PBS Video, 4401 Sunset Boulevard, Los Angeles, CA 90027. Companion volume: *The Creative Spirit*, by D. Goleman, P. Kaufman, & M. Ray (New York, Dutton, 1992).

Detroit Head Start Inspired by the Reggio Approach. (1996). The Merrill-Palmer Institute, Wayne State University, 71-A E. Ferry Ave., Detroit, MI 48202.

Early Learning in Reggio Emilia, Italy. (1993). Distributed by Project Apples, 27 Horrabin Hall, College of Education, Western Illinois University, Macomb, IL 61455, Phone (309) 298-1634. Narration by Brenda Fyfe.

Jed Draws His Bicycle: A Case of Drawing to Learn. (1995). By G. Forman. Performanetics Press, 19 The Hollow, Amherst MA 01002, Fax: (413) 253-0898.

The Long Jump: A video analysis of small group projects in early education as practiced in Reggio Emilia, Italy. (1991). By G. Forman & L. Gandini. Performanetics Press, 19 The Hollow, Amherst, MA 01002, Fax (413) 253-0898.

To Build a Bridge in Clay. (1994). Available from Education Products, The Model Early Learning Center, 800 Third Street, NE, Washington, DC 20002.

To Make a Portrait of a Lion [Per Fare il Ritratto di un Leone]. (1987). Comune di Reggio Emilia. Distributed by Reggio Children USA, Washington, DC 20005-3105, Phone (202) 265-9090.

SLIDE SETS

Environment, Projects, and Learning to Use Materials. Three sets of 40 slides each, illustrating the adaptation of the Reggio Emilia approach at the Model Early Learning Center in Washington, DC. Available from Education Products, The Model Early Learning Center, 800 Third Street NE, Washington, DC 20002.

Open Window. (1994). Portfolio of 36 slides showing the schools of Reggio Emilia and children at work in them. Produced by the Comune di Reggio Emilia. Distributed by Reggio Children USA, Washington, D.C. 20005-3105, Phone (202) 265-9090, Fax (202) 265-9161.

St. Louis–Reggio Collaborative for the Study and Adaptation of the Reggio Approach. A set of 34 slides from three schools portraying the children, teachers, and parents of the St. Louis–Reggio Collaborative. Available through St. Michael's School, 6345 Wydown Blvd., St. Louis, MO 63105. Phone (314) 721-4422. Fax (314) 721-4670.

NEWSLETTER

Innovations in early education: The international reggio exchange. The Merrill-Palmer Institute, 71A East Ferry Avenue, Detroit, Michigan 48202, Phone (313) 872-1790, Fax (313) 577-0995.

rechild, Reggio Children newsletter. Distributed by REGGIO CHILDREN S.r.l. Piazza della Vittoria 6, Reggio Emilia 42100, Italy, Fax 011-39-522-455621.

EXHIBIT

The Hundred Languages of Children: Narratives of the Possible. (1987). Created by Department of Early Education, Reggio Emilia, Italy. Contact: Reggio Children USA, 1341 G Street, NW Suite 400, Washington, DC 20005, Phone (202) 265-9090, Fax (202) 265-9161, or exhibit curator Pamela Houk, Dayton Art Institute, PO Box 941, Dayton, OH 45401.

ELECTRONIC MAIL

REGGIO-L Listserv. To subscribe to the REGGIO-L electronic discussion group on the Internet: Send a message to: listserv@postoffice.cso.uiuc.edu. Leave the subject line blank. In the body of the message, type: subscribe REGGIO-L YourFirstName YourLastName in the first line of the message area.

The ERIC Clearinghouse on Elementary and Early Childhood Education (ERIC/EECE) maintains a collection of information and resources related to Reggio Emilia and the Reggio Emilia approach on the clearinghouse Web site. The URL for the home page of the ERIC/EECE Web site is: http://ericps.ed.uiuc.edu/ericeece.html

The URL for the special section on Reggio Emilia is: http://ericps.ed.uiuc.edu/eece/reggio.html. In this Reggio Emilia section of the Web site are resources that include bibliographies of ERIC Documnets, journal articles, and other publications.

Author Index

A
Azer, S. 452, *453*

B
Balbo, L. 153n, *157*
Barden, M. 261, *281*, 440, *452*
Bates, J. 315, *333*
Becchi, E. 22, *24*
Bellah, R. N. 296, 307, *310*
Bell, R. M. 183, *198*
Bennett, M. J. 296, *311,* 446, *453*
Berger, P. 239, *259*
Berk, L. E. 262, 270, 271, 272, 273, *281,* 408, *416*
Berrigan, C. 200, *214*
Bohlen, C. 8, *24*
Bowman, B. T. 296, *310*
Bredekamp, S. 261, 262, *281,* 296, *310,* 408, *416,* 440, 450, 451, *452*
Broberg, A. G. 460, *466*
Brooks, J. G. 263, *281*
Brooks, M. G. 263, *281*
Brown, A. 272, *281*
Brown, A. L. 239, 246, *259*
Brown, C. S. 246, *259*
Brown, O. 405, *416*
Bruner, J. 35, *45,* 87, *96,* 133, *137,* 240, *259,* 265, 270, *281*

C
Cadwell, L. 435, *436, 437*
Cambi, F. 18, *24*
Carr, W. 86, *96*
Cecchini, M. 200, 201, *214*
Chafel, J. A. 304, *310*
Chard, S. 406, *416*
Chard, S. C. 28, *45*
Chattin-McNichols, J. 338, *357*
Ciari, B. 21, 22, *24*
Cobb, P. 263, 277, *281*
Cochran, M. 460, *465*
Cochran-Smith, M. 276, *281*
Cohen, D. L. 5, *24*
Colton, A. B. 405, *417*
Copple, C. 262, *281*
Corsaro, W. A. 5, 22, *24,* 264, 265, 271, *281,* 315, *333*
Costa, S. 421, *437*
Costley, J. 452, *453*
Cuffaro, H. 276, *281*

D
Della Peruta, F. 18, 20, *24*
Derman-Sparks, L. 306, *310*
Devlin, J. 435, *437*
De Vries, R. 262, 263, *281*
Dewey, J. 280, *281,* 307, *311,* 315, *332*
Dixon, V. 452, *453*
Doise, W. 239, *259*
Driver, R. 263, *282*
Drummond, M. J. 276, 278, *282*
Duckworth, E. *282*
Dunn, S. 241, *259*

E
Eder, D. 271, *281*
Edwards, C. P. 8, *24,* 179, 188, *198,* 265, 266, *282, 284,* 304, *311,* 406, 408, *416,* 440, *453,* 458, *466*
Eisner, E. W. *282,* 314, *332,* 421, *437*
Elgas, P. 271, *282,* 315, 317, *333*
Emiliani, F. 5, 22, *24*
Entzminger, E. 422, *437*
Evangelou, D. 41, *45*

F
Fernie, D. 271, *282,* 313, 315, 316, 317, *332, 333*

Ferrara, R. 272, *281*
Feuerstein, R. 338, *357*
Filippini, T. 164, *177,* 181, *198, 237,* 269, *282*
Floden, R. E. 263, 270, 272, 280, *284*
Forman, E. A. 240, 246, *259, 282*
Forman, G. 248, 249, *259,* 266, 276, *282,* 360, 371, 373, *374,* 406, 408, 409, *416,* 434, *437,* 440, *453*
Fosnot, C. 276, *282,* 406, *416*
Friere, P. 279, *282*
Fullan, M. G. 421, 425, 426, *437*
Fuller, F. 405, *416*
Fyfe, B. 240, *259,* 420, 422, 427, 434, 435, *436, 437*

G
Gaetano, Y. 297, 306, *312*
Gallimore, R. 240, *260,* 273, *284*
Gandini, L. 179, *198,* 240, *259,* 266, 267, *282,* 309, *311,* 342, *357,* 406, 408, *416,* 423, *437,* 458, *466*
Gardner, H. 96, *96,* 240, 248, *259,* 269, *282,* 338, *357*
Garmston, R. 421, *437*
Garrison, J. 272, 280, *282*
Gatto, J. T. 297, *311*
Gee, J. 241, *259*
Geertz, C. 408, *416*
Genser, A. 452, *453*
Gerber, M. 324, 325, *333*
Gergen, K. 315, *333*
Ghedini, P. O. 20, *24*
Glazer, S. M. 246, *259*
Goffin, S. G. 296, *311*
Goldhaber, J. 408, *416*
Goncu, A. 264, *284*
Goodenough, W. H. 314, *333*
Goodman, I. 452, *453*
Goodman, K. 241, *259*
Goodnow, J. J. 265, *282*
Graham, S. 263, *282*
Greenberg, P. 302, *311*
Green, J. 315, *333*
Greene, M. 279, *282*
Greenman, J. 169, *177*

H
Hale, J. E. 297, *311*
Hall, G. 421, *437*
Harel, I. 241, *259*
Harkness, S. 266, *282, 284*
Harris, K. R. 263, *282*
Hartmann, J. A. 41, *45*
Hawkins, D. 78, 86, *96*
Hawkins, F. P. 37, *45*
Hellman, J. A. 8, *24,* 183, *198*
Hill, F. 373, *374*
Hill, T. 296, *311*
Hord, S. 421, *437*
Howes, C. 442, *454*
Hulling-Austin, L. 421, *437*
Hwang, C. P. 460, *466*

I
Inagaki, K. 33, *45*
Isaacs, S. 246, *259*

J
Jankowicz, A. D. 239, *259*
Jones, E. 309, *311,* 451, *453*

K
Kafai, Y. 241, *259*
Kahn, A. J. 5, *24*
Kamerman, S. B. 5, *24*
Kamii, C. 263, *282*
Kantor, R. 271, *282,* 313, 315, 316, 317, *332, 333*
Katz, L. G. 28, 41, 43, *45,* 405, 406, *416*
Kessel, F. 265, *282*
Kessler, S. 262, *283*
Killion, J. P. 276, *283*
Klein, M. 315, 317, *333*
Kohlberg, L. 262, *281*
Kostelnik, M. 444, *453*
Kuhn, T. 263, *283*
Kushner, D. 249, *259*

L
Ladson-Billings, G. 297, *311*
Lambert, L. 421, *437*
Lamb, M. E. 460, *466*
Larsen, R. 241, *259*
LeeKeenan, D. 304, *311,* 444, *453*
Levine, J. M. 270, 272, *283*
Lewin, A. W. 337, *357*
Liston, D. P. 405, *417*
Lombardi, J. 452, *453*
Lucchini, E. 19, *24*
Luckmann, T. 239, *259*
Lytle, S. L. 276, *281*

M
Madsen, R. 296, *310*

Malaguzzi, L. 55, *96,* 137, *137,* 172, 173, *177,* 188, *198,* 230, 275, 277, 278, 279, *283,* 207, *311,* 440, 446, *453*
Mallory, B. L. 200, *214,* 262, *283,* 296, *311*
Masiello, T. 264, *284*
Matthews, G. B. 273, *283*
McCleary, I. D. 200, 201, *214*
McGimsey, B. 452, *453*
McPhail, J. 246, *259*
Mead, M. 265, *283*
Metz, K. E. 273, *283*
Meyer, L. 315, 317, *333*
Miles, M. B. 421, *437*
Miller 264, 265, *281*
Miller, P. J. 265, *282*
Minick, N. *282*
Mistry, J. 264, *284*
Moll, L. 257, *259*
Moran, M. J. 407, *416*
Morgan, G. 450, 452, *453*
Moshman, D. 280, *283*
Mosier, C. 264, *284*
Mugny, G. 239, *259*
Musatti, T. 19, *25*

N

New, R. S. 5, 22, *25,* 200, *214,* 261, 262, 265, 275, 276, 278, *283,* 296, *311,* 408, *416*
Nimmo, J. W. 179, *198,* 298, 302, 303, 304, 309, *311,* 444, *453*
Nuthall, G. 40, *45*

O

Oja, S. N. 405, *416*
Olesen, V. 314, *333*
Olmstead, P. 21, 23, *25,* 460, *466*

P

Palincsar, A S. 239, 246, *259*
Parten, M. 316, *333*
Pelo, A. 306, *311*
Perret-Clemont, A. N. 239, *259*
Pessoa, F. 80, *96*
Phillips, C. B. 296, *311,* 442, *453*
Phillips, D. C. 263, *283,* 442, *454*
Piaget, J. 81, 82, *97,* 240, 244, *259,* 315, 316, 324, *333*
Pistillo, F. 5, 20, 21, 23, *25*
Powell, D. 441, *453*
Prawat, R. S. 263, 270, 272, 280, *284*
Prawat, R. W. *283*
Putnam, R. D. 8, *25,* 183, *198*

R

Rabitti, G. 37, *45,* 180, 181, 186, *198*
Radziszewska, B. 264, *284*
Rankin, B. 215, 231, 233, *237,* 304, *311*
Reed, K. 296, *311*
Reisman, B. 441, *453*
Resnick, L. B. 270, 272, *283,* 337, *357*
Rinaldi, C. 28, *45,* 105, *112,* 240, 245, *259,* 408, *416*
Rizzo, T. 270, *284,* 315, *333*
Robins, K. 200, *214*
Rodari, G. *97*
Rogoff, B. 265, 265, 266, 270, 272, *284,* 414, *417*
Ross, G. *260*
Ross, H. 5, *25*
Rubenstein, T. S. 315, 326, *333*
Rutherford, W. 421, *437*

S

Saltz, R. 5, 19, *25*
Sanders, R. S. 430, *437*
Scheper-Hughes, N. 314, *333*
Schlecty, P. 42, *45*
Schon, D. A. 414, *417*
Schwartz, M. *466*
Scott, P. 263, *282*
Scuola, di Barbiana, *25*
Skrtic, T. M. 43, *45*
Smagorinsky, P. 277, *284*
Smith, D. 408, *416*
Smith, E. *284*
Smulyan, L. 405, *416*
Snook, I. 40, *45*
Solisken, J. 247, *259*
Sortino, S. 408, *416*
Spaggiari, S. 269, *284*
Sparks-Langer, G. M. 405, *417*
Spradley, J. P. 315, *333*
Steiegelbauer, S. 421, *437*
Sternberg, K. J. 460, *466*
Stewart, E. C. 296, *311,* 446, *453*
Stone, C. A. 273, *282, 284*
Stott, F. M. 296, *310*
Strange, J. 435, *437*
Stubbs, M. 241, *259*
Sullivan, W. W. 296, *310*
Super, C. 266, *282, 284*
Swadener, B. B. 262, *283*
Swidler, A. 296, *310*

T

Tannen, D. 248, *260*

Tarini, E. 279, *403*
Tharp, R. 452, *454*
Tharp, R. G. 240, *260,* 273, *284*
Tierney, R. 246, *260*
Tipton, S. M. 296, *310*
Todnem, G. R. 276, *283*
Tudge, J. 239, *260*

U
Ulivieri, S. 18, *24*

V
Van Manen, M. 406, *417*
Vartuli, S. 422, *437*
Vecchi, V. 268, 275, *284,* 307, *311*
von Glaserfeld, E. 240, *250*
Vygotsky, L. S. 83, *97,* 239, 244, *260,* 270, 272, 274, *284,* 315, 324, 326, *333*

W
Wallat, C. 315, *333*
Warfield-Coppock, N. 310, *311*
Weikart, D. P. 21, 23, *25,* 460, *466*
Wertheimer, M. 68, *97*
Wertsch, J. V. 239, 244, *260,* 264, 270, *284*
Whaley, K. 271, *282,* 315, 326, *333*
Whitebook, M. 442, *454*
Whiting, B. B. 265, *284,* 304, *311,* 458, *466*
Whiting, J. 265, *284*
Willette, J. 247, *259*
Williams, D. 317, *333*
Williams, L. R. 296, 297, 306, *312*
Wilson, J. 247, *259*
Winsler, A. 262, 270, 271, 272, 273, *281,* 408, *416*
Winterhoff, P. A. 239, *260*
Wood, D. *260*

Z
Zan, B. 263, *281*
Zeichner, K. M. 405, *417*

Subject Index

A

A. Sophie Rogers Lab School, discussed, 313–332

adults. *see also* parents; teachers

relationships with children, 36–38, 92, 140–141

role of in learning, 81, 272, 377–378, 379

Advisory Council

children's understanding of, 99

duties and officers of, 103–104

advocacy

for co-construction and community support, 255–257

relation to teaching, 183

Agazzi, Rosa, 60

Alerta Approach, 306

amiability, in school environment, 63–64

The Amusement Park for the Birds, 268

anti-bias curriculum, 306

apprenticeship, 266

art. *see also* drawing

created by children, 145–146

ownership of, 298–299

art instruction, 35, 140

Asili Nido. see infant-toddler centers

assessore, duties and responsibilities, 128

atelier. see also environment

background for, 23

mini-ateliers facilities, 64, 87, 172–173

research and provocation within, 73–75

role in education, 64, 87, 172, 174–175

role in preprimary school, 140–143

teacher development in, 139

atelierista

background for, 23

documentation use by, 39, 175–176

in process of change, 427–431

relationship with teachers, 142–143, 146–147, 172, 218

role of, 139–147

autism, 203, 209

autonomy

communication affecting, 69

development of, 206, 296

B

baby boomers, 53

Bambini (Children), 56

Bell, Ted, 335

Bicycle Project, 378–388

The Biology of Knowledge (Piaget), 81

birth rate, relation to family structure, 102–103

Bovet, Pierre, 59

Bowlby, John, 61

boys. *see also* children

project collaboration procedures, 224–225, 229–231

thinking process, compared to girls, 220–221

Bruner, Jerome, 81, 133

C

Carr, Wilfred, 86

Catholic Church, influence on education, 18, 20–21, 52, 54–55, 60, 61, 72, 100

cerebral palsy, 209–211

change

administrative concerns for, 431–435

atelierista role in, 427–431

childhood images. *see also* early childhood lore

affect on *pedagogista*, 128–129

affecting childhood education, 77–80, 296

children. *see also* boys; girls

as "activists", 306

as author and inventor, 67
class group continuity for, 267, 303–304
in community, 295–310
contemporary appreciation of, 102–103, 108, 110–111
differences among, 79–80
documentation opportunities for, 122
"egocentric" nature of, 296
peer group forces affecting, 265
as peers, playmates, provocateurs, 270–272
predisposition for relationships, 15, 62, 110, 155–157, 205–206
as protagonist, 110, 180, 274, 287, 297, 457
reintegration of, 457
rights of, 8, 57–58, 114, 161, 164
self-identity construction, 304–305, 306
sensitivity to adults, 37–38
as social actor, 296–297
as social beings, 62
as "social constructivist", 115, 118
as source of curriculum, 51, 88–90
Christian Democratic Party, 21
Ciari, Bruno, 21–22, 54
circularity
principle of, 83–84
of teachers' role, 183
city. *see also* community
education within, 87, 164–167
City Project, 315–324
City in the Rain Project, 167, 359
City in the Snow Project, 359–374
civil meaning, child's rights to, 8, 57–58
classroom. *see also* environment
choices for children in, 87
as cultures, 314–315
organization of, 64, 172
relationship organization within, 69
co-construction. *see also* knowledge construction
principles of, 255–257
cognition. *see also* learning
collaborative, 270–271
situated, 337–338
cognitive psychology, 263–264
collaboration. *see* cooperation; relationships
collaborative learning. *see also* learning
project approach framework, 405–416
collectivity. *see also* cooperation
background for, 21–22
in project creation, 10
in teaching, 9, 414–415
College School Project, 419–436
professional development system, 420–427
communalism
children's participation in, 41
space affecting, 172–173
communication. *see also* discussion; listening; negotiation
factors affecting, 74, 170, 239–240, 268
graphic languages use in, 34
in Model Early Learning Center, 340
"pedagogy of communication", 109–110
communication networks, development of, 68–69
community
children's activities in, 52, 124–125, 166
child's place in, 295–310
description of, 297
documentation use for, 12
educational responsibilities of, 111
as model for preschool program, 40–41, 252
community consciousness, 9
community participation
constraints on, 297–308
in educational organization, 99–106, 122, 164–167, 233, 252–257, 269
community-based management, 7
discussed, 99–102
community-teacher partnership, in school governance, 99–111
competition, 302–305
conflict
intellectual, 300–301
sociocognitive, 270–272
conflict resolution. *see also* negotiation
between children and adults, 297
negotiation affecting, 94
relation to creativity, 76
socialization enhanced in, 115–116, 320–321
teacher's role in, 194–197
conservation of length task, 229
constructivism. *see also* social constructivism
of Piaget, 82
theory for, 262–275
constructivist psychology, 8
cooperation. *see also* negotiation; reciprocity; relationships
and co-construction, 254–255, 316
curriculum affecting, 41, 252, 331–332
demonstrated in classroom, 70, 94–95, 186, 267–268, 376
factors affecting, 168, 170
and shared control, 182–186
and subjectivity, 143–144
corporation, as model for education, 41–43

creativity
  beliefs and principles for, 75–77
  relation to meaning, 81
  universality of, 143–144
crèches, 18
cross-modal representation, 368
The Crowd Project, 123–124
cultural diffusion, 458
culture
  classroom as, 69
  environment for expression of, 143
  as forum, 133
  of schooling, 266–267, 276
  and space, 167–169
  symbols representing, 93
curiosity, enhancement of, 155
curriculum
  based on negotiated learning, 251–252
  children as source of, 51, 88–90
  classification of children affecting, 79–80
  emergent and informal, 41
  negotiation of, 315
  zone of proximal development affecting, 272–273
curriculum planning. *see also* planning
  challenge and meaning for, 252
  for dinosaur project, 215–236
  and reconnaissance, 87–88
  for "special rights" children, 204
  teachers' role in, 118–119, 134–135

D

Dads and Their Work Project, 388–403
Dalton School, 59
Dance of World Making, 285–293
democracy
  in education, 83, 252, 268
  tradition of in Emilia Romagna, 8–9
design
  and description, 243–245, 399
  negotiated learning through, 239, 240, 241–242
Dewey, John, 57, 59, 78
Diana School, 165, 191, 209
differences
  affecting children, 79–80
  recognition and acceptance of, 205–208, 302–305
Dinosaur Project, 215–236
disabled and handicapped children
  provisions for, 5
  "special rights" children, 199–214
  bodyguard model, 202
  declaration of intent, 204
  definitions, 200
  psychologist-pedagogista responsibilities, 202–203
discourse. *see also* communication
  negotiated learning through, 239, 241, 243, 246–247, 253
discussion. *see also* communication; negotiation
  documentation of, 220–221
  relation to graphic representation, 91–93
  teachers' participation in, 120, 135–136, 186, 189–191, 255
dispenser of occasions, teachers' role as, 181, 182–183, 192
documentation
  affect on relationships, 121–122
  of artwork, 298–299
  and discourse, 243
  discussed, 10–12, 120–121, 323–324, 330, 331–332
  and displays, 245–246
  graphic materials inclusion in, 34
  mutual criticism of, 189–191
  negotiated learning through, 239, 241–242
  of project discussions, 220–221
  role of *atelier* in, 141–142
  role of in education, 23, 38–40, 70, 95, 185, 186, 252–257, 268, 346, 370, 373, 378, 409–412, 447, 464
  and space, 175–176
  for "special rights" children, 203–204
drawing. *see also* art; graphic languages
  as design, 241, 243–244
  learning by use of, 124, 392, 398
  life-size, 225–232
  for projects, 219–220, 363–370
  realistic and imaginative, 35
  of sounds, 368
  use of in communication, 34

E

early childhood education, reconsidered in the U.S., 439–452
early childhood lore. *see also* childhood images
  constraints from, 295–310
early childhood programs
  contemporary appreciation for, 108
  corporate and industrial model, 41–43
  family and community model, 40–41
  first city-run schools, 51–54
  organizational chart of, 101

reconsideration of, 448–451
education
objectives of, 82–83
social services relation to, 5
educational and caring spaces. *see also* environment
discussed, 161–177
educational choices, relation to organization, 62–70
educational levels, 79–80
elementary school, transition to, 155
Emilia Romagna, 8–9
emotions, exploration and expression of, 28, 208–209, 301–302, 461–462
enthusiasm. *see also* motivation
enhancement of, 155, 389–390
environment. *see also atelier*; *piazza*
amiability in, 63–64
educational and caring spaces, 161–177
historical consideration for, 22
influence of on education, 40, 266–267
for Model Early Learning Center, 340
epistemology, 240
educational concerns with, 82
Esperienze per Una Nuova Scuola dell'Infanzia (Experiences for a New School for Young Children), 54–55
European Community, educational study committee, 19–20
expectations
of children, 68, 235–236, 257
for project success, 90–91
experience
childrens' participation in, 115, 367
creativity enhanced within, 76
mediation of, 338
remembering and revisiting, 247–248
experimentation
in curriculum, 89–90
opportunities for, 207
in project selection, 33
expertise, acknowledgement and sharing of, 302–305
experts, consultation with, 105

F

factory educational model, 42–43
family. *see also* father; mother; parents
as model for preschool program, 40–41, 43–44
role of in education, 59, 69–70, 102, 305–306
Fascism. *see also* politics
influence on education, 18–19, 20–21, 59
father. *see also* adults; men; parents
role for in parenting, 151–152, 153
feelings. *see* emotions
Ferrière, Adolfe, 59
La Festa dell'Acqua (Water Party), 149–150
forum
culture as, 133
public function of, 87
Freinet, Celestine, 59

G

Gambetti, Amelia, 341–342, 345–346, 352, 356
Gardner, Howard, 81
gender roles, 273, 464
"genetic law" (Vygotsky), 270
gestione sociale. see community-based management
girls
project collaboration procedures, 223–224, 228–229
thinking process, compared to boys, 220–221
Goodman, Nelson, 67
government, role in infant-toddler management, 100–101
Grammatica della Fantastica (The Grammar of Fantasy), 54
graphic languages. *see also* symbolic representation
encouragement for use of, 28
exploration of in *atelier*, 64, 140–141
use of in communication, 34, 35, 139–140
graphic representation, relation of discussion to, 91–93
groups. *see also* relationships; small groups
children's experience in, 170, 325
dynamics of, 463–464
for peer support, 424–425
project creation by, 219
Guilford, J.P., 75

H

Hawkins, David, 78, 81
holidays, celebration of, 106
human potential
waste of in educational system, 77–78
zone of proximal development for, 83–84
The Hundred Languages of Children, 12, 23, 122, 344, 359
discussed, 9–12

I

ideas. *see also* knowledge construction
children's search for, 184
exchange of, 165, 304, 458
graphic representation of, 92
identity
affirmation of, 107
construction of, 207
of educational system, 141
reinforcement and recognition of, 68–69, 139–140, 304, 306
of teachers, 180
If...(poem), 293
images, communication with, 287–288
individual, relationship with sociocultural context, 264
individualism. *see also* differences
development of, 296
and ownership, 298
industry, as model for education, 41–43
infancy, duration of, 80
infant-toddler centers (*Asili Nido*)
background, 18–20, 61
basic educational principles, 114–115
community-based management of, 100
contemporary facilities for, 5, 62, 174
in lab school
curriculum and materials, 324–325, 330
Gluing Project, 326–329
relationships, 325–326
parents' involvement with, 104–106, 130–131, 149–152
Inhelder, Barbel, 82
intellectual development, 7
interventions. *see also* provocation
principles for, 79, 187–189, 230, 319, 321–324
Io chi siamo philosophy, 219, 265–270, 297

K

Kamehameha Elementary Education Project (KEEP), 273
"knot" identification, teacher's responsibility for, 187
knowledge. *see also* cognition
intuitive, 372–373
theory of, 239
knowledge construction. *see also* cognition; ideas
co-constructed, 170–171, 183–184, 249, 399, 408–409, 457
motivation for, 249
processes for, 115, 119, 208, 264, 270, 376
socially mediated, 276, 280

L

La Gestione Sociale nella Scuola dell'Infanzia (Community-based Management in the Preprimary School), 55
La Villetta School, 149–157, 166
lab school. *see* A. Sophie Rogers Lab School
labs, for teacher development, 105–106
language
and dialect, 50–51
and symbols, 248–249
Law 1044, 19
learning. *see also* curriculum
adult understanding of, 140–141
in group context, 115, 302–305
mediated, 338
multilevel/multimodal, 10
negotiated, 239–258
components of, 242
relation to teaching, 82–83
and relationships, 66–68
spiraling, 182–186
learning theory, meaning construction, 81
left-wing politics, 8, 21
Letter to a Teacher, 22
Lewin, Ann, 339–342, 346–347, 350, 353–354, 356–357
listening. *see also* communication
documentation affecting, 121–122
and hearing, 249–250
processes for, 120–121, 376
teachers' responsibilities for, 181–182
L'Occhio se Salta il Muro (When the Eye Jumps Over the Wall), 12
The Long Jump, 268

M

maintenance, children's responsibility for, 41
"markers of affiliation", 271
marketplace, 87, 173
Marks Meadow Elementary School, City in the Snow Project, 359–374
mathematics, education about, 53, 89
mealtimes, 152–153
meaning
and creativity, 75–77
documentation of, 39
in language, 249
negotiation of, 133, 239–240, 270–271, 408, 413

meaning construction, 81. *see also* knowledge construction
  documentation enhancing, 122
  shared procedures for, 133–134
measurement
  in dinosaur project, 225–232
  education about, 53, 89–90
meetings. *see also* groups
  for family involvement, 105–106, 131, 153, 306
  for teachers and staff, 423
men. *see also* fathers; parents
  non-availability of for teaching, 71
mirrors, in school environment, 206–207, 267
Model Early Learning Center (MELC), 335–357
Montessori, Maria, 20, 60
Moscovici, Serge, 85
mother-child relationship. *see also* women
  impacts to, 61
motivation
  factors affecting, 67, 155
  for knowledge construction, 249
  project as trigger for, 90–91
Movement of Cooperative Education (MCE), 21
Mugny, Gabriel, 85
multiple intelligences theory, 338
mutual criticism, among teachers, 189–191

N

A Nation at Risk, 335
National Center for Research (CNR), 50
The National Learning Center (TNLC), 336
National Liberation Committee (CLN), 50
National Organization for Maternity and Infancy (ONMI), 18
negotiation. *see also* conflict resolution; cooperation; reciprocity
  of curriculum, 315
  discovery of other by use of, 94
  individual and group, 208
  of learning, 239–258
  of meaning, 133, 239–240, 270–271, 408, 413
  relation to creativity, 76
  social skills enhanced with, 153
neighborhood. *see* community
The New Education (Bovet), 59
number, education about, 53, 89–90

O

observation, processes for, 120–121, 376
open education, 28
organization
  by relationship, 69
  organizational chart of early childhood education, 101
  relation to educational choices, 62–70, 163, 267
  to support collaboration, 255

P

painting. *see also* drawing; graphic languages
  use of in communication, 34
parents. *see also* family; father; mother
  at Model Early Learning Center, 351, 354–356
  changing role of, 107–108
  documentation use for, 12, 39, 120–121, 252–254
  involvement with schools, 7, 43–44, 74, 102–106, 110–111, 130, 149–157, 185, 252–254, 441
  relationship with child, 62
  single-parent admission priority, 201–202
  of "special rights" children, 203–204
participatory appropriation, 273
pedagogista, role in education, 64, 121, 127–137, 445–446
photographic masks, 249–251
photographs
  for documentation, 254, 330, 397
  as symbol and document, 162
Piaget, Jean, 81–82, 244
piazza. *see also* environment
  role of in education, 40, 64, 164–166, 171
planning. *see also* curriculum planning
  definitions for, 113
  and design, 241
  requirements for teachers, 208, 255, 461
play
  emotional expression in, 28
  practical substitutes for, 20
  spontaneous, 35
  to promote development, 274
"Plowden Years", 28
politics
  Fascism, 18–19, 20–21, 59
  left-wing, 8, 21
  relation to teaching, 183, 278
portfolios, and documentation, 246
Portrait of a Lion, 344
positivism, 278

practice, theory relation to, 84–90, 119–120, 261–280
prediction, documentation enhancing, 122
preprimary schools (*Scuole dell'Infanzia*)
  atelier role in, 140–143
  background, 20–24
  basic educational principles, 114–115
  community-based management of, 100
  contemporary facilities for, 5
  parents' involvement with, 104–106
  schedules and staffing, 9
presepi, 18
problem identification, teacher's responsibility for, 187, 379
problem solving
  discussion affecting, 189–190
  environment for, 373
  intervention affecting, 188–189
  theory affecting, 278, 464
progettazione
  discussed, 113–125, 132–135
  processes for, 189, 268
Progetto Ascanio, 23
progressive educational philosophy, 8, 27–28
Project Approach Framework for Teacher Education (PAFTE), for collaborative learning, 405–416
project work
  childrens' contributions to, 33
  inclusion in curriculum, 27–28, 268, 374
  in *mini-ateliers*, 64
projects
  Bicycle Project, 378–388
  City Project, 315–324
  City in the Rain, 167, 359
  City in the Snow, 359–374
  The Crowd Project, 123–134
  Dads and Their Work Project, 388–403
  "didactic projects" for "special rights" children, 204
  Dinosaur Project, 215–236
  expectations for success of, 90–91
  and learning encounters, 251–252
  processes for, 122–124, 185
  Snow Explorations, 427–431
protagonist
  child as, 110, 180, 274, 287, 297, 457
  citizens as, 8
"Protection and Assistance of Infancy" legislation, 18
provocation. *see also* interventions
  in *atelier*, 73–75
  by children, 270–272
  by teachers, 182–183, 218, 273, 302, 322, 380, 396, 447
  and understanding, 250–251

R

rainstorm, exploring in project, 166–167, 359–360
reciprocity. *see also* cooperation; negotiation
  in projects, 217, 230–231, 234–235
  in school relationships, 441–442
reconnaissance, and curriculum planning, 87–88, 461
records. *see also* documentation
  of parent involvement, 253–255
REGGIO CHILDREN S.r.l., 23–24
Reggio Emilia
  background, 5–6
  early childhood education system organizational chart, 101
  philosophy
    educational approaches, 60–62
    inspiration, 58–59, 60
    1960s educational situation, 59–60
  principles
    communication networks, 68–69
    family involvement, 69–70
    relationship-based education, 64–66
    learning and relationships, 66–68
    organization and educational choices, 62–63
  schedules and staffing, preprimary schools, 9
  teachers
    collegial work of, 71
    creativity genesis and meaning, 75–77
    formation and reformation of, 72–73
    training for, 71–72
Reggio Emilia approach
  adapting for study and practice, 419–436
  discussed, 7–8
  guiding principles, 461–465
  historical context, 17–24
relationships. *see also* teacher-child relationships
  affect on learning, 141
  children's predisposition for, 15, 62, 110, 155–157, 205–206
  in community-based management, 102
  content requirements for, 36
  creativity enhanced within, 76
  documentation affecting, 121–122
  "genetic law" of, 270
  hierarchial, 71

importance of, 287, 289
and learning, 66–68
pedagogista within, 129
role of in education, 64–66, 68–69, 115, 268–269, 305–306
in small groups, 94
representation. *see also* graphic representation
in project, 371–372
research
atelier use for, 74–75
by teachers, 86–87, 119, 276, 408–409
documentation use for, 10–12, 39
in library, 221–222
for projects, 319–320
rights of children
examples of, 8, 57–58, 114, 161, 164
"special rights" children, 199–214
Robinson school, 51–54
Rodari, Gianni, 54
rope, 255–256

S

satisfaction
achievement of as educational goal, 66
as goal for contemporary women, 62
school of knowing, connected to school of expressing, 77
"school-city" committees, 100
Scuola di Barbiana, 22
Scuole dell'Infanzia. see preprimary schools
self-examination
by children, 207
by teachers, 189–191
simulation, learning by, 364–366
small groups. *see also* groups
at Model Early Learning Center, 340
communication affecting, 69
discussed, 94–95
emphasis on, 41, 206, 304, 461
pairs, 320
for parent-teacher meetings, 105
in project learning, 7, 268, 316–317, 377, 392
snow explorations, 427–431
social attention, cycles of, 319–320
social constructivism. *see also* constructivism
children's role in, 115, 118, 264
enhancement in schools, 119, 162–163
and negotiated learning, 239–240, 315–316
teachers' support with, 130, 407–408
theory for, 338
social services
public demand for, 53
relation to education, 5, 170
socialization, childrens' participation in, 115, 180
society. *see* community
sociocultural context
for classrooms as cultures, 314–315
individual relationship with, 264, 265–270
sounds, drawing of, 368
space. *see also* environment
and culture, 167–169
for different ages and development levels, 174–175
and documentation, 175–176
as educational element, 162–164
and social exchange, 170–173
and time, 169–170
"special rights" children, discussed, 199–214
spiraling, of teachers' role, 183
Spitz, Rene, 61
subjectivity
and cooperation, 143–144
social forces for, 107
supermarket study, 29–32
symbol
as catalyst, 371
definition of, 92–93
and language, 248–249
symbolic representation. *see also* graphic languages
as basis for intellectual development, 7, 303
cross-modal representation, 368
discussed, 93
self-expression using, 114, 162
symbolization
cycles of, 362–370
multiple, 409
relation to meaning and communication, 240

T

teacher behaviors
dispute metamorphosis, 194–195
dispute resolution, 196–197
getting children started, 192–193
instruction in tool use and technique, 193–194
interventions, 79, 187–189, 230, 319, 321–324
provocations, 182–183, 218, 273, 302, 322, 380, 396, 447
teacher compensation, 448–449

teacher development
  in *atelier*, 139
  in College School Project, 420–427
  documentation affecting, 120
  in-service and out-of-classroom training, 130, 132
  labs for, 105–106
  project approach framework for, 405–416
  reconsideration of, 49, 442–447
  support for, 72–73
teacher training
  considerations for, 71–72, 140
  for "special rights" children, 204–205
teacher-child continuity, benefits of, 7, 40–41, 303–304, 307
teacher-child ratio, in preprimary schools, 22
teacher-child relationships
  content of, 36–37
  strength of, 154, 441–442
teachers
  adjustments required by, 69–70
  at Model Early Learning Center, 343–344, 348–349, 350–352, 354
  co-teaching pairs, 71, 185, 444–445
  collegial work of, 71
  creativity genesis and meaning, 75–77
  as dispenser of occasions, 181, 182–183, 192
  formation and reformation of, 72–73
  industrial model for, 42
  relationship with *atelierista*, 142–143, 146–147
  relationships with parents, 105, 130, 253
  role in curriculum planning, 118–119
  role in education, 179–198
    definitions, 180–181
    listening responsibilities, 181–182
    mutual criticism and self-examination, 189–191
    special difficulties, 187–189
    spiraling learning and shared control, 182–186
    teacher behavior examples, 191–197
  support processes for, 129–132
  training of, 71–72
teaching
  as reflective praxis, 275–277
  relation to learning, 82–83
  and space, 177
television, 53
tests and evaluations, 208
theory
  legitimization of, 277–278
  for Model Early Learning Center, 337–338
  relation to practice, 84–90, 119–120, 261–280
time
  cyclical alterations in, 183
  incorrect appreciation of, 80
  modification of, 351
  relation to child, 307–308, 376–377
  and space, 169–170
tool use, instruction in, 193–194
Torrance, Paul, 75
Tutto Ha Un' Ombra Meno Le Formich (Everything Has a Shadow Except Ants), 147

U

United States
  affinity between Reggio Emilia philosophy, 261, 262
  art representations treatment in, 34, 35
  corporate educational models, 41–43
  developmentally appropriate practice, 235
  early childhood education reconsidered, 439–452
  educational environment considerations in, 163
  Reggio Emilia approach in, 13
  school culture supports in, 276
  teacher-child relationships, 36–38

V

Villa Cella, 49–50
visual languages. *see* graphic languages
vocabulary, factors affecting growth of, 124
voice, and language, 248
vulnerabilities, revelation of, 346
Vygotsky, Lev, 57, 67, 83–84, 244, 264, 270, 272

W

Winnetka schools, 375–403
  Bicycle Project, 378–388
  Dads and Their Work Project, 388–403
  key principles, 376–378
  philosophy of, 376
women. *see also* family; mother; parents
  in contemporary society, 22
  desires of for children's education, 58
  identity development for, 139–140
  mother-child relationship, 61
  role in early preschools, 49–50
  social choices for, 62
  as teachers, 71, 145

words
    distinguishing between, 249–250
    familiar and special, 415
    power of, 91–92
work sessions, parent-teacher, 105

Z

Zerosei (Zero to Six), 56
zone of proximal development
    advantages of, 83–84
    discussed, 272–275, 280